CLASSICAL MYTHOLOGY

Fifth Edition

Mark P.O. Morford
University of Virginia

Robert J. Lenardon
*Ohio State University,
Emeritus
Siena College*

Longman *Publishers USA*

Classical Mythology, fifth edition

Longman, 10 Bank Street, White Plains, N.Y. 10606

Associated companies:
Longman Group Ltd., London
Longman Cheshire Pty., Melbourne
Longman Paul Pty., Auckland
Copp Clark Longman Ltd., Toronto

Acquisitions editor: Virginia L. Blanford
Development editor: Susan G. Alkana
Production editor: Halley Gatenby
Cover and text designs: A Good Thing Inc.
Cover art: *Aurora,* artist unknown. New England (possibly Massachusetts),
    ca. 1820, formerly called *Chariot in the Clouds* and *Venus Drawn by Doves.*
    Watercolor and gold paper collage on silk; $14\frac{1}{2} \times 14\frac{1}{4}$ in. See page 47.
Text art: A Good Thing Inc.
Photo research: Aerin Csigay
Production supervisor: Richard Bretan

Library of Congress Cataloging-in-Publication Data

Morford, Mark P. O., Date.
    Classical mythology / Mark P.O. Morford, Robert J. Lenardon. —
5th ed.
        p.   cm.
    Includes bibliographical references and index.
    ISBN: 0-8013-1488-7
    ISBN: 0-8013-1138-1 (pbk.)
    1. Mythology, Classical.   I. Lenardon, Robert J., Date.
II. Title.
BL722.M67   1994
292.1'3—dc20   94-18932
                                                             CIP

345678910-MA-98979695

CLASSICAL
MYTHOLOGY

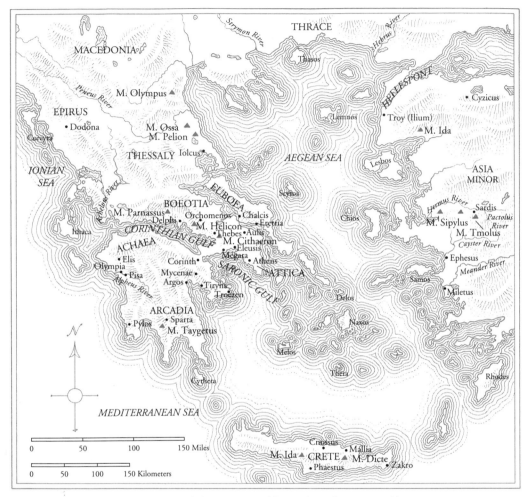

Greece and the Aegean. (© *Laszlo Kubinyi, 1994.*)

Dedicated to the memory of
WILLIAM ROBERT JONES,
teacher, scholar, and friend

CONTENTS

ILLUSTRATIONS
AND WORKS OF ART

Color Plates

Other Works of Art

Maps

Charts and Other Diagrams

PREFACE

The years since the publication of the fourth edition of *Classical Mythology* have brought far-reaching changes in modes of access to and dissemination of information. We have thoroughly revised the book in the light of these changes, with the primary goal of making it more useful, flexible, and contemporary.

New to This Edition

We have shortened the text in many places and have added new subheadings to present a clearer organization to each chapter. We have transferred less vital information to the notes and eliminated altogether many obscure variants of myths which have proved unenlightening to students. The Introduction and chapters in Part III have been extensively rewritten, and Chapter 25, "The Survival of Classical Mythology in Art and Literature," has been reorganized. We have added two sections on the civic uses of mythology in connection with the temple of Zeus at Olympia and the Periclean buildings on the Acropolis at Athens. Finally, the new glossary provides brief identifications of people and places.

Throughout, we have attempted to be responsive to current educational concerns without abandoning our fundamental reliance on the primary sources, in the belief that they are the foundation for the study of classical mythology.

Illustrations

The number of illustrations has been expanded to 109, of which 22 are color plates. We have substantially revised and expanded the photo captions, undertaking new research and incorporating the results of recent scholarship. Details of size and medium have been added to give some idea of the scale of the original work. The illustrations are an integral part of the book, and by themselves give a wide-ranging survey of changing attitudes over the centuries to the relationship between the written word and the visual image. The interaction of word and image has been a dynamic force in the continuing tradition of *Classical Mythology*. In addition, some maps have been expanded and all have been redrawn.

Companion

For the first time, a separate *Companion to Classical Mythology* will be offered to both students and instructors in the classical mythology classroom. The *Companion* will include some material removed from earlier editions of the text itself, in particular a discography of music on Greek and Roman themes available now on CD. In addition, the *Companion* will contain expanded bibliographical and interpretive material, summaries of key myths, and derivations of contemporary words from Greek and Roman roots. Perhaps most significant, the *Companion* will provide students of classical mythology with access to vastly enhanced contextual resources in the form of computer-aided, interactive modes of study. Through a special arrangement with Yale University Press and the developers of *Perseus,* the *Companion* will include paths through the *Perseus* CD-ROM keyed to every chapter of *Classical Mythology.* We hope that these paths will allow readers of *Classical Mythology* to immerse themselves in the archival, artistic, and archaeological resources that the *Perseus* program offers.

Acknowledgments

The authors are grateful to many friends and colleagues for suggestions and help. We are especially grateful to the Longman Publishers USA for its renewed commitment to this book, made evident by the vigorous and sensitive support of Roth Wilkofsky and the editorial skill of Susan Alkana, who has helped us immeasurably in the complex work of a major revision with patience and enthusiasm. We are grateful to the following reviewers, who provided critical commentary on this revision: O. Kimball Armayor, University of Alabama; James R. Baron, The College of William & Mary; Joseph Cotter, The Pennsylvania State University; Robert Eisner, San Diego State University; Alain M. Gowing, University of Washington; Robert James Griffin, Western

Michigan University; Karelisa Hartigan, University of Florida; Jackson P. Hershbell, University of Minnesota at Minneapolis; Maria C. Pantelia, University of New Hampshire; Terry Papillon, Marquette University; Michael L. Robertson, California State University at Sacramento; and C. Brian Rose, University of Cincinnati.

Dedication

This edition is dedicated to the memory of Martha Morford, whose critical acumen and profound knowledge of the history of art have been a constant support to the authors.

PREFACE TO
THE FIRST EDITION

Our experience in teaching courses in classical mythology to large undergraduate classes has convinced us of the need for a new and comprehensive survey that will be useful to readers who have little or no background of classical knowledge. We must acknowledge our debt to predecessors in the field, most especially the works of Röscher, Preller, Robert, and Rose. Our method, however, has taken us beyond these convenient but secondary sources to the classical authors themselves. The compendium of the second century A.D. attributed to Apollodorus has been drawn upon where legends could not be conveniently found in earlier authors, but we have preferred where possible to make extensive use of Homer, Hesiod, the *Homeric Hymns,* Pindar and the Lyric Poets, and the tragedians, among Greek authors; among Latin authors, of Vergil and Ovid. We have provided our own translations of many of the original passages, so that the reader may have knowledge of the classical sources upon which modern discussion of the legends is based. It has proved more practical to give extensive translations in Part I, most especially of passages from the *Homeric Hymns* to the various gods; in dealing with saga and local legends (Part II) we have resorted more to paraphrase in the interests of conciseness and clarity, although even here we have included a generous amount of the classical sources in translation. In writing the book we have each taken the major responsibility for certain sections—Professor Lenardon for the Introduction, Part I and Chapter 24, and Professor Morford for Parts II and III (other than Chapter 24) and the illustrations; we have each read and criticized the other's contributions and take joint responsibility for the whole.

Consistency in spelling has proved impossible to attain. In general we have adopted Latinized forms (*Cronus* for *Kronos*) or spellings generally accepted in English-speaking countries (*Heracles,* not *Herakles*); the Greek final *-ōs* has been kept, as in *Minos.* In doubtful cases we have accepted the spelling given by Gordon Kirkwood in his *Short Guide to Classical Mythology* (New York, 1959). We have generally used the Greek forms of names where there is a separate Latin equivalent (Aphrodite, not Venus); this rule obviously does not apply in the chapter on Roman Legends. The index provides cross-references to both the Greek and Roman names.

We have received help and encouragement from many colleagues, students, and friends. Our colleague, the late Professor W. Robert Jones, until his death in 1968, gave generously to us of his time and wisdom. Mr. Gordon Hill and the late Mr. Charles Hillard, of David McKay's, were more patient and encouraging than we deserved; Miss Ellen B. Karge and Mr. Charles A. McCloud were helpful in providing material for the writing of Chapter 24. Dr. Arta Johnson has provided patient and detailed criticism of the manuscript and has undertaken the labor of compiling the index. Mrs. Mark Morford has helped us in selecting the illustrations and in typing much of the manuscript, while Mrs. Colette Armstrong, Mrs. Nicholas Genovese, and Miss Joann Phillips typed the remaining parts of the manuscript. To all these persons we extend our thanks.

INTRODUCTION

DEFINITIONS AND INTERPRETATIONS OF MYTH

The word *myth* comes from the Greek word *mythos,* which means "word," "speech," "tale," or "story," and that is essentially what a myth is: a story. Some would limit this broad definition by insisting that the story must have proven itself worthy of becoming traditional.[1] A myth may be a story that is narrated orally but usually it is eventually given written form. A myth also may be told by means of no words at all, for example, through painting, sculpture, music, dance, and mime, or by a combination of various media as in the case of drama, song, opera, or the movies.

Many specialists in the field of mythology, however, are not satisfied with such broad interpretations of the term *myth.* They attempt to distinguish "true myth" (or "myth proper") from other varieties and seek to draw distinctions in terminology between myth and other words often used synonymously, such as *legend, saga,* and *folktale.*[2]

Myth, Saga or Legend, and Folktale

Myth is a comprehensive (but not exclusive) term for stories primarily concerned with the gods and humankind's relations with them; **saga,** or **legend** (and we use the words interchangeably), has a perceptible relationship to history; however fanciful and imaginative, it has its roots in historical fact.[3] These two categories underlie the basic division of the first two parts of this book into "The Myths of Creation: the Gods" and "The Greek Sagas: Greek Local Legends."

Interwoven with these broad categories are **folktales,** which are often tales of adventure, sometimes peopled with fantastic beings, and enlivened by ingenious strategies on the part of the hero; their object is primarily but not necessarily solely to entertain. Rarely, if ever, do we find a pristine, uncontaminated example of any one of these forms. Yet the traditional categories of myth, folktale, and legend or saga are useful guides as we try to impose some order upon the multitudinous variety of classical tales.[4]

How loose these categories are can be seen, for example, from the legends of Odysseus or of the Argonauts, which contain elements of history but are full of stories that may be designated as myths and folktales. The criteria for definition merge and the lines of demarcation blur.

Comparative Mythology

The impossibility of establishing a satisfactory definition of *myth* has not deterred scholars from developing comprehensive theories on the meaning and interpretation of myth, usually to provide bases for a hypothesis about origins. Useful surveys of the principal theories are easily available,[5] so that we shall attempt to touch upon only a few theories that are likely to prove especially fruitful or are persistent enough to demand attention. One thing is certain: no single theory of myth can cover all kinds of myths. The variety of traditional tales is matched by the variety of their origins and significance, so that no monolithic theory can succeed in achieving universal applicability. Definitions will tend to be either too limiting or so broad as to be virtually useless. In the last analysis definitions are enlightening because they succeed in identifying particular characteristics of different types of stories and thus provide criteria for classification.

Comparisons among the various stories told throughout the ages, all over the world, have become influential in establishing definitions and classifications. In the modern study of comparative mythology, much emphasis tends to be placed upon stories told by preliterate and primitive societies and too often the developed literature of the Greeks and Romans has virtually been ignored. It was not always so; for pioneers in the field, such as Frazer (identified below), classical mythology was understandably fundamental. Yet classical mythology developed from something less sophisticated than the form in which we find it in, say, Homer or Euripides. Although it may be difficult and at times impossible to ascertain with any certainty the precise details of earlier versions of a classical story,[6] its universal, thematic character remains.

True, it can be misleading, to press analogies and parallels in the legends of widely divergent societies, especially where, as in Greek mythology, even our earliest literary sources (Homer and Hesiod) appear after a lengthy period of evolution, far removed from the myths' primitive origins. It is equally misleading to posit a "primitive" mentality as if it were something childlike and simple, in contrast to the "sophisticated" mentality of more advanced societies such as the Greeks'.[7] In fact, anthropologists have proved how far the myths of primitive societies reflect the complexities of social family structures; and their tales, however they may be compared to the classical, are far from being merely alogical and mystical.

Despite these warnings, we may assert that the comparative study of myths, especially by anthropologists (as opposed to philologically trained classicists), has been one of the most fruitful approaches to the interpretation of myths. Despite its faults, Sir J. G. Frazer's *The Golden Bough* remains a pioneering monument in the field. It is full of comparative data on kingship and ritual, but its value is lessened by Frazer's ritualist interpretation of myth (explained later) and by his eagerness to establish dubious analogies between myths of primitive tribes and classical myths.

The application of comparative methods to the classical myths in particular will be discussed at more length below, after we have examined significant definitions, explanations, and classifications of myths.

Myth and Religion

Foremost and most compelling is the distinction between true myth and saga and folktale described above, that is, true myth is primarily concerned with the gods, religion, and the supernatural. Most Greek and Roman stories (comprising Part 1 of this book, and actually a substantial portion of Part 2) reflect this universal preoccupation with creation, the nature of god and humankind, the afterlife and other spiritual concerns.

Thus mythology and religion are inextricably entwined. One tale or another once may have been believed at some time by certain people; specific creation stories and mythical conceptions of deity may still be considered true today and provide the basis for devout religious belief in a contemporary society. In fact, any collection of material for the comparative study of world mythologies will be dominated by the study of texts that are, by nature, religious.

Since, as we have seen, the Greek word for myth means "word," "speech," or "story," for a critic like Aristotle it became the designation for the plot of a play; thus, it is easy to understand how a popular view would equate myth with fiction. In everyday speech the most common association of the words *myth* and *mythical* is with what is incredible and fantastic. How often do we hear the expression, "It's a myth," uttered in derogatory contrast with such laudable concepts as reality, truth, science, and the facts.

Therefore important distinctions may be drawn between stories that are perceived as true and those that are not.[8] The contrast between myth and reality has been a major philosophical concern since the time of the Pre-Socratics. Myth is a many-faceted personal and cultural phenomenon created to provide a reality and a unity to what is transitory and fragmented in the world that we experience—the philosophical vision of the afterlife in Plato and any religious conception of a god are mythic, not scientific, concepts. Myth provides us with absolutes in the place of ephemeral values and a comforting perception of the world that is necessary to make the insecurity and terror of existence bearable.[9]

It is disturbing to realize that our faith in absolutes and factual truth can be easily shattered. "Facts" change in all the sciences; textbooks in chemistry, physics, and medicine are sadly (or happily, for progress) soon out of date. It is embarrassingly banal but fundamentally important to reiterate the platitude that myth, like art, is truth on a quite different plane from that of prosaic and transitory factual knowledge. Yet myth and factual truth need not be mutually exclusive, as some so emphatically insist. A story embodying eternal values may contain what was imagined, at any one period, to be scientifically correct in every factual detail; and the accuracy of that information may be a vital component of its mythical raison d'être. Indeed one can create a myth out of a factual story, as a great historian must do: any interpretation of the facts, no matter how credible, will inevitably be a mythic invention. On the other hand, a different kind of artist may create a nonhistorical myth for the ages, and whether it is factually accurate or not may be quite beside the point.[10]

Myth in a sense is the highest reality; and the thoughtless dismissal of myth as untruth, fiction, or a lie is the most barren and misleading definition of all. The dancer and choreographer Martha Graham, sublimely aware of the timeless "blood memory" that binds our human race and that is continually revoked by the archetypal transformations of mythic art, offers a beautifully concise summation: as opposed to the discoveries of science that "will in time change and perhaps grow obsolete . . . art is eternal, for it reveals the inner landscape, which is the soul of man."[11]

Myth and Society: Bronislav Malinowski

Important in the development of modern theories is the work of Bronislav Malinowksi, who was stranded among the Trobriand Islanders (off New Guinea) during World War I; he used his enforced leisure to study the Trobrianders.[12] His great discovery was the close connection between myths and social institutions, which led him to explain myths not in cosmic or mysterious terms, but as "charters" of social customs and beliefs. To him myths were related to practical life, and they explained existing facts and institutions by reference to tradition: the myth confirms (i.e., is the "charter" for) the institution, custom, or belief. Clearly such a theory will be valid only for certain myths (e.g., those involving the establishment of a ritual), but any theory that excludes the speculative element in myth is bound to be too limited.

Myth and Ritual: Robert Graves

This brings us to the ritualist interpretation of myth, a most influential and persistent theory, which underlies Robert Graves's definition of "true myth," which for him is "the reduction to narrative shorthand of ritual mime performed in public festivals, and in many cases recorded pictorially on temple walls, vases, seals, bowls, mirrors, chests, shields, tapestries, and the like";[13] he distinguishes this true myth from twelve other categories, such as philosophical allegory, satire or parody, minstrel romance, political propaganda, theatrical melodrama, and realistic fiction. It is perceptive of Graves to realize that literary distinctions may be as enlightening as any other type of classification for classical mythology. Yet stated most bluntly, this theory says that "myth implies ritual, ritual implies myth, they are one and the same."[14] True, many myths are closely connected with rituals, and the theory is valuable for the connection it emphasizes between myth and religion; but it is patently untenable to connect *all* true myth with ritual.

Rationalism versus Metaphor, Allegory, and Symbolism

The desire to rationalize classical mythology arose far back in classical antiquity, and is especially associated with the name of Euhemerus (ca. 300 B.C.), who claimed that the gods were men deified for their great deeds.[15] The supreme god Zeus, for example, was once a mortal king in Crete who deposed his father, Cronus. At the opposite extreme from Euhemerism is the metaphorical interpretation of stories. Antirationalists, who favor metaphorical interpretations, believe that traditional tales hide profound meanings. At its best the metaphorical approach sees myth as allegory (allegory is to be defined as sustained metaphor), where the details of the story are but symbols of universal truths. At its worst the allegorical approach is a barren exercise in cryptology: to explain the myth of Ixion and the Centaurs in terms of clouds and weather phenomena is hardly enlightening and not at all ennobling.[16]

Allegorical Nature Myths: Max Müller

An influential theory of the nineteenth century was that of Max Müller: myths are nature myths, all referring to meteorological and cosmological phenomena. This is, of course, an extreme development of the allegorical approach; and it is hard to see how or why *all* myths can be explained as allegories of, for example, day replacing night, winter succeeding summer, and so on. True, some myths are nature myths; and certain gods, for example Zeus, represent or control the sky and other parts of the natural order; yet it is just as true that a great many more myths have no such relationship to nature.[17]

Myth and Etiology

Another universalist theory says that a myth should be interpreted narrowly as an explication of the origin of some fact or custom. Hence the theory is called *etiological,* from the Greek word for cause *(aitia).* In this view, the mythmaker is a kind of primitive scientist, using myths to explain facts that cannot otherwise be explained within the limits of society's knowledge at the time. This theory, again, is adequate for some myths, for example, those that account for origin of certain rituals (Graves) or cosmology (Müller); but interpreted literally and narrowly it does not allow for the imaginative or metaphysical aspects of mythological thought.

Yet, if one does not interpret *etiological* too literally and narrowly but defines—or better, replaces—it with the adjective *explanatory,* interpreted in its most general sense, one perhaps may find at last the most applicable of all the monolithic theories. Myths usually try to explain matters physical, emotional, and spiritual not only literally and realistically but figuratively and metaphorically as well. Myths attempt to explain the origin of our physical world: the earth and the heavens, the sun, the moon, and the stars; where human beings came from and the dichotomy between body and soul; the source of beauty and goodness, and of evil and sin; the nature and meaning of love; and so on. It is difficult to tell a story that does not reveal, and at the same time somehow explain, something; and the imaginative answer usually is in some sense or other scientific or theological. The major problem with this universal etiological approach is that it does nothing to identify a myth specifically and distinguish it clearly from any other form of expression, whether scientific, religious, or artistic.

Myth and Psychology: Freud and Jung

Sigmund Freud   The metaphorical approach has taken many forms in the present century through the theories of the psychologists and psychoanalysts, most especially those of Sigmund Freud and Carl Jung. We need to present at least some of their basic concepts, which have become essential for any understanding of mythic creativity. Freud's views were not completely new of course (the concept of "determinism," for example, "one of the glories of Freudian theory" is to be found in Aristotle),[18] but his formulation and analysis of the inner world of humankind bear the irrevocable stamp of genius.

Certainly methods and assumptions adopted by comparative mythologists—the formulations of the structuralists and the modern interpretation of mythological tales as imaginative palliative and directive formulations, created to make existence in this real world tolerable—all these find a confirmation and validity in premises formulated by Freud. The endless critical controversy in our post-Freudian world merely confirms his unique contribution.

Among Freud's many important contemporaries and successors, Jung (deeply indebted to the master but a renegade) must be singled out because of the particular relevance of his theories to a fuller appreciation of the deep-rooted recurring patterns of mythology. Among Freud's greatest contributions are his emphasis upon sexuality (and in particular infantile sexuality), his theory of the unconscious, his interpretation of dreams, and his identification of the Oedipus complex (although the term *complex* belongs to Jung). Freud has this to say about the story of King Oedipus:

> *His fate moves us only because it might have been our own, because the oracle laid upon us before our birth the very curse which rested upon him. It may be that we are all destined to direct our first sexual impulses toward our mothers, and our first impulses of*

> *hatred and resistance toward our fathers; our dreams convince us
> that we were. King Oedipus, who slew his father Laius and wedded
> his mother Jocasta, is nothing more or less than a wish-fulfill-
> ment—the fulfillment of the wish of our childhood. But we, more
> fortunate than he, in so far as we have not become psychoneurotics,
> have since our childhood succeeded in withdrawing our sexual
> impulses from our mothers, and in forgetting the jealousy of our
> fathers. . . . As the poet brings the guilt of Oedipus to light by his
> investigation, he forces us to become aware of our own inner selves,
> in which the same impulses are still extant, even though they are
> suppressed.*[19]

This Oedipal incest complex is here expressed in the masculine form, of a man's behavior in relationship to his mother; but it also could be expressed in terms of the relationship between daughter and father; the daughter turns to the father as an object of love and becomes hostile to her mother as her rival. This is for Jung an Electra complex.

Dreams for Freud are the fulfillments of wishes that have been repressed and disguised. In order to protect sleep and relieve poten-tial anxiety, the mind goes through a process of what is termed "dream-work," which consists of three primary mental activities: "condensation" of elements; "displacement" of elements in terms of allusion and a difference of emphasis; and "representation," the transmission of elements into imagery or symbols, which are many, varied, and often sexual. Something similar to this process may be discerned in the origin and evolution of myths; it also provides insight into the mind and the methods of the creative artist, as Freud himself was well aware in his studies.[20]

Thus Freud's discovery of the significance of dream-symbols led him and his followers to analyze the similarity between dreams and myths. Symbols are many and varied and often sexual (e.g., objects like sticks and swords are phallic). Myths, therefore, in the Freudian interpretation, reflect people's waking efforts to systematize the inco-herent visions and impulses of their sleep world. The patterns in the imaginative world of children, savages, and neurotics are similar, and these patterns are revealed in the motifs and symbols of myth.

As can be seen from Freud's description (quoted above), one of the basic patterns is that of the Oedipus story, in which the son kills the father in order to possess the mother. From this pattern Freud propounded a theory of our archaic heritage, in which the Oedipal drama was played out by a primal horde in their relationship to a primal father. The murder and the eating of the father led to important tribal and social developments, among them deification of the father figure, the triumph of patriarchy, and the establishment of a totemic system, whereby a sacred animal was chosen as a substitute for the slain father. Most important of all, from the ensuing sense of guilt and sin for parricide emerges the conception of God as Father who must be appeased and to whom atonement must be made. In fact, according to Freud, the Oedipus complex has inspired the beginning not only of religion but also of all ethics, art, and society.

It is clear that Freud's connection between dreams and myths is illuminating for many myths, if not for all. In addition to the story of Oedipus one might single out, for example, the legend of the Minotaur or the saga of the House of Atreus, both of which deal with some of the most persistent, if repressed, human fears and emotions and, by their telling, achieve a kind of catharsis.

Carl Jung Jung went beyond the mere connection of myths and dreams to interpret myths as the projection of what he called the "collective unconscious" of the race, that is, a revelation of the continuing psychic tendencies of society. Jung made a distinction between the personal unconscious and the collective unconscious: the personal concerns matters of an individual's own life; the collective embraces political and social questions involving the group. Dreams therefore may be either personal or collective.

Thus myths contain images or "archetypes" (to use Jung's term, which embraces Freud's concept of symbols), traditional expressions of collective dreams, developed over thousands of years, of symbols upon which the society as a whole has come to depend. For Jung the Oedipus complex was the first archetype that Freud discovered. There are many such archetypes in Greek mythology and in dreams. Here are some of the ways in which Jung thought about archetypes, the collective unconscious, and mythology. An archetype is a kind of dramatic abbreviation of the patterns involved in a whole story or situation, including the way it develops and how it ends; it is a behavior pattern, an inherited scheme of functioning. Just as a bird has the physical and mental attributes of a bird and builds its nest in a characteristic way, so human beings by nature and by instinct are born with predictable and identifiable characteristics.[21] In the case of human behavior and attitudes, the patterns are expressed in archetypal images or forms. The archetypes of behavior with which human beings are born and which find their expression in mythological tales are called the "collective unconscious." Therefore, "mythology is a pronouncing of a series of images that formulate the life of archetypes."[22] Heroes like Heracles and Theseus are models who teach us how to behave.[23]

Here are a few examples of archetypes. The *anima* is the archetypal image of the female that each man has within him; it is to this concept that he responds (for better or for worse) when he falls in love. Indeed the force of an archetype may seize a person suddenly, as when one falls in love at first sight. Similarly, the *animus* is the archetypal concept of the male that a woman instinctively harbors within her. The old wise man and the great mother and symbols or signs of various sorts are also among the many Jungian archetypes. These appear in the dreams of individuals or are expressed in the myths of societies.

The great value of Jung's concept is that it emphasizes the psychological dependence of all societies (sophisticated as well as primitive) upon their traditional myths, often expressed also in religion and ritual. But Jung's theories, like those we have already examined, have their limitations; they are not the only key to an understanding of mythology.

The Structuralists: Lévi-Strauss, Propp, and Burkert

Claude Lévi-Strauss More recently, the structural theories of Claude Lévi-Strauss have enriched the anthropological approach to myth, and they invite us to observe Malinowski's most important concept, that is, the connection between myth and society.[24]

Lévi-Strauss sees myth as a mode of communication, like language or music. In music it is not the sounds themselves that are important but their *structure*, that is, the relationship of sounds to other sounds. In myth it is the narrative that takes the part of the sounds of music, and the structure of the narrative can be perceived at various levels and in different codes (e.g., culinary, astronomical, and sociological). From this it follows that no one version of a myth is the "right" one; all versions are valid, for myth, like society, is a living organism in which all the parts contribute to the existence of the whole. As in an orchestral score certain voices or instruments play some sounds, while the whole score is the sum of the individual parts, so in a myth the different, partial versions combine to reveal its total structure, including the relationship of the different parts to each other and to the whole.

Lévi-Strauss's method is therefore rigorously analytical, breaking down each myth into its component parts. Underlying his analytical approach are basic assumptions, of which the most important is that all human behavior is based on certain unchanging patterns, whose structure is the same in all ages and in all societies. Second, he assumes that society has a consistent structure and therefore a functional unity in which every component plays a meaningful part. As part of the working of this social machine, myths are derived ultimately from the structure of the mind. And the basic structure of the mind, as of the myths it creates, is *binary;* that is, the mind is constantly dealing with pairs of contradictions or opposites. It is the function of myth to mediate between these opposing extremes—raw/cooked, life/death, hunter/hunted, nature/culture, and so on. "Mythical thought always progresses from the awareness of oppositions towards their resolution."[25] Myth, then, is a mode by which a society communicates and through which it finds a resolution between conflicting opposites. The logical structure of a myth provides a means by which the human mind can avoid unpleasant contradictions and thus, through mediation, reconcile conflicts that would be intolerable if unreconciled. Lévi-Strauss would maintain that all versions of a myth are equally authentic for exploring the myth's structure.

The theories of Lévi-Strauss have aroused passionate controversy among anthropologists and mythographers. His analysis of the Oedipus myth, for example, has been widely criticized. Yet whatever one's judgment may be, there is no doubt that this structural approach can illuminate a number of Greek myths, especially with regard to the function of "mediating." But it is open to the same objections as other comprehensive theories, that it establishes too rigid, too universal a concept of the functioning of the human mind. Indeed, the binary functioning of the human mind and of human society may be common, but it has not been proved to be either universal or necessary. Finally, Lévi-Strauss draws most of his evidence from primitive and preliterate cultures, and his theories seem to work more convincingly for them than for the literate mythology of the Greeks. His approach is better applied, for example, to the early Greek succession myths than to the Sophoclean, literate version of the legends of Oedipus and his family. We should all the same be aware of the potential of structuralist theories and be ready to use them as we seek to make meaningful connections between the different constituent elements of a myth, or between different myths that share constituent elements.

Vladimir Propp   The structural interpretation of myth was developed, long before the work of Lévi-Strauss, by Vladimir Propp in his study of the Russian folktale.[26] Like Lévi-Strauss, Propp analyzed traditional tales into their constituent parts, from which he deduced a single, recurrent structure applicable to all Russian folktales. Unlike Lévi-Strauss, however, he described this structure as linear, that is, having an unchanging temporal sequence, so that one element in the myth always follows another and never occurs out of order. This is significantly different from the pattern in Lévi-Strauss's theory, where the elements may be grouped without regard to time or sequence.

Propp divided his basic structure into thirty-one functions or units of action (which have been defined by others as *motifemes,* on the analogy of morphemes and phonemes in linguistic analysis). These functions are constants in traditional tales: the characters may change, but the functions do not. Further, these functions always occur in an identical sequence, although not all the functions need appear in a particular tale. Those that do, however, will always occur in the same sequence. Finally, Propp states that "all fairy tales are of one type in regard to their structure."[27]

Propp was using a limited number (100) of Russian folktales of one sort only, that is, the Quest. Yet his apparently strict analysis has proven remarkably adaptable and valid for other sorts of tales in other cultures. The rigid sequence of functions is too inflexible to be fully applicable to Greek myths that have a historical dimension (e.g., some of the tales in the Trojan cycle of saga), where the "facts" of history, so far as they can be established, may have a sequence independent of structures whose origins lie in psychological or cultural needs.

On the other hand, Propp's theories are very helpful in comparing myths that are apparently unrelated, showing, for example, how the same functions appear in the myths, no matter what names are given to the characters who perform them. Mythological names are a strain on the memory. Merely to master them is to achieve very little, unless they can be related in some meaningful way to other tales, including tales from other mythologies. Dreary memorization, however, becomes both easier and purposeful if underlying structures and their constituent units can be perceived and arranged logically and consistently.

A very simple example would be the structural elements common to the myths of Heracles, Theseus, Perseus, and Jason, whose innumerable details can be reduced to a limited sequence of functions. It is more difficult to establish the pattern for, say, a group of stories about the mothers of heroes (e.g., Callisto, Danaë, Io, and Antiope). Yet they resolve themselves into a clear sequence of five functions: (1) the girl leaves home; (2) the girl is secluded (beside a river, in a tower, in a forest, etc.); (3) she is made pregnant by a god; (4) she suffers punishment or rejection or a similar unpleasant consequence; and (5) she is rescued, and her son is born.[28]

We can say definitely that in most cases it is helpful to the student to analyze a myth into its constituent parts. There should be four consequences:

1. A perceptible pattern or structure will emerge.
2. It will be possible to find the same structure in other myths, thus making it easier to organize the study of myths.
3. It will be possible to compare the myths of one culture with those of another.
4. As a result of this comparison, it will be easier to appreciate the development of a myth prior to its literary presentation.

Structuralism need not be—indeed, cannot be—applied to all classical mythology, nor need one be enslaved to either Lévi-Strauss or the more rigid but simpler structure of Propp's thirty-one functions; it basically provides a means toward establishing a rational system for understanding and organizing the study of mythology.

Walter Burkert   Walter Burkert has persuasively attempted a synthesis of structural theories with the more traditional approaches to classical mythology.[29] In defining a theory of myth he developed four theses, which are in part based upon structural theories and in part meet the objection that these theories are not adequate for many Greek myths as they have come down to us after a long period of development. According to Burkert, classical myths have a "historical dimension" with "successive layers" of development, during which the original tale has been modified to fit the cultural or other circumstances of the time of its retelling. This will be less true of a tale that has sacred status, for it will have been "crystallized" in a sacred document—for example, the myth of Demeter in the *Homeric Hymn to Demeter.* In contrast, many Greek myths vary with the time of telling and the teller—for example, the myths of Orestes or Meleager appear differently in Homer from their treatment in fifth-century Athens or in Augustan Rome.

Burkert therefore believes that the structure of traditional tales cannot be discovered without taking into account cultural and historical dimensions. With regard to the former, the structure of a tale is shaped by its human creators and by the needs of the culture within which it is developed. Therefore the structure of a tale is "ineradicably anthropomorphic" and fits the needs and expectations of both the teller and the audience. (Indeed, as Burkert points out, this is why good tales are so easy to remember: "There are not terribly many items to memorize, since the structure has largely been known in advance.") Further—and here we approach the historical dimension—a tale has a use to which it is put, or, expressed in another way, "Myth is traditional tale applied."

This refinement of the structural theory allows for the development of a tale to meet the needs or expectations of the group for whom it is told—family, city, state, or culture group, for example. A myth, in these terms, has reference to "something of collective importance." This further definition meets a fundamental objection to many earlier "unitary" theories of myth. If myth is a sacred tale or a tale about the gods, how do we include, for example, the myths of Oedipus or Achilles? Similar objections can easily be made to other theories that we have been describing. The notions of "myth applied" and "collective importance" avoid the objection of rigid exclusivity, while they allow for the successive stages in the historical development of a myth without the Procrustean mental gymnastics demanded by the theories of Lévi-Strauss.

Here, then, are the four theses of Burkert's modified synthesis of the structural and historical approaches:

1. Myth belongs to the more general class of traditional tale.
2. The identity of a traditional tale is to be found in a structure of sense within the tale itself.
3. Tale structures, as sequences of motifemes, are founded on basic biological or cultural programs of actions.
4. Myth is a traditional tale with secondary, partial reference to something of collective importance.

These theses form a good working basis upon which to approach the interpretation of myth. They make use of the significant discoveries of anthropologists and psychologists, while they allow flexibility in exploring the structure of classical myths. Finally, they take account of the historical development of myths and of the culture within which they were told. It will be useful to refer to these theses when studying individual traditional tales.

Feminism and Mythology

Feminist critical theories have led to many new, and often controversial, interpretations of classical myths. They approach mythology from the perspective of women and interpret the myths by focusing especially on the psychological and social situation of their female characters. These theories share with structuralism a focus on the binary nature of human society and the human mind, especially in the opposition (or complementary relationship) of female and male. Social criticism of the male-centered world of Greek mythology goes back at least to Sappho, who, in her *Hymn to Aphrodite,* used the image of Homeric warfare to describe her emotions, and in her poem on Anaktoria contrasts what she loves, another human being, with what conventional men love, the panoply of war.[30] In 1942 the French philosopher Simone Weil took basically the same approach in her essay on the *Iliad* (translated by Mary McCarthy as *The Iliad, or the Poem of Force*), focusing on the issues of violence, power, and domination, fundamental to Homeric mythology.

More recently feminist scholars have used the critical methods of narratology and deconstruction to interpret the traditional tales, associating them with the theories of psychologists (especially Freud) and comparative anthropologists. Many feminist interpretations have compelled readers to think critically about the social and psychological assumptions that underly approaches to mythology, and they have led to original and stimulating interpretations of many myths, especially where the central figure is female. The work of feminist scholars has led to greater flexibility and often (although by no means always) greater sensitivity in modern readings of classical literature. Nevertheless, some scholars (among them leading classical feminists) have warned against the tendency to interpret classical myths in the light of contemporary social and political concerns. For example, Marilyn Katz criticizes those who object on moral grounds to the apparent infidelity of Odysseus to his wife, saying that "such an interpretation . . . imports into the poem our own squeamish disapproval of the double standard."[31]

The Comparative Study of Classical Mythology

We have established that, over the past few decades, comparative mythology has been used extensively for the understanding of the myths of any one culture. Greek mythology, largely because of the genius of the authors who told the stories in their literary form, has too often in the past been considered as something so unusual that it can be set apart from other mythologies. It is true that the sophisticated versions of Greek and Roman authors are clearly to be differentiated from many preliterate tales gathered from other cultures by anthropologists. Yet the work of the stucturalists has shown that classical myths share fundamental characteristics with traditional tales everywhere. It is important to be aware of this fact and to realize that there are many successive layers in the development of Greek and Roman myths before their crystallization in literary form. Often, and especially in structural interpretations, the earlier stages of a myth are discovered to have been rooted in another culture, or at least show the influence of other mythologies.

For example, there are obvious parallels between the Greek creation and succession myths and myths of Near Eastern cultures.[32] The myth of the castration of Uranus by Cronus is better understood if we compare it with the Hittite myth of Kumarbi, in which Anu, the sky-god, is castrated by Kumarbi, who rises against him. Kumarbi swallows Anu's genitals, spits them out when he cannot contain them, and is finally replaced by the storm-god. The structure of this tale is paralleled by the myth of Uranus, castrated by Cronus, who, in his turn, cannot hold what he has swallowed (in this case, his children) and is eventually replaced by the sky-god Zeus. Some details in the two tales, of course, are different, but the basic functions (kingship, revolt, castration, swallowing, regurgitation, replacement by a new king) are the same and occur in the same sequence. Thus the basic structure is the same and a better understanding of the origin and purpose of the Greek myth, as narrated by Hesiod, is achieved by comparison with the older myth from Near Eastern culture. Whether direct influence can be proved (and scholars do not agree on this point), the structural similarities do at least show how Greek myths are to be studied in conjunction with those of other cultures.

As another example we may take the work of Joseph Campbell. He has done much to popularize the study of comparative mythology, and for this we are grateful, even though we wish that, in his popularizations at least, he paid more serious attention to the Greeks and the Romans. Perhaps he will appeal most of all to those who seek to recognize the kindred spiritual values that may be found through a comparison of the myths and legends of various peoples over the centuries.[33]

Some Conclusions and a Definition of Classical Myth

Our survey of different interpetations of myth is intended to show that there is something of value to be found in a study of various approaches; and we have included only a selection from a wide range of possibilities. There are others that might be explored; belief in the importance and validity of diverse interpretations naturally varies from reader to reader. About this conclusion, however, we are convinced: it is impossible to develop any one theory that will be meaningfully applicable to *all* myths; there is no identifiable Platonic Idea or Form of a myth, embodying characteristics copied or reflected in the mythologies of the world. The many interpretations of the origin and nature of myths are primarily valuable for highlighting the fact that myths embrace different kinds of stories which may be classified in numerous different ways.

We realize fully the necessity for the study of comparative mythology and appreciate its many attractive rewards; but we are also wary of its dangers: oversimplification, distortion, and the reduction of an intricate masterpiece to a chart of leading motifs. Greek and Roman mythology is unique, but not so unique that we can set it apart from other mythologies. In other words, it will illuminate other mythologies drawn from primitive and preliterate societies, just as they will help us understand the origin, development, and meaning of classical literature. We must, however, be aware of the gulf that separates the primitive legends gathered by anthropologists from the sophisticated mythological thinking that evolved among the Greeks and Romans. Even our earliest literary sources (Homer, Hesiod, and the lyric poets) provide artistic presentations of intellectual, emotional, and spiritual values and concepts in influential works of the highest order. Greek and Roman mythology shares similar characteristics with the great literatures of the world, which have evolved mythologies of their own, whether or not they have borrowed thematic material from the ancients. Classical mythology has at least as much (if not more) in common with English and American literature (not to mention French and German, among others)[34] as it does with preliterate comparisons and archaic artifacts.

Since the goal of this book is the transmission of the myths themselves as recounted in the Greek and Roman periods, literary myth is inevitably our primary concern. Many of the important myths exist in multiple versions of varying quality, but usually one ancient treatment has been most influential in establishing the prototype or archetype for all subsequent art and thought. Whatever other versions of the Oedipus story exist,[35] the dramatic treatment by Sophocles has established and imposed the mythical pattern for all time—he is the poet who forces us to see and feel the universal implications. Although his art is self-conscious, literary, and aesthetic, nevertheless the myth *is* the play. We cannot provide complete texts of Greek tragedy, but insofar as possible the original text of the dominant version of a myth will be translated in this book. We believe that a faithful translation or even a paraphrase of the sources is far better than a bald and eclectic retelling in which the essential spirit and artistic subtlety of literary myth is obliterated completely for the sake of scientific analysis. It is a commonplace to say that myths are by nature good stories, but some are more childish, confused, and repetitious than others; the really good ones are usually good because they have survived in a form molded by an artist.

There are two indisputable characteristics of the literary myths and legends of Greek and Roman mythology: their artistic merit and the inspiration they have afforded to others. We have, for example, from the ancient world touching renditions of the story of Orpheus and Eurydice. The number of retellings of their tale in Western civilization has been legion (in every possible medium), and it seems as though the variations will go on forever.[36] Thus we conclude with a short definition that concentrates upon the gratifying tenacity of the classical tradition, inextricably woven into the very fabric of our culture:

A **classical myth** *is a story that, through its classical form, has attained a kind of immortality because its inherent archetypal beauty, profundity, and power have inspired rewarding renewal and transformation by successive generations.*

THE HISTORICAL BACKGROUND

As we have already seen, the historical dimension is a prominent feature of Greek legend or saga, and an outline of the historical background will be helpful for a fuller understanding.[37] Our knowledge of the early history of Greece and the Aegean is constantly changing, thanks to the fresh discoveries of archaeologists and other scholars. Consequently our view of Greek religion and mythology has been (and will continue to be) modified by new knowledge, not least in the area of legends that cluster around the sagas of Mycenae and Troy.

The foundations of modern archaeological work in the Mycenaean world were laid by the brilliant pioneer, Heinrich Schliemann, who, because of his love of Greek antiquity in general and Homer in particular, was inspired by a faith in the ultimate historical authenticity of Greek legend.[38] In the 1870s he went to Troy, Mycenae, and Tiryns and confirmed the reality of the wealth, grandeur, and power of the cities, kings, and heroes of Minoan-Mycenaean saga. Sir Arthur Evans followed at the turn of the century, unearthing the splendid and grand complex of the Palace of Minos at Cnossus in Crete. A whole new world had been opened up.

For a long time, it was believed that Greece had not been inhabited before the Neolithic period. But we know today that the country was settled in Paleolithic times (before 70,000 B.C.). With the present state of excavation and study, our knowledge of this early period remains tentative. Evidence for the Neolithic period (ca. 6000–3000 B.C.) is more abundant. Archaeology has revealed settled agricultural communities (i.e., outlines of houses, pottery, tools, and graves). It is conjectured that the Neolithic inhabitants came from the east and the north. For our purposes it is noteworthy that evidence of religion seems apparent; particularly significant are little female idols, their sexuality exaggerated by the depiction of swollen belly, buttocks, and full breasts. Male figures also are found (some ithyphallic), although in far fewer numbers. Was a fertility mother-goddess worshiped in this early period, and perhaps already associated with a male consort? The interpretation of prehistoric icons for an understanding of the worship of gods and goddesses in patriarchal and matriarchal societies has become a subject of intense scrutiny.[39]

The Bronze Age

The Stone Age gave way to the Bronze Age in Greece, Crete, and the Islands with an invasion from the east (the movement was from Asia Minor across the Aegean to the southern Peloponnesus up into Greece). This people was responsible for the building of the great Minoan civilization of Crete. The Bronze Age is divided into three major periods: Early, Middle, and Late; these periods are also labeled according to geographical areas. Thus the Bronze Age in Crete is designated as Minoan (from the tradition of King Minos); for the Islands the term is Cycladic (the Cyclades are the islands that encircle Delos); in Greece it is called Helladic (Hellas is the Greek name for the country). The Late Bronze Age on the mainland (i.e., the late Helladic period) is also identified as the Mycenaean Age, from the citadel of power (Mycenae) dominant in Greece during this period. The chronology with the terminology is as follows:[40]

3000–2000 B.C.	Early Bronze Age	Early Minoan Early Cycladic Early Helladic
2000–1600 B.C.	Middle Bronze Age	Middle Minoan Middle Cycladic Middle Helladic
1600–1100 B.C.	Late Bronze Age	Late Minoan Late Cycladic Late Helladic; also the Mycenaean Age

Minoan Civilization

The Minoan civilization grew to maturity in the Middle Bronze Age and reached its pinnacle of greatness in the following period (1600–1400 B.C.). The palace at Cnossus was particularly splendid (although another at Phaestus is impressive, too). The excavations confirm the tradition (as interpreted later, for example, by Thucydides) that Cnossus was the capital of a great thalassocracy and that Minoan power extended over the islands of the Aegean and even the mainland of Greece. Tribute was in all probability exacted from her allies or her subjects; the complex plan of the palace at Cnossus suggests the historical basis for the legend of the Minotaur. The fact that Cnossus had no walls (unlike the fortress citadels of Hellas) suggests that her security depended upon ships and the sea. The sophistication of Minoan art and architecture implies much about the civilization, but more particularly the painting and the artifacts reflect a highly developed sense of religion, for example, the importance of the bull in ritual, the dominant role of a snake-goddess, the sacred significance of the double axe.[41] It seems fairly clear that the worship of a fertility mother-goddess was basic in Minoan religion.

About 1400 B.C., Cretan power was eclipsed (archaeology reveals signs of fire and destruction) and the focus of civilization shifted to the mainland of Greece. Did the Greeks overthrow Cnossus and usurp the Minoan thalassocracy? Was an earthquake solely responsible for the eclipse of this island power? Theories abound, but there is no general agreement except insofar as scholars may be divided into two groups: those who stress the dominant influence of the Minoans on the mainland civilization and refuse to attribute the downfall of Crete to a Mycenaean invasion as against those who argue for Mycenaean (Greek) encroachment and eventual control of the island. We incline to the latter view.

Excavations on the island of Thera (modern Santorini, about seventy miles northwest of Crete) have unearthed exciting new finds, among them interesting frescoes, and have indicated clear signs of destruction by earthquakes in the Minoan-Mycenaean period which may be dated ca. 1600 B.C.; it is conjectured that these same earthquakes were responsible for the disintegration of power on the island of Crete. In particular the discovery in the 1960s of a palace at Zakros in eastern Crete has indicated that perhaps it was destroyed at the same time as the disturbances occurred on Thera. Thus archaeologists have turned to the mythical tale about Atlantis (recorded by Plato in his *Critias* and *Timaeus* on the authority of Egyptian priests), a great island culture that vanished into the sea; conflict between Atlantis and Attica for control of the sea had broken out when earthquake and flood caused the astonishing disappearance of Atlantis. Does this Platonic legend reflect in any way the actual destruction of Thera, or of Crete itself, and the subsequent encroachment of Mycenaean power?[42] Again no certain answer is forthcoming.

The Mycenaean Age

On the mainland of Greece, the Middle Bronze Age (or Middle Helladic period) was ushered in by an invasion from the north and possibly the east. These Nordic Indo-Europeans are the first Greeks (i.e., they spoke the Greek language) to enter the peninsula; gradually they created a civilization (usually called Mycenaean) that reached its culmination in the Late Helladic period (1600–1100 B.C.).[43] They learned much from the Minoans; their painting, palaces, and pottery are strikingly similar, but there are some significant differences. Schliemann was the first to excavate at Mycenae, the kingdom of the mythological family of Atreus, corroborating the appropriateness of the Homeric epithet, "rich in gold." Cyclopean walls typically surround the complex palace of the king and the homes of the aristocracy; the entrance to Mycenae was particularly splendid, graced as it was with a relief on which two lions or lionesses flanking a column were sculptured—presumably the relief was of political and religious significance, perhaps the emblem of the royal family. A circle of shaft graves within the citadel, set off in ritual splendor, has revealed a hoard of treasures—masks of beaten gold placed on the faces of the corpses, exquisite jewelry, and beautifully decorated weapons. Larger (and later) tholos tombs (also typical of Mycenaean civilization elsewhere and confirming a belief in the afterlife) built like huge beehives into the sides of hills below the palace complex were dramatically and erroneously identified by Schliemann as both the treasury of Atreus and the tomb of Clytemnestra.

Schliemann's discoveries established the certainty of a link between the traditional tales of Greek saga, especially those contained in the Homeric poems, and the actual places named in the poems, for example Mycenae. Archaeologists have proved that these places were prosperous centers during the Mycenaean Age, and the distinction must be appreciated between the legends of heroes associated with Mycenaean palaces (Agamemnon at Mycenae, Heracles at Tiryns, Oedipus at Thebes, and Nestor at Pylos, to name four such heroes) and the actual world revealed by archaeologists. Carl Blegen's discovery of the Mycenaean palace at Pylos settled once and for all the controversy over its site and established the plan of the palace, with its well-preserved megaron (i.e., central room with an open hearth); and his conclusion seems inevitable that this is the palace of the family of Nestor. It is difficult to imagine to what families, other than those of the legends, these citadels could have belonged. Yet, of course, we must be wary of a naive belief in the details of the poetic tradition.

In religion there were important differences between the Minoans and the Mycenaeans. The northern invaders of 2000 B.C. worshiped in particular a sky-god, Zeus; and in general their religious attitudes were not unlike those mirrored in the world of Homer's celestial Olympians. How different from the spiritual atmosphere of the Minoans dominated by the conception of a fertility mother-goddess, with or without a male counterpart! At any rate, Greek mythology seems to accommodate and reflect the union of these two cultures, as we shall see in Chapter 1.

Linear B

Clay tablets inscribed with writing have been found on the mainland (an especially rich hoard was found at Pylos). These tablets were baked hard in the conflagrations that destroyed these Mycenaean fortresses when they fell before the onslaught of the invaders.[44] The key to the decipherment of the Linear B tablets was discovered in 1952 by Michael Ventris, who was killed in 1956 in an accident. His friend and collaborator, John Chadwick, has written for the layperson a fascinating account of their painstaking and exciting work on the tablets, one of the most significant scholastic and linguistic detective stories of this or any other age.[45] Important for our study is the finding of the names of familiar deities of classical Greece, Zeus and Hera (listed as a pair), Poseidon, Hermes, Athena, Artemis, Eileithyia (Eleuthia in the tablets), and the name Dionysus (a startling discovery, since it has usually been assumed that the worship of Dionysus did not come to Greece until later); also identified is an early form of the word *paean,* which was later applied as a title or epithet for Apollo. Similarly, Enualios appears, a name identified in classical times with Ares. The word *potnia* (mistress or lady) is frequent, and thus support is added to the theory that the Mycenaeans as well as the Minoans worshiped a goddess of the mother-fertility type and that the concept of chthonian deities that this implies was merged with that of the Olympians. The gods are listed in the tablets as the recipients of offerings (i.e., of animals, olive oil, wheat, wine, and honey), which suggests ritual sacrifice and ceremonial banquets.

Schliemann and Wilhelm Dörpfeld (his contemporary and successor) were pioneers at Troy. Carl Blegen was the next archaeologist to provide a significant re-examination of the site; since Blegen's time, excavations have been renewed in the 1990s by a team of archaeologists, led by Manfred Korfmann from the University of Tübingen and C. Brian Rose, like Blegen before him, from the University of Cincinnati.[46]

Troy 1 was settled in the Early Bronze Age (ca. 3500 B.C.), and there continued to be successive settlements (at least nine) on the site for a long period of history. The Romans restored the city on a large scale in the first century A.D., it was flourishing in the time of Constantine the Great (in the fourth century), and it survived until the late 12th/early 13th century. Of the seven major settlements in the Minoan-Mycenaean period (Troy 1–7) identified by Blegen, Troy 2 is particularly interesting because of treasure Schliemann claimed to have found at that level. A famous picture shows Schliemann's wife Sophia decked out in some of the jewelery from this treasure, which was taken from Turkey to Berlin and then disappeared during World War II; in the 1990s, it was rediscovered in the basement of the Pushkin Museum in Moscow.

The collapse of Troy 6 is dated ca. 1300–1250 B.C. by the new excavators. They are not yet able to determine whether its fall was caused by earthquake or invasion or a combination of both. The fortification walls of Troy 6 are particularly impressive, and Dörpfeld identified this settlement as the great city of King Priam. According to Blegen, however, Troy 6 was destroyed by an earthquake, and it is the next city, Troy 7 (Troy 7a to be exact), that was Priam's city, since for Blegen the evidence seemed to provide signs of a siege and fire, indicative of the Trojan War; for him, the fall of Troy 7a (not Troy 6) belonged ca. 1250 B.C.[47]

And so, sad to say, absolute archaeological and historical proof for the identification of Priam's city and the reality of the Trojan War has yet to be found and, indeed, may never be found. Nevertheless the temptation is overwhelming to conjecture that the excavated Troy (whether Troy 6 or Troy 7) must be the city of Priam that fell to the Greeks; as for chronology, the date of the conflict was ca. 1250–1200 B.C., not too far from the traditionally accepted date of 1184 B.C.

Among the exciting finds made by the recent excavators are signs of a clay wall (about 14 feet thick) more than 1,300 feet beyond the previously known citadel with its inner city and walls, as well as traces of buildings indicating that a Bronze Age settlement existed between the central fortress and this outer wall. But investigation is very preliminary and has yet to be substantiated; if it is, we shall have greater proof that Troy 6 could certainly have been of a magnitude and significance worthy of the power of Priam celebrated in the heroic tradition. From the conjecture that the Trojans probably charged tolls for those traveling through the Dardanelles or Hellespont, serious economic causes may be easily conjured up to explain a conflict between the Mycenaeans and the Trojans.

In the epic cycle of saga, the great leaders of the Mycenaean kingdoms banded together to sail against Troy and, even though the historical facts remain a matter of conjecture, the romance of this poetic legend has a reality too. Until it is disproven with certainty (an unlikely prospect), we have every right to believe that there once was an Agamemnon and a Clytemnestra, a Hector and an Andromache and an Achilles, who lived and died, no matter how fictitious the details of the story that they inspired; and handsome Paris and beautiful Helen ran away together in the grip of Aphrodite, providing the inciting cause for a great war that has become immortal. The final results of the reexcavation of Troy will, we fervently hope, provide some secure answers at last.

End of the Mycenaean Age

For Blegen, the destruction of Troy 7b (ca. 1100 B.C.) marked the troublesome period of transition from the Late Bronze Age to the Age of Iron. The Greeks, we are to assume, returned from Troy in triumph. Yet not long after their return, the Mycenaean Age in Greece was brought to a violent end, perhaps precipitated by internal dissension. The widely held theory that the destruction was entirely the work of Dorians invading from the north and east, has been questioned. Some historians not very convincingly associate the destruction of the Mycenaean kingdoms with the "sea peoples" mentioned in an Egyptian inscription put up by the pharaoh Rameses III in the twelfth century B.C., but there is still no certainty about the details of the end of the Bronze Age in Greece.

Darkness descends upon the history of Greece, a darkness that is only gradually dispelled with the emergence of the two great Homeric epics, the *Iliad* and the *Odyssey,* in the ninth and eighth centuries B.C. The stories of the earlier period were kept alive by oral recitation, transmitted by bards like those described in the epics themselves. "Homer" almost certainly belongs to Asia Minor or one of the islands (e.g., Chios) off the coast. In the cities of this area in this period, we find that monarchy is the prevailing institution; significantly enough, the social and political environment for the bard of this later age is not unlike that of his predecessors in the great days of Mycenae.

Most important for the appreciation of the cumulative nature of the growth of the legends is the realization that there were two major periods of creative impetus, one before the destruction of Mycenaean civilization and one after. The Homeric poems maintain the fiction of the Bronze Age, but they portray far more their own Age of Iron. To mention but one example, archaeology shows us that burial was prevalent in the Mycenaean Age, but in Homer cremation is common. The saga of the Argonauts reflects an interest in the Black Sea that is historical—but was this interest Mycenaean, or do the details belong to the later age of Greek colonization (ca. 800–600 B.C.)? The legend as we have it must be a composite product of both eras. The Theseus story blends in splendid confusion Minoan-Mycenaean elements with facts of the later historical period of monarchy in Athens.

The Homeric poems were eventually set down in writing; this was made possible by the invention of an alphabet. The Greeks borrowed the symbols of the Phoenician script and used them to create a true alphabet, distinguishing by each sign individual vowels and consonants, unlike earlier scripts (such as Linear B) in which syllables are the only linguistic units. This stroke of genius, by the way, is typically Greek in its brilliant and inventive simplicity; surely no one of our countless debts to Greek civilization is more fundamental. Is the invention of the Greek alphabet and the setting down of the Homeric epics coincidental? Presumably the dactylic hexameter of epic poetry cannot be reproduced in the clumsy symbols of Linear B. At any rate, when tradition tells us that the legendary Cadmus of Thebes taught the natives to write, we may wonder whether he is supposed to have instructed them in Mycenaean Linear B or in the later Greek alphabet.

SOURCES FOR CLASSICAL MYTHOLOGY

Traditional tales were handed down orally until they were stabilized in a written form that spread over a wide area. The geography and topography of the Greek world often made communications by land and sea difficult, and these natural tendencies to cultural separatism were enhanced by tribal, ethnic, and linguistic variations. The Greek myths, therefore, varied greatly from place to place, as did the cults of individual gods. With the coming of writing, perhaps in the eighth century, "standard" versions of myths began to be established, but the sophistication of succeeding generations of poets led also to ingenious variations. Even in the central myths of Athenian drama—whose stories were well known to and expected by their audiences—substantial variations are found, as, for example, in the legends of Electra. The problem of variations is especially acute in saga, where differing literary versions and local variations (often based on local pride in the heroic past) make it virtually impossible to identify a "standard" version. This is especially the case with local heroes like Theseus at Athens. Nevertheless, there is a body of recognized principal sources for classical mythology from which major versions may be identified.

Greek Sources

Pride of place goes to Homer (to use the name of the poet to whom the *Iliad* and the *Odyssey* are ascribed), whose poems stabilized the myths of the Olympian gods and exercised an unparalleled influence on all succeeding Greek and Roman writers. The *Iliad* is much more than the story of the wrath of Achilles or the record of an episode in the tenth year of the Trojan War, for it incorporates many myths of the Olympian and Mycenaean heroes, while its picture of the gods has ever since been the foundation of literary and artistic representations of the Olympian pantheon. The poems themselves, which developed over centuries of oral tradition, perhaps took something like their final form in the eighth century, the *Iliad* being somewhat earlier than the *Odyssey*. The written text was probably stabilized at Athens under the tyranny of Pisistratus during the second half of the sixth century. Our debt to Homeric mythology and legend will be apparent in this book.

Important also for the Olympian gods and the organization of Olympian theology and theogony are the works of Hesiod, the Boeotian poet of the late eighth century, perhaps as late as 700. His *Theogony* is our most important source for the relationship of Zeus and the Olympians to their predecessors, the Titans, and other early divinities; it also records how Zeus became supreme and organized the Olympian pantheon. Hesiod's *Works and Days* also contains important mythology. Thus substantial portions of these works appear in translation or paraphrase in the earlier chapters.

The thirty-three *Homeric Hymns* are a body of poems composed in honor of Olympian deities, most of which embody at least one myth of the god or goddess. Four (those to Demeter, Apollo, Hermes, and Aphrodite) are several hundred lines long and are the most significant sources for those gods' myths; others are very short indeed and appear to be preludes for longer compositions that have not survived. Because of their importance we have have translated all these hymns complete.[48] The *Homeric Hymns* were composed at widely different times, some perhaps as early as the eighth or seventh century, some (for example, the *Hymn to Ares*) as late as the fourth century or Hellenistic times.

Another group of archaic poets whose work is an important source for mythology are the lyric poets, who flourished, especially in the islands of the Aegean Sea, during the seventh and sixth centuries. The lyric tradition was continued in the complex victory *Odes* of the Theban poet Pindar during the first half of the fifth century and in the dithyrambs of his rival and contemporary, Bacchylides of Cos. The lyric choruses of the Athenian tragedians also enshrine important versions of myths.

In the fifth century, the flourishing of the Greek city-states led to the creation of great literature and art, nowhere more impressively than at Athens. Here the three great writers of tragedy, Aeschylus (who died in 456), Sophocles, and Euripides (both of whom died in 406), established the authoritative versions of many myths and sagas: a few examples are the *Oresteia* of Aeschylus for the saga of the House of Atreus; the Theban plays of Sophocles for the saga of the family of Laius; and the *Bacchae* of Euripides (translated in large part in Chapter 11) for the myths of Dionysus.

After the fifth century, the creative presentation of myths in Greek literature gave way to more contrived versions, many of which were composed by the Alexandrian poets in the third century. Neither the *Hymns* of Callimachus nor the hymn to Zeus of Cleanthes has great value as a source for myth, but the epic, *Argonautica,* of Apollonius of Rhodes (ca. 260) is the single most important source for the saga of the Argonauts. Other Alexandrian versions of the classical myths are discussed below in Chapter 25.

The principal Greek prose sources are the historians and the mythographers. Of the former, Herodotus is preeminent, although some myths are recorded in Thucydides (last quarter of the fifth century). Herodotus (born ca. 485) traveled widely, both within the Greek world and to Persia and Egypt, and he recorded traditional tales wherever he went. Some of his stories contain profound and universal truths of the sort we would associate with myth as well as history; his account of the meeting between Solon and Croesus, which we have translated in Chapter 4, is a perfect example of the developed "historical myth," giving us insight into Greek interpretations of god and fate that arose out of their factual and mythical storytelling.

The mythographers were late compilers of handbooks of mythology. Of these, the work ascribed to Apollodorus with the title *Biblio-theca,* which is still valuable, perhaps was composed around A.D. 120. The *Periegesis* of Pausanias (ca. A.D. 150) is a description of Greece containing many myths in its accounts of religious sites and their works of art.

The philosophers, most notably Plato (fourth century B.C.), used myth for didactic purposes, and Plato himself developed out of the tradition of religious tales "philosophical myth" as a distinct literary form. His myth of Er, for example, is a philosophical allegory about the soul and its existence after death. It is important as evidence for beliefs about the Underworld, and its religious origins go back to earlier centuries, in particular to the speculations of Pythagorean and Orphic doctrine. The Roman poet Vergil (identified below), in his depiction of the afterlife, combines more traditional mythology developed out of Homer with mythical speculations about rebirth and reincarnation found in philosophers like Plato. Thus by translating all three authors—Homer, Plato, and Vergil—on the Realm of Hades (Chapter 13) we have a composite and virtually complete summary of the major mythical and religious beliefs about the afterlife evolved by the Greeks and Romans.

One late philosopher who retold archaic myths for both philosophical and satirical purposes was the Syrian author Lucian (born ca. A.D. 120), who wrote in Greek. His satires, often in dialogue form, present the Olympian gods and the old myths with a good deal of humor. Despite his satirical purpose, his dialogues are still valuable, particularly "The Judgment of Paris," found in Chapter 17.

Roman Sources

The Greek authors are the foundation of our knowledge of classical myth. Nevertheless, the Roman authors were not merely derivative. Vergil (70–19 B.C.) developed the myth of the Trojan hero Aeneas in his epic, the *Aeneid.* In so doing, he preserved the saga of the fall of Troy, a part of the Greek epic cycle now lost to us. He also developed the legend of the Phoenician queen Dido, and told a number of myths and tales associated with particular Italian localities, such as the story of Hercules at Rome. Several passages from Vergil appear in Chapter 24 as well as Chapter 13.

Vergil's younger contemporary Ovid (43 B.C.–A.D. 17) is the single most important source for classical mythology after Homer, and his poem *Metamorphoses* (completed ca. A.D. 8) has probably been more influential even than Homer as a source for representations of the classical myths in literature and art. A kind of epic, the poem includes more than two hundred legends arranged in a loose chronological framework from the Creation down to Ovid's own time. Many of the most familiar stories come from Ovid, for example, the stories of Echo and Narcissus, Apollo and Daphne, and Pyramus and Thisbe. Ovid's poem on the Roman religious calendar, *Fasti*, is a unique source for the myths of the Roman gods, although he completed only the first six months of the religious year. A great deal from Ovid, in direct translation or in paraphrase, is an inevitable inclusion.

The historian Livy (59 B.C.–A.D. 17) recorded the foundation myths of Rome in the first book of his *Ab Urbe Condita*. He is the source for many of the legends from Roman history that are closer to myth than history. Other Roman writers had antiquarian interests, but none wrote continuous accounts comparable with Livy's.

Later in the first century A.D., there was a literary renaissance during the reign of the emperor Nero (54–68). The tragedies of Seneca present important versions of several myths, most notably those of Phaedra and Hippolytus, Medea, and Thyestes, the last named being the only surviving full-length version of the myth.

In the generation following Seneca, there was a revival of epic. The *Argonautica* of Valerius Flaccus (ca. 80) and the *Thebaid* of Statius (d. 96) are important versions of their respective sagas. After this time, there are few original works worth notice. One exception is a novel by the African rhetorician Apuleius (b. 123) formally titled *Metamorphoses* but better known to us as *The Golden Ass*. This is our source for the tale of Cupid and Psyche, while its final book is invaluable for its account of the mysteries of Isis.

Interest in mythology continued to be shown in a number of handbooks of uncertain date. We have mentioned the *Bibliotheca* of Apollodorus in Greek; in Latin, compendia were written by Hyginus (perhaps in the mid-second century) and Fulgentius (perhaps an African bishop of the sixth century). This tradition was revived during the Renaissance, especially in Italy, and we discuss some of the important handbooks of mythology in Chapter 25.

The Eclectic Variety of the Sources

It is readily apparent that this literary heritage offers infinite variety. The religious tales of Hesiod contrast with the sophisticated stories of Ovid. The historical legend of Herodotus differs in character from the legendary history of Homer. The philosophical myth of Plato and the romantic storytelling of Apuleius reveal contrasting spiritual hues. The dramatic environments of Aeschylus and Seneca are worlds apart. Yet *all* these authors from different periods and with diverse art provide the rich, eclectic heritage from which a survey of Graeco-Roman mythology must be drawn.

Translations

All the Greek and Roman works named here (except for the late Latin handbooks of mythology) are available in inexpensive translations. The Loeb series includes texts with facing translations, the latter of widely varying quality and readability. The translations published by Penguin and by the University of Chicago Press are generally both reliable and in some cases distinguished. But there is considerable choice, and some plays are available individually. A particularly good buy is *Ten Plays by Euripides,* in very readable translations by Moses Hadas and John McLean—all the plays of Euripides that one usually reads and all in one volume![49]

SELECT BIBLIOGRAPHY

The modern bibliography is endless, and we offer only a few of the more helpful works. Bibliographical information is also given in the footnotes throughout and at the end of Chapters 14, 25, and 26. Handbooks and surveys are listed on p. 649.

Bibliography and Teaching

O'Connor, J. F., and Rowland, R. J. *Teaching Classical Mythology,* Education Papers 5. New York, American Philological Association, 1987. An extremely helpful collection of opinions about content and method with significant, updated bibliography.

Peradotto, John. *Classical Mythology: An Annotated Bibliographical Survey.* Urbana: American Philological Association, 1973. An invaluable and inexpensive guide in which the subject is neatly categorized and books are evaluated; a good starting point.

Interpretation, Analysis, and Comparative Studies

Bremmer, J., ed. *Interpretations of Greek Mythology.* New Jersey: Barnes & Noble, 1986. A collection of essays.

Burkert, Walter. *Structure and History in Greek Mythology and Ritual.* Berkeley: University of California Press, 1979; paperback, 1982. By far the best explanation of the significance of structural theories.

Detienne, Marcel. *The Creation of Mythology.* Chicago: University of Chicago Press, 1986.

Edmunds, Lowell, ed. *Approaches to Greek Myth.* Baltimore: Johns Hopkins University Press, 1989. A collection of essays.

Fontenrose, Joseph. *The Ritual Theory of Myth.* Berkeley: University of California Press, 1971.

Frazer, James G. *The New Golden Bough, a New Abridgement of the Classic Work.* Edited by Theodor H. Gaster. New York: Criterion Books, 1959; Mentor Books, 1964.

Kirk, G. S. *Myth: Its Meaning and Function in Ancient and Other Cultures.* Berkeley: University of California Press, 1970. Valuable for its critical views of comparative studies.

————. *The Nature of Greek Myths.* Baltimore: Penguin Books, 1974. Useful for its treatment of different approaches to myth.

Leach, E. *Claude Lévi-Strauss.* New York: Viking Press, 1970. A good exposition of Lévi-Strauss; in the chapter "The Structure of Myth," Leach offers structural analysis of several Greek myths.

Lévi-Strauss, Claude. *The Savage Mind.* Chicago: University of Chicago Press, 1966 [1962].

————. *The Raw and the Cooked.* Translated by J. and D. Weightman. New York: Harper & Row, 1969. Volume 1 of the four volumes of *Mythologiques;* its "Overture" is the best introduction to Lévi Strauss.

Propp, Vladimir. *Morphology of the Folktale.* 2d ed. Translated by Lawrence Scott. Austin: University of Texas Press, 1968 [1928]. The pioneer work in the structural theory of myth.

Puhvel, Jaan. *Comparative Mythology.* Baltimore: Johns Hopkins University Press, 1987. A study of the prehistoric origins of mythical patterns in India, Iran, Greece, Rome, and elsewhere.

Sebeok, T. A., ed. *Myth: A Symposium.* Bloomington: Indiana University Press, 1971. A collection of essays on the major approaches to the interpretation of myth.

Thompson, Stith. *Motif-index of Folk-literature.* 6 vols. Bloomington: Indiana University Press, 1966. The basic reference book for folktale motifs.

Vernant, J.-P. *Myth and Society in Ancient Greece.* Translated by J. Lloyd. New York: Zone Books, 1990 [1974].

Myth, Religion, and the Occult

Burkert, Walter. *Greek Religion.* Cambridge: Harvard University Press, 1985 [1977].

————. *Homo Necans, The Anthropology of Ancient Greek Sacrificial Ritual and Myth.* Berkeley: University of California Press, 1983 [1972]. Chapters deal with "Sacrifice, Hunting, and Funerary Rituals"; "Werewolves around the Tripod Kettle"; "Dissolution and New Year's Festival"; "Anthesteria" (festival of Dionysus); and "Eleusis."

Detienne, Marcel, and Vernant, Jean-Pierrre. *The Cuisine of Sacrifice among the Greeks.* Chicago: University of Chicago Press, 1989. Essays on blood sacrifice.

Dodds, E. R. *The Greeks and the Irrational.* Berkeley: University of California Press, 1951.

Dowden, Ken. *Death and the Maiden: Girls' Initiation Rites in Greek Mythology.* New York: Routledge, 1989.

Ferguson, John. *Among the Gods: An Archaeological Exploration of Greek Religion.* New York: Routledge, 1990.

Guthrie, W. K. C. *The Greeks and Their Gods.* Boston: Beacon Press, 1955. The best introductory survey of Greek religion.

James, E. O. *Seasonal Feasts and Festivals.* New York: Barnes & Noble, 1961.

Kerenyi, C. *The Gods of the Greeks.* New York: Grove Press, 1960.

Luck, Georg, ed. *Arcana Mundi: Magic and the Occult in the Greek and Roman Worlds.* Baltimore: Johns Hopkins University Press, 1985. A collection of ancient texts, translated and annotated.

Malinowski, B. *Magic, Science and Religion.* New York: Doubleday, 1955. Includes "Myth in Primitive Psychology" (1926).

Mikalson, Jon D. *Athenian Popular Religion.* Chapel Hill: University of North Carolina Press, 1983. Subjects include divine intervention and divination, the gods and human justice, the afterlife, piety and impiety.

Nilsson, M. P. *A History of Greek Religion.* 2d ed. New York: Norton, 1963. An excellent, scholarly introduction.

———. *The Mycenaean Origin of Greek Mythology.* New York: Norton, 1963 [1932].

Rice, David G., and Stambaugh, John E. *Sources for the Study of Greek Religion.* Atlanta, Ga.: Scholars Press, 1979. Translations of texts and inscriptions dealing with "The Olympian Gods," "Heroes," "Public Religion," "Private Religion," "Mystery Cults," and "Death and Afterlife."

Rose, H. J. *Religion in Greece and Rome.* New York: Harper & Row, 1959. Originally published as *Ancient Greek Religion* (1946) and *Ancient Roman Religion* (1948).

Myth and Psychology

Bolen, Jean Shinoda. *Goddesses in Everywoman, A New Psychology of Women.* New York: Harper & Row, 1984. A psychologist provides archetypal descriptions of the Greek and Roman goddesses and shows how they provide meaningful patterns for the understanding of the character, behavior, and personality of women today.

———. *Gods in Everyman: A New Psychology of Men's Lives and Loves.* New York: Harper & Row, 1989. A sequel for men.

Eisner, Robert. *The Road to Daulis: Psychoanalysis, Psychology, and Classical Mythology.* New York: Syracuse University Press, 1987. Chapters include "Oedipus and His Kind," "Electra and Other Monsters," and "Apollo and His Boys."

Evans, Richard I. *Dialogue with C. G. Jung.* 2d ed. New York: Praeger, 1981. Basic concepts clearly presented through Jung's own words.

Jung, C. G., et al. *Man and His Symbols.* New York: Dell, 1968. Only the first essay ("Approaching the Unconscious") is by Jung.

Mullahy, Patrick. *Oedipus Myth and Complex, A Review of Psychoanalytic Theory.* New York: Grove Press, 1955. An excellent survey.

Schneiderman, Leo. *The Psychology of Myth, Folklore, and Religion.* Chicago: Nelson-Hall, 1981. Chapters include "The Mystical Quest," "The Cult of Fertility," and "Jason and the Totem."

Woolger, Jennifer Barker, and Woolger, Roger J. *The Goddess Within: A Guide to the Eternal Myths That Shape Women's Lives.* New York: Fawcett Columbine, 1987. The major goddesses considered as types, with a bibliography of novels and plays and a list of movies (on video), identifying characters that embody these types.

Feminism and Mythology

Clark, G. *Women in the Ancient World.* Greece and Rome Surveys 21. New York: Oxford University Press, 1989.

Fantham, E. "Women in Antiquity: a Selective (and Subjective) Survey." *Échos du Monde Classique* 30 (1986): 1–24.

Foley, H. P., ed. *Reflections of Women in Antiquity.* New York: Gordon and Breach, 1981. First published in *Women's Studies* 8, nos. 1–2 (1981).

Lefkowitz, Mary R. *Women in Greek Myth.* Baltimore: Johns Hopkins University Press, 1986.

Pomeroy, Sarah B. *Goddesses, Whores, Wives, and Slaves.* New York: Schocken, 1975. See especially Chapters 2 and 6.

Winkler, John J. *Constraints of Desire, The Anthropology of Sex and Gender in Ancient Greece.* New York: Routledge, 1990. See pp. 129–161 and 232–233 for "Penelope's Cunning and Homer's."

Two scholarly journals, *Arethusa* and *Helios,* are especially receptive to feminist scholarship. *Arethusa* 6 (1973) and 11 (1978) have been mostly reprinted in J. J. Peradotto and J. P. Sullivan, eds., *Women in the Ancient World: The Arethusa Papers* (Albany: State University of New York, 1984). *Helios* 12, no. 2 (1985) contains a debate on "Classical Studies vs. Women's Studies," by Marilyn Skinner, Mary Lefkowitz, and Judith Hallett.

Historical Background

Alsop, Joseph. *From the Silent Earth.* New York: Harper & Row, 1964.

Blegen, Carl W. *Troy and the Trojans.* New York: Praeger, 1963.

Bury, J. B., and Meiggs, R. *A History of Greece.* London: Macmillan, 1975. This revision is the fourth edition of the durable history first published by Bury in 1900.

Cambridge Ancient History. 3d ed. Vols. 1 and 2. Cambridge: Cambridge University Press, 1970–1975. The standard work of reference in English, with chapters by various authorities. These volumes cover the early history of the Aegean world and the Near East and Bronze Age Greece.

Chadwick, John. *The Mycenaean World.* Cambridge and New York: Cambridge University Press, 1976.

Finley, M. I. *Early Greece: The Bronze and Archaic Ages.* Rev. ed. New York: Norton, 1981. A short account on the subject with conclusions that are sometimes controversial.

Mellersh, H. E. *The Destruction of Knossos: The Rise and Fall of Minoan Crete.* New York: Weybright & Talley, 1970.

Vermeule, Emily. *Greece in the Bronze Age.* Chicago: University of Chicago Press, 1964.

Wood, Michael. *In Search of the Trojan War.* New York: Facts on File Publications, 1984. Based on the BBC Television series, this is the best survey available for the general reader.

Iconography and Religion

Dexter, Miriam Robbins. *Whence the Goddesses: A Source Book.* Elmsford, N.Y.: Pergamon Press, 1990. A history of goddesses through a comparison of the iconography with the literary tradition.

Ehrenberg, Margaret. *Women in Prehistory.* Norman: University of Oklahoma Press, 1989. The role of women from the Paleolithic to the Iron Age, with a consideration of matriarchy in Minoan Crete.

Gimbutas, Marija. *Goddesses and Gods of Old Europe, 7000–3500 B.C.: Myths and Cult Images.* New and updated ed. Berkeley: University of California Press, 1982. A study of figurines, which includes analysis of "Mistresses of Waters," "The Great Goddess of Life," "Death and Regeneration," and the "Year God."

———. *The Language of the Goddesses.* Foreword by Joseph Campbell. New York: Harper & Row, 1989. An analysis of the symbols in the archaeological evidence under the major categories of "Life-Giving," "The Renewing and Eternal Earth," "Death and Regeneration," "Energy and Unfolding."

THE MYTHS

OF CREATION:

THE GODS

MYTHS OF CREATION

here were many myths about creation among the Greeks and
Romans, and these myths have many parallels in other mythologies, such as Egyptian, Sumerian, Babylonian, and Hebraic.
Homer (ca. 800 B.C.)[1] has the Titans Oceanus and Tethys (identified
below) responsible for the origin of the gods (*Iliad* 14. 201) and reflects
a primitive belief in the geographical nature of the universe as a flat disc
with hills, touched at its rim by the vast dome of the heavens. The deity
Oceanus is the stream of ocean that encircles the earth (Figure 22.2,
p. 477). But Homer does not by any means provide a complete account
of genesis. Hesiod (ca. 700), as far as we can tell, was the first to give
literary expression to a systematic explanation of how the gods, the
universe, and humankind came into being. At any rate his, the earliest
account to survive, may be considered the classic Greek version. The
genealogical scheme is presented in his *Theogony*, while his *Works
and Days* adds significant details.

Creation According to Hesiod

In the opening of the *Theogony*, Hesiod devotes many lines to the
beauty and power of the Muses, with particular emphasis upon their
ability to inspire the infallible revelation of the poet. This ardent invocation to the Muses is no mere artistic convention but the utterance
of a prophetic visionary.[2] Hesiod's vehement sincerity may be illustrated by these lines from the *Theogony* (22–34):

They, the Muses, once taught Hesiod beautiful song, while he was
shepherding his flocks on holy Mount Helicon; these goddesses of
Olympus, daughters of aegis-bearing Zeus first of all spoke this
word to me, "Oh, you shepherds of the fields, base and lowly

things, little more than bellies, we know how to tell many
falsehoods that seem like truths but we also know, when we so
desire, how to utter the absolute truth."

Thus they spoke, the fluent daughters of great Zeus. Plucking a
branch, to me they gave a staff of laurel, a wondrous thing, and
into me they breathed a divine voice, so that I might celebrate
both the things that are to be and the things that were before; and
they ordered me to honor, in my song, the race of the blessed
gods who exist forever, but always to sing of them themselves, the
Muses, both first and last.

Hesiod's attention to the Muses is steeped in a religious aura of
divinely inspired revelation. As he begins his genesis, Hesiod asks the
Muses, "Tell me how first gods, earth, rivers, the boundless sea . . .
the shining stars, and the wide heavens above came into being." This
is their answer (*Theogony* 116–25):

Verily, very first of all Chaos came into being, but then Gaia wide-
bosomed, secure foundation of all forever, and dark Tartarus in the
depth of the broad land and Eros, the most beautiful of all the
immortal gods, who loosens the limbs and overcomes judgment
and sagacious counsel in the breast of gods and all humans. From
Chaos, Erebus [the gloom of Tartarus] and black Night came into
being; but from Night were born Aether [the right upper
atmosphere] and Day, whom Night bore when she became
pregnant after mingling in love with Erebus.

The Greek word *Chaos* suggests a "yawning void." Exactly what
it means to Hesiod is difficult to establish.[3] His account of creation,
fraught with interpretative problems, begins paratactically, that is,
very first of all Chaos (not a deity particularly, but a beginning or a
first principle, perhaps a void) came into being (or was), but then

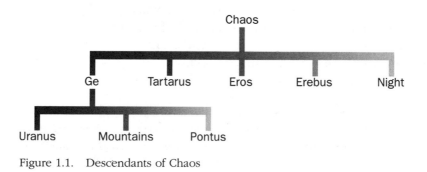

Figure 1.1. Descendants of Chaos

(next) came Gaia (Gaea or Ge, Earth),[4] and the others, all presumably out of Chaos, just as Hesiod actually states that "from Chaos" came Erebus and dark Night. Tartarus is a place deep in the depths of the earth (*Theogony* 713 ff.); Erebus is the gloomy darkness of Tartarus; later it may be equated with Tartarus itself.

The Primacy and Mystery of Eros

Love, typically a potent force in tales of creation and procreation, inevitably appears early in the *Theogony*. Hesiod, as we have just seen, characterizes the most beautiful Eros by one of his many descriptive touches, which strive to lift his didacticism to the realm of poetry. For the Romans, Eros was called Cupid (or Amor).

Another myth of creation is found in *The Birds,* a comedy by the fifth-century playwright Aristophanes. For all its mock heroism and burlesque of religious and philosophical speculation, this account reflects earlier theory and illustrates both the multiplicity of versions and the primacy of Eros. A chorus of birds proves that the birds are much the oldest of all the gods by the following tale (683 ff.):

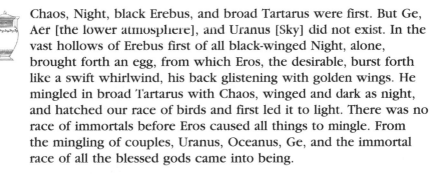

Chaos, Night, black Erebus, and broad Tartarus were first. But Ge, Aer [the lower atmosphere], and Uranus [Sky] did not exist. In the vast hollows of Erebus first of all black-winged Night, alone, brought forth an egg, from which Eros, the desirable, burst forth like a swift whirlwind, his back glistening with golden wings. He mingled in broad Tartarus with Chaos, winged and dark as night, and hatched our race of birds and first led it to light. There was no race of immortals before Eros caused all things to mingle. From the mingling of couples, Uranus, Oceanus, Ge, and the immortal race of all the blessed gods came into being.

The Eros responsible for this fury of procreation may very well be the same Eros who is, in the later tradition, appropriately called Phanes (the one who first shone forth or gave light to creation) and Protogonus (first-born). If so, we have in Aristophanes a parody of a myth that was the basis of a religion ascribed to Orpheus in which the world-egg was a dominant symbol. Orpheus and Orphism are discussed in Chapter 14 and with them other religions similar in nature, designated generically as mystery religions.[5] The link between myth and profound religious thought and experience in the ancient world is a continuing and fascinating theme.

Creation According to Ovid

Ovid, a Roman poet who wrote some seven hundred years after Hesiod, provides another classic account of genesis, different in important respects from that of Hesiod. Ovid is eclectic in his sources, which include not only Hesiod but many other writers, in particular, Empedocles, a fifth-century philosopher, who theorized that four basic elements (earth, air, fire, and water) are the primary materials of the universe.

Ovid's Chaos *(Metamorphoses* 1. 1-75) is not a gaping void but rather a crude and unformed mass of elements in strife from which a god (not named) or some higher nature formed the order of the universe.[6] Ovid's poem *Metamorphoses,* which concentrates upon stories that involve transformations of various sorts, could very well provide a basic text for a survey of mythology. We shall on occasion reproduce Ovid's versions, since it is often his poetic, sensitive, and sophisticated treatment that has dominated subsequent tradition. But we must remember that Ovid is Roman and late and that his mythology is far removed in spirit and belief from that of earlier conceptions. Mythology for him is little more than inspirational, poetic fodder, however successful and attractive the end product may be. Both the poetic and the real worlds of Hesiod and Ovid are poles apart.

The Sacred Marriage of Uranus (Sky) and Gaia (Earth)

But let us return to Hesiod's *Theogony* (126-210). "Gaia (Earth) first brought forth starry Uranus (Sky or Heaven), equal to herself, so that he might surround and cover her completely and be a secure home for the blessed gods forever." Thus Gaia, alone, without the sweet union of love, produced Uranus and also the Mountains and Pontus (the Sea). But afterwards she lay with Uranus and bore the Titans. In addition to the Titans, Uranus and Gaia (Father Sky and Mother Earth) bore Brontes (Thunder), Steropes (Lightning), and Arges (Bright), who were called Cyclopes (Orb-Eyed) because each Cyclops had only

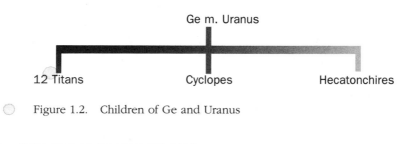

Figure 1.2.   Children of Ge and Uranus

one eye in the middle of his forehead; they in their might and skill forged the thunder and lightning.[7] Uranus and Ge also bore Cottus, Briareus, and Gyes, who were even more overbearing, strong, and monstrous than the Cyclopes; they each had a hundred arms and hands and fifty heads and were named the Hecatonchires (Hundred-Handed or -Armed).

For Hesiod, it appears, the first deity is female, a basic, matriarchical concept of mother earth and her fertility as primary and divine; comparative studies of iconography from primitive societies provide abundant evidence to confirm this archetype of the primacy of the feminine.[8] The male sky-god Uranus (another fundamental conception), produced by Earth herself, emerges, at least in this beginning, as her equal partner; in matriarchal societies, he is reduced to a subordinate; in patriarchal societies he becomes the supreme god.

So it is then that the personification and deification of sky and earth as Uranus and Ge and their physical union represent basic recurring themes in mythology. Uranus is the male principle, a god of the sky; Ge, the female goddess of fertility and the earth. Worship of them may be traced back to very early times; sky and rain, earth and fertility are fundamental concerns and sources of wonder to primitive agricultural peoples. The rain of Uranus might, for example, be imagined as his seed that fertilizes the hungry earth and makes her conceive. Thus develops the archetypal concept of a "sacred" or "holy marriage," a translation of the Greek phrase *hieros gamos.* The sky-god and the earth-goddess appear again and again under various names and guises (for example, Uranus and Ge, Cronus and Rhea, and Zeus and Hera) to enact this holy rite.

The worship of the female earth divinity has many important facets, whether or not she assumes the dominant role in the partnership with her male consort. But whatever her name and however varied her worship, she is significant in all periods, either maintaining her own identity or lurking behind, influencing, and coloring more complex and sophisticated concepts of female deity. Ge, Themis, Cybele, Rhea, Hera, Demeter, and Aphrodite are all, either wholly or in part, divinities of fertility.[9] Certainly the emotional, philosophical, religious, and intellectual range of the worship of the mother-goddess is vast. It may run the gamut from frenzied orgiastic celebrations with the castration of her devoted priests to a sublime belief in spiritual communion and personal redemption; from a blatant emphasis upon the sexual attributes and potency of the female to an idealized vision of love, motherhood, and virgin birth.[10]

The *Homeric Hymn to Earth, Mother of All* (30), in its invocation of Gaia gives us the essentials of her primary archetype:

About Earth, I will sing, all-mother, deep-rooted and eldest, who nourishes all that there is in the world: all that go on the divine land, all that sail on the sea and all that fly—these she nourishes from her bountifulness. From you, reverend lady, mortal humans have abundance in children and in crops, and it is up to you to give them their livelihood or take it away. Rich and fortunate are those whom you honor with your kind support. To them all things are bounteous, their fields are laden with produce, their pastures are covered with herds and flocks, and their homes are filled with plenty. These rule with good laws in cities of beautiful women and much happiness and wealth attend them. Their sons glory in exuberant joy and their daughters, with carefree hearts, play in blossom-laden choruses and dance on the grass over the soft flowers. These are the fortunate whom you honor, holy goddess, bountiful deity.

Hail, mother of the gods, wife of starry Uranus. Kindly grant happy sustenance in return for my song and I will remember both you and another song too.

The Titans and Their Descendants: Ocean, Sun, Moon, and Dawn

The Titans, children of Uranus and Ge, are twelve in number: Oceanus, Coeus, Crius, Hyperion, Iapetus, Theia, Rhea, Themis, Mnemosyne, Phoebe, Tethys, and the last-born, Cronus, "wily and most terrible, who hated his lusty father" (*Theogony* 137–138). They are for the most part deifications of various aspects of nature, and important for their progeny, although a few assume some significance in themselves. In the genealogical labyrinth of mythology, all lineage may be traced back to the Titans and to the other powers originating from Chaos. From these beginnings Hesiod continues to create a universe both real and imagined, physical and spiritual, peopled with gods, demigods, deified or personified abstractions, animals, monsters, and mortals; we cannot list them all here, but we shall select the most important figures. The Titans are best considered in pairs, since there are six males and six females; and the inevitable, incestuous matings of some of these brothers and sisters produce cosmic progeny.

Oceanus and the Oceanids Oceanus and his mate, Tethys, produced numerous children, the Oceanids, three thousand daughters and the same number of sons, spirits of rivers, waters, and springs, many with names and some with mythological personalities.[11] Hesiod provides an impressive list, but he admits (*Theogony* 369–370) that it is diffi-

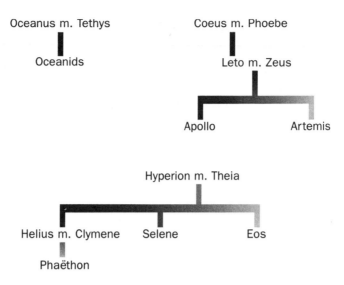

Figure 1.3.   Descendants of Titans. For the children of Cronus and Rhea and other marriages and offspring of Zeus, see Figure 3.1, p. 77.

cult for a mortal to name them all, although people know those belonging to their own area.

Hyperion and Helius, Gods of the Sun   The Titan Hyperion is a god of the sun, more important than his sister and mate, Theia. They are the parents of Helius, Selene, and Eos. Helius, like his father, is a sun-god. Duplication of divinities is common in the early scheme of things; they may exist side by side, or their names and personalities may be confused. Very often the younger generation will dominate the older and usurp its power.

The conventional picture of the sun-god is in harmony with the Homeric conception of geography described at the beginning of this chapter. The sun-god dwells in the East, crosses the dome of the sky with his team of horses, descends in the West into the stream of Oceanus, which encircles the earth, and sails back to the East, chariot and all. The *Homeric Hymn to Helius* (31) offers a glowing picture. Euryphaëssa (the word means "widely shining"), given as the wife of Hyperion and mother of Helius, is probably just another name for Theia.

Now begin to sing, O Muse Calliope, daughter of Zeus, about shining Helius, whom ox-eyed Euryphaëssa bore to the son of Earth and starry Uranus. For Hyperion married glorious Euryphaëssa, his own sister, who bore him beautiful children, rosy-fingered Eos and Selene of the lovely hair and weariless Helius like the deathless ones, who shines for mortals and immortal gods as he drives his horses. The piercing gaze of his eyes flashes out of his golden helmet. Bright beams radiate brilliantly from his temples and the shining hair of his head frames a gracious countenance seen from afar. The exquisite, finely wrought robe that clothes his body shimmers in the blast of the winds. Mighty stallions are under his control. Then he stays his golden-yoked chariot and horses and stops there at the peak of the heavens, until the time when he again miraculously drives them down through the sky to the Ocean.

Hail, lord, kindly grant a happy sustenance. From you I have begun and I shall go on to celebrate the race of mortal men, the demigods, whose achievements the Muses have revealed to mortals.

Phaëthon, Son of Helius   A well-known story concerns Phaëthon (whose name means "shining"), the son of Helius by one of his mistresses, Clymene. According to Ovid's account (*Metamorphoses* 1. 747–779; 2. 1–366), Phaëthon was challenged by the accusation that the Sun was not his real father at all. His mother, Clymene, however, swore to him that he was truly the child of Helius and told him that he should, if he so desired, ask his father, the god himself.

Ovid describes in glowing terms the magnificent palace of the Sun, with its towering columns, gleaming with gold and polished ivory. Phaëthon, awed by the grandeur, is prevented from coming too close to the god because of his radiance; Helius, however, confirms Clymene's account of Phaëthon's parentage, lays aside the rays that shine around his head, and orders his son to approach. He embraces him and promises on an oath sworn by the Styx (dread river of the Underworld) that the boy may have any gift that he likes so that he may dispel his doubts once and for all. Phaëthon quickly and decisively asks that he be allowed to drive his father's chariot for one day.

Helius tries in vain to dissuade Phaëthon and he must abide by his dread oath. He reluctantly leads the youth to his chariot, fashioned exquisitely by Vulcan,[12] of gold, silver, and jewels that reflect the brilliant light of the god. The chariot is yoked; Helius anoints his son's face as protection against the flames, places the rays on his head, and with heavy heart advises him on his course and the management of the horses.

Phaëthon, young and inexperienced, is unable to control the four winged horses who speed from their usual path. The chariot races to the heights of heaven, creating havoc by the intensity of the heat, then hurtles down to earth. Ovid delights in his description of the destruction; among the many transformations that result because of the heat, the Ethiopians at this time acquired their dark skins and Libya became a desert. Earth herself is ablaze and unable to endure her fiery anguish any longer.

Jupiter in answer to Earth's prayer hurls his thunder and lightning and shatters the car, dashing Phaëthon to his death. The river Eridanus receives and bathes him, and nymphs bury him with the following inscription upon his tomb: "Here is buried Phaëthon, charioteer of his father's car; he could not control it, yet he died after daring great deeds."[13]

Selene, Goddess of the Moon   Selene, daughter of Hyperion and Theia, is a goddess of the moon. Like her brother Helius, she drives a chariot, although hers usually has only two horses. The *Homeric Hymn to Selene* (32) presents a picture.

Tell in song about the moon in her long-winged flight, Muses, skilled in song, sweet-voiced daughters of Zeus, the son of Cronus. The heavenly gleam from her immortal head radiates onto earth. The vast beauty of the cosmos emerges under her shining radiance. The air, unlit before, glistens and the rays from her golden crown offer illumination whenever divine Selene, having bathed her beautiful skin, put on her far-glistening raiment, and yoked the powerful necks of her shining team, drives forward her beautifully maned horses at full speed in the evening; in mid-month brightest are her beams as she increases and her great orbit is full. From the heavens she is fixed as a sure sign for mortals.

Once Zeus, the son of Cronus, joined in loving union with her; she became pregnant and bore a daughter, Pandia, who had exceptional loveliness among the immortal gods.

Hail, kind queen with beautiful hair, white-armed goddess, divine Selene. From you I have begun and I shall go on to sing of mortal demigods whose achievements minstrels, servants of the Muses, celebrate in songs from loving lips.

Selene and Endymion   Only one famous myth is linked with Selene, and that concerns her love for the handsome youth Endymion, who is usually depicted as a shepherd. On a still night Selene saw Endymion asleep in a cave on Mt. Latmus (in Caria). Night after night, she lay down beside him as he slept. There are many variants to this story, but in all the outcome is that Zeus granted Endymion perpetual sleep with perpetual youth. This may be represented as a punishment (although sometimes Endymion is given some choice) because of Selene's continual absence from her duties in the heavens, or it may be the fulfillment of Selene's own wishes for her beloved.

Apollo, Sun-God, and Artemis, Moon-Goddess   Many stories about the god of the sun, whether he be called Hyperion, Helius, or merely the Titan, were transferred to the great god Apollo, who shares with them the same epithet, Phoebus, which means "bright." Although Apollo was, in all probability, not originally a sun-god, he came to be considered as such. Thus Phaëthon may become the son of Apollo, as sun-god. Similarly Apollo's twin sister Artemis became associated with the moon, although originally she probably was not a moon-goddess. Thus Selene and Artemis merge in identity, just as do Hyperion, Helius, and Apollo; and Selene and Artemis also are decribed by the adjective "bright," Phoebe (the feminine form of Phoebus).[14] Therefore the lover of Endymion becomes Artemis (or Roman Diana).

Eos, Goddess of the Dawn, and Tithonus   Eos (the Roman Aurora), the third child of Hyperion and Theia, is goddess of the dawn, and like her sister Selene drives a two-horsed chariot. Her epithets in poetry are appropriate, for instance, rosy-fingered and saffron-robed. She is an amorous deity. Aphrodite, the goddess of love, caused her to long perpetually for young mortals because she caught her mate Ares in Eos' bed[15] but her most important mate was Tithonus, a handsome youth of the Trojan royal house. Eos carried off Tithonus; their story is simply and effectively told in the *Homeric Hymn to Aphrodite* (5. 218–238), which is translated in its entirety in Chapter 7.

> Eos went to Zeus, the dark-clouded son of Cronus, to ask that Tithonus be immortal and live forever. Zeus nodded his assent and accomplished her wish. Poor goddess, she did not think to ask that her beloved avoid ruinous old age and retain perpetual youth. Indeed as long as he kept his desirable youthful bloom, Tithonus took his pleasure with early-born Eos of the golden throne by the stream of Oceanus at the ends of the earth. But when the first gray hairs sprouted from his beautiful head and noble chin, Eos avoided his bed. But she kept him in her house and tended him, giving him food, ambrosia, and lovely garments. When hateful old age oppressed him completely and he could not move or raise his limbs, the following plan seemed best to her. She laid him in a room and closed the shining doors. From within his voice flows faintly and he no longer has the strength that he formerly had in his supple limbs.

Aurora, artist unknown. Watercolor and gold paper collage on silk, ca. 1820; $14\frac{1}{2} \times 14\frac{1}{4}$ in. The goddess in this painting, formerly called *Venus Drawn by Doves,* has been identified as Aurora (Eos) by verses that accompany other copies, beginning: "Hail, bright Aurora, fair goddess of the morn! / Around thy splendid Car the smiling Hours submissive wait attendance." Her chariot is drawn by doves and winged cupids fly around it. Aurora is dressed in early nineteenth-century clothing, appropriate for the American landscape to which she brings the light of a new day. *(Abby Aldrich Rockefeller Folk Art Collection, Williamsburg, Virginia. Reproduced by permission.)*

Later writers add that eventually Tithonus was turned into a grasshopper.

The Castration of Uranus and the Birth of Aphrodite

We must now return to Hesiod (*Theogony* 155–210), and his account of the birth of the mighty goddess of love, Aphrodite (the Roman Venus). The children of Uranus and Ge (the twelve Titans, including the last-born, wily Cronus, who especially hated his father; the Cyclopes; and the Hecatonchires) all were despised by their father from the beginning.

 As each of his children was born, Uranus hid them all in the depths of Ge and did not allow them to emerge into the light. And he delighted in his wickedness. But huge Earth in her distress groaned within and devised a crafty and evil scheme. At once she created gray adamant and fashioned a great sickle and confided in her dear children. Sorrowing in her heart she urged them as follows: "My children born of a presumptuous father, if you are willing to obey, we shall punish his evil insolence. For he was the first to devise shameful actions."

Thus she spoke. Fear seized them all and not one answered. But great and wily Cronus took courage and spoke to his dear mother: "I shall undertake and accomplish the deed, since I do not care about our abominable father. For he was the first to devise shameful actions."

Thus he spoke. And huge Earth rejoiced greatly in her heart. She hid him in an ambush and placed in his hands the sickle with jagged teeth and revealed the whole plot to him. Great Uranus came leading on night and desirous of love lay on Ge, spreading himself over her completely. And his son from his ambush reached out with his left hand and in his right he seized hold of the huge sickle with jagged teeth and swiftly cut off the genitals of his own dear father and threw them so that they fell behind him. And they did not fall from his hand in vain. Earth received all the bloody drops that fell and in the course of the seasons bore the strong Erinyes and the mighty giants (shining in their armor and carrying long spears in their hands) and nymphs of ash trees (called Meliae on the wide earth).

When first he had cut off the genitals with the adamant and cast them from the land on the swelling sea, they were carried for a long time on the deep. And white foam arose about from the immortal flesh and in it a maiden grew. First she was brought to holy Cythera, and then from there she came to sea-girt Cyprus. And she emerged a dread and beautiful goddess and grass rose under her slender feet.

Gods and human beings call her Aphrodite, and the foam-born goddess because she grew amid the foam *(aphros)*, and Cytherea of the beautiful crown because she came to Cythera, and Cyprogenes because she arose in Cyprus washed by the waves. She is called too Philommedes (genital-loving) because she arose from the genitals.[16] Eros attended her and beautiful desire followed her when she was born and when she first went into the company of the gods. From the beginning she has this honor, and among human beings and the immortal gods she wins as her due the whispers of girls, smiles, deceits, sweet pleasure, and the gentle delicacy of love.

The stark power of this passage is felt even in translation. The real yet anthropomorphic depiction of the vast Earth enveloped sexually by the surrounding Sky presents its own kind of poetic power. The transparent illustration of basic motives and forces in human nature, through this brutal allegory of Aphrodite's birth, provides fertile material for modern psychology: the youngest son whose devotion to his mother is used by her against the father, the essentially sexual nature of love, the terror of castration. The castration complex of the Freudians is the male's unconscious fear of being deprived of his sexual potency, which springs from his feeling of guilt because of his unrecognized hatred of his father and desire for his mother. Hesiod provides literary documentation for the elemental psychic conscience of humankind Finally, Hesiod, with characteristic simplicity, suggests Aphrodite's powers of fertility by a brief and beautiful image, "and grass rose under her slender feet."

Is it Hesiod's art that gets to the essence of things or is it that he is close to the primitive expression of the elemental in human nature? It is a commonplace to say that, although elements of the more grotesque myths may be detected in Greek literature, they were humanized and refined by the Greeks and transformed by their genius. Yet it is also true that these primitive elements were retained deliberately and consciously because of the horror, shock, and revelation they contain. The Greeks did not suppress the horrible and horrifying; they selected from it and used it boldly with profound insight and sensitivity. Thus Hesiod's account may reflect a primitive myth, the ultimate origins of which we can never really know, but his version gives it meaning with an artistry that is far from primitive.

Cronus (Sky) and Rhea (Earth) and the Birth of Zeus

Cronus united with his sister Rhea, who gave birth to Hestia, Demeter, Hera, Hades, Poseidon, and Zeus. Cronus devoured all these children, except Zeus, as Hesiod relates (*Theogony* 453–506):

 Great Cronus swallowed his children as each one came from the womb to the knees of their holy mother, with the intent that no other of the illustrious descendants of Uranus should hold kingly power among the immortals. For he learned from Ge and starry

Uranus that it was fated that he be overcome by his own child. And so he kept vigilant watch and lying in wait he swallowed his children.

A deep and lasting grief took hold of Rhea and when she was about to bring forth Zeus, father of gods and men, then she entreated her own parents, Ge and starry Uranus, to plan with her how she might bring forth her child in secret and how the avenging fury of her father, Uranus, and of her children whom great Cronus of the crooked counsel swallowed, might exact vengeance. And they readily heard their dear daughter and were persuaded, and they counseled her about all that was destined to happen concerning Cronus and his stout-hearted son. And they sent her to the town of Lyctus in the rich land of Crete when she was about to bring forth the youngest of her children, great Zeus. And vast Ge received him from her in wide Crete to nourish and foster.

Carrying him from Lyctus, Ge came first through the swift black night to Dicte. And taking him in her hands she hid him in the deep cave in the depths of the holy earth on thickly wooded Mt. Aegeum.[17] And she wrapped up a great stone in infant's coverings and gave it to the son of Uranus, who at that time was the great ruler and king of the gods. Then he took it in his hands, poor wretch, and rammed it down his belly. He did not know in his heart that there was left behind, in the stone's place, his son unconquered and secure, who was soon to overcome him and drive him from his power and rule among the immortals.

Cronus and Rhea are deities of sky and earth, doublets of Uranus and Gaea, whose power they usurp, and their union represents the reenactment of the universal sacred marriage. But in the tradition Cronus and Rhea have a more specific reality than their parents. Cronus appears in art as a majestic and sad deity, sickle in hand. He rules, as we shall see, in a golden age among mortals; and after he is deposed by Zeus, he retires to some distant realm, sometimes designated as the Islands of the Blessed, one of the Greek conceptions of paradise. Cronus is called Saturn by the Romans.

Rhea, too, has a definite mythical personality, although basically yet another mother-goddess of earth and fertility. She sometimes is equated with Cybele, an Oriental goddess who intrudes upon the classical world; the worship of Rhea-Cybele involved frenzied devotion and elements of mysticism. Her attendants played wild music on drums and cymbals and she was attended by animals. The *Homeric*

Hymn to the Mother of the Gods (14), pays tribute to this aspect of Rhea's nature:

> Through me, clear-voiced Muse, daughter of great Zeus, sing a hymn to the mother of all gods and all mortals too. The din of castanets and drums, along with the shrillness of flutes, are your delight, and also the cry of wolves, the roar of glaring lions, the echoing mountains and the resounding forests.
>
> So hail to you and, at the same time, all the goddesses in my song.

Religious and Historical Interpretations

Of great mythological significance is Hesiod's account of the birth of Zeus on the island of Crete.[18] We can detect in this version some of the basic motives in the creation of myth, especially when we take into account later variations and additions. From these we learn that after Rhea brought forth Zeus in a cave on Mt. Dicte, he was fed by bees and nursed by nymphs on the milk of a goat named Amalthea. Curetes (the word means "young men") guarded the infant and clashed their spears on their shields so that his cries would not be heard by his father, Cronus. These attendants and the noise they make suggest the frantic devotees of a mother-goddess: Ge, Rhea, or Cybele. The myth is etiological in its explanation of the origin of the musical din and ritual connected with her worship.

Like many myths, the story of the birth of Zeus on Crete accommodates an actual historical occurrence: the amalgamation of at least two different peoples or cultures in the early period. When the inhabitants of Crete began to build their great civilization and empire (ca. 3000), the religion they developed (insofar as we can ascertain) was Mediterranean in character, looking back to earlier Eastern concepts of a mother-goddess. The northern invaders who entered the peninsula of Greece (ca. 2000), bringing with them an early form of Greek and their own gods (chief of whom was Zeus), built a significant Mycenaean civilization on the mainland, but it was strongly influenced by the older, more sophisticated power of Crete. The myth of the birth of Zeus reads very much like an attempt to link by geography and genealogy the religion and deities of both cultures. Zeus, the Nordic male god of the Indo-Europeans, is born of Rhea, the Oriental goddess of motherhood and fertility.

Two dominant strains in the character of subsequent Greek thought can be understood at least partly in terms of this thesis.

W. K. C. Guthrie clearly identifies this dual aspect of the religion of classical Greece in the contrast between the Olympian gods of Homer and the cult of the mother-goddess Demeter at Eleusis:

> *The Mother-goddess is the embodiment of the fruitful earth, giver of life and fertility to plants, animals and men. Her cult takes certain forms, involving at least the more elementary kinds of mysticism, that is, the belief in the possibility of a union between the worshipper and the object of his worship. Thus the rites may take the form of adoption as her son or of sexual communion. Orgiastic elements appear, as in the passionate, clashing music and frenzied dancing employed by the followers of Rhea or Cybele. . . . What an essentially different atmosphere we are in from that of the religion of the Achaean heroes described by Homer. There we are in clear daylight, in a world where the gods are simply more powerful persons who might fight for or against one, with whom one made bargains or contracts. The Achaean warrior did not seek to be born again from the bosom of Hera. He was indeed the reverse of a mystic by temperament.[19]*

We can detect the ramifications of this paradox again and again in many places, but perhaps we feel it most clearly in the mysticism and mathematics that permeate Greek philosophical attitudes: the numbers of Pythagoras and the immortality of the soul in Orphic doctrine; the dichotomy of Platonic thought and Socratic character in the search for clarity and definition through rational argument coupled with the sound of an inner voice, the depths of a trance, and divine revelation in terms of the obscure and profound symbols of religious myth. God is a geometer and a mystic.

ZEUS' RISE TO POWER: THE CREATION OF MORTALS

2

The Titanomachy: Zeus Defeats His Father, Cronus

When Zeus had grown to maturity, Cronus was beguiled into bringing up all that he had swallowed, first the stone and then the children.[1] Zeus then waged war against his father with his disgorged brothers and sisters as allies: Hestia, Demeter, Hera, Hades, and Poseidon. Allied with him as well were the Hecatonchires and the Cyclopes, for he had released them from the depths of the earth, where their father, Uranus, had imprisoned them. The Hecatonchires were invaluable in hurling stones with their hundred-handed dexterity, and the Cyclopes forged for him his mighty thunder and lightning. On the other side, allied with Cronus, were the Titans—with the important exception of Themis and her son Prometheus, both of whom allied with Zeus. Atlas, the brother of Prometheus, was an important leader on the side of Cronus.

The battle was of epic proportions, Zeus fighting from Mt. Olympus, Cronus from Mt. Othrys. The struggle is said to have lasted ten years.[2] An excerpt from Hesiod conveys the magnitude and ferocity of the conflict (*Theogony* 678–721):

The boundless sea echoed terribly, earth resounded with the great roar, wide heaven trembled and groaned, and high Olympus was shaken from its base by the onslaught of the immortals; the quakes came thick and fast and, with the dread din of the endless chase and mighty weapons, reached down to gloomy Tartarus.

Thus they hurled their deadly weapons against one another. The cries of both sides as they shouted reached up to starry heaven, for they came together with a great clamor. Then Zeus did not

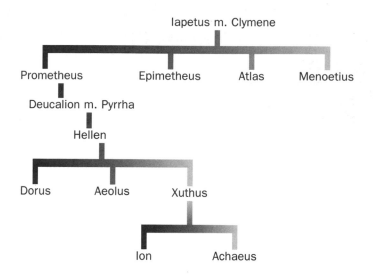

Figure 2.1.   The Family of Prometheus. The mother of Prometheus is Ge-Themis according to Aeschylus.

hold back his might any longer, but now immediately his heart was filled with strength and he showed clearly all his force. He came direct from heaven and Olympus hurling perpetual lightning, and the bolts with flashes and thunder flew in succession from his stout hand with a dense whirling of holy flame. Earth, the giver of life, roared, everywhere aflame, and on all sides the vast woods crackled loudly with the fire. The whole of the land boiled, and as well the streams of Ocean, and the barren sea. The hot blast engulfed the earth-born Titans and the endless blaze reached the divine aether; the flashing gleam of the thunder and lightning blinded the eyes even of the mighty. Unspeakable heat possessed Chaos.

The sight seen by the eyes and the sound heard by the ears were as if earth and wide heaven above collided; for the din as the gods met one another in strife was as great as the crash that would have arisen if earth were dashed down by heaven falling on her from above. The winds mingled the confusion of tremor, dust, thunder, and the flashing bolts of lightning (the shafts of great Zeus) and carried the noise and the shouts into the midst of both sides. The terrifying clamor of fearful strife arose, and the might of their deeds was shown forth. They attacked one another and fought relentlessly in mighty encounters until the battle was decided.

The Hecatonchires (Cottus, Briareus, and Gyes), insatiate of battle, were among the foremost to rouse the bitter strife; they hurled three hundred rocks, one right after another, from their staunch hands and covered the Titans with a cloud of missiles and sent them down far beneath the broad ways of the earth to Tartarus and bound them in harsh bonds, having conquered them with their hands even though they were great of spirit. The distance from earth to gloomy Tartarus is as great as that of heaven from earth.

The Hecatonchires guarded the Titans imprisoned in Tartarus. Atlas was punished with the task of holding up the sky. Some say that after Zeus became secure in power he eventually relented and gave the Titans their freedom.

The Gigantomachy: Zeus Defeats the Giants and Typhoeus

Another threat Zeus had to face came from giants that Earth produced to challenge the new order of the gods, or that had been born when the blood from the mutilation of Uranus fell upon the ground; these monstrous creatures are called Gegeneis, which means "earthborn." The many details of the battle vary, but it is generally agreed that the struggle was fierce and ended with the imprisonment of the giants under the earth, usually in volcanic regions where they betray their presence by the violence of their natures. Thus, for example, the giant Enceladus writhes under volcanic Mt. Aetna in Sicily.

One of the most vicious of the monsters who opposed Zeus was the dragon Typhoeus (or Typhaon or Typhon). He sometimes joins others in their conflict with the gods, or he may do battle alone, as in Hesiod's account (*Theogony* 820–880):

> When Zeus had driven the Titans from heaven, vast Gaea brought forth the youngest of her children through the love of Tartarus and the agency of golden Aphrodite. The hands of the mighty god were strong in any undertaking and his feet were weariless. From the shoulders of this frightening dragon a hundred snake heads grew, flickering their dark tongues; fire blazed from the eyes under the brows of all the dreadful heads, and the flames burned as he glared. In all the terrible heads voices emitted all kinds of amazing sounds; for at one time he spoke so that the gods understood, at another his cries were those of a proud bull bellowing in his invincible might; sometimes he produced the pitiless roars of a courageous lion, or again his yelps were like those of puppies, wondrous to hear, or at another time he would hiss; and the great mountains resounded in echo.

> Now on that day of his birth an irremediable deed would have been accomplished and he would have become the ruler of

mortals and immortals, if the father of gods and men had not taken swift notice and thundered loudly and fiercely; the earth resounded terribly on all sides and as well the wide heaven above, the sea, the streams of Ocean, and the depths of Tartarus. Great Olympus shook under the immortal feet of the lord as he rose up and earth gave a groan. The burning heat from them both, with the thunder and lightning, scorching winds, and flaming bolts reached down to seize the dark-colored sea. The whole land was aboil and heaven and the deep; and the huge waves surged around and about the shores at the onslaught of the immortals, and a quake began its tremors without ceasing.

Hades who rules over the dead below shook, as did the Titans, the allies of Cronus, in the bottom of Tartarus, from the endless din and terrifying struggle. When Zeus had lifted up the weapons of his might, thunder and lightning and the blazing bolts, he leaped down from Olympus and struck, and blasted on all sides the marvelous heads of the terrible monster. When he had flogged him with blows, he hurled him down, maimed, and vast earth gave a groan. A flame flared up from the god as he was hit by the bolts in the glens of the dark craggy mountain where he was struck down. A great part of vast earth was burned by the immense conflagration and melted like tin heated by the craft of artisans in open crucibles or like iron which although the hardest of all is softened by blazing fire and melts in the divine earth through the craft of Hephaestus. Thus the earth melted in the flame of the blazing fire. And Zeus in the rage of his anger hurled him into broad Tartarus.

From Typhoeus arise the winds that blow the mighty rains; but not Notus, Boreas, and Zephyr[3] who brings good weather, for they are sprung from the gods and a great benefit for mortals. But the others from Typhoeus blow over the sea at random; some fall upon the shadowy deep and do great harm to mortals, raging with their evil blasts. They blow this way and that and scatter ships and destroy sailors. Those who encounter them on the sea have no defense against their evil. Others blowing over the vast blossoming land destroy the lovely works of mortals born on earth, filling them with dust and harsh confusion.[4]

The attempt of the giants Otus and Ephialtes to storm heaven by piling the mountains Olympus, Ossa, and Pelion upon one another is sometimes linked to the battle of the giants or treated as a separate attack upon the power of Zeus. In fact there is considerable confusion in the tradition concerning details and characters in the battle of the giants (Gigantomachy) and the battle of the Titans (Titanomachy). Both conflicts may be interpreted as reflecting the triumph of the more benign powers of nature over the more wild powers or of civilization over savagery. Historically, it is likely that they represent the fact of conquest and amalgamation when, in about 2000, the Greek-speaking invaders brought with them their own gods, with Zeus as their chief, and triumphed over the deities of the existing peoples in the peninsula of Greece.

The Creation of Mortals

Various versions of the birth of mortals existed side by side in the ancient world. Very often they are the creation of Zeus alone, or of Zeus and the other gods. Sometimes immortals and mortals spring from the same source. A dominant tradition depicts Prometheus as the creator of man; and sometimes woman is created later and separately through the designs of Zeus.

After describing the creation of the universe and animal life out of the elements of Chaos, Ovid tells about the birth of mortals, depicting the superiority and lofty ambition of this highest creature in the order of things (*Metamorphoses* 1. 76–88); Ovid's "man" *(homo)* epitomizes the human race.

 Until now there was no animal more godlike than these and more capable of high intelligence and able to dominate all the rest. Then man was born; either the creator of the universe, originator of a better world, fashioned him from divine seed, or earth, recently formed and separated from the lofty aether, retained seeds from its kindred sky and was mixed with rain water by Prometheus, the son of Iapetus, and fashioned by him into the likeness of the gods who control all.[5] While other animals look down to the ground, man was given a lofty visage and ordered to look up to the sky and fully erect lift his face to the stars. Thus earth that had been crude and without shape was transformed and took on the figure of man unknown before.

The Four or Five Ages

Ovid goes on to describe the four ages: gold, silver, bronze, and iron. We prefer, however, to excerpt Hesiod's earlier account of these ages, which for him are five in number, since he feels compelled to include the historical age of heroes. After he has recounted the story of Pandora and her jar, his introduction to the description of the five ages suggests both the multiplicity of versions of the creation of mortals and the futility of even attempting to reconcile the diverse accounts (*Works and Days* 106–201).

If you like, I shall offer a fine and skillful summary of another tale
and you ponder it in your heart: how gods and mortal humans
came into being from the same origin.

The Age of Gold

At the very first the immortals who have their homes on Olympus
made a golden race of mortal humans. They existed at the time
when Cronus was king in heaven, and they lived as gods with
carefree hearts completely without toil or trouble. Terrible old age
did not come upon them at all, but always with vigor in their
hands and their feet they took joy in their banquets removed from
all evils. They died as though overcome by sleep. And all good
things were theirs; the fertile land of its own accord bore fruit
ungrudgingly in abundance. They in harmony and in peace
managed their affairs with many good things, rich in flocks and
beloved of the blessed gods. But then the earth covered over this
race. Yet they inhabit the earth and are called holy spirits, who are
good and ward off evils, as the protectors of mortal beings, and
are providers of wealth, since they keep watch over judgments
and cruel deeds, wandering over the whole earth wrapped in air.
For they have these royal prerogatives.

The Age of Silver

Then those who have their home on Olympus next made a second
race of silver, far worse than the one of gold and unlike it both
physically and mentally. A child was brought up by the side of his
dear mother for a hundred years, playing in his house as a mere
baby. But when they grew up and reached the measure of their
prime they lived for only a short time and in distress because of
their senselessness. For they could not restrain their wanton
arrogance against one another and they did not wish to worship
the blessed immortals or sacrifice at their holy altars, as is
customary and right for human beings. Then in his anger, Zeus,
the son of Cronus, hid them away because they did not give the
blessed gods who inhabit Olympus their due. Then the earth
covered over this race too. And they dwell under the earth and are
called blessed by mortals, and although second, nevertheless
honor attends them also.

The Age of Bronze

Father Zeus made another race of mortal humans, the third, of
bronze and not at all like the one of silver; terrible and mighty
because of their spears of ash, they pursued the painful and
violent deeds of Ares. They did not eat bread at all but were
terrifying and had dauntless hearts of adamant. Great was their

might, and unconquerable hands grew upon their strong limbs out of their shoulders. Of bronze were their arms, of bronze were their homes, and they worked with bronze implements. Black iron there was not. When they had been destroyed by their own hands, they went down into the dark house of chill Hades without leaving a name. Black death seized them, although they were terrifying, and they left the bright light of the sun.

The Age of Heroes

But when the earth covered over this race too, again Zeus, the son of Cronus, made still another, the fourth on the nourishing earth, valiant in war and more just, a godlike race of heroic men, who are called demigods, and who preceded our own race on the vast earth. Evil war and dread battle destroyed some of them under seven-gated Thebes in the land of Cadmus as they battled for the flocks of Oedipus; the end of death closed about others after they had been led in ships over the great depths of the sea to Troy for the sake of Helen of the beautiful hair. Some, father Zeus, the son of Cronus, sent to dwell at the ends of the earth where he has them live their lives; these happy heroes inhabit the Islands of the Blessed with carefree hearts by the deep swirling stream of Ocean. For them the fruitful earth bears honey-sweet fruit that ripens three times a year. Far from the immortals Cronus rules as king over them; for the father of gods and men released him from his bonds. Honor and glory attend these last in equal measure.

The Age of Iron

Far-seeing Zeus again made still another race who live on the nourishing earth. Oh, would that I were not a man of the fifth generation but either had died before or had been born later. Now indeed the race is of iron. For they never cease from toil and woe by day, nor from being destroyed in the night. The gods will give them difficult troubles, but good will be mingled with their evils. Zeus will destroy this race of mortals too, whenever it comes to pass that they are born with gray hair on their temples. And a father will not be in harmony with his children nor his children with him, nor guest with host, nor friend with friend, and a brother will not be loved as formerly. As they grow old quickly they will dishonor their parents, and they will find fault, blaming them with harsh words and not knowing respect for the gods, since their right is might. They will not sustain their aged parents in repayment for their upbringing. One will destroy the city of another. No esteem will exist for the one who is true to an oath or just or good; rather mortals will praise the arrogance and evil of the wicked. Justice will be might and shame will not exist. The evil person will harm the better, speaking against him unjustly and he will swear an oath besides. Envy, shrill and ugly and with evil delight, will attend all human beings in their woe. Then Aidos and Nemesis both[6] will forsake them and go, their beautiful forms shrouded in white, from the wide earth to Olympus among the company of the gods. For mortals sorry griefs will be left and there will be no defense against evil.

The bitterness and pessimism of this picture of his own age of iron are typical of Hesiod's general crabbed, severe, and moral outlook. But his designation of the five ages reflects a curious blend of fact and fiction. Historically his *was* the age of iron, introduced into Greece at the time of the invasions that brought the age of bronze to a close. Hesiod's insertion of an age of heroes reflects the fact of the Trojan War, which he cannot ignore.

This conception of the deterioration of the human race has been potent in subsequent literature, both ancient and modern. The vision of a paradise in a golden age when all was well inevitably holds fascination for some, whether imagined as long ago or merely in the good old days of their youth.[7]

It would be wrong to imply that this theory of the degeneration of the human race was the only one current among the Greeks and Romans. Prometheus' eloquent testimony in Aeschylus' play, translated on pp. 66–67, listing his gifts to humans, rests upon the belief in progressive stages from savagery to civilization.[8]

Prometheus against Zeus

In the *Theogony* (507–616) Hesiod tells the stories of Prometheus and his conflict with Zeus, with the human race as the pawn in this gigantic clash of divine wills. He begins with the birth of Prometheus and explains how Prometheus tricked Zeus (507–569):

 Iapetus led away the girl Clymene, an Oceanid, and they went together in the same bed; and she bore to him a child, stout-hearted Atlas; she also brought forth Menoetius, of very great renown, and devious and clever Prometheus, and Epimetheus,[9] who was faulty in judgment and from the beginning was an evil for mortals who work for their bread. For he was the first to accept from Zeus the virgin woman he had formed. Far-seeing Zeus struck arrogant Menoetius with his smoldering bolts and hurled him down into Erebus because of his presumption and excessive pride. Atlas stands and holds the wide heaven with his head and tireless hands through the force of necessity at the edge of the earth, and in the sight of the clear-voiced Hesperides; this fate Zeus in his wisdom allotted him.

And Zeus bound devious and wily Prometheus with hard and inescapable bonds, after driving a shaft through his middle; and roused up a long-winged eagle against him that used to eat his immortal liver. But all the long-winged bird would eat during the whole day would be completely restored in equal measure during the night. Heracles, the mighty son of Alcmene of the lovely ankles, killed it and rid the son of Iapetus from this evil plague and released him from his suffering, not against the will of Olympian Zeus who rules from on high, so that the renown of Theban-born Heracles might be still greater than before on the bountiful earth. Thus he respected his famous son with this token of honor. Although he had been enraged, the mighty son of Cronus gave up the anger that he had held previously because Prometheus had matched his wits against him.

For when the gods and mortals quarreled at Mecone,[10] then Prometheus with quick intelligence divided up a great ox and set the pieces out in an attempt to deceive the mind of Zeus. For the one group in the dispute he placed flesh and the rich and fatty innards on the hide and wrapped them all up in the ox's paunch; for the other group he arranged and set forth with devious art the white bones of the ox, wrapping them up in white fat.

Then the father of gods and men spoke to him: "Son of Iapetus, most renowned of all lords, my fine friend, how partisan has been your division of the portions!" Thus Zeus whose wisdom is immortal spoke in derision. Wily Prometheus answered with a gentle smile, as he did not forget his crafty trick. "Most glorious Zeus, greatest of the gods who exist forever, choose whichever of the two your heart in your breast urges." He spoke with crafty intent.

But Zeus whose wisdom is immortal knew and was not unaware of the trick. And he foresaw in his heart evils for mortals, which would be accomplished. He took up in both his hands the white fat, and his mind was enraged, and anger took hold of his heart as he saw the white bones of the ox arranged with crafty art. For this reason the races of human beings on earth burn the white bones for the immortals on the sacrificial altars.

Zeus the cloud-gatherer was greatly angered and spoke to him: "Son of Iapetus, my fine friend, who know thoughts that surpass those of everyone, so you have then not yet forgotten your crafty arts." Thus Zeus whose wisdom is immortal spoke in anger. From this time on he always remembered the deceit and did not give the power of weariless fire out of ash trees to mortals who dwell on the earth.

But the noble son of Iapetus tricked him by stealing in a hollow fennel stalk the gleam of weariless fire that is seen from afar. High-thundering Zeus was stung to the depths of his being and angered in his heart as he saw among mortals the gleam of fire seen from afar.

The Creation of Pandora

Hesiod goes on to describe the dread consequence of Zeus' anger at Prometheus for his theft of fire (*Theogony* 570–616):

 Immediately he contrived an evil thing for mortals in recompense for the fire. The renowned lame god, Hephaestus, fashioned out of earth the likeness of a modest maiden according to the will of the son of Cronus. Bright-eyed Athena clothed and arrayed her in silvery garments and with her hands arranged on her head an embroidered veil, wondrous to behold. And Pallas Athena put around her head lovely garlands of budding flowers and greenery. And she placed on her head a golden crown that the renowned lame god himself made, fashioning it with his hands as a favor to his father, Zeus. On it he wrought much intricate detail, wondrous to behold, of the countless animals which the land and the sea nourish; many he fixed on it, amazing creations, like living creatures with voices; and its radiant loveliness shone forth in profusion.

When he had fashioned the beautiful evil in recompense for the blessing of fire, he led her out where the other gods and mortals were, exulting in the raiment provided by the gleaming-eyed daughter of a mighty father. Amazement took hold of the immortal gods and mortals as they saw the sheer trick, from which human beings could not escape. For from her is the race of the female sex, the ruinous tribes of women, a great affliction, who live with mortal men, helpmates not in ruinous poverty but in excessive wealth, just as when in overhanging hives bees feed the drones, conspirators in evil works; the bees each day the whole time to the setting of the sun are busy and deposit the white honeycombs, but the drones remain within the covered hives and scrape together the toil of others into their own belly. Thus in the same way high-thundering Zeus made women, conspirators in painful works, for mortal men.

He also contrived a second evil as recompense for the blessing of fire; whoever flees marriage and the troublesome deeds of women and does not wish to marry comes to ruinous old age destitute of anyone to care for him. He does not lack a livelihood while he is living but, when he has died, distant relatives divide up the inheritance. And again even for the one to whom the fate of acquiring a good and compatible wife in marriage falls as his lot, evil continually contends with good throughout his life. Whoever begets mischievous children lives with a continuous sorrow in his breast; in heart and soul the evil is incurable. Thus it is not possible to go beyond the will of Zeus nor to deceive him. For not even the goodly Prometheus, son of Iapetus, got out from under his heavy wrath and a great bondage held him fast, even though he was very clever.

Once again Hesiod's dominant note is despair. He provides another dismal account of Prometheus in the *Works and Days* (47–105); despite some minor repetitions it is worth quoting for its elaboration of the theft of fire and its variations on the creation of woman. The evil is now specifically named; she is Pandora, which means "all gifts," and she has a jar (see Color Plate 18).[11]

Zeus, angered in his heart, hid the means of human livelihood because wily Prometheus deceived him. And so he devised for human beings sorrowful troubles. He hid fire. Then the good son of Iapetus, Prometheus, stole it for human beings from wise Zeus in a hollow reed, without Zeus who delights in thunder seeing it.

But then Zeus the cloud-gatherer was roused to anger and spoke to him: "Son of Iapetus, who know how to scheme better than all others, you are pleased that you stole fire and outwitted me—a great misery for you and men who are about to be. As recompense for the fire I shall give them an evil in which all may take delight in their hearts as they embrace it."

Thus he spoke and the father of gods and men burst out laughing. He ordered renowned Hephaestus as quickly as possible to mix earth with water and to implant in it a human voice and strength and to fashion the beautiful and desirable form of a maiden, with a face like that of an immortal goddess. But he ordered Athena to teach her the skills of weaving at the artful loom, and golden Aphrodite to shed grace about her head and painful longing and sorrows that permeate the body. And he commanded the guide Hermes, slayer of Argus, to put in her the mind of a bitch and the character of a thief.

Thus he spoke and they obeyed their lord Zeus, son of Cronus. At once the famous lame god molded out of earth the likeness of a modest maiden according to the will of Zeus. Bright-eyed Athena clothed and arrayed her, and the Graces and mistress Persuasion adorned her with golden necklaces. The beautiful-haired Seasons crowned her with spring flowers, and Pallas Athena fitted out her body with every adornment. Then the guide and slayer of Argus contrived in her breast lies and wheedling words and a thievish nature, as loud-thundering Zeus directed. And the herald of the gods put in her a voice, and named this woman Pandora, because all who have their homes on Olympus gave her a gift, a bane to men who work for their bread.

But when the Father had completed this sheer impossible trick he sent the swift messenger of the gods, the renowned slayer of Argus, to bring it as a gift for Epimetheus. And Epimetheus did not think about how Prometheus had told him never to accept a gift from Olympian Zeus but to send it back in case that in some way it turned out to be evil for mortals. But he received the gift and when indeed he had the evil he realized.

Previously the races of human beings used to live completely free from evils and hard work and painful diseases, which hand over mortals to the Fates. For mortals soon grow old amidst evil. But the woman removed the great cover of the jar with her hands and scattered the evils within and for mortals devised sorrowful troubles.

Hope alone remained within there in the unbreakable home under the edge of the jar and did not fly out of doors. For the lid of the jar stopped her before she could, through the will of the cloud-gatherer Zeus who bears the aegis. But the other thousands of sorrows wander among human beings, for the earth and the sea are full of evils. Of their own accord diseases roam among human beings some by day, others by night bringing evils to mortals in silence, since Zeus in his wisdom took away their voice. Thus it is not at all possible to escape the will of Zeus.

Interpretations of the Myths of Prometheus and Pandora

The etiology of the myth of Prometheus is perhaps the most obvious of its many fascinating elements. It explains procedure in the ritual of sacrifice and the origin of fire; in the person of Pandora the existence of evil and pain in the world is accounted for. Prometheus himself is the archetype of the culture god or hero ultimately responsible for all the arts and sciences.[12] Prometheus is also the archetype of the divine or heroic trickster (cf. Hermes and Odysseus).

The elements in the myth of the creation of woman also reveal attitudes common among early societies. Like Eve, for example, Pandora is created after man and she is responsible for his troubles. Why should this be so? The answer is complex, but inevitably it must lay bare the prejudices and mores inherent in the social structure. But some detect as well the fundamental truths of allegory and see the woman and her jar as symbols of the drive and lure of procreation, the womb and birth and life, the source of all our woes.[13]

Details in the story of Pandora are disturbing in their tantalizing ambiguity. What is Hope doing in the jar along with countless evils? If it is a good, it is a curious inclusion. If it too is an evil, why is it stopped at the rim? What then is its precise nature, whether a blessing or a curse? Is Hope the one thing that enables human beings to survive the terrors of this life and inspires them with lofty ambition? Yet is it also by its very character delusive and blind, luring them on to prolong their misery? It is tempting to see in Aeschylus' play *Prometheus Bound* an interpretation and elaboration: human beings were without hope until Prometheus gave it to them along with the benefit of fire. The hope Prometheus bestows on mortals is both blind and a blessing. The pertinent dialogue between Prometheus and the chorus of Oceanids runs as follows (248–252):

 PROMETHEUS: I stopped mortals from foreseeing their fate.

CHORUS: What sort of remedy did you find for this plague?

PROMETHEUS: I planted in them blind hopes.

CHORUS: This was a great advantage that you gave mortals.

PROMETHEUS: And besides I gave them fire.

Fundamental to both Hesiod and Aeschylus is the conception of Zeus as the oppressor of humankind and Prometheus as its benefactor. In Aeschylus the clash of divine wills echoes triumphantly through the ages. His portrait, more than any other, offers the towering image of Prometheus as the Titan, the bringer of fire, the vehement and wearless champion against oppression, the mighty symbol for art, literature, and music of all time.

Aeschylus' *Prometheus Bound*

Aeschylus' play *Prometheus Bound* begins with Strength (Kratos) and Force (Bia), brutish servants of an autocratic Zeus, having brought Prometheus to the remote and uninhabited land of Scythia. Hephaestus accompanies them. Kratos urges the reluctant Hephaestus to obey the commands of Father Zeus and bind Prometheus in bonds of steel and pin him with a stake through his chest to the desolate crags. It was Hephaestus' own brilliant "flower" of fire, deviser of all the arts, that Prometheus stole, and for this error ("sin" is not an inappropriate translation) he must pay to all the gods "so that he might learn to bear the sovereignty of Zeus and abandon his love and championship of mortals" (10–17).

Aeschylus, with great skill and economy, provides us with the essentials for the conflict and the mood of the play. The violent struggle pits a harsh, young, and angry Zeus against the defiant determination of a glorious and philanthropic Prometheus.[14]

Hephaestus in contrast to savage Strength and Force is sensitive and humane; he curses his craft, hates the job he has to do, and pities the sleepless torment of Prometheus. Hephaestus also expresses an important theme of the play in his realization that Zeus has seized supreme rule of gods and mortals only recently: "The mind of Zeus is inexorable; and everyone is harsh when he first comes to power." The contrast is presumably intended to foreshadow the later Zeus, who will learn benevolence through experience, wisdom, and maturity. Certainly Zeus, fresh from his triumphant defeat of his father and the Titans, might indeed be uneasy and afraid. He may suffer the same fate as Cronus or Uranus before him; and Prometheus, his adversary, knows the terrifying secret that might lead to Zeus' undoing: Zeus must avoid the sea-nymph Thetis in his amorous pursuits, for she is destined to bear a son mightier than his father. In his knowledge of this lies Prometheus' defiant power and the threat of Zeus' ultimate downfall.

The first utterance of Prometheus after Strength, Force, and Hephaestus have done their work is glorious, capturing the universality of his great and indomitable spirit (88–92):

O divine air and sky and swift-winged breezes, springs of rivers and countless laughter of sea waves, earth, mother of everything, and all-seeing circle of the sun, I call on you. See what I, a god, suffer at the hands of the gods.

In the course of the play, Prometheus expresses his bitterness because, although he with his mother fought on the side of Zeus against the Titans, his only reward is torment. It is typical of the tyrant to forget and turn against his former allies. Prometheus lists the many gifts he has given to humankind for whom he suffers now (442–506):

PROMETHEUS: Listen to the troubles that there were among mortals and how I gave them sense and mind, which they did not have before. I shall tell you this not out of any censure of humankind but to explain the good intention of my gifts. In the beginning they had eyes to look, but looked in vain, and ears to hear, but did not hear, but like the shapes of dreams they wandered in confusion the whole of their long life. They did not know of brick-built houses that face the sun or carpentry, but dwelt beneath the ground like tiny ants in the depths of sunless caves. They did not have any secure way of distinguishing winter or blossoming spring or fruitful summer, but they did everything without judgment, until I showed them the rising and the setting of the stars, difficult to discern.

And indeed I discovered for them numbers, a lofty kind of wisdom, and letters and their combination, an art that fosters memory of all things, the mother of the Muses' arts. I first harnessed animals, enslaving them to the yoke to become reliefs for mortals in their greatest toils, and I led horses docile under the reins and chariot, the delight of the highest wealth and luxury. No one before me discovered the seamen's vessels which with wings of sail are beaten by the waves. Such are the contrivances I, poor wretch, have found for mortals, but I myself have no device by which I may escape my present pain.

CHORUS: You suffer an ill-deserved torment, and confused in mind and heart are all astray; like some bad doctor who has fallen ill, you yourself cannot devise a remedy to effect a cure.

PROMETHEUS: Listen to the rest, and you will be even more amazed at the kinds of skills and means that I devised; the greatest this: if anyone fell sick, there existed no defense, neither food nor drink nor salve, but through lack of medicines they wasted away until I showed them the mixing of soothing remedies by which they free themselves from all diseases. I set forth the many ways of the prophetic art. I was the first to determine which dreams would of necessity turn out to be true, and I established for them the difficult interpretation of sounds and omens of the road and distinguished the precise meaning of the flight of birds with crooked talons, which ones are by nature lucky and propitious, and what mode of life each had, their mutual likes, dislikes, and association; the smoothness of the innards and the color of the bile that would meet the pleasure of the gods, and the dappled beauty of the liver's lobe. I burned the limbs enwrapped in fat and the long shank and set mortals on the path to this difficult art of sacrifice, and made clear the fiery signs, obscure before. Such were these gifts of mine. And the benefits hidden deep within the earth, copper, iron, silver, and gold—who could claim that he had found them before me? No one, I know full well, unless he wished to babble on in vain.

In a brief utterance learn the whole story: all arts come to mortals from Prometheus.

When Hermes, Zeus' messenger, appears in the last episode, Prometheus is arrogant and insulting in his refusal to bow to the threats of even more terrible suffering and reveal his secret. The play ends with the fulfillment of the promised torment; the earth shakes and cracks, thunder and lightning accompany wind and storm as Prometheus, still pinned to the rock, is plunged beneath the earth by the cataclysm; there he will be plagued by the eagle daily tearing his flesh and gnawing his liver. Prometheus' final utterance echoes and affirms the fiery heat and mighty spirit of his first invocation: "O majesty of earth, my mother, O air and sky whose circling brings light for all to share. You see me, how I suffer unjust torments."

Io, Zeus, and Prometheus

In order to appreciate Aeschylus' depiction of Zeus and his vision of the final outcome of the conflict between Zeus and Prometheus,[15] we must introduce the story of Io, a pivotal figure in *Prometheus Bound*.[16] In the series of exchanges between Prometheus and the various characters who come to witness his misery, the scene with Io is particularly significant in terms of eventual reconciliation and knowledge.

Io was loved by Zeus; she was a priestess of Hera and could not avoid detection by the goddess. Zeus failed to deceive Hera, who in retaliation turned Io into a white cow,[17] and to guard her new possession, she set Argus over her. Argus, whose parentage is variously given, had many eyes (the number varies from four in Aeschylus to one hundred in Ovid) and was called Argus Panoptes (the all-seeing); because his eyes never slept all at once, he could have Io under constant surveillance. Zeus therefore sent Hermes to rescue Io; Hermes lulled Argus to sleep by telling him stories, and then cut off his head—hence his title Argeiphontes, or slayer of Argus. Hera set Argus' eyes in the tail of the peacock, the bird with which she is especially associated. Io still could not escape Hera's jealousy; Hera sent a gadfly that so maddened her that she wandered miserably over the whole world until finally she came to Egypt. There by the Nile, Zeus restored her human form, and she gave birth to a son, Epaphus.[18]

In *Prometheus Bound*, Aeschylus describes Io's sufferings in some detail to illustrate the ultimate wisdom, justice, and mercy of an all-powerful Zeus. In agony because of the stings of the gadfly and tormented by the ghost of Argus, Io flees over the earth in mad frenzy. She asks why Zeus has punished her, an innocent victim of Hera's brutal resentment, and longs for the release of death. This is how the uncomprehending Io tells Prometheus of her anguish (645–682):

Again and again in the night, visions would appear to me in my
room and entice me with seductive words: "O blessed maiden,
why do you remain a virgin for so long when it is possible for you
to achieve the greatest of marriages? For Zeus is inflamed by the
shafts of desire and longs to make love to you. Do not, my child,
reject the bed of Zeus but go out to the deep meadow of Lerna
where the flocks and herds of your father graze, so that the
longing of the eye of Zeus may be requited." I, poor wretch, was
troubled every night by such dreams until at last I dared to tell my
father about them. He sent numerous messengers to Delphi and
Dodona to find out what he must do or say to appease the gods;
and they returned with difficult and obscure answers, cryptically
worded. At last an unambiguous injunction was delivered to
Inachus, clearly ordering him to evict me from his house and city
to wander without a home to the ends of the earth; if he did not
comply, the fiery thunderbolt of Zeus would strike and annihilate
his whole race.

In obedience to this oracle of Apollo, my father, unwilling as was
I, expelled and drove me from my home; indeed the bridle bit of
Zeus forcefully compelled him to do such things. Straightway my
body was changed and my mind distorted; with horns, as you can
see, and pursued by the sharp stings of a gadfly, I rushed in
convulsive leaps to the clear stream of Cerchnea and the spring of
Lerna. The giant herdsman Argus, savage in his rage, accompanied
me, watching with his countless eyes my every step. A sudden
unexpected fate deprived him of his life; but I, driven mad by the
stings of the gadfly, wander from land to land under the scourge
of god.

As the scene continues, Prometheus foretells the subsequent
course of Io's wanderings. Eventually she will find peace in Egypt,
where (848–851):

 Zeus will make you sane by the touch of his fearless hand—the
touch alone; and you will bear a son, Epaphus, "Him of the
Touch," so named from his begetting at the hand of Zeus.

Aeschylus' version of the conception of Epaphus is religious. Io
has been chosen by Zeus and has suffered at the hands of Hera for
the fulfillment of a destiny and she will conceive not through rape
but by the gentle touch of the hand of god. Prometheus, with the
oracular power of his mother, foresees the generations descended
from Io, the culmination of his narrative being the birth of the great

hero Heracles, who will help Zeus in the final release of Prometheus. Thus the divine plan is revealed and the absolute power of almighty Zeus is achieved; in mature confidence he will rest secure, without fear of being overthrown, as the supreme and benevolent father of both gods and mortals.

As Aeschylus' other plays on Prometheus survive only as titles and fragments, we do not know how he conceived details in the ultimate resolution. From Hesiod (above, p. 61) we know that Heracles, through the agency of Zeus, was responsible for killing the eagle and releasing Prometheus—after Prometheus had revealed the fatal secret about mating with Thetis. Conflicting and obscure testimony has Chiron, the centaur, involved in some way, as Aeschylus seems to predict; Chiron, wounded by Heracles, gives up his life and his immortality in a bargain for the release of Prometheus.[19]

Zeus and Lycaon and the Wickedness of Mortals

Prometheus had a son, Deucalion, and Epimetheus had a daughter, Pyrrha. Their story, from Ovid's *Metamorphoses,* involves a great flood sent by Zeus (Jupiter) to punish mortals for their wickedness. In the passage below Jupiter tells an assembly of the gods how he, a god, became a man to test the truth of the rumors of human wickedness in the age of iron. There follows an account of Jupiter's anger at the evil of mortals, in particular Lycaon (1. 211–252).

"Reports of the wickedness of the age had reached my ears; wishing to find them false, I slipped down from high Olympus and I, a god, roamed the earth in the form of a man. Long would be the delay to list the number of evils and where they were found; the iniquitous stories themselves fell short of the truth. I had crossed the mountain Maenalus, bristling with the haunts of animals, and Cyllene, and the forests of cold Lycaeus; from these ridges in Arcadia I entered the realm and inhospitable house of the tyrant Lycaon, as the dusk of evening was leading night on.

"I gave signs that a god had come in their midst; the people began to pray but Lycaon first laughed at their piety and then cried: 'I shall test whether this man is a god or a mortal, clearly and decisively.' He planned to kill me unawares in the night while I was deep in sleep. This was the test of truth that suited him best. But he was not content even with this; with a knife he slit the throat of one of the hostages sent to him by the Molossians and, as the limbs were still warm with life, some he boiled until tender and others he roasted over a fire. As soon as he placed them on the table, I with a flame of vengeance brought the home down upon its gods, worthy of such a household and such a master.

"Lycaon himself fled in terror, and when he reached the silence of the country he howled as in vain he tried to speak. His mouth acquired a mad ferocity arising from his basic nature, and he turned his accustomed lust for slaughter against the flocks and now took joy in their blood. His clothes were changed to hair; his arms to legs; he became a wolf retaining vestiges of his old form. The silver of the hair and the violent countenance were the same; the eyes glowed in the same way; the image of ferocity was the same.[20]

"One house had fallen but not one house only deserved to perish. Far and wide on the earth the Fury holds power; you would think that an oath had been sworn in the name of crime. Let all quickly suffer the penalties they deserve. Thus my verdict stands."

Some cried approval of the words of Jove and added goads to his rage, others signified their assent by applause. But the loss of the human race was grievous to them all and they asked what the nature of the world would be like bereft of mortals, who would bring incense to the altars, and if Jupiter was prepared to give the world over to the ravagings of animals. As they asked these questions the king of the gods ordered them not to be alarmed, for all that would follow would be his deep concern; and he promised a race of wondrous origin unlike the one that had preceded.

The Flood

Set upon destroying humankind, Jupiter rejects the idea of hurling his thunderbolts against the world because he fears they may start a great conflagration that could overwhelm the universe. As Ovid continues the story, the god has decided on a different means of punishment: a great flood (260–290). The motif of the Flood is one of the most important and universal in myth and legend.[21]

 A different punishment pleased him more: to send down from every region of the sky torrents of rain and destroy the human race under the watery waves. Straightway he imprisoned the North Wind, and such other blasts as put storm clouds to flight in the caves of Aeolus, and let loose the South Wind who flew with drenched wings, his dread countenance cloaked in darkness black as pitch; his beard was heavy with rain, water flowed from his hoary hair, clouds nestled on his brow, and his wings and garments dripped with moisture. And as he pressed the hanging clouds with his broad hand, he made a crash, and thence thick rains poured down from the upper air. The messenger of Juno, Iris, adorned in varied hues, drew up the waters and brought nourishment to the clouds. The crops were leveled and the farmers' hopeful prayers lay ruined and bemoaned the labor of the long year in vain destroyed.

Nor was the wrath of Jove content with his realm, the sky. His brother Neptune of the sea gave aid with waves as reinforcements. He called together the rivers and, when they had entered the dwelling of their master, said: "Now I cannot resort to a long exhortation. Pour forth your strength, this is the need—open wide your domains, and all barriers removed, give full rein to your streams." This was his command. They went back home and opened wide their mouths for their waters to roll in their unbridled course over the plains. Neptune himself struck the earth with his trident; it trembled and with the quake laid open paths for the waters. The streams spread from their course and rushed over the open fields and swept away, together and at once, the trees and crops, cattle, human beings, houses, and their inner shrines with sacred statues. If any house remained and was able to withstand being thrown down by so great an evil, yet a wave still higher touched its highest gables, and towers overcome lay submerged in the torrent.

Deucalion and Pyrrha

Ovid provides further elaborate and poetical description of the ravages of the terrible flood and then concentrates upon the salvation of the pious couple, Deucalion (the Greek Noah) and his wife, Pyrrha, and the repopulation of the world (311–421).

 The greatest part of life was swept away by water; those whom the water spared were overcome by slow starvation because of lack of food.

The territory of Phocis separates the terrain of Thessaly from that of Boeotia, a fertile area when it was land, but in this crisis it had suddenly become part of the sea and a wide field of water. Here a lofty mountain, Parnassus by name, reaches with its two peaks up to the stars, the heights extending beyond the clouds. When Deucalion with his wife was carried in his little boat to this mountain and ran aground (for the deep waters had covered the rest of the land) they offered worship to the Corycian nymphs,[22] the deities of the mountain, and prophetic Themis, who at that time held oracular power there. No man was better than

Deucalion nor more devoted to justice, and no woman more reverent towards the gods than his wife, Pyrrha.

When Jupiter saw the earth covered with a sea of water and only one man and one woman surviving out of so many thousands of men and women, both innocent and both devout worshipers of deity, he dispelled the clouds, and after the North Wind had cleared the storm, revealed the earth to the sky and the upper air to the world below. The wrath of the sea did not endure and the ruler of the deep laid aside his trident and calmed the waves. He summoned the sea-god Triton, who rose above the waters, his shoulders encrusted with shellfish; he ordered him to blow into his resounding conch shell and by this signal to recall the waves and the rivers. Triton took up the hollow horn which grows from the lowest point of the spiral, coiling in ever widening circles. Whenever he blows into his horn in the middle of the deep, its sounds fill every shore to east and west. Now too, as the god put the horn to his lips moist with his dripping beard and gave it breath, it sounded the orders of retreat and was heard by all the waves on land and on the sea, and as they listened all were checked.

Once more the sea had shores and streams were held within their channels, rivers subsided, and hills were seen to rise up. Earth emerged and the land grew in extent as the waves receded. And after a length of time the tops of the woods were uncovered and showed forth, a residue of mud left clinging to the leaves. The world had been restored.

When Deucalion saw the earth devoid of life and the profound silence of its desolation, tears welled up in his eyes as he spoke to Pyrrha thus: "O my cousin, and my wife, the only woman left, related to me by family ties of blood, then joined to me in marriage, now danger itself unites us. We two alone are the host of the whole world from east to west; the sea holds all the rest. Besides assurance of our life is not yet completely certain. Even now the clouds above strike terror in my heart. What feelings would you have now, poor dear, if you had been snatched to safety by the Fates without me? In what way could you have been able to bear your fear alone? Who would have consoled you as you grieved? For I, believe me, would have followed, if the sea had taken you, dear wife, and the sea would have taken me with you. How I wish I might be able to repopulate the earth by the arts of my father and infuse the molded clods of earth with life. As it is, the race of mortals rests in just us two—thus have the gods ordained—and we remain the only vestiges of human beings." Thus he spoke and they wept.

They decided to pray to the goddess Themis and seek help
through her holy oracles with no delay. Together they approached
the waves of the river Cephisus, which, although not yet clear,
was cutting its accustomed course. When they had drawn water
and sprinkled their heads and clothes, they turned their steps from
there to the temple of the goddess; its pediments were discolored
with vile moss and its altars stood without fire. As they reached
the steps of the temple, both fell forward on the ground, and in
dread awe implanted kisses on the cold stone. They spoke as
follows: "If the divine majesty is won over and made soft by just
prayers, if the anger of the gods is turned aside, tell, O Themis, by
what art the loss of the human race may be repaired and give
help, O most gentle deity, in our drowned world."

The goddess was moved and gave her oracle: "Go away from my
temple, cover your heads and unloose the fastenings of your
garments, and toss the bones of the great mother behind your
back." For a long time they were stupefied at this; Pyrrha first
broke the silence by uttering her refusal to obey the orders of the
goddess; with fearful prayer she begged indulgence, for she feared
to hurt the shade of her mother by tossing her bones. But all the
while they sought another explanation and mulled over, alone and
together, the dark and hidden meaning of the obscure words given
by the oracle. Then the son of Prometheus soothed the daughter
of Epimetheus with pleasing words: "Unless my ingenuity is
wrong, oracles are holy and never urge any evil; the great parent is
the earth; I believe that the stones in the body of earth are called
her bones. We are ordered to throw these behind our backs."

Although the Titan's daughter was moved by the interpretation of
her husband, her hope was still in doubt; to this extent they both
distrusted heaven's admonitions. But what harm would there be in
trying? They left the temple, covered their heads, unloosed their
garments, and tossed the stones behind their steps as they were
ordered. The stones (who would believe this if the antiquity of
tradition did not bear testimony?) began to lose their hardness and
rigidity and gradually grew soft and in their softness assumed a
shape. Soon as they grew and took on a more pliant nature, the
form of a human being could be seen, in outline not distinct, most
like crude statues carved in marble, just begun and not sufficiently
completed. The part of the stones that was of earth dampened by
some moisture was converted into flesh; what was solid and
unable to be so transformed was changed into bone; what once
had been a vein in the stone remained with the same name; in a
short time, through the will of the gods, the stones hurled by the
hands of the man assumed the appearance of men, and those cast
by the woman were converted into women. Hence we are a hard

race and used to toils and offer proof of the origin from which we were sprung.

The earth of her own accord produced other animals of different sorts, after the moisture that remained was heated by the fire of the sun; and the mud and soggy marshes began to swell because of the heat, and fertile seeds of things began to grow nourished by the life-giving earth, as in a mother's womb, and gradually took on a certain form.

Deucalion and Pyrrha had a son Hellen, the eponymous ancestor of the Greek people; for the Greeks called themselves Hellenes and their country Hellas.[23]

Succession Myths and Other Motifs

Babylonian, Hurrian, Hittite, and Phoenician literature has many parallels to Hesiod's account of genesis. One of the most striking is the archetypal motif known as the Succession Myth. In the Babylonian epic of creation, which begins with the words by which it is entitled (*Enuma Elish*, "When above"), three of the ruling gods, Anu, Ea, and Marduk, play roles similar to those of Uranus, Cronus, and Zeus in the conflict for power; and Marduk, like Zeus, attains ultimate control by defeating a monster, Tiamat, who thus resembles Typhoeus. Likewise among Hurrian-Hittite stories, two known as *Kingship in Heaven* and *Songs of Ullikummi* reveal common thematic patterns; especially startling is the episode that tells how Kumarbi defeats Anu by biting off his genitals, a brutal act not unlike the castration of Uranus by Cronus.[24]

Among the many themes inherent in the character and career of Zeus himself, the following deserve special emphasis. Like that of many another god or hero, his life as an infant is both precarious and charmed, progressing in accordance with the motif of the Divine Child. He grows up close to nature and the world of animals; and, with special care and training, he emerges to overthrow his father and face all his challenges. Very special on the list of his triumphs is the slaying of a dragon. By killing Typhoeus, Zeus, the supreme god, may be proclaimed as the archetypal dragonslayer—one of the most powerful and symbolic of all divine and heroic achievements.

THE TWELVE OLYMPIANS: ZEUS, HERA, AND THEIR CHILDREN

3

Thus Zeus is established as lord of gods and men. He is supreme, but he does share his powers with his brothers. Zeus himself assumes the sky as his special sphere; Poseidon, the sea; and Hades, the Underworld. Sometimes the three are said to have cast lots for their realms. Zeus takes his sister Hera as his wife; she reigns by his side as his queen and subordinate. His sisters Hestia and Demeter share in divine power and functions, as we shall see, and the other major gods and goddesses are also given significant prerogatives and authority as they are born.

And so a circle of major deities (fourteen in number) comes into being; their Greek and Roman names are as follows: Zeus (Jupiter), Hera (Juno), Poseidon (Neptune), Hades (Pluto), Hestia (Vesta), Hephaestus (Vulcan), Ares (Mars), Apollo, Artemis (Diana), Demeter (Ceres), Aphrodite (Venus), Athena (Minerva), Hermes (Mercury), and Dionysus (Bacchus).[1] This list was reduced to a canon of twelve Olympians by omitting Hades (whose specific realm is under the earth) and replacing Hestia with Dionysus, a great deity who comes relatively late to Greece.

Hestia, Goddess of the Hearth and Its Fire

Although her mythology is meager, Hestia is important. She rejected the advances of both Poseidon and Apollo and vowed to remain a virgin; like Athena and Artemis, then, she is a goddess of chastity.[2] But she is primarily the goddess of the hearth and its sacred fire; her name, *Hestia,* is the Greek word for hearth. Among primitive peoples fire was obtained with difficulty, kept alive, and revered for its basic

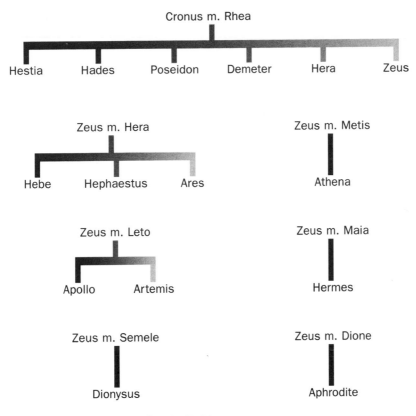

Figure 3.1. The Lineage of Major Deities.

importance in daily needs and religious ceremony. The hearth too was the center first of the family and then of the larger political units: the tribe, the city, and the state. Transmission of the sacred fire from one settlement to another represented a continuing bond of sentiment and heredity. Thus both the domestic and the communal hearth were designated as holy, and the goddess herself presided over them. Hestia often gained precedence at banquets and in sacrificial ritual; for as the first-born of Cronus and Rhea she was considered august, one of the older generation of the gods.

There are two *Homeric Hymns to Hestia*. Number 24 briefly calls on her as the manifestation of the protecting flame of the sacred hearth in a temple:

 Hestia, you who tend the hallowed house of the far-shooter Apollo in holy Pytho, liquid oil always drips from your hair.[3] Come to this house; enter in sympathetic support, along with Zeus, the wise counselor. Grant as well a pleasing grace to my song.

In number 29, Hestia is invoked as the protectress of the hearth in the home; the poet appeals to the god Hermes as well, since both deities protect the house and bring good fortune.

Hestia, you have as your due an everlasting place in the lofty homes of immortal gods and human beings who walk on earth—the highest of honors and a precious right. For without you, there are no banquets for mortals where one does not offer honey-sweet wine as a libation to Hestia, first and last.

And you, Hermes, the slayer of Argus, son of Zeus and Maia, messenger of the blessed gods, bearer of a golden staff and giver of good things, along with revered and beloved Hestia, be kind and help me. Come and inhabit beautiful homes, in loving harmony. For since you both know the splendid achievements of mortals on earth, follow in attendance with intelligence and beauty.

Hail, daughter of Cronus, you and Hermes, bearer of a golden staff; yet I shall remember you both and another song too.

The Diverse Character of Zeus

Zeus is an amorous god; he mates with countless goddesses and mortal women, and his offspring are legion. Most genealogies demanded the glory and authority of the supreme god himself as their ultimate progenitor. Along with this necessity emerged the character of a Zeus conceived and readily developed by what might be called a popular mythology. This Zeus belonged to a monogamous society in which the male was dominant; however moral the basic outlook, the standards for the man were different from those for the woman. Illicit affairs were possible and even, if not officially sanctioned, were at least condoned for men, but under no circumstances tolerated for women. Thus Zeus is the glorified image not only of the husband and father, but also of the lover. The gamut of Zeus' conquests will provide a recurrent theme.

As the picture evolves, Zeus' behavior may be depicted as amoral or immoral or merely a joke—the supreme god can stand above conventional standards. At other times he will act in harmony with them, and more than once he must face the shrewish harangues of his wife, Hera, and pay at least indirectly through pain and suffering wrought by his promiscuity.

Yet this same Zeus (as we shall see below in his worship at Dodona and Olympia) becomes the one god, and his concerns envelop the whole sphere of morality for both gods and humankind. He is the wrathful god of justice and virtue, upholding all that is sacred and holy in the moral order of the universe. This Zeus we discuss at greater length in Chapter 4. In the literature, the portrayal of Zeus depends upon both the period and the intent and purpose of individual authors. The conception of deity is multifaceted, infinitely varied, and wondrously complex.

We are already familiar with Zeus the god of the sky, the cloud-gatherer of epic. The etymological root of his name means "bright" (as does that of Jupiter). His attributes are thunder and lightning, and he is often depicted about to hurl them. The king of gods and men is a regal figure represented as a man in his prime, usually bearded. He bears as well the aegis, a word meaning "goat skin" that originally designated merely the cloak of a shepherd. For Zeus it is a shield with wonderful and miraculous protective powers.[4] The majestic eagle and mighty oak were sacred to Zeus.

Zeus and Hera

The union of Zeus and Hera represents yet another enactment of the sacred marriage between the sky-god and earth-goddess; this is made clear in the lines from Homer (*Iliad* 14. 346–351) that describe their lovemaking:

The son of Cronus clasped his wife in his arms and under them the divine earth sprouted forth new grass, dewy clover, crocuses, and hyacinths, thick and soft, to protect them from the ground beneath. On this they lay together and drew around themselves a beautiful golden cloud from which the glistening drops fell away.

Hera has little mythology of her own, being important mainly as Zeus' consort and queen; yet she has great power. The *Homeric Hymn to Hera* (12) makes this power very clear:

I sing about golden-throned Hera, whom Rhea bore, immortal queen, outstanding in beauty, sister and wife of loud-thundering Zeus; she is the illustrious one whom all the blessed ones throughout high Olympus hold in awe and honor, just as they do Zeus who delights in his lightning and thunder.

Hera consistently appears as the vehement wife and mother who will punish and avenge the romantic escapades of her husband; she consistently acts with matronly severity, the severe champion of morality and marriage.[5] In art Hera is depicted as regal and matronly, often with attributes of royalty.

Homer describes her as ox-eyed and white-armed, both epithets presumably denoting her beauty. The appropriateness of "white-armed" seems self-evident; and if we mistranslate "ox-eyed" as "doe-eyed," perhaps the complimentary nature of that adjective becomes clear. The peacock is associated with Hera; this is explained by her role in the story of Io (told in Chapter 2). Argos was a special center for her worship, and a great temple was erected there in her honor. Hera was worshiped less as an earth-goddess than as a goddess of women, marriage, and childbirth, functions she shares with other deities.

The Sanctuary of Zeus at Olympia

Olympia is a sanctuary beside the river Alpheus, in the territory of the Peloponnesian city of Elis. By the time of the reorganization of the Olympic Games in 776,[6] Zeus had become the principal god of the sanctuary, and his son Heracles was said to have founded the original Olympic Games, one of the principal athletic festivals in the ancient world.[7] An earlier cult of the hero Pelops and his wife, Hippodamia (see pp. 340–342), continued, nevertheless, along with the worship of Zeus and Hera, whose temples were the principal buildings of the sanctuary at the peak of its greatness.

The temple of Hera was older, while the temple of Zeus was built in the fifth century with a monumental statue of Zeus placed inside.[8] The statue and the sculptures on the temple itself together formed a program in which religion, mythology, and local pride were articulated on a scale paralleled only by the sculptures of the Parthenon at Athens.

On the west pediment was displayed the battle of the Greeks and the centaurs at the wedding of a son of Zeus, the Lapith king Pirithoüs, a myth that also appears in the metopes of the Parthenon. The central figure in the pediment is another son of Zeus, Apollo, imposing order on the scene of violence and chaos (illustrated on p. 190).

The east pediment shows the scene before the fateful chariot race between Pelops and Hippodamia and her father Oenomaüs. Zeus himself is the central figure, guaranteeing the success of Pelops in the coming race and the winning of Hippodamia as his wife.

The Twelve Labors of Heracles were carved in the metopes of the Doric frieze (each about 1.6 meters in height), six above the entrance porch to the inner chamber (cella, or naos) at each end of the temple. The climax of the Labors, above the east porch, was the local myth of the cleansing of the stables of Augeas, king of Elis. In this labor

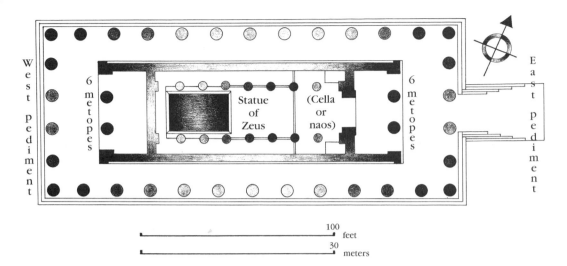

Figure 3.2. Plan of the Temple of Zeus at Olympia. *(After W. B. Dinsmoore.)*

(and in three others) Athena is shown helping the hero, and in the labors of the Nemean Lion and Cerberus, Hermes is the helper.

The most complex union of myth and religion was in the statue of Zeus, carved by the Athenian sculptor Pheidias, and the most admired of all ancient statues. It was huge (over 12 meters in height), and its surfaces were made of precious materials, gold (for the clothing and ornaments) and ivory (for the flesh). It inspired awe on those who saw it; although nothing remains of the statue today, we can reconstruct its appearance.[9] Zeus was seated on his throne, carrying a figure of Nike (Victory) in his right hand, and in his left hand a scepter, on which perched his eagle. On the feet of the throne were depicted the myths of the Theban sphinx and the killing of the children of Niobe by Apollo and Artemis. Also part of the structure of the throne was a representation of Heracles fighting the Amazons, and Heracles appeared again in the paintings on a screen that enclosed the underpart of the throne, performing two of his labors (the Apples of the Hesperides and the Nemean Lion), as well as freeing Prometheus. Significant among the many other mythological details were the carved reliefs on the base of the throne; here the Olympian gods accompanied the miraculous birth of Aphrodite from the sea. In front of the staue was a reflecting pool of olive oil.

Thus in the temple and its statue, at the heart of the greatest of Panhellenic sanctuaries, myths of human and divine struggle and victory, of destruction and creation, combined to honor Zeus as the supreme god of civilization.

The Oracles at Olympia and Dodona

Dodona (in northern Greece) as well as Olympia was an important center for the worship of Zeus, and both were frequented in antiquity for their oracular responses.

The traditional methods for eliciting a response from the god were by the observation and interpretation of omens, for example, the rustling of leaves, the sound of the wind in the branches of his sacred oaks, the call of doves, and the condition of burnt offerings. At Olympia inquiries were usually confined to the chances of the competitors in the games. Eventually at Dodona, through the influence of the oracle of Apollo at Delphi, a priestess would mount a tripod and deliver her communications from the god.[10] Here leaden tablets have been found inscribed with all kinds of questions posed by the state and the individual. The people of Corcyra ask Zeus to what god or hero they should pray or sacrifice for their common good; others ask if it is safe to join a federation; a man inquires if it is good for him to marry; another, whether he will have children from his wife. There are questions about purchases, health, and family.

Children of Zeus and Hera: Eileithyia, Hebe, Hephaestus, and Ares

Eileithyia, Goddess of Childbirth   Zeus and Hera have four children: Eileithyia, Hebe, Hephaestus, and Ares. Eileithyia is a goddess of childbirth, a role she shares with her mother Hera; at times mother and daughter merge in identity. Artemis (as we shall see in Chapter 8) is another important goddess of childbirth.

Hebe and Ganymede, Cupbearers to the Gods   Hebe is the goddess of youthful bloom (the literal meaning of her name). She is a servant of the gods as well.[11] Hebe is primarily known as the cupbearer for the deities on Olympus. When Heracles wins immortality, she becomes his bride. Some versions explain that she resigned from her position to marry. Late authors claim that she was discharged for clumsiness.

The Trojan prince Ganymede shares honors with Hebe as cupbearer of the gods; according to some he replaces her. The *Homeric Hymn to Aphrodite* (5. 202–217), translated in its entirety in Chapter 7, tells how Zeus carried off Ganymede, the handsome son of Tros:

Indeed Zeus in his wisdom seized and carried off fair-haired Ganymede because of his beauty, so that he might be in the company of the gods and pour wine for them in the house of Zeus, a wonder to behold, esteemed by all the immortals, as he draws the red nectar from a golden bowl. But a lasting sorrow gripped the heart of Tros, for he had no idea where the divine whirlwind had taken his dear son. Indeed he mourned for him unceasingly each and every day and Zeus took pity on the father and gave him as recompense for his son brisk-trotting horses, the kind which carry the gods. These he gave him to have as a gift.

And at the command of Zeus, Hermes, the guide and slayer of Argus, told everything and how Ganymede would be immortal and never grow old, just like the gods. When Tros heard this message from Zeus, he no longer continued his mourning but rejoiced within his heart and joyfully was borne by the horses that were as swift as a storm.

In some accounts an eagle, not a whirlwind, carries Ganymede away. This myth, for some, represents the spiritual calling of a young man by god; others attribute homosexual desire to a bisexual Zeus, thus having the supreme god mirror yet another human passion.[12]

Hephaestus, the Divine Artisan Hephaestus, the next child of Zeus and Hera to be considered, is a god of creative fire and a divine smith. His divine workshop is often placed in heaven or on Olympus. All that this immortal craftsman produces excites wonder; his major role in mythology is to create things of extraordinary beauty and utility, often elaborately wrought. One of his masterpieces, the shield of Achilles, is described in exquisite detail by Homer. Hephaestus even has attendants fashioned of gold that look like living young women; these robots can move with intelligence and speak with knowledge. He is indeed the master artisan. Sometimes his forge is under the earth; and as he labors all covered with soot and sweat, he may be attended by the three Cyclopes, whom we already know as the ones who create the thunder and lightning of Zeus.[13]

Hephaestus and the goddess Athena were often linked together as benefactors of wisdom in the arts and crafts and champions of progress and civilization. Their joint worship was particularly significant in Athens, and in the *Homeric Hymn to Hephaestus* (20) they are invoked together as archetypal, divine culture figures like Prometheus.

Sing, clear-voiced Muse, about Hephaestus, renowned for his intelligence, who, with bright-eyed Athena, taught splendid arts to human beings on earth. Previously they used to live in mountain caves, like animals, but now, because of Hephaestus, renowned for his skill, they have learned his crafts and live year round with ease and comfort in their own houses.

Be kind, Hephaestus, and give me both excellence and prosperity.

The god Hephaestus was lame from birth. One story maintains that Hera was ashamed of his deformity and cast him down from Olympus or heaven.[14] He was rescued and eventually returned home. We are also told that he was hurled to earth on another occasion, this time by Zeus. Hephaestus lands on the island of Lemnos, which in classical times was an important center of his worship, Other volcanic regions (e.g., Sicily and its environs) were also associated with this divine smith; these places bore testimony to the fire and smoke that at times would erupt from his forge.

At the close of Book 1 of the *Iliad,* Hephaestus himself recounts the episode of Zeus' anger against him. We excerpt this passage because it illustrates many things: the character of Hephaestus; his closeness to his mother Hera; the tone and atmosphere instigated by an episode in the life of the Olympian family; Zeus as the stern father in his house; his difficult relations with his wife; the uneasy emotions of the children while they witness the quarrel of their parents.

The sea-goddess Thetis has come to Zeus on Olympus to ask that he grant victory to the Trojans until the Achaean Greeks honor her son Achilles and give him recompense for the insult that he has suffered. As Thetis clasps the knees of Zeus and touches his chin in the traditional posture of a suppliant (see Color Plate 1), Zeus agrees to her wishes with these words (*Iliad* 1. 517–611):

"A bad business indeed if you set me at variance with Hera and she reviles me with reproaches. She always abuses me, even as it is, in the presence of the immortal gods and says that I help the Trojans in battle. But you now must withdraw, lest Hera notice anything. These things you have asked for will be my concern until I accomplish them. Come now, I shall nod my assent to you so that you may be convinced. For this from me is the greatest pledge among the immortals; for no promise of mine is revocable or false or unfulfilled to which I give assent with the nod of my head." He spoke and the son of Cronus with his dark brows nodded to her wishes; and the ambrosial locks flowed round the immortal head of the lord and he made great Olympus tremble.[15]

After the two had made their plans, they parted; then she leaped into the deep sea from shining Olympus and Zeus returned to his own house. All the gods rose together from their places in the presence of their father and no one dared to remain seated as he entered but all stood before him. Thereupon he sat down on his throne. But Hera did not fail to observe that silver-footed Thetis, daughter of the old man of the sea, had taken counsel with him. Immediately she addressed Zeus, the son of Cronus, with cutting remarks: "Which one of the gods this time has taken counsel with you, crafty rogue? Always it is dear to you to think secret thoughts and to make decisions apart from me and never yet have you dared say a word openly to me about what you are thinking."

Then the father of men and gods answered her: "Hera, do not hope to know all that I say; it would be difficult for you even though you are my wife. But whatever is fitting that you should hear, then not anyone either of gods nor of mortals will know it before you. But do not pry or ask questions about each and every thing to which I wish to give thought apart from the gods."

And then ox-eyed Hera in her majesty replied: "Most dread son of Cronus, what kind of answer is this you have given? I have not pried too much or asked questions before but completely on your own you plan whatever you wish. Yet now I am terribly afraid in my heart that silver-footed Thetis, daughter of the old man of the sea, has won you over; for early this morning she sat by your side and grasped your knees and I believe that you nodded your oath that you would honor Achilles and destroy many by the ships of the Achaeans."

The cloud-gatherer Zeus spoke to her in answer: "You always believe something and I never escape you; nevertheless you will be able to accomplish nothing, but you will be farther removed from my heart; and this will be all the more chill an experience for you. If what you say is so, its fulfillment is what I desire. But sit down in silence, and obey what I say; for now all the gods in Olympus will be of no avail when I come closer and lay my invincible hands upon you." Thus he spoke and ox-eyed lady Hera was afraid, and she sat down in silence wrenching her heart to obedience, and the gods of heaven were troubled in the house of Zeus.

But Hephaestus renowned for his art began to make a speech to them showing his concern for his dear mother, Hera of the white arms. "This will be a sorry business indeed and not to be endured any longer, if you two quarrel on account of mortals and bring wrangling among the gods. There will be no further pleasure in the excellent feast when baser instincts prevail. I advise my mother, even though she is prudent, to act kindly toward my dear father Zeus so that he will not be abusive again and disturb our banquet. Just suppose he, the Olympian hurler of lightning, wishes to blast us from our seats. For he is by far the strongest. But you touch him with gentle words; immediately then the Olympian will be kindly toward us.''

Thus he spoke and springing up he placed a cup with two handles in the hand of his mother and spoke to her: "Bear up, mother dear, and endure, although you are hurt, so that I may not see you struck before my eyes, and then even though you are dear and I am distressed I shall not be able to help. For the Olympian is hard to oppose. Previously on another occasion when I was eager to defend you, he grabbed me by the feet and hurled me from the divine threshold. And I fell the whole day and landed on Lemnos when the sun was setting, and little life was left in me. There Sintian men took care of me at once after my fall.''

Thus he spoke. And the goddess Hera of the white arms smiled and as she smiled she received the cup from his hand. He drew sweet nectar from a mixing bowl and poured it like wine for all the other gods from left to right. Then unquenchable laughter rose up among the blessed gods as they saw Hephaestus bustling about the house.

In this way then the whole day until the sun went down they feasted, nor was anyone's desire for his share of the banquet found wanting nor of the exquisite lyre that Apollo held nor of the Muses, who sang in harmony with beautiful voice. But when the bright light of the sun set they went to bed each to his own home which the renowned lame god Hephaestus had built by his skill and knowledge. Olympian Zeus, the hurler of lightning, went to his own bed where he always lay down until sweet sleep would come to him. There he went and took his rest and beside him was Hera of the golden throne.

Hephaestus, Aphrodite, and Ares Hephaestus is a figure of amusement as he hobbles around acting as the cupbearer to the gods in the scene above, on Olympus; but he is a deadly serious figure in his art and in his love. His wife is Aphrodite,[16] and theirs is a strange and tempestuous marriage: the union of beauty and deformity, the intellectual and the sensual. Aphrodite is unfaithful to her husband and turns to the virile Ares, handsome and whole, brutal and strong. Homer with deceptive simplicity lays bare the psychological implications in a tale about the eternal triangle that remains forever fresh in its humanity and perceptions.

In Book 8 (266–366) of the *Odyssey,* the bard Demodocus sings of the love affair between Ares and Aphrodite and the suffering of Hephaestus (see Color Plate 13):

He took up the lyre and began to sing beautifully of the love of Ares and Aphrodite with the fair crown: how first they lay together by stealth in the home of Hephaestus. He gave her many gifts and defiled the marriage bed of lord Hephaestus. But soon Helius, the Sun, came to him as a messenger, for he saw them in the embrace of love, and Hephaestus when he heard the painful tale went straight to his forge planning evil in his heart. He put his great anvil on its stand and hammered out chains that could not be broken or loosened so that they would hold fast on the spot.

When he had fashioned this cunning device in his rage against Ares, he went directly to his chamber where the bed was and spread the many shackles all around the bedposts and hung them suspended from the rafters, like a fine spider's web that no one could see, not even the blessed gods, for they were very cunningly made. When he had arranged the whole device all about the bed, he pretended to journey to the well-built citadel of Lemnos, which of all lands was by far the most dear to him.

But Ares of the golden reins was not blind in his watch and as he saw Hephaestus leave he went straight to the house of the craftsman renowned for his art, eager for love with Cytherea of the fair crown. She was sitting, having just come from her mighty father, the son of Cronus, when Ares came into the house; he took her hand and spoke out exclaiming: "My love, come let us go to bed and take our pleasure, for Hephaestus is no longer at home but he has gone now, probably to visit Lemnos and the Sintian inhabitants with their barbarous speech." Thus he spoke and to her the invitation seemed most gratifying; they both went and lay down on the bed. And the bonds fashioned by ingenious Hephaestus poured around them, and they were not able to raise or move a limb. Then to be sure they knew that there was no longer any escape.

The renowned lame god came from close by; he had turned back before he had reached the land of Lemnos, for Helius watched from his lookout and told him the story. Hephaestus made for his home, grieving in his heart, and he stood in the doorway and wild rage seized him; he cried out in a loud and terrible voice to all the gods: "Father Zeus and you other blessed gods who live forever, come here so that you may see something that is laughable and cruel: how Aphrodite the daughter of Zeus always holds me in contempt since I am lame and loves the butcher Ares because he is handsome and sound of limb, but I was born a cripple. I am not to blame for this nor is anyone else except both my parents who I wish had never begotten me. You will see how these two went into my bed where they lay down together in love. As I look at them I am overcome by anguish. I do not think that they will still want to lie here in this way for even a brief time, although they are so very much in love, and very quickly they will no longer wish to sleep side by side, for my cunning and my bonds will hold them fast until her father pays back all the gifts that I gave to him for this hussy because she was his daughter and beautiful, but she is wanton in her passion.

Thus he spoke and the gods assembled at his house with the floor of bronze. Poseidon the earthshaker came and Hermes the helpful runner, and lord Apollo the far-shooter. But the goddesses in their modesty stayed at home one and all. The blessed gods, dispensers of good things, stood at the door and unquenchable laughter rose up among them as they saw the skill of ingenious Hephaestus. And one would speak to another who was next to him as follows: "Bad deeds do not prosper; the slow overtakes the swift, since now Hephaestus who is slow and lame has caught by his skill Ares, even though he is the swiftest of the gods who inhabit Olympus. Therefore he must pay the penalty for being caught in adultery." This was the sort of thing that they said to one another.

And lord Apollo, son of Zeus, spoke to Hermes: "Hermes, son of Zeus, runner and bestower of blessings, would you wish to lie in bed by the side of golden Aphrodite, even though pressed in by mighty shackles?" Then the swift runner Hermes answered: "I only wish it were so, lord Apollo, far-shooter. Let there be three times the number of shackles and you gods looking on and all the goddesses, I still would lie by the side of golden Aphrodite."

Thus he spoke and a laugh rose up among the immortal gods. But Poseidon did not laugh; he relentlessly begged Hephaestus, the renowned smith, to release Ares and addressed him with winged words: "Release him. I promise you that he will pay all that is fitting in the presence of the immortal gods, as you demand." Then the renowned lame god answered: "Do not demand this of me, Poseidon, earthshaker; pledges made on behalf of worthless characters are worthless to have and to keep. How could I hold you fast in the presence of the immortal gods, if Ares gets away and escapes both his debt and his chains?" Then Poseidon the earthshaker answered: "Hephaestus, if Ares avoids his debt and escapes and flees, I myself will pay up." Then the renowned lame god replied: "I cannot and I must not deny your request."

Thus speaking Hephaestus in his might released the chains. And when they both were freed from the strong bonds, they immediately darted away, the one went to Thrace and the other, laughter-loving Aphrodite, came to Paphos in Cyprus where are her sanctuary and altar fragrant with sacrifices. There the Graces bathed her and anointed her with divine oil, the kind that is used by the immortal gods, and they clothed her in lovely garments, a wonder to behold.

A funny story yet a painful one; glib in its sophisticated and ironic portrayal of the gods, but permeated with a deep and unshakable moral judgment and conviction. The Greeks particularly enjoyed the fact that the lame Hephaestus by his intelligence and craft outwits the nimble and powerful Ares.

Ares, God of War   Ares himself, the god of war, is the last child of Zeus and Hera to be considered. His origins probably belong to Thrace, an area with which he is often linked. Aphrodite is usually named as his cult partner; several children are attributed to them, the most important being Eros. Dawn (Eos) was one of his mistresses, and we have already mentioned (in Chapter 1) Aphrodite's jealousy.

In character Ares is generally depicted as a kind of divine swash-buckler. He is not highly thought of, and at times he appears as little more than a butcher. The more profound moral and theological aspects of war were taken over by other deities, especially Zeus or Athena. Zeus' response to Ares after he has been wounded by Diomedes (Ares sometimes gets the worst of things even in battle) is typical of the Greek attitude toward him (*Iliad* 5. 889–891, 895–898).

Do not sit beside me and complain, you two-faced rogue. Of all the gods who dwell on Olympus you are the most hateful to me, for strife and wars and battles are always dear to you. . . . Still I shall not endure any longer that you be in pain, for you are of my blood and your mother bore you to me. But if you were born of some other of the gods, since you are so destructive you would have long since been thrown out of Olympus.

The Greeks felt strongly about the brutality, waste, and folly of war, all of which are personified and deified in the figure of Ares. Yet they inevitably developed an appreciation (if that is the right word) of the harsh realities that Ares could impose and the various aspects of warfare that he might represent. After all, throughout much of their history the Greeks (like us) were plagued by war; and in the pages of the great historian Thucydides we see most clearly of all that despicable war is the harshest of teachers. The Greeks *did* worship Ares, Athena, and Zeus as divine champions in righteous conflict.

The *Homeric Hymn to Ares* (8), a relatively late composition with its astrological reference to the planet Ares, invokes with more compassion a god of greater complexity who is to provide an intelligent and controlled courage.[17]

Ares—superior in force, chariot-rider, golden-helmeted, shield-bearer, stalwart in battle, savior of cities, bronze-armored, strong-fisted, unwearingly relentless, mighty with the spear, defense of Olympus, father of the war-champion Nike [Victory], ally of Themis [Right], tyrant against the rebellious, champion for the righteous, sceptred king of manhood—as you whirl your fiery red sphere among the planets in their seven courses through the air, where your blazing steeds keep you forever above the third orbit,[18] hear me, helper of mortals, giver of vigorous youth; from above shed upon my life a martial ferocity, so that I may be able to drive off bitter cowardice from my person, and then again a radiant gentleness so that I may be able to bend to my will the treacherous impulse of my spirit to rush to the attack and check the keen fury of my passion which drives me to engage in the chilling din of battle.

You, blessed one, give me the strength to keep within the harmless constraints of peace and flee from the strife of enemies and violence of fateful death.

Other Children of Zeus: The Muses and the Fates

The Nine Muses, Daughters of Zeus and Memory (Mnemosyne)
We shall conclude this chapter with two of Zeus' many affairs, because of the universal significance of the offspring. He mates with the Titaness Mnemosyne (Memory), and she gives birth to the Muses, the patronesses of literature and the arts; thus allegorically Memory with divine help produces inspiration. The home of the Muses is often located in Pieria in northern Thessaly near Mt. Olympus,[19] or about the fountain Hippocrene on Mt. Helicon in Boeotia. The Muses (their name means "the reminders") may originally have been water spirits with the power of prophecy and then inspiration, imagined from the babbling of waters as they flow. They are supreme in their fields, and those who dare to challenge them meet with defeat and punishment. In this respect they resemble Apollo, with whom they are often associated. The number of the Muses is not consistent, but later authors usually identify nine of them, each with a specific function, although assignments will vary. Calliope presides over epic poetry; Clio, history (or lyre playing); Euterpe, lyric poetry (or tragedy and flute playing); Melpomene, tragedy (or lyre playing); Terpsichore,

choral dancing (or flute playing); Erato, love poetry (or hymns to the gods and lyre playing); Polyhymnia, sacred music (or dancing); Urania, astronomy; Thalia, comedy.

In the *Homeric Hymn to the Muses and Apollo* (25), the great deity Apollo is invoked along with them because as god of music, poetry, and the arts he is often their associate.

> With the Muses, let me begin, and with Apollo and Zeus. For through the Muses and far-shooting Apollo, human beings on earth are poets and musicians; but through Zeus, they are kings. Blessed are the ones whom the Muses love; sweet is the sound that flows from their lips.
>
> Hail, children of Zeus, and give honor to my song; yet I shall remember you and another song too.

The Three Fates, Daughters of Zeus and Themis Zeus is sometimes said to be the father of the Fates (Greek, *Moirai;* Latin, *Moerae*) as a result of his union with Themis. Night and Erebus are also said to be their parents. The Fates are originally birth spirits who often came to be depicted as three old women responsible for the destiny of every individual. Clotho (Spinner) spins out the thread of life, which carries with it the fate of each human being from the moment of birth; Lachesis (Apportioner) measures the thread; and Atropos (Inflexible), sometimes characterized as the smallest and most terrible, cuts it off and brings life to an end. On occasion they can be influenced to alter the fate decreed by their labors, but usually the course of the destiny that they spin is irrevocable.

Fate is often thought of in the singular (Greek, *Moira*; Latin, *Moera*), in a conception that is much more abstract and more closely linked to a profound realization of the roles played by Luck or Fortune (Tyche) and Necessity (Ananke) in the scheme of human life. The relation of the gods to destiny is variously depicted and intriguing to analyze in the literature. According to some authors Zeus is supreme and controls all, but others portray a universe in which even the great and powerful Zeus must bow to the inevitability of Fate's decrees. The depth of this feeling of the Greeks for the working of Moira or the Moirai cannot be overemphasized. It provides a definite and unique tone and color to the bulk of their writing. One thinks immediately of Homer or Herodotus or the tragedians, but no major author was untouched by fascination with the interrelation of god, mortals, and fate and the tantalizing interplay of destiny and free will.[20]

In the brief *Homeric Hymn to the Supreme Son of Cronus* (23), Zeus is invoked as the intimate confidant of Themis; for Zeus and

Themis were the parents not only of the Fates but also of the Hours (Horae)[21] and (appropriately for this hymn) of Good Order (Eunomia), Justice (Dike), and Peace (Eirene).

 About Zeus, I will sing, the best and greatest of the gods, far-seeing ruler and accomplisher, who confides his words of wisdom to Themis, as she sits and leans close. Be kind, far-seeing son of Cronus, most glorious and most great.

ANTHROPOMORPHISM AND GREEK HUMANISM

4

The Nature of the Gods

By now the nature of the anthropomorphic conception of deity that evolved among the Greeks and the Romans should be evident. The gods are generally depicted as human in form and character; but although they look and act like humans, very often their appearance and their actions are to some extent idealized. Their beauty is beyond that of ordinary mortals, their passions more grand and intense, their sentiments more praiseworthy and touching; and they can embody and impose the loftiest moral values in the universe. Yet these same gods can mirror the physical and spiritual weaknesses of human counterparts: they can be lame and deformed or vain, petty, and insincere; they can steal, lie, and cheat, sometimes with a finesse that is exquisitely divine.

The gods usually live in houses on Mt. Olympus or in heaven; a very important distinction, however, is to be made between those deities of the upper air and the upper world (the Olympians) and those of the realm below, appropriately named chthonian (i.e., of the earth). They eat and drink, but their food is ambrosia and their wine nectar. Ichor (a substance clearer than blood) flows in their veins. Just as they can feel the gamut of human emotion, so too they can suffer physical pain and torment. They are worshiped in shrines and temples and sanctuaries; they are honored with statues, placated by sacrifices, and invoked by prayers.

In general the gods are more versatile than mortals. They are able to move with amazing speed and dexterity, appear and disappear in a moment, and change their shape at will, assuming various forms—human, animal, and divine. Their powers also are far greater than those of mortals. Yet gods are seldom omnipotent, except possibly for Zeus himself, and even Zeus may be made subject to Fate or the Fates. Their knowledge, too, is superhuman, if on occasion limited. Omniscience is most often reserved as a special prerogative of Zeus and Apollo, who communicate their knowledge of the future to mortals. Most important of all, the gods are immortal; in the last analysis, their immortality is the one divine characteristic that most consistently distinguishes them from mortals.

Very often one or more animals are associated with a particular deity. For Zeus, it is the eagle; for Ares, the boar; for Athena, the owl; for Aphrodite, the dove, sparrow, or goose; and so forth. In addition a deity who desires to do so can take the form of an animal. There is no concrete evidence, however, to show that the Greeks at an early period ever worshiped animals as sacred.

The Divine Hierarchy

Many of the preceding remarks apply for the most part only to the highest order of divinity in the Greek pantheon. Such wondrous and terrible creations as the Gorgons or Harpies, who populate the universe to the enrichment of mythology and saga, obviously represent a different category of the supernatural. Of a different order, too, are the divine spirits who animate nature. These beings are usually depicted as nymphs, beautiful young girls who love to dance and sing and, in some cases, are extremely amorous. Very often nymphs act as attendants for one or more of the major gods or goddesses. The Muses are a kind of nymph, and so are the Nereids and Oceanids, although some of them assume virtually the stature of deity. More typically, nymphs are rather like fairies, extremely long-lived but not necessarily immortal.[1]

Demigods are another class of superhuman beings, or better, a superior kind of human being—that is, supermen. They are the offspring of mixed parentage, the union of a god with a mortal, who may or may not be extraordinary.[2] Demigods are therefore limited in their powers, which are rather less than those of full-fledged gods; and they are mortals, often little more than figures made larger than life because of their tragic and epic environment.

Heroes sometimes are demigods, but the terminology is not easy to define precisely. Mortals like Oedipus and Amphiaraus are not, strictly speaking, demigods, although they are far from ordinary beings. They may be called heroes, and certainly they become so after death, honored with a cult largely because of the spiritual intensity of their lives and the miraculous nature of their deaths; they thus assume a divine status. Heracles, too, is a hero and a demigod but he is an exception because he joins the company of the immortal gods on Olympus as a reward for his glorious attainments in this world. The difficulty in establishing absolute definitions is complicated because of the use of the designation "hero" in the vocabulary of literary criticism. Achilles is a demigod, that is, the son of a mortal Peleus and the nymph-goddess Thetis. His powers are extraordinary, but it is ultimately as a mortal, the dramatic and epic hero of the *Iliad,* that he is to be judged.

It is apparent that a hierarchy of divinities existed in the Greek pantheon. The Olympians along with the major deities of the lower world represent as it were a powerful aristocracy. Although individual gods and goddesses may be especially honored in particular places (e.g., Athena in Athens, Hera in Argos, Hephaestus in Lemnos, Apollo in Delos and Delphi), in general the major divinities were universally recognized throughout the Greek world. At the top is Zeus himself, the king, the father of both gods and mortals, the supreme lord.

Zeus and Monotheism

We have already seen the popular anthropomorphic conception of Zeus as the father, husband, and lover; and we know too the primary sphere of his power: the sky and the upper air, with their thunder, lightning, and rain. Zeus also becomes the god who upholds the highest moral values in the order of the universe—values that he absorbs unto himself or that are divided among and shared by other deities. He is the god who protects the family, the clan, and the state, championing the universal moral and ethical responsibilities that these human associations entail. He protects suppliants, imposes ties of hospitality, upholds the sanctity of oaths; in a word, he is the defender of all that is right or just in the mores of advanced civilization.

Thus a monotheistic cast in the conception of Zeus is evident from the beginning; as it evolves, it may be linked closely to the standard depictions of an anthropomorphic Zeus or imagined in terms of more abstract philosophical and religious theories of a supreme power. Many selections from many authors could be quoted to bear testimony to the variety and complexity of Greek conceptions of the nature of the one god. A few examples must suffice.

Hesiod, who preaches a hard message of righteousness and warns of the terror of Zeus' punishment of the wicked, sounds very much like a severe prophet of the Old Testament. The opening section of his *Works and Days* includes the following lines (3-7):

Through Zeus, who dwells in a most lofty home and thunders from on high and by his mighty will, mortals are both known and unknown, renowned and unrenowned; for easily he makes them strong and easily he brings them low; easily he makes the overweening humble and champions the obscure; easily he makes the crooked straight and strikes down the haughty.

Xenophanes, a poet and philosopher of the pre-Socratic period, was vehement in his attack on the conventional anthropomorphic depictions of the gods:

 Homer and Hesiod have ascribed to the gods all that is shameful and reproachful among mortals: stealing, adultery, and deception. [frag. 11]

But mortals think that gods are born and have clothes and a voice and a body just like them. [frag. 14]

The Ethiopians say that their gods are flat-nosed and black and the Thracians that theirs are fair and ruddy. [frag. 16]

But if cattle and horses and lions had hands and could create with their hands and achieve works like those of human beings, horses would render their conceptions of the gods like horses, and cattle like cattle, and each would depict bodies for them just like their own. [frag. 15]

One god, greatest among gods and mortals, not at all like them, either in body or in mind. [frag. 23]

The chorus of Aeschylus' *Agamemnon* (160–161) calls upon god by the name of Zeus with words that illustrate beautifully the universality of this supreme deity: "Zeus, whoever he may be, I call on him by this name, if it is pleasing to him to be thus invoked."

It is important to realize that monotheism and polytheism are not mutually exclusive, and that human religious experience usually tends (as Xenophanes observes) to be anthropomorphic. It would be absurd to deny that Christianity in its very essence is monotheistic, but its monotheism too rests upon a hierarchical conception of the spiritual and physical universe, and its standard images are obviously cast in anthropomorphic molds: for example, there is one God in three divine persons, God the Father, the Son, and the Holy Ghost; there are angels, saints, devils, and so on. This does not mean that the Christian philosopher and layperson view the basic tenets of their religion in exactly the same way; ultimately each vision of deity is personal, as abstract and sublime for one as it is human and compassionate for another. Among

Christian sects alone there are significant variations in dogma and ritual; and of course, there are those who do not believe at all. The range from devout belief to agnosticism and atheism was as diverse and rich in the ancient world as it is in our world. The tendency in a brief survey such as this is to oversimplify and distort.

Greek Humanism

The anthropomorphism of the Greeks is almost invariably linked to their role as the first great humanists. Humanism (the Greek variety or, for that matter, any other kind) can mean many things to many people. Standard interpretations usually evoke a few sublime (although hackneyed) quotations from Greek literature. The sophist Protagoras is said to have proclaimed (presumably challenging absolute values by voicing new relativistic attitudes): "Man is the measure of all things"; a chorus in Sophocles' *Antigone* sings out exultantly: "Wonders are many but none is more wonderful than man"; and Achilles' judgment of the afterlife in Homer's *Odyssey* (translated on pp. 274-275) quoted out of context seems to affirm the glories of this life as opposed to the dismal gloom of the hereafter:

> I should prefer as a slave to serve another man, even if he had no property and little to live on, than to rule all those dead who have done with life.

With words such as these ringing in one's ears, it seems easy to postulate a Greek worship (even idolatry) of the human in a universe, where mortals pay the gods the highest (but surely dubious) compliment of casting them in their own image.

Whatever truths this popular view may contain, it is far too one-dimensional and misleading to be genuinely meaningful and fair. Greek literature and thought are shot through with an awesome reverence for the supremacy of god, a tragic realization of the irony of man's dilemma as the plaything of fate, and a profound awareness of the pain and suffering of human existence, however glorious the triumphant heights to which mortals may attain in the face of dreadful unccrtaintics and tcrrors.

Myth, Religion, and Philosophy

Another word of caution is in order about generalizations concerning Greek religious attitudes. It has been claimed that the Greeks had no Bible or strict dogma and (incredible as it may seem) no real sense of sin, or that they were innocently free and tolerant in their acceptance of new gods—what difference does one more make to a polytheist? One should not merely repeat stories (many of them from Ovid) and make pronouncement upon the spiritual adequacy or inadequacy of the theological convictions they are supposed to represent. Mythology, philosophy, and religion are inextricably entwined, and one must try to look at all the evidence. Homer offered to the Greeks a literary bible of humanism that could on occasion be quoted (as Shakespeare is for us) like scripture; the mystery religions provided a dogma and ritual of a more exacting nature. Certainly Hesiod pronounces his divine revelation with a vehement biblical authority.

Priests and priestesses devoted their lives to the service of the gods. The city-states upheld—by custom, tradition, and law—strict moral and ethical codes of behavior. If the stories of opposition to the new god Dionysus rest upon any stratum of historical truth, a foreign message of salvation was not always readily or easily accommodated, and one could be put to death (in Athens, of all places) on a charge of impiety. The Greeks thought profoundly about god, the immortality of the soul, and the meaning and consequences of vice and virtue. The Platonic myth of Er (translated in Chapter 13) is a terrifying vision of heaven and hell; as such it is a religious document. Along with much other evidence, it shows that Greek philosophical thought can hold its own with that of any of the so-called higher religions.

The Legendary History of Herodotus

The historian Herodotus perhaps best represents Greek humanistic and religious attitudes in their clearest and most succinct form when he relates the story of Solon, Croesus, and Cyrus. Fortunately, episodes in this drama may be easily excerpted here, for they illustrate many things. Monotheism and polytheism are shown resting compatibly side by side. The jealous god of Solon is not unlike the wrathful deity of the Old Testament, a god who makes manifest to mortals that it is better to be dead than alive. The divine is able to communicate with mortals in a variety of ways; one can understand the simple and sincere belief in Apollo and Delphi possible in the sixth century B.C. There is a fascinating interplay between the inevitability of fate or destiny and the individuality of human character and free will.

Much that is Homeric has colored the Herodotean view, not least of all a compassion, tinged with a most profound sadness and pity, for the human condition. Homeric and dramatic, too, is the simple elucidation of the dangers of hubris and the irrevocable vengeance of Nemesis—the kernel, as it were, of a theme that dominates Greek tragedy. Herodotus' conception of god and his message of knowledge through suffering are strikingly Aeschylean. The story of the death of Atys is most Sophoclean in its movement and philosophy, and Croesus (like Oedipus) fulfills his inevitable destinies in terms of his character; each step that he takes in his blind attempts to avoid his fate brings him closer to its embrace. As Herodotus tells it, we have a complete drama conceived and beautifully executed within the structure of the short story.

But let Herodotus' art speak for itself. He is neither professional theologian nor philosopher, yet by his molding of traditional tales he sums up the spiritual essence of an age of faith and shows how history, mythology, and religion are for him inextricably one. The story of Solon's meeting with Croesus is found in Book 1 of Herodotus (30–46):

 And so Solon set out to see the world and came to the court of Amasis in Egypt and to Croesus at Sardis. And when he arrived, Croesus received him as a guest in his palace. Three or four days later at the bidding of Croesus, servants took Solon on a tour of his treasuries, pointing out that all of them were large and wealthy. When he had seen and examined them all to suit his convenience, Croesus asked the following question: "My Athenian guest, many stories about you have reached us because of your wisdom and your travels, of how you in your love of knowledge have journeyed to see many lands. And so now the desire has come over me to ask if by this time you have seen anyone who is the happiest." He asked this expecting that he was the happiest of human beings, but Solon did not flatter him at all but following the truth said: "O king, Tellus the Athenian."

Croesus, amazed at this reply, asked sharply: "How do you judge Tellus to be the most happy?" And Solon said: "First of all he was from a city that was faring well and he had beautiful and good children and to all of them he saw children born and all survive, and secondly his life was prosperous, according to our standards, and the end of his life was most brilliant. When a battle was fought by the Athenians against their neighbors near Eleusis, he went to help and after routing the enemy died most gloriously, and the Athenians buried him at public expense there where he fell and honored him greatly." Thus Solon provoked Croesus as he listed the many good fortunes that befell Tellus, and he asked whom he had seen second to him, thinking certainly that he would at least win second place.

Solon said: "Cleobis and Biton. They were Argives by race and their strength of body was as follows: both similarly carried off prizes at the festivals and as well this story is told. The Argives celebrated a festival to Hera and it was absolutely necessary that the mother of these boys be brought by chariot to the temple.[3] But the oxen had not come back from the fields in time, and the youths, because it was growing late, yoked themselves to the chariot and conveyed their mother, and after a journey of five miles they arrived at the temple. When they had done this deed, witnessed by the whole congregation, the end of life that befell them was the very best. And thereby god showed clearly how it is better for a human being to be dead than alive.[4] For the Argive men crowded around and congratulated the youths for their strength and the women praised their mother for having such fine sons. And the mother was overjoyed at both the deed and the praise and standing in front of the statue prayed to the goddess to give to her sons, Cleobis and Biton, who had honored her greatly, the best thing for a human being to obtain. After this prayer, when they had sacrificed and feasted, the two young men went into the temple itself to sleep and never more woke up, but the end of death held them fast. The Argives had statues made of them and set them up in Delphi since they had been the best of men.[5]

Thus Solon assigned the second prize of happiness to these two and Croesus interrupted in anger: "My Athenian guest, is our happiness so dismissed as nothing that you do not even put us on a par with ordinary men?" And he answered: "O Croesus, you ask me about human affairs, who know that all deity is jealous and fond of causing troubles. For in the length of time there is much to see that one does not wish and much to experience. For I set the limit on life at seventy years; these seventy years comprise 25,200 days, if an intercalary month is not inserted. But if one wishes to lengthen every other year by a month, so that the seasons will occur when they should, the months intercalated in the seventy years will number thirty-five and these additional months will add 1,050 days. All the days of the seventy years will total 26,250; and no one of them will bring exactly the same events as another.

"And so then, O Croesus, a human being is completely a thing of chance.[6] To me you appear to be wealthy and king of many subjects; but I cannot answer the question that you ask me until I know that you have completed the span of your life well. For the one who has great wealth is not at all more fortunate than the one who has only enough for his daily needs, unless fate attend him and, having everything that is fair, he also end his life well. For many very wealthy men are unfortunate and many with only moderate means of livelihood have good luck. Indeed the one who is very wealthy but unfortunate surpasses the lucky man in two respects only, but the man of good luck surpasses the wealthy but unlucky man in many. The latter [wealthy but unlucky] is better able to fulfill his desires and to endure a great disaster that might befall him, but the other man [who is lucky] surpasses him in the following ways. Although he is not similarly able to cope with doom and desire, good fortune keeps these things from him, and he is unmaimed, free from disease, does not suffer evils, and has fine children and a fine appearance. If in addition to these things he still ends his life well, this is the one whom you seek who is worthy to be called happy. Before he dies do not yet call him happy, but only fortunate.

"Now it is impossible that anyone, since he is a man, gather unto himself all these blessings, just as no country is self-sufficient providing of itself all its own needs, but possesses one thing and lacks another. Whichever has the most, this is the best. Thus too no one human person is self-sufficient, for he possesses one thing but lacks another. Whoever continues to have most and then ends his life blessedly, this one justly wins this name from me, O king. One must see how the end of everything turns out. For to be sure, god gives a glimpse of happiness to many and then casts them down headlong."

Solon did not find favor with Croesus by his words. He was sent away as one of no account, since Croesus was very much of the opinion that a man must be ignorant who sets aside present goods and bids one look to the end of everything.

After the departure of Solon, a great Nemesis from god took hold of Croesus, very likely because he considered himself to be the happiest of all men. Straightway a dream stood before him as he slept, which made clear to him the truth of the evils that were to come about in connection with his son. Croesus had two sons, one of whom was dumb, the other by far the first in all respects among youths of his own age. His name was Atys. The dream indicated to Croesus that this Atys would die struck by the point of an iron weapon. When he woke up he thought about the dream and was afraid; he got his son a wife and, although the boy was accustomed to command the Lydian forces, he no longer sent him out on any such mission; and javelins and spears and all such weapons that men use in war he had removed from the men's quarters and piled up in the women's chambers, for fear that any that were hanging might fall on his son.

While they had on their hands arrangements for the marriage, there came to Sardis a man seized with misfortune, his hands polluted with blood, a Phrygian by race and of the royal family. This man came to the palace of Croesus, and according to the traditions of the country begged to obtain purification, and Croesus purified him. The ritual of cleansing is similar for the Lydians and the Hellenes.[7] When Croesus had performed the customary rites, he asked from where he came and who he was in the following words: "My fellow, who are you and from where in Phrygia have you come to my hearth? What man or woman have you killed?" And he answered: "O king, I am the son of Gordias, the son of Midas, and I am called Adrastus. I killed my brother unintentionally and I come here driven out by my father and deprived of everything."

Croesus answered him with these words: "You happen to be from a family of friends, and you have come to friends where you will want for nothing while you remain with us. It will be most beneficial to you to bear this misfortune as lightly as possible." So Adrastus lived in the palace of Croesus.

At this very same time a great monster of a boar appeared in Mysian Olympus, and he would rush down from this mountain and destroy the lands of the Mysians; often the Mysians went out against him but did him no harm and rather suffered from him. Finally messengers of the Mysians came to Croesus and spoke as follows: "O king, the greatest monster of a boar has appeared in our country and destroys our lands. We are not able to capture him despite our great effort. Now then we beseech you to send your son to us and with him a picked company of young men and dogs so that we may drive him out of our land."

They made this plea, but Croesus remembering the dream spoke the following words: "Do not mention my son further; for I will not send him to you; he is newly married and this now is his concern. I shall, however, send along a select group of Lydians and all my hunting equipment and hounds, and I shall order them as they go to be most zealous in helping you drive the beast from your land."

This was his answer, and the Mysians were satisfied with it when the son of Croesus, who had heard their request, broke in on them. Croesus still refused to send his son along with them and the young man spoke to him as follows: "O father, previously the finest and most noble pursuits were mine—to win renown in war and in the hunt. But now you have barred me from both, although you have not seen any lack of spirit or cowardice in me. Now how must I appear in the eyes of others as I go to and from the agora? What sort of man will I seem to my fellow citizens, what sort to my new bride? What kind of husband will she think she has married? So either let me go to the hunt or explain and convince me that it is better for me that things be done as you wish."

Croesus answered with these words: "My child, I do not do this because I have seen in you cowardice or any other ugly trait, but the vision of a dream stood over me in sleep and said that your life would be short; for you will die by means of the sharp point of an iron weapon. And so in answer to the vision I urged this marriage on you and do not send you away on the present enterprise, being on my guard if in any way I might be able to steal you from fate for my own lifetime. For you happen to be my one and only child; for the other boy is deaf and I do not count him as mine."[8]

The young man answered: "O father, I forgive you for taking precautions for me since you have seen such a vision. But you do not understand; the meaning of the dream has escaped you and it is right for me to explain. You say that the dream said that I would die by the point of an iron weapon. But what sort of hands does a boar have? And what sort of iron point that you fear? For if it said that I would die by a tusk or tooth or some other appropriate attribute, you should do what you are doing. But as it is, the instrument is a weapon's point; and so then let me go since the fight is not against men."

Croesus answered: "My child, you have won me over with your interpretation of the dream; and so since I have been won over by you I reverse my decision and let you go to the hunt."

After these words Croesus sent for the Phrygian Adrastus; when he arrived he spoke as follows to him: "Adrastus, I did not reproach you when you were struck down by an ugly misfortune, I cleansed you, received you in my palace, and offered you every luxury. Now then since you owe me good services in exchange for those that I have done for you, I ask that you be a guardian of my boy while he hastens out to the hunt, in case some malicious robbers turn up on the journey to do you harm. Furthermore you should go where you will become famous for your deeds, for it is your hereditary duty and you have the strength and prowess besides."

Adrastus answered: "Ordinarily I would not go out to this kind of contest, for it is not fitting that one under such a misfortune as mine associate with companions who are faring well, nor do I have the desire and I should hold myself back for many reasons. But now, since you urge me and I must gratify you (for I owe you a return for your good services), I am ready to do this; expect that your boy, whom you order me to guard, will come back home to you unharmed because of his guardian."

This was the nature of his answer to Croesus, and afterward they left equipped with a band of picked young men and dogs. When they came to the mountain Olympus they hunted the wild beast, and after they had found him they stood in a circle round about and hurled their weapons. Then the stranger, the guest and friend who had been cleansed of murder, who was called Adrastus, hurled his javelin at the boar, but missed him, and hit the son of Croesus, who, struck by the point of the weapon, fulfilled the prediction of the dream; someone ran to Croesus, as a messenger of what had happened, and when he came to Sardis he told him of the battle and the fate of his child.

Croesus was greatly distressed by the death of his son and was even more disturbed because the very one whom he himself had purified had killed him. Overcome by his misfortune, Croesus called terribly on Zeus the Purifier, invoking him to witness that he had suffered at the hands of the stranger and guest-friend; he called on him too as god of the hearth and as god of friendship, giving this same god these different names: god of the hearth because he did not realize that he received in his palace and nourished as a guest the murderer of his son, and god of friendship because he sent him along as a guardian and found him to be his greatest enemy.

Afterward the Lydians arrived with the corpse and the murderer followed behind. He stood before the dead body and stretching forth his hands surrendered himself to Croesus; he bade Croesus slaughter him over the corpse, telling of his former misfortune and how in addition to it he had destroyed the one who had cleansed him, and life for him was not worth living. Croesus heard and took pity on Adrastus although he was enmeshed in so great a personal evil, and he spoke to him: "I have complete justice from yourself, my guest and friend, since you condemn yourself to death. You are not the one responsible for this evil (except insofar as you did the deed unwillingly), but some one of the gods somewhere who warned me previously of the things that were going to be."

Croesus now buried his son as was fitting; and Adrastus, the son of Gordias, the son of Midas, this murderer of his own brother and murderer of the one who purified him, when the people had gone and quietness settled around the grave, conscious that he was the most oppressed by misfortune of mankind, slaughtered himself on the tomb.

Croesus' personal and domestic tragedy was compounded by his political downfall. Daily the power of Cyrus the Great and the Persians was growing; and as they extended their empire to the west, Croesus' own kingdom of Lydia eventually was absorbed. In this crisis, Croesus consulted various oracles and came to believe that the one of Apollo at Delphi alone could speak the truth. He sent magnificent offerings to Delphi and inquired of the oracle whether or not he should go to war with the Persians. The Delphic reply is perhaps the most famous oracle of all time, typically ironic in its simple ambiguity: if Croesus attacked the Persians he would destroy a mighty empire. Croesus, of course, thought he would destroy the empire of the Persians; instead he brought an end to his own. Through Croesus' suffering the wisdom of Solon was confirmed. Herodotus tells of the fall of Sardis (the capital of Lydia) and the fate of Croesus, its king, and his other son, "a fine boy except that he could not speak" (1. 85-88):

 When the city was taken, one of the Persians made for Croesus to kill him, not knowing who he was; now Croesus saw the man coming but he did not care, since in the present misfortune it made no difference to him if he were struck down and died. But the boy, this one who was dumb, when he saw the Persian attacking, through fear of the terrible evil that was to happen broke into speech and cried: "Soldier, do not kill Croesus." This was the first time that he had uttered a sound but afterward he could speak for the rest of his life.

The Persians then held Sardis and took Croesus himself captive after he had ruled for fourteen years and been besieged for fourteen days, and as the oracle predicted, he brought to an end his own mighty empire. The Persians took Croesus and led him to Cyrus, who had a great pyre erected and ordered Croesus bound in fetters to mount it and along with him twice seven children of the Lydians. Cyrus intended either to offer them as the first fruits of the booty to some one of the gods, perhaps in a desire to fulfill a vow, or having learned that Croesus was a god-fearing man placed him on the pyre wishing to see if any of the gods would save him from being burned alive. At any rate this is what Cyrus did, but to Croesus as he stood on the pyre came the realization (even though he was in such sore distress) that the words of Solon had been spoken under god's inspiration: "No one of the living is happy!"

As this occurred to him he sighed and groaned and broke the lengthy silence by calling out three times the name of Solon. When Cyrus heard this he bade interpreters ask Croesus who this was whom he invoked, and they came up and asked the question. For a time Croesus did not answer, but eventually through compulsion he said: "The man I should like at all costs to converse with every tyrant."

Since his words were unintelligible to them, they asked again and again what he meant; annoyed by their persistence, he told how Solon the Athenian first came to him, and after having beheld all his prosperity made light of it by the nature of his talk, and how everything turned out for him just as Solon had predicted, with words that had no more reference to Croesus himself than to all human beings and especially those who in their own estimation considered themselves to be happy. As Croesus talked, the fire was kindled and began to burn the outer edges of the pyre. When Cyrus heard from his interpreters what Croesus had said, he changed his mind, reflecting that he too was a human being who was surrendering another human being while still alive to the fire; besides he feared retribution, and realizing how nothing in human affairs is certain and secure, he ordered the burning fire to be quenched as quickly as possible and Croesus and those with him taken down from the pyre. And they made the attempt but were unable to master the flames.

Then, according to the Lydian version of the story, when Croesus learned of Cyrus' change of heart as he saw all the men trying to put out the fire but no longer able to hold it in check, he shouted aloud calling on Apollo, if ever he had received from him any gift that was pleasing, to stand by him and save him from the present evil. In tears he called on the god and suddenly out of the clear and calm atmosphere storm clouds rushed together, burst forth in violent torrents of rain, and quenched the fire.

Thus Cyrus knew that Croesus was beloved by god and a good man. He brought him down from the pyre and asked: "Croesus, what man persuaded you to march against my land and become my enemy instead of my friend?" And he answered: "O king, these things I have done are to your good fortune but my own misfortune. The god of the Hellenes is responsible since he incited me to war. For no one is so senseless as to prefer war instead of peace. In time of peace sons bury their fathers, but in war fathers bury their sons. But it was somehow the pleasure of the gods that this be so." These were his words, and Cyrus released him and sat by his side and held him in great respect, and both he and all those around him looked on him with wonder.

Thus Croesus became the wise and benevolent counselor of Cyrus. In the concluding pages of this minisaga (Herodotus 1. 90–91), Croesus sends to inquire of the priestess of Apollo why the oracle had misled him. "It is impossible even for god to escape destined fate" the priestess replies, and then tells of the ways in which Apollo indeed tried to ameliorate Croesus' fated misfortune.

 Apollo saved him from burning. And it was not right that Croesus find fault with the oracle that he received. For Apollo warned that if he marched against Persia he would destroy a great empire. He should, if he were going to act wisely with respect to this reply, have sent again to ask whether his own empire or that of Cyrus was meant. If he did not understand the reply and he did not press the question, he should see himself as the one to blame. . . . When he [Croesus] heard he agreed that it was his own fault and not that of the god.

Interpretations of Herodotean Legend

The Herodotean account gives us a glimpse into the fascinating world of legendary history. How can one possibly with complete confidence isolate the facts from the fiction in the epic context of Herodotus' literary art? The name of Croesus' son Atys means "the one under the influence of Ate" (a goddess of doom and destruction), and he has links, too, in cult and in story, with Attis and Adonis. Adrastus may be connected to the mythological concept of Nemesis or Adrasteia (Necessity), and the name Adrastus can be translated "the one who cannot escape," that is, "the one who is doomed." Incidents in the tale recall those of the legendary Calydonian boar hunt. Is there anyone today who has enough faith in miracles to believe that Apollo saved Croesus from a fiery death?

Yet there *are* parts of the myth that perhaps may be true. Despite chronological problems, Solon could have met Croesus, although not at the time Herodotus imagines;[9] Croesus probably had a son named Atys who died young. But the historian Herodotus could never be satisfied with this prosaic truth alone. His stories (wrought with exquisite art) must illustrate a different level of emotional and spiritual truth that illuminates character and elucidates philosophy. The life of Tellus the Athenian, the happiest of men, reveals the character and the values of those Greeks who fought and won in great battles like that of Marathon, defending their country against the Persian invaders in the first quarter of the fifth century B.C.; god will punish their king Xerxes for his sinful hubris, just as he did Croesus, Xerxes' prototype. Herodotus explains through his manipulation of traditional tales (military numbers, strategy, and "facts" will come later) why the Greeks defeated the Persians. These are truths, too, but of another order, and they are the essence of mythic art.

POSEIDON, SEA DEITIES, GROUP DIVINITIES, AND MONSTERS

5

Poseidon, the great god of waters in general and of the sea in particular, was by no means the first or only such divinity. As we have seen, Pontus (the Sea) was produced by Ge in the initial stages of creation; and two of the Titans, Oceanus and Tethys, bore thousands of children, the Oceanids. In addition Pontus mated with his mother, Ge, and begat (among other progeny, discussed below) Nereus, the eldest of his children, who was gentle, wise, and true, an old man of the sea with the gift of prophecy. Nereus in turn united with Doris (an Oceanid) who bore him fifty daughters, the Nereids; three of these mermaids should be singled out: Thetis, Galatea, and Amphitrite.

Peleus and Thetis

We have already mentioned that Thetis was destined to bear a son mightier than his father. Zeus learned this secret from Prometheus and avoided mating with Thetis; she married instead a mortal named Peleus, who was hard pressed to catch his bride. For Thetis possessed the power of changing shape and transformed herself into a variety of states (e.g., a bird, tree, tigress) in rapid succession, but eventually she was forced to succumb. Peleus and Thetis celebrated their marriage with great ceremony (though she later left him; see p. 367), and their son Achilles did indeed become mightier than his father.

Acis, Galatea, and Polyphemus

Galatea, another Nereid, was loved by the Cyclops Polyphemus, a son of Poseidon. Ovid's account (*Metamorphoses* 13. 750–897) presents a touching rendition of their story, playing upon the incongruity

Nereid, by Georges Braque (1882–1963). Incised plaster, 1931–1932; $73\frac{1}{4} \times 51$ in. This is part of a series of mythological figures incised on large slabs of black-painted plaster. A Nereid (whose name, SAO, is added in Greek letters), rides upon a sea horse, while curving lines, reminiscent of ancient Greek and Etruscan techniques of engraving, represent other marine animals and the waves. *(Fondation Marguerite et Aimée Maeght, 06570 St. Paul, France. © 1994 Artists Rights Society [ARS], New York/ ADAGP, Paris.)*

of the passion of the monstrous and boorish giant for the delicate nymph. Repelled by his attentions, she loved Acis, handsome son of Faunus and a sea-nymph, Symaethis, daughter of the river-god, Symaethus, in Sicily. Overcome by emotion, Polyphemus attempted to mend his savage ways; he combed his hair with a rake and cut his beard with a scythe.

Ovid's Galatea tells how the fierce Cyclops would sit on the cliff of a promontory jutting out to the sea, where he would lay down his staff (a huge pine-trunk the size of a ship's mast) and take up his pipe of a hundred reeds. Hiding below in the arms of her beloved Acis, Galatea would listen to his song. First he would extravagantly describe her magnificent beauty, then bitterly lament her adamant rejection of him and continue with an offer of many rustic gifts. His tragicomic appeal concludes as follows (839–897):

"Now Galatea, come, don't despise my gifts. Certainly I know what I look like; just recently I saw myself in the reflection of a limpid pool, and I was pleased with the figure that I saw. Look at what a size I am! Jupiter in the sky doesn't have a body bigger than mine—you are always telling me that someone or other named Jove reigns up there. An abundance of hair hangs over my rugged features and, like a grove of trees, overshadows my shoulders; and don't think my body ugly because it bristles with the thickest and coarsest of hair. A tree without leaves is ugly; ugly is a horse, if a bushy mane doesn't cover its tawny neck; feathers cover birds and their own wool is an adornment for sheep; for a man a beard and shaggy hair are only fitting. So there is one eye in the middle of my forehead. What of it? Doesn't the great Sun see all these things here on earth from the sky? Yet the sun has only a single eye.

"Furthermore, my father Neptune rules over your waters and he is the one I give you as a father-in-law. Only have pity and listen to the prayers of my supplication! I succumb to you alone. I am scornful of Jove, of his sky and his devastating thunder; but I am afraid of you; your wrath is more deadly than his thunderbolt. I should better endure this contempt of yours, if you would run away from everybody; but why do you reject me and love Acis? Why do you prefer Acis to my embraces? Yet he may be allowed to please himself and you as well—but I don't want him to be pleasing to you! Just let me have the chance. He will know then that my strength is as huge as the size of my body. I'll tear out his living innards and I'll scatter his dismembered limbs over the land and the waves of your waters—in this way may he mingle in love with you! For I burn with a fiery passion that, upon being rejected, flames up the more fiercely and I seem to carry Mt. Aetna, with all its volcanic force, buried in my breast. And you, Galatea, remain unmoved."

After such complaints made all in vain, he rose up (for I saw it all) and was unable to stand still, but wandered the woods and his familiar pastures, like a bull full of fury when his cow has been taken away from him. Then the raging Cyclops saw me and Acis, who were startled by such an unexpected fright. He shouted, "I see you and I'll make this loving union of yours your last." That voice of his was as great as a furious Cyclops ought to have; Aetna trembled at his roar. But I was terrified and dove into the waters nearby. My Symaethian hero had turned his back in flight and cried, "Bring help to me, Galatea, help, my parents, and take me, about to die, to your watery kingdom!"

The Cyclops, in hot pursuit, hurled a section torn out of the mountain. Although only a mere edge of that jagged mass struck Acis, it buried him completely, but it was through me that Acis appropriated to himself the watery power of his ancestry—the only solution allowed by the Fates. Red blood began to trickle from out the mass that had buried him, and in a short time the red of the blood began to disappear and it became the color of a stream made turbid by an early rain, and in a while the water cleared. Then the mass that had been thrown upon him split open and, through the cleft, a reed, green and slender, rose up and the hollow opening in the rock resounded with the leaping waves. Suddenly a wonderful thing happened—up to his waist in the midst of the waves there stood a youth, the sprouting horns on his brow wreathed with pliant reeds. Except that he was bigger and his whole face the bluish green of water, this was Acis indeed turned into a river-god.

Poseidon and Amphitrite

The third Nereid, Amphitrite, is important mainly as the wife of Poseidon; like her sister Thetis she proved a reluctant bride, but Poseidon finally was able to win her. As husband and wife they play roles very much like those enacted by Zeus and Hera; Poseidon has a weakness for women, and Amphitrite with good cause is angry and vengeful. They had a son, Triton, a merman, human above the waist, fish-shaped below. He is often depicted blowing a conch shell, a veritable trumpeter of the sea;[1] he can change shape at will (see Color Plate 14).

Proteus

The sea divinity Proteus, probably another of the older generation of gods, is often named as the attendant of Poseidon or even as his son. Like Nereus, he is an old man of the sea who can foretell the future; he can also change shape. It is easy to see how the identities of Nereus, Proteus, and Triton could be merged. Confusion among sea divinities and duplication of their characteristics are everywhere apparent.[2]

The Appearance and Character of Poseidon

Poseidon is similar in appearance to his brother Zeus, a majestic, bearded figure, but he is generally more severe and rough; besides, he carries the trident, a three-pronged fork resembling a fisherman's spear. By his very nature Poseidon is ferocious. He is called the supporter of the earth but the earthshaker as well, and as a god of earthquakes he exhibits his violence by the rending of the land and the surge of the sea. By a mere stroke of his trident he may destroy and kill. His relentless anger against Odysseus for the blinding of Polyphemus provides a dominant theme in the *Odyssey*. *The Homeric Hymn to Poseidon* (22) attempts to appease his anger.

> About Poseidon, a great god, I begin to sing, the shaker of the earth and of the barren sea, ruler of the deep and also over Mt. Helicon and the broad town of Aegae.[3] A double honor, the gods have allotted to you, O Earthshaker—to be both a tamer of horses and a savior of ships. Hail, dark-haired Poseidon, who surrounds the earth and, O blessed god, be of kind heart and protect those who sail your waters.

The origins of Poseidon are much disputed. If his trident represents what was once a thunderbolt, then he was in early times a god of the sky. More attractive is the theory that he was once a male spirit of fertility, a god of earth who sent up springs. This fits well with his association with horses and bulls (he either creates them or makes them appear) and explains the character of some of his affairs. He mated with Demeter in the form of a stallion; he pursued her while she was searching for her daughter, and her ruse of changing into a mare to escape him was to no avail. Thus we have the union of the male and female powers of the fertility of the earth.[4] It nevertheless should be remembered that standard epithets of the sea are "barren" and "unharvested" as opposed to the fecundity of the land. The suggestion that Poseidon's horses are the mythical depiction of the white-caps of the waves is not convincing, at least in terms of origins.

The important story of the contest between Poseidon and Athena for control of Athens and its surrounding territory, Attica, is told in Chapter 6 in connection with the sculpture of the west pediment of the Parthenon.

Scylla and Charybdis

Poseidon made advances to Scylla, the daughter of Phorcys and Hecate. Amphitrite became jealous and threw magic herbs into Scylla's bathing place. Thus Scylla was transformed into a terrifying monster, encircled with a ring of dogs' heads;[5] her home was a cave in the Straits of Messina between Sicily and Italy. With her was Charybdis, the daughter of Poseidon and Ge, a formidable and voracious ally whom Zeus had cast into the sea by his thunderbolt; three times a day she drew in mountains of water and spewed them out again. Scylla and Charybdis have been rationalized into natural terrors faced by mariners when they sailed through the straits. Certainly many of the tales about the gods of the waters are reminiscent of the yarns spun by fishermen, sailors, and the like, whose lives are involved with the sea and with travel.

The Progeny of Pontus and Ge

Pontus and Ge produced legions of descendants. Notice how elements of the fantastic and the grotesque appear again and again in the nature of the progeny associated with the sea and the deep.

In addition to Nereus, Pontus and Ge had two more sons, Thaumas and Phorcys, and two daughters, Ceto and Eurybie. Thaumas mated with Electra (an Oceanid) to produce Iris and the Harpies. Iris is the

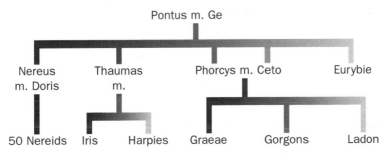

Figure 5.1. Descendants of the Sea.

goddess of the rainbow (her name means "rainbow"). She is also a messenger of the gods, sometimes the particular servant of Hera, with Hermes' offices then confined to Zeus. She is fleet-footed and winged, as are her sisters, the Harpies, but the Harpies are much more violent in nature. In early sources, they are conceived of as strong winds (their name means "the snatchers"), but later they are depicted in literature and in art as birdlike creatures with the faces of women, often terrifying and a pestilence.[6]

Phorcys and his sister Ceto produce two groups of children, the Graeae and the Gorgons. The Graeae (Aged Ones) are three sisters, personifications of old age; their hair was gray from birth, but in their general aspect they appeared swanlike and beautiful. They had, however, only one eye and one tooth, which they were forced to share among themselves.

The Graeae knew the way to their sisters, the Gorgons, also three in number (Stheno, Euryale, and Medusa), whose hair writhed with serpents. They were of such terrifying aspect that those who looked upon them turned to stone. Gorgons are a favorite theme in Greek art, especially in the early period; they leer out most disconcertingly with a broad archaic smile, tongue protruding in the midst of a row of bristling teeth. Medusa is the most important Gorgon; Poseidon was her lover. When Perseus beheaded her, she was pregnant; from her corpse sprang a winged horse, Pegasus, and a son, Chrysaor (He of the Golden Sword).

Phorcys and Ceto also bore a dragon named Ladon; he helped the lovely Hesperides (Daughters of Evening), who guarded a wondrous

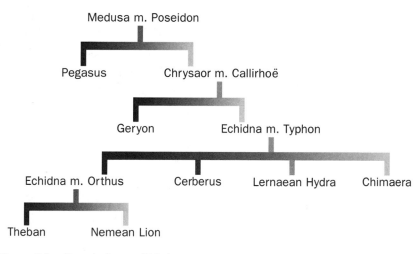

Figure 5.2.   Descendants of Medusa.

tree that grew golden fruit, far away in the west, and passed their time in beautiful singing.

Chrysaor mated with an Oceanid, Callirhoë, and produced the monsters Geryon and Echidna (half nymph and half snake). Echidna united with Typhon and bore Orthus (the hound of Geryon), Cerberus (the hound of Hades), the Lernaean Hydra, and the Chimaera. Echidna and Orthus produced the Theban Sphinx and the Nemean Lion. These monsters will appear later in saga.

ATHENA

The Birth of Athena

The *Homeric Hymn* (28) tells the story of Athena's birth.

I begin to sing about Pallas Athena, renowned goddess, with bright
eyes, quick mind, and inflexible heart, chaste and mighty virgin,
protectress of the city, Tritogeneia. Wise Zeus himself gave birth
to her from his holy head and she was arrayed in her armor of war,
all-gleaming in gold, and every one of the immortals was gripped
with awe as they watched. She quickly sprang forth from the
immortal head in front of aegis-bearing Zeus, brandishing her sharp
spear. And great Olympus shook terribly at the might of the bright-
eyed goddess, and the earth round about gave a dread groan and the
dark waves of the deep seethed. But suddenly the sea became calm,
and the glorious son of Hyperion halted his swift-footed horses all
the while that the maiden Pallas Athena took the divine armor from
her immortal shoulders, and Zeus in his wisdom rejoiced.

So hail to you, child of aegis-bearing Zeus; yet I shall remember
both you and another song too.

Hesiod (*Theogony* 886–898) tells how Zeus had swallowed his
consort Metis (her name means "wisdom") after he had made her
pregnant with Athena; he was afraid that Metis would bear a son who
would overthrow him.

Zeus, king of the gods, first took as his wife Metis, who was very
wise indeed among both gods and mortals. But when she was
about to give birth to the bright-eyed goddess Athena, then Zeus
treacherously deceived her with wheedling words and swallowed

The Birth of Athena. Detail of an Athenian black-figure amphora, sixth century B.C.; height $15\frac{1}{2}$ in. Athena emerges fully armed from the head of Zeus, who is seated on his throne holding the thunderbolt. At the left stand Hermes and Apollo (with his kithara), and to the right are Eileithyia, gesturing towards the newborn goddess whose birth she has assisted, and Ares. Beneath the throne is a sphinx. *(Courtesy of Museum of Fine Arts, Boston.)*

her down into his belly at the wise instigations of Gaea and starry Uranus. These two gave Zeus this advice so that no other of the eternal gods might rule supreme as king in his place. For Metis was destined to bear exceptional children: first, the keen-eyed maiden Athena, Tritogeneia, the equal of her father in might and good counsel, and then she was to give birth to a son of indomitable spirit who would become the king of both gods and mortals.

Variations in the story of Athena's birth have Hephaestus split Zeus' head open with an axe to facilitate the birth[1] some add to the dread awe of the occasion by having Athena cry out thunderously as she springs to life in full panoply. This myth (whatever its etiology in terms of the physical manifestations of the thunderstorm) establishes the close bond between Zeus and his favorite daughter and allegorizes the three basic characteristics of the goddess Athena: her prowess,

her wisdom, and the masculinity of her virgin nature, sprung ultimately not from the female but from the male.

The Sculpture of the Parthenon

The Parthenon was the great temple to Athena Parthenos (*parthenos*,
meaning "virgin," was a standard epithet of Athena) on the Acropolis
at Athens. It was built between 447 and 438 B.C., and it embodied the
Greek (and specifically Athenian) courage and piety over the Persians,
who had sacked the Acropolis in 480 and destroyed the Old Parthenon. Like the temple of Zeus at Olympia (described on pp. 80–81),
the Parthenon was decorated with a complex program of sculpture
in which mythology and religion glorified the city and its gods, above
all honoring Athena, whose great statue was housed in the temple.
The whole program was directed by Pheidias, creator of the statue
of Zeus at Olympia.

The east pediment of the Parthenon immortalized the dramatic
moment of the birth of Athena, who stood in the center before the
throne of Zeus, from whose head she had just sprung full grown and
fully armed. Hephaestus, who had assisted in the birth, and Hera were
probably present, while the announcement of the birth was brought
to other divine figures waiting to observe the miracle. At the corners,

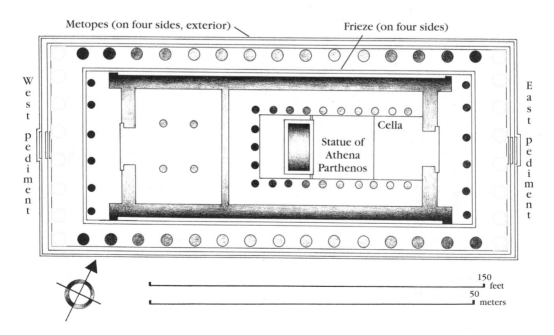

Figure 6.1. Plan of the Parthenon. *(After J. Travlos.)*

to set the divine event in cosmic time, were the horses of Helius, rising from the sea, and of Selene, sinking into it.

As at Olympia, the west pediment was a scene of violent action, celebrating the victory of Athena in her contest with Poseidon for control of Athens and Attica. The central figures pull away from each other as they produce the gifts with which they vied, and to each side were figures of divinities and heroic kings of early Athens who attended the contest. Athena with her spear created an olive tree; Poseidon with his trident, a salt spring. Athena was proclaimed victor.[2] Poseidon continued to be worshiped (in conjunction with the Athenian hero Erechtheus) in the nearby sanctuary of the Erechtheum (described on pp. 451–452).[3] There the marks of Poseidon's trident were enshrined and Athena's olive tree continued to grow.

There were two friezes on the Parthenon. The exterior Doric frieze consisted of 92 metopes (each 1.2 meters high), 32 on each of the long sides and 14 on the short ones. On the south were reliefs of the battle of the Lapiths and Centaurs, also the subject of the west pediment of the temple of Zeus at Olympia. On the north side the subject was probably the sack of Troy, while on the east it was the Gigantomachy (the battle of the Olympian gods against the giants), and on the west the battle of the Greeks and the Amazons. Thus the mythical themes of the metopes reinforced the idea of the triumph of Greek courage over the barbarians, and of the Greek gods over their predecessors.

The second, Ionic, frieze ran continuously round the outer wall of the cella, or naos (the interior part of the temple that housed the statue of Athena and the treasury). It shows the people of Athens moving in procession as they celebrate the festival of the Panathenaea in honor of their goddess. Athenian men and women are shown as marshals, attendants, horsemen, hoplites, and assistants in the worship of Athena, along with the animals for the ritual sacrifice.[4] At the climax of the procession, on the east side (i.e., over the entrance to the part of the cella housing the statue) the ceremonial robe (*peplos*) was presented to the priestess of Athena,[5] and nearby sat the Olympian immortals enthroned, taking part in the joyous celebration of civic piety.[6]

In the cella of the Parthenon stood a monumental statue, the Athena Parthenos. The original by Pheidias is completely lost but reconstructions (like the one illustrated on p. 121) may be made with some accuracy.[7] Like Pheidias' later masterpiece at Olympia, the surfaces of the statue were made of gold and ivory, and its decoration contained a program related to the architectural sculptures already described that witnessed to the honor and glory of the goddess and the city she

Figure 6.2. Sectional Drawing of the East End of the Parthenon Showing Relationship of Frieze, Metopes, and Pediment. *(After N. Yalouris.)*

protected. It was nearly twelve meters high and in front of it was a reflecting pool. The standing goddess held a figure of Nike (Victory) in her right hand, and her armor included a helmet decorated with sphinxes, the aegis with the head of Medusa, a shield, and a spear, beside which was a serpent (representing the chthonic divinity Erechtheus). The shield was decorated with the battle of the Amazons on the exterior, and the Gigantomachy on the interior; on the rims of her sandals were reliefs of the battle with Centaurs (all themes repeated from the metopes). The relief on the base of the statue showed the creation of Pandora.

In the sculpture of the Parthenon, mythology and religion combine with local pride to glorify the gods and civilization of the Greeks and to celebrate the city and its citizens under the protection of Athena.

Athena Parthenos. Reconstruction by N. Leipen of the original by Pheidias, 447–438 B.C.; about one-tenth full size. The original cult-statue stood some thirty-eight feet tall, its gold and ivory gleaming in the half-light as the worshiper entered the cella with its double row of columns and reflecting pool. Pheidias focused on the majesty of the city's goddess, and the reliefs on her shield, sandals, and statue-base all are symbols of the victory of order over disorder in the human and divine spheres. The atmosphere of civic grandeur is far from the intimate emotion of the *Mourning Athena* on p. 126. *(Courtesy of the Royal Ontario Museum, Toronto, Canada.)*

Pallas Athena Tritogeneia

Athena's title, Tritogeneia, is obscure. It seems to refer to a region sometimes associated with her birth, the river or lake Triton, or Tritonis, in Boeotia or in Libya. Some scholars see in this link the possibility that Athena was, at least in her origins, at one time a goddess of

Athena. Detail from an Attic red-figure amphora by the Andocides Painter, ca. 520 B.C.; height of vase 22½ in. Athena is armed with helmet, spear, and shield, and her aegis is tasseled with snakes, with a Gorgon's head at the center. On the vase she stands at the left watching Heracles and Apollo struggling for the Pythian tripod (see p. 437 and illustration on p. 438). *(Staatliches Museum, Berlin, Photograph courtesy of Hirmer Verlag, München.)*

waters or of the sea. We are told that soon after her birth Athena was reared by Triton (presumably the god of this body of water, wherever it may be). Now Triton had a daughter named Pallas, and Athena and the girl used to practice the arts of war together. But on one occasion they quarreled and, as Pallas was about to strike Athena, Zeus intervened on behalf of his daughter by interposing the aegis. Pallas was startled, and Athena took advantage of her surprise and wounded and killed her. Athena was distraught when she realized what she had done; in her grief she made a wooden image of the girl and decked it with the aegis. Cast down by Zeus, this statue, called the Palladium, fell into the territory of the Trojans, who built a temple to house it in honor. The Palladium in saga carries with it the destiny of the city of Troy. In honor of her friend, Athena took the name Pallas for herself. A more likely etiology is that the word *Pallas* means "maiden" and is but another designation of Athena's chastity, just as she is called *Parthenos,* "virgin," or (like Persephone) *Kore,* "girl."

Athena and Arachne

The famous story of Arachne bears testimony to the importance of Athena as the patroness of women's household arts, especially spinning and weaving. In Ovid's account (*Metamorphoses* 6. 5–145) Athena has, of course, become the Roman Minerva.

 Minerva turned her mind to Arachne's destruction, for she had heard that her fame as a worker in wool equaled her own. Arachne's birth and position brought her no distinction—it was her skill that did. Idmon of Colophon was her father, who dyed the thirsty wool with Ionian purple; her mother, who also was of low birth like her husband, had died. Yet their daughter, Arachne, for all that she was born in a lowly family living at lowly Hypaepa, pursued her quest for fame throughout the cities of Lydia by her work.

The nymphs of Tmolus often left their vineyards, the nymphs of Pactolus often left their waters—to see and wonder at Arachne's handiwork. Nor was their pleasure merely in seeing her finished work, but also in observing her at work, such delight was in her skill. Whether at the beginning she gathered the unworked wool into balls, or worked it with her fingers and drew out lengths of fleece like clouds, or with swift-moving thumb turned the smooth spindle, or whether she used her embroidering needle—you would know that Minerva had taught her. Yet she would not admit this; jealous of her great teacher, she said, "Let her compete with me; if she wins I deny her nothing."

Minerva disguised herself as an old woman, white-haired and supporting herself upon a stick, and spoke as follows: "Not everything that old age brings is to be avoided; experience comes with the passing years. Do not despise my advice! Let your ambition be to excel mortal women at weaving; give place to the goddess and pray for her forgiveness for your rash words! She will pardon you if you pray." Arachne glowered at her; leaving her half-finished work and with difficulty restraining herself from blows, she openly showed her anger by her expression, as she attacked disguised Minerva with these words: "You old fool, enfeebled by advanced old age. Too long a life has done you no good! Keep your advice for your sons' wives (if you have any) and your daughter. I can think for myself, and you need not think your advice does any good—you will not change my mind. Why does not the goddess herself come? Why does she refuse to compete with me?"

Then Minerva cried: "She has come!" and throwing off her diguise she showed herself as she was, the goddess Minerva. The nymphs and women of Lydia worshiped her divine presence; Arachne alone felt no awe. Yet she blushed; a sudden flush stole over her face in spite of herself and as suddenly faded, like the red glow of the sky when Dawn first glows just before the heavens begin to whiten with the sun's rising. Obstinately she held to her course and rushed to destruction in her foolish desire for the prize. Jupiter's daughter resisted no more; she offered her no more advice; no more did she put off the competition.

Ovid goes on to describe the weaving contest. Each weaves a tapestry at her loom with surpassing skill, depicting scenes from mythology. Minerva displays her contest with Neptune for the lordship of Attica and adds four subordinate scenes of mortals who challenged gods and were turned by them into other shapes. The whole was framed by an olive-tree motif: "with her own tree she concluded her work."

Heedless of the lessons of Minerva's legends, Arachne depicted scenes of the gods' less honorable amorous conquests—where Jupiter, Neptune, Apollo, Bacchus, and Saturn deceived goddesses and mortal women. As she completed her tapestry with a design of trailing ivy, Minerva's anger burst forth. Ovid continues:

Minerva could find no fault with the work, not even Envy herself could. Angered by Arachne's success, the golden-haired goddess tore up the embroidered tapestry with its stories of the gods' shameful deeds. With the boxwood shuttle she beat Arachne's face repeatedly. In grief Arachne strangled herself, stopping the passage of life with a noose. Minerva pitied her as she was hanging and raised her up with these words: "Stubborn girl, live, yet hang! And—to make you anxious for the future—may the same punishment be decreed for all your descendants."

With these words Minerva sprinkled her with the juice of a magic herb. As the fateful liquid touched her, Arachne's hair dropped off; her nose and ears vanished, and her head was shrunken; her whole body was contracted. From her side thin fingers dangled for legs, and the rest became her belly. Yet still from this she lets the thread issue forth and, a spider now, practices her former weaving art.

This story also illustrates the severe, moral earnestness of this warrior maiden that is often only too apparent.

The Character and Appearance of Athena

Athena is a goddess of many other specific arts, crafts, and skills (military, political, and domestic), as well as the deification of wisdom and good counsel in a more generic and abstract conception. She is skilled in the taming and training of horses, interested in ships and chariots, and the inventor of the flute. This latter invention was supposed to have been inspired by the lamentations (accompanied by the hiss of serpents) uttered by the surviving Gorgons after the death of Medusa. But Athena quickly grew to dislike the new instrument because her beautiful features became distorted when she played, and so she threw it away in disgust. Marsyas, the satyr, picked up the instrument with dire consequences, as we shall see in Chapter 9. In Athens Athena was worshiped along with Hephaestus as patroness of all arts and crafts.

Athena is often represented in art with her attributes as a war goddess: helmet, spear, and shield (the aegis, on which the head of the Gorgon Medusa may be depicted). Sometimes she is attended by a winged figure (*Nike*, Victory) bearing a crown or garland of honor and success. Athena herself, as Athena Nike, represented victorious achievement in war, and a simple but elegant temple of Athena Nike stood on a bastion to the right of the entrance to the Acropolis. The brief *Homeric Hymn to Athena* (11) invokes her as a deity of war (like Ares).

I begin to sing about Pallas Athena, city-guardian, who with Ares is concerned about the deeds of war—the din of fighting and battles and the sacking of cities; she also protects the people as they leave and return.

Hail, goddess, give us good luck and good fortune.

Pallas Athena is beautiful with a severe and aloof kind of loveliness that is masculine and striking. One of her standard epithets is *glaukopis,* which may mean gray- or green-eyed, but more probably refers to the bright or keen radiance of her glance rather than to the color of her eyes. Possibly, too, the adjective may be intended to mean

Mourning Athena. Marble relief from the Acropolis, ca. 460 B.C.; height 21 in. Athena is a young woman, with helmet and spear, but without aegis and shield. She gazes at a stele (an upright stone slab), on which may have been inscribed the names of Athenians killed in the previous year's fighting. The folds of her skirt follow her body and do not fall straight. The title and purpose of the work are unknown, but it shows how closely the goddess was concerned with the life and death of her citizens. *(Acropolis Museum, Athens. Courtesy of Alinari/Art Resource, New York.)*

owl-eyed, or of owlish aspect or countenance; certainly Athena is at times closely identified with the owl (particularly on coins). The snake is also associated with her, sometimes appearing coiled at her feet or on her shield. This association (along with those of the owl and the olive tree) suggests that perhaps Athena originally was (like so many others) a fertility goddess, even though her character as a virgin dominates later tradition.

In fact her character is usually impeccable. Unlike another virgin goddess, Artemis, to whom men made advances (although at their dire peril), Athena remained sexually unapproachable. The attempt of Hephaestus on her honor (in the early saga of Athens, p. 449) confirms the purity and integrity of her convictions. It would be a misconception, however, to imagine Athena only as a cold and formidable virago who might easily elicit one's respect but hardly one's love. This Valkyrie-like maiden does have her touching moments, not only in her close and warm relationship with her father, Zeus, but also in her devout loyalty and steadfast protection of more than one hero (e.g., Telemachus and Odysseus, Heracles, Perseus, and Bellerophon).

Either alone or coupled with Apollo, Athena can be made the representative of a new order of divinity—the younger generation of the gods championing progress and the advanced enlightenment of civilization. As the agent of Zeus, Athena brings the *Odyssey* to a close by answering the primitive demand for blood evoked by the relatives of the suitors and establishing the divine and universal validity of the justice meted out by Odysseus. In Aeschylus' *Oresteia* she is on the side of Apollo for the acquittal of Orestes through the due process of law in Athens before the court of the Areopagus (which the goddess is said to have created), appeasing and silencing, presumably forever, the old social order of family vendetta represented by the Furies.

APHRODITE AND EROS

7

As we have seen, Hesiod describes the birth of Aphrodite after the castration of Uranus and derives her name from the Greek word for foam, *aphros.* Hesiod also links the goddess closely with Cythera (see Color Plate 15) and Cyprus; the latter was especially associated with her worship, particularly in its city of Paphos. Thus Aphrodite is called both Cytherea and Cypris. Another version of her birth gives her parents as Zeus and Dione. Dione is little more than a name to us, but a curious one, since it is the feminine form of the name Zeus (which in another form is Dios).

Aphrodite Urania and Aphrodite Pandemos

This double tradition of Aphrodite's birth suggested a basic duality in her character or the existence of two separate goddesses of love: Aphrodite Urania or Celestial Aphrodite sprung from Uranus alone, ethereal and sublime; Aphrodite Pandemos (Aphrodite of All the People, or Common Aphrodite) sprung from Zeus and Dione and essentially physical in nature. Plato's *Symposium* elaborates upon this distinction and claims that Aphrodite Urania, the older of the two, is stronger, more intelligent, and spiritual, whereas Aphrodite Pandemos, born from both sexes, is more base, and devoted primarily to physical satisfaction.[1] It is imperative to understand that the Aphrodite who sprang from Uranus (despite her sexuality in Hesiod's account) becomes, for philosophy and religion, the celestial goddess of pure and spiritual love and the antithesis of Aphrodite, daughter of Zeus and Dione, the goddess of physical attraction and procreation. This distinction between sacred and profane love is one of the most potent archetypes in the history of civilization.

The Nature and Appearance of Aphrodite

The *Homeric Hymn to Aphrodite* (10) with its brief glimpse of Aphrodite reminds us of her cult places, Cyprus and Cythera, and adds a third island, Salamis.

 I shall sing about Cyprus-born Cytherea, who gives mortals sweet gifts; on her lovely face, smiles are always suffused with the bloom of love.

Hail, goddess, mistress of well-built Salamis and sea-girt Cyprus. Give me a desirable song. Yet I shall remember you and another song too.

In general Aphrodite is the goddess of beauty, love, and marriage. Her worship was universal in the ancient world, but its facets were varied. At Corinth temple harlots were kept in Aphrodite's honor; at Athens this same goddess was the staid and respectable deity of marriage and married love. The seductive allurement of this goddess was very great; she herself possessed a magic girdle with irresistible powers of enticement. In the *Iliad* Hera borrows it with great effect upon her husband, Zeus.

The gamut of the conceptions of the goddess of love is reflected in sculpture as well as literature. Archaic idols, like those of other fertility goddesses, are grotesque in their exaggeration of her sexual attributes. In early Greek art she is rendered as a beautiful woman, usually clothed. By the fourth century she is portrayed nude (or nearly so), the idealization of womanhood in all her femininity; the sculptor Praxiteles was mainly responsible for establishing the type—sensuous in its soft curves and voluptuousness.[2] As so often in the ancient world, once a master had captured a universal conception, it was repeated endlessly with or without significant variations. Everyone knows the *Venus di Milo* or one of the many other extant copies, although Praxiteles' originals have not survived.

Attendants of Aphrodite

The Graces (Charites) and the Hours or Seasons (Horae) are often associated with Aphrodite as decorative and appropriate attendants. The Graces, generally three in number, are personifications of aspects of loveliness. The Horae, daughters of Zeus and Themis, are sometimes difficult to distinguish from the Graces, but they eventually emerge with clearer identity as the Seasons; thus they usually are thought of as a group of two, three, or four. Horae means "hours" and therefore "time" and thus ultimately "seasons." The *Homeric Hymn to Aphrodite* (6) focuses upon the decking out of the goddess by the Horae, whom we call in this context the Hours.

> I shall sing about beautiful and revered Aphrodite of the golden crown, who holds as her domain the battlements of all sea-girt Cyprus. The moist force of the West Wind Zephyrus as he blows brought her there amidst the soft foam on the waves of the resounding sea. The gold-bedecked Hours gladly received her and clothed her in divine garments. On her immortal head they placed a finely wrought crown of gold and in her pierced earlobes, flowers of copper and precious gold. About her soft neck and silvery breasts they adorned her with necklaces of gold, the kind that beautify the Hours themselves whenever they go to the lovely dancing choruses of the gods and to the home of their father. Then after they had bedecked her person with every adornment they led her to the immortals, who greeted her when they saw her and took her in their welcoming hands; and each god prayed that she would be his wedded wife and he would bring her home, as he marveled at the beauty of violet-crowned Cytherea.
>
> Hail, sweet and winning goddess with your seductive glance; grant that I may win victory in the contest and make my song fitting. Yet I shall remember you and another song too.

The Phallic Priapus

The more elemental and physical aspects of Aphrodite's nature are seen in her son, Priapus.[3] His father may be Hermes, Dionysus, Pan, Adonis, or even Zeus. Priapus is a fertility god, generally depicted as deformed and bearing a huge and erect phallus. He is found in gardens and at the doors of houses. He is part scarecrow, part bringer of luck, and part guardian against thieves; therefore he has something in common with Hermes. He also resembles Dionysus and Pan (two of his other reputed fathers), and is sometimes confused with them or their retinues. Whatever the origins of Priapus in terms of sincere and primitive reverence for the male powers of generation, stories about him usually came to be comic and obscene. In the jaded society of later antiquity, his worship meant little more than a cult of sophisticated pornography.

Pygmalion

Although many stories illustrate the mighty power of Aphrodite, the story of Pygmalion has provided a potent theme in subsequent literature. Ovid tells how Aphrodite (Venus in his version) was enraged with the women of Cyprus because they dared to deny her divinity; in her wrath, the goddess caused them to be the first women to prostitute themselves, and as they lost all their sense of shame it was easy to turn them into stone. Ovid goes on to relate the story of Pygmalion and the result of his disgust for these women (*Metamorphoses* 10. 243–297).

Pygmalion saw these women leading a life of sin and was repelled by the many vices that nature had implanted in the feminine mind. And so he lived alone without a wife for a long time, doing without a woman to share his bed. Meanwhile he fashioned happily a statue of ivory, white as snow, and gave it a beauty surpassing that of any woman born; and he fell in love with what he had made. It looked like a real maiden who you would believe was alive and willing to move, had not modesty prevented her. To such an extent art concealed art; Pygmalion wondered at the body he had fashioned and the flames of passion burned in his breast. He often ran his hands over his creation to test whether it was real flesh and blood or ivory. And he would not go so far as to admit that it was ivory. He gave it kisses and thought that they were returned; he spoke to it and held it and believed that his fingers sank into the limbs that he touched and was afraid that a bruise might appear as he pressed her close.

Sometimes he enticed her with blandishments, at other times he brought her gifts that please a girl: shells and smooth pebbles, little birds, flowers of a thousand colors, lilies, painted balls, and drops of amber, the tears wept by Phaëthon's sisters who had been changed into trees. He also clothed her limbs with garments, put rings on her fingers, draped long necklaces around her neck, dangled jewelry from her ears, hung adornments on her breast. All was becoming, but she looked no less beautiful naked. He placed her on his bed with covers dyed in Tyrian purple and laid her down, to rest her head on soft pillows of feathers as if she could feel them.

The most celebrated feast day of Venus in the whole of Cyprus arrived; heifers, their crooked horns adorned with gold, were slaughtered by the blow of the axe on their snowy necks, and incense smoked. When he had made his offering at the altar, Pygmalion stood and timidly prayed: "If you gods are able to grant everything, I desire for my wife. . . ." He did not dare to say "my ivory maiden." Golden Venus herself was present at her festival and understood what his prayers meant. As an omen of her kindly will a tongue of flame burned bright and flared up in the air.

When he returned home Pygmalion grasped the image of his girl and lay beside her on the bed and showered her with kisses. She seemed to be warm. He touched her with his lips again and felt her breasts with his hands. At his touch the ivory grew soft, and its rigidity gave way to the pressure of his fingers; it yielded just as Hymettan wax when melted in the sun is fashioned into many shapes by the working of the hands and made pliable. He is stunned but dubious of his joy and fearful he is wrong. In his love he touches this answer to his prayers. It was a body; the veins throbbed as he felt them with his thumb. Then in truth Pygmalion was full of prayers in which he gave thanks to Venus. At last he presses his lips on lips that are real and the maiden feels the kisses she is given and as she raises her eyes to meet his she sees both her lover and the sky.

The goddess is present at the marriage that she has made, and now when the crescent moon had become full nine times, Pygmalion's wife gave birth to Paphos, and from him the place got its name.

Galatea is the name given to Pygmalion's beloved in later versions of the tale.

Aphrodite and Adonis

In the most famous of her myths Aphrodite is confused with the great Phoenician goddess Astarte; they have in common as their love a young and handsome youth named by the Greeks Adonis.[4] Perhaps the best-known version of the story of Aphrodite and Adonis is told by Ovid. Paphos (the son of Pygmalion and Galatea) had a son, Cinyras. Myrrha, the daughter of Cinyras, fell desperately in love with her own father. Tormented by her sense of shame and guilt, the poor girl was on the point of suicide, but she was rescued just in time by her faithful nurse, who eventually wrenched the secret from her. Although the old woman was horrified by what she learned, she preferred to help satisfy the girl's passion rather than to see her die.

It was arranged that the daughter should go to the bed of her father without his knowing her identity, and their incestuous relations continued for some time until Cinyras in dismay found out with whom he had been sleeping. In terror Myrrha fled from the wrath of her father. As he pursued her she prayed for deliverance and was changed into a myrrh tree, which continually drips with her tears. Myrrha had become pregnant by her father, and from the tree was born a beautiful son named Adonis, who grew up to be a most handsome youth and keen hunter. At the sight of him Aphrodite fell desperately in love.

She warned Adonis against the dangers of the hunt, telling him to be especially wary of any wild beasts that would not turn and flee but stood firm (see Color Plate 10). Ovid's story continues as follows (*Metamorphoses* 10. 708–739):

These were the warnings of Venus and she rode away through the air in her chariot yoked with swans. But Adonis' courageous nature stood in the way of her admonitions. By chance his dogs followed the clear tracks of a wild boar and frightened it from its hiding place. As it was ready to come out of the woods, the son of Cinyras hit a glancing blow on its side. With its crooked snout the savage beast immediately dislodged the blood-stained spear and made for the frightened youth as he fled for safety. The boar buried its tusk deep within his groin and brought him down on the yellow sand, dying.

As Venus was being borne through the air in her light chariot on the wings of swans (she had not yet reached Cyprus), she heard the groans of the dying boy from afar and turned the course of her white birds toward them. When she saw from the air above his lifeless body lying in his own blood, she rushed down, and rent her bosom and her hair and beat her breast with hands not meant to do such violence. She complained against the Fates, crying: "But still everything will not be subject to your decrees; a memorial of my grief for you, Adonis, will abide forever. The scene of your death will be recreated annually with the ritual of my grief performed. But your blood will be transformed into a flower. O Persephone, you were allowed at one time to change the limbs of the maiden Mentha into the fragrant mint—will I be begrudged then the transformation of my hero, the son of Cinyras?"

With these words she sprinkled fragrant nectar on his blood which, at the touch of the drops, began to swell just like a gleaming bubble in the rain. In no longer than an hour's time a flower sprang from the blood, red as the thick skin of the fruit of the pomegranate that hides the seeds within. Yet the flower is of brief enjoyment for the winds (which give it its name, anemone) blow upon it; with difficulty it clings to life and falls under the blasts and buffeting.

Ovid's story predicts the rites associated with the worship of Adonis involving ceremonial wailing and the singing of dirges over the effigy of the dead youth. Obviously we have here once again a rendition of a recurrent theme: the Great Mother and her lover, who dies as vegetation dies and comes back to life again. Another version of the myth makes this even clearer.

Venus Discovering the Dead Adonis, by a Neapolitan follower of José de Ribera (1591–1652). Oil on canvas, ca. 1650; $72\frac{1}{2} \times 94$ in. Whereas Veronese shows Venus and Adonis before the tragedy (Color Plate 10), Ribera's follower represents Ovid's narrative of Venus descending from her dove-drawn chariot to mourn over her dead lover. The scene is full of dramatic emotion, focused by brilliant light on the gesture of Venus and the body of Adonis, and amplified by the brooding figure of a shepherd on the right and the animals in the corners—Adonis' hound and the unyoked doves of Venus. (© *The Cleveland Museum of Art, Mr. and Mrs. William H. Marlatt Fund, 65.19.*)

When Adonis was an infant, Aphrodite put Adonis in a chest and gave it to Persephone to keep. Persephone looked inside; and once she saw the beauty of the boy, she refused to give him back. Zeus settled the quarrel that ensued by deciding that Adonis would stay with Persephone below one part of the year and with Aphrodite in the upper world for the other part. It is possible to detect similarities between Easter celebrations of the dead and risen Christ in various parts of the world and those in honor of the dead and risen Adonis. Christianity, too, absorbed and transformed the ancient conception of the sorrowing goddess with her lover dying in her arms to that of the sad Virgin holding in her lap her beloved Son.

Cybele and Attis

Parallels to the figures of Aphrodite and Adonis can readily be found in the Phrygian story of Cybele and Attis, yet another variation of the eternal myth of the Great Mother and her lover that infringed upon the Graeco-Roman world.[5] Cybele was sprung from the earth, originally a bisexual deity but then reduced to a female. From the severed organ, an almond tree arose. Nana, the daughter of the god of the river Sangarios, picked a blossom from the tree and put it in her bosom; the blossom disappeared, and Nana found herself pregnant. When a son, Attis, was born, he was exposed and left to die, but a he-goat attended him. Attis grew up to be a handsome youth, and Cybele fell in love with him; however, he loved another, and Cybele in her jealousy drove him mad. In his madness, Attis castrated himself and died.[6] Cybele repented and obtained Zeus' promise that the body of Attis would never decay.

In her worship, Cybele was followed by a retinue of devotees who worked themselves into a frenzy of devotion that could lead to self-mutilation.[7] The orgiastic nature of her ritual is suggested by the frantic music that accompanied her: the beating of drums, the clashing of cymbals, and the blaring of horns. The myth explains why her priests (called Galli) were eunuchs. It is also easy to see how the din that attended Cybele could be confused with the ritual connected with another mother-goddess, Rhea, whose attendants long ago hid the cries of the infant Zeus from his father, Cronus, by the clash of their music.

Like Adonis, Attis is another resurrection-god, and their personalities become merged in the tradition. Like Adonis, Attis may die not through his self-inflicted wounds but by the tusk of a boar. Furthermore Attis, like Adonis, comes back to life with the rebirth of vegetation.

We have evidence of springtime ceremonies at which the public mourned and rejoiced for the death and rebirth of Attis. We can ascertain, too, the nature of the secret and mystic rites that were also a part of his worship. Frazer provides a compelling reconstruction:

> *Our information as to the nature of these mysteries and the date of their celebration is unfortunately very scanty, but they seem to have included a sacramental meal and a baptism of blood. In the sacrament the novice became a partaker of the mysteries by eating out of a drum and drinking out of a cymbal, two instruments of music which figured prominently in the thrilling orchestra of Attis. The fast which accompanied the mourning for the dead god may perhaps have been designed to prepare the body of the communi-*

cant for the reception of the blessed sacrament by purging it of all that could defile by contact the sacred elements. In the baptism the devotee, crowned with gold and wreathed with fillets, descended into a pit, the mouth of which was covered with a wooden grating. A bull, adorned with garlands of flowers, its forehead glittering with gold leaf, was then driven on to the grating and there stabbed to death with a consecrated spear. Its hot reeking blood poured in torrents through the apertures, and was received with devout eagerness by the worshipper on every part of his person and garments, till he emerged from the pit, drenched, dripping, and scarlet from head to foot, to receive the homage, nay the adoration of his fellows as one who had been born again to eternal life and had washed away his sins in the blood of the bull. For some time afterwards the fiction of a new birth was kept up by dieting him on milk like a newborn babe.[8]

The regeneration of the worshiper took place at the same time as the regeneration of his god, namely at the vernal equinox. We are obviously once again in the exotic realm of the mystery religions; this one, like the others, rests upon a common fundamental belief in immortality.

The myth of Aphrodite and Adonis, like that of Cybele and Attis, depicts the destruction of the subordinate male in the grip of the eternal and all-dominating female, through whom resurrection and new life may be attained.

Aphrodite and Anchises

An important variation on the same theme is illustrated by the story of Aphrodite and Anchises. In this instance the possibility of the utter debilitation of the male as he fertilizes the female is a key element; Anchises is in dread fear that he will be depleted and exhausted as a man because he has slept with the immortal goddess. As the story is told in the *Homeric Hymn to Aphrodite* (5) we are given ample evidence of the mighty power of the goddess in the universe and a rich and symbolic picture of her devastating beauty. Here Aphrodite is a fertility goddess and mother as well as a divine and enticing woman, epitomizing the lure of sexual and romantic love.

The *Homeric Hymn* begins by telling us that there are only three hearts that the great goddess of love is unable to sway: those of Athena, Artemis, and Hestia. All others, both gods and goddesses, she can bend to her will. So great Zeus caused Aphrodite herself to fall in love with a man, because he did not want her to continue her boasts that she in her power had joined the immortal gods and goddesses in love with mortals to beget mortal children but had experienced no such humiliating coupling herself. Although it is this major theme of the union between Aphrodite and Anchises that needs emphasis in this context, the hymn is translated in its entirety; thus its integral beauty and power are preserved.

Muse, tell me about the deeds of Cyprian Aphrodite, the golden goddess who excites sweet desire in the gods and overcomes the races of mortal humans, the birds of the sky and all animals, as many as are nourished by the land and sea; all these are touched by beautifully crowned Cytherea.

Yet she is not able to seduce or ensnare the hearts of three goddesses. First there is the daughter of aegis-bearing Zeus, bright-eyed Athena; for the deeds of golden Aphrodite give her no pleasure. She enjoys the work of Ares—fights, battles, and wars—and splendid achievements. She first taught craftsmen on the earth to make war-chariots and carriages fancy with bronze. She also teaches beautiful arts to soft-skinned maidens in their homes by instilling the proper skill in each of them.

Next, laughter-loving Aphrodite is never able to subdue in love Artemis, the goddess of the noisy hunt, with shafts of gold; for she enjoys her bow and arrows and killing animals in the mountains, and also the lyre, dancing choruses, thrilling cries, shady groves, and the cities of just mortals.

Finally, the deeds of Aphrodite are not pleasing to the modest maiden Hestia, who was the first of Cronus' children and again the last, by the will of aegis-bearing Zeus.[9] Poseidon and Apollo wooed this revered virgin, but she did not want them at all and firmly said no. She touched the head of her father, aegis-bearing Zeus, and swore that she would be a virgin all her days, this goddess of goddesses—and her oath has been fulfilled. Father Zeus has given her beautiful honor, instead of marriage. In the middle of the home she sits and receives the richest offering, in all the temples of the gods she holds her respected place, and among all mortals she is ordained as the most venerable of deities.

Yet Zeus put into the heart of Aphrodite herself sweet longing for Anchises, who at that time was tending cattle on the high ranges of Mt. Ida with its many streams. In beauty he was like the immortals; and so when laughter-loving Aphrodite saw him, she fell in love, and a terrible longing seized her being. She went to Paphos in Cyprus and entered her fragrant temple. For her precinct and fragrant altar are there. After she went in, she closed the shining doors; inside the Graces (Charites) bathed her and rubbed her with ambrosial oil, the kind used by the eternal gods, and she emerged perfumed in its heavenly sweetness.

When she was beautifully clothed in her lovely garments and adorned with gold, laughter-loving Aphrodite left fragrant Cyprus and hastened to Troy, pressing swiftly on her way, high among the clouds. And she came to Ida, the mother of beasts, with its many springs, and crossed the mountain straight for the hut of Anchises. Gray wolves, bright-eyed lions, bears, and swift panthers, ravenous after deer, followed her, fawning. When she saw them, she was delighted within her heart and filled their breasts with desire; and they all went together in pairs to their beds, deep in their shadowy lairs.

She came to the well-built shelter and found him in his hut, left alone by the others, the hero Anchises, who had in full measure the beauty of the gods. All the rest were out following the cattle in the grassy pastures, but he, left alone by the others, paced to and fro playing a thrilling melody on his lyre. The daughter of Zeus, Aphrodite, stood before him, assuming the form of a beautiful young virgin, so that Anchises might not be afraid when he caught sight of her with his eyes. After Anchises saw her, he pondered as he marveled at her beautiful form and shining garments. For she wore a robe that was more brilliant than the gleam of fire, and she was adorned with intricate jewelry and radiant flowers, and about her soft throat were exquisite necklaces beautifully ornate and of gold. The raiment about her tender breasts shone like the moon, a wonder to behold.

Desire gripped Anchises and he addressed her: "Hail to you, O lady, who have come to this dwelling, whoever of the blessed gods you are, Artemis or Leto or golden Aphrodite or well-born Themis or gleaming-eyed Athena; or perhaps you who have come here are one of the Graces, who are the companions of the gods and are called immortal, or one of the nymphs, who haunt the beautiful woods or inhabit this beautiful mountain, the streams of rivers, and the grassy meadows. I shall build an altar for you on a high mound in a conspicuous spot and I shall offer you beautiful sacrifices in all seasons. Be kindly disposed toward me and grant that I be a preeminent hero among the Trojans; make my offspring flourish in the time to come and allow me myself to live well for a long time and see the light of the sun, happy among my people, and reach the threshold of old age."

Then Aphrodite, the daughter of Zeus, answered him: "Anchises, most renowned of earthborn men, I tell you that I am not any one of the gods. Why do you compare me to the immortals? No, I am a mortal and my mother who bore me was a mortal woman; my father, Otreus, who rules over all Phrygia with its fortresses, has a famous name; perhaps you have heard of him. But I know your language as well as I know our own, for a Trojan nurse reared me in my home in Phrygia; she took me from my mother when I was a very little child and brought me up. And so to be sure I readily understand your language. Now Hermes, the slayer of Argus, with his golden wand, snatched me away from the choral dance in honor of Artemis, the goddess of the golden arrows, who delights in the sounds of the hunt. We were a group of many nymphs and virgins such as suitors pursue, and in a vast throng we circled round about. From here the slayer of Argus with his golden wand snatched me away and whisked me over many places, some cultivated by mortals, others wild and unkempt, through which carnivorous beasts stalk from their shadowy lairs. I thought that I should never set foot again on the life-giving earth. But he told me that I should be called to the bed of Anchises as his lawful wife and that I should bear splendid children to you. And when he had explained and given his directions, then indeed he, the mighty slayer of Argus, went back again among the company of the gods.

"But I have come to you and the force of destiny is upon me. I implore you, by Zeus and by your goodly parents (for they could not be base and have such a son as you), take me, pure and untouched by love, as I am, and present me to your father and devoted mother and to your brothers who are born from the same blood. I shall not be an unseemly bride in their eyes but a fitting addition to your family. And send a messenger quickly to Phrygia, home of swift horses, to tell my father and worried mother. They will send you gold enough and woven raiment; accept their many splendid gifts as their dowry for me. Do these things and prepare the lovely marriage celebration which both mortal humans and immortal gods cherish."

As she spoke thus, the goddess struck Anchises with sweet desire and he cried out to her: "If, as you declare, you are mortal, and a mortal woman is your mother, and Otreus is your renowned father, and you have come here through the agency of Hermes and are to be called my wife all our days, then no one of the gods or mortals will restrain me from joining with you in love right here and now, not even if the archer god Apollo himself were to shoot his grief-laden shafts from his silver bow. After I have once gone up into your bed, O maiden, fair as a goddess, I should even be willing to go below into the house of Hades."

As he spoke he clasped her hand, and laughter-loving Aphrodite turned away and with her beautiful eyes downcast crept into his bed, with its fine coverings, for it had already been made with soft blankets; on it lay the skins of bears and loud-roaring lions that

Anchises had slain in the lofty mountains. And then when they went up to his well-wrought bed, Anchises first removed the gleaming ornaments, the intricate brooches and flowers and necklaces; and he loosened the belt about her waist and took off her shining garments and set them down on a silver-studded chair. Then by the will of the gods and of fate he, a mortal man, lay with an immortal goddess, without knowing the truth.

At the time when herdsmen turn their cattle and staunch sheep back to their shelter from the flowery pastures, Aphrodite poured upon Anchises a sleep that was sound and sweet, and she dressed herself in her lovely raiment. When the goddess of goddesses had clothed her body beautifully, she stood by the couch and her head reached up to the well-wrought beam of the roof, and from her cheeks shone the heavenly beauty that belongs to Cytherea of the beautiful crown. She roused Anchises from sleep and called out to him with the words: "Get up, son of Dardanus; why do you sleep so deeply? Tell me if I appear to you to be like the person whom you first perceived with your eyes."

Thus she spoke, and he immediately awoke and did as he was told. When he saw the neck and the beautiful eyes of Aphrodite, he was afraid and looked down turning his eyes away and he hid his handsome face in his cloak and begged her with winged words: "Now from the first moment that I have looked at you with my eyes, O goddess, I know you are divine; and you did not tell me the truth. But I implore you, by aegis-bearing Zeus, do not allow me to continue to dwell among mortals, still alive but enfeebled; have pity, for no man retains his full strength who sleeps with an immortal goddess."

Then Aphrodite, the daughter of Zeus, replied: "Anchises, most renowned of mortal men, be of good courage and do not be overly frightened in your heart. For you need have no fear that you will suffer evil from me or the other blessed ones; indeed you are beloved by the gods. And you will have a dear son who will rule among the Trojans; and his children will produce children in a continuous family succession. His name will be Aeneas, since I am gripped by a dread anguish[10] because I went into the bed of a man, although among mortals those of your race are always most like the gods in beauty and in stature."

Aphrodite is upset because she can no longer taunt the gods with the boast that she has caused them to love mortals while she alone has never succumbed. She continues to try to justify her actions by glorifying the family of Anchises. She tells the story of Ganymede, who was beautiful and made immortal by Zeus, and relates the sad tale of handsome Tithonus, also of the Trojan royal family, who was beloved by Eos and granted immortality. Aphrodite's son Aeneas, of course, emerges eventually as the great hero of the Romans. Here is the conclusion of the *Homeric Hymn to Aphrodite.*

"Indeed Zeus in his wisdom seized and carried off fair-haired Ganymede because of his beauty, so that he might be in the company of the gods and pour wine for them in the house of Zeus, a wonder to behold, esteemed by all the immortals, as he draws the red nectar from a golden bowl. But a lasting sorrow gripped the heart of Tros, for he had no idea where the divine whirlwind had taken his dear son. Indeed he mourned for him unceasingly each and every day, and Zeus took pity on the father and gave him as recompense for his son brisk-trotting horses, the kind which carry the gods. These he gave him to have as a gift. And at the command of Zeus, Hermes, the guide and slayer of Argus, told everything and how Ganymede would be immortal and never grow old, just like the gods. When Tros heard this message from Zeus, he no longer continued his mourning but rejoiced within his heart and joyfully was borne by the horses that were as swift as a storm.

"So also golden-throned Eos carried off Tithonus, one of your race, and like the immortals. Eos went to Zeus, the dark-clouded son of Cronus, to ask that Tithonus be immortal and live forever. Zeus nodded his assent and accomplished her wish. Poor goddess, she did not think to ask that her beloved avoid ruinous old age and retain perpetual youth. Indeed as long as he kept his desirable youthful bloom, Tithonus took his pleasure with early-born Eos of the golden throne by the stream of Oceanus at the ends of the earth. But when the first gray hairs sprouted from his beautiful head and noble chin, Eos avoided his bed. But she kept him in her house and tended him, giving him food, ambrosia, and lovely garments. When hateful old age oppressed him completely and he could not move or raise his limbs, the following plan seemed best to her. She laid him in a room and closed the shining doors. From within his voice flows faintly and he no longer has the strength that he formerly had in his supple limbs.

"I should not choose that you, Anchises, be immortal and live day after day like him; but, if you could live on and on a beautiful man, as you are now, and if you could be called my husband, then grief would not cloud my anxious heart. Now, however, soon you will be enveloped by pitiless old age, which depleting and destructive, stands beside all human beings and is despised by the gods.

"Besides, among the immortal gods there will be disgrace for me, continually and forever, because of you. Before this happened,

they used to dread the jeers and schemes with which I used to
mate all the immortal gods with mortal women at one time or
another; for they were all subject to my will. But now no more
will I be able to open my mouth about this power of mine among
the gods, since driven quite out of my mind, wretched and
blameless, I have been utterly insane—I have gone to bed with a
mortal and I carry his child in my womb.

"When our baby first sees the light of the sun, deep-bosomed
mountain nymphs who inhabit this great and holy mountain will
bring him up. They are not the same as either mortals or
immortals; they live a long time and eat ambrosial food and also
with the immortals they join in beautiful choruses of dancers. The
Sileni and the keen-eyed slayer of Argus make love to them in the
depths of desireful caves. When they are born, pines and high-
topped oaks are born along with them on the nourishing earth,
beautiful and flourishing trees that stand towering on the high
mountains; mortals call their groves sacred and do not cut them
down with an axe. Yet when the fate of death stands at their side,
these trees first begin to wither in the earth and then their
enveloping bark shrivels and their branches fall off. Together with
the trees the souls of their nymphs leave the light of the sun.

"These nymphs will have my son by their side to bring up. When
he has first been touched by the enticing bloom of youth, the
goddesses will bring the boy here to show you. Yet so that I may
go over with you all that I intend, I shall come back again with my
son, about the fifth year. Certainly when you first behold with
your eyes this flourishing child, you will rejoice at the sight, for he
will be very much like a god; and you will bring him to windy
Troy. If any mortal person asks who the mother was who carried
him under her girdle, remember to say what I tell you. Say she is
the daughter of one of the nymphs, beautiful as a flower, who
inhabits this forest-covered mountain. If you speak out and boast
like a fool that you were joined in love with lovely-crowned
Cytherea, Zeus in his anger will strike you with a smoldering
thunderbolt. Everything has been told to you; take it all to heart.
Refrain from naming me and be intimidated by the anger of the
gods." Having spoken thus, she soared upward to windy heaven.

Hail, goddess, guardian of well-built Cyprus; I began with you and
now I shall go on to another hymn.

Eros

Eros, the male counterpart of Aphrodite, shares many of her characteristics. He too had a dual tradition for his birth. He may be the early
cosmic deity in the creation myths of Hesiod and the Orphics or the

son of Aphrodite, his father being Ares. At any rate he is often closely associated with the goddess as her attendant. Eros, like Aphrodite, may represent all facets of love and desire, but often he is the god of male homosexuality, particularly in the Greek classical period. He is depicted as a handsome young man, the embodiment and idealization of masculine beauty.

The *Symposium* of Plato

The *Symposium* of Plato provides a most profound analysis of the manifold nature and power of love, especially in terms of a conception of Eros. The dialogue tells of a select gathering at the house of Agathon, a dramatic poet, on the day after the customary celebration with the members of his cast in honor of his victory with his first tragedy. The topic at this most famous of dinner parties is that of love. Each guest in turn is asked to expound on the subject. The speeches of Aristophanes and Socrates, both of whom are present, are by far the most rewarding in their universal implications.[11]

Aristophanes' Speech in the Symposium

Aristophanes' speech (*Symposium* 14-16 [189A-193E]) follows those of Pausanias and Eryximachus, two of the other guests.

 Men seem to me to have failed completely to comprehend the power of Eros, for if they did comprehend it, they would have built to him the greatest altars and temples and offered the greatest sacrifices, whereas he is given none of these honors, although he should have them most of all. For he is the most friendly to man of all the gods, his helper and physician in those ills, which if cured, would bring about the greatest happiness for the human race. Therefore I shall try to initiate you into the nature of his power, and you will be the teachers of others.

But first you must understand the nature of mortals and what experiences they have suffered. For our nature long ago was not the same as it is now but different. In the beginning humankind had three sexes, not two, male and female, as now; but there was in addition, a third, which partook of both the others; now it has vanished and only its name survives. At that time there was a distinct sex, the androgynous both in appearance and in name, partaking of the characteristics of both the male and the female, but now it does not exist, except for the name, which is retained as a term of reproach.

Furthermore every human being was in shape a round entity, with back and sides forming a circle; he had four hands, an equal number of feet, one head, with two faces exactly alike but each looking in opposite directions, set upon a circular neck, four ears, two sets of genitals and everything else as one might imagine from this description. He walked upright just as we do now in whichever direction (backward or forward) he wished. When they were anxious to run, they made use of all their limbs (which were then eight in number) by turning cartwheels, just like acrobats, and quickly carried themselves along by this circular movement.

The sexes were three in number and of such a kind for these reasons; originally the male was sprung from the sun, the female from the earth, and the third, partaking of both male and female, from the moon, because the moon partakes of both the sun and the earth; and indeed because they were just like their parents, their shape was spherical and their movement circular. Their strength and might were terrifying; they had great ambitions, and they made an attack on the gods. What Homer relates about Ephialtes and Otus and their attempt to climb up to heaven and assail the gods is told also about these beings as well.

Zeus and the other gods took counsel about what they should do, and they were at a loss. They could not bring themselves to kill them (just as they had obliterated the race of the giants with blasts of thunder and lightning), for they would deprive themselves of the honors and sacrifices which they received from mortals, nor could they allow them to continue in their insolence. After painful deliberation Zeus declared that he had a plan. "I think that I have a way," he said, "whereby mortals may continue to exist but will cease from their insolence by being made weaker. For I shall cut each of them in two, and they will be at the same time both weaker and more useful to us because of their greater numbers, and they will walk upright on two legs. If they still seem to be insolent and do not wish to be quiet, I shall split them again and they will hop about on one leg."

With these words he cut human beings in two, just as one splits fruit which is to be preserved or divides an egg with a hair. As he bisected each one, he ordered Apollo to turn the face with the half of the neck attached around to the side that was cut, so that man, by being able to see the signs of his bisection, might be better behaved; and he ordered him to heal the marks of the cutting. Apollo turned the face around and drew together the skin like a pouch with drawstrings on what is now called the belly and tied it in the middle making a single knot, which is called the navel. He smoothed out the many other wrinkles and molded the chest using a tool like that of cobblers when they smooth out the wrinkles in the leather on their last. But he left a few on their bellies around their navels as a reminder of their experience of long ago.

And so when their original nature had been split in two, each longed for his other half, and when they encountered it they threw their arms about one another and embraced in their desire to grow together again and they died through hunger and neglect of the other necessities of life because of their wish to do nothing separated from each other. Whenever one of a pair died, the other that was left searched out and embraced another mate, either the half of a whole female (which we now call woman) or of a male. Thus they perished, and Zeus in his pity devised another plan: he transferred their genitals to the front (for until now they had been on the outside, and they begot and bore their offspring not in conjunction with one another but by emission into the earth, like grasshoppers).

And so Zeus moved their genitals to the front and thereby had them reproduce by intercourse with one another, the male with the female. He did this for two reasons: if a man united with a woman they would propagate the race and it would survive, but if a male united with a male, they might find satisfaction and freedom to turn to their pursuits and devote themselves to the other concerns of life. From such early times, then, love for one another has been implanted in the human race, a love that unifies in his attempt to make one out of two and to heal and restore the basic nature of humankind.

Each of us therefore is but a broken tally, half a man, since we have been cut just like the side of a flatfish and made two instead of one. All who are a section halved from the beings of the common sex (which was at that time called androgynous) are lovers of women; many adulterers come from this source, including women who love men and are promiscuous. All women who are a section halved from the female do not pay any attention to men but rather turn to women; lesbians come from this source. All who are a section halved from the male pursue males; and all the while they are young, since they are slices, as it were, of the male, they love men and take delight in lying by their side and embracing them; these are the best of boys and youths because they are the most manly in nature. Some say that they are without shame, but they do not tell the truth. For they behave the way they do not through shamelessness but through courage, manliness, and masculinity as they cling to what is similar to them.

Here is a great proof of what I say. Only men of this sort proceed to politics when they grow up. Once they are men they love boys and do not turn their thoughts to marriage and procreation naturally but are forced to by law or convention; it is enough for them to spend their lives together unmarried. In short, then, a man like this is a lover of men as a boy and a lover of boys as a man, always clinging to what is akin to his nature. Therefore whenever anyone of this sort and every other kind of person encounters the other half that is actually his, then they are struck in an amazing way with affection, kinship, and love, virtually unwilling to be separated from each other for even a short time. These are the ones who spend their whole life together, although they would not be able to tell what they wish to gain from each other. No one would imagine that it is on account of their sexual association that the one enjoys intensely being with the other; clearly the soul of each desires something else, which it cannot describe but only hint at obscurely.

Suppose Hephaestus, his tools in hand, were to stand over them as they lay together and ask: "O mortals, what is it that you wish to gain from one another?" Or when they were at a loss for an answer he were to ask again: "Is this what you desire, to be together always as much as possible so as never to be separated from each other night and day? If this is what you desire, I am willing to fuse and weld you together so that the two of you may become one and the same person and as long as you live, you may both live united in one being, and when you die, you may die together as one instead of two, united even in the realms of Hades. Just see if this would be enough to satisfy your longing." We know that there is not one person who, after hearing these words, would deny their truth and say that he wanted something else, but he would believe that he had heard exactly what he had desired for a long time—namely, to be melted in unison with his beloved, and the two of them become one. The reason is that our ancient nature was thus and we were whole. And so love is merely the name for the desire and pursuit of the whole.

Previously, as I have said, we were one, but now because of our wickedness we have been split by the god (just as the Arcadians have been split up by the Spartans).[12] There is too the fear that if we do not behave properly toward the gods we may again be bisected, just as dice that are divided as tallies, and go around like the figures cut in profile on steles, split right along their noses. For this reason all mortals must be urged to pay reverence to the gods so that we may avoid suffering further bisection and win what Eros has to give as our guide and leader. Let no one act in opposition to him—whoever does incurs the enmity of the gods. For if we are reconciled and friendly to the god of love, we shall find and win our very own beloved, an achievement few today attain.

Eryximachus is not to suppose in ridicule of my speech that I am referring only to Pausanias and Agathon, since they perhaps happen to be of the class of those who love males by nature. I am referring rather to all men and women when I say that the happiness of our race lies in the fulfillment of love; each must find the beloved that is his and be restored to his original nature. If this ancient state was best, of necessity the nearest to it in our present circumstances must be best—namely, to find a beloved who is of one and the same mind and nature. It is right to praise Eros as the god responsible; he helps us most in our present life by bringing us to what is kindred to us and offers us the greatest hopes for the future. If we pay reverence to the gods, he will restore us to our ancient nature and with his cure make us happy and blessed.

Aristophanes concludes by again imploring Eryximachus not to ridicule his speech; and indeed, in the last analysis, we cannot help but take it very seriously. The invention, the wit, and the absurdity are all typical of the comic playwright, but so is the insight that they so brilliantly elucidate. We do not know how much belongs to the genius of Plato, but it would be difficult to imagine anything more in character for Aristophanes. With or without the outspoken glorification of love between males (inspired perhaps by the company present and certainly preliminary to Plato's own message in Socrates' subsequent speech), we have a vision of the basic need of one human being for another that is astonishingly like our own.

Who can ever forget Hephaestus as he stands before the two lovers and asks what they hope to gain from each other? After all Aristophanes refers to all men and women when he says that happiness lies in the fulfillment of love and each must find the appropriate beloved. The archetypal concept of love as a sensual and romantic striving for a blessed completeness or wholeness is basic and universal;[13] and who can deny that the complex nature of this most fundamental physical and psychological drive is here laid bare, with a ruthless penetration that is disconcertingly familiar to us, however much the scientific quest for precise definition and vocabulary since the time of Freud has replaced the symbols of mythic art.

Socrates' Speech in the *Symposium*

In Socrates' speech, which provides the dramatic and philosophical climax of the dialogue, we move from the conception of love that is elemental and essentially physical to a sublime elucidation of the highest spiritual attainments that Eros can inspire. Another myth is evoked, this time to establish the true nature of the divine being, in opposition to the misconceptions of the previous speakers. Socrates tells how he was instructed in the true nature of Eros by a woman of Mantinea called Diotima. She makes him realize that Eros is neither good and beautiful nor bad and ugly, but in nature lies somewhere between the two. Therefore he is not a god. Socrates continues his argument quoting from his conversation with Diotima (*Symposium* 23 [202D–204C]):

"What then might love be," I said, "a mortal?" "Not in the least," she replied. "But what is he then?" "As I told you earlier, he is not mortal or immortal but something between." "What then, O Diotima?" "A great spirit, O Socrates; for every spirit is intermediate between god and human beings." "What power does he have?" I asked. "He interprets and conveys exchanges between gods and human beings, prayers and sacrifices from human beings to gods, and orders and gifts in return from gods to human beings; being intermediate he fills in for both and serves as the bond uniting the two worlds into a whole entity. Through him proceeds the whole art of divination and the skill of priests in sacrifice, ritual, spells, and every kind of sorcery and magic. God does not have dealings with mortals directly, but through Love all association and discourse between the two are carried on, both in the waking hours and in time of sleep. The one who is wise in such matters as these is a spiritual being, and he who is wise in other arts and crafts is his inferior. These spirits are many and of every kind and one of them is Eros."

"Who were his father and mother?" I asked. "Although it is a rather long story, I shall tell you," she replied. "When Aphrodite was born, the gods held a feast and among them was Resourcefulness (*Poros*), the son of Cleverness (*Metis*), and while they were dining, Poverty (*Penia*) came and stood about the door to beg, since there was a party.[14] Resourcefulness became intoxicated with nectar (for wine did not yet exist) and went into the garden of Zeus where, overcome by his condition, he fell asleep. Then Poverty, because of her own want and lack of resourcefulness, contrived to have a child by Resourcefulness, and she lay by his side and conceived Eros. And so Eros became the attendant and servant of Aphrodite, for he was begotten on her birthday and he is by nature a lover of beauty and Aphrodite is beautiful.

"Since Eros then is the son of Resourcefulness and Poverty, he is fated to have the following kind of character. First of all, he is continually poor, and far from being soft and beautiful as many believe, he is hard and squalid, without shoes, without a home, and without a bed; he always sleeps on the ground, in doorways, and on the street. Thus he has his mother's nature, with want as his constant companion. On the other hand, like his father, he lays his plots to catch the beautiful and the good; being vehement and energetic, he is a dread hunter, always weaving some scheme; full of resource, he has a passion for knowledge and is a lover of wisdom during all his life, a clever wizard, sorcerer, and sophist. He is not immortal nor is he mortal, but at one time he flourishes and lives whenever he is successful, and at another he dies all in the same day, but he will come back to life again because of his nature inherited from his father—what he acquires slips away from him again, and so Eros is never either poor or rich and he is in a state between wisdom and ignorance. This is the way he is. No one of the gods loves wisdom and longs to become wise, because he is wise; and so with any other who is wise—he does not love wisdom. On the other hand, the ignorant do not love wisdom or long to become wise. Ignorance is a difficult thing for this very reason, that the one who is neither beautiful nor good nor wise is completely satisfied with himself. The one who does not think he is lacking in anything certainly does not desire what he does not think he lacks."

"O Diotima," I asked, "who are those who love wisdom if not the wise or the ignorant?" "By now certainly it would be clear even to a child," she replied, "that they are those who are in a state between desire and wisdom, one of whom is Eros. To be sure wisdom is among the most beautiful of things and Eros is love of beauty; and so Eros must be a lover of wisdom, and being a lover of wisdom he lies between wisdom and ignorance. The nature of his birth is the reason for this. He springs from a wise and resourceful father and a mother who is not wise and without resources. This then, my dear Socrates, is the nature of this spirit. The conception you had of Eros is not surprising. You believed, to infer from what you said, that Love was the beloved (the one who is loved) and not the lover (the one who loves). For this reason, I think, Love appeared to you to be all beautiful. For that which is loved is that which actually is beautiful and delicate, perfect and most happy, but that which loves has another character, of the kind that I have described."

Diotima goes on to explain the function, purpose, and power of Eros in human life. Love and the lover desire what they do not possess, namely, the beautiful and the good, and the ultimate goal of their pursuit is happiness. Love finds particular expression in the procreation of what is beautiful, both physically and spiritually; and all humans in their quest to bring forth beauty and knowledge are thereby touched by a divine harmony with the immortal. Procreation is the closest means by which the human race can attain to perpetuity and immortality; love, then, is a love of immortality as well as of the beautiful and the good.

Animals as well as humans seek to perpetuate themselves and thereby become immortal. But for humans there are various stages in the hierarchy of love. The lowest is that of the animal inspired by the desire for children of the body, but as one ascends, there is the realization of the possibility of producing children of the mind. Who would not prefer the poetic offspring of a Homer or a Hesiod and the more lasting glory and immortality that they have achieved? Just as on the rungs of a ladder we proceed from one step to another, so initiates into the mysteries of love move from the lower to the higher.

Love begins with the physical and sensual desire for the beautiful person or the beautiful thing. From the specific object one moves to the generic conception of beauty, which is wondrous and pure and universal. It is the love of this eternal beauty (and with it the goodness and wisdom it entails) that inspires the pursuit of philosophy in the philosopher.

Diotima sums up by describing the final stages of initiation and revelation, sustaining the vocabulary of the mysteries (28 [210A–C]):

> It is necessary for the one proceeding in the right way toward his goal to begin, when he is young, with physical beauty; and first of all, if his guide directs him properly, to love one person, and in his company to beget beautiful ideas and then to observe that the beauty in one person is related to the beauty in another. If he must pursue physical beauty, he would be very foolish not to realize that the beauty in all persons is one and the same. When he has come to this conclusion, he will become the lover of all beautiful bodies and will relax the intensity of his love for one and think the less of it as something of little account. Next he will realize that beauty in the soul is more precious than that in the body, so that if he meets with a person who is beautiful in his soul, even if he has little of the physical bloom of beauty, this will be enough and he will love and cherish him and beget beautiful ideas that make the young better, so that he will in turn be forced to see the beauty in morals and laws and that the beauty in them all is related.

This then is the Platonic Eros, a love that inspires the philosopher to self-denial in the cause of humanity and in the pursuit of true wisdom. Presumably this philosophic Eros can ultimately be aroused from any type of love, heterosexual as well as homosexual (both male and female); the crucial issue is that it be properly directed and become transformed from the erotic to the intellectual. According to Plato in his *Republic*, certain men as well as certain women can attain the highest goals of the true philosopher king. As we have just learned, this cannot be achieved without the sensual and sublime impetus of Eros. Whatever the physical roots, the spiritual import is universal, kindred to the passionate love of God that pervades all serious religious devotion. Aristotle too thinks in Platonic terms when he describes his god as the unmoved mover, the final cause in the universe, who moves as a beloved moves the lover.

How far we have come from the traditional depiction of Eros as the handsome young athlete who attends Aphrodite! Even more remote is the image that later evolved of Eros as Cupid, a chubby mischievous little darling with wings and a bow and arrow. He still attends Aphrodite; and although the wounds he inflicts can inspire a passion that is serious and even deadly, too often he becomes little more than the cute and frivolous deus ex machina of romantic love.

Cupid and Psyche

Finally, the story of Cupid and Psyche remains to be told. It is given its classic form by Apuleius, a Roman author of the second century A.D., in his novel *Metamorphoses, or The Golden Ass* (4. 28–6. 24). One's first impressions about a tale uniting Cupid (or Eros) with Psyche (Soul) should inevitably be Platonic; but whatever philosophical profundities, Platonic or otherwise, have been detected in Apuleius' allegory, popular and universal motifs common to mythology in general and folktale, fairy tale, and romance in particular, emerge with striking clarity: for example, the mysterious bridegroom, the taboo of identification, the hostile mother figure, the jealous sisters, the heroine's forgetfulness, the imposition of impossible labors accomplished with divine assistance, among them descent into the very realm of Hades, and the triumph of romantic love. In this tale, which begins "Once upon a time," and ends "happily ever after," Cupid appears as a handsome young god with wings. Here is a summary of Apuleius' version.

Once upon a time, a certain king and queen had three daughters, of whom Psyche, the youngest, was by far the most fair. In fact many believed that she was Venus reincarnated and paid her such adulation that the goddess became outraged. And so Venus ordered her son Cupid to make Psyche fall in love with the most base and vile of mankind; instead, Cupid himself fell in love with Psyche. Psyche's inferior sisters had easily found husbands, but Psyche remained unmarried since she was admired by all with the awe that is inspired by divinity. Her father suspected that a god's wrath was responsible. He consulted Apollo, who demanded that Psyche be decked out like a corpse and placed on a mountaintop to be wed by a terrifying serpent.

Therefore Psyche, amid the rites of a funeral for a living bride, was left on a mountaintop to meet a fate that she finally accepted with resignation. Psyche fell into a deep sleep, and the gentle breezes of Zephyrus wafted her down to a beautiful valley. When she awoke, she entered a magnificent palace, where her every wish was taken care of. And when Psyche went to bed, an anonymous bridegroom visited her, only to depart quickly before sunrise. Thus Psyche spent her days—and her nights—in the palace.

Meanwhile, her sisters set out in search of her; but her mysterious husband continually warned her not to respond to them when they approached. Alone in her prison all day, Psyche besought her husband each night to allow her to see her sisters and give them gold and jewels. He finally consented on the condition that she must not, despite her sisters' urgings, try to learn his identity. When the sisters arrived and interrogated her, Psyche kept her secret—although she did say that her husband was a very handsome young man.

The sisters returned home with the riches that Psyche had given them, but in their hearts they nursed an all-consuming jealousy. The mysterious bridegroom warned Psyche of her sisters' treachery: their purpose was to persuade her to look upon his face; if she did so, she would never see him again. He also told her that she was pregnant, and if she kept their secret, their child would be divine; if she did not, it would be mortal. Nevertheless, he granted Psyche's appeal to see her sisters once again. In answer to their questions, Psyche revealed that she was pregnant. The sisters once again returned home laden with gifts, but more jealous than ever; they now suspected that Psyche's lover must be a god and her expected child divine.

The evil sisters visited Psyche a third time; this time they told her that her husband really was the monstrous serpent of the oracle and that she would be devoured when the time of her pregnancy was completed. Psyche was horrified and, believing that she was sleeping with the monster, forgot the warnings of her husband and took her sisters' advice. She was to hide a sharp knife and a burning lamp; when the monster was asleep, she was to slash it in the neck.

In anguish, Psyche made her preparations; in the night her husband made love to her and then fell asleep. As she raised the lamp, knife in hand, she saw the sweet, gentle, and beautiful Cupid. Overcome by the sight, her first impulse was to take her own life, but this she was unable to do. Spellbound by Cupid's beauty, she gazed at his lovely wings and fondled the bow and quiver that lay at the foot of their bed; she pricked her thumb on one of the arrows and drew blood. Overcome by desire, she kissed her husband passionately. Alas, the lamp dropped oil on the god's right shoulder. Cupid leaped out of bed and attempted to fly away at once; Psyche caught hold of his right leg and soared aloft with him, but her strength gave way and she fell to earth. Before flying away, Cupid admonished her from a nearby cypress: he had ignored Venus' command, he said, and had taken her as his love; he had warned her; his flight was penalty enough; and her sisters would pay for what they had done.

Psyche attempted to commit suicide by throwing herself in a nearby river; but the gentle stream brought her safely to its bank. She was advised by Pan to forget her grief and win back Cupid's love. In her wanderings, she came to the very city where one of her sisters lived. Psyche told her sister what had happened, but added that Cupid would marry the sister if she hastened to his side. The sister called on Zephyrus to carry her from a mountaintop to Cupid's palace, but as she leaped into the air she fell and perished on the rocks below. Psyche then found her way to her other sister, who died in the same manner.

Psyche wandered in search of Cupid; he lay in his mother's bedroom, moaning because of his burn; Venus, learning of what had happened, rushed to her son's side, berated him for his behavior, and vowed revenge. In a rage, Venus left to pursue Psyche, but eventually abandoned her search. She approached Jupiter, who agreed to send Mercury to make a public proclamation for the capture of Psyche. When she was brought before Venus, the goddess denounced and abused her. In addition Venus imposed upon the poor girl a series of impossible tasks.

First, Psyche was ordered to sort out before nightfall a vast heap of mixed grains (wheat, barley, and the like). In this endeavor, an ant came to her rescue and summoned his army to isolate each different grain.

The next day Venus ordered Psyche to go to a riverbank where dangerous sheep with thick golden fleeces grazed and to bring back some of their wool. This time, a reed murmured instructions. She was to wait until the sheep had stopped their frenzied wandering under the blazing sun; and when they had lain down to rest, she was to shake from the trees under which they passed the woolly gold clinging richly to the branches. And so she accomplished the task.

Still not satisfied, Venus ordered Psyche to go to the top of a high mountain, from which dark water flowed—water that ultimately fed the Underworld stream of Cocytus. Psyche was to bring back a jar filled with this chill water; among the terrors to be faced was a dragon. The eagle of Jupiter swooped down and filled the jar for Psyche.

Angrier now than ever, Venus imposed the ultimate task—descent into the realm of Hades. Psyche was ordered to take a box to Persephone and ask her to send back in it a fragment of her own beauty. In despair Psyche decided to throw herself off a high tower. But the tower spoke to her and gave her specific directions to the Underworld and instructions about what she was and was not to do. Among the stipulations was that she provide herself with sops to mollify Cerberus and money to pay the ferryman Charon. Most important, the tower warned Psyche not to look into the box. Psyche did everything that she had been told, but she could not resist looking into the box.

Psyche Is Brought to Olympus by Mercury, by Raphael (1483–1520) and assistants. Fresco, 1518. This is the eastern half of the fresco painted on the vault of the loggia of the Villa Farnesina, which is sixty feet long. The other half shows the wedding banquet. Both scenes closely follow the narrative of Apuleius. Here Mercury introduces Psyche on the left, while the assembled gods attend as Jupiter, on the right, judges Cupid, to whose left stands Venus. Around Jupiter are (from the right) Juno, Minerva, Diana, and Neptune. The fresco was designed to give the illusion of a tapestry, and its floral border was painted by Giovanni da Udine. *(Palazzo della Farnesina, Rome. Courtesy of Alinari/Art Resource, New York.)*

Inside the box was not beauty but the sleep of the dark night of the Underworld; by this deathlike sleep Psyche was enveloped.

By now cured of his burn, Cupid flew to Psyche's rescue. He put sleep back into the box and reminded Psyche that her curiosity once again had gotten the better of her. She was to go and complete her task. Cupid then appealed to Jupiter, who agreed to ratify his marriage with Psyche; since Psyche was made one of the immortals, Venus was appeased. Here is how Apuleius describes the glorious wedding feast on Olympus that marked the happy ending of the story of Cupid and Psyche (*Metamorphoses* 6. 23-24):

Immediately a wedding feast appeared. The bridegroom took the highest place, embracing Psyche. So Jupiter with his own Juno took his place and then, in order, the other gods. Then Jupiter's cupbearer, the shepherd boy Ganymede, brought him a cup of nectar, the wine of the gods, and Bacchus gave nectar to the others. Vulcan cooked the feast; the Hours decorated everything with roses and other flowers. The Graces sprinkled the scent of balsam, and the Muses played and sang. Apollo sang to the cithara and Venus danced in all her beauty to the music; the tableau was so fitting for her that the Muses accompanied her with choral odes or played upon the tibia; a satyr and Pan played the pipes.

So, with all due ceremony, Psyche was married to Cupid and, in due time, a daughter was born to them, whom we call Pleasure (*Voluptas*).

Sappho's Aphrodite

It is impossible to survey the mythological concepts of love without including the poetic vision of Sappho of Lesbos, the poetess of love in antiquity. Only a little of her work has survived, but the critical acclaim for her artistry glows undiminished. We know practically nothing with certainty about her life and career. She was devoted to Aphrodite and to the girls with whom she was associated. But we cannot even confidently speak about a cult of the goddess, and her relations with her loved ones can legitimately be imagined only from the meager remains of her poetry. Her circle has been interpreted as everything from a finishing school for girls in the Victorian manner to a hotbed of sensuality.

Sappho's invocation to Aphrodite has real meaning for us in this context because it illustrates beautifully the passionate intensity that infuses so much of Greek art within the disciplined control of artistic form. It reminds us too of the sincerity of the conception of the goddess that was possible in the seventh and sixth centuries B.C. Too often our sensibilities are numbed by the later artificial and conventional stereotypes to which the gods are reduced, once all genuine belief is gone. There can be no question about the intense reality of Aphrodite in the following lines—which even a prose translation cannot obliterate completely.

Exquisitely enthroned, immortal Aphrodite, weaver of charms, child of Zeus, I beg you, reverend lady, do not crush my heart with sickness and distress. But come to me here, if ever once before you heard my cry from afar and listened and, leaving your father's house, yoked your chariot of gold. Beautiful birds drew you swiftly from heaven over the black earth through the air between with the rapid flutter of their downy wings.

Swiftly they came and you, O blessed goddess, smiling in your immortal beauty asked what I wished to happen most of all in my frenzied heart. "Who is it this time you desire that Persuasion entice to your love? Who, O Sappho, has wronged you? For if she runs away now, soon she will follow; if she rejects your gifts, she will bring gifts herself; if she does not now, soon she will love, even though she does not wish it."

Come to me now too and free me from my harsh anxieties; all that my heart longs for, accomplish. You, your very self, stand with me in my conflict.

ARTEMIS

8

The *Homeric Hymn to Artemis* (27) draws the essential features of her character and appearance: beautiful, chaste, virgin of the hunt, armed with bow and arrows.

 I sing about Artemis of the golden arrows, chaste virgin of the noisy hunt, who delights in her shafts and strikes down the stag, the very own sister of Apollo of the golden sword. She ranges over shady hills and windy heights, rejoicing in the chase as she draws her bow, made all of silver, and shoots her shafts of woe. The peaks of the lofty mountains tremble, the dark woods echo terribly to the shrieks of wild beasts, and both the earth and fish-filled sea are shaken. But she with dauntless heart looks everywhere to wreak destruction on the brood of animals. But when the huntress, who delights in her arrows, has had her fill of pleasure and cheered her heart, she unstrings her curved bow and makes her way to the great house of her dear brother, Phoebus Apollo, in the rich land of Delphi, where she supervises the lovely dances of the Muses and the Graces. After she has hung up her unstrung bow and arrows, she takes first place and, exquisitely attired, leads the dance. And they join in a heavenly choir to sing how Leto of the beautiful ankles bore two children who are by far the best of the immortals in sagacious thought and action.

Hail, children of Zeus and Leto of the lovely hair; yet I shall remember you and another song too.

The shorter *Homeric Hymn to Artemis* (9) dwells upon the closeness of Artemis and Apollo and their cult places in Asia Minor. The river Meles flows near Smyrna, where there was a temple of Artemis; and Claros was the site of a temple and oracle of Apollo.

Artemis the Huntress. Roman copy in marble of a Greek bronze of the late fourth century B.C.; height 78 in. Artemis appears both as huntress, taking an arrow from her quiver, and as protectress of animals, as she grasps the leaping stag. Her short skirt, sandals, and loose clothing are appropriate for the activity of the hunt. *(Musée du Louvre, Paris. Courtesy of Alinari/Art Resource, New York.)*

 Sing, O Muse, about Artemis, the virgin who delights in arrows, sister of Apollo, the far-shooter, and nursed together with him. She waters her horses at the river Meles, thick with rushes, and swiftly drives her chariot, made all of gold, through Smyrna to Claros, rich in vines; here Apollo of the silver bow sits and waits for the goddess who shoots from afar and delights in her arrows.

So hail to you, Artemis, with my song and at the same time to all the other goddesses as well; yet I begin to sing about you first of all and, after I have made my beginning from you, I shall turn to another hymn.

The Birth of Artemis and Apollo

The goddess Leto mated with Zeus and bore the twin deities Artemis and Apollo. The story of Apollo's birth on the island of Delos is recounted in Chapter 9 in the version given by the *Homeric Hymn to Apollo*.[1] Traditionally Artemis is born first and is able to help with the delivery of her brother, Apollo, thus performing one of her primary functions as a goddess of childbirth early in her career (a role she shares with Hera and Eileithyia, as we have seen).

On other occasions too, Artemis is closely linked with Apollo, both appearing as vehement and haughty agents of destruction with their shafts of doom. Sudden death (particularly of the young) was often attributed to these two deities, Artemis striking down the girls, Apollo the boys.

Niobe and Her Children

One of the most famous exploits of Artemis and Apollo concerns Niobe and her children, told at length by Ovid (*Metamorphoses* 6. 148–315).

The women of Thebes bestowed great honor upon Leto and her twin children, crowning their heads with laurel and offering up incense and prayers in obedience to an injunction by the goddess herself. Niobe, however, was enraged by the whole proceedings and rashly boasted that she was more deserving of tribute than Leto. After all she was rich, beautiful, and the queen of Thebes.[2] Besides, Leto had borne only two children, whereas Niobe was the mother of seven sons and seven daughters. Indeed Niobe was so confident in the abundance of her blessings that she felt that she could afford to lose some of them without serious consequences.

Leto was enraged at such hubris and complained bitterly to Artemis and Apollo. Together the two deities swiftly glided down to the palace of Thebes to avenge the insulted honor of their mother. Apollo struck down all the sons of Niobe with his deadly and unerring arrows, and Artemis in turn killed all her daughters. Just as Artemis was about to shoot the last child, Niobe in desperation shielded the girl and pleaded that this one, her youngest, be spared. While she was uttering this prayer, she was turned to stone; and a whirlwind whisked her away to her homeland, Phrygia, where she was placed on a mountain-top. Tears continue to trickle down from her marble face as she wastes away.[3]

Actaeon

Several stories illustrate the hallowed purity of the goddess Artemis. A famous one concerns Actaeon,[4] an ardent hunter who lost his way and by accident (or was it fate?) had the misfortune to see Artemis (Diana in Ovid's version) naked (*Metamorphoses* 3. 138–255):

 Actaeon first tinged with grief the happiness of his grandfather, Cadmus. A stag's horns grew on his head, and his hounds feasted on their master's flesh. Yet, if you look closely, you will find that his guilt was misfortune, not a crime; what crime indeed lies in an innocent mistake?

There was a mountain on which had fallen the blood of beasts of many kinds. It was midday, when shadows are at their shortest and the Sun is midway in his course. Young Actaeon calmly called his fellow huntsmen as they tracked the game through the depths of the pathless forest: "My friends, our nets and spears are wet with the blood of our prey; we have had luck enough today! Dawn's saffron-wheeled chariot will bring another day tomorrow and then we will renew the chase. The Sun now stands midway 'twixt east and west and with his hot rays parches the earth. Stop now the hunt, and take in the knotted nets!" His men obeyed and halted from their labors.

A vale there was called Gargaphië, sacred to the huntress Diana; clothed with a dense growth of pine and pointed cypress, it had at its far end a woodland cave which no human hand had shaped. . . . on the right from a murmuring spring issued a stream of clearest water, and around the pool was a grassy bank. Here would the woodland goddess rest when weary from the hunt and bathe her virgin body in the clear water. That day she came there and to one of her nymphs handed her hunting spear, her quiver and bow, and the arrows that were left. Upon another's waiting arms she cast her cloak, and two more took off her sandals. . . . Other nymphs[5] fetched water and poured it from ample urns. And while Diana thus was being bathed, as she had been many times before, Actaeon, Cadmus' grandson, his labors left unfinished, came to the grotto uncertain of his way and wandering through the unfamiliar wood; so fate carried him along. Into the dripping cave he went, and the nymphs, when they saw a man, beat their breasts and filled the forest with their screams.

Surrounding Diana they shielded her with their bodies, but the goddess was taller than they and her head o'ertopped them all. Just as the clouds are tinged with color when struck by the rays of the setting sun, or like the reddening Dawn, Diana's face flushed when she was spied naked. Surrounded by her nymphs she turned and looked back; wishing that her arrows were at hand, she used what weapons she could and flung water over the young man's face and hair with these words, foretelling his coming doom: "Now you may tell how you saw me naked—if you can tell!" And with this threat she made the horns of a long-lived stag[6] rise on his head where the water had struck him; his neck grew long and his ears pointed, his hands turned to hooves, his arms to legs, and his body she clothed with a spotted deerskin. And she made him timid; Autonoë's valiant son ran away in fear and as he ran wondered at his speed. He saw his horned head reflected in a pool and tried to say "Alas"—but no words would come. He sobbed; that at least was a sound he uttered, and tears flowed down his new-changed face.

Only his mind remained unchanged. What should he do? Go home to the royal palace? Or hide in the woods? Shame prevented him from the one action, fear from the other. While he stood undecided his hounds saw him. Blackfoot and clever Tracker first raised the hue and cry with their baying, the latter a Cretan hound, the former of Spartan pedigree. Then the rest of the pack rushed up, swifter than the wind, whose names it would take too long to give.[7] Eager for the prey, they hunt him over rocks and cliffs, by rough tracks and trackless ways, through terrain rocky and inaccessible. He fled, by ways where he had often been the pursuer; he fled, pursued by his own hounds! He longed to cry out "Actaeon am I; obey your master!" He longed—but could utter no words; and the heavens echoed to the baying hounds. First Blackie gored his back; then Hunter followed, while Hill-hound gripped Actaeon's shoulder with his teeth. These three had been slower to join the chase but had outstripped the pack along mountain shortcuts; while they held back their master, the pack came up and all sank their teeth into his body. His whole body was torn by the hounds; he groaned, a sound which was not human nor yet such as a stag could make.

The hills he knew so well echoed with his screams; falling on his knees, like a man in prayer, he dumbly looked at them in entreaty, for he had no human arms to stretch out to them. But the huntsmen, ignorant of the truth, urge on the pack with their usual cries; they look round for Actaeon and loudly call his name as if he were not there. At the sound of his name he lifts his head; they think it a pity that he is not there, too slow to see the sight of the stag at bay. He could indeed wish he were not there! But he is; he

The Death of Actaeon. Athenian red figure krater by the Pan Painter, ca. 460 B.C.; height $14\frac{1}{2}$ in. Artemis shoots Actaeon, who falls in agony as his hounds tear him. Actaeon is shown in fully human form, and the small size of the hounds compels the viewer to focus on the human figure and his divine antagonist. The scene of the consequences of chastity violated is made the more poignant by the reverse of this vase which shows the lustful god Pan pursuing a shepherd. *(Courtesy of Museum of Fine Arts, Boston. James Fund and Special Contribution.)*

could wish to be the spectator, not the victim, of his hounds' cruel jaws. Completely encircling him, with jaws biting deep, they tear in fact their master's flesh when he seems to be a stag. Only when his life has ebbed out through innumerable wounds, was it said that the vengeance was satisfied of the huntress Diana.

Opinions varied about the deed. Some thought the goddess had been more cruel than just; others approved, and said that her severity was worthy of her virgin chastity. Each view had good reasons to support it.

Callisto and Arcas

The same insistence on purity and chastity, the same vehemence against defilement of any sort, appear again in the story of Callisto, one of the followers of Artemis (or Diana, as Ovid tells it; *Metamorphoses* 2. 409-507):

 As Jupiter journeyed back and forth to Arcadia, he saw the Arcadian girl Callisto, and the fires of love were kindled in his bones. She did not care to draw out the unworked wool or to change her hair's style. She would pin her dress with a brooch, keep her hair in place with a white ribbon; with a smooth spear in her hand or a bow, she marched in Diana's troops. No other girl who trod the Arcadian hills was dearer to the goddess—but no one's power can last for long!

High in the heaven rode the Sun beyond the middle of his course, when Callisto came to a wood that no one throughout the years had touched. Here she took off the quiver from her shoulder and unstrung the pliant bow; she lay upon the grassy ground, her head resting upon the painted quiver. Jupiter saw her, tired and unprotected. "My wife," said he, "will never discover this affair, and if she does—well, the prize is worth her anger." So he disguised himself to look like Diana and said: "Dear girl, my follower, upon which mountain did you hunt?" Callisto sprang up from the turf. "Hail, goddess," said she, "greater in my opinion than Jupiter—and let him hear my words!"

Jupiter smiled as he heard this, glad that Diana was preferred to himself; he kissed the girl, more warmly than a maiden should. He cut short Callisto's tale of the forest hunt with an embrace, and as he forced her showed who he really was. Callisto fought against him with all a woman's strength—Juno's anger would have been lessened could she have seen her—but who is weaker than a girl, and who can overcome Jupiter? He won; to the heavens he flies and she hates the wood that knows her shame; as she fled from it, she almost forgot to take her quiver and arrows and the bow that she had hung up.

Diana saw her as she moved with her followers along the heights of Maenalus, flushed with pride at the beasts she had killed, and called her. Callisto hid, afraid at first that Jupiter in disguise was calling her. But as she saw the nymphs and goddess go on together she knew it was no trick, and joined the band. Poor Callisto! How hard it is not to show one's guilt in one's face! She could hardly lift her eyes from the ground; no longer did she stay close to Diana's side nor be the first of all her followers. In silence she blushed and showed her shame; if Diana had not been a maiden, she could have known Callisto's guilt by a thousand signs. They say that the nymphs realized it.

The horned moon was waxing for the ninth time when Diana, weary from the chase and tired by the sun, her brother's flaming heat, reached a cool wood; here flowed a babbling stream, gliding over its smooth and sandy bed. She praised the place; she dipped her feet into the water and it pleased her. "No man is here to spy on us," she cried: "let us bathe naked in the stream!" Callisto blushed; the others took off their clothes; she alone held back. And as she delayed, they stripped her, and then her naked body and her guilt were plain to see. She stood confused, trying to hide her belly with her hands; but Diana cried: "Be off from here! Do not defile these sacred waters!" and expelled her from her band.

Long before, Juno had known the truth and put off revenge until the time was ripe. She saw no cause to wait now; Callisto's son, Arcas (his very name caused Juno pain), had been born, and when Juno's cruel gaze fell on him she cried: "So only this was left, you whore; for you to be pregnant and by this birth make known the wrong I suffer and my husband's shameful act! But I will have my revenge! I will take away the beauty that pleases you so much and gives my husband, you flirt, such pleasure."

And as she spoke she seized Callisto's hair and threw her to the ground. Callisto spread her arms in suppliant prayer; her arms began to bristle with black hair, her hands to be bent with fingers turning to curved claws; she used her hands as feet and the face that once delighted Jupiter grew ugly with grinning jaws. Her power of speech was lost, with no prayers or entreaties could she win pity, and a hoarse and frightening growl was her only utterance.

Yet Callisto's human mind remained even when she had become a bear; with never-ceasing moans she made known her suffering; lifting what once had been her hands to heaven she felt Jupiter's ingratitude, although she could not with words accuse him. Poor thing! How often was she afraid to sleep in the solitary forest before her former home; how often did she roam in the lands that once were hers! How often was she pursued over the rocky hills by the baying hounds; how often did the huntress run in fear from the hunters! Often she hid herself (forgetting what she was) and though a bear, shrank from the sight of bears; wolves scared her, although her father Lycaon had become one.

One day Arcas, now nearly fifteen years old and ignorant of his parentage, was out hunting; as he picked a likely covert and crisscrossed the forests of Mt. Erymanthus with knotted nets, he came upon his mother. She saw him and stood still, like one who sees a familiar face. He ran away, afraid of the beast who never took her gaze from him (for he knew not what she was); he was on the point of driving a spear though her body, eager as she was to come close to him. Then almighty Jupiter prevented him; he averted Arcas' crime against his mother and took them both on the wings of the wind to heaven and there made them neighboring stars.

Callisto became the Great Bear (Arctus, or Ursa Major); Arcas the Bear Warden (Arctophylax, or Arcturus, or Boötes). Ursa Major was also known as Hamaxa (the Wain). The story of Callisto is typical of a group of myths that provide etiology for individual stars or constellations. These stories (most of which belong to late antiquity) are told about various figures in mythology, and several of them, in one way or another, cluster about Artemis herself.

Orion

One such story concerns Orion, a composite figure about whom many tales are related with multiple and intricate variations.[8] He is traditionally a mighty and amorous hunter and often associated with the island of Chios and its king, Oenopion (the name means "wine-face"; Chios was famous for its wines). The many versions play upon the following themes. Orion woos the daughter of Oenopion, Merope; he becomes drunk and is blinded by the king, but he regains his sight through the rays of the sun-god, Helius. While he is clearing the island of wild beasts as a favor for Oenopion, he encounters Artemis and tries to rape her. In her anger the goddess produces a scorpion out of the earth that stings Orion to death.[9] Both can be seen in the heavens. Some say that Orion pursued the Pleiades (daughters of the Titan Atlas and Pleione, an Oceanid), and they were all transformed into constellations; with Orion was his dog, Sirius, who became the Dog Star.

Origins of Artemis

The origins of Artemis are obscure. Although she is predominantly a virgin goddess, certain aspects of her character suggest that originally she may have had fertility connections.[10] Artemis' interest in childbirth and in the young of both humans and animals seems to betray concerns that are not entirely virginal. At Ephesus in Asia Minor, a statue of Artemis depicts her in a robe of animal heads, which in its upper part exposes what appears to be (but may not be) a ring of multiple breasts. We should remember, too, that Artemis became a goddess of the moon in classical times. As in the case of other goddesses worshiped by women (e.g., Hera), this link with the moon may be associated with the lunar cycle and women's menstrual period.

Artemis, Selene, and Hecate

As a moon-goddess, Artemis is sometimes closely identified with Selene and Hecate. Hecate is clearly a fertility deity with definite chthonian characteristics. She can make the earth produce in plenty, and her home is in the depths of the Underworld. She is a descendant of the Titans and in fact a cousin of Artemis.[11] Hecate is a goddess of roads in general and crossroads in particular, the latter being considered the center of ghostly activities, particularly in the dead of night. Thus the goddess developed a terrifying aspect; triple-faced statues depicted the three manifestations of her multiple character as a deity of the moon: Selene in heaven, Artemis on earth, and Hecate in the realm of Hades. Offerings of food (known as Hecate's suppers) were left to placate her, for she was terrible both in her powers and in her person—a veritable Fury, armed with a scourge and blazing torch and accompanied by terrifying hounds. Her skill in the arts of black magic made her the patron deity of sorceresses (like Medea) and witches. How different is the usual depiction of Artemis, young, vigorous, wholesome, and beautiful! In the costume of the huntress, she is ready for the chase, armed with her bow and arrow; an animal often appears by her side, and crescent moonlike horns rest upon her head; the torch she holds burns bright with the light of birth, life, and fertility. Whatever the roots of her fertility connections, the dominant conception of Artemis is that of the virgin huntress. She becomes, as it were, the goddess of nature itself, not always in terms of its teeming procreation, but instead often reflecting its cool, pristine, and virginal aspects. As a moon-goddess too (despite the overtones of fecundity), she can appear as a symbol, cold, white, and chaste.

Artemis versus Aphrodite: Euripides' *Hippolytus*

In her role as a goddess of chastity, Artemis provides a ready foil for the voluptuous sensuality of Aphrodite. Artemis in this view becomes at one and the same time a negative force, representing the utter rejection of love and also a positive compulsion toward purity and asceticism. No one has rendered the psychological and physiological implications of this contrast in more human and meaningful terms than the poet Euripides in his tragedy *Hippolytus*.

As the play begins, Aphrodite is enraged (and she tells us so in a typically Euripidean prologue); her power is great and universal, yet she is vehemently spurned by Hippolytus, who will have absolutely nothing to do with her. The young man must certainly pay for this hubris, and the goddess uses his stepmother, Phaedra, to make certain that he will. Phaedra is the second wife of Theseus, the father of Hippolytus, and Aphrodite impels the poor woman to fall desperately in love with her stepson. Phaedra's nurse wrests the fatal secret of her guilty love from her sick and distraught mistress and makes the tragic mistake of taking it upon herself to inform the unsuspecting Hippolytus. The boy is horrified; the thought of physical love for any woman is for him traumatic enough; a sexual relationship with the wife of his father would be an abomination.

In her disgrace Phaedra commits suicide; but first she leaves a note that falsely incriminates Hippolytus, whose death is brought about by the curse of his enraged father, Theseus, a heroic extrovert who has never really understood the piety of his son. Artemis appears to her beloved follower Hippolytus as he lies dying. She promises him, in return for a lifetime of devotion that has brought about his martyrdom, that she will get even by wreaking vengeance upon some favorite of Aphrodite, and she will establish a cult in honor of Hippolytus as well—virgin maidens will pay tribute to him by dedicating their shorn tresses and lamenting his fate by their tears and their songs.[12] Theseus realizes his error too late; he must suffer the consequences of his rash and hasty judgment against Hippolytus; but in the end father and son find understanding and reconciliation.

At the close of the play we are left with a fascinating chain of enigmas in the Euripidean manner. Is Hippolytus a saint or a foolish and obstinate prig? Has he destroyed himself through the dangerous, if not impossible, rejection of the physical? Are men at the mercy of ruthless and irrational forces inherent in their very nature, which they deify in terms of ruthless and vindictive women? Certainly the two goddesses play upon the basic character of the human protagonists. Aphrodite uses the essentially sensual Phaedra, and Artemis responds to the purity of Hippolytus' vision. Each human being is created in his god's image, or each creates his own god according to his own nature.

At any rate, the prayer with which Euripides introduces us to Hippolytus defines the essential nature of the young man and of Artemis;

he stands before a statue of the goddess offering her a diadem of flowers (*Hippolytus* 73–87):

 For you, my mistress, I bring this garland which I have fashioned of flowers plucked from a virgin meadow untouched by iron implements, where no shepherd has ever presumed to graze his flock—indeed a virgin field which bees frequent in spring. Purity waters it like a river stream for those who have as their lot the knowledge of virtue in everything, not through teaching but by their very nature. These are the ones for whom it is right to pluck these flowers, but those who are evil are forbidden. My dear lady, accept from my holy hand this garland to crown your golden hair. I alone of mortals have this privilege: I am with you and converse with you, for I hear your voice, although I do not see your face. As I have begun life in your grace, may I so keep it to the end.[13]

APOLLO

9

The Birth of Apollo

As has been told in the previous chapter, Zeus mated with Leto and she conceived the twin gods, Artemis and Apollo. The *Homeric Hymn to Apollo* (3) concentrates in its first part (1–178: To Delian Apollo) on the story of how Delos became the site of Apollo's birth. The hymn begins with a scene of the gods in the home of Zeus (1–29):

> I shall not forget far-shooting Apollo but remember him before whom the gods tremble when he comes to the home of Zeus. They all spring up from their seats as he approaches and draws his shining bow, and Leto alone remains beside Zeus, who delights in thunder. But then she unstrings his bow and closes his quiver and, taking them from his mighty shoulders, hangs them on a column of his father's house from a golden peg. She leads him to a chair and sits him down, and his father welcomes his dear son by giving him nectar in a gold cup. Then the other deities sit down in their places and the lady Leto rejoices because she has borne a son who is a mighty archer. Rejoice, O blessed Leto, since you have borne splendid children, lord Apollo and Artemis, who take delight in arrows; Artemis you bore in Ortygia and Apollo in rocky Delos as you leaned against the great and massive Cynthian hill, right next to the palm tree near the stream of the Inopus.
>
> How then shall I celebrate you in my song—you who are in all ways the worthy subject of many hymns? For everywhere, O Phoebus, music is sung in your honor, both on the mainland where heifers are bred and on the islands. All mountaintops give you pleasure and the lofty ridges of high hills, rivers flowing to the sea, beaches sloping to the water, and harbors of the deep. Shall I

sing about how Leto gave you birth against Mt. Cynthus on the rocky island, on sea-girt Delos? On either side a dark wave was driven towards the land by shrill winds. From your beginning here, you rule over all mortals [including those to whom Leto came when she was in labor].

Leto had roamed far and wide in her search for a refuge where she might give birth to Apollo. The hymn continues with a long and impressive list of cities and islands to emphasize the extent of her wanderings; she visited all those who lived in these places (30–139):[1]

Crete and the land of Athens, the islands of Aegina and Euboea famous for its ships, and Aegae, Eiresiae, and Peparethus by the sea, Thracian Athos, the tall peaks of Pelion, Thracian Samos, the shady hills of Ida, and Scyros, Phocaea, the sheer mountain of Autocane, well-built Imbros, hazy Lemnos, and holy Lesbos, seat of Macar, the son of Aeolus, and Chios, most shimmering of the islands that lie in the sea, craggy Mimas, the tall peaks of Corycus, gleaming Claros, the steep mountain of Aesagea, rainy Samos, the sheer heights of Mycale, Miletus and Cos, the city of Meropian mortals, and steep Cnidos, windy Carpathos, Naxos, Paros, and rocky Rhenaea.

Leto approached these many places in labor with the far-shooting god in the hope that some land might want to make a home for her son. But they all trembled and were very much afraid; and not one of them, even the more rich, dared to receive the god Phoebus, until lady Leto came to Delos[2] and asked with winged words: "Delos, if you would like to be the home of my son, Phoebus Apollo, and to establish for him a rich temple—do not refuse, for no one else will come near you, as you will find out, and I do not think that you will be rich in cattle and sheep or bear harvests or grow plants in abundance—if you would then have a temple of Apollo, the far-shooter, all people will congregate here and bring hecatombs, and the aroma of rich sacrifices will rise up incessantly and your inhabitants will be nourished by the hands of foreigners."

Thus she spoke; Delos rejoiced and said to her in answer: "Leto, most renowned daughter of great Coeus, I should receive your son, the lord who shoots from afar, with joy, for the terrible truth is that I have a bad reputation among human beings, and in this way I should become greatly esteemed. But I fear this prediction (and I shall not keep it from you): they say that Apollo will be someone of uncontrollable power, who will mightily lord it over both immortal gods and mortal humans on the fruitful earth. And so I am dreadfully afraid in the depths of my heart and soul that when he first looks upon the light of the sun he will be contemptuous of me (since I am an island that is rocky and barren) and overturn me with his feet and push me down into the depths of the sea where the surge of the great waves will rise mightily above me. And he will come to another land that pleases him, where he will build his temple amidst groves of trees. But sea monsters will find their dens in me, and black seals will make me their home without being disturbed, since I will be without human inhabitants. But if, O goddess, you would dare to swear to me a great oath that he will build here first of all a very beautiful temple to be an oracle for men; then after he has done this, let him proceed to extend his prestige and build his sanctuaries among all people; for to be sure his wide renown will be great."

Thus Delos spoke. And Leto swore the great oath of the gods: "Now let Gaea and wide Uranus above bear witness and the flowing waters of the Styx (this is the greatest and most dread oath that there is for the blessed gods), in truth a fragrant altar and sacred precinct of Apollo will be established here forever, and he will honor you above all."

When she had ended and sworn her oath, Delos rejoiced greatly in the birth of the lord who shoots from afar. But Leto for nine days and nine nights was racked by desperate pains in her labor. All the greatest of the goddesses were with her—Dione, Rhea, righteous Themis, and sea moaning Amphitrite—and others too, except for white-armed Hera; for she sat at home in the house of Zeus the cloud-gatherer. Eileithyia, the goddess of pangs of childbirth, was the only one who had not heard of Leto's distress, for she sat on the heights of Olympus beneath golden clouds through the wiles of white-armed Hera, who kept her there because she was jealous that Leto of the beautiful hair was about to bear a strong and noble son.

But the goddesses on the well-inhabited island sent Iris away to fetch Eileithyia, promising her a great necklace strung with golden threads, over thirteen feet long. They ordered her to call Eileithyia away from white-armed Hera so that Hera might not be able to dissuade the goddess of childbirth from going. When Iris, swift-footed as the wind, heard their instructions, she ran on her way and quickly traversed all the distance between. And when she came to sheer Olympus, home of the gods, immediately she called Eileithyia out of the house to the door and addressed her with winged words, telling her everything just as the goddesses who have their homes on Olympus had directed.

Thus she moved Eileithyia to the depths of the heart in her breast, and like timid doves they proceeded on their journey. As soon as

Eileithyia, goddess of the pangs of childbirth, came to Delos, the pains of labor took hold of Leto, and she was anxious to give birth. And she threw her arms about the palm tree and sank on her knees in the soft meadow, and the earth beneath her smiled. The baby sprang forth to the light, and all the goddesses gave a cry. There, O mighty Phoebus, the goddesses washed you with lovely water, holily and purely, and wrapped you in white swaddling clothes, splendid and new, fastened round about with a golden cord. And his mother did not nurse Apollo of the gold sword, but Themis from her immortal hands gave him nectar and delicious ambrosia. And Leto rejoiced because she had borne a strong son who carries a bow.

But after you had tasted the divine food, O Phoebus, then no longer could golden cords hold you in your restlessness or bonds keep you confined, but they all were undone. And straightway Phoebus Apollo exclaimed to the immortal goddesses: "Let the lyre and curved bow be dear to my heart, and I shall prophesy to human beings the unerring will of Zeus." With these words Phoebus, the far-shooter with unshorn hair, strode on the ground that stretches far and wide; all the goddesses were amazed, and the whole of Delos blossomed, laden with gold like the top of a mountain with woodland flowers, as she beheld the son of Zeus and Leto, in her joy that the god had chosen her among all islands and mainland sites to be his home, and loved her most of all in his heart.

The conclusion of this first part of the *Homeric Hymn to Apollo* tells about the great festival to Apollo at Delos, the amazing chorus of maidens, the Deliades, who can sing in all dialects, and about the poet himself, the blind bard from the island of Chios (140–178).

And you yourself, O lord Apollo, far-shooter of the silver bow, come at times to the steep Cynthian hill of Delos, and on other occasions you wander among other islands and other peoples; indeed many are your temples and wooded groves, and every vantage point, highest peak of lofty mountains, and river flowing to the sea, is dear to you. But, O Phoebus, your heart is delighted most of all with Delos, where the long-robed Ionians gather with their children and their revered wives. In commemoration of you they will take pleasure in boxing and dancing and song when they celebrate your festival. And anyone who might encounter the Ionians while they are thus assembled together would say that they were immortal and ageless, for he would perceive grace in them all and be delighted in his heart as he beheld the men and the beautifully robed women, the swift ships, and the abundant possessions.

In addition to this, there would be the maidens who serve the far-shooting god, the Deliades, a great and wondrous sight, whose renown will never perish. They sing their hymn to Apollo first of all and then to Leto and Artemis, who delights in her arrows, and they remember the men and women of old and enchant the assembled throng with their songs. They know how to imitate the sounds and sing in the dialects of all human beings. So well does their beautiful song match the speech of each person that one would say he himself were singing.

But come now Apollo with Artemis, and be propitious. Farewell, all you Delian maidens. Remember me hereafter when someone of earthborn mortals, a stranger who has suffered, comes here and asks: "Maidens, what man do you think is the sweetest of the singers who frequent this place and in whom do you delight most of all?" Then all of you answer that I am the one: "A blind man who lives in rocky Chios; all his songs are the best forevermore."[3]

I will bring your renown wherever I roam over the earth to the well-inhabited cities of humans; and they will believe since it is true. Yet I shall never cease to hymn the praises of Apollo, god of the silver bow, whom Leto of the beautiful hair bore.

Apollo and Delphi

Some believe that this first part of the lengthy *Hymn to Apollo* was originally a separate composition, a hymn to Delian Apollo. The second part of the hymn, which is translated in the appendix to this chapter, would have been recited as a song to Pythian Apollo, the god of Delphi.[4] Filled with a wealth of mythological information, it tells how Apollo descended from Mt. Olympus and made his way through northern and central Greece, finally discovering the proper spot for the foundation of his oracle among humankind at Crisa under snow-capped Parnassus. Apollo laid out his temple and then slew a she-dragon by the fair-flowing stream nearby. The name of the site was henceforth called Pytho (and Apollo, the Pythian) because the rays of the sun made the monster rot. (The Greek verb *pytho* means "I rot.")[5]

A cogent historical reconstruction of the conflicting evidence[6] suggests that originally the site was occupied by an oracle of the great mother-goddess of the Minoan-Mycenaean period, sometimes known as Ge-Themis. The slaying of the dragon (the traditional manifestation of a deity of earth), therefore, represents the subsequent conquest by Hellenic or Hellenized Apollo. For murdering the dragon, Zeus sent Apollo into exile in Thessaly for nine years (his punishment presumably mirrors the religious dictates of ancient society).[7]

The omphalos, an archaic stone shaped like an egg, which was kept in the temple during the classical period, seems to confirm an early habitation of the site.[8] Legend has it that this omphalos (the word means "navel") signified that Delphi actually occupied the physical center of the earth (certainly it was in many ways the spiritual center of the ancient world). Zeus was said to have released two eagles who flew from opposite ends of the earth and met exactly at the site of Apollo's sanctuary—a spot marked out for all to see by the stone omphalos with two birds perched on either side.

The hymn to Pythian Apollo concludes with a curious and interesting story. After he had established his sanctuary at Crisa, Apollo was concerned about recruiting attendants to his service. He noticed a ship passing, manned by Cretans from Cnossus, on its way to sandy Pylos. Phoebus Apollo transformed himself into a dolphin and immediately sprang aboard. At first the men tried to throw the monster into the sea, but such was the havoc it created that they were awed to fearful submission. Speeded on by a divine wind, the ship would not obey the efforts of the crew to bring it to land. Finally, after a lengthy course, Apollo led them to Crisa, where he leaped ashore and revealed himself as a god amid a blaze of fiery brightness and splendor. He addressed the Cretan men, ordering them to perform sacrifices and pray to him as Apollo Delphinius. Then he led them to his sanctuary, accompanying them on the lyre as they chanted a paean in his honor. The hymn ends with the god's prediction of the prestige and wealth that is to come to his sanctuary as he instructs the Cretan band, who are placed in charge.

The story links the early cult of Apollo with Crete, explains the epithet Delphinius in terms of the Greek word for dolphin, and provides an etymology for Delphi as the name of the sanctuary. As god of sailors and of colonization (his oracle played a primary role as the religious impetus for the sending out of colonies), Apollo was worshiped under the title Delphinius. The hymn as a whole confirms the universality of the worship of Apollo and the importance of his outstanding cult centers, certainly at Delos but above all at Delphi.

The sanctuary of Apollo at Delphi is representative of the nature and character of other Panhellenic sites elsewhere.[9] The sacred area was built on the lower slopes of Mt. Parnassus, about two thousand feet above the Corinthian Gulf. It is an awe-inspiring spot to this day. For anyone walking along the Sacred Way up to the great temple of the god, it is not difficult to sense the feelings of reverence and exaltation that filled the heart and the soul of the ancient believer. The excavations have laid bare the foundations of the many and varied types of monuments along the winding path that were set up by individuals and city-states in honor and gratitude. Small temples (called treasuries) were a particularly imposing type of dedication, erected to house expensive and precious offerings. Among the major buildings of the sanctuary were a stadium, a theater, and of course the great temple of Apollo himself.

The Pythian Games, which were celebrated every four years, included (after 582 B.C.) both physical and intellectual competitions. Footraces, chariot races, and musical, literary, and dramatic presentations were among the events that combined to make the festival second only to that of Zeus at Olympia. The sanctuary and the celebrations reflect much that is characteristic of Greek life and thought. The numerous triumphant dedications of victory in war mirror the narrow particularism and vehement rivalry among individual city-states, while the fact of the festivals themselves, to which *all* Greeks might come to honor gods common to their race, reveals the strivings toward a wider and more humane vision. Certainly the sense of competition in both athletics and the arts was vital to the Greek spirit. The importance of both the physical and the aesthetic also suggests a fundamental duality made one and whole in the prowess and intellectuality of the god Apollo himself. The *Odes* of Pindar, written to celebrate the glorious victors in the athletic competitions, have proven to be among the most sublime lyrical outpourings of the human spirit. Physical excellence intensified a sense of physical beauty that inspired Greek artists to capture in sculpture and in painting the realism and idealism of the human form. The crystallization of the Doric, Ionic, and Corinthian orders of architecture in the construction of sublime architectural forms was also inspired by religious as well as civic devotion. The spiritual and human impetus to great feats of body and mind is among the most wondrous achievements of the Greek religious experience.

The Oracle and the Pythia at Delphi

The Panhellenic sanctuary of Delphi was above all an oracle.[10] People from all over the Greek world (and even beyond) came to Apollo with questions of every sort, both personal and political. Herodotus' story of Solon and Croesus, translated in Chapter 4, bears testimony to the prestige of the god, already well established in the sixth century, and provides primary evidence for the nature and form of his responses as well.

The exact oracular procedures followed cannot be determined precisely because our sources are inadequate. The Pythia (prophetess of Apollo) uttered the responses of the god. Her seat of prophecy was the tripod, a bowl supported by three metal legs. A tripod was a utensil of everyday life; a fire could be lit beneath or inside the bowl, and it could be used for many obvious practical purposes. The tripod at Delphi was both a symbol and a source of divine prophetic power. Ancient pottery depicts Apollo himself seated on the bowl; his Pythian priestess who does likewise becomes his mouthpiece. In a frenzy of inspiration she utters her incoherent ravings. A priest or prophet nearby will transcribe them into intelligible prose or verse (usually dactylic hexameters) to be communicated to the inquirer.

The Pythia herself underwent certain initial ceremonies to ensure purification and inspiration, among them a ritual cleansing with the sacred water of the famous Castalian spring. Some of our sources maintain that the Pythia's inspiration came from the vaporous outpourings from a chasm or cave and depict the priestess seated on the tripod above some such cleft or opening.

Unfortunately, the west end of Apollo's temple (where she uttered her responses) is so badly preserved in the excavations that it cannot be reconstructed with certainty; therefore we cannot be sure where the Pythia may have been placed.

The inquirer who came to the temple with his question for the god had to go through certain prescribed ceremonies that were in the nature of a fee.[11] First he had to offer an expensive sacred cake on the altar outside the temple; and once he had entered, he was required to sacrifice a sheep or goat, a portion of which went to the Delphians. After these preliminaries, he could enter the holy of holies, the innermost shrine of the temple, where he took his seat. The chief priest or prophet addressed the questions to the Pythia (who may have been in an area separated from the inquirer) and interpreted her answers.[12]

In early times, according to tradition, the Pythia was a young virgin. On one occasion an inquirer fell in love with one and seduced her. From then on, only mature women (probably over fifty years old) could become priestesses; whatever the nature of their previous lives (they could have been married), purity was required once they had been appointed to serve the god for life. At times one from among at least three women could be called upon to prophesy, and there were probably more in reserve.[13]

Inevitably one must wonder about the religious sincerity of the priests and priestesses at Delphi. Was it all a fraud? There is no good reason to think so. Many people have believed in the possibility of god communicating with mortals in marvelous ways. And belief in a medium, a person with special mantic gifts, is by no means unique to the Greeks. The Pythia presumably was chosen because of her special nature and religious character—she was susceptible to supernatural callings. It is true that the oracle was often on the side of political expediency and that the ambiguity of the responses was notorious. Apollo's obscure epithet, Loxias, was thought to bear testimony to the difficult and devious nature of his replies. But only a glance at the life and career of Socrates shows the sincere and inner religious meaning that an intellectually devout person is able to wrest from the material trappings of established institutions in any society. According to Plato's *Apology,* Socrates' friend Chaerephon went to Delphi to ask who was the wisest of men. The answer was "Socrates"; and when the philosopher learned this, he could not rest until he had determined the meaning of the response and proved the god right. If we are to take the *Apology* at all literally and historically (and why not?), this message from Apollo provided a turning point for Socrates in his missionary-like zeal to make men and women think of eternal moral and ethical values in terms of their immortal souls.

The Cumaean Sibyl

The Pythia is the specific title given to the priestess of Apollo at Delphi. A more generic term for prophetess was *Sibyl,* and many Sibyls were found at various places in various periods in the ancient world. Originally the title was probably the proper name (Sibylla) of an early prophetess. At any rate, the Sibyls at Cumae were among the most famous mediums of antiquity.[14] The description of the Cumaean Sibyl as she prophesies to Aeneas helps us understand the nature of the communication of a prophetess with her god, even though we must allow for poetic imagination.[15] The innermost shrine of the temple is a cavern from which the responses issue (Vergil, *Aeneid* 6. 42–51):

 The vast end of the temple, built in Euboean stone, is cut out into a cavern; here are a hundred perforations in the rock, a hundred mouths from which the many utterances rush, the answers of the Sibyl. They had come to the threshold, when the virgin cried: "Now is the time to demand the oracles, the god, behold, the god!" She spoke these words in front of the doors and her countenance and color changed; her hair shook free, her bosom heaved, and her heart swelled in wild fury; she seemed of greater stature, and her cries were not mortal as she was inspired by the breath of the god drawing nearer.

Later follows the metaphor of a wild horse trying to throw its rider (77-82, 98-101):

Not yet willing to endure Apollo, the prophetess raged within the cavern in her frenzy, trying to shake the mighty god from her breast; all the more he wore out her ravings, mastering her wild heart and fashioning her to his will by constraint. Now the hundred mouths of the cavern opened wide of their own accord and bore the responses of the prophetess to the breezes. . . . The Cumaean Sibyl chants her terrifying riddles and, from the innermost shrine of the cavern, truth resounded, enveloped in obscurity, as Apollo applied the reins to her raving and twisted the goad in her breast.

Earlier in the *Aeneid* (3. 445) the seer Helenus warned Aeneas that the Sibyl wrote her prophecies on leaves that were carefully arranged. But when the doors of the cavern were opened, these leaves were scattered by the wind so that those who had come for advice left without help and hated the dwelling of the Sibyl. Thus Aeneas asks (6. 74-76) that the Sibyl utter the prophecies herself and not entrust them to the leaves. All this may be an oblique reference to some characteristic of the Sibylline books (collections of prophecies of the Sibyls often consulted by the Romans) and the way in which they were interpreted.[16]

Ovid has the Sibyl tell Aeneas the story of her fate (*Metamorphoses* 14. 132-153):

Eternal life without end would have been given me if I had yielded my virginity to Phoebus Apollo who loved me. He hoped that I would and desired to bribe me with gifts, so he said: "Virgin maid of Cumae, choose what you desire; you will attain whatever it is." I picked up a heap of sand, showed it to him and asked for the vain wish that I might have as many birthdays as the individual grains in my hand. I forgot to ask for continuous youth along with the years. He would have given me both, long life and eternal youth, if I had succumbed to his love. But I despised Phoebus' gift and I remain unmarried. And now the happier time of youth is gone and sick old age has come with its feeble steps and I must endure it for a long time.

For now as you see I have lived through seven generations; there remain for me to witness three hundred harvests, three hundred vintages in order to equal in years the number of grains of sand.[17] The time will be when length of days will have reduced me from my former stature and make me small, and my limbs consumed by age will be diminished to the tiniest weight. And I shall not seem like one who was pleasing to a god and loved by him. Even Phoebus himself perhaps either will not recognize me or will deny that he once desired me; I shall be changed to such an extent that I shall be visible to no one, but I shall be recognized by my voice; the Fates will leave me my voice.

In another version the Sibyl became a tiny thing suspended in a bottle. Boys asked: ''Sibyl, what do you want?'' Her answer was: ''I want to die.''[18]

Apollo and Cassandra

Priam's daughter Cassandra, a pathetic figure in the Trojan saga, was another of Apollo's loves and another prophetess. When she agreed to give herself to Apollo, as a reward the god bestowed upon her the power of prophecy. But Cassandra then changed her mind and rejected his advances. Apollo asked for one kiss and spat into her mouth. Although he did not revoke his gift, Cassandra was thereafter doomed to prophesy in vain, for no one would believe her.

Apollo and Marpessa

Apollo also attempted to win Marpessa, daughter of Evenus, a son of Ares. She was also wooed by Idas, one of the Argonauts, who carried her off in his chariot against the will of her father. Evenus unsuccessfully pursued the pair, then in his anger and heartbreak committed suicide. Subsequently Apollo, who had also been a suitor for Marpessa's hand, stole her away from Idas in similar fashion. Ultimately the two rivals met face to face in conflict over the girl. At this point Zeus intervened and ordered Marpessa to choose between her lovers. She chose Idas because he was a mortal, for she was afraid that the undying and eternally handsome god Apollo would abandon her when she grew old.

Apollo and Cyrene

Nearly all of Apollo's numerous affairs are tragic; he is perhaps the most touchingly human and the most terrifyingly sublime of all the Greek gods. A notable exception is his success with Cyrene, an athletic nymph, with whom he fell in love as he watched her wrestling with a lion. He whisked her away to Libya in his golden chariot, to the very site of the city that would be given her name, and she bore him a son, Aristaeus.[19]

Apollo and Daphne

The story of Apollo's love for Daphne explains why the laurel (the Greek word *daphne* means "laurel") was sacred to him. Ovid's version is the best known *(Metamorphoses* 1. 452–567):

Daphne, daughter of Peneus, was the first object of Apollo's love. It was not blind fate that brought this about, but Cupid's cruel anger. Apollo, flushed with pride at his victory over Python, had seen Cupid drawing his bow and taunted him: "What business of yours are brave men's arms, young fellow? The bow suits *my* shoulder; *I* can take unerring aim at wild animals or at my enemies. I it was who laid low proud Python, though he stretched over wide acres of ground, with uncounted arrows. You should be content with kindling the fires of love in some mortal with your torch; do not try to share my glory!"

To him Cupid replied: "Although your arrows pierce every target, Apollo, mine will pierce you. Just as all animals yield to you, so your glory is inferior to mine." And as he spoke he quickly flew to the peak of shady Parnassus and from his quiver drew two arrows. Different were their functions, for the one, whose point was dull and leaden, repelled love; the other—golden, bright, and sharp— aroused it. Cupid shot the leaden arrow at Peneus' daughter, while he pierced Apollo's inmost heart with the golden one.

Straightway Apollo loved, and Daphne ran even from the name of "lover." Companion of Diana, her joy was in the depths of the forests and the spoils of the chase; a headband kept her flowing hair in place. Many suitors courted her, while she cared not for love or marriage; a virgin she roamed the pathless woods. Her father often said, "My daughter, you owe me a son-in-law and grandchildren"; she, hating the marriage torch as if it were a disgrace, blushed and embraced her father saying, "Allow me, dearest father, always to be a virgin. Jupiter granted this to Diana." Peneus granted her prayer; but Daphne's beauty allowed her not to be as she desired and opposed her wish.

Apollo loved her; he saw her and desired to marry her. He hoped to achieve his desire, misled by his own oracle. Even as the stubble burns after the harvest, or a hedge catches fire from a careless traveler's embers, so the god burned with all-consuming fire and fueled his love with fruitless hope. He sees her hair lying unadorned upon her neck and says, "What if it were adorned?" He sees her flashing eyes like stars; he sees her lips—and merely to see is not enough. He praises her fingers, hands, arms, and shoulders half-bared; those parts which are covered he thinks more beautiful.

Swifter than the wind, Daphne runs from him and stays not to hear him call her back: "Stay, nymph! Stay, daughter of Peneus, I pray! I am not an enemy who pursues you. Stay, nymph! A lamb runs like this from the wolf, a hind from the lion, doves with fluttering wings from the eagle. Each kind runs from its enemy: love makes me pursue! Oh, take care you do not fall; let not the thorns scratch those legs that never should be marred and I be the cause of your hurt! Rough is the place where you run; run more slowly, I beg, and I will pursue more slowly. Yet consider who loves you; I am not a mountain peasant; I am not an uncouth shepherd who watches here his flocks and herds. Unheeding you know not whom you try to escape, and therefore do you run. I am lord of Delphi, of Claros, Tenedos, and royal Patara; Jupiter is my father! I show the future, the past, the present; through me came the harmony of lyre and song! Unerring are my arrows, yet one arrow is yet more unerring and has wounded my heart, before untouched. The healing art is mine; throughout the world am I called the Bringer of Help; the power of herbs is mine to command. Ah me! for no herb can remedy love; the art which heals all cannot heal its master!"

Even as he spoke, Daphne fled from him and ran on in fear; then too she seemed lovely—the wind laid bare her body, and her clothes fluttered as she ran and her hair streamed out behind. In flight she was yet more beautiful. Yet the young god could not bear to have his words of love go for nothing; driven on by love he followed at full speed. Even as a Gallic hound sees a hare in an empty field and pursues its prey as it runs for safety—the one seems just to be catching the quarry and expects each moment to have gripped it; with muzzle at full stretch it is hot on the other's tracks; the other hardly knows if it has been caught and avoids the snapping jaws—so the god chased the virgin: hope gave him speed; her speed came from fear. Yet the pursuer gains, helped by the wings of love; he gives her no respite; he presses hard upon her and his breath ruffles the hair upon her neck.

Now Daphne's strength was gone, drained by the effort of her flight, and pale she saw Peneus' waters. "Help me, Father," she cried, "if a river has power; change me and destroy my beauty which has proved too attractive!" Hardly had she finished her prayer when her limbs grew heavy and sluggish; thin bark

Apollo and Daphne, attributed to Antonio del Pollaiuolo (1433–1498). Oil on panel; $11\frac{5}{8} \times 7\frac{7}{8}$ in. Apollo, in the guise of a young Florentine nobleman, has just caught up with Daphne. Her left leg is rooted in the ground and her arms have already become leafy branches, while she looks down at the god with a mysterious smile. The painter has caught the interaction of movement and fixity that permeates Ovid's narrative, while the tragedy is set in a jewellike Tuscan landscape. *(National Gallery, London. Reproduced by courtesy of the Trustees.)*

enveloped her soft breasts; her hair grew into leaves, her arms into branches. Her feet, which until now had run so swiftly, held fast with clinging roots. Her face was the tree's top; only her beauty remains.

Even in this form Apollo loves her; placing his hand on the trunk he felt the heart beating beneath the new-formed bark. Embracing

Apollo and Daphne, by Gian Lorenzo Bernini (1598–1680). Marble, 1624; height 96 in. Like Pollaiuolo, Bernini has chosen the moment when swift movement is stopped. The sculptor brilliantly incorporates the psychological tensions of Ovid's narrative, frozen in the moment of metamorphosis. The contrast between Apollo, adapted from the famous *Apollo Belvedere*, and the agitated emotions of Daphne serves to heighten the tragedy. On the base (not shown) are inscribed Ovid's description of the metamorphosis (*Metamorphoses* 1. 519–521) and two Latin lines by the future Pope Urban VIII: "Every lover who pursues the joys of fleeing beauty fills his hands with leaves or plucks bitter berries." *(Galleria Borghese, Rome, Italy. Courtesy of Alinari/ Art Resource, New York.)*

the branches, as if they were human limbs, he kisses the wood; yet the wood shrinks from his kisses. "Since you cannot be my wife," said he, "you shall be my tree. Always you shall wreathe my hair, my lyre, my quiver. You shall accompany the Roman generals when the joyous triumph hymn is sung and the long procession climbs the Capitol . . . and as my young locks have never been shorn, so may you forever be honored with green leaves!" Apollo's speech was done: the new-made laurel nodded her assent and like a head bowed her topmost branches.

Apollo and Hyacinthus

Apollo was also susceptible to the love of young men.[20] His devotion to Hyacinthus, a handsome Spartan youth from Amyclae, is well known from Ovid's account; the great god neglected his other duties in order to be in the company of his beloved (*Metamorphoses* 10. 174–219):

The Titan sun was almost midway between the night that had passed and the one to come—equidistant from both—when Apollo and the boy took off their garments and glistening with olive oil began to compete with the broad discus. Phoebus made the first throw. He poised the discus and hurled it so far into the air that the clouds were scattered by its course and only after a long time, because of its own sheer weight, did it fall back again to solid earth. His throw exhibited great skill combined with great strength. Straightway Hyacinthus under the impulse of his enthusiasm, heedless of all but the game, made a dash to pick up the discus. But it bounced back, O Hyacinthus, as it hit the hard earth and struck you full in the face.[21] The god turned as pale as the boy himself. He took up the limp body in his attempt to revive him, frantically staying the flow of blood from the sad wound and applying herbs to sustain the life that was ebbing away. His arts were to no avail; the wound was incurable. Just as when someone in a garden breaks off violets or brittle poppies or lilies that cling to their tawny stems, and suddenly these flowers droop and fade and cannot support the tops of their heavy heads which look down to the ground, so dropped the head of the dying boy and his neck, once strength was gone, gave way to the burden of its weight and sank on his shoulder.

Phoebus cried: "You slip away, cheated of your youthful prime. Your wound that I look upon accuses me. You are my grief and my guilt—my own hand is branded with your death! I am the one who is responsible. But what fault was mine? Can it be called a fault to have played a game with you, to have loved you? O that I could give you my life as you deserve or die along with you. But we are bound by fate's decree. Yet you will always be with me, your name will cling to my lips, forever remembering. You will be my theme as I pluck my lyre and sing my songs and you, a new flower, will bear markings in imitation of my grief; and there will come a time when the bravest of heroes will be linked to this same flower and his name will be read on its petals."

While Apollo spoke these words from his unerring lips, lo and behold, the blood that had poured upon the ground and stained the grass ceased to be blood and a flower arose, of a purple more brilliant than Tyrian dye; it took the shape of a lily and differed only in color, for lilies are silvery white. Apollo, although responsible for so honoring Hyacinthus, was not yet satisfied. The god himself inscribed his laments upon the petals and the flower bears the markings of the mournful letters *AI AI*.[22] Sparta was proud to claim Hyacinthus as her son and his glory endures to this day; every year a festival, the Hyacinthia, is celebrated in his honor with ceremonies ancient in their traditions.

Apollo, Coronis, and Asclepius

Several stories emphasize Apollo's role as a god of medicine, which is taken over in large part by his son Asclepius. And this brings us to Apollo's affair with Coronis, the last we shall tell. Coronis (in Ovid's version) was a lovely maiden from Larissa in Thessaly whom Apollo loved; in fact she was pregnant with his child. Unfortunately the raven, Apollo's bird, saw Coronis lying with a young Thessalian and told all to the god (*Metamorphoses* 2. 600-634):

 When Apollo heard this charge against Coronis, the laurel wreath slipped from his head, his expression changed, and the color drained from his cheeks. As his heart burned with swollen rage, he took up his accustomed weapons and bent his bow to string it; with his unerring arrow he pierced the breast which he had so often embraced. She gave a groan as she was struck; and when she drew the shaft from her body, red blood welled up over her white limbs. She spoke: "You could have exacted this punishment and I have paid with my life, after I had borne your child; as it is, two of us die in one." With these words her life drained away with her blood; the chill of death crept over her lifeless corpse.

Too late, alas, the lover repented of his cruel punishment. He hated himself because he had listened to the charge against her and had been so inflamed. He hated his bow and his arrows and his hands that had so rashly shot them. He fondled her limp body and strove to thwart the Fates; but his efforts came too late, and he applied his arts of healing to no avail. When he saw that his attempts were in vain and the pyre was being built and saw her limbs about to be burned in the last flames, then truly (for it is forbidden that the cheeks of the gods be touched by tears) Apollo uttered groans that issued from the very depths of his heart, just as when a young cow sees the mallet poised above the right ear of her suckling calf to shatter the hollow temples with a crashing blow. He poured perfumes upon her unfeeling breast, clasped her in his embrace, and performed the proper rites so just and yet unjust. Phoebus could not bear that his own seed be reduced to the same ashes, but he snatched his son out of the flames from the womb of his mother and brought him to the cave of the centaur Chiron. The raven, who hoped for a reward for the truth of his utterances, Apollo forbade evermore to be counted among white birds. Meanwhile the centaur was happy to have the divine infant as a foster child and delighted in such an honorable task.

Thus, like many another mythological figure, Asclepius was trained by the wise and gentle Chiron, and he learned his lessons well, particularly in the field of medicine. When he grew up, he refined this science and raised it by transforming it into a high and noble art (just as the Greeks themselves did in actual fact, particularly in the work of the great fifth-century physician, Hippocrates, with his medical school at Cos). Asclepius married and had several children, among them doctors such as Machaon (in the *Iliad*) and more shadowy figures such as Hygeia or Hygieia (Health).

The *Homeric Hymn to Asclepius* (16) is a short and direct appeal to the mythical physician.

 About the healer of sicknesses, Asclepius, son of Apollo, I begin to sing. In the Dotian plain of Argos, goddess-like Coronis, daughter of King Phlegyas, bore him, a great joy to mortals, a soother of evil pains.

So hail to you, lord; I pray to you with my song.

So skilled a physician was Asclepius (he was worshiped as both a hero and a god) that when Hippolytus died, Artemis appealed to him to restore her devoted follower to life. Asclepius agreed and succeeded in his attempt; but he thus incurred the wrath of Zeus who hurled him into the lower world with a thunderbolt for such a disruption of nature.

The *Alcestis* of Euripides

Apollo was enraged by the death of his son; he did not, of course, turn against Zeus, but he killed the Cyclopes who had forged the lethal thunderbolt. Because of his crime, he was sentenced (following once again the pattern of the human social order and its codes concerning blood-guilt) to live in exile for a year under the rule of Admetus, the beneficent king of Pherae in Thessaly. Apollo felt kindly toward his master, and when he found out that Admetus had only a short time to live, he went to the Moirai and induced them, with the help of wine, to allow the king a longer life. But they imposed the condition that someone must die in his place. Admetus, however, could find no one willing to give up his or her life on his behalf (not even his aged parents) except his devoted wife, Alcestis; and he accepted her sacrifice.

In his fascinating and puzzling play *Alcestis* (it is difficult to find general agreement on the interpretation of this tragicomedy), Euripides presents a touching and ironic portrait of the devoted wife. She is, however, rescued from the tomb in the nick of time by the good services of Heracles, who happens to be a visitor in the home of Admetus and wrestles with Death himself (*Thanatos*) for the life of Alcestis.

Apollo's Musical Contest with Marsyas

Apollo's skill as a musician has already been attested. Two additional stories concentrate more exclusively upon the divine excellence of his art and the folly of inferiors who challenged it. The first concerns Marsyas, the satyr (as we have previously mentioned) who picked up the flute after it had been invented and then discarded by Athena. Although the goddess gave Marsyas a thrashing for taking up her instrument, he was not deterred by this and became so proficient that he dared to challenge Apollo himself to a contest. The condition imposed by the god was that the victor could do what he liked with the vanquished. Of course Apollo won, and he decided to flay Marsyas alive. Ovid describes the anguish of the satyr (*Metamorphoses* 6. 385–400):

 Marsyas cried out: "Why are you stripping me of my very self? Oh no, I am sorry; the flute is not worth this torture!" As he screamed, his skin was ripped off all his body and he was nothing but a gaping wound. Blood ran everywhere, his nerves were laid bare and exposed, and the pulse of his veins throbbed without any covering. One could make out clearly his pulsating entrails and the vital organs in his chest that lay revealed. The spirits of the countryside and the fauns who haunt the woods wept for him; and so did his brothers, the satyrs and nymphs and all who tended woolly sheep and horned cattle on those mountains—and Olympus, dear to him now, wept as well. The fertile earth grew wet as she received and drank up the tears that fell and became soaked to the veins in her depths. She formed of them a stream which she sent up into the open air. From this source a river, the clearest in all Phrygia, rushes down between its sloping banks into the sea. And it bears the name of Marsyas.

Apollo's Musical Contest with Pan

Apollo was involved in another musical contest, this time with the god Pan, and King Midas of Phrygia acted as one of the judges (Ovid *Metamorphoses* 11. 146-193):

 Midas, in his loathing for riches,[23] found a retreat in the woods and the country and worshiped Pan, the god who always inhabits mountain caves. But his intelligence still remained limited, and his own foolish stupidity was going to harm him once again as it had before. There is a mountain, Tmolus, that rises high in its steep ascent with a lofty view to the sea; on one side it slopes down to Sardis, on another to the little town of Hypaepa. Here while he was singing his songs to his gentle nymphs and playing a dainty tune on his pipes made of reeds and wax, Pan dared to belittle the music of Apollo compared to his own.

And so he engaged in an unequal contest, with Tmolus as judge. This elderly judge took his seat on his own mountain and freed his ears of trees; only the oak remained to wreathe his dark hair, and acorns hung down around his hollow temples. He turned his gaze upon the god of flocks and said: "Now the judge is ready." Pan began to blow on his rustic pipes; and Midas, who happened to be nearby as he played, was charmed by the tune. When Pan had finished, Tmolus, the sacred god of the mountain, turned around to face Phoebus, and his forests followed the swing of his gaze. The golden head of Apollo was crowned with laurel from Parnassus, and his robe, dyed in Tyrian purple, trailed along the ground. His lyre was inlaid with precious stones and Indian ivory; he held it in his left hand with the plectrum in his right. His very stance was the stance of an artist. Then he played the strings with knowing hand; Tmolus was captivated by their sweetness and ordered Pan to concede that his pipes were inferior to the lyre.

The judgment of the sacred mountain pleased everyone except

Midas; he alone challenged the verdict and called it unjust. At this the god of Delos could not bear that such stupid ears retain their human shape. He made them longer, covered them with white shaggy hair, and made them flexible at their base so that they could be twitched. As for the rest of him he remained human; in this one respect alone he was changed, condemned to be endowed with the ears of a lumbering ass.

Midas of course wanted to hide his vile shame, and he attempted to do so by covering his head with a purple turban. But his barber, who regularly trimmed his long hair, saw his secret. He wanted to tell about what he had seen, but he did not dare reveal Midas' disgrace. Yet it was impossible for him to keep quiet, and so he stole away and dug a hole in the ground. Into it, with the earth removed, he murmured in a low whisper that his master had ass's ears. Then he filled the hole up again, covering up the indictment he had uttered and silently stole away from the scene. But a thick cluster of trembling reeds began to grow on the spot; in a year's time, as soon as they were full grown, they betrayed the barber's secret. For, as they swayed in the gentle south wind, they echoed the words that he had buried and revealed the truth about his master's ears.

Thus if one listened carefully to the wind whistling in the reeds he could hear the murmur of a whisper: "King Midas has ass's ears."[24]

The Nature of Apollo

The facets of Apollo's character are many and complex. His complex nature sums up the many contradictions in the tragic dilemma of human existence. He is gentle and vehement, compassionate and ruthless, guilty and guiltless, healer and destroyer. The extremes of his emotion are everywhere apparent. He acts swiftly and surely against Tityus, who dared to attempt the rape of Leto, and for this crime is punished (as we see later) in the realm of Hades. As he shot down Tityus with his arrows, he acted the same way against Niobe, this time in conjunction with his sister, Artemis (see pp. 159–160). Can one ever forget Homer's terrifying picture of the god as he lays low the Greek forces at Troy with a plague in response to the appeal of his priest Chryses (*Iliad* 1. 43–52)?

 Phoebus Apollo . . . came down from the peaks of Olympus, angered in his heart, wearing on his shoulders his bow and closed quiver. The arrows clashed on his shoulders as he moved in his rage, and he descended just like night. Then he sat down apart from the ships and shot one of his arrows; terrible was the clang made by his silver bow. First he attacked the mules and the swift hounds, but then he let go his piercing shafts against the men themselves and struck them down. The funeral pyres with their corpses burned thick and fast.

Yet this same god is the epitome of Greek classical restraint, championing the proverbial Greek maxims: "Know thyself"; and "Nothing too much." He knows by experience the dangers of excess. From a sea of blood and guilt, Apollo brings enlightenment, atonement, and purification wherever he may be, but especially in his sanctuary at Delphi.

The origins of Apollo are obscure. He may have been one of the gods brought into Greece by the northern invaders of 2000 B.C.; if

Apollo. Marble detail from the west pediment of the temple of Zeus at Olympia, ca. 460 B.C.; height of complete figure approx. 120 in. This is the head of the central figure in the pediment (see p. 80). Son of Zeus, he imposes peace on the drunken brawl of the Lapiths and Centaurs at the wedding of Pirithoüs (also the subject of the metopes on the south side of the Parthenon). The ancient traveler Pausanias thought that the figure was Pirithoüs, but no modern scholars accept his interpretation. *(Olympia Museum, Greece. Courtesy of Alinari/Art Resource, New York.)*

not, he was probably very soon absorbed by them in the period 2000–1500. Some scholars imagine Apollo as originally the prototype of the Good Shepherd with his many protective powers and skills, especially those of music and medicine.[25] As we have seen in Chapter 1, he becomes a sun-god and usurps the power of Hyperion and of Helius.

For many, Apollo appears to be the most characteristically Greek god in the whole pantheon—a gloriously conceived anthropo-morphic figure, perhaps epitomized best of all in the splendid depic-tion of the west pediment of the great temple of Zeus at Olympia (illustrated on p. 190). Here Apollo stood with calm intelligent strength, his head turned to one side, his arm upraised against the raging turmoil of the battle between the Centaurs and Lapiths by which he is surrounded.

By stressing certain aspects of his character and ignoring others, Apollo may be presented as the direct antithesis of the god Dionysus. In the persons of these two deities, the rational (Apollonian) and irrational (Dionysiac) forces in human psychology, philosophy, and religion are dramatically pitted against one another. Some scholars maintain that Apollo represents the true and essential nature of the Greek spirit, as reflected in the poetry of Homer, in contrast to the later, foreign intrusion of the mysticism of Dionysus. Whatever kernel of truth this view may hold, it must be realized that by the sixth and fifth centuries B.C. Dionysus had become an integral part of Greek civilization. By the classical period, he was as characteristically Greek as Apollo, and *both* deities actually reflect a basic duality inherent in the Greek conception of things. We have already detected in Chapter 1 this same dichotomy in the union of the mystical and mathematical that was mirrored in the amalgamation of two cultures (the Nordic and the Mediterranean) in the Minoan and Mycenaean periods.

Just as Apollo may be made a foil for Dionysus, so he may be used as a meaningful contrast to the figure of Christ. Each in his person and his life represents, physically and spiritually, two quite different concepts of meaning and purpose both in this world and in the next. Apollo and Christ do indeed afford a startling and revealing antithesis.

Here now is the brief *Homeric Hymn to Apollo* (21):

Phoebus, about you even the swan sings clearly as it wings its way and alights on the bank along the swirling river, Peneus; and about you the sweet-voiced minstrel with his lovely sounding lyre always sings both first and last.

So hail to you, lord; I propitiate you with my song.

APPENDIX TO CHAPTER 9

The *Homeric Hymn to Apollo*
(3. 179–546: To Pythian Apollo)

O lord, you hold Lycia and charming Maeonia and Miletus, desirable city on the sea; but you yourself rule mightily over Delos, washed by the waves.

The renowned son of Leto, dressed in divine and fragrant garments, goes to rocky Pytho, as he plays upon his hollow lyre; at the touch of his golden pick, the lyre makes a lovely sound. From there, as swift as thought, he soars from earth to Olympus, to the house of Zeus and the company of the other gods. Immediately the immortals are obsessed with the lyre and song. The Muses, all together, harmonize with their charming voices and celebrate the endless gifts enjoyed by the gods and the sufferings inflicted by these immortals that human beings must bear, as they live foolish and helpless lives, unable to find a defense against old age and a cure for death.

Also the Graces with beautiful hair, and the cheerful Hours, and Harmonia, Hebe, and Aphrodite, daughter of Zeus, dance together, holding hands at the wrist; and with them sings a goddess who is not slight or homely but awesome to behold and wondrously beautiful, Artemis, who delights in her arrows, sister to Apollo. Among them too, Ares and the keen-eyed slayer of Argus join in the merriment, and Apollo continues to play his beautiful music on the lyre, as he steps high and stately. The radiance from his glittering feet and glistening robe envelop him in splendor. Both golden-haired Leto and wise Zeus watch their dear son playing his music among the immortal gods and rejoice in their mighty hearts.

Shall I sing about you as a suitor in your love affairs? How you went to woo the daughter of Azan along with godlike Ischys, the son of Elatus famous for his horses, or with Phorbas, the son of Triops, or with Ereuthus or with Leucippus for the wife [to be] of Leucippus, you on foot and he from his chariot; indeed he was not a rival inferior to Triops.[26]

Or shall I sing about how at first you went over all the earth, seeking a location for your oracle for the human race, O far-shooting Apollo?[27] First you came down from Olympus to Pieria and went past sandy Lectus and Enienae and through the territory of the Perrhaebi. Soon you came to Iolcus and entered Cenaeum in Euboea, famous for its ships, and you stood on the Lelantine plain; but it did not please your heart to build a temple amidst forest groves. From there you crossed the Euripus, far-shooting

Apollo, and made your way along the holy green mountains, and quickly you went on from here to Mycalessus and grassy Teumessus and reached the forest-covered home of Thebe; for no one of mortals as yet lived in holy Thebes, nor were there yet at that time paths or roads running through the wheat-bearing plain of Thebes; but it was overgrown with trees.

From there you went further, O far-shooting Apollo, and came to Onchestus, with its spendid grove of Poseidon. Here, while the newly broken colt, worn out with drawing the beautiful chariot, slows down to get its wind, the noble driver springs out of his seat to the ground and makes his own way. Without guidance, the horses for a time knock about the empty chariot; and, if they smash it in the forest grove, the horses are taken care of but the chariot is put at a tilt and left there. For in this way from the very first the holy rite was enacted. They pray to the god, lord of the shrine, who then keeps the chariot as his allotted portion.[28] From there you went further, far-shooting Apollo, and then you came upon the beautifully flowing river, Cephisus, which pours its sweet-running water from Lilaea; you crossed it, and from many-towered Ocalea you arrived at grassy Haliartus. Then you went to Telphusa; here was a propitous place that you found pleasing for making a forest grove and a temple. You stood very near her and spoke these words: "Telphusa, here I intend to build a very beautiful temple, an oracle for mortals. Here all those who live in the rich Peloponnesus, in Europe, and on the sea-girt islands will bring perfect hecatombs and consult the oracle. To them I shall deliver my answers and ordain infallible counsel in my wealthy temple."

Thus Phoebus Apollo spoke and laid out the foundations, wide and very long overall. But Telphusa, upon seeing his actions, became deeply incensed and spoke: "Phoebus, lord and far-worker, I shall give you this warning to think about. Since you intend to build a very beautiful temple here, to be an oracle for mortals, who will always bring perfect hecatombs, I will speak out and you take my words to heart. The clatter of swift horses and the sounds of mules being watered at my holy spring will always annoy you; here any person will prefer to look at the well-made chariots and the noisy swift-footed horses rather than at your great temple and the many treasures inside. But if you were to listen to me (you are better and stronger than I am and your might is the greatest), build in Crisa, beneath the slopes of Mt. Parnassus, where beautiful chariots will not clatter and no noise will be made by swift-footed horses around your well-built altar. So there hordes of renowned mortals will bring gifts to you as IePaeon,[29] and you will rejoice greatly in your heart to receive the beautiful sacrifices of the people living roundabout." Thus Telphusa spoke and convinced the far-shooter, so that renown in her land should go to Telphusa herself and not to Apollo.

From there you went further, far-shooting Apollo, and you reached the town of the hubristic people, the Phlegyae, who have no concern for Zeus and live on earth in a beautiful glen near the Cephisean lake. You darted away from here quickly and came to mountain ridges and arrived at Crisa beneath snowy Mt. Parnassus. Its foothills turn towards the west, and its rocky cliffs hang from above over the hollow glade that stretches below. Here the lord Phoebus Apollo decreed that he would make his lovely temple and he said: "Here I intend to build a very beautiful temple, an oracle for mortals. Here all those who live in the rich Peloponnesus, in Europe, and on the sea-girt islands will bring perfect hecatombs and consult the oracle. To them I shall deliver my answers and ordain infallible counsel in my wealthy temple."

Thus Phoebus Apollo spoke and laid out the foundations, wide and very long overall. On these foundations Trophonius and Agamedes, the sons of Erginus, both dear to the immortal gods placed a threshold of stone; and countless numbers of men built up with finished blocks of stone the temple, to sing about forever. There was a beautifully flowing spring nearby, where the lord, son of Zeus, killed with his mighty bow a she-dragon, a huge, bloated, and fierce monster who had done many evils to mortals on earth, to mortals themselves and to their thin-shanked flocks; for she was a bloodthirsty scourge.

Once she received, from golden-throned Hera to bring up, Typhaon, another terrible and cruel scourge for mortals;[30] this was when Hera became angry with father Zeus and gave birth to the monster because the son of Cronus bore renowned Athena from his head. Lady Hera was quickly enraged and she spoke among the immortals: "Hear from me, all you gods and all you goddesses, how Zeus, the cloud-gatherer, first begins to dishonor me, when he has made me his dear and trusting wife. Apart from me, just now, he has given birth to keen-eyed Athena, who is outstanding among all the blessed immortals. But my son, Hephaestus, whom I myself bore, with his withered feet, was a weakling among the immortals—a shame to me and a disgrace on Olympus. I grabbed him myself with my own hands and threw him out and he fell into the wide sea. But silver-footed Thetis, daughter of Nereus, accepted him and with her sisters took care of him. (How I wish that she had done some other favor for the blessed gods!) Villain, crafty deceiver, what other scheme will you devise now? How do you dare, all alone, to give birth to keen-eyed Athena? Would I not have borne a child by you? To be sure I was the one called your very own among the immortals who hold the wide heaven. Watch out now that I don't devise some evil for you in the future. Indeed I will contrive how a son of mine will be born, who will be outstanding among the immortals, without any shame to our sacred marriage vow, either yours or mine. I shall not go near your bed, but separated from you I shall associate with the immortal gods."

Thus she spoke and went apart from the gods, angered in her heart. Then straightway ox-eyed lady Hera prayed and struck the ground with the flat of her hand and uttered this invocation: "Earth and wide Heaven, hear me now, and you, Titan gods dwelling beneath the earth in vast Tartarus, from whom both mortals and gods are descended—all of you listen to me and give me, without Zeus as father, a child in no way inferior to him in might. But let him be as much stronger than Zeus as all-seeing Zeus is stronger than Cronus." Thus she called out and lashed the ground with her mighty hand. The life-giving Earth was moved; and, when Hera saw this, she rejoiced in her heart. For she believed that her prayer would be answered.

From this time then, for a whole year, she never approached the bed of wise Zeus, nor did she ever, as before, sit on her intricate throne and by his side devise shrewd plans. But ox-eyed lady Hera remained in her temples, filled with her worshipers, and took delight in their offerings. Yet when the months and days were completed and the seasons had passed as the full year came round, she gave birth to a terrible scourge for mortals, cruel Typhaon, like neither a god nor a human being. Ox-eyed lady Hera at once took and gave him, an evil, to the evil she-dragon, who accepted him, Typhaon, who used to inflict many sufferings on the renowned tribes of human beings. As for the she-dragoness, whoever opposed her met the fatal day of death, until lord Apollo, the far-shooter, struck her with a mighty arrow. Racked by bitter pain, she lay gasping frantically for breath and writhing on the ground. An unspeakable and terrifying sound arose as she twisted and rolled in the forest; breathing out blood, she gave up her life, and Phoebus Apollo vaunted over her:

"Now rot here on the ground that nourishes mortals. You shall not live any longer to be the evil ruin of human beings who eat the fruit of the all-fostering earth and who will bring perfect hecatombs to his place." Thus he spoke, boasting; and darkness covered her eyes and the holy might of Helius caused her to rot there. Because of this, now the place is named Pytho, and they call its lord by the title, Pythian, since the mighty glare of the burning sun made the monster rot on the very spot.

Then Phoebus Apollo knew in his heart why the beautifully flowing spring, Telphusa, had tricked him. In anger he went to her and quickly he was there; standing very near her, he said: "Telphusa, you were not about to deceive my intelligence and keep this desirable place for you to put forth your beautifully flowing water. Here, to be sure, will be my glory, and not only yours." He spoke and lord Apollo, the far-worker, pushed on top of her a massive shower of rocks and hid her flowing stream; and he built an altar in the forest grove very near her beautifully flowing fountain. There all pray to Apollo under the name Telphusian because he shamed the stream of holy Telphusa.

Then Phoebus Apollo thought deeply about what people he would bring in as his priests who would serve him in rocky Pytho. While he was thinking this over, he noticed a swift ship on the wine-dark sea. On it were many fine men, Cretans from Minoan Cnossus, who perform sacrifices to their lord and make known the pronouncements of Phoebus Apollo of the golden sword, whatever oracle he gives from his laurel beneath the slopes of Parnassus. These men were sailing in their black ship to sandy Pylos and the people in Pylos for trade and profit. But Phoebus Apollo intercepted them on the sea and leaped onto their swift ship in the shape of a dolphin and lay there, a huge and dread monster. None of the men understood, nor did they recognize the dolphin as the god, and they wanted to throw it overboard. But he kept making the entire ship quake and its timbers quiver. They were afraid and sat in silence on the hollow black ship; and they did not slacken the ropes or the sail of their dark-prowed ship. But as they had fixed their course by the oxhide ropes, so they sailed on, and a fierce south wind drove the swift ship from behind.

First they sailed by Malia and the coast of Laconia and came to Taenarum, a sea-crowned town, and the land of Helius, who makes mortals glad, where the thick-fleeced sheep of lord Helius pasture always and inhabit a pleasurable country.[31] They wanted to bring the ship ashore, disembark, and study the great marvel and watch with their own eyes whether the monster would remain on the deck of the hollow ship or leap back into the swell of the sea, full of fish. But the well-built ship did not obey their directions but made its way along the fertile Peloponnesus; lord Apollo, the far-worker, easily directed it with a breeze. The ship, continuing its course, came to Arena, lovely Argyphea, and Thryon, the ford of the river Alpheus, and well-built Aepy and Pylos and the inhabitants of Pylos; and it went past Cruini and Chalcis and past Dyme and splendid Elis, where the Epei hold power. When it was sailing towards Pherae, jaunty in a wind from Zeus, beneath the clouds appeared the steep mountain of Ithaca and Dulichium and Same and wooded Zacynthus. But when it had passed the whole coast of the Peloponnesus, then to be sure, as they turned toward Crisa, there loomed before them the vast gulf whose length cuts off the rich Peloponnesus. A west wind, strong, clear, and vehement, came out of the sky by Zeus' decree and speeded the ship along so that it might complete its fast course over the briny water of the sea as quickly as possible. Then indeed they were sailing back towards the dawn and the sun. Lord Apollo, son of Zeus, was their guide, and they came to the conspicuous harbor of vine-clad Crisa, where the seafaring ship was grounded on the sands.

There lord Apollo, the far-worker, leaped out of the ship like a star at midday. His person was engulfed by a shooting fiery shower and his splendor reached to the heavens. He made his way, amidst precious tripods, to his innermost sanctuary. Then he caused a blaze to flare up and his arrows were bathed in a brilliance that encompassed the whole of Crisa. The wives and the lovely-dressed daughters of the Crisaeans cried out in amazement at the spectacular sight of Apollo; for the god instilled an awesome fear in each of them. Thereupon, swift as thought, he made a flying leap back onto the ship, in the form of a man in his prime, strong and vigorous, with his hair flowing about his broad shoulders. Uttering winged words, he spoke to them.

"Strangers, who are you? From where do you sail the watery paths? Is barter your goal, or do you roam recklessly, like pirates over the deep, who hazard their lives as they wander bringing evil to strangers. Why do you sit this way, despondent? Why don't you disembark and take your gear from your black ship to land? This is the right thing for enterprising men to do whenever they come from the sea to shore in their black ship; they are worn out and weary and straightway overcome by the desire for luscious food."

Thus he spoke and put spirit in their breasts and the leader of the Cretans said in answer: "Stranger, indeed you do not look at all like mortals in your appearance and stature, but like the immortal gods. Good health and all hail, may the gods give you prosperity! Tell me this truly so that I may understand fully: What territory, what land is this? What people live here? For we were sailing the great seas, with other intentions, bound for Pylos from Crete, where we are proud to have been born; yet now we have arrived here with our ship, in a different way and by another course, not at all willingly, and anxious to return; but someone of the immortals has taken us here, against our wishes."

Then Apollo, the far-worker, spoke in answer: "Strangers, who used to live in wooded Cnossus before, now no longer will you return again to your lovely city, beautiful homes, and dear wives;

but each of you here will keep my rich temple, honored by many mortals. I say proudly that I am Apollo, son of Zeus, and I took you to this place over the wide expanse of the sea. I intend you no harm, but you will keep my rich temple here, greatly esteemed and honored by all human beings; and you will know the counsels of the immortals, by whose will you always will be honored continually all your days. But come, as quickly as possible obey me in what I say. First let down the sails and loosen the ropes of ox-hide; then draw the swift ship up from the water onto dry land and remove your possessions and gear from the well-balanced ship; and build an altar on the shore of the sea; and, kindling a fire, make an offering of white barley. Then pray, standing around the altar. As I first leaped aboard your swift ship on the hazy sea in the form of a dolphin, so pray to me as Delphinius; furthermore, the altar itself will be Delphinius and overlooking[32] forever. Next, take your meal by the swift black ship and make a libation to the blessed gods who hold Olympus. But when you have satisfied your desire for luscious food, come with me and sing the IePaean until the time when you arrive at the place where you will keep my rich temple."

So Apollo spoke, and they readily listened to him and obeyed. First they let down the sails and loosened the ropes of ox-hide; and, lowering the mast by the forestays, they brought it to rest on the mast-holder. They themselves disembarked on the seashore and drew the swift ship up from the water onto dry land. They built an altar on the shore of the sea; and, kindling a fire, they made an offering of white barley; and they prayed, as he ordered, standing around the altar. Then they took their meal by the swift black ship and made a libation to the blessed gods who hold Olympus. But when they had satisfied their desire for food and drink, they got up and went with their leader, lord Apollo the son of Zeus, who held his lyre in his hands and played a lovely tune, as he stepped high and stately. The Cretans followed, marching to his rhythm, and they sang the IePaean, like the Cretan paean singers and those in whose breasts the divine Muse has placed sweet song.

With weariless feet they reached the mountain-ridge and quickly arrived at Parnassus itself and the desirable place where they were going to live, honored by human beings. Apollo who had led them there pointed out his sacred sanctuary and rich temple. And the spirit was aroused in their dear breasts; and the leader of the Cretans questioned him with these words: "O lord, since you have brought us far from our loved ones and our fatherland—so was it somehow your wish—how then shall we live now? This we ask you to explain. This place is desirable neither as a vineyard nor as a pasture."

And Apollo, the son of Zeus, smiling upon them, said: "Foolish, wretched mortals, who prefer heartfelt care, hard work, and trouble; I shall give you a message of comfort, and take it in earnest. Even if each of you, holding a knife in his right hand, were to slaughter sheep continuously, still the supply would not be exhausted with all that the renowned tribes of human beings bring to me here. Guard my temple and receive the human hordes who gather here, and above all point out to them my directions and keep my ordinances in your hearts. But if anyone is foolish enough to pay no heed and disobey, if there will be any idle word or deed or hubris, which is usually the case among mortal humans, then other men will be masters over you and you will be forced to submit to their might all your days. Everything has been told to you; store it in your hearts."

So farewell, son of Zeus and Leto. Yet I shall remember you and another song too.

HERMES

10

The Birth and Childhood of Hermes

The *Homeric Hymn to Hermes* (18) concentrates upon the story (repeated at the beginning of the much more lengthy and important hymn that follows) of how Zeus became the father of Hermes as the result of his union with Maia, one of the Pleiades, the daughters of Atlas and Pleione.

> I sing about Hermes, the Cyllenian slayer of Argus, lord of Mt. Cyllene and Arcadia rich in flocks, the messenger of the gods and bringer of luck, whom Maia, the daughter of Atlas, bore, after uniting in love with Zeus. She in her modesty shunned the company of the blessed gods and lived in a shadowy cave; here the son of Cronus used to make love to this nymph of the beautiful hair in the dark of night, without the knowledge of immortal gods and mortal humans, when sweet sleep held white-armed Hera fast.
>
> So hail to you, son of Zeus and Maia. After beginning with you, I shall turn to another hymn. Hail, Hermes, guide and giver of grace and other good things.

The more famous *Homeric Hymn to Hermes* (4) tells the story of the god's birth and childhood with delightful charm and disarming candor; here is a most artful depiction of this mischievous divine child, who invents the lyre and steals Apollo's cattle:

> Sing, O Muse, of the son of Zeus and Maia, lord of Mt. Cyllene and Arcadia rich in flocks, the messenger of the gods and bringer of luck, whom Maia of the beautiful hair bore after uniting in love with Zeus. She in her modesty shunned the company of the

blessed gods and lived within a shadowy cave; here the son of Cronus joined in love with this nymph of the beautiful hair in the dark of night, without the knowledge of immortal gods and mortal humans, while sweet sleep held white-armed Hera fast. But when the will of Zeus had been accomplished and her tenth month was fixed in the heavens, she brought forth to the light a child, and a remarkable thing was accomplished; for the child whom she bore was devious, winning in his cleverness, a robber, a driver of cattle, a guide of dreams, a spy in the night, a watcher at the door, who soon was about to manifest renowned deeds among the immortal gods.

Maia bore him on the fourth day of the month. He was born at dawn, by midday he was playing the lyre, and in the evening he stole the cattle of far-shooting Apollo. After he leaped forth from the immortal limbs of his mother, he did not remain lying in his sacred cradle; but he sprang up and looked for the cattle of Apollo. When he crossed the threshold of the high-roofed cave, he found a tortoise and obtained boundless pleasure from it.

Hermes Invents the Lyre

Indeed Hermes was the very first to make the tortoise a minstrel. He happened to meet it in the very entranceway, waddling along as it ate the luxurious grass in front of the dwelling. When Zeus' son, the bringer of luck, saw it, he laughed and said at once: "Already a very good omen for me; I shall not be scornful. Greetings; what a delight you appear to me, lovely in shape, graceful in movement and a good dinner companion. Where did you, a tortoise living in the mountains, get this speckled shell that you have on, a beautiful plaything? Come, I shall take you and bring you inside. You will be of some use to me and I shall do you no dishonor. You will be the very first to be an advantage to me, but a better one inside, since the out-of-doors is dangerous for you. To be sure, while you are alive you will continue to be a charm against evil witchcraft, but if you were dead, then you would make very beautiful music."[1]

Thus he spoke and lifted the tortoise in both hands and went back into his dwelling carrying the lovely plaything. Then he cut up the mountain-dwelling tortoise and scooped out its life-marrow with a knife of gray iron. As swiftly as a thought darts through the mind of a man whose cares come thick and fast or as a twinkle flashes from the eye, thus glorious Hermes devised his plan and carried it out simultaneously. He cut to size stocks of reeds, extended them across the back and through the tortoise shell and fastened them securely. In his ingenuity he stretched the hide of an ox all around and affixed two arms to which he attached a bridge and then he extended seven tuneful strings of sheep gut.

When he had finished, he took up the lovely plaything and tried it by striking successive notes. It resounded in startling fashion under his hand, and the god accompanied his playing with a beautiful song, improvising at random just as young men exchange banter on a festive occasion. He sang about Zeus, the son of Cronus, Maia with the beautiful sandals, and their talk in the intimacy of their love, and proclaimed aloud the renown of his birth. He honored too the handmaids of the nymph, her splendid home, and the tripods and the ample cauldrons it contained. He sang of these things, but his heart was set on other pursuits. He took the hollow lyre and set it down in his sacred cradle; for he craved for meat and leaped out of the fragrant hall to a place where he could watch, since he was devising in his heart sheer trickery such as men who are thieves plan in the dead of black night.

Hermes Steals Apollo's Cattle

Helius, the Sun, with his horses and chariot was descending to earth and the stream of Ocean, when Hermes came hurrying to the shady mountains of Pieria[2] where the immortal cattle of the blessed gods have their home, grazing on the lovely untouched meadows. The sharp-sighted son of Maia, the slayer of Argus, cut off from the herd fifty loud-bellowing cattle and drove them over sandy ground reversing their tracks as they wandered. For he did not forget his skill at trickery, and he made their hoofs go backward, the front ones last and the back ones first; he himself walked straight ahead. For quickly, by the sandy seashore, he wove sandals of wicker, a wonderful achievement, beyond description and belief; he combined twigs of myrtle and tamarisk and fastened together bundles of the freshly sprouting wood which he bound, leaves and all, under his feet as light sandals. The glorious slayer of Argus made them so, as he left Pieria, improvising since he was hastening over a long journey.[3]

But an old man, who was working in a luxuriant vineyard, noticed him coming to the plain through Onchestus with its beds of grass. The renowned son of Maia spoke to him first: "Old man, digging about with stooped shoulders, you will indeed have much wine when all these vines bear fruit, if you listen to me and earnestly remember in your heart to be blind to what you have seen and deaf to what you have heard and to keep silent, since nothing of your own has been harmed in any way." He said only this much and pushed the sturdy head of cattle on together. Glorious Hermes drove them over many shady mountains, echoing hollows, and flowery plains.

The greater part of divine night, his dark helper, was over; and the break of day that calls men to work was soon coming on, and bright Selene, daughter of lord Pallas, the son of Megamedes,[4] had climbed to a new watchpost, when the strong son of Zeus drove the broad-browed cattle of Phoebus Apollo to the river Alpheus. They were unwearied when they came to the lofty shelter and the watering places that faced the splendid meadow. Then, when he had fed the loud-bellowing cattle well on fodder, he drove them all together into the shelter, as they ate lotus and marsh plants covered with dew. He gathered together a quantity of wood and pursued with diligent passion the skill of producing fire. He took a good branch of laurel and trimmed it with his knife, and in the palm of his hand he grasped a piece of wood; and the hot breath of fire rose up.[5] Indeed Hermes was the very first to invent fire sticks and fire. He took many dry sticks which he left as they were and heaped them up together in a pit in the ground. The flame shone forth, sending afar a great blaze of burning fire.

While the power of renowned Hephaestus was kindling the fire, Hermes dragged outside near the blaze two horned cattle, bellowing, for much strength went with him. He threw them both panting upon their backs onto the ground and bore down upon them. Rolling them over, he pierced through their life's marrow; he followed up this work with more, cutting the meat rich in fat and spearing the pieces with wooden spits, and roasted all together the flesh, choice parts from the back, and the bowels that enclosed the black blood. He laid these pieces on the ground and stretched the hides on a rugged rock, and thus still even now they are there continually long afterward, despite the interval of time. Next Hermes in the joy of his heart whisked the rich bundles away to a smooth flat rock and divided them into twelve portions that he allotted, adding a choice piece to each, making it wholly an honorable offering.

Then glorious Hermes longed for the sacred meat of the sacrifice, for the sweet aroma made him weak, even though he was an immortal. But his noble heart did not yield, although his desire was overwhelming to gulp the offering down his holy throat.[6] But he quickly put the fat and all the meat away in the cave with its lofty roof, setting them up high as a testimony of his recent childhood theft, and he gathered up wood for the fire and destroyed all the hoofs and the heads in the blaze. When the god had accomplished all that he had to do, he threw his sandals into the deep-eddying stream of the Alpheus; he put out the embers and hid the black ashes in the sand. Thus he spent the whole night as the beautiful light of Selene shone down on him. Swiftly then he went back to the divine peaks of Cyllene and encountered no one at all (neither blessed gods nor mortal humans) on his long journey, and dogs did not bark.

Hermes, the luck-bringer, son of Zeus, slipped sideways past the lock into his house, like the gust of a breeze in autumn, and went directly through the cave to his luxurious inner chamber, stepping gently on his feet, for he did not make a sound as one would walking upon the floor. Glorious Hermes quickly got into his cradle and wrapped the blankets about his shoulders like a helpless baby and lay toying with his fingers at the covers on his knees; at his left side he kept his beloved lyre close by his hand.

But the god did not escape the notice of his goddess mother, who spoke to him: "You devious rogue, in your cloak of shameless guile, where in the world have you come from in the nighttime? Now I am convinced that either Apollo, son of Leto, by his own hands will drag you with your sides bound fast right out the door or you will prowl about the valleys, a robber and a cheat. Be gone then! Your father begat you as a great trouble for mortals and immortal gods!"

Hermes answered her with clever words: "Mother, why do you throw this up at me, as to a helpless child who knows in his heart very little of evil, a fearful baby, frightened of his mother's chiding? But I shall set upon whatever work is best to provide for me and you together. We two shall not endure to stay here in this place alone, as you bid, apart from the immortals without gifts and prayers. Better all our days to live among the gods, rich and full in wealth and plenty, than to sit at home in the shadows of this cave! And I shall go after divine honor just as Apollo has. And if my father does not give it to me, to be sure I shall take my honor myself (and I can do it) which is to be the prince of thieves. And if the glorious son of Leto search me out, I think he will meet with another even greater loss. For I shall go to Pytho and break right into his great house and I shall seize from within plenty of very beautiful tripods and bowls and gold and gleaming iron and an abundance of clothing. You will be able to see it all, if you like." Thus they conversed with each other, the son of aegis-bearing Zeus and the lady Maia.

Apollo Confronts Hermes

As Eos, the early-born, sprang up from the deep-flowing waters of Ocean, bringing light to mortals, Apollo was on his way and came to Onchestus, a very lovely grove sacred to loud-roaring Poseidon, who surrounds the earth. There he found the old man, who on the path within was feeding the animal that guarded his vineyard. The glorious son of Leto spoke to him first: "Old man, who pull the weeds and briars of grassy Onchestus, I have come here from Pieria looking for some cattle from my herd—all cows, all with curved horns. The bull, which was black, fed alone away from the others; keen-eyed dogs followed behind, four of them, of one mind like humans. They were left behind, both the dogs and the bull—a truly amazing feat. But just as the sun had set, the cows went out of the soft meadow away from the sweet pasture. Tell me this, old fellow, have you seen a man passing along the road with these cows?"

The old man spoke to him in answer: "My friend, it is hard to tell everything that one sees with one's eyes. For many wayfarers pass along the road; some travel intent on much evil, others on much good. To know each of them is difficult. But, good sir, the whole day long until the sun set I was digging about in my fruitful vineyard and I thought that I noticed a child, I do not know for sure; whoever the child was, he, an infant, tended the fine-horned cattle and he had a stick. He walked from side to side as he drove them backward and kept their heads facing him."

Thus the old man spoke; after Apollo had heard his tale, he went more quickly on his way. He noticed a bird with its wings extended, and from this sign he knew at once that the thief was a child born of Zeus, the son of Cronus. So lord Apollo, the son of Zeus, eagerly hastened to holy Pylos in search of his shambling cows, his broad shoulders enshrouded in a dark cloud. When the archer-god spied the tracks he cried out: "Why, indeed, here is a great marvel that 1 see with my eyes. These are definitely the tracks of straight-horned cows, but they are turned backward toward the asphodel meadow. And these here are not the prints of a man or a woman or gray wolves or bears or lions; nor are they, I expect, those of a shaggy-maned centaur or whoever makes such monstrous strides with its swift feet. On this side of the road the tracks are strange but on the other side they are even stranger."

With these words lord Apollo, the son of Zeus, hurried on and came to the forest-clad mountain of Cyllene and the deeply shaded cave in the rock where the immortal nymph bore the child of Zeus, the son of Cronus. A lovely odor pervaded the sacred mountain, and many sheep ranged about grazing on the grass. Then the archer-god, Apollo himself, hurried over the stone threshold down into the shadowy cave.

When the son of Zeus and Maia perceived that far-shooting Apollo was in a rage about his cattle, he sank down into his fragrant blankets. As ashes hide a bed of embers on logs of wood, so Hermes buried himself in his covers when he saw the archer-god. He huddled head and hands and feet tightly together as though just bathed and ready for sweet sleep, but he was really wide awake, and under his arm he held his lyre. The son of Zeus and Leto knew both the beautiful mountain nymph and her dear son, the little boy enveloped in craft and deceit, and he was not fooled. He looked in every corner of the great house. He took a shining key and opened three chambers full of nectar and lovely ambrosia, and in them too lay stored much silver and gold and many of the nymph's garments, rich in their hues of purple and silver, such as are found in the sacred dwellings of the blessed gods.

Then, when the son of Leto had searched every nook in the great house, he addressed glorious Hermes with these words: "You, O child, lying in the cradle, inform me about my cattle and be quick or soon the two of us will be at variance and it will not be nice. For I shall take hold of you and hurl you down into the terrible and irrevocable darkness of murky Tartarus; neither your mother nor your father will release you to the light above, but you will wander under the earth, a leader among little people."

Hermes answered him craftily: "Son of Leto, what are these harsh words you have spoken? Have you come here looking for cattle of the field? I have not seen a thing, I do not know a thing, I have not heard a word from anyone. I cannot give information nor can I win the reward. Do I look like a man of brawn, a cattle rustler? That is not my line; I am interested rather in other things: sleep, milk from my mother's breast, baby blankets about my shoulders and warm baths. Do not let anyone find out how this dispute came about. It would indeed be a source of great amazement among the immortals that a newborn child should bring cattle of the field right through the front door of his house. What you say is pretty unlikely. I was born yesterday, my feet are tender and the ground is rough beneath them. If you wish, I shall swear a great oath by the head of my father; I pledge a vow that I am not guilty myself and that I have not seen anyone else who might be the one who stole your cows—whatever cows are, for I have only heard about them now for the first time."

Thus Hermes spoke, his eyes twinkling and his brows raised as he looked all about, and gave a long whistle to show how fruitless he considered Apollo's quest. But far-shooting Apollo laughed softly and spoke to him: "Oh splendid, you sly-hearted cheat; from the way that you talk I am sure that many a time you have broken into the better homes during the night and reduced more than one poor fellow to extremities by grabbing everything in the house without a sound. And you will distress many a shepherd in the mountain glens, when greedy after meat you come upon their herds of cattle and their woolly sheep. But come on now, if you do not want to sleep your last and longest sleep, get down out of your cradle, you comrade of black night. For this then you will have as your prerogative hereafter among the gods: you will be called forevermore the prince of thieves.''

Thus Phoebus Apollo spoke and took hold of the child to carry him away. At that very moment the mighty slayer of Argus had an idea; as he was being lifted in Apollo's hands he let go an omen, a bold and servile messenger from his belly, a hearty blast, and right after it he gave a violent sneeze. And when Apollo heard, he dropped glorious Hermes out of his hands to the ground and sat in front of him; even though he was eager to be on his way he spoke with taunting words: "Rest assured, son of Zeus and Maia, in your swaddling clothes, with these omens I shall find my sturdy head of cattle by and by, and furthermore you will lead the way." Thus he spoke.

Hermes and Apollo Bring Their Case before Zeus

And Cyllenian Hermes gave a start and jumped up pushing the blanket away from both his ears with his hands, and clutching it around his shoulders he cried out: "Where are you taking me, O far-shooter, most vehement of all the gods? Is it because of the cows that you are so angry and assault me? Oh, oh, how I wish the whole breed of cattle might perish! For I did not steal your cows and I have not seen anyone else who has—whatever cows are, for I have only heard about them now for the first time. Let us have the case decided before Zeus, the son of Cronus.''

Thus as they quarreled over each and every point, Hermes, the shepherd, and the splendid son of Leto remained divided. The latter spoke the truth and not without justice seized upon glorious Hermes because of the cattle; on the other hand the Cyllenian wished to deceive the god of the silver bow by tricks and by arguments. But when he in his ingenuity found his opponent equally resourceful, he hastened to walk over the sandy plain in front with the son of Zeus and Leto behind. Quickly these two very beautiful children of Zeus came to their father, the son of Cronus, on the top of fragrant Olympus. For there the scales of justice lay ready for them both.

A happy throng occupied snow-capped Olympus, for the deathless gods had assembled with the coming of golden-throned Dawn. Hermes and Apollo of the silver bow stood before the knees of Zeus, and he who thunders from on high spoke to his glorious son with the question: "Phoebus, where did you capture this delightful booty, a child newly born who has the appearance of a herald? This is a serious business that has come before the assembly of the gods.''

Then lord Apollo, the archer, replied: "O father, you, who scoff at me for being the only one who is fond of booty, are now going to hear a tale that is irrefutable. After journeying for a long time in the mountains of Cyllene I found a child, this out-and-out robber here; as sharp a rogue I have not seen either among gods or mortals who cheat their fellows on earth. He stole my cows from the meadow in the evening and proceeded to drive them along the shore of the loud-sounding sea making directly for Pylos. The tracks were of two kinds, strange and marvelous, the work of a clever spirit. The black dust retained the prints of the cattle and showed them leading into the asphodel meadow. But this rogue I have here, an inexplicable wonder, did not cross the sandy ground on his feet or on his hands; but by some other means he smeared the marks of his amazing course as though someone had walked on oak saplings. As long as he followed the cattle across the sandy ground, the tracks stood out very clearly in the dust. But when he had covered the great stretch of sand, his own course and that of the cows quickly became imperceptible on the hard ground. But a mortal man noticed him driving the herd of cattle straight for Pylos. When he had quietly penned up the cows and slyly confused his homeward trail by zigzagging this way and that, he nestled down in his cradle, obscure as the black night, within the darkness of the gloomy cave, and not even the keen eye of an eagle would have spied him. He kept rubbing his eyes with his hands as he devised his subtle wiles, and he himself immediately maintained without a qualm: "I have not seen a thing, I do not know a thing and I have not heard a word from anyone. I cannot give information nor can I win the reward." Thus Phoebus Apollo spoke and then sat down.

And Hermes in answer told his side of the story, directing his words pointedly to Zeus, the ruler of all the gods. "Father Zeus, I shall indeed tell you the truth. For I am honest and I do not know how to lie. He came to our house today as the sun was just rising, in search of his shambling cattle. He brought none of the blessed gods as witnesses or observers and with great violence ordered me to confess; he made many threats of hurling me down into wide Tartarus, since he is in the full bloom of his glorious prime, while I was born only yesterday (as he too well knows himself) and do not look at all like a cattle rustler or a man of brawn. Believe me (for you claim to be my own dear father too) that I did not drive his cows home nor even cross the threshold—so may I prosper, what I tell you is the truth. I deeply revere Helius and the other gods; I love you and I am in dread of this fellow here. You know yourself that I am not guilty—I shall swear a great oath besides—no, by these beautifully ornate portals of the gods. Somehow, someday, I will pay him back, even though he is mighty, for his ruthless behavior. Be on the side of a defenseless baby." Thus the Cyllenian slayer of Argus spoke, blinking in innocence, and he held his baby blanket on his shoulder and would not let it go.

Zeus gave a great laugh as he saw the devious child knowingly and cleverly make his denials about the cattle. He ordered the two of them to act in accord and make a search; Hermes, in his role of guide, was to lead without any malicious intent and point out the spot where he had hidden away the mighty herd of cattle. The son of Cronus nodded his head and splendid Hermes obeyed, for the will of aegis-bearing Zeus easily persuaded him.

The Reconciliation between Hermes and Apollo

The two very beautiful sons of Zeus hastened together to sandy Pylos, crossed the river Alpheus, and came to the lofty cave where the animals were sheltered in the nighttime. Then, while Hermes went into the rocky cavern and drove the mighty head of cattle out into the light, the son of Leto looked away and noticed the cowhides on the steep rock and immediately asked glorious Hermes: "O sly rogue, how were you, a newborn infant, able to skin two cows? I do indeed wonder at the strength that will be yours in the future; there is no need to wait for you to grow up, O Cyllenian, son of Maia."

Thus he spoke and fashioned with his hands strong bonds out of willow.[7] But they grew up in that very spot on the ground under their feet; and twisting and twining together, they readily covered over all the cattle of the field at the will of the trickster Hermes, while Apollo watched in wonder. Then the mighty slayer of Argus looked away to the ground, fire flashing from his eyes, in his desire to get out of his predicament. But it was very easy for him, just as he wished, to soften the far-shooting son of Leto, even though he was strong; he took up the lyre in his left hand and tried it by striking successive notes. The instrument resounded in startling fashion and Phoebus Apollo laughed with delight as the lovely strains of the heavenly music pierced his being, and sweet yearning took hold of his heart while he listened.

The son of Maia, growing bold as he played so beautifully, took his stand on the left side of Phoebus Apollo and began to sing a song—and lovely was the ensuing sound of his voice—fashioned on the theme of the immortal gods and the dark earth and how in the beginning they came into being and how each was allotted his due. Of the gods he honored first of all Mnemosyne, mother of the Muses, for she honored him, the son of Maia, as one of her own. The splendid son of Zeus paid tribute to each of the other immortal gods according to age and birth, mentioning all in the proper order, as he played the lyre on his arm.

But an irresistible desire took hold of Apollo, heart and soul, and he spoke up, interrupting with winged words: "Cattle slayer, contriver, busy worker, good companion at a feast, this skill of yours is worth fifty cows—I think that we soon will be peacefully reconciled. Come now, tell me, ingenious son of Maia, was this wonderful achievement yours from birth or did one of the gods or mortal humans give you this noble gift and teach you inspired song? For this newly uttered sound I hear is wonderful, and I tell you that no one, either mortal or god who dwells on Olympus, has ever before known it, except you, you trickster, son of Zeus and Maia. What skill! What Muse's art! What salve for sorrow and despair! It gives the choice of three blessings together all at once: joy and love and sweet sleep. I follow the Olympian Muses who delight in dancing, the swelling beat of music, and the lovely tune of flutes, yet never have I been as thrilled by such clever delights as these at young men's feasts. I marvel, O son of Zeus, at your charming playing. Since you know such a glorious skill, even though you are little, sit down, my boy, and listen to what I intend. For you yourself and your mother will have renown among the immortal gods. And I shall vow this to you truly: By this spear of cornel wood, I shall make you a renowned and prosperous guide among the immortal gods, and I shall give you splendid gifts and to the end I shall not deceive you."

Hermes answered him with clever words: "Archer-god, your questions are well considered; I do not begrudge your taking up my art. You will know it this very day. I want us to be friends, alike in what we think and what we say. You know all things in your heart, for you, son of Zeus, sit in the first place among the immortals, brave and strong. Zeus in his wisdom loves you as he rightly should and has granted you splendid gifts. And they say that you have acquired from the mouth of Zeus honors and, O archer-god, from him too every kind of divine oracular power. I know then that you are very rich in these gifts and you have only to make the choice of whatever you desire to learn. So, since your heart is set on playing the lyre, sing and play and be merry; accept this gift from me; and you, my dear friend, bestow glory upon me. With this clear-voiced companion in your hands,[8] sing beautifully and well, knowing the art of proper presentation. Then with confidence take it to a luxurious feast and lovely dance and splendid revel, a thing of joy both night and day. Whoever makes demands of it after acquiring skill and knowledge is informed with sounds of every sort to delight the mind, for it is played by gentle familiarity and refuses to respond to toilsome drudgery. And whoever through lack of skill is from the first vehement in his demands is answered in return with wild and empty notes that clang upon the air. But you have only to make the choice of learning whatever you desire. To you I give this gift, splendid son of Zeus, and we both shall feed the cattle of the field on the pastures in the mountain and the plain where horses also graze. Even you, shrewd bargainer that you are, ought not to be violently angry.''

With these words he held out the lyre, and Phoebus Apollo accepted it. And he entrusted to Hermes the shining whip that he had and put him in charge of cattle herds. The son of Maia accepted this with joy. The far-shooting lord Apollo, the glorious son of Leto, took the lyre in his left hand and tried it by striking successive notes. It sounded in startling fashion at his touch and the god sang a beautiful song in accompaniment.

Afterward the two of them turned the cows out into the sacred meadow and they, the very beautiful sons of Zeus, hastened back to snow-capped Olympus, all the while taking delight in the lyre. Zeus in his wisdom was pleased and united them both in friendship; Hermes has loved the son of Leto steadfastly, and he still does even now, as is evident from the pledges made when Hermes entrusted his lovely lyre to the archer-god and Apollo took it on his arm and learned how to play. But Hermes himself fashioned another instrument and learned another art, producing the sound of pipes that are heard from afar.[9]

Then the son of Leto said to Hermes, "I fear, cunning guide, that you may steal my lyre and my curved bow; for you have from Zeus the prerogative of establishing the business of barter among people on the nourishing earth. Yet if, for my sake, you would deign to swear the great oath of the gods, either by a nod of your head or by the mighty waters of the river Styx, you would do everything that would satisfy my heart's desire." Then the son of Maia nodded and promised that he would never steal a thing from all that the far-shooter possessed and that he would never come near his mighty house. In turn Apollo, the son of Leto, nodded in loving friendship that no one else among mortals would be more dear, neither god nor mortal sprung from Zeus, and said, "I shall pledge that this bond between us will be trusted and honored both in my heart and that of all the gods. Besides I will give you in addition a very beautiful golden staff of prosperity and wealth, three-branched and protective; it will keep you safe while, in the name of all the gods, you accomplish by word and by deed the good things which I declare that I learn from the divine voice of Zeus.

"As for this gift of prophecy which you mention, O best of Zeus' sons, it is not allowed by god that you or any other of the immortals learn what the mind of Zeus knows; but I have pledged, vowed, and sworn a mighty oath that no other one of the eternal gods (apart from me) should know the infinite wisdom of Zeus. You, my brother, with your rod of gold, do not bid me reveal any of the divine plans which far-seeing Zeus is devising. I shall hurt some and help others, as I cause great perplexity for the masses of unhappy human beings. The person will profit from my utterance who comes under the guidance of the flight and the cry of my birds of true omen. This is the one who will profit from my utterance and whom I will not deceive; but the one who trusts the birds of meaningless chatter will seek to find out my prophecies and to know more than the eternal gods, quite against my will. I declare that for this one the journey will be in vain but I would take his gifts anyway.

"I shall tell you another thing, son of illustrious Maia and aegis-bearing Zeus, O divine luck-bringer of the gods: indeed, certain holy sisters have been born, three virgins, glorying in their swift wings and having on their heads a sprinkling of white barley, and they live under a ridge of Mt. Parnassus;[10] set apart, they are masters of divination, an art I practiced while still a lad tending cattle and my father did not mind. Then from their home they fly from one place to another and feed from every honeycomb until it is empty. When they have eaten the yellow honey, they become inspired and willingly desire to speak the truth; but if they are deprived of the sweet food of the gods, they gather in a swarm and tell lies. These sisters I give to you; enquire of them carefully and take pleasure in your heart. If then you inform mortal persons, they will listen to what you say often, if they are fortunate. Have these things, son of Maia, and care for the horned oxen of the field, the toiling mules and the horses."

Thus he spoke, and from heaven father Zeus himself added a final pledge to his words: he ordered that glorious Hermes be the lord of all birds of good omen, fierce-eyed lions, boars with gleaming tusks, dogs, and every flock and herd that the wide earth nourishes; and that he alone would be the ordained messenger to Hades, who, although he accepts no gifts, will grant this, by no means the least of honors.

So lord Apollo loved the son of Maia in an all-encompassing friendship; and Zeus, the son of Cronus, bestowed on him a beguiling charm. He associates with mortals and immortals. On occasion he gives profit or help to a few, but for the most part he continually deceives human beings by the horde in the blackness of night.

So hail to you, son of Zeus and Maia; yet I shall remember both you and another song too.

This artful hymn to Hermes has been much admired; the English poet Shelley himself was one of its translators. The glib and playful treatment of both Hermes and Apollo is often labeled typically Greek.[11] It is typically Greek only if we mean by typical *one* of the many brilliant facets of Hellenic genius and a suggestion of the wide variety and scope in the conception of deity. Sincere profundity in religion and philosophy are as typically Greek as wit and facetious sophistication.

The Nature of Hermes and His Worship

Many of Hermes' characteristics and powers are evident from the poem. The Greek admiration for cleverness is readily apparent; it is this same admiration that condones the more dubious traits of the hero Odysseus. Anthropomorphism and liberalism are both pushed to their extreme in the depiction of the god Hermes as a thief and in the implication that thieves too must have their patron deity. Divine Hermes, like Prometheus, represents another (albeit extreme) example of the archetypal trickster.

The similarities between Hermes and Apollo are equally apparent. The origins of both were probably rooted in the same pastoral society of shepherds with their interest in flocks, music, and fertility. The two are alike in appearance, splendid examples of vigorous and handsome masculinity. But Hermes is the younger and more boyish, the idealization and patron of youths in their late teens; his statue belonged in every gymnasium.

Hermes is perhaps best known as the divine messenger, often delivering the dictates of Zeus himself; as such he wears a traveler's hat (*petasus*) and carries a herald's wand (*caduceus*), which sometimes bears two snakes entwined. Wings may be depicted on his hat, his sandals, and even his wand. Thus he is also the god of travelers and roads. As the guide of souls (*psychopompos*) to the realm of Hades under the earth, he provides another important function, which reminds us once again of his fertility connections.

Statues of Hermes, called *herms*, (singular, *herm*), were common in the ancient world; they also suggest fertility. They were square pillars equipped with male genitals; on top of each was the head of Hermes. These phallic statues probably marked areas regarded as sacred or designated, at least originally, the bounds of one's home or

Mercury, by Giovanni Bologna (known as Giambologna, 1529–1608). Bronze, 1576; height 25 in. Giambologna has taken the classical attributes of Hermes—the petasus, caduceus, and winged sandals—and combined them with the nude figure of a running man to create a masterpiece of Late Renaissance Mannerism. *(Museo Nazionale del Bargello, Florence. Courtesy of Alinari/Art Resource, New York.)*

property. They were intended to bring prosperity and luck. In the classical period, a herm might be found outside any house; and these herms could be taken very seriously.[12]

Hermaphroditus and Salmacis

Among the adventures and affairs of Hermes, his union with Aphrodite is important because of their offspring, Hermaphroditus, whose story is told by Ovid (*Metamorphoses* 4. 285–388):

Let me tell you how the fountain Salmacis got its bad reputation and why it weakens and softens limbs touched by its enervating waters.[13] This power of the fountain is very well known; the reason for it lies hidden. A son was born to Mercury and Venus, and Naiads brought him up in the cave of Mt. Ida. You could recognize his mother and father in his beauty and his name also came from them. As soon as he reached the age of fifteen, he left the hills of his homeland. When he had departed from Ida, the mountain that had nurtured him, he took delight in wandering over unknown lands and in seeing unknown rivers; his zeal made the hardships easy.

Then he came to the cities of the Lycians and their neighbors the Carians. There he saw a pool of water that was clear to the very bottom with no marsh reeds, barren sedge, or sharp-pointed rushes to be seen. The water was transparent in its clarity, and the edge of the pool was surrounded by fresh turf and grass that was always green.

A nymph lived here; but one who was not inclined to hunt and not in the habit of bending the bow or contending in the chase. She alone of the Naiads was unknown to swift Diana. It is told that her sisters often said to her: "Salmacis, take up a javelin or a lovely painted quiver; vary the routine of your idleness with the strenuous exercise of the hunt." She did not take up the javelin or the lovely painted quiver and did not vary the routine of her idleness with the strenuous exercise of the hunt. Instead she would only bathe her beautiful limbs in her fountain and often comb out her hair with a comb of boxwood and look into the water to see what suited her best; and then she would clothe her body in a transparent garment and recline on the soft leaves or the soft grass. Often she picked flowers.

Salamacis was picking flowers as it happened when she saw the boy Hermaphroditus. As soon as she saw him she desired to have him. Although she was anxious to hasten to him, she did not approach until she had composed herself, arranged her garment, and assumed a beautiful countenance. When she looked as attractive as she ought, she began to speak as follows: "Lovely boy, most worthy to be believed a god; if you are a god, you could be Cupid; if a mortal, blessed are your parents, and happy your brother and fortunate indeed your sister, if you have one, and the nurse who gave you her breast. But by far the most blessed of all is your betrothed, if she exists, whom you will consider worthy of marriage. If you have such a beloved, let my passion be satisfied in secret but if you do not, let me be the one and let us go together to our marriage bed." With this the nymph was silent.

A blush flared up in the boy's face, for he did not know what love was. But the flush of red was becoming; his was the color of apples hanging in a sunny orchard or of tinted marble or of the moon, a reddish glow suffusing its whiteness. . . . To the nymph, as she demanded without end at least the kisses of a sister and brought her hand to touch his ivory neck, he exclaimed: "Are you going to stop or am I to flee and leave you and your abode?" Salmacis was frightened and replied: "I give over to you free access to this place, my guest and friend." She turned her step away and pretended to depart, though still with a glance back. She concealed herself in a hidden grove of bushes, dropping on bended knees. But he moved on the deserted grass from one spot to another, confident that he was not being watched and gradually dipped his feet as far as the ankles in the playful waves.

Taken by the feel of the captivating waters, with no delay he threw off the soft clothes from his body. Then to be sure Salmacis was transfixed, enflamed with desire for his naked form. Her eyes too were ablaze just as if the radiant orb of the glowing sun were reflected in their mirror. With difficulty she endured the agony of waiting, with difficulty she held off the attainment of her joy. Now she longed to embrace him, now in her frenzy she could hardly contain herself. He swiftly struck his hollow palms against his sides and plunged into the pool and as he moved one arm and then the other he glistened in the limpid water like an ivory statue or a lily that one has encased within clear glass. The nymph cried out: "I have won, he is mine!" And she flung off all her clothes and threw herself into the middle of the waves. She held him as he fought and snatched kisses as he struggled; she grasped him with her hands and touched his chest and now from this side and now from that enveloped the youth.

Finally she encircled him as he strove against her in his desire to escape, like a serpent which the king of birds has seized and carried aloft, and which as it hangs binds the eagle's head and feet and with its tail enfolds the spreading wings, even as ivy is wont to weave around tall trunks of trees or as the octopus grabs and holds fast its enemy in the deep with tentacles let loose on every side. Hermaphroditus, the descendant of Atlas, endured and denied the nymph the joys that she had hoped for. She continued her efforts, and her whole body clung to him as though they were glued together. She cried: "You may fight, cruel villain, but you will not escape. May the gods so ordain and may we never be separated in future time, you from me or me from you." The gods accepted her prayer.

For their two bodies were joined together as they entwined, and in appearance they were made one, just as when one grafts branches on a tree and sees them unite in their growth and become mature together; thus, when their limbs united in their close embrace, they were no longer two but a single form that could not be called girl or boy and appeared at the same time neither one, but both. And so, when he saw that the limpid waters into which he had gone as a man had made him half a man and in them his limbs had become enfeebled, Hermaphroditus stretched out his hands and prayed in a voice that was no longer masculine: "Father and mother, grant this gift to your son who bears both your names. Let whatever man who enters this pool come out half a man and let him suddenly become soft when touched by its waves." Both parents were moved and granted the wish of their child, who was now of a double nature, and they tainted the waters with this foul power.

Statues of Hermaphroditus and hermaphrodites became common in the fourth century and in the following Hellenistic period, when Greek masters strove to vary their repertoires with fascinating and brilliantly executed studies in the realistic, erotic, and unusual.[14]

DIONYSUS, PAN, ECHO, AND NARCISSUS

The Birth, Childhood, and Origins of Dionysus

The traditional account of the birth of Dionysus (Bacchus)[1] runs as follows. Disguised as a mortal, Zeus was having an affair with Semele, a daughter of Cadmus. When Hera found out, her jealousy led her to get even. She appeared to Semele disguised as an old woman and convinced her rival that she should ask her lover to appear in the full magnificence of his divinity. Semele first persuaded Zeus to swear that he would grant whatever she might ask of him, and then revealed her demand. Zeus was unwilling but was obliged to comply, and Semele was burned to a cinder by the splendor of his person and the fire of his lightning flash. The unborn child, being divine was not destroyed in the conflagration; Zeus saved his son from the ashes of his mother and sewed him up in his own thigh, from which he was born again at the proper time.[2]

Various nurses are associated with the infant Dionysus, in particular certain nymphs of Nysa, a mountain of legendary fame located in

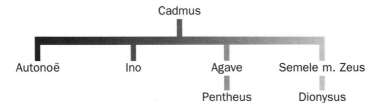

Figure 11.1. The Children of Cadmus. A fuller genealogy for the House of Cadmus is given in Figure 15.2, p. 322.

The Indian Triumph of Dionysus. Roman marble sarcophagus, mid-second century A.D.: width (without lid) 92 in., height 39 in.; lid, width 93 in., height 12½ in. Dionysus rides on a chariot drawn by panthers. He is preceded by by satyrs, maenads, sileni, and animals, among which elephants and lions are prominent. He has come from India, bringing happiness and fertility to the Greek world. On the lid are reliefs of the death of Semele, the birth of Dionysus from the thigh of Zeus, and his nurture by the nymphs of Nysa. The sarcophagus is one of seven found in the tomb of the family of the Calpurnii Pisones in Rome. *(Walters Art Gallery, Baltimore.)*

various parts of the ancient world. Ino, Semele's sister, is traditionally singled out as one who cared for the god when he was a baby.[3] When Dionysus reached manhood, he carried the message of his worship far and wide, bringing happiness and prosperity to those who would listen and madness and death to those who dared oppose. The tradition of his arrival in Greece makes clear that he is a latecomer to the Olympian pantheon. His origins lie in Thrace and ultimately Phrygia.[4]

The *Bacchae* of Euripides

Dionysus is basically a god of vegetation in general, and in particular of the vine, the grape, and the making and drinking of wine. But his person and his teaching eventually embrace very much more. The best source for the profound meaning of his worship and its most universal implications is found in Euripides' *Bacchae* (The Bacchic Women). Whatever one makes of the playwright's depiction of the rites in a literal sense, the sublimity and terror of the spiritual message are inescapable and timeless.

The play opens with Dionysus himself, who has come in anger to Thebes; his mother's integrity has been questioned by her own relatives, and the magnitude and power of his very godhead have been challenged and repudiated; the sisters of Semele claim (and Pentheus agrees) that she became pregnant because she slept with a mortal and that Cadmus was responsible for the story that Zeus was the father of her child; as a result Zeus killed her with a blast of lightning. (1–63):

DIONYSUS: I, Dionysus, the son of Zeus, have come to this land of the Thebans; my mother Semele, the daughter of Cadmus, gave birth to me, delivered by a fiery blast of lightning. I am here by the stream of Dirce and the waters of the Ismenus, not as a god but in disguise as a man. I see here near the palace the shrine that commemorates my mother, who was struck dead by the lightning blast, and the ruins of her home, smoldering yet from the flame of Zeus' fire that still lives—the everlasting evidence of Hera's outrage against my mother. I am pleased with Cadmus for setting this area off as a holy sanctuary dedicated to his daughter, and I have enclosed it round about with the fresh greenery of the clustering vine.

I left the fertile plains of gold in Lydia and Phrygia and made my way across the sunny plateaus of Persia, the walled towns of Bactria, the grim land of the Medes, rich Arabia, and the entire coast of Asia Minor, where Hellenes and non-Hellenes live together in teeming cities with beautiful towers. After having led my Bacchic dance and established my mysteries in these places, I have come to this city of the Hellenes first.

I have raised the Bacchic cry and clothed my followers in the fawnskin and put into their hands the thyrsus—my ivy-covered shaft—here in Thebes first of all Greece, because my mother's sisters claim (as least of all they should) that I, Dionysus, was not begotten of Zeus but that Semele became pregnant by some mortal man and through the clever instigations of Cadmus laid the blame on Zeus; they gloatingly proclaim that Zeus because of her deception struck her dead.

And so these same sisters I have stung with madness, driving them from their homes, and they inhabit Mt. Cithaeron, bereft of sense; I have compelled them to take up the symbols of my rituals, and all the women of Thebes—the entire female population—I have driven from their homes in frenzy. Together with the daughters of Cadmus they sit out in the open air on rocks under the evergreens. For although it does not wish to, this city must learn full well that it is still not completely schooled in my Bacchic mysteries and I must defend the reputation of my mother Semele by showing myself to mortals as the god whom she bore to Zeus.

Cadmus has handed over the prerogatives of his royal power to his daughter's son, Pentheus, who fights against my godhead, thrusting me aside in sacrifices and never mentioning my name in prayers. Therefore I shall show myself as a god to him and all the Thebans. And when I have settled matters here, I shall move on to another place and reveal myself. If the city of Thebes in anger tries by force to drive the Bacchae down from the mountains, I shall join them in their madness as their war commander. This then is why I have assumed a mortal form and changed myself into the likeness of a man.

O you women whom I have taken as companions of my journey from foreign lands, leaving the Lydian mountain Tmolus far behind, come raise the tambourines, invented by the great mother Rhea, and by me, and native to the land of Phrygia. Come and surround the royal palace of Pentheus and beat out your din so that the city of Cadmus may see. I will go to my Bacchae on the slopes of Cithaeron, where they are, and join with them in their dances.

The chorus of women that follows reveals the exultant spirit and mystic aura surrounding the celebration of their god's mysteries (64–167)

CHORUS: Leaving Asia and holy Mt. Tmolus, we run in sweet pain and lovely weariness with ecstatic Bacchic cries in the wake of the roaring god Dionysus. Let everyone, indoors or out, keep their respectful distance and hold their tongue in sacred silence as we sing the appointed hymn to Bacchus.

Happy is the one who, blessed with the knowledge of the divine mysteries, leads a life of ritual purity and joins the holy group of revelers, heart and soul, as they honor their god Bacchus in the mountains with holy ceremonies of purification. He participates in mysteries ordained by the great mother, Cybele herself, as he follows his god, Dionysus, brandishing a thyrsus.

Run, run, Bacchae, bringing the roaring god, Dionysus, son of a god, out of the Phrygian mountains to the spacious streets of Hellas.

Once when his mother carried him in her womb, the lightning bolt flew from the hand of Zeus and she brought the child forth prematurely with the pains of a labor forced on her too soon, and she gave up her life in the fiery blast. Immediately Zeus, the son of Cronus, took up the child and enclosed him in the secret recess of his thigh with fastenings of gold, and hid him from Hera thus in a second womb. When the Fates had so decreed, Zeus bore the bull-horned god and wreathed his head with a crown of serpents, and so the Maenads hunt and catch wild snakes and twine them in their hair.

O Thebes, crown yourself with ivy, burst forth luxuriant in verdant leaves and lovely berries; join the Bacchic frenzy with branches torn from trees of oak or fir and consecrate your cloak of dappled fawnskin with white tufts of purest wool. Be reverent with the violent powers of the thyrsus. Straightway the whole land will dance its way (whoever leads the sacred group represents the roaring god himself) to the mountain, to the mountain where the crowd of women waits, driven from their labors at the loom by the maddening sting of Dionysus.

O secret chamber on Crete, holy cavern where Zeus was born, attended by the Curetes![5] Here the Corybantes with their three-crested helmets invented this drum of hide stretched tight for us and their ecstatic revels mingled its tense beat with the sweet alluring breath of the Phrygian flutes, and they put it into the hand of mother Rhea, so that she might beat an accompaniment to the cries of her Bacchic women. The satyrs in their frenzy took up the drum from the mother-goddess and added it to the music of their dances during the festivities in which Dionysus delights.

How sweet it is in the mountains when, out of the rushing throng, the priest of the roaring god falls to the ground in his quest for blood and with a joyful cry devours the raw flesh of the slaughtered goat. The plain flows with milk and wine and the nectar of bees; but the Bacchic celebrant runs on, brandishing his pine torch, and the flame streams behind with smoke as sweet as Syrian frankincense. He urges on the wandering band with shouts and renews their frenzied dancing, as his delicate locks toss in the breeze.

Amid the frantic shouts is heard his thunderous cry: "Run, run, Bacchae, you the pride of Tmolus with its streams of gold. Celebrate the god Dionysus on your thundering drums, honoring this deity of joy with Phrygian cries and shouts of ecstasy, while the melodious and holy flute sounds its sacred accompaniment as you throng, to the mountain, to the mountain."

Every Bacchanal runs and leaps in joy, just like a foal that frisks beside her mother in the pasture.

The scene that follows (215–313) is fraught with tragic humor and bitter irony. Cadmus (retired king) and Tiresias (priest of the traditional religion) welcome the new god with motives that are startling in their blatant pragmatism. In their joyous rejuvenation, these two old men, experienced realists, present just the right foil for the introduction of the doomed Pentheus, who, in his mortal blindness, dares to challenge the god, his cousin, Dionysus.

TIRESIAS: Who attends at the gate? Summon Cadmus from the house, the son of Agenor, who came from Sidonia and fortified the city of the Thebans. Let someone go and announce that Tiresias wants to see him. He already knows for what reason I have come. I made an agreement with him, even though I am old and he is even older, to make myself a thyrsus, wear a fawnskin, and crown my head with shoots of ivy.

CADMUS: My dearest friend, I knew your voice from inside the palace, and recognized the wise words of a wise man. I have come ready with the paraphernalia of the god. For since Dionysus, who has revealed himself to mortals as a god, is the son of my daughter, I must do everything in my power to magnify his greatness. Where should we go to join the others in the dance, shaking our gray heads in ecstasy? Tell me, an old man, Tiresias, for you are old too and wise. I shall never grow tired by night or by day as I strike the ground with my thyrsus. It will be a sweet pleasure to forget that we are old.

TIRESIAS: You experience the same sensations as I do, for I feel young again and I shall attempt the dance

CADMUS: Shall we not proceed to the mountain by chariot?

TIRESIAS: No, the god would not have as appropriate an honor.

CADMUS: I will lead the way for you, two old men together.

TIRESIAS: The god will lead the two of us there without any difficulty.

CADMUS: Are we to be the only men of the city to dance in honor of Bacchus?

TIRESIAS: We are the only ones who think the way one should; the others are wrong and perverse.

CADMUS: We delay too long; give me your hand.

TIRESIAS: Here it is, take hold and join our hands together.

CADMUS: Being a mere mortal, I am not scornful of the gods.

TIRESIAS: About the gods we have no new wise speculations. The ancestral beliefs that we hold are as old as time, and they cannot be destroyed by any argument or clever subtlety invented by profound minds. How could I help being ashamed, one will ask, as I am about to join in the dance, at my age, with an ivy wreath on my head? The god does not discriminate whether young or old must dance in his honor, but he desires to be esteemed by all alike and wishes his glory to be magnified, making no distinctions whatsoever.

CADMUS: Since you are blind, Tiresias, I shall be a prophet for you, and tell you what I see. Pentheus, the son of Echion, to whom I have given my royal power in Thebes, comes in haste to this palace. How excited he is; what news has he to tell us?

PENTHEUS: Although I happened to have been away from Thebes, I have heard of the new evils that beset the city; the women have abandoned our homes on the pretense of Bacchic rites, and gad about on the dark mountainside honoring by their dances the new god, Dionysus, whoever he is. Bowls full of wine stand in the midst of each group, and they sneak away one by one to solitary places where they satisfy the lust of males. Their pretext is that they are Maenad priestesses, but they put Aphrodite ahead of Bacchus. All those I have caught are kept safe with their hands tied by guards in the state prison. The others, who still roam on the mountain, I shall hunt out, including my own mother, Agave, and her sisters, Ino and Autonoë, the mother of Actaeon. And when I have bound them fast in iron chains, I shall soon put an end to this evil Bacchism.

They say too that a stranger has come here from Lydia, some wizard and sorcerer, with scented hair and golden curls, who has the wine-dark charms of Aphrodite in his eyes. He spends both night and day in the company of young girls, enticing them with his Bacchic mysteries. If I catch him here in my palace, I'll cut off his head and put a stop to his thyrsus-pounding and head-tossing. That fellow is the one who claims that Dionysus is a god, who was once sewn up in the thigh of Zeus, when he was in fact destroyed by the fiery blast of lightning along with his mother, because she lied and said that Zeus had been her husband. Whoever this stranger may be, does he not deserve to hang for such hubris?

But here is another miracle—I see the prophet Tiresias in a dappled fawnskin, and my mother's father, a very funny sight, playing the Bacchant with a wand of fennel reed. I refuse, sir, to stand by and see you behave so senselessly in your old age. You are my grandfather; won't you toss away your garland of ivy and rid your hand of the thyrsus?

You persuaded him, Tiresias. Why? By introducing this new divinity among people do you hope that he will afford you an additional source of income from your omens and your sacrifices? If it were not for your gray hairs, you would not escape being bound and imprisoned along with the Bacchae for initiating evil rites. As far as women are concerned, I maintain that whenever the gleam of wine is in their feasts, there can be nothing further that is wholesome in their ceremonies.

CHORUS: What sacrilege, sir! Do you not have respect for the gods and Cadmus, who sowed the seeds from which the earthborn men arose; are you the son of Echion, who was one of them, bringing shame on your own family?

TIRESIAS: Whenever a wise man takes a good theme for his argument, it is no great task to speak well. You seem to be a man of intelligence from the glibness of your tongue, but there is no good sense in your words. A headstrong man who is powerful and eloquent proves to be a bad citizen because he is wanting in intelligence. This new divinity whom you laugh at—I could not begin to tell you how great he will become throughout Hellas. . . .[6]

Pentheus, believe me; do not be overly confident that force is all-powerful in human affairs, and do not think that you are wise when the attitude that you hold is sick. Receive the god into the city, pour him libations, crown your head, and celebrate his worship.

Tiresias goes on to argue that self-control is a question of one's own nature and character. Dionysus is not immoral; he cannot corrupt a chaste woman or restrain a promiscuous one. Besides, the god (just like Pentheus himself) is happy to receive the homage of his people.

Cadmus reinforces Tiresias' appeal for reason and control. Pentheus must be sick to defy the god; and even if he were right and Dionysus were an impostor, he should be willing to compromise and lie in order to save the honor of Semele and the whole family. But Pentheus is young and adamant; he accuses his peers of folly and madness and directs one of his henchmen to smash Tiresias' place of augury (after all has he not himself desecrated his own priestly office?) and to hunt down the effeminate foreigner who has corrupted the women of Thebes.

A guard brings in the exotic stranger who has come with his new religion (in reality he is Dionysus himself), and Euripides presents the first of three interviews between the god and the man which turn upon the ironic reversal of their positions. Pentheus, believing himself triumphant, is gradually but inevitably caught in the net prepared for him by Dionysus. The calm and sure strength of the god plays beautifully upon the neurotic impulsiveness of the mortal (433–518):

GUARD: Pentheus, here we are, having hunted the quarry you sent us after, and our efforts have not been unsuccessful. But we found this wild beast tame—he did not attempt to flee, but gave me his hands willingly; he did not even turn pale, but kept the flush of wine in his cheeks. With a smile he bade me tie him up and lead him away and waited for me, thus making my task easy. I was taken aback and said: "O stranger, I do not arrest you of my own free will but at the orders of Pentheus who has sent me."

About the Bacchae whom you seized and bound and imprisoned—they are freed and have gone and dance about the glens calling on their god, Bacchus. The bonds fell from their feet of their own accord, and the locks on the door gave way untouched by mortal hands. This man who has come to our city of Thebes is full of many miraculous wonders—and what else will happen is your concern, not mine.

PENTHEUS: Untie his hands. Now that he is in my trap, he is not nimble enough to escape me. Well, stranger, you are not unattractive physically—at least to women—and, after all, your purpose in Thebes is to lure them. Your flowing locks that ripple down your cheeks so seductively prove that you are no wrestler. Your fair complexion too is cultivated by avoiding the rays of the sun and by keeping in the shade so that you may ensnare Aphrodite with your beauty. But first tell me where you come from.

DIONYSUS: I can answer your question easily and simply. I am sure you have heard of the mountain of Tmolus with its flowers.

PENTHEUS: I have; its range encircles the city of Sardis.

DIONYSUS: I am from there; Lydia is my fatherland.

PENTHEUS: How is it that you bring these mysteries of yours to Hellas?

DIONYSUS: Dionysus, the son of Zeus, has directed me.

PENTHEUS: Is there a Zeus in Lydia who begets new gods?

DIONYSUS: No, he is the same Zeus who wedded Semele here in Thebes.

PENTHEUS: Did he bend you to his service, an apparition in the night, or did you really see him with your own eyes?

DIONYSUS: We saw each other face to face and he gave me his secrets.

PENTHEUS: What is the nature of these secrets of yours?

DIONYSUS: It is not lawful for the uninitiated to know them.

PENTHEUS: What advantage is there for those who do participate?

DIONYSUS: It is not right for you to learn this, but the knowledge is worth much.

PENTHEUS: Your answer is clever, designed to make me want to hear more.

DIONYSUS: An impious man is abhorred by the god and his mysteries.

PENTHEUS: You say that you saw the god clearly; well then what did he look like?

DIONYSUS: He looked as he wished; I had no control over his appearance.

PENTHEUS: Once again you have sidetracked me cleverly with an answer that says nothing.

DIONYSUS: The words of the wise seem foolish to the ignorant.

PENTHEUS: Have you come here first of all to introduce your god?

DIONYSUS: Every foreigner already dances his rituals.

PENTHEUS: Yes, of course, for they are far inferior to Hellenes.

DIONYSUS: Customs differ, but in these rituals the foreigners are superior.

PENTHEUS: Do you perform your holy rites by night or by day?

DIONYSUS: By night for the most part; darkness adds to the solemnity.

PENTHEUS: For women it is treacherous and corrupt.

DIONYSUS: One may find, if one looks for it, shameful behavior by daylight too.

PENTHEUS: You must be punished for your evil sophistries.

DIONYSUS: And you for your ignorance and blasphemy against the god.

PENTHEUS: How bold our Bacchant is and how facile his retorts.

DIONYSUS: What punishment must I suffer? What terrible thing will you do to me?

PENTHEUS: First I shall cut your pretty locks.

DIONYSUS: My hair is sacred; it belongs to the god.

PENTHEUS: Hand over your thyrsus then.

DIONYSUS: Take it away from me yourself. I carry it for Dionysus; it really belongs to him.

PENTHEUS: I shall close you up in a prison.

DIONYSUS: The god himself will free me, whenever I wish.

PENTHEUS: As you call on him when you take your stand amid your Bacchic women, I suppose.

DIONYSUS: Even now he is near at hand and sees what I endure.

PENTHEUS: Where is he? My eyes cannot see him.

DIONYSUS: Here with me. But you in your blasphemy cannot perceive him for yourself.

PENTHEUS: Guards, seize him; he is making a fool of me and of all Thebes.

DIONYSUS: I tell you not to bind me—I am the sane one, not you.

PENTHEUS: My orders are to bind you, and I have the upper hand.

DIONYSUS: You do not know what life you live, what you do, or who you are.

PENTHEUS: I am Pentheus, the son of Agave; my father is Echion.

DIONYSUS: Your name, Pentheus, which means sorrow, is appropriate for the doom that will be yours.

PENTHEUS: Get out of here—Guards, imprison him in the neighboring stables where he may find his secret darkness—do your mystic dances there. And the women you have brought with you as accomplices in your evil I shall either keep as slaves myself to work the loom or sell them to others—this will stop their hands from beating out their din on tambourines.

DIONYSUS: I will go, since what is not destined to be, I am not destined to suffer. But Dionysus, who you say does not exist, will exact vengeance for your insolence. For as you do me wrong and imprison me, you do the same to him.

Pentheus confidently follows Dionysus into the prison. But the god miraculously frees himself amid fire, earthquake, and the destruction of the entire palace. He explains to the chorus how he has escaped from Pentheus' evil clutches, maintaining throughout the fiction of his role as the god's disciple. Quite typically Dionysus is associated with or transformed into an animal (616-636):

DIONYSUS: I have made a fool of Pentheus—he thought that he was tying me up, yet he did not so much as lay a finger on me but fed on empty hopes. In the chamber where he led me a prisoner, he found a bull. It was the knees and hoofs of this animal that he tried to bind, fuming and raging, biting his lips, and dripping with sweat, while I sat calmly close by his side and watched. In this crisis Bacchus arrived and made the building shake and raised a flame up from the tomb of his mother. When Pentheus saw it, he thought that the palace was on fire and rushed this way and that, calling on the servants to bring water. The entire household joined in the work but their toil was for nothing. Pentheus, thinking that I had got away, abandoned his efforts and seized a dark sword and rushed inside the palace in pursuit.

Then Dionysus created an illusion in the courtyard (I am telling you what I believe happened) and Pentheus made a dash for it, jabbing and stabbing at the sunny air, imagining he was butchering me. Bacchus had even greater humiliation for him than this. He razed the whole palace to the ground; all lies shattered for him as he beholds the most bitter results of my imprisonment. Worn out and exhausted, he has dropped his sword; a mere mortal, he dared to go to battle against a god.

As Dionysus coolly finishes his account, Pentheus appears, bewildered, angry, and, despite his experience, still relentlessly aggressive. A brief exchange between the two is interrupted by the arrival of a messenger, who reports what he and others have seen of the Bacchic women and their worship in the mountains; at first a calm, peaceful scene full of miracles, then madness and bloodshed when the interlopers are detected—a grim foreshadowing of what is in store for Pentheus (678–774):

MESSENGER: I had just reached the hill country with my pasturing herds by the time that the sun had risen and was warming the earth with its rays. And I saw the women, who had arranged themselves in three groups; Autonoë led one, your mother, Agave, the second, and Ino, the third. All were stretched out asleep, some reclined on beds of fir, others rested their heads on oak leaves, having flung themselves down at random but with modesty; and they were not, as you said they would be, intoxicated with wine and the music of the flute, bent on satisfying their lust in solitary places.

When your mother heard the sounds of our horned cattle, she stood up in the midst of the Bacchae, and cried out to rouse them from their sleep, and they threw off the heavy slumber from their eyes and jumped up—amazing in their orderliness, young and old (many still unwed). The first thing they did was to loosen their hair to their shoulders and tie up their fawnskins if any of the fastenings had come loose; and they made a belt for the dappled fur with snakes that licked their cheeks. Some held in their arms the young of the wild, a gazelle or wolf cubs, and those who had left their newborn babes at home gave them white milk from breasts that were still full.

And they put on crowns of ivy, oak, and flowering vine. One took her thyrsus and struck it against a rock, and from it a gush of dewy water welled up; another hit the solid earth with her wand, and from the spot the god sent forth a spring of wine. Those who thirsted for milk scraped the earth with their fingertips and produced white streams; and from each thyrsus, wreathed in ivy, dripped sweet drops of honey. And so, if you had been there to see these things, you would have invoked with prayers the god whom you now blame.

We herdsmen and shepherds gathered together to discuss and argue about the strange and wondrous actions. One of the group, who always goes into town and has a way with words, spoke to us all: "You who inhabit the sacred mountain heights, how would you like to hunt down Agave, the mother of Pentheus, in her revels and do the king a favor?" What he said seemed good to us, so we hid ourselves in a leafy thicket and waited in ambush. At the appointed time they began their Bacchic revels, shaking their thyrsus and calling on the god, the son of Zeus, with one voice "Iacchus, Bromius!" The whole mountain and animals joined in their ecstasy and there was nothing that remained unmoved by the dance.

It happened that Agave, as she leaped and ran, came close to me, and I leaped out of the ambush where I had hidden myself, bent on seizing her. But she cried aloud: "O my swift-running hounds, we are being hunted by these men; so follow me, follow, armed with your thyrsus in your hands."

And so we fled and escaped being torn into pieces by the Bacchae, but with their bare hands they attacked our cattle grazing on the grass. You could see one of them wrenching apart a bellowing cow, its udders full. Others ripped apart the calves, and you could see ribs and cloven hoofs being scattered high and low, and from the pines the pieces hung dripping with blood. Bulls, arrogant before as they raged with their horns, were laid low, dragged bodily to the ground by the countless hands of girls; and their flesh was stripped from their bodies more quickly than you, O king, could wink your eyes.

Like birds propelled aloft by the speed of their course, the Bacchae ranged across the stretch of plain along the stream of the Asopus, which affords the Thebans a rich harvest. Like a hostile army they descended upon the villages of Hysiae and Erythrae, nestled low on the slopes of Cithaeron, and devastated them. They snatched children from their homes, and all the booty (including bronze and iron) that they carried off on their shoulders did not fall onto the dark earth, although it was not fastened. They bore fire on their hair and it did not burn. The villagers, enraged by the plundering of the Bacchae, rushed to arms.

Then, my king, there was a terrifying sight to behold. The weapons that the villagers threw did not draw any blood, but when the Bacchae hurled the thyrsus from their hands they inflicted wounds on many. Women routed men—a feat not to be accomplished without the power of some god. Back they came to where they sallied forth, to the very streams which the god made gush for them. They washed their hands of blood, and snakes licked the stains from their cheeks.

And so, my lord, receive into the city this god, whoever he is. He is great in many respects but especially in his reputed gift to mortals, about which I have heard, the grape, our remedy for pain and sorrow. With no more wine, there could be no more love and no other pleasure for humankind besides.

Pentheus refuses to listen to the pleas of the messenger. He is determined to rush to arms for an assault on the Bacchae. But the stranger, Dionysus, finds a way to restrain him by appealing to Pentheus' basic nature and psychology—in general, the complex neurosis that stems from his repressions, in particular, his prurient preoccupation with sex and his desire to see the orgies that he insists are taking place (811–861):

DIONYSUS: Would you like to see the women banded together in the mountains?

PENTHEUS: Yes, indeed. I would give a ton of gold for that.

DIONYSUS: Why are you driven by such a great desire to see them?

PENTHEUS: Actually, it would pain me to see them drunk.

DIONYSUS: Nevertheless you would be pleased to see what is painful to you?

PENTHEUS: To be sure, if I watched in silence crouched beneath the firs.

DIONYSUS: But they will track you down, even if you go in secret.

PENTHEUS: Then I shall go openly; what you say is right.

DIONYSUS: You will undergo the journey then? Let me lead you.

PENTHEUS: Come, as quickly as possible; I begrudge you this delay.

DIONYSUS: Then dress up in a fine linen robe.

PENTHEUS: What is this? Am I to change from a man to a woman?

DIONYSUS: If you are seen there as a man, they will kill you.

PENTHEUS: Again, what you say is right. You are like some sage of long ago.

DIONYSUS: Dionysus gives me this inspiration.

PENTHEUS: In the garb of a woman? But shame holds me back!

DIONYSUS: You are no longer interested in watching the Maenads?

PENTHEUS: What dress did you say that you would put on me?

DIONYSUS: I shall set on your head a long flowing wig.

PENTHEUS: And what is the next feature of my outfit?

DIONYSUS: A robe that falls to your feet, and a band around your head.

PENTHEUS: What else will you give me?

DIONYSUS: A thyrsus in your hand and a dappled fawnskin cloak.

PENTHEUS: I cannot bring myself to put on the costume of a woman.

DIONYSUS: But if you attack the Bacchae in battle, you will shed blood.

PENTHEUS: This is true; I must first go as a spy.

DIONYSUS: To be sure, it is wiser than to hunt out evil by evil.

PENTHEUS: How shall I get out of the city without being seen?

DIONYSUS: We shall take a deserted route, and I shall lead the way.

PENTHEUS: Anything, rather than have the Bacchae laugh at me. I shall go into the house and make preparations that are for the best.

DIONYSUS: So be it, and I am at your side ready for everything.

PENTHEUS: I am going inside; I shall either proceed with arms or follow your instructions.

DIONYSUS: Women, this man is ready to be caught in the net. He will go to the Bacchae, and he will pay the penalty with his life. Dionysus, now do your work; for you are not far away. We shall exact our retribution. First we shall inflict upon him delirious madness and drive him out of his wits; in his right mind, he would not want to dress up in the costume of a woman; but once driven from reason he will put it on. My desire is to make him the laughingstock of the Thebans as they see him led in a woman's garb through the city in return for the terrible threats that he uttered before. I go now to deck out Pentheus in the dress with which he will go down to the realm of Hades, slaughtered by the hands of his mother. He will know Dionysus as the son of Zeus and a deity of his own right, among humankind most dread and most gentle.

The dressing of Pentheus in the garb of the Bacchae suggests the ceremonial decking out of the sacrificial victim. By the ritual of donning his costume, Pentheus falls under the spell and the power of the god, eventually to be offered up to him. The chorus sings of the joys of their worship and the justice of their triumph over impiety; and at the end of their song, Dionysus exerts final and complete mastery over Pentheus, who is delirious (912–970):

 DIONYSUS: Pentheus, I call on you, the one who desires to see what he should not see and hastens upon what he should not do. Come forward out of the house, let me behold you dressed in the garb of a woman, a Bacchic Maenad, about to go as a spy on your mother and her group.

PENTHEUS: I think that I see two suns, and the image of Thebes with its seven gates appears double. You look like a bull as you lead me forward, with horns growing out of your head. Were you then an animal? Now, indeed, you have become a bull.

DIONYSUS: The god walks with us; he is on our side although he was not kindly disposed before. Now you see what you should see.

PENTHEUS: Tell me how I look. Do I not have the bearing of Ino or my mother, Agave?

DIONYSUS: Looking at you I seem to see those very two. But this lock here that I had fixed under your hairband has fallen out of place.

PENTHEUS: I shook it loose indoors while I was tossing my head back and forth like a Bacchic reveler.

DIONYSUS: Well we, whose concern is to serve you, shall put it back in place. Bend your head.

PENTHEUS: Fine, you deck me out properly, for I am now dedicated to you.

DIONYSUS: Your belt is loose and the folds of your dress do not hang straight to your ankles.

PENTHEUS: They are not straight at the right foot but here on the left the dress hangs well at the heel.

DIONYSUS: You will, I am sure, consider me the best of your friends, when contrary to your expectation you witness the temperance of the Bacchae.

PENTHEUS: Shall I be more like one of the Bacchae if I hold my thyrsus in my right or my left hand?

DIONYSUS: You should hold it in your right hand, and raise it and your right foot at the same time.

PENTHEUS: Will I be able to lift up on my shoulders Mt. Cithaeron with its glens full of Bacchae?

DIONYSUS: You will, if you wish; before your mind was not sound, but now it is as it ought to be.

PENTHEUS: Let us take crowbars, or shall I thrust my shoulder or my arm under the peaks and crush them with my hands?

DIONYSUS: Do not destroy the haunts of the nymphs and the places where Pan does his piping.

PENTHEUS: Your words are right; women must not be overcome by force; I will hide myself among the firs.

DIONYSUS: You will find the hiding place that you should, coming upon the Maenads as a crafty spy.

PENTHEUS: Indeed I can see them now in the bushes like birds held fast in the enticing coils of love.

DIONYSUS: Yes, of course, you go on a mission to guard against this very thing. Maybe you will catch them, if you yourself are not caught first.

PENTHEUS: Take me through the middle of Thebes, for I am the only man among them who dares this deed.

DIONYSUS: You alone bear the burden of toil for this city—you alone. And so the struggle which must be awaits you. Follow me, I shall lead you there in safety, but another will lead you back.

PENTHEUS: My mother.

DIONYSUS: A spectacle for all.

PENTHEUS: It is for this I am going.

DIONYSUS: You will be carried home.

PENTHEUS: What luxury you are suggesting.

DIONYSUS: In the hands of your mother.

PENTHEUS: You insist upon pampering me.

DIONYSUS: Pampering of sorts.

PENTHEUS: Worthy of such deserts, I follow you.

Pentheus imagines he will return in a splendid carriage, with his mother by his side. This terrifying scene is built on more than this one irony and laden with a multiplicity of ambiguities. Pentheus the transvestite imagines, like a child, loving care at the hands of his mother. How bitter now appear the earlier taunts of Pentheus against Cadmus and Tiresias. In his delirium, does Pentheus really see the god in his true and basic character—a beast? Or does his vision spring from his own warped interpretation of the bestial nature of the worship?

A messenger arrives to tell of Pentheus' horrifying death (1043–1152):

MESSENGER: When we had left the town of Thebes behind and crossed the stream of the Asopus, we made our way up the slopes of Cithaeron, Pentheus and I (for I followed with my master) and the stranger who led us to the scene.

First we took a position in a grassy glen, with silent footsteps and not a word, so that we might see and not be seen. It was a valley surrounded by cliffs, watered by streams, and shaded by pines; here Maenads sat, their hands occupied in their joyous tasks. Some were restoring a crown of ivy on a thyrsus that had lost its foliage; others, happy as fillies let loose from their painted yokes, were singing Bacchic hymns in answering refrains.

But poor Pentheus, who could not see this crowd of women, said: "My friend, from where I stand I am too far away to see these counterfeit Maenads clearly, but if I climbed up a towering pine on the hillside, I could properly behold the orgies of the Maenads." Then and there I saw the stranger do wondrous things. He took hold of the very top branch of a pine that reached up to the sky and pulled it down, down, down to the black earth. And it was bent like a bow or the curving line of the circle of a wheel. Thus the stranger grabbed the mountain pine with his hands and bent it to the ground, a feat no mortal could accomplish.

He sat Pentheus on the topmost branches and let the tree go, sliding it through his hands until it was upright again, slowly and carefully so that he might not dislodge him. It towered straight to towering heaven, with our king perched on top. He could be seen more clearly by the Maenads than he could see them. He was just becoming visible, seated aloft, when the stranger was no longer to be seen, and from heaven a voice (I imagine that of Dionysus) cried aloud: "O women, I bring the man who made a mockery of you and me and our mysteries; now take vengeance on him."

As the voice spoke these words, a blaze of holy fire flashed between heaven and earth. The air grew still, every leaf in the wooded glen stood silent, and no sound of a beast was to be heard. The women had not made out the voice clearly, and they stood up straight and looked around. He called again, and when the daughters of Cadmus understood the clear command of Bacchus, they rushed forth as swift as doves in their relentless course, his mother, Agave, her sisters, and all the Bacchae. With a madness inspired by the breath of the god, they darted over the glen with its streams and rocks. When they saw the king seated in the pine tree, they first climbed on the rock cliff that towered opposite and hurled stones at him with all their might and pelted him with branches of pines. Others hurled the thyrsus through the air at Pentheus, a pitiable target.

But they were unsuccessful, for the poor wretch sat trapped and helpless, too high for even their fanaticism. Finally with a lightning force they ripped off oak branches and tried to use them as levers to uproot the tree. But when these efforts too were all in vain, Agave exclaimed: "Come, O Maenads, stand around the tree in a circle and grab hold of it, so that we may catch the climbing beast and prevent him from revealing the secret revels of the god." And they applied a thousand hands and tore up the tree out of the earth. And from his lofty seat Pentheus fell hurtling to the ground with endless cries; for he knew what evil fate was near.

His mother as priestess was the first to begin the slaughter. She fell on him and he ripped off the band from his hair so that poor Agave might recognize him and not kill him, and he cried out as he touched her cheek: "Mother, it is your son, Pentheus, whom you bore in the home of Echion. Have pity on me for my sins and do not kill me, your son."

But Agave was not in her right senses; her mouth foamed and her eyes rolled madly as the god Bacchus held her in his power. And Pentheus could not reach her. She seized his left arm below the elbow and placing her foot against the ribs of her ill-fated son, wrenched his arm out of his shoulder. It was not done through her own strength, but the god made it easy for her hands. From the other side, Ino clawed and tore at his flesh, and Autonoë and the whole pack converged on him. All shouted together, he moaning with what breath remained, they screaming in triumph. One carried an arm, another a foot with the boot still on; his ribs were stripped clean and they all with blood-drenched hands tossed the flesh of Pentheus among them like a ball. His body lies scattered, some pieces under hard rocks, others in the shady depths of the woods—not easy to find.

His mother has taken his poor head and affixed it on the point of her thyrsus; she carries it like that of a mountain lion through the depths of Cithaeron, leaving her sisters and their Maenad bands. She comes within these walls, exulting in her ill-fated prey and calling on Bacchus, her partner in the hunt, her comrade in the chase, her champion of victory, who gave her tears as her reward. And so I am leaving now, before Agave reaches the palace, to get away from this misfortune. Temperance and reverence for the gods are best, the wisest possessions, I believe, that exist for mortals who will use them.

Agave returns and awakens to the horror of her deed; the concluding scenes affirm the divine power of Dionysus. There are serious textual problems in the last section of the play; and a medieval work, the *Christus Patiens,* that drew upon Euripides, is of some help—an interesting fact that rivets our attention to the parallels between Dionysus and Christ.

The pathos and horror of the butchering of Pentheus have led some to advance a sympathetic view of the rash king as an ascetic martyr, killed in his crusade against the irrational tide of religious fanaticism. But too much in the makeup of this young man suggests the myopic psychopath who is unable to accept human nature as it is and foolishly tries to suppress it. The basic impulses toward both the bestial and the sublime are terrifyingly and wondrously interrelated; Dionysus is after all the god of mob fury and religious ecstasy and anything in between. Was the celebration of his worship a cry for release from the restraints of civilized society and a return to the mystic purity and abounding freedom of nature, or was it merely a deceptive excuse for self-indulgence in an orgy of undisciplined passion?[7]

The Nature of Dionysus, His Retinue, and His Religion

The *Homeric Hymn to Dionysus* (1)[8] gives some variant information about Dionysus' birth, derives his name from Zeus (Dios) and the mountain Nysa (which is here placed in Egypt), and establishes the universal power of his worship.

O divinely born god, sewn in Zeus' thigh,[9] some say it was on Dracanum, some in windy Icarus, some at the deep flowing Alpheus,[10] where Semele, made pregnant by Zeus who delights in the lightning, gave birth to you. Others say, O lord, that you were born in Thebes. They are all wrong; the father of both gods and men gave you birth, away from people and hidden from white-armed Hera.

There is a certain mountain, Nysa, very high and with verdant forests, far from Phoenicia, near the streams of Egypt.[11]

" . . . and they will set up many statues in temples; and as things are three, mortals always, everywhere, will sacrifice perfect hecatombs to you in triennial festivals."[12] The son of Cronus spoke and nodded with his dark brows; and the divine hair of our lord flowed down around his immortal head and he made great Olympus shake. Thus speaking, wise Zeus nodded confirmation with his head.

Be kind, you, sewn in Zeus' thigh, who drive women mad. We bards sing of you as we begin and end our song. It is utterly impossible for anyone who is forgetful of you to remember how to sing his holy song.

So hail to you, Dionysus, sewn in Zeus' thigh, along with your mother, Semele, whom indeed they call Thyone.

Another *Homeric Hymn to Dionysus* (26) tells us more about the god:

I begin to sing about ivy-crowned, loud-crying Dionysus, glorious son of Zeus and renowned Semele. The nymphs with beautiful hair took him to their bosoms from the lord his father and nurtured him tenderly in the vales of Mt. Nysa. By the grace of his father, he grew up in a fragrant cave, to be counted among the immortals. But when the goddesses had brought up this muchhymned god, then indeed he used to wander, heavily wreathed in ivy and laurel, among the woodland haunts of the forest. The nymphs followed along, with him as leader, and the sound of their cries filled the vast forest.

So hail to you, Dionysus, rich in grape clusters; grant that we may in our joy go through these seasons again and again for many years.

The essential characteristics of Dionysiac religion are an ecstatic spiritual release through music and dance,[13] the possession by the god of his followers, the rending apart of the sacrificial animal, and the eating of the raw flesh (*omophagy*, a kind of ritual communion, since the god was believed to be present in the victim). The religious congregation (the holy *thiasus*) was divided into groups, often with a male leader for each, who played the role of the god. The Bacchae, or maenads, are the female devotees, mortal women who become possessed. In mythology they are more than human, nymphs rather than mere mortals.

Their mythological male counterparts are satyrs, who are, like them, spirits of nature; they, however, are not completely human but part man and part animal, possessing various attributes of a horse or a goat—a horse's tail and ears, a goat's beard and horns—although in the later periods they are often depicted as considerably more humanized. Satyrs dance and sing and love music; they make wine and drink it, and they are perpetually in a state of sexual excitement. One of their favorite sports is to chase maenads through the woods. Animal skins and garlands are traditional attributes of Bacchic revelers (although satyrs are usually nude); maenads, in particular, carry the thyrsus, a pole wreathed with ivy or vine leaves, pointed at the top to receive a pine cone. As we have seen, it is a magic wand that evokes miracles; but if necessary it can be converted into a deadly weapon.

Sileni also attend Dionysus; they often cannot be distinguished from satyrs, although some of them are older (*papposileni*) and even more lecherous. Yet others are old and wise, like Silenus himself, the tutor of Dionysus. A story tells how once one of them was made drunk by adding wine to the water of a spring; when he was brought to King Midas, this silenus philosophized that the best fate for human beings was not to be born at all, the next best to die as soon as possible after birth, a typical example of Greek pessimism, and wisdom reminiscent of Solon and Herodotus.[14] Dionysus and his retinue are favorite subjects in Greek art.

As the male god of vegetation, Dionysus was, as we should expect,

Maenad. Interior of an Attic kylix by the Brygos Painter, ca. 480 B.C. diameter $11\frac{1}{4}$ in. This lively white-ground painting (the cup is signed by the potter Brygos) shows a maenad in violent motion, holding a thyrsus in her right hand and a small leopard in her left. A leopardskin is fastened over her dress and a wreath of serpents encircles her head. *(Antikensammlungen, Munich. Photograph courtesy of Hirmer Verlag, München.)*

associated with a fertility goddess; his mother, Semele, was a full-fledged earth deity in her own right before she became Hellenized. The story of Zeus' birth on Crete, with the attendants who drowned out his infant cries by their frenzied music, suggests contamination with Dionysiac ritual. Certainly Euripides associates Bacchic mysticism with the ritual worship of both Rhea and Cybele. Dionysus'

Dionysus with Satyrs and Maenads. Athenian black-figure amphora, sixth century B.C.; height 18¾ in. Dionysus, wreathed with ivy, holds a horn-shaped wine cup in his left hand and looks back at the satyr on the left who is carrying off a maenad playing a double-flute. A second satyr on the right carries off a maenad with castanets, who raises her arms and looks back at the god. Vine leaves and bunches of grapes trail in the background and frame Dionysus. *(British Museum, London. Reproduced by permission of the Trustees.)*

"marriage" with Ariadne, saving her after she was deserted by Theseus on the island of Naxos (see pp. 461–463), not only provides an example of the union of the male and female powers of vegetation but also illustrates allegorically his powers of redemption. Dionysus represents the sap of life, the coursing of the blood through the veins, the throbbing excitement and mystery of sex and of nature; thus he is a god of ecstasy and mysticism.

Another myth told about his birth even more clearly established him in this role as a god of the mysteries. Zeus mated with his daughter Persephone, who bore a son, Zagreus, which is another name for Dionysus. In her jealousy, Hera then aroused the Titans to attack the child. These monstrous beings, their faces whitened with chalk, attacked the infant as he was looking in a mirror (in another version, they beguiled him with toys and cut him to pieces with knives). After the murder, the Titans devoured the dismembered corpse.[15] But the heart of the infant god was saved and brought to Zeus by Athena, and Dionysus was born again—swallowed by Zeus and begotten on Semele. Zeus was angry with the Titans and destroyed them with his thunder and lightning; but from their ashes humankind was born.

Surely this is one of the most significant myths in terms of the philosophy and religious dogma that it provides. By it human beings are endowed with a dual nature—a body gross and evil (since we are sprung from the Titans) and a soul that is pure and divine (for after all the Titans had devoured the god). Thus basic religious concepts (which lie at the root of all mystery religions) are accounted for: sin, immortality, resurrection, life after death, reward, and punishment. It is no accident that Dionysus is linked with Orpheus and Demeter and the message that they preached. He is in his person a resurrection-god; the story is told that he went down into the realm of the dead and brought back his mother, who in this account is usually given the name Thyone.

In the emotional environment of Dionysiac ecstasy are to be found the essence and spirit of Greek drama. Theories concerning the origins of this genre in its relationship to Dionysus are legion. But it is a fact that tragedy and comedy were performed at Athens in a festival in his honor. It is difficult to agree with those who feel that this connection was purely accidental. Certainly Aristotle's treatise dealing with the nature of tragedy in terms of a catharsis of pity and fear takes for granted emotions and excitement that are essentially Bacchic. [16]

Dionysus and Icarius and Erigone

Dionysus, however, can be received amid peace and joy. In Attica, in the days of King Pandion, a man named Icarius was most hospitable to the god, and as a reward he was given the gift of wine. But when the people first felt the effects of this blessing, they thought they had been poisoned, and they turned upon Icarius and killed him. Erigone, his devoted daughter, accompanied by her dog Maira, searched every-where for her father. When she found him, she hanged herself in grief. Suffering and plague ensued for the people until, upon Apollo's advice, they initiated a festival in honor of Icarius and Erigone.

Dionysus' Gift to Midas of the Golden Touch

We have learned above how the philosophical Silenus was captured and brought to King Midas.[17] Midas recognized the satyr at once as a follower of Dionysus and returned him to Dionysus. The god was so delighted that he gave the king the right to choose any gift he would like for himself. Midas foolishly asked that whatever he should touch might be turned into gold. At first Midas was delighted with his new power, when he saw that he could transform everything into gleaming riches by the mere touch of his hand. But the blessing quickly became a curse, for he could no longer eat or drink; any morsel or drop that he brought to his lips became a solid mass of gold. Midas' greed turned to loathing; in some accounts, even his beloved daughter was transformed. He begged the god's forgiveness for his sin and release from his accursed power. Dionysus took pity and ordered the king to cleanse himself of the remaining traces of his guilt in the source of the river Pactolus, near Sardis. Midas obeyed, and the power of transforming things into gold passed from his person into the stream, whose sands forevermore were sands of gold.

Dionysus and the Pirates

In *Homeric Hymn to Dionysus* (7) the god is abducted by pirates who mistake him for a mortal (see Color Plate 2). The ensuing events aboard ship offer a splendid picture of Dionysus' power and majesty and remind us of fundamental elements in the nature of his character and worship: miracles, bestial transformation, violence to enemies, and pity and salvation for those who understand.[18]

I shall sing of how Dionysus, the son of renowned Semele, appeared as a man in the first bloom of youth on a projecting stretch of shore by the sea that bears no harvest. His hair, beautiful and dark, flowed thickly about his head, and he wore on his strong shoulders a purple cloak. Before long foreign pirates, led on by evil fate, appeared swiftly over the sea, dark as wine, in a ship with fine benches of oars. As soon as they saw him, they nodded one to the other and, quickly jumping out, seized him at once and put him on board ship, delighted in their hearts. For they thought that he was the son of kings, who are cherished by Zeus, and wanted to bind him in harsh bonds. But the bonds fell far from his hands and feet and did not hold him as he sat with a smile in his dark eyes.

When the helmsman saw this he called aloud to his comrades: "Madmen, who is this mighty god whom you have seized and attempt to bind? Not even our strong ship can carry him, for this is either Zeus or Apollo of the silver bow or Poseidon, since he is not like mortal men but like the gods who have their homes on Olympus. But come, let us immediately set him free on the dark shore; do not lay hands on him for fear that he become angered in some way and rouse up violent winds and a great storm."

So he spoke, but the commander of the ship rebuked him scornfully: "Madman, check the wind, and while you are at it seize the tackle and hoist the sail. I expect that he will come with us to Egypt or Cyprus or the northern Hyperboreans or farther. But at his destination he will eventually tell us about his friends and all his possessions and his brothers, since a divine power has put him in our hands." When he had spoken, the mast and sail were hoisted on the ship; the wind breathed into the midst of the sail and the men made the ropes tight all around.

But soon deeds full of wonder appeared in their midst. First of all a sweet and fragrant wine flowed through the black ship, and a divine ambrosial odor arose. Amazement took hold of all the sailors as they looked, and immediately a vine spread in all directions up along the very top of the sail, with many clusters hanging down; dark ivy, luxuriant with flowers, entwined about the mast, and lovely fruit burst forth, and all the oarpins bore garlands. When they saw this, they ordered the helmsman to bring the ship to land. But then the god became a terrifying lion in the upper part of the ship and roared loudly, and in the middle of the ship he created a shaggy-necked bear, thus manifesting his divine credentials. The bear stood up raging, while on the upper deck the lion glared and scowled.

The sailors fled into the stern and stood in panic around the helmsman, who had shown his right sense. The lion sprang up suddenly and seized the commander of the ship, but the sailors when they saw this escaped an evil fate and leaped all together into the shining sea and became dolphins.

The god took pity on the helmsman and saved him and made him happy and fortunate in every way, saying: "Be of good courage, you who have become dear to my heart. I am loud-crying Dionysus, whom my mother, Semele, daughter of Cadmus, bore after uniting in love with Zeus."

Hail, son of Semele of the beautiful countenance; it is not at all possible to forget you and compose sweet song.

Pan

The god Pan has much in common with the satyrs and sileni of Dionysus.[19] He is not completely human in form but part man and part goat—he has the horns, ears, and legs of a goat; he will join in Bacchic revels, and he is full of spirit, impulsive, and amorous. His parents are variously named: his mother is usually some nymph or other; his father is very often Hermes or Apollo. Like them, he is a god of shepherds and a musician.

Pan is credited with the invention of his own instrument, the panpipe (or in Greek, *syrinx*); Ovid tells the story with brevity and charm (*Metamorphoses* 1. 689–712). Syrinx was once a lovely nymph, devoted to Artemis, who rejected the advances of predatory satyrs and woodland spirits. Pan caught sight of her, and as he pursued her she was transformed into a bed of marsh reeds. The wind blowing through them produced a sad and beautiful sound, and Pan was inspired to cut two of the reeds, fasten them together with wax, and thus fashion a pipe on which he could play.

Pan's haunts are the hills and the mountains, particularly those of his homeland, Arcadia, and came to be especially honored in Athens.[20]

Pan had other loves besides Syrinx.[21] His passion for the nymph Echo also ended tragically. She fled from his advances, and Pan spread such madness and "panic" among a group of shepherds (a particular feat to which he was prone) that they tore her to pieces. All that remained was her voice.

The *Homeric Hymn to Pan* (19) presents a memorable account of his birth and his revels; in this case his father is Hermes and his mother Dryope, the daughter of Dryops.

Tell me, O Muse, about the dear son of Hermes—Pan, goat-footed, two-horned, lover of musical clangor—who wanders through wooded meadows together with a chorus of nymphs dancing along the heights of sheer rock. They call upon Pan, the splendid shaggy-haired god of shepherds, who has for his domain every snowy ridge, and mountaintops and rocky summits. He roams this place and that through dense thickets; sometimes he is tempted by soft streams, and then again he passes among sheer rocks and climbs up to the highest peak that overlooks the flocks. Often he moves across gleaming high mountains; often, among the slopes, he presses on and, sharply on the outlook, kills animals.

Then, in the evening only, returning from the chase, he plays a lovely tune upon his pipe of reeds. Not even the nightingale, the bird who pours forth her sad lament in honeyed song amidst the petals of flower-laden spring, could surpass him in melody. With him then the clear-voiced mountain nymphs, moving on nimble feet, sing by a dark-watered spring; and Echo's wails reverberate around the mountaintop. The god Pan dances readily here and there among the chorus and then slips easily into their midst. He wears a spotted pelt of a lynx on his back, and his heart is delighted by his piercing tunes in a soft meadow where the crocus and fragrant hyacinth blooming at random mingle in the grass.

They sing hymns about the blessed gods and high Olympus, and, above the rest, they single out Hermes, the bringer of luck. They sing how he is the swift messenger for all the gods and how he came into Arcadia, full of springs and mother of flocks, the place where his sacred precinct is located. There, even though he was a god, he tended the shaggy fleeced sheep, in the service of a mortal. For a melting longing seized Hermes, and his passion to make love to the daughter of Dryops,[22] the nymph with the beautiful hair, intensified; and he brought to its fulfillment a fruitful marriage.

Dryope bore to Hermes in their house a dear son, a marvel to behold right from his birth, a goat-footed, two-horned baby who loved music and laughter. But his mother was startled and fled, and she abandoned the child, for she was frightened when she saw his coarse features and full beard. Hermes, the luck-bringer, took him at once and clasped him in his arms; and the god felt extremely happy. Quickly he covered the child in the thick skin of a mountain hare and went to the homes of the immortals and sat him down beside Zeus and the other gods and showed them the boy. All the immortals were delighted in their hearts, and especially Bacchic Dionysus; and they called him Pan because he delighted the hearts of them all.[23]

So hail to you, lord. I pray to you with my song, and I shall remember both you and another song too.

Echo and Narcissus

We know that because she rejected him Pan caused Echo to be torn to pieces so that only her voice remained. A more famous story about Echo concerns her love for Narcissus. Ovid's version is as follows (*Metamorphoses* 3. 342–510):

The river-god Cephisus once embraced the nymph Liriope in his winding stream and, enveloping her in his waves, took her by force. When her time had come, the beautiful Liriope bore a child with whom even as a baby the nymphs might have fallen in love. And she called him Narcissus. She consulted the seer Tiresias, asking whether her son would live a long time to a ripe old age; his answer was: "Yes, if he will not have come to know himself." For a long time this response seemed to be an empty prophecy, but as things turned out, its truth was proven by the unusual nature of the boy's madness and death.

The son of Cephisus had reached his sixteenth year and could be looked upon as both a boy and a young man. Many youths and many maidens desired him, but such a firm pride was coupled with his soft beauty that no one (either boy or girl) dared to touch him. He was seen once as he was driving the timid deer into his nets by the talkative nymph, who had learned neither to be silent when another is speaking nor to be the first to speak herself, namely the mimic Echo.

At that time Echo was a person and not only a voice; but just as now, she was garrulous and was able to use her voice in her customary way of repeating from a flood of words only the very last. Juno brought this about because, when she might have been able to catch the nymphs lying on the mountain with her Jove, Echo knowingly detained the goddess by talking at length until the nymphs could run away. When Juno realized the truth, she exclaimed: "The power of that tongue of yours, by which I have been tricked, will be limited; and most brief will be the use of your voice." She made good her threats; Echo only gives back the words she has heard and repeats the final phrases of utterances.

And so she saw Narcissus wandering through the secluded countryside and burned with passion; she followed his footsteps furtively, and the closer she pursued him, the nearer was the fire that consumed her, just like the tops of torches, smeared with sulphur, that catch fire and blaze up when a flame is brought near. O how often she wanted to approach him with blandishments and tender appeals! Her very nature made this impossible, for she was not allowed to speak first. But she was prepared to wait for his utterances and to echo them with her own words—this she could do.

By chance the boy became separated from his faithful band of companions and he cried out: "Is there anyone there?" Echo replied "There!" He was dumbfounded and glanced about in all directions; then he shouted at full voice: "Come!" She called back to him with the same word. He looked around but saw no one approaching; "Why do you run away from me?" he asked. She echoed his words just as he spoke them. He was persistent, beguiled by the reflection of the other's voice, and exclaimed: "Come here and let us get together!" Echo replied, "Let us get together," and never would she answer any other sound more willingly. She emerged from the woods, making good her very words and rushed to throw her arms about the neck of her beloved. But he fled and in his flight exclaimed, "Take your hands off me; I would die before I let you possess me." She replied with only the last words "Possess me."

Thus spurned, Echo hid herself in the woods where the trees hid her blushes; and from that time on she has lived in solitary caves. Nevertheless, her love clung fast and grew with the pain of rejection. Wakeful cares wasted away her wretched body, her skin became emaciated, and the bloom and vigor of her whole being slipped away on the air. Her voice and her bones were all that was left. Then only her voice remained; her bones, they say, were turned into stone. From that time on, she has remained hidden in the woods; she is never seen on the mountains, but she is heard by everyone. The sound of her echo is all of her that still lives.

Narcissus had played with her so, just as he had previously rejected other nymphs sprung from the waves or the mountains, and as well males who had approached him. Thereupon one of those scorned raised up his hands to the heavens and cried: "So may he himself fall in love, so may he not be able to possess his beloved!" The prayer was a just one, and Nemesis heard it.

There was a spring, its clear waters glistening like silver, untouched by shepherds, mountain goats, and other animals, and undisturbed by birds, wild beasts, and falling tree branches. Grass grew round about, nourished by the water nearby, and the woods protected the spot from the heat of the sun. Here the boy lay down, tired out by the heat and his quest for game and attracted by the pool and the beauty of the place. While he was trying to quench his thirst, it kept coming back again and again, and as he continued to drink, he was captivated by the reflection of the beauty that he saw.

He fell in love with a hope insubstantial, believing what was only an image to be real and corporeal. He gazed in wonder at himself, clinging transfixed and emotionless to what he saw, just like a statue formed from Parian marble. From his position on the ground he looked at his eyes, twin stars, and his hair, worthy of both Bacchus and Apollo, and his smooth cheeks, his ivory neck, and the beauty of his face, a flush of red amid snowy whiteness. He marveled at all the things that others had marveled at in him. Unwise and unheeding, he desired his very self, one and the same person approving and being approved, seeking and being sought, inflaming and being inflamed. How many times he bestowed vain kisses on the deceptive pool! How many times he plunged his arms into the midst of the waters to grasp the neck that he saw! But he could not catch hold of himself in their embrace. He did not understand what he was looking at, but was inflamed by what he saw, and the same illusion that deceived his eyes aroused his passion.

Poor deluded boy, why do you grasp at your fleeting reflection to no avail? What you seek is not real; just turn away and you will lose what you love. What you perceive is but the reflection of your own image; it has no substance of its own. With you it comes and stays, and with you it will go, if you can bear to go. No concern for food or rest could drag him away from his post, but stretched out on the shady grass he looks at this deceptive beauty with insatiable gaze and destroys himself through his own eyes. He raised himself up a little and stretching out his arms to the surrounding woods exclaimed:

"Has there ever been anyone smitten by more cruel a love? Tell me, O trees, for you know since you have provided opportune haunts for countless lovers. In the length of your years, in the many ages you have lived, can you remember anyone who has wasted away like me? I behold my beloved, but what I see and love I cannot have; such is the frustration of my unrequited passion. And I am all the more wretched because it is not a vast sea or lengthy road or impregnable fortress that separates us. Only a little water keeps us from each other. My beloved desires to be held, for each time that I bend down to kiss the limpid waters, he in return strains upward with his eager lips. You would think that he could be touched; it is such a little thing that prevents the consummation of our love. Whoever you are, come out to me here. Why, incomparable boy, do you deceive me? When I pursue you, where do you go? Certainly you do not flee from my youthful beauty, for nymphs loved me too. You promise me some kind of hope by your sympathetic looks of friendship. When I stretch forth my arms to you, you do the same in return. When I laugh, you laugh back, and I have often noted your tears in response to my weeping. And as well you return my every gesture and nod; and, as far as I can surmise from movements of your lovely mouth, you answer me with words that never reach my ears. I am you! I realize it; my reflection does not deceive me; I burn with love for myself, I am the one who fans the flame and bears the torture. What am I to do? Should I be the one to be asked or to ask? What then shall I ask for? What I desire is with me; all that I have makes me poor. O how I wish that I could escape from my body! A strange prayer for one in love, to wish away what he loves! And now grief consumes my strength; the time remaining for me is short, and my life will be snuffed out in its prime. Death does not weigh heavily upon me, for death will bring an end to my misery. I only wish that he whom I cherish could live a longer time. As it is, we two who are one in life shall die together!''

He finished speaking and, sick with longing, turned back again to his own reflection. His tears disturbed the waters and caused the image in the pool to grow less distinct. When he saw it disappearing he screamed: "Where are you going? Stay here, do not desert me, your lover. I cannot touch you—let me look at you, give me this nourishment at least in my misery and madness." As he grieved, he tore his garment in its upper part and beat his bare chest with his marble-white hands. And his chest when struck took on a rosy tinge, as apples usually have their whiteness streaked with red, or grapes in various clusters when not yet ripe are stained with purple. As soon as he beheld himself thus in the water that was once again calm, he could endure it no further; but, as yellow wax is wont to melt under the touch of fire and the gentle frost under the warmth of the sun, so he was weakened and destroyed by love, gradually being consumed in its hidden flame. His beautiful complexion, white touched with red, no longer remained nor his youthful strength, nor all that he had formerly looked upon with such pleasure. Not even his body, which Echo had once loved, was left.

When Echo saw what he had become, she felt sorry, even though she had been angry and resentful. Each time that the poor boy exclaimed "Alas," she repeated in return an echoing "Alas." And as he struck his shoulders with his hands, she gave back too the same sounds of his grief. This was his last cry as he gazed into the familiar waters: "Alas for the boy I cherished in vain!" The place repeated these very same words. And when he said "Farewell," Echo repeated "Farewell" too. He relaxed his weary head on the green grass; night closed those eyes that had so admired the beauty of their owner. Then too, after he had been received in the home of the dead below, he gazed at himself in the waters of the Styx. His sister Naiads wept and cut off their hair and offered it to their brother; the Dryads wept, and Echo sounded their laments.

> Now the pyre and streaming torches and the bier were being
> prepared, but the corpse was nowhere to be seen. They found
> instead a yellow flower with a circle of white petals in its center.

This tragic story of self-love and self-destruction has cast a particularly potent spell upon subsequent literature and thought. Narcissism is, as we all know, an important psychological concept; yet how typical of classical poetry is Ovid's insight: it is in answer to a male lover's prayer that Narcissus suffers, and thus the essentially homosexual nature of narcissistic love is illuminated.[24]

DEMETER AND THE ELEUSINIAN MYSTERIES

The Myth of Demeter and Persephone

There are two *Homeric Hymns to Demeter*. Number 13 is a very short prelude.

I begin to sing about the holy goddess Demeter of the beautiful hair, about her and her very lovely daughter Persephone. Hail, goddess; preserve this city and lead my song.

The lengthy and powerful *Homeric Hymn to Demeter* (2), by contrast, is of the utmost importance; it begins with Hades' abduction of Persephone at the will of Zeus:

I begin to sing about the holy goddess, Demeter of the beautiful hair, about her and her daughter, Persephone of the lovely ankles, whom Hades snatched away; loud-thundering Zeus, who sees all, gave her to him.

Alone, away from Demeter of the golden scepter and goodly crops, Persephone was playing with the deep-bosomed daughters of Oceanus and picking flowers along a soft meadow: beautiful roses, crocuses, violets, irises, and hyacinths; and Earth at the will of Zeus to please Hades, the host of many, produced as a snare for the fair maiden a wonderful and radiant narcissus, an awesome sight to all, both immortal gods and mortal humans. From its stem a hundred blossoms sprouted forth, and their odor was most sweet. All wide heaven above, the whole earth below, and the swell of the salt sea laughed. The girl was astounded and reached out with both her hands together to pluck the beautiful delight.

Demeter. Marble, second half of the fourth century B.C.; height 58 in. This is the cult-statue from the sanctuary of Demeter at Cnidus in Asia Minor. She is shown seated and heavily draped. Her solemn gaze and matronly clothing are consistent with the Demeter of the *Homeric Hymn to Demeter.* (*British Museum, London. Reproduced by permission of the Trustees.*)

And the wide-pathed Earth yawned in the Nysaean plain, and the lord and host of many, who goes by many names, the son of Cronus, rushed at her with his immortal horses. And he snatched her up in his golden chariot and carried her away in tears.

She shouted with shrill cries and called on father Zeus, the son of Cronus, the highest and the best, but no one of the immortals or of mortals—not even the olive trees laden with their fruit—heard her voice except for the daughter of Persaeus [Perses], Hecate, her hair brightly adorned, who listened from her cave as she thought kindly thoughts, and lord Helius, the splendid son of Hyperion. These two heard the maid call on the son of Cronus, father Zeus; but he sat apart, away from the gods, in his temple with its many suppliants, receiving beautiful holy offerings from mortals. By the counsel of Zeus, his brother and her uncle Hades, the son of Cronus, who bears many names, the lord and host of many, led her off with his immortal horses against her will.

As long as the goddess could behold the earth, starry heaven, the deep flowing sea full of fish, the rays of the sun, and still hoped to see her dear mother and the race of everlasting gods, hope soothed her great heart, although she was distressed. But the peaks of the mountains and the depths of the sea echoed with her immortal voice, and her lady mother heard her.

Demeter's Grief, Anger, and Retaliation

Sharp pain seized Demeter's heart, and she tore the headdress about her ambrosial hair with her own dear hands and threw off the dark covering from both her shoulders, and she rushed in pursuit, just like a bird, over land and water. But no one—either of gods or mortals—wished to tell what had really happened—not even a bird came to her as a messenger of truth. For nine days, then, lady Demeter roamed over the earth holding burning torches in her hands and in her grief did not eat any ambrosia or drink sweet nectar, nor did she bathe her body. But when dawn brought on the light of the tenth day, Hecate, a torch in hand, met her and gave her some news as she exclaimed: "Lady Demeter, bringer of goodly gifts in season, who of the heavenly gods or mortals carried off Persephone and troubled your dear heart? For I heard her voice but did not see with my eyes who it was. I am telling you the whole truth quickly."

Thus Hecate spoke, and the daughter of Rhea of the beautiful hair did not answer but swiftly rushed away with her, holding burning torches in her hands. They came to Helius, the lookout for both gods and human beings, and stood before his horses, and the goddess of goddesses spoke: "Helius, do at least have respect for me, a goddess, if I have ever by word or by deed gladdened your heart and your spirits. Through the barren air I heard the piercing cry of the girl whom I bore, a sweet daughter, illustrious in her beauty, as though she were being violated; yet I saw nothing with my eyes. But since you look down from the divine aether with your rays on all the earth and sea, tell me truthfully if you have seen my dear child at all and who, either of gods or mortals, has seized her alone, away from me, by force against her will and made away."

Thus she spoke. And the son of Hyperion answered her: "Demeter, regal daughter of Rhea of the beautiful hair, you will know the truth. For indeed I revere you greatly and I pity you in your grief for your daughter of the lovely ankles. No other of the immortals is to blame except the cloud-gatherer Zeus, who gave her to his own brother Hades to be called his lovely wife. And he seized her and with his horses carried her away to the gloomy depths below as she cried aloud. But, O goddess, desist from your great lament; you should not thus bear an unrelenting anger to no avail. Indeed Hades, the ruler over many, is not an unseemly husband for your daughter; he is your own brother and born from the same blood; and as for honor, when at the first power was divided three ways, his lot was to be made lord of all those with whom he dwelt."

Thus he spoke and called out to his horses. And at his cry they nimbly bore the swift chariot, just like long-winged birds. But a more dread and terrible grief possessed Demeter's heart, and thereafter she was angry with the son of Cronus, Zeus, enwrapped in clouds; she kept away from the gatherings of the gods and high Olympus; and for a long time she went among the cities and rich fields of human beings, disguising her beautiful form.

Demeter Comes to Eleusis and the Palace of Celeus

No one of men or deep-bosomed women who saw her recognized her until she came to the home of wise Celeus, who at that time was ruler of fragrant Eleusis. Grieving in her dear heart, she sat near the road by the Maiden Well, from which the people drew their water; she was in the shade, for an olive tree grew overhead. Her appearance resembled that of a very old woman long past her days for childbearing and the gifts of garland-loving Aphrodite; she was like the nurses for the children of law-pronouncing kings or the housekeepers in their echoing halls.

The daughters of Celeus, of the family of Eleusis, saw her there as they came after the easily drawn water so that they might bring it in their bronze pitchers to the dear home of their father. There were four of them, just like goddesses in their youthful bloom, Callidice and Cleisidice and lovely Demo and Callithoë, who was the oldest of them all. They did not know Demeter, for it is difficult for mortals to recognize the gods; and standing near they spoke winged words: "Who are you, old woman, of those born long ago? Where are you from? Why have you come away from the city and not approached the houses there, in whose shadowy halls dwell women just like you and younger, who would welcome you in word as well as in deed?"

Thus they spoke. And she, the queenly goddess, answered with these words: "Dear children, whoever you are of women, I bid you greeting, and I shall tell you my tale. To be sure it is not inappropriate to relate the truth to you who have asked. My name is Doso, for my lady mother gave it to me. Now then I have come from Crete over the broad back of the sea—not willingly but against my wishes, for by force pirates carried me away. Then they put in at Thoricus, where the women and the men together disembarked; they were busy with their meal beside the cables of the ship, but my heart had no desire for the delicious food. I hastened away over the black land and escaped from my overbearing masters so that they might not sell me, whom they had not bought, and reap a profit from me. And so I have come here after my wanderings, and I have no idea at all what land this is or who inhabit it. But may all those who dwell in homes on Olympus grant that you have husbands and bear children just as parents desire. But you maidens pity me now and show concern until, dear children, I come to the home of a man and woman to perform for them zealously the tasks appropriate for an elderly woman like me; I could hold a newborn child in my arms and care for him well, make my master's bed in the recess of his well-built chambers, and teach the women their tasks."

Thus spoke the goddess, and at once the virgin maiden Callidice, the most beautiful of the daughters of Celeus, answered: "Good woman, we mortals, even though we suffer, must bear what the gods bestow, for indeed they are much the stronger. I shall help you with the following advice, and I shall tell you the names of the men who have great honor and power here and who are foremost among the people and guard the battlements of our city by their counsels and firm judgments. There is clever Triptolemus and Dioclus and Polyxeinus and noble Eumolpus and Dolichus and our own brave father. All of these have wives who take care of their homes, and no one of them at the very first sight of your person would dishonor you or turn you out of his house, but they will welcome you, for to be sure you are like one of the gods. But if you wish, stay here, so that we may go to our father's house and tell our mother, the deep-bosomed Metaneira, the whole story in the hope that she will bid you come to our place and not search for the homes of the others. She cherishes in our well-built house an only son, born late, a darling long prayed for. If you were to bring him up and he attained the measure of his youth, you would easily be the envy of any woman who saw you. Such are the great rewards that would be yours for your care."

Thus she spoke, and Demeter nodded her head in agreement. And the girls filled their shining pitchers with water and carried them away happy. Quickly they came to the great house of their father and told their mother at once what they had seen and heard. She enjoined them to go with all speed and to hire the woman at any price. Just as deer or heifers bound along the meadow when in the springtime they have had their fill of pasture, thus they hurried along the hollow wagon path, holding up the folds of their lovely garments, and their hair, which was like the flower of the crocus, danced about their shoulders. And they found the illustrious goddess where they had left her earlier and thereupon led her to the dear house of their father; she followed behind with her head veiled, distressed at heart, and the dark robe grazed the slender feet of the goddess.

Soon they arrived at the house of Celeus, a man cherished by Zeus, and passed through the vestibule to where their lady mother sat by the pillar that supported the sturdy roof, holding her son, just a baby, in her lap. Her daughters ran to her, but the goddess stood at the threshold; her head reached up to the beams and she filled the doorway with a divine radiance. Then awe and reverence and fear seized Metaneira, and she sprang up from her couch and bade her guest be seated, but Demeter, the giver of goodly gifts in season, did not wish to sit on the splendid couch but waited in silence with her beautiful eyes downcast, until [the servant] Iambe in her wisdom set out for her a chair, artfully made, and threw a silvery fleece over it; then Demeter sat down, holding her veil over her face with her hands.

For a long time she remained seated without a sound, grieving; she did not by word or action acknowledge anyone; but without a smile, not touching food or drink, she sat wasted with longing for her deep-bosomed daughter, until Iambe in her wisdom resorted to many jests and jokes and brought the holy lady around to smile and laugh and bear a happy heart (thereafter too Iambe was to cheer her in her anguish). And Metaneira filled a cup with wine as sweet as honey and offered it, but she refused saying that it was not right for her to drink red wine. But she ordered them to mix meal and water with tender mint and give it to her to drink. Metaneira mixed the potion and gave it to the goddess as she had ordered. And the great lady Demeter took it for the sake of the holy rite.[1]

Demeter Nurses Demophoön

Beautifully robed Metaneira was the first to speak among them: "Greetings, O lady, I expect that you are not born of base parents but of noble ones. Majesty and grace shine clearly in your eyes as though from the eyes of royalty who mete out justice. But we mortals, even though we suffer, must bear what the gods bestow, for the yoke lies on our necks. Yet now since you have come here, as much as I have will be yours. Nurse this child, whom the immortals gave me late in life, fulfilling my desperate hopes and endless prayers. If you were to bring him up and he attained the measure of his youth, you would easily be the envy of any woman who saw you. Such are the great rewards that would be yours for your care." Then Demeter of the beautiful crown replied to her: "Sincere greetings to you, also, O lady, and may the gods afford you only good. I shall take the boy gladly, as you bid, and tend to him, and I have good hopes that he will not be harmed or destroyed by any evil charms, for I know much more potent remedies and effective antidotes for harmful spells."

Thus she spoke, and with her immortal hands she took the child to her fragrant bosom. And his mother rejoiced in her heart. Thus she nursed in the house the splendid son of wise Celeus, Demophoön, whom beautifully robed Metaneira bore. And he grew like a god, not nourished on mortal food but anointed by Demeter with ambrosia, just as though sprung from the gods, and she breathed sweetness upon him as she held him to her bosom. At night she would hide him in the might of the fire, like a brand, without the knowledge of his dear parents. It was a source of great wonder to them that he grew and flourished before his time, for he was like the gods to look upon. And she would have made him immortal and never to grow old if beautifully robed Metaneira in her foolishness had not seen what was happening, as she watched in the night from her fragrant chamber. Great was her dismay, and she gave a shriek and struck both her thighs, terrified for her child. Amid her groans she uttered winged words: "Demophoön, my child, this stranger buries you within the blazing fire to my anguish and grievous pain."

Thus she spoke in agony, and the goddess of goddesses, Demeter of the beautiful crown, grew angry as she listened; with her immortal hands she snatched from the fire the dear son whom Metaneira had borne in her house, blessing beyond hope, and threw him down on the floor. Demeter was dreadfully angry in her heart as she spoke to beautifully robed Metaneira: "Mortals are ignorant and stupid who cannot foresee the fate both good and bad that is in store. Thus you in your foolishness have done a thing that cannot be remedied. I call to witness by the relentless waters of the river Styx, the oath of the gods, that I would have made your dear child immortal and never to grow old all his days, and I would have granted him imperishable honor; but now, as it is, he will not be able to escape death and the Fates. Yet imperishable honor will always be his because he has lain on my knees and slept in my arms. But when the years go by and he has reached his prime, the new generation of Eleusinians will continually engage in dread wars and battles all their days. I am Demeter, esteemed and honored as the greatest benefit and joy to mortals and immortals. Now then, let all the people build to me a great temple and an altar with it, below the town and its steep wall, on the rising hill above the well, Kallichoron. And I myself shall teach my rites, so that performing them with reverence you may propitiate my heart.''

Thus the goddess spoke and cast aside her old age, transforming her size and appearance. Beauty breathed around and about her, and a delicious odor was wafted from her fragrant garments. The radiance from the immortal person of the goddess shone far and wide, and her golden hair flowed down on her shoulders. The sturdy house was filled with her brilliance as though with a lightning flash. She disappeared from the room, and at once Metaneira's knees gave way; for a long time she was speechless and did not even remember at all to pick up her late-born son from the floor. But his sisters heard his pitiful cries and sprang down from their beds, spread well with covers; one of them then picked up the child in her arms and took him to her bosom, another stirred the fire, and a third hastened on her delicate feet to rouse their mother from her fragrant chamber. They gathered around the frantic child and bathed him with loving care. But his spirits were not soothed, for the nurses who tended him now were indeed inferior.

The whole night long, trembling with fear, they made their supplication to the illustrious goddess, and as soon as dawn appeared they told the truth to Celeus, whose power was great, just as Demeter the goddess of the beautiful crown had commanded. Then Celeus called the many people to an assembly and bade them build a splendid temple to Demeter of the lovely hair and an altar on the rising hill. They listened to him as he spoke and immediately complied and did as they were told. And the child flourished by divine destiny.

Hades and Persephone and Her Eating of the Pomegranate

When they had finished and ceased from their labor, each made his way homeward. But golden Demeter remained sitting there quite apart from all the blessed gods, wasted with longing for her deep-bosomed daughter. And she caused human beings a most terrible and devastating year on the fruitful land. The earth would not send up a single sprout, for Demeter of the lovely crown kept the seed covered. In vain the oxen dragged the many curved ploughs through the fields, and much white barley was sown in the earth to no avail. Now she would have destroyed the entire human race by cruel famine and deprived those who have their homes on Olympus of their glorious prestige from their gifts and sacrifices, if Zeus had not noticed and taken thought in his heart. First he roused golden-winged Iris to summon Demeter of the lovely hair, desirable in her beauty.

Thus he ordered. And Iris obeyed Zeus, the dark-clouded son of Cronus, and on swift feet traversed the interval between. She came to the citadel of fragrant Eleusis and found dark-robed Demeter in her temple. She spoke to her, uttering winged words: "Demeter, father Zeus, whose knowledge is imperishable, commands you to join the company of the eternal gods. Come now, let not the word I bring from Zeus be unaccomplished."

Thus she spoke in supplication, but Demeter's heart was unswayed. Thereupon father Zeus sent down to her all the blessed gods who exist forever; and they came one by one, calling out her name and offering her many very beautiful gifts and whatever honors she would like to choose for herself among the immortals. But no one was able to sway her mind and her heart from her anger, and she stubbornly rejected all appeals. She maintained that she would never set foot on fragrant Olympus or allow fruit to sprout from the earth until she saw with her own eyes her lovely daughter.

Then loud-thundering Zeus, who sees all, sent the slayer of Argus, Hermes, with his golden wand to Erebus to appeal to Hades with gentle words and bring chaste Persephone up from the murky depths to the light, so that her mother might desist from anger when she saw her daughter with her own eyes. Hermes did not disobey, and straightway he left the realms of Olympus and swiftly rushed down to the depths of the earth. He encountered the lord Hades within his house, sitting on a couch with his modest wife, who was very reluctant because of her longing for her mother. And Demeter far away brooded over her designs to thwart the actions of the blessed gods.

The mighty slayer of Argus stood near and said: "Hades of the dark hair, ruler of the dead, father Zeus has ordered me to bring to him from Erebus august Persephone, so that her mother may see her with her own eyes and desist from her wrath and dread anger against the immortals. For she is devising a great scheme to destroy the feeble tribes of earthborn men by keeping the seed hidden under earth and ruining the honors that are bestowed on the immortals. She clings to her dire wrath and does not associate with the gods but remains on the rocky citadel of Eleusis sitting apart within her fragrant temple."

Hades and Persephone. Terra-cotta plaque, ca. 460 B.C.; height 10¼ in. This is one of a series of small votive reliefs from the sanctuary of Persephone at Locri (in southern Italy). The divinities of the Underworld sit enthroned holding emblems connected with their worship—grain, parsley, a cock, a bowl. In front stands a lamp with a tiny cock on it, and another cock stands beneath Persephone's throne. *(Museo Nazionale, Reggio. Photograph courtesy of Hirmer Verlag; München.)*

Thus he spoke. And Hades, the lord of those below, smiled with furrowed brows and did not disobey the commands of Zeus the king; and he hastily ordered wise Persephone: "Go, Persephone, to the side of your dark-robed mother, with a gentle and loving heart in your breast. Be not distraught. I among the immortals shall not be an unworthy husband for you, since I am the full brother of your father, Zeus. While you are here with me you will rule over all that lives and moves and you will hold the greatest honors among the immortals. Those who wrong you and do not propitiate your power by performing holy rites and sacrifices and offering appropriate gifts will find eternal retribution.''

Thus he spoke. And wise Persephone was delighted and jumped up quickly in her joy. But her husband secretly gave her the honey-sweet fruit of the pomegranate to eat, taking thought for himself that she should not remain all her days above with august, dark-robed Demeter. Hades, host of many, then yoked his immortal horses to the front of his golden chariot, which Persephone mounted; the mighty slayer of Argus, Hermes, took the reins and whip in his hands and drove them up and away from the palace; the pair of horses readily sped along and easily covered their long journey. Neither the sea nor streams of rivers nor grassy glens nor mountaintops impeded the onrush of the immortal horses as they cut through the deep air above them in their course. The charioteer brought them to a halt in front of the fragrant temple where Demeter of the lovely crown waited.

Demeter's Ecstatic Reunion with Persephone

At the sight of her daughter, she rushed out like a maenad down a mountain thick with woods. When Persephone on the other side saw the beautiful eyes of her mother, she leaped down from the chariot with its horses and ran, throwing her arms about her neck in an embrace. But while Demeter still had her dear child in her arms, suddenly her heart sensed some treachery; trembling with dread she let go her loving embrace and asked quickly: ''My child, have you eaten any food while you were below? Speak up, do not hide anything so that we both may know. If you have not, even though you have been in the company of loathsome Hades, you will live with me and your father, Zeus the cloud-gatherer, son of Cronus, in honor among all the immortals. But if you have eaten anything, you will return again beneath the depths of the earth and live there a third part of each year; the other two-thirds of the time you will spend with me and the other immortals. When the spring blooms with all sorts of sweet-smelling flowers, then again you will rise from the gloomy region below, a great wonder for gods and mortals. But tell me, too, by what trick the strong host of many deceived you?''

The very beautiful Persephone then said in answer: ''To be sure, mother, I shall tell you the whole truth. When Hermes, the bringer of luck and swift messenger, came from my father, the son of Cronus, and the other gods of the sky, saying that I was to come up from Erebus in order that you might see me with your own eyes and desist from your wrath and dread anger against the immortals, I immediately jumped up in my joy. But Hades swiftly put in my mouth the fruit of the pomegranate, a honey-sweet morsel, and compelled me to eat it by force against my will. I shall tell you too how he came and carried me down to the depths of the earth through the shrewd plan of my father, the son of Cronus, going through it all as you ask.

"We were all playing in a lovely meadow: Leucippe, Phaeno, Electra, Ianthe, Melite, Iache, Rhodeia, Callirhoë, Melobosis, Tyche, Ocyrhoë beautiful as a flower, Chryseïs, Ianeira, Acaste, Admete, Rhodope, Pluto, lovely Calypso, Styx and Urania, charming Galaxaura,[2] and Pallas the battle-rouser and Artemis delighting in arrows.

"We were playing and gathering lovely flowers in our hands, a mixed array of soft crocuses, irises, hyacinths, roses in full bloom, and lilies, wonderful to behold, and a narcissus, which the wide earth produced, in color yellow of a crocus. I plucked it joyously, but the earth beneath opened wide and thereupon the mighty lord, the host of many, leaped up and carried me away in his golden chariot beneath the earth despite my violent protests—my cries were loud and shrill. I tell you the whole truth, although the story gives me pain."

Thus they then in mutual love and tender embraces greatly cheered each other's heart and soul the whole long day. Their grief was assuaged as they exchanged their joys. Hecate, her hair brilliantly arrayed, approached them and frequently embraced the holy daughter of Demeter. From that time on, regal Hecate became the lady and attendant of Persephone.

Demeter Restores Fertility and Establishes the Mysteries

Loud-thundering Zeus, who sees far and wide, sent as a messenger to them Rhea of the lovely hair to lead dark-robed Demeter among the company of the gods, and he promised to grant her the honors that she would choose among the immortal gods, and he consented that her daughter live a third part of the revolving year in the gloomy depths below and the other two-thirds by the side of her mother and the other immortals. Thus he ordered, and the goddess Rhea did not disobey the message of Zeus. She quickly rushed down from the heights of Olympus and came to the Rharian plain, previously very fertile, but now not fertile at all, standing leafless and barren. The white seed was hidden through the machinations of Demeter of the lovely ankles. But soon thereafter, with the burgeoning of spring, long ears of grain would be luxuriant and the rich furrows too along the ground would be laden with grain, some already bound in sheaves.

Rhea came from the barren air to this place first of all, and the goddesses beheld each other gladly and rejoiced in their hearts. Rhea, her hair brilliantly arrayed, spoke to Demeter thus: "Come here, my daughter; loud-thundering Zeus, who sees far and wide, summons you to join the company of the gods, and he has promised to grant you whatever honors you would like among the immortals, and he has consented that your daughter live a third part of the revolving year in the gloomy depths below and the other two-thirds with you and the other gods. Thus he said it would be accomplished and nodded his head in assent. But come, my child, and be obedient; do not persist in your relentless anger against Zeus, the dark-clouded son of Cronus. But quickly make grow for human beings the life-bringing fruit in abundance."

Thus she spoke, and Demeter of the lovely crown obeyed. Quickly she caused fruit to spring up from the fertile plains, and the whole wide land was laden with leaves and flowers. She went to the kings who minister justice (Triptolemus, Diocles, the rider of horses, the mighty Eumolpus, and Celeus, the leader of the people) and showed them the performance of her holy rites and taught her mysteries to them all, Triptolemus and Polyxeinus and Diocles besides—holy mysteries that one may not by any means violate or question or express. For the great reverence due to the gods restrains one's voice.

Happy is the one of mortals on earth who has seen these things. But those who are uninitiated into the holy rites and have no part never are destined to a similar joy when they are dead in the gloomy realm below.

But when the goddess of goddesses had ordained all these things, they made their way to Olympus among the company of the other gods. There they dwell beside Zeus, who delights in the thunder, august and holy goddesses. Greatly happy is the one of mortals on earth whom they dearly love; straightway they send, as a guest to his great house, Plutus, who gives wealth to human beings.

Come now you who hold power over the land of fragrant Eleusis, sea-girt Paros, and rocky Antron, lady and queen Demeter, the giver of good things in season, both yourself and your daughter, very beautiful Persephone, kindly grant me a pleasing substance in reward for my song. Yet I shall remember both you and another song too.

Interpretations of the Hymn

The myth of Demeter and Persephone represents another variation of a fundamental and recurring theme—the death and rebirth of vegetation as a metaphor or allegory for spiritual resurrection. In the New Testament (John 13. 24), this archetype is expressed in this way: "Unless a grain of wheat falls into the earth and dies, it remains alone;

but if it dies it bears much fruit." In this Greek hymn, the allegory is rendered in terms of the touching emotions of mother and daughter; more often the symbols and metaphors involve the relationship between a fertility goddess (see Color Plate 19) and her male partner, either lover or son (e.g., Aphrodite and Adonis, Cybele and Attis, Semele and Dionysus). Demeter is often imagined as the goddess of the ripe grain; Persephone then is the deity of the budding tender shoots. They are invoked together as the "two goddesses." Persephone (who is often called merely *Kore*, a name meaning "girl") is the daughter of Demeter and Zeus, who enact once again the sacred marriage between earth-goddess and sky-god. This is a hymn permeated by religious and emotional allegories about death and rebirth, resurrection, and salvation. The nurturing of the infant Demophoön is a particularly revealing parable: those nourished, like this child, at the bosom of the divine mother Demeter will attain a glorious and happy immortality, their impure physical mortality cleansed away by the fire. The *Homeric Hymn to Demeter* also illustrates the grim character of Hades in his method of obtaining a wife and provides the mythological reasons for Hecate's prominence as a goddess of the Underworld. Hades' basic character as a fertility god is evident from the location of his realm, the violence of his nature, and his link with horses. He is thus a god of agricultural wealth (compare his names, Pluto or Dis, among the Romans); but he should not be confused with Plutus (Wealth) mentioned in the last lines of the hymn, another deity of agricultural plenty and prosperity (and thus wealth in general), the offspring of Demeter and Iasion.

Triptolemus

Triptolemus, who also appears in the concluding lines of the hymn, is generally depicted as the messenger of Demeter when she restored fertility to the ground. He is the one who taught and spread her arts of agriculture to new lands at that time and later, often traveling in a magical car drawn by winged dragons, a gift of Demeter. He is sometimes either merged in identity with the infant Demophoön (variant spelling is Demophon) of the hymn or said to be his brother; in Plato, Triptolemus is a judge of the dead.

The Eleusinian Mysteries

This hymn to Demeter is of major importance because it provides the most significant evidence that we have for the nature of the worship of Demeter at Eleusis. The town of Eleusis is about fourteen miles west of Athens; the religion and ceremony that developed in honor of Demeter and her daughter had its center here, but the city of Athens too was intimately involved. This religion was of a special kind, not the general prerogative of everyone but open only to those who wished to become initiates; these devotees were sworn to absolute secrecy and faced dire punishments if they revealed the secret rites.[3] This does not imply that initiation was confined to a select few. In early times, membership was inevitably limited to the people of Eleusis and Athens; but soon participants came from all areas of the Hellenic world, and eventually from the Roman Empire as well.

This religion was not restricted to men; women, children, and even slaves could participate. Appropriately, the religious celebration that evolved was given the name of the Eleusinian mysteries. Demeter, then, along with other Hellenic deities, is the inspiration for a kind of worship that is generally designated as the mystery religions (compare Dionysus and Apollo in the religion of Orpheus, or aspects of the devotion to Aphrodite and Adonis or Cybele and Attis). In fact, Orpheus himself is credited with originating the mysteries. Although there must have been differences among the various mystery religions (some of them probably quite marked) obvious to the ancient world, we have difficulty today in distinguishing precisely among them. It seems fairly certain that the major common denominator is a belief in the immortality of the soul and a future life.

The mysteries at Eleusis were kept secret so successfully that scholars are by no means agreed about what can be said with any certainty, particularly about the highest and most profound elements of the worship. The sanctuary at Eleusis has been excavated,[4] and buildings connected with the ceremonies have been found, most important among them being the temple of Demeter, where the final revelation of the mysteries was celebrated.[5] But no evidence has been unearthed that might dispel the secrecy with absolute certainty once and for all. The priests in charge of the rites presumably transmitted orally what Demeter was said to have taught.

It is impossible to know just how much of the ritual is revealed in the *Hymn to Demeter*. It would be presumptuous to imagine that the most profound secrets are here for all to read, and we cannot be sure how much may be inferred from what is directly stated. That elements of the ceremonies are indicated cannot be denied, but presumably these are only the elements that were witnessed or revealed to all, not only to the initiated. Thus we have prescribed by the text such details as an interval of nine days, fasting, the carrying of torches, the exchange of jests, the partaking of the drink *Kykeon,* the wearing of a special dress (e.g., the veil of Demeter); even precise geographical indications (e.g., the Maiden Well and the site of the temple) are designated.

The emotional tone of the poem, too, might set the key for a mystic performance in connection with the celebrations. The anguish of Demeter, her frantic wanderings and search, the traumatic episode with Demophoön, the miraculous transformation of the goddess, the thrilling reunion between mother and daughter, the blessed return of vegetation to a barren earth—these are some of the obvious emotional and dramatic highlights.

On the basis of our inadequate evidence, the following tentative outline of basic procedures in the celebration of the Eleusinian mysteries may be presented; ultimate revelation and meaning are matters of more tenuous conjecture. Two major compulsory stages had to be undertaken: (1) participation in the Lesser Mysteries, involving preliminary steps in initiation; (2) advancement to the Greater Mysteries, which entailed full initiation into the cult. A third stage, not required but possible, entailed participation in the highest rites.[6] It is immediately apparent that these mysteries are basically different from the festivals celebrated in the Panhellenic sanctuaries at Olympia and Delphi, which were open to all, without secrecy or initiation or a fundamental mystic philosophy, however religious the tone that oracular response and devotion to a god might set.

Two major priestly families were connected with Eleusis.[7] Among the many important priesthoods and assistant officials, the highest was that of the Hierophant; this priest alone could reveal to the worshipers the ultimate mysteries that entailed the showing of the *Hiera*, the sacred objects—his title means "he who reveals the *Hiera*." Prominent too was the priestess of Demeter, who lived in a sacred house. Many of the priests received a fixed sum of money from each initiate as a fee for their services. The initiate was sponsored and directed by a patron.[8]

The Lesser Mysteries were held in Athens, usually once a year in early spring. Precise details are unknown, but the general purpose was certainly the preliminary preparation of the initiates for subsequent advancement to higher things. Ceremonies probably focused upon ritual purification, involving sacrifices, prayer, fasting, and cleansing by water.

The Greater Mysteries were held annually during the months of September and October. A holy truce was declared for a period of fifty-five days, and heralds were sent to issue invitations to states. Both Athens and Eleusis were involved in the festivities. Preliminary to the festival proper was the day on which the *Hiera* were taken out of the temple of Demeter in Eleusis and brought to Athens amid great pomp and ceremony. The splendid procession, headed by the priests and priestesses who carried the *Hiera* in sacred caskets bound by ribbons, was met officially in Athens and escorted in state to the sanctuary of Demeter in the city (the Eleusinion).

The next day began the formal celebration of the Greater Mysteries, which continued through eight days, the ceremonies culminating in Eleusis, with a return to Athens on the ninth. The first day saw the people summoned to an assembly in the Athenian agora; those who were pure and knew Greek were invited by proclamation to participate in the mysteries. On the second day all participants were ordered to cleanse themselves in the sea. The following day (the third) was devoted to sacrifices and prayers. The fourth day was spent honoring the god of healing, Asclepius, who according to tradition had in previous times arrived late for initiation. So on this day other latecomers could enroll.

The festivities in Athens culminated on the fifth day in a brilliant procession back to Eleusis. Priests and laymen wended their prescribed way, crowned with myrtle and carrying mystic branches of myrtle tied with wool strands.[9] Heading the procession was a wooden statue of Iacchus (very likely another name for the god Dionysus) escorted in a carriage. At some stages of the journey, abuse, jest, insults, and scurrilous language were exchanged, perhaps in part to instill humility in the throng. Prayers were chanted and hymns sung; torches were carried and lit as night fell, and the sacred procession reached the sanctuary of Demeter in Eleusis.

The sixth and seventh days brought the initiates to the secret core of the mysteries, and it seems safe to assume that much of the ritual was performed in remembrance of the episodes described in the *Hymn to Demeter*. Thus there was a fast (certain foods, such as pomegranates and beans were prohibited) and a vigil; the fast was probably ended by the drinking of the prescribed drink, the *Kykeon,* whatever its significance.

The heart of the ceremonies, which were celebrated in Demeter's temple, apparently involved three stages: a dramatic enactment, the revelation of sacred objects, and the uttering of certain words. What were the themes of the dramatic pageant? Probably it focused upon incidents from the story of Demeter and her wanderings and other episodes recorded in the hymn, all designed to elicit a religious catharsis. Some have suggested scenes of an Orphic character involving a simulated trip to the Underworld, with fabricated apparitions of terror and sublimity as the action moved from Hell (Tartarus) to Paradise (Elysium). That no underground chambers have been found in the excavations does not necessarily invalidate this theory. We do not know whether the initiates merely witnessed the drama or actually participated in it. Eventually the culmination was the awesome exhibition by the Hierophant himself of the holy objects, bathed in a radiant light as he delivered his mystic utterances. The highest stage of all, which was not required for full initiation, entailed further revelation of some sort. The eighth day concluded the ceremonies; the ninth brought the return to Athens, this time with no organized procession. The following day the Athenian council heard a full report on the conduct of the ceremonies.

Conjectures about the exact nature of the highest mysteries have been legion. Comments by the Fathers of the Christian Church have been brought to witness, but their testimony has been rightly viewed with grave suspicion because it was probably rooted in prejudice, stemming from ignorance and hostility. No one of them had ever been initiated into the mysteries, and surprisingly enough, those Christian converts who had been initiated seem to have continued to take their pledges of secrecy very seriously. It has been claimed that the ultimate revelation was connected with the transformation of the Eleusinian plain into a field of golden grain (as in the hymn); the heart of the mysteries consisted of no more than showing an ear of grain to the worshipers. Thus we actually *do* know the secrets; or, if you like, they are really not worth knowing at all in terms of serious religious thought. Yet this ear of grain may, after all, realistically and allegorically represent the enigma of the mystery itself. Others insist upon an enactment of the holy marriage in connection with the ceremonies, imagining not a spiritual but a literal sexual union between the Hierophant and the Priestess of Demeter. The *Hiera* too might be the female pudenda; and, since Dionysus may be linked with Demeter and Kore, the male phallus as well. These holy objects were witnessed, or even manipulated, by the initiates in the course of the ritual. But there is no good evidence to argue with any certainty for such orgiastic procedures. The *Hiera,* as has been conjectured, could have been merely sacred and antique relics handed down from the Mycenaean Age.

It is difficult to agree with those who assert that Dionysus was completely excluded from the worship of Demeter at Eleusis. Iacchus has good claims to be Dionysus. And the myth of Zagreus-Dionysus, which provides the biblical authority for Orphism (see pp. 305–306), makes Persephone his mother. Any spiritual message in the cult at Eleusis must have, in common with Dionysiac cults, a belief in the immortality of the soul and in redemption. If a doctrine similar to that of Orphism is also involved, it need not spring directly from Orphism. The confusion arises because all the mystery religions (whatever their precise interrelation)[10] did in fact preach certain things in common.

The death and rebirth of vegetation as deified in Demeter and Kore surely suggest a belief in the afterlife. After all this is the promise of the hymn: "But the one who is not initiated into the holy rites and has no part never is destined to a similar joy when he is dead in the gloomy realm below." If at some future time, only obscure evidence remained for the ritual of the Christian mass, scholars might imagine all sorts of things and miss completely the religious and spiritual doctrine upon which it rests. The words uttered by the Hierophant could have ordained spiritual direction and hope. But there was no church body as such for the followers of Demeter, in the sense that they were required to return each year; we know of no sacred writings like those, say, of Orphism. George Mylonas's conclusions after years of study and thought are worthy of the deepest respect:

> *Whatever the substance and meaning of the Mysteries was, the fact remains that the cult of Eleusis satisfied the most sincere yearnings and the deepest longings of the human heart. The initiates returned from their pilgrimage to Eleusis full of joy and happiness, with the fear of death diminished and the strengthened hope of a better life in the world of shadows: "Thrice happy are those of mortals, who having seen those rites depart for Hades; for to them alone is it granted to have true life there; to the rest all there is evil," Sophocles cries out exultantly. And to this Pindar with equal exultation answers: "Happy is he who, having seen these rites goes below the hollow earth; for he knows the end of life and he knows its god-sent beginning." When we read these and other similar statements written by the great or nearly great of the ancient world, by the dramatists and the thinkers, when we picture the magnificent buildings and monuments constructed at Eleusis by great political figures like Peisistratos, Kimon, Perikles, Hadrian, Marcus Aurelius and others, we cannot help but believe that the Mysteries of Eleusis were not an empty, childish affair devised by shrewd priests to fool the peasant and the ignorant, but a philosophy of life that possessed substance and meaning and imparted a modicum of truth to the yearning human soul. That belief is strengthened when we read in Cicero that Athens has given nothing to the world more excellent or divine than the Eleusinian Mysteries. Let us recall again that the rites of Eleusis were held for some two thousand years; that for two thousand years civilized humanity was sustained and ennobled by those rites. Then we shall be able to appreciate the meaning and importance of Eleusis and of the cult of Demeter in the pre-Christian era. When Christianity conquered the Mediterranean world, the rites of Demeter, having perhaps fulfilled their mission*

to humanity, came to an end. The "bubbling spring" of hope and inspiration that once existed by the Kallichoron well became dry and the world turned to other living sources for sustenance. The cult that inspired the world for so long was gradually forgotten, and its secrets were buried with its last Hierophant.[11]

Finally, a word of caution about the usual generalizations put forth concerning the dichotomy between the mystery religions and the state religions of antiquity. The argument runs something like this. The formal state religions were sterile or very soon became so; people's hope and faith lay only in the vivid experience offered by the mysteries. Whatever the general truth of this view, it must be noted that for classical Greece, at any rate, the lines are not so distinct. Ceremonies connected with Demeter at Eleusis are tied securely to the policies of the Athenian state. The *archon basileus* (an Athenian official in charge of religious matters in general) directed the celebrations for Demeter in Athens. The Athenian council as a political body was very much concerned about the festival. The pomp and procession involved are startlingly similar to the pageant connected with the Panathenaic festival in honor of Athena, a civic function, whatever its spiritual import. The ''church'' at Eleusis and the Athenian state were, to all intents and purposes, one.[12]

VIEWS OF THE AFTERLIFE: THE REALM OF HADES

13

Homer's Book of the Dead

The earliest surviving account of the realm of Hades appears in Book 11 of the *Odyssey*. Homer's geographical and spiritual depiction is fundamental to subsequent elaborations and thus deserves to be excerpted at some length. Odysseus is telling the Phaeacians and their king Alcinoüs of his visit to the Underworld where he must consult the seer Tiresias about how to reach Ithaca, his homeland (12–99):

> Our ship came to the farthest realm of deep-flowing Oceanus, where the country of the Cimmerians lies shrouded in cloud and mist. Bright Helius never looks down on them with his rays, either when he ascends to starry heaven or returns to earth; but dire night covers these poor mortals. Here we beached our ship, and after putting the animals ashore, we went along the stream of Oceanus until we came to the place that Circe had indicated. Here two of my men, Perimedes and Eurylochus, held the sacrificial victims, and I drew my sharp sword from my side and dug a pit about eighteen inches square. Around it I poured a libation to all the dead, first with a mixture of honey and milk, then with sweet wine, and a third time with water; over this I sprinkled white barley. I then supplicated the many strengthless spirits of the dead, promising that once I had come to Ithaca I should sacrifice, in my own halls, a barren heifer, the very best I had, and heap the sacrificial pyre with the finest things and offer separately to Tiresias alone a jet-black sheep that was outstanding among my flocks.[1]
>
> When I had finished entreating the host of the dead with prayers and supplications, I seized the victims and cut their throats, and

their dark blood flowed into the pit. Then the souls of the dead who had departed swarmed up from Erebus:[2] young brides, unmarried boys, old men having suffered much, tender maidens whose hearts were new to sorrow, and many men wounded by bronze-tipped spears and wearing armor stained with blood. From one side and another they gathered about the pit in a multitude with frightening cries. Pale fear took hold of me, and then I urgently ordered my companions to flay the animals which lay slaughtered by the pitiless bronze and burn them and pray to the gods, to mighty Hades and dread Persephone. But I myself drew my sword from my side and took my post and did not allow the strengthless spirits of the dead to come near the blood before I had questioned Tiresias.

But first the soul of my comrade Elpenor came up. For he had not yet been buried in the wide earth.[3] We had left his body in Circe's palace, unwept and unburied, since other toil had oppressed us. I wept at seeing him and pitied him and calling out addressed him with winged words: "Elpenor, how have you come in this gloomy realm? You arrived on foot sooner than I in my black ship."

Thus I spoke; and he replied with a groan: "Royal son of Laertes, clever Odysseus, a divine and evil destiny and too much wine were my undoing. When I went to sleep in Circe's palace, I forgot to climb down the long ladder and fell headlong from the roof; my neck was severed from my spine and my soul came down to the realm of Hades.[4] Since I know that when you leave this house of Hades you will stop with your fine ship at Circe's island of Aeaea, I beseech you by those whom you left behind far away, by your wife and father who took care of you as a child, and by Telemachus, your only son whom you left at home in your palace, do not turn away and go back leaving me unwept and unburied for future time, or I may become the cause of wrathful vengeance from the gods upon you. But burn my body with all the armor that I have and pile up a mound for me on the shore of the gray sea, the grave of an unfortunate man, so that posterity too may know. Do these things for me and plant on the mound the oar with which I rowed alongside my companions while I was alive."

Thus he spoke. And I addressed him in answer: "My poor friend, I shall accomplish to the full all your wishes." So we two faced each other in sad conversation, I holding my sword over the blood and on the other side the shade of my companion recounting many things. The soul of my dead mother came up next, daughter of great-hearted Autolycus, she who was alive when I went to sacred Ilium. I cried when I saw her and pitied her in my heart. Still even though I was deeply moved I did not allow her to come near the blood before I had questioned Tiresias.

Then the soul of Theban Tiresias came up, bearing a golden scepter. He knew me and spoke: "Royal son of Laertes, clever Odysseus, why, why, my poor fellow, have you left the light of the sun and come to see the dead and their joyless land? But step back from the pit, and hold aside your sharp sword so that I may drink the blood and speak the truth to you." So he spoke; and I drew back my silver-studded sword and thrust it into its sheath. After he had drunk the dark blood, then the noble seer spoke to me.[5]

Tiresias then tells Odysseus what destiny has in store for him; after the seer has prophesied, Odysseus asks how he can enable his mother, Anticlea, to recognize him (141–159):

"I see there the soul of my dead mother, and she stays near the blood in silence and has not dared to look at her own son face to face nor speak to him. Tell me, O prince, how may she recognize that I am her son?" Thus I spoke. And he addressed me at once with the answer: "I shall tell you simple directions which you must follow. Any one of the dead you allow to come near the blood will speak to you clearly, but anyone you refuse will go back away from you." With these words the soul of Prince Tiresias went into the home of Hades, after he had uttered his prophecies.

But I remained steadfast where I was until my mother came up and drank the dark blood. Immediately then she knew me and in her sorrow spoke winged words: "My son, how have you come, while still alive, below to this gloomy realm which is difficult for the living to behold? For great rivers and terrible waters lie between, first Oceanus which, if one does not have a sturdy ship, he cannot in any way cross on foot."

Anticlea and Odysseus continue their conversation, questioning each other. Finally she reveals to her son that is was heartache and longing for him that brought her life to an end. At this Odysseus cannot restrain himself (204–234):

Troubled in spirit I wished to embrace the soul of my dead mother; three times I made the attempt, as desire compelled me, three times she slipped through my hands like a shadow or a dream. Sharp pain welled up from the depths of my heart, and speaking I addressed her with winged words: "O my mother, why do you not stay for me so eager to embrace you, so that we both may throw our arms about each other, even in Hades' realm, and take comfort in chill lamentation? Or has august Persephone conjured up this phantom for me so that I may groan still more in my grief?"

Thus I spoke, and she my lady mother answered at once: "O my poor child, ill-fated beyond all men; Persephone, daughter of Zeus, does not trick you at all; but this is the doom of mortals when they die, for no longer do sinews hold bones and flesh together, but the mighty power of blazing fire consumes all, as soon as the life breath leaves our white bones and the soul like a dream flutters and flies away. But as quickly as possible make your way back to the light, but understand all these things so that you may in the future tell them to your wife." Thus we two exchanged words; then women came up (for august Persephone compelled them), all of whom were the wives or daughters of noble men. And they gathered all together about the dark blood. But I deliberated how I might speak to each one individually, and upon reflection this seemed to me the best plan. I drew my sharp sword from my sturdy side and did not allow them to drink the dark blood all at the same time. And they came up one by one and each explained her lineage and I questioned them all.

The parade of beautiful women that follows is packed with mytho-logical and genealogical information that has little meaning for us in this context. At the end Persephone drives away the souls of these illustrious ladies. A lengthy interview follows between Odysseus and Agamemnon, who tells bitterly of his murder at the hands of his wife, Clytemnestra, and her lover, Aegisthus, and remains suspicious and hostile toward all women. Then the souls of Achilles and Patroclus and the greater Ajax appear. The soul of Achilles addresses Odysseus next (Patroclus does not speak). We must excerpt two portions of their conversation to establish more completely the tone and human-ity of Homer's conception. The first reveals Achilles' despair (473–491):

"Royal son of Laertes, clever and indomitable Odysseus, what still greater exploit have you ingeniously devised? How have you dared to come down to Hades' realm where spirits without body or sense dwell, shadows of mortals worn out by life?" Thus he spoke, and I addressed him in answer, "O Achilles, son of Peleus, by far the mightiest of the Achaeans, I came down to Hades' realm to ask the seer Tiresias if he might tell me some way by which I might return to rocky Ithaca. For I have not yet come near Achaea nor yet reached my homeland, but I always have misfortunes. But no man either before or after is more fortunate than you, Achilles. Previously while you lived, we Argives heaped honors on you equal to those of the gods, and now being in this place you have great power among these shades. So, Achilles, do not be at all distressed, even though you are dead."

Thus I spoke, and he at once addressed me in answer: "Do not speak to me soothingly about death, glorious Odysseus; I should prefer as a slave to serve another man, even if he had no property and little to live on, than to rule over all these dead who have done with life."

Achilles goes on to inquire about his son, Neoptolemus; and when Odysseus has given details of how the boy has proven himself a man worthy of his father, Achilles in his pride feels a surge of joy illumine his gloomy existence (538-544):

The soul of swift-footed Achilles [Odysseus goes on to relate] made its way in great strides over the plain full of asphodel, rejoicing because I said that his son was a renowned hero. Other souls of the dead stood grieving, and each recounted his sorrows. Only the soul of Ajax, son of Telamon, stood apart.

Ajax, who committed suicide because Odysseus was awarded the armor of Achilles rather than he, will not respond to Odysseus' appeals (563-600):

Instead he followed the dead spirits into Erebus, where perhaps he might have spoken to me or I to him. But desire in my breast wished to see the souls of the other dead.

There I saw Minos, the splendid son of Zeus, sitting with a gold scepter in his hand and pronouncing judgments for the dead, and they sitting and standing asked the king for his decisions within the wide gates of Hades' house.

And I saw next the giant hunter Orion, driving together on the plain of asphodel the wild beasts which he himself had killed on the lonely mountains, having in his hand a bronze club that was always unbreakable. And I saw Tityus, son of revered Earth, lying on the ground covering a vast area. Two vultures sitting on either side of him tore into his body and ate at his liver, and his hands could not keep them off. For he had assaulted Leto, the renowned consort of Zeus, as she was going through Panopeus, a city of beautiful dancing places, to Pytho.[6]

And also I saw Tantalus enduring harsh sufferings as he stood in a pool that splashed to his chin. He strained to quench his thirst but was not able; for every time the old man leaned eagerly to take a drink, the water was swallowed up and gone and about his feet the black earth showed, dried up by some divine power. Tall and leafy trees dangled fruit above his head: pears, pomegranates, apples, sweet figs, and olives, growing in luxuriant profusion. But whenever he reached out to grasp them in his hands, the wind snatched them away to the shadowy clouds.[7]

And also I saw Sisyphus enduring hard sufferings as he pushed a huge stone; exerting all his weight with both his hands and feet he kept shoving it up to the top of the hill. But just when he was about to thrust it over the crest then its own weight forced it back and once again the pitiless stone rolled down to the plain. Yet again he put forth his strength and pushed it up; sweat poured from his limbs and dust rose up high about his head.[8]

Odysseus next sees the phantom of Heracles—the real Heracles is with his wife, Hebe, among the immortal gods. Heracles tells how he too was ill-fated while he lived, performing labors for an inferior master.

Homer's Book of the Dead ends when hordes of the shrieking dead swarm up and Odysseus in fright makes for his ship to resume his journey.

Countless difficulties beset any interpretation of the Homeric view of the afterlife, many of them linked to the nature of the composition of the *Odyssey* as a whole and of this book in particular. Discrepancies are apparent, and explanations must finally hinge upon one's views on the much wider problems of the Homeric question. Does the Book of the Dead reflect different attitudes and concepts put together by one man or by several, at one time or over a period of years—even centuries? Basic to the account, perhaps, is a cult of the dead—seen in the sacrificial ceremonies performed at the trench and in the serious note of moral compulsion to provide burial for one who has died. But as the description proceeds, there is much that is puzzling. Odysseus apparently remains at his post while the souls come up; if so, how does he witness the torments of the sinners and the activities of the heroes described? Are they visions from the pit of blood, or is this episode an awkward addition from a different treatment that had Odysseus actually tour the realm of Hades? Certainly the section listing the women who come up in a group conveys strongly the feelings of an insertion, written in the style of the Boeotian epic of Hesiod. As the book begins, the stream of Oceanus seems to be the only barrier, but later Anticlea speaks of other rivers to be crossed.

Thus the geography of the Homeric Underworld is vague, and similarly the classification of those who inhabit it is obscurely defined, particularly in terms of the precision that is evident in subsequent literature. Elpenor, among those who first swarm up, may belong to a special group in a special area, but we cannot be sure. Heroes like Agamemnon and Achilles are together, but they do not clearly occupy a separate paradise; the meadow of asphodel they inhabit seems to refer to the whole realm, not to an Elysium such as we find described by Vergil. One senses, rather, that all mortals end up together pretty much in the same place, without distinction. Since Odysseus thinks that Achilles has power among the shades as great as that which he had among the living, perhaps some prerogatives are assigned or taken for granted. A special hell for sinners may be implied (at least they are listed in a group), but it is noteworthy that these sinners are extraordinary indeed, great figures of mythological antiquity who dared great crimes against the gods. Apparently ordinary mortals do not suffer so for their sins. Homer does not seem to present an afterlife of judgment and reward and punishment, and Minos presumably acts as a judge among the dead, settling their disputes there very much as he did in real life.

The tone and mood of the Homeric afterlife are generally more consistent. Vague and fluttering spirits, with all the pursuits, passions, and prejudices they had while alive, drift aimlessly and joylessly in the gloom; the light and hope and vigor of the upper world are gone. Philosophical and religious thought, shot through with moral earnestness and righteous indignation, will soon bring about sublime and terrifying variations in this picture.

Plato's Myth of Er

Plato concludes the last book of his great dialogue, the *Republic,* with the myth of Er. This vision of the afterlife is steeped in religious and philosophical concepts; and although figures from mythology are incorporated, the symbolic and spiritual world depicted is far removed from that of Homer. Addressing Glaucon, Socrates makes this clear as he begins (614B–616B):

 I shall not tell a tale like that of Odysseus to Alcinoüs, but instead my story is of a brave man, Er, the son of Armenius, a Pamphylian, who at one time died in war; after ten days, when the bodies—by now decayed—were taken up, his alone was uncorrupted. He was brought home, and on the twelfth day after his death placed on a funeral pyre in preparation for burial. But he came back to life and told what he had seen in the other world. He said that, after his soul had departed, it traveled with many and came to a divine place, in which there were two openings in the earth next to each other, and opposite were two others in the upper region of the sky.

In the space between these four openings sat judges who passed sentence: the just they ordered to go to the right through one of the openings upward in the sky, after they had affixed their judgments in front of them; the unjust they sent to the left through one of the downward openings, bearing on their backs indications of all that they had done; to Er when he approached they said that he must be a messenger to human beings about the afterlife and commanded him to listen and watch everything in this place.

To be sure he saw there the souls, after they had been judged, going away through the opening either in the heaven or in the earth, but from the remaining two openings he saw some souls coming up out of the earth, covered with dust and dirt, and others descending from the second opening in the sky, pure and shining. And they kept arriving and appeared as if they were happy indeed to return after a long journey to the plain that lay between. Here they encamped as though for a festival, and mutual acquaintances exchanged greetings; those who had come from the earth and those from the sky questioned one another. The first group recounted their experiences, weeping and wailing as they recalled all the various things they had suffered and seen in their journey under the earth, which had lasted one thousand years; the others from the sky told in turn of the happiness they had felt and sights of indescribable beauty.

O Glaucon, it would take a long time to relate everything. But he did say that the essential significance was this: everyone had to suffer an appropriate penalty for each and every sin ten times over, in retribution for the number of times and the number of persons he had wronged; that is, he must make one full payment once every hundred years (since this is considered the span of human life) so that he might pay in full for all his wrongs, tenfold in one thousand years. For example, if any were responsible for the deaths of many or betrayed and enslaved cities or armies or were guilty of any other crime, they would suffer torments ten times over for all these sins individually, but on the other hand, if they had done good deeds and were just and holy, in the same proportion they were given a worthy reward. About those who died immediately after birth and those who had lived a short time he said other things not worth mentioning.

He described still greater retribution for honor or dishonor toward gods and parents and for murder. He told how he was near one spirit who asked another where Ardiaeus the Great was. This Ardiaeus had been tyrant in a city of Pamphylia a thousand years before this time, and he was said to have killed his aged parents and older brother and to have committed many other unholy deeds. The reply was that he had not and would not come back to the plain. For to be sure this was one of the terrifying sights that we witnessed.

When we were near the mouth and about to come up, after experiencing everything else, we suddenly saw Ardiaeus and others, most of whom were tyrants, but there were also some ordinary persons who had committed great wrongs. They all thought that they would at last ascend upward, but the mouth would not let them; instead it gave forth a roar, whenever any who were so incurable in their wickedness or had not paid sufficient penalty attempted to come up. Then indeed wild men, fiery of aspect, who stood by and understood the roar, seized some of them and led them away, but they bound Ardiaeus and the others, head, hand, and foot, threw them down, and flayed them; they dragged them along the road outside the mouth combing their flesh like wool with thorns, making clear to others as they passed the reason for the punishment and that they were being led away to be hurled down to Tartarus.

Of all the many and varied terrors that happened to them there, by far the greatest for each was that he might hear the roar as he came up, and when there was silence each ascended with the utmost joy. The judgments then were such as these: punishments for some and again rewards for others in due proportion.

The souls who have completed their cycle of one thousand years spend seven days on the plain and then proceed on another journey, accompanied by Er. Four days later they arrive at a place from which they behold a beam of light that extends like a pillar through all of heaven and earth. After another day's journey, they can see that this light provides as it were a bond or chain to hold the universe together; from this chain of light extends the spindle of Necessity *(Ananke)* by which all the revolving spheres are turned. The next section of the myth presents a difficult, cosmological explanation of the universe, with its circles of fixed stars and revolving planets, the earth being at the center.[9]

Then Plato's account of Er, as Socrates relates it, continues with a description of the harmony of the spheres (617B-621D):

The spindle turned on the knees of Necessity. A Siren was perched aloft each of the circles and borne along with it, uttering a single sound on one musical note; from all eight came a unified harmony. Round about at equal distances sat three others, each on a throne, the Fates (Moirai), daughters of Necessity, in white robes with garlands on their heads, Lachesis, Clotho, and Atropos, singing to the music of the Sirens: Lachesis of the past, Clotho of the present, and Atropos of the future. Clotho touches with her right hand the outside circle of the spindle and helps turn it; with her left Atropos moves the inner circles in the same way, and Lachesis touches and moves both, alternating with each hand.

Immediately after the souls arrived, they had to approach Lachesis. First of all a prophet arranged them in order; and then, after taking from the knees of Lachesis lots and examples of lives, he mounted a lofty platform and spoke: "Hear the word of Lachesis, maiden daughter of Necessity. Ephemeral souls, this is the beginning of another cycle of mortal life fraught with death. A divinity will not allot himself to you, but you will choose your divinity.[10] Let one who has drawn the first lot choose a life, which will be his by necessity. Virtue is without master; each man has a greater or lesser share, insofar as he honors or dishonors her. The blame belongs to the one who makes the choice; god is blameless."

With these words, he cast the lots among them all, and each picked up the one that fell near him. Only Er was not allowed to participate. It was clear to each when he had picked up his lot what number he had drawn. Next he placed the examples of lives on the ground in front of them, many more than those present and of every kind; lives of all living creatures and all human beings. Among them lives of tyrants, some complete, others cut short and ending in poverty, exile, and destitution. There were lives of illustrious men, renowned for form and beauty or strength and physical achievement, others for family and the virtues of their ancestors; in the same way were lives of unknown or disreputable men; and so it was for women. But the disposition of the soul was not included, because with its choice of another life it too of necessity became different, but the other qualities were mixed with one another, wealth and poverty, sickness and health, and intermediate states.

Herein to be sure, as it seems, my dear Glaucon, lies all the risk; therefore each one of us must seek to find and understand this crucial knowledge; he must search if he can hear of and discover one who will make him capable of knowing; he must distinguish the good life from the wicked and choose always in every situation from the possibilities the better course, taking into account all that has now been said. He must know how these qualities, individually or combined, affect virtue in a life; what beauty mixed with poverty or wealth achieves in terms of good and evil, along with the kind of state of soul that it inspires; and what high and low birth, private status, public office, strength, weakness, intelligence, stupidity, and all such qualities, inherent or acquired, achieve in combination with one another, so that after deliberation he may be able to choose from all of these between the worse and better life, looking only to the effect upon the nature of his soul.

By the worse life I mean that leading the soul to become more unjust, by the better, that leading it to become more just. All other considerations he will ignore. For we have seen that this is the most crucial choice for a human being living or dead. Indeed one must cling to this conviction even when he comes to the realm of Hades, so that here, just as in the other world, he may not be overwhelmed by wealth and similar evils and succumb to acts like those of a tyrant, committing many incurable evils, and besides suffering still greater ones himself, and so that he may know how to choose a life that follows the mean in such circumstances, and to avoid the excess in either direction, both in this life and in every future life, as far as he is able. For in this way a person becomes most fortunate and blessed.

Then indeed Er, the messenger from the afterlife, reported that the prophet spoke as follows: "Even for the one who comes last, there lies a life that is desirable and not evil, if he chooses intelligently and lives it unflinchingly. Let not the one who chooses first be careless, nor the last discouraged." After he had spoken, the one who had drawn the first lot immediately went up and chose the most extreme tyranny, and he made his choice out of senselessness and greed and did not look closely at everything, and he did not notice that his life entailed the fate of eating his own children and other evils. And when he examined his choice at leisure, he beat his breast and lamented that he had not abided by the warnings of the prophet. For he did not accept the responsibility for these evils, but he blamed fate and the gods and everything rather than himself. He was one of those who had come down from the sky and had lived his previous life in a city with an orderly political constitution and adopted virtue through habit rather than wisdom.

Generally speaking, the number of those who came down from the sky and were caught in this kind of predicament was not small, since they were untrained in suffering. But many of those from earth, since they had themselves suffered and seen others suffer, did not make their choice on impulse. Because of this and because of the chance of the lot, for many souls there occurred a change from an evil to a good fate or the reverse. For if one always pursues wisdom with all his strength each time he takes a life in the world and if the lot of choosing does not fall to him among the last, it is likely, from all that has been reported, that not only will he be happy in life but also his journey after death from the plain and back will not be under the earth and hard, but easy and upward to the sky.

Er said that to watch each soul as he chose his life was a worthwhile sight, piteous, laughable, and wondrous. For the most part, they made their choices on the basis of their experiences in their previous lives. He saw the soul that had been that of Orpheus choose the life of a swan through hatred of the female sex because of his death at their hands, not wishing to be born again of woman. And he saw the soul of Thamyras select the life of a nightingale, and a swan decide to change to the life of a human, and other musical creatures make similar decisions. The soul that drew the twentieth lot chose the life of a lion; this was the soul of Ajax, son of Telamon, avoiding a human life because he remembered the judgment concerning Achilles' armor. After him came the soul of Agamemnon; he too through hatred of the human race because of his sufferings changed to the life of an eagle. The choice of the soul of Atalanta fell in the middle of the proceedings; she saw great honors attached to the life of a male athlete and took it, not being able to pass it by. He saw after her the soul of Epeus, the son of Panopeus, assuming the nature of a craftswoman, and far away among the last the soul of the ridiculous Thersites taking the form of an ape.

In his fated turn, the soul of Odysseus, who had drawn the last lot, went to choose; remembering his former toils he sought to be free from ambition; he looked a long time and with difficulty found the quiet life of an ordinary man lying somewhere disregarded by the others and, when he saw it, he made his choice gladly and said that he would have done the same thing even if the first lot had fallen to him. In the same way, souls of wild animals exchanged forms or entered human beings, the unjust changing to savage beasts, the just to tame ones; and all kinds of combinations occurred.

When all the souls had chosen lives, they proceeded in order according to their lots to Lachesis. She gave to each the divinity *(daimon)* he had chosen to accompany him as a guardian for his life and to fulfill his choices. This divinity first led the soul to Clotho, under her hand as it turned the revolving spindle, to ratify the fate each had chosen after drawing his lot. He touched her and then led the soul to the spinning of Atropos, thus making the events on the thread of destiny unalterable. From here without turning back they went under the throne of Necessity and passed beyond it. When all the souls and their guardian divinities had done this, they proceeded together to the plain of the river of forgetfulness (Lethe) through a terrible and stifling heat. For it was devoid of trees and all that the earth grows.

Now that it was evening, they encamped by the river of forgetfulness, whose water no container can hold. It is necessary for all to drink a fixed amount of the water, but some do not have the wisdom to keep from drinking more than this amount. As one drinks one becomes forgetful of everything. In the middle of the night when they were asleep there was thunder and an earthquake, and then suddenly just like shooting stars they were borne upward, each in a different direction to his birth. Er himself was prevented from drinking the water. He does not know where and how he returned to his body, but suddenly opening his eyes he saw that he was lying on the funeral pyre at dawn.

Thus, O Glaucon, the myth has been preserved and has not perished. We should be saved if we heed it, and we shall cross the river of forgetfulness well and not contaminate our souls. But if we all agree in believing the soul is immortal and capable of enduring all evils and all good, we shall always cling to the upward path and in every way pursue justice with wisdom, so that we may be in loving reconciliation with ourselves and the gods, and so that when we carry off the prizes of justice, just like victors in the games collecting their rewards, both while we are here and in the thousand-year journey we have described, we may fare well.

This vision of an afterlife, written in the fourth century B.C., comes from various sources about which we can only conjecture. We must also allow for the inventive genius of Plato himself in terms of his own philosophy. The numerical intervals (e.g., the journey of a thousand years) are reminiscent of Pythagoras and the belief in the transmigration of the soul; reward and punishment, with ultimate purification, is usually identified as Orphic. Since this myth of revelation concludes the *Republic* with proof of divine immortality, problems abound in connection with its precise interpretation. How much was intended to be accepted literally? Is Er's story an allegory filled with profound symbols hiding the universal truths it wishes to disclose?

In his *Phaedo,* Plato provides another vision of the afterlife in which he explains (114B–C) how true philosophers eventually are released from the cycle of reincarnation; those who have lived a life of exceptional holiness and purify themselves sufficiently through their pursuit of philosophy live entirely as souls in the hereafter in beautiful dwellings, which are not easy to describe.

For the purposes of our sketch of the development of the Greek and Roman concept of the afterlife, it is important to stress that a heaven and a hell are clearly depicted for the soul of every mortal; and in addition to the upward and downward paths that must be traversed, special tormentors exist and a special place of torment (Tartarus) in which the greatest sinners are placed forever.[11] In such a conception lies the mythical and biblical basis for the mystery religions of antiquity, whether their god be Demeter or Dionysus and their prophet Orpheus or Plato.[12] Ties with Christian sentiments are not hard to see, despite the obvious differences. More specific links are provided by the early Christian identification of Er as an ancestor of St. Joseph and by the fact that these early Christians, in their championship of free will, seized upon the admonition of Lachesis: "This blame belongs to him who makes the choice; god is blameless."

Vergil's Book of the Dead

In Book 6 of the *Aeneid,* Vergil paints his sad and prophetic picture of the Underworld in shadowy halftones fraught with tears and pathos. His sources are eclectic, but his poetic vision is personal and unique. Despite the centuries of oral and written tradition and the Roman chauvinism of his depiction, Homeric and Platonic elements are often still distinctly evident. At Cumae, in Italy, the Sibyl, prophetess of Apollo, tells Aeneas what the requirements are to visit his father in the realm of Hades. He must get a golden bough, sacred to Proserpine (i.e., Persephone), and bury his comrade, Misenus. It is easy to descend to the Underworld; the task is to retrace one's steps to the upper air; only a special few have managed this. While his men are preparing a funeral pyre for Misenus, Aeneas goes in search of the bough (186–204):

> As Aeneas gazed at the vast woods, it happened that he uttered a prayer: "If only the golden bough would show itself to me in so immense a forest. For the priestess told all that was true—alas, too true—about your need for burial, Misenus." At that moment, as it happened, twin doves came flying from the sky under his very eyes and settled on the green ground. Then the great hero recognized his mother's birds and in his joy prayed: "Be leaders, if there is some way, and direct your course to the grove where the branch rich in gold shades the fertile earth; O goddess mother do not fail me in this crisis."
>
> Thus he spoke and stopped in his tracks, watching what sign they gave and what course they took. They would stop to feed and then fly ahead, always permitting Aeneas to keep them in sight as he followed. When they approached the foul odor coming up from Lake Avernus, they quickly flew higher; and gliding through the liquid air the doves settled down together on the longed-for tree, where the tawny gleam of gold flickered through the branches.

Aeneas eagerly breaks off the golden bough; after the funeral rites for Misenus have been completed, he takes it to the Sibyl (237–322):

 There was a deep and rocky cave with a huge yawning mouth sheltered by the black lake and the darkness of the forest; no birds at all were able to wing their way overhead, so great and foul an exhalation poured up to the vault of heaven from the lake. Its name, Avernus, deriving from the Greek, means birdless. Here first of all the priestess set four black bullocks and poured wine over their heads; between their horns she cut the tips of bristles and placed them on the sacred fire as first libations, calling aloud on Hecate, who holds power both in the sky above and in the depths of Erebus. Attendants applied their knives and caught the warm blood in bowls. Aeneas himself slaughtered with his sword a black-fleeced lamb for Night, the mother of the Eumenides, and her great sister, Earth; and for you, Proserpine, a barren cow; then he built an altar in the night for the Stygian king and placed on the flames the whole carcasses of bulls, pouring rich oil over their entrails. Lo, at the first rays of the rising sun, the ground rumbled and the wooded ridges began to move and she dogs appeared howling through the gloom as the goddess approached from the Underworld.

The Sibyl cried: "Keep back, keep back, you who are unhallowed; withdraw completely from this grove. But you, Aeneas, enter the path and seize your sword from its sheath. Now there is need for courage and a stout heart." This much she spoke and threw herself furiously into the cave. Aeneas, without fear, matched the steps of his leader as she went.

You gods who rule over spirits, silent shades, depths of Chaos, Phlegethon, and vast realms of night and silence, let it be right for me to speak what I have heard; by your divine will let me reveal things buried deep in earth and blackness.

They went, dim figures in the shadows of the lonely night, through the empty homes and vacant realms of Dis, as though along a road in woods by the dim and treacherous light of the moon, when Jupiter has clouded the sky in darkness, and black night has robbed objects of their color. At the entrance itself, in the very jaws of Orcus, Grief and avenging Cares have placed their beds; here dwell pale Diseases, sad Old Age, Fear, evil-counseling Hunger, foul Need, forms terrible to behold, and Death and Toil; then Sleep, the brother of Death, and Joys evil even to think about, and opposite on the threshold, death-dealing War, the iron chambers of the Eumenides, and insane Discord, her hair entwined with snakes and wreaths of blood.

CAPTIONS FOR COLOR PLATES 1–11

1. *Jupiter and Thetis,* by J. A. D. Ingres (1780–1867). Oil on canvas, 1811; 136 × 101 in. In this huge painting Jupiter is enthroned among the clouds with his attributes, the scepter and the eagle. Thetis kneels and touches Jupiter's chin in a gesture of supplication. To the left Juno (Hera) appears threateningly, and reliefs of the battle of gods and giants decorate the base of Jupiter's throne.

2. *Dionysus.* Kylix by Exekias, ca. 530 B.C.; diameter $4\frac{1}{2}$ in. The scene depicts the story told in the *Homeric Hymn to Dionysus.* The god reclines on the pirates' ship, round whose mast a grape-laden vine entwines itself. The crew have leaped overboard and have been transformed into dolphins.

3. *The Death of Sarpedon.* Athenian red-figure krater by Euphronios, ca. 510 B.C.; height 18 in. The winged gods, Sleep (Hypnos, *left*) and Death (Thanatos, *right*), carry the body from the battlefield under the guidance of Hermes, as two Greek warriors look on. The gods wear armor (note the chain mail of Thanatos), but the corpse of Sarpedon has been stripped. This vase is one of the masterpieces of Athenian vase-painting.

4. *Dionysus and Ariadne.* Bronze krater (the Derveni Krater), second half of the fourth century B.C.; height $35\frac{1}{2}$ in. The krater, which held the ashes of a Thessalian nobleman, was discovered at Derveni, not far from Thessalonike, in 1962. The reliefs on the central panel show Dionysus, naked, seated on a rock with his leg over Ariadne's thigh. She draws her veil aside, the gesture of a bride accepting her husband. Behind Dionysus is a panther, and birds, animals, vines, and ivy ornament the neck and body of the krater. Figures of Maenads flank the divine pair, and in the upper register the seated Dionysus gestures towards a sleeping Maenad. The handles, in the form of serpents, frame the head of a horned god to the left and of Heracles (with lionskin over his head) to the right.

5. *Christus Apollo.* Vault mosaic, third century A.D.; height of vault 72 in. Christ is shown with the attributes of the sun-god (Apollo or Helius), ascending into the vault of the sky on a chariot drawn by four white horses (two are missing from the damaged part). The rays emanating from his head form a cross. Across the background trails the ivy of Dionysus, another pagan symbol of immortality used in early Christian art. This vault mosaic is in a Christian tomb in the cemetery beneath the basilica of St. Peter's in the Vatican.

6. *The Lycurgus Cup.* Glass, early fourth century A.D.; height $6\frac{1}{2}$ in. The Thracian king Lycurgus is trapped in the vine of Dionysus (who appears on the other side of the cup, along with a nymph, a satyr, and Pan), as a punishment for his persecution of the god. The axe with which he tried to cut down the vine lies useless behind his left foot. This "cage cup" is carved from green glass, which is translucent red when placed in front of light. The glass has been undercut to show the agony of Lycurgus in high relief. The gilt-bronze rim is a nineteenth-century addition.

7. *The Rape of Helen by Paris,* attributed to a follower of Fra Angelico. Oil on wood, ca. 1450; 20 × 24 in. The companions of Paris carry Helen (distinguished by her central position and headdress) and three of her companions from a temple (as related by Dares Phrygius) to a waiting ship, accompanied by a cupid in the foreground. Paris may be the central figure in the group on the left. This octagonal painting was originally a panel in a wedding chest, perhaps as a warning of the dangers of marital infidelity.

PLATE 10   *Venus and Adonis,* by Paolo Veronese (Paolo Caliari). *([Madrid, Spain, Prado] Scala/Art Resource, NY.)*

PLATE 11   *The Discovery of the Infant Erichthonius,* by Peter Paul Rubens. *(Courtesy of the Collections of the Prince of Liechtenstein, Vaduz Castle.)*

8. *The Return of Odysseus,* by Pintoricchio (Bernardo Betti, 1454–1513). Fresco transferred to canvas, 1509, 60 × 50 in. As in Plate 7 the characters are shown in Renaissance dress. To the left sits Penelope at her loom, with Euryclea beside her; above her head are the bow and quiver of Odysseus. Telemachus runs to greet his mother, and behind him are a young suitor (note the falcon on his wrist), the seer Theoclymenus, and Eumaeus. Odysseus, disguised as a beggar, is coming through the door on the right. In the background is the ship of the Phaeacians; to its left is Odysseus' boat being shattered by Poseidon, and, in the wooded landscape beyond, Odysseus meets Circe, while his men root around as pigs. This fresco was originally painted for a wall in a room of the Ducal Palace in Siena.

9. *The Feast of the Gods,* by Giovanni Bellini (1430–1516), with additions by Titian. Oil on canvas, 1514; 67 × 74 in. Painted when the artist was eighty-four years old, this painting has been called "both mysterious and comic." Its subject is the attempt of Priapus to rape the nymph Lotis (cf. Ovid, *Fasti* 1. 391–440 and 6. 319–346, where the intended victim is Vesta), shown on the right. The gods appear as young Renaissance men and women: Jupiter (drinking from a cup) is in the center, Mercury (wearing a helmet) reclines in the left center foreground, and a group consisting of a satyr, Silenus, and Dionysus (kneeling on one knee) is on the left. Between Dionysus and Silenus is the donkey whose braying woke Lotis.

10. *Venus and Adonis,* by Paolo Veronese (Paolo Caliari, 1528–1588). Oil on canvas, 1584; $83\frac{1}{2}$ × 75 in. Adonis sleeps in the lap of Venus, who fans him with a small flag. A cupid restrains one of the hounds, eager for the hunt that will bring the death of Adonis. Veronese transforms the text of Ovid (*Metamorphoses* 10. 529–559), and the last moments of the lovers together are enriched by the splendid colors of their robes, while the darkening sky foreshadows the tragedy.

11. *The Discovery of the Infant Erichthonius,* by Peter Paul Rubens (1577–1640). Oil on canvas, ca. 1616; 85 × 125 in. Rubens has painted the moment when Aglauros has opened the basket containing Erichthonius and shows him to her sisters, Pandrosos (on the right) and Herse (on the left) with a brilliant red robe. Cupid gestures towards her as the future bride of Mercury. Behind is a fountain of the many-breasted Artemis, whose fertility is echoed by the herm of the lascivious god Pan, on the left. The identity of the old woman is not known.

In the middle, a huge and shady elm spreads its boughs, aged arms in which empty Dreams are said to throng and cling beneath all the leaves. There were also many different forms of beasts and monsters: Centaurs had their haunt in the doorway, Scyllas with twofold form, hundred-handed Briareus, the creature of Lerna hissing dreadfully, the Chimaera armed with flames, Gorgons, Harpies, and the shade of triple-bodied Geryon. Suddenly Aeneas, startled by fear, snatched his sword and threatened them with his drawn blade as they approached. If his wise companion had not warned that these insubstantial lives without body flitted about with but the empty shadow of a form, he would have rushed in and smitten the shades with his weapon for nothing.

From here is a path that leads to the waters of Acheron, a river of Tartarus, whose seething flood boils turbid with mud in vast eddies and pours all its sand into the stream of Cocytus.[13] A ferryman guards these waters, Charon, horrifying in his terrible squalor; a mass of white beard lies unkempt on his chin, his eyes glow with a steady flame, and a dirty cloak hangs from his shoulders by a knot. He pushes his boat himself by a pole, tends to the sails, and conveys the bodies across in his rusty craft; he is now older, but for a god old age is vigorous and green. Here a whole crowd poured forth and rushed down to the bank: mothers and men, the bodies of great-souled heroes finished with life, boys and unmarried girls, young men placed on the pyres before the eyes of their parents, as many as the leaves that drop and fall in the forest at the first cold of autumn or as the birds that flock to land from the stormy deep, when winter puts them to flight across the sea and sends them to sunny lands. They stood pleading to be the first to cross and stretched out their hands in longing for the farther shore. The grim boatman accepted now these and now those, but he drove others back and kept them at a distance from the sandy shore.

Aeneas, who was moved by the tumult, asked in wonder: "Tell me, O virgin Sibyl, the meaning of this gathering at the river. What do these souls seek? By what distinction do some retire from the bank, while others are taken across the murky stream?" The aged priestess answered him briefly as follows: "Son of Anchises, and most certainly a descendant of the gods, you see the deep pools of Cocytus and the marshes of the Styx, the river by which the gods fear to swear falsely. This one group here consists of those who are poor and unburied.[14] The ferryman is Charon. The others whom he takes across are those who have been buried. Charon is not allowed to transport them over the hoarse-sounding waters to the dread shore if their bones have not found rest in proper burial; but a hundred years they wander and flit about this bank before they come back at last to the longed-for waters to be admitted to the boat." The son of Anchises stopped in his tracks and stood thinking many thoughts, pitying in his heart the inequity of the fate of human beings.

Among those who have not received burial Aeneas sees his helmsman Palinurus, who had fallen overboard on their voyage from Africa; he managed to reach the coast of Italy, but once he came ashore tribesmen killed him. The interview is reminiscent of the exchange between Odysseus and Elpenor in human emotion and religious sentiment. The Sibyl comforts Palinurus with the prediction that he will be buried by a neighboring tribe. The book continues (384–449):

Aeneas and the Sibyl proceed on their way and approach the river. When the ferryman spied them from his post by the river Styx, coming through the silent grove and turning their steps toward the bank, he challenged them first with unprovoked abuse: "Whoever you are who approach our river in arms, explain why you have come but answer from there, do not take another step. This is the place of the shades, of sleep and drowsy night; it is forbidden to carry living bodies in my Stygian boat. To be sure, I was not happy to accept Heracles and Theseus and Pirithoüs when they came to these waters, although they were of divine descent and invincible strength. Heracles by his own hand sought and bound in chains the guardian dog of Tartarus and dragged it away trembling from the throne of the king himself. The other two attempted to abduct the queen from the chamber of Dis."

The priestess of Apollo answered briefly: "No such plots this time; be not dismayed; our weapons bear no violence; let the huge doorkeeper howl forever and strike terror into the bloodless shades; let Proserpine remain safe and pure within the house of Pluto, her uncle. Trojan Aeneas, outstanding in goodness and valor, descends to the shades below to his father. If the sight of such great virtue and devotion does not move you, at least recognize this bough."

She revealed the bough that lay hidden in her robe, and at this his heart that was swollen with anger subsided. Not a word more was uttered. He marveled at the hallowed gift of the fateful branch, which he had not seen for a long time, and turned his dark-colored boat around to approach the shore. Then he drove away the souls that were sitting on the long benches, cleared the gangway, and at the same time took the mighty Aeneas aboard; the leaky seams groaned under his weight and let in much of the swampy water. At last Charon disembarked the seer and the hero safe and sound on the further shore amid shapeless mud and slimy sedge.

Huge Cerberus, sprawling in a cave facing them, made these regions echo with the howling from his three throats. When the prophetess saw his necks bristling with serpents she threw him a cake of meal and honey drugged to make him sleep. He opened wide his three throats in ravenous hunger and snatched the sop; his immense bulk went limp and spread out on the ground, filling the whole of the vast cavern. With the guard now buried in sleep, Aeneas made his way quickly over the bank of the river of no return.

Immediately, on the very threshold, voices were heard and a great wailing and the souls of infants weeping who did not have a full share of sweet life but a black day snatched them from the breast and plunged them into bitter death. Next to them were those who had been condemned to die by a false accusation. To be sure their abode has not been assigned without an allotted jury, and a judge, Minos, is the magistrate; he shakes the urn and draws lots for the jury, summons the silent court, and reviews the lives and the charges. Right next is an area occupied by an unhappy group who were guiltless but sought death by their own hand and hating the light abandoned their lives. How they wished now even for poverty and hard labor in the air above! But fate stands in the way and the hateful marsh binds them with its gloomy waters, and the Styx flowing round nine times imprisons them.

Not far from here spread out in all directions were the fields of Mourning, as they are named. Here those whom relentless and cruel love had wasted and consumed hide themselves in secret paths in the woods of myrtle; even in death itself their anguish does not leave them. In this place he saw Phaedra, Procris, and unhappy Eriphyle displaying the wounds inflicted by a cruel son, and Evadne, Pasiphaë, and with them Laodamia and Caeneus, who had been changed into a boy and now once again was a woman.

Here Aeneas meets Dido, queen of Carthage, who has recently committed suicide because of her love for Aeneas and his betrayal. He addresses her in sad, piteous, and uncomprehending tones; but she refuses to answer and turns away to join the shade of her former husband, Sychaeus.

From here Aeneas and his guide move on to the last group and farthest fields, reserved for those renowned in war, who had been doomed to die in battle and were much lamented by those on earth. Tydeus, Parthenopaeus, Adrastus, and many, many others come to meet Aeneas. Trojan heroes crowd around him, but the Greek warriors from Troy flee in terror. Aeneas converses with Deïphobus, the son of Priam who married Helen after the death of Paris. Deïphobus tells the story of his death at the hands of Menelaus and Odysseus through the treachery of Helen. Their talk is interrupted by the Sibyl, who complains that they are wasting what brief time they have; it is now already past midday on earth and night is coming on (540-543):

This is the place where the road divides and leads in two directions: our way is to the right and extends under the ramparts of Dis to Elysium, but the left path leads to the evil realms of Tartarus, where penalties for sin are exacted.

We must look at Vergil's conception of hell, Tartarus, and paradise, Elysium or the Elysian Fields (548-579):

Suddenly Aeneas looked back to the left and saw under a cliff lofty fortifications enclosed by a triple wall around which flowed Phlegethon, the swift stream of Tartarus, seething with flames and rolling clashing rocks in its torrent. He saw in front of him a huge door, with columns of solid adamant that no human force nor even the gods who dwell in the sky would have the power to attack and break through. Its tower of iron stood high against the winds; and one of the Furies, Tisiphone, clothed in a bloody robe, sat guarding the entrance, sleepless day and night. From within he heard groans and the sound of savage lashes, then the grating of iron and the dragging of chains. Aeneas stood in terror absorbed by the din. "Tell me, virgin prophetess, what is the nature of their crimes? What penalties are imposed? What is this great wail rising upward on the air?"

Then she began to speak: "Renowned leader of the Trojans, it is not permitted for anyone who is pure to cross the threshold of the wicked. But when Hecate put me in charge of the groves of Avernus, she herself taught me the penalties exacted by the gods and went through them all. Cretan Rhadamanthus presides over this pitiless kingdom; he punishes crimes and recognizes treachery, forcing each to confess the sins committed in the world above, atonement for which each had postponed too long, happy in his futile stealth, until death. At once the avenging fury, Tisiphone, armed with a whip, leaps on the guilty and drives them with blows; as she threatens with her fierce serpents in her left hand, she summons the phalanx, her savage sisters. Then at last the sacred gates open wide, turning with strident horror on their creaking hinges. Do you see what kind of sentry sits at the entrance? What forms are watching in the threshold? The monstrous Hydra, more fierce than the Furies with its fifty black and gaping throats, has its home within. Then Tartarus itself yawns deep under the shades, extending straight down twice as far as the view upward to the sky and celestial Olympus.''

In Tartarus Vergil places the Homeric sinners Tityus, Sisyphus, and possibly Tantalus; but there is difficulty in the text and its interpretation. Tityus is the only one of the three named directly. Other criminals identified by Vergil are the Titans, who were hurled to the very bottom of Tartarus by the thunderbolts of Jupiter; the sons of Aloeus, Otus and Ephialtes,[15] who tried to storm heaven and seize Jupiter himself; Salmoneus, who was foolish enough to play the role of Jupiter and claim divine honors; Theseus and Pirithoüs; Phlegyas;[16] and Ixion. Ixion is one of the more famous sinners condemned to Tartarus; he is punished by being bound to a wheel that eternally revolves.[17]

Vergil's Tartarus is not a hell just for heroic sinners of mythological antiquity; in it all who are guilty suffer punishment. It is important to realize fully the ethical standards he applies. The nature of sin is clearly summed up by the Sibyl as she continues; just as clear is the moral conviction that assigns happiness to the good in the paradise of Elysium (608–751):

"Here are imprisoned and await punishment those who hated their brothers while they were alive or struck a parent and devised guile against a dependent or who hovered over their acquired wealth all alone and did not share it with their relatives (these misers were the greatest throng), and those who were killed for adultery or took up arms in an impious cause and were not afraid to betray the pledges made to their masters. Do not seek to learn the nature of the crime and fate of each and every sinner and the punishment in which he is submerged. Some roll a huge rock, others hang stretched on the spokes of a wheel; Theseus sits in his misery and will remain sitting forever; wretched Phlegyas admonishes all as he bears testimony in a loud voice among the shades: 'Be warned! Learn justice and not to despise the gods.' This one sold his country for gold, set up a tyrannical despot, made laws and revoked them for a price. This one invaded the bedroom of his daughter in forbidden incestuous marriage.

"All dared enormous crime and were successful in the attainment of their daring. I should not be able to recount all the forms of wickedness or enumerate all the names of the punishments if I had a hundred tongues and a hundred mouths.''

After the aged priestess of Phoebus had uttered these words, she continued: "But come now, proceed on your way and accomplish the task you have undertaken. Let us hurry. I see opposite fortifications of Pluto's palace erected by the forges of the Cyclopes and the vaulted arch of its door where we have been ordered to lay down this gift!'' She had spoken, and making their way together through the gloom of the path they hurried over the space between and approached the gates. Aeneas reached the entrance, sprinkled himself with fresh water, and placed the bough on the threshold.

When this had been done and the gift had been given to the goddess, then at last they came to the happy places, the pleasant green glades of the Woods of the Fortunate, the home of the blessed. Here air that is more pure and abundant clothes the plains in soft-colored light and they have their own sun and their own stars. Some exercise their limbs on the grassy wrestling grounds, vie in sport, and grapple on the yellow sand. Others dance in a chorus and sing songs; and the Thracian priest, Orpheus, in his long robe, accompanies their measures on the seven strings of his lyre, plucking them now with his fingers, now with an ivory quill. Here is the ancient Trojan line of King Teucer, a most beautiful race, great-souled heroes born in better years, and Ilus, Assaracus, and Dardanus, the founder of Troy.

Aeneas marvels at the unreal arms of the heroes and their chariots nearby. The spears stand fixed in the ground, and horses browse freely everywhere on the plain. The same pleasure that they had in their chariots and arms and in tending their sleek horses follows them after they have been laid in the earth. Behold he sees others feasting to the right and to the left on the grass and singing a happy paean in a chorus amidst a fragrant grove of laurel, from which the full stream of the Eridanus River rolls through the woods in the upper world.[18]

Here in a group were those who suffered wounds while fighting for their country, and the priests who remained pure while they lived, and the poets who were devout in their art and whose words were worthy of their god, Phoebus Apollo, or those who made life better by their discoveries in the arts and the sciences and who through merit made others remember them. All of these wore around their temples a snowy white garland; the Sibyl spoke to them as they surrounded her, singling out Musaeus especially: "Tell my happy souls and you, O illustrious poet, what region, what place does Anchises inhabit? We crossed the great rivers of Erebus and have come on his account." Musaeus replied in these few words: "No one has a fixed abode; we inhabit shady groves living in meadows fresh with streams along whose banks we recline. But if the desire in your heart so impels you, cross over this ridge; I shall show you an easy path." He spoke and walked ahead of them pointing out the shining fields below; then they made their way down from the height.

Father Anchises was eagerly contemplating and surveying souls that were secluded in the depths of a green valley and about to enter upon the light of the upper air. It happened that he was reviewing the whole number of his own dear descendants; the fate, fortune, character, and exploits of Roman heroes. When he saw Aeneas coming toward him over the grass, he quickly extended both his hands and a cry escaped his lips as the tears poured down his cheeks: "At last you have come, and your long-awaited devotion to your father has overcome the hard journey. Is it granted to me to see your face, to hear your voice, to speak to you as of old? I have been pondering your visit, thinking about when it would be, counting out the time, and my anxiety has not gone unrewarded. I receive you here after your travels over so many lands and so many seas, harried by so many dangers! How much I feared that Dido in her African kingdom might do you some harm!"

Aeneas replied: "The vision of you in your sadness appearing to me again and again compelled me to pursue my way to this realm. My ships are moored on the Italian shore. Give me, give me your right hand, father, do not shrink from my embrace." As he was speaking, his face was moist with many tears. Three times he attempted to put his arms around his father's neck, three times he reached in vain as the phantom escaped his hands as light as a breeze, like a fleeting vision of the night.[19] Meanwhile, Aeneas saw in this valley set apart a secluded grove and the rustling thickets of a wood and the stream of Lethe, which flowed by the serene abodes. Around the river countless tribes and peoples were flitting, just as when bees settle on different flowers in a meadow in the calm heat of summer and swarm about the white lilies; the whole plain was filled with a murmuring sound.

Aeneas, who did not understand, gave a sudden shudder at the sight; and seeking reasons for it all, he asked what the river was in the distance and what crowd of men filled its banks. Then father Anchises replied: "The souls to which bodies are owed by Fate at the stream of the river Lethe drink waters that release them from previous cares and bring everlasting forgetfulness. Indeed I have desired for a long time to tell you about these souls, to show them before your very eyes, and to list the number of my descendants; now all the more may you rejoice with me that you have found Italy." "O father, am I to think that some souls go from here to the upper air and enter sluggish bodies again? What is this dread desire of these poor souls for light?" "To be sure I shall tell you and not hold you in suspense." Thus Anchises replied and proceeded step by step to reveal the details in order.

"In the first place, a spirit within sustains the sky, the earth, the waters, the shining globe of the moon, and the Titan sun and stars; this spirit moves the whole mass of the universe, a mind, as it were, infusing its limbs and mingled with its huge body. From this arises all life, the race of mortals, animals, and birds, and the monsters that the sea bears under its marble surface. The seeds of this mind and spirit have a fiery power and celestial origin, insofar as the limbs and joints of the body, which is of earth, harmful, and subject to death, do not make them dull and slow them down. Thus the souls, shut up in the gloomy darkness of the prison of their bodies, experience fear, desire, joy, and sorrow, and do not see clearly the essence of their celestial nature.

"Moreover, when the last glimmer of life has gone, all the evils and all the diseases of the body do not yet completely depart from these poor souls; and it is inevitable that many ills, for a long time encrusted, become deeply ingrained in an amazing way. Therefore they are plied with punishments and they pay the penalties of their former wickedness. Some spirits are hung suspended to the winds; for others the infection of crime is washed by a vast whirlpool or burned out by fire. Each of us suffers his own shade.[20]

"Then we are sent to Elysium, and we few occupy these happy fields, until a long period of the circle of time has been completed and has removed the ingrown corruption and has left a pure ethereal spirit and the fire of the original essence. When they have completed the cycle of one thousand years, the god calls all these in a great throng to the river Lethe, where, of course, they are made to forget so that they might begin to wish to return to bodies and see again the vault of heaven."

Anchises then leads Aeneas and the Sibyl to a mound from which they can view the souls as they come up, and he points out to them with affection and pride a long array of great and illustrious Romans who are to be born. The book ends with Aeneas and his guide leaving by the gate of ivory; why Vergil has it so, no one knows for sure (893–899):

 "There are twin gates of Sleep; one is said to be of horn, through which easy exit is given to the true shades. The other is gleamingly wrought in shining ivory, but through it the spirits send false dreams up to the sky." After he had spoken, Anchises escorted his son and the Sibyl and sent them out by the gate of ivory. Aeneas made his way to his ships and rejoined his companions.

Vergil wrote in the second half of the first century B.C., and variations and additions are apparent when his depiction is compared to the earlier ones of Homer and Plato. There are, of course, many other sources for the Greek and Roman conception of the afterlife, but none are more complete or more profound than the representative visions of these authors, and a comparison of them gives the best possible insight into the general nature and development of the ancient conception both spiritually and physically.

Vergil's geography is quite precise. Aeneas and the Sibyl go through various regions. First of all a neutral zone contains those who met an untimely death (infants, suicides, and persons condemned unjustly); next the Fields of Mourning are inhabited by victims of unrequited love and warriors who fell in battle. The logic of these allocations is not entirely clear. Is a full term of life necessary for complete admission to the Underworld? Then appear the crossroads to Tartarus and the Fields of Elysium. The criteria for judgment are interesting; like many another religious philosopher and poet, Vergil must decide who will merit the tortures of his hell or the rewards of his heaven on the basis both of tradition and of personal conviction. Other writers vary the list.[21] Some have observed that the tortures inflicted are often imaginative and ingenious, involving vain and frustrating effort of mind and body, and therefore characteristically Greek in their sly inventiveness. Perhaps so, but depicted as well is sheer physical agony through scourging and fire. Attempts made to find a logic in the meting out of a punishment to fit the crime are only sometimes successful.[22]

Vergil's paradise is very much an idealization of the life led by Greek and Roman gentlemen; and the values illustrated in the assignment of its inhabitants are typical of ancient ethics: devotion to humankind, to country, to family, and to the gods. Yet despite the Greek and Roman coloring of the picture, the morality is universal and germane to all humanity and civilization. In Elysium, too, details supplement the religious philosophy of Plato, which has been labeled Orphic and Pythagorean in particular and mystic in general. The human body is of earth—evil and mortal; the soul is of the divine upper aether—pure and immortal. It must be cleansed from contamination and sin. Once again we are reminded of the myth of Dionysus, which explains the dual nature of human beings in terms of their birth from the ashes of the wicked Titans (the children of Earth) who had devoured the heavenly god Dionysus.

Presumably in the cycle of rebirth and reincarnation, the weary chain is ultimately broken; and we are no longer reborn into this world, but join the oneness of divinity in the pure spirit of the upper air.

Traditional Elements of Hades' Realm

Some identification and clarification of the various names and terminology linked with the Underworld are in order. The realm as a whole may be called Tartarus or Erebus, although these are also the names given solely to the region of torment, as opposed to Elysium or the Elysian Fields. Sometimes the realm of paradise is located elsewhere in some remote place of the upper world, such as the Islands of the Blessed.

There are usually three judges of the Underworld: Minos, Rhadamanthys (or Rhadamanthus), and Aeacus, whose duties are variously assigned. Aeacus is sometimes relegated to more menial tasks; in comedy he appears as the gatekeeper. The rivers are generally five in number, with appropriate names: Styx (the river of hate); Acheron (of woe); Lethe (of forgetfulness); Cocytus (of wailing); Pyriphlegethon or Phlegethon (of fire). For philosophical and religious conceptions of the afterlife and the belief in the transmigration of souls and rebirth, the River of Forgetfulness (Lethe) assumes great importance. It was a custom to bury the dead with a coin in the mouth to provide the ferryman Charon with his fare.[23] Hermes Psychopompus often plays the role of guide for the souls from this world to the next.

Hades, king of the Underworld, is also called Pluto or (in Latin) Dis, which means the wealthy one, referring to him either as a god of earth and fertility or as a deity rich in the numbers of those who are with him. The Romans called him and his realm Orcus, which probably means "the one or the place that constrains or confines." Sometimes Hades (this word may mean "the unseen one") is given no name at all or is addressed by some complimentary epithet, as is the custom with all dreadful deities or spirits—including the devil. Hades and his realm and its inhabitants are in general called *chthonian,* that is, of the earth, as opposed to the bright world of the Olympian gods of the upper air; and Hades himself may even be addressed as Chthonian Zeus. His queen is Persephone.

In Hades' realm, we may find either our heaven (Elysium) or our hell (Tartarus). Tradition developed a canon of mythological sinners who suffer there forever: Tityus, with vultures tearing at his liver; Ixion, bound to a revolving wheel; the Danaids, vainly trying to carry water in sievelike containers; Sisyphus, continually rolling a rock up a hill; and Tantalus, tantalized by food and drink.[24]

The Furies (Erinyes) usually have their home in the realm of Hades; so does Hecate, who sometimes resembles them in appearance and in character. Hesiod, as we have seen, tells how the Furies were born from the blood that fell onto the earth after the castration of Uranus; according to others, they are the offspring of Night. Both versions are appropriate in terms of their sphere and their powers. They vary in number, but they may be reduced to three with specific names: Allecto, Megaera, and Tisiphone. In literature and art they are depicted as formidable, bearing serpents in their hands or hair, and carrying torches and scourges. They are the pitiless and just avengers of crime, especially murder; blood guilt within the family is their particular concern, and they may relentlessly pursue anyone who has killed a parent or close relative. It has been conjectured that originally they were thought of as the ghosts of the murdered seeking vengeance on the murderer or as the embodiment of curses called down upon the guilty.

The Furies very definitely represent the old moral order of justice within the framework of primitive society, where the code of "an eye for an eye and a tooth for a tooth" is meted out by the personal vendetta of the family or the clan. This is Aeschylus' conception of them in his dramatic trilogy, the *Oresteia.* The Furies persecute Orestes after he murders his mother (who has murdered his father), but eventually their role is taken over by a new regime of right: the Areopagus, the court of Athens, decides Orestes' case through the due process of law; and it is significant that Apollo and Athena (the new generation of progressive deities) join forces with the justice of advanced civilization. The last play in the trilogy is called the *Eumenides,* which means the "kindly ones"; this is the name for the Furies as they were worshiped in Athens, after having finally been appeased and put to rest once and for all.[25]

The Christian concept of Satan should not be confused with the ancient portrayal of Hades, who is not fighting with his brother Zeus for our immortal souls. We all end up in his realm, where we may or may not find our heaven or our hell. The only exceptions are those who (like Heracles) are specifically made divinities and therefore allowed to join the gods in heaven or on Olympus. Hades, to be sure, is terrible and inexorable in his severity, but he is not in himself evil or our tormentor; we may fear him as we fear death and its possible consequences, which we cannot avoid. But he does have assistants, such as the Furies, who persecute with devilish and fiendish torments.[26] Hades' wife and queen of his realm, Persephone, is considered in the previous chapter.

The profundity and intensity of the Greek and Roman visions of an afterlife have been all-pervasive in the art and literature of Western civilization. Dante, the great Italian poet of the fourteenth century, was steeped in its radiance, which he suffused with Christian imagination and dogma, albeit taking Vergil as his guide.

It would be misleading to imply that all Greek and Roman literature treats the realm of Hades and the afterlife so seriously. One thinks immediately of Aristophanes' play the *Frogs,* in which the god Dionysus rows across the Styx to the accompaniment of a chorus croaking *brekekekex koax koax;* his tour of the Underworld is different and at times hilarious.[27]

ORPHEUS AND ORPHISM: MYSTERY RELIGIONS IN ROMAN TIMES

14

Orpheus and Eurydice

Ovid tells the story of Orpheus and Eurydice as follows (*Metamorphoses* 10. 1–85; 11. 1–66):

Hymen, god of marriage, wrapped in his saffron-colored cloak, left the wedding of Iphis and Ianthe and made his way through the vast tracts of air to the shores of the Thracian Cicones; he came at the call of Orpheus, but in vain, for although he was to be sure present at the marriage of Orpheus to Eurydice, he did not smile or bless the pair or give good omens. Even the torch he held kept sputtering with smoke that drew tears and would not burn despite vigorous shaking. The outcome was even more serious than this ominous beginning. For while the new bride was wandering through the grass accompanied by a band of Naiads, she was bitten on the ankle by a serpent and collapsed in death.

After Orpheus, the bard of the Thracian mountains, had wept his fill to the breezes of the upper world, he dared to descend to the Styx by the entrance near Taenarus so that he might rouse even the shades.[1] Past the tenuous multitudes of ghosts beyond the grave, he approached Persephone and her lord, who rule this unlovely realm of shadows, and sang his song as he plucked the strings of his lyre: "O deities of the world below the earth, into which all of us who are mortal return, if it is right and you allow me to utter the truth, laying aside evasion and falsehood, I did not come down to see the realms of Tartarus or to bind the triple neck, bristling with serpents, of the monstrous hound descended from Medusa; the cause of my journey is my wife; she stepped on a snake, and its venom coursing through her veins stole from her the bloom of her years. I wanted to be able to endure, and I admit that I have tried; but Love has conquered. He is a god who is well known in the world above; I suspect that he is famous even here as well (although I do not know for sure); if the story of the abduction of long ago is not a lie, Love also brought you two together.

"By these places full of fear, by this yawning Chaos, and by the silent vastness of this kingdom, reweave I pray the thread of Eurydice's destiny cut off too soon! We pay everything to you, and after tarrying but a little while, we hasten more slowly or more quickly to this one abode. All of us direct our course here, this is our very last home, and you hold the longest sway over the human race. Eurydice too, when she in her ripe age has gone through the just allotment of her years, will fall under your power; I ask as a gift her return to me. If the Fates refuse this reprieve for my wife, it is sure that I do not wish to return either. Take joy in the death of us both!"

As he made this plea and sang his words to the tune of his lyre, the bloodless spirits wept; Tantalus stopped reaching for the receding waters, the wheel of Ixion stopped in wonder, the vultures ceased tearing at the liver of Tityus, the Danaid descendants of Belus left their urns empty, and you, O Sisyphus, sat on your stone. Then for the first time, the story has it, the cheeks of the Eumenides were moist with tears as they were overcome by his song, and the king who rules these lower regions and his regal wife could not endure his pleas or their refusal. They called Eurydice; she was among the more recent shades and she approached, her step slow because of her wound. Thracian Orpheus took her and with her the command that he not turn back his gaze until he had left the groves of Avernus, or the gift would be revoked.

Through the mute silence, they wrest their steep way, arduous, dark, and thick with black vapors. They were not far from the border of the world above; here frightened that she might not be well and yearning to see her with his own eyes, through love he turned and looked, and with his gaze she slipped away and down. He stretched out his arms, struggling to embrace and be embraced, but unlucky and unhappy he grasped nothing but the limp and yielding breezes. Now as Eurydice was dying for a second time, she did not reproach her husband; for what complaint should she have except that she was loved? She uttered for the very last time a farewell that barely reached his ears and fell back once more to the same place.

Orpheus, Eurydice, and Hermes. Marble relief, Roman copy of a Greek original of the fifth century B.C.; height $46\frac{1}{2}$ in. This panel was originally part of a parapet placed around the Altar of the Twelve Gods in the Agora at Athens. It shows the moment when Orpheus has looked back at Eurydice and they part forever. Hermes Psychopompos has his hand on Eurydice's wrist, ready to lead her back to the Underworld—a poignant contrast with the tender placement of Eurydice's left hand on her husband's shoulder. The names of the figures appear above them, Orpheus' being written right to left. *(Museo Nazionale, Naples. Photograph courtesy of the Bettmann Archive.)*

At the second death of his wife, Orpheus was stunned. . . . The ferryman kept Orpheus back as he begged in vain, wishing to cross over once again; yet he remained seated on the bank for seven days, unkempt and without food, the gift of Ceres; anxiety, deep grief, and tears were his nourishment as he bewailed the cruelty of the gods of Erebus. He then withdrew to the mountains of Thrace, Rhodope, and windswept Haemus. Three times the Titan sun had rounded out the year with the sign of watery Pisces, and Orpheus the while had fled from love with all women, either because of his previous woe or because he had made a pledge. Many women were seized with passion for union with the bard and many in anguish were repulsed. He was the originator for the Thracian peoples of turning to the love of young men and of enjoying the brief spring of their youth and plucking its first flowers. . . .

While the Thracian bard was inducing the woods, the rocks, and the hearts of the wild beasts to follow him, Ciconian women, their frenzied breasts clad in animal skins, spied Orpheus from the top of a hill as he was singing to his lyre. One of them, her hair tossing in the light breeze, exclaimed: "Ah look, here is the one who despises us." And she hurled her weapon, wreathed with foliage, straight at the face of Apollo's son as he sang, and it made its mark but did not wound. The weapon of another was a stone, which as it hurtled was overcome in midair by the harmony of voice and lyre and fell prone at his feet like a suppliant apologizing for so furious an assault. But their hostility grew more bold, and restraint was abandoned until the Fury of madness held absolute sway. All weapons would have been softened by his song, but the great clamor, the Phrygian flutes with their curved pipes, the drums, the pounding, and the Bacchic shrieks drowned out the sound of his lyre.

Then at the last the stones that could not hear grew red with the blood of the poet. But first the maenads seized the hordes of birds still spellbound by the singer's voice, the serpents, and the throng of beasts, all testimonies to the triumph of his song. And then they turned with bloody hands on Orpheus himself, like birds that throng together if at any time they see the owl of night abroad by day. They made for the bard, just as the stag about to die is prey for the dogs in the morning sand of the amphitheater, and they flung the verdant leafy thyrsus, not made for such deadly purpose. Some hurled clods of earth, others branches ripped from trees, still others stones.

So that weapons might not be wanting for their fury, it happened that oxen were working the earth, yoked to the ploughshare; and nearby sturdy farmers were digging the hard fields with much sweat preparing for the harvest. When they saw the throng, they fled leaving behind the tools with which they worked. Hoes, heavy mattocks, and long rakes lay scattered through the empty fields. The madwomen snatched them up; and after they had torn apart the oxen that threatened with their horns, they rushed back again to mete out the poet's fate. In their sacrilege they destroyed him as he stretched out his hands and spoke then for the first time in vain with a voice that touched no one. And through that mouth, which was heard, god knows, by stones and understood by bestial senses, his soul breathed forth receding on the winds.

For you, O Orpheus, for you the trees let fall their leaves and shorn of foliage made lament. They say too that rivers swelled with their own tears, and the Naiads and Dryads changed their robes to black and wore their hair disheveled. His limbs lie scattered in various places; his head and lyre you got, O river Hebrus; and—O wonder—while they floated in midstream, the lyre made some plaintive lamentation, I know not what, the lifeless tongue murmured laments too, and the banks lamented in reply. And then they left his native Thracian river and were carried out to sea, until they reached Methymna on the island of Lesbos. Here they were washed ashore on foreign sands, and a savage snake made for the mouth and hair soaked with the dripping foam. At last Phoebus Apollo appeared and stopped the serpent as it prepared to make its bite and froze hard its open mouth and gaping jaws, just as they were, in stone.

The shade of Orpheus went down below the earth and recognized all the places he had seen before; he looked amid the fields of the pious and found Eurydice, and clasped her in his eager arms. Here now they walk together side by side, sometimes he follows her as she precedes, sometimes he goes ahead and safely now looks back at his Eurydice.

As Ovid continues the story, we learn that Bacchus was distressed at the loss of the poet who sang his mysteries; he punished the Thracian women by turning them into trees and then abandoned Thrace all together.

The other major classical version of the story of Orpheus and Eurydice is Vergil's.[2] Most, but not all, of the details are similar, although the poetic timbre is different. According to Vergil, Eurydice stepped on the snake while running away from the unwelcome advances of Aristaeus.[3] Thus Ovid and Vergil represent the tradition for the tragic love story of Orpheus and Eurydice, a paean to the devotion of lover and beloved, husband and wife. Their eternal myth has been recreated again and again with imagination, beauty, and profundity

Orpheus and Eurydice, by Isamu Noguchi (1904–1988). Scenic model, 1948. In this model for a scene from the ballet *Orpheus,* with choreography by Balanchine and music by Stravinsky, Orpheus charms all the Underworld by his music, so that, according to Noguchi, "glowing rocks, like astral bodies, levitate." *(Photograph by Rudolph Burckhardt. Courtesy of the Isamu Noguchi Foundation, Inc.)*

whether it be in an opera by Gluck or a movie by Cocteau. Orpheus has become the archetype of the poet and musician, and the great and universal power of art.

Life of Orpheus, Religious Poet and Musician

There is another very important side to Orpheus' character, of which we can only catch glimpses today because of the inadequacy of our evidence. Orpheus was considered the founder of a religion, a prophet, who with his priests and disciples committed to writing holy words that provided a bible for dogma, ritual, and behavior. Variations and inconsistencies in the tradition make it difficult to know this Orpheus and his religion precisely, but the general nature of their character and development can be discerned, despite the frustrating contradictions and obscurities.[4] Some of the significant "facts" that can be isolated from the diverse accounts are as follows.

Orpheus' home was in Thrace; his mother was one of the Muses, usually Calliope; his father was either Oeagrus, a Thracian river-god, or the great god Apollo, whom he followed. He wooed and won Eurydice, a Dryad, by the charm of his music. When she died, he went to Hades to fetch her but failed. Orpheus was one of the members of Jason's Argonautic expedition.[5] He had a son or a pupil, Musaeus, who assumed many of the characteristics of Orpheus himself. Among the versions of his death, several prove interesting in the quest for the historical religious teacher. He is said to have been struck down by the thunderbolt of Zeus because in his mysteries he taught things unknown before; he also is said to have died through a conspiracy of his countrymen, who would not accept his teachings.

The common tradition (which both Ovid and Vergil reflect) makes the women of Thrace responsible for his death. But the reasons for their hostility vary: they were angry because he neglected them after the death of Eurydice, or refused to initiate them into his mysteries, or enticed their husbands away from them. Sometimes the women are followers of Dionysus, expressly directed against Orpheus by their god, for Dionysus in his attempts to convert Thrace to his religion met the opposition of Orpheus, a devoted follower of Apollo the sun-god, and sent his maenads to tear the bard to pieces. According to some, the fragments of his body were buried by his mother and sister Muses in Thrace or in the region of Mt. Olympus. His head and lyre were claimed by Lesbos (as already explained by Ovid), where a shrine was erected in his honor. The head became an oracular source, but its prophecies were suppressed by Apollo. A temple of Bacchus was built over the spot where the head was buried.[6]

In these conflicting speculations, a fundamental and puzzling duality is evident. Orpheus is linked in one way or another to both Apollo and Dionysus. Was there a *real* Orpheus, a missionary in Thrace who met his death violently? Did he champion Apollo against Dionysus or Dionysus against Apollo? Did he compromise and adapt the religion of the Oriental Dionysus to that of Hellenic Apollo, taking from both and preaching a message that was new and convincing, at least to some?

However one would like to interpret the evidence, this duality cannot be ignored. The music, magic, and prophecy suggest Apollo, as does the championship of civilization, but Apollo silenced the oracle of Orpheus, whose sermon of gentleness and peace has none of the violence of the archer-god. On the other hand, Orpheus' music is the antithesis of the clashing din of Bacchus; and the tales of his misogyny could imply a religion that at some period was confined to men, in contrast to the worship of Dionysus with its appeal to women. At the same time, Orphic initiation and mysteries are by their very nature Dionysiac. Other elements in the legends of both Orpheus and Dionysus are strikingly parallel: Orpheus is torn to pieces like Dionysus himself (at the hands of the Titans), or like Pentheus, who also opposed the god and met destruction of the hands of his Maenads. Like Orpheus, Dionysus descended to the Underworld, in his case to fetch his mother, Semele; indeed, a less common variant has Orpheus successful (like Dionysus) in his pursuit of Eurydice.[7]

There is nevertheless a well-established tradition that the historic Orpheus was not a god but a hero who lived, suffered, and died; his tomb was sacred, and he had a cult. He was in this view a prophet, a priest, or if you like, a saint, whose god was Apollo or Dionysus or both. Such a belief is ultimately subjective; but by the fifth century B.C. he *was* accepted as a human religious teacher, whose doctrine was communicated in sacred writings attributed to him and believed to be much earlier in time. Tablets were said to be found in the mountains of Thrace inscribed with his writing, prescribing potent charms, incantations, and spells. In the fourth century, Plato quotes hexameter lines of Orpheus and tells of priests who preached his message of salvation. Later, Orpheus is credited with songs about the gods and the origin of all things. The hymns that have come down to us under Orpheus' name[8] were given their present form in the early centuries of our era; in fact this corpus of *Orphic Hymns* may have been composed (rather than compiled) in the second or third century A.D. It is of little help for reconstructing early Orphic doctrine.[9]

The Orphic Bible

Dominant in the pantheon of Orphism was Dionysus, very often under the name of Zagreus. Although we hear about initiation into mysteries and a ritual life of purity demanded by the Orphics, we do not know their details. The shedding of blood and the eating of flesh seem to have been important prohibitions inspired by a fundamental belief in the transmigration of the soul and the sanctity of all life. It is possible to reconstruct the basic themes of the Orphic theogony, with its myth of Dionysus crucial to the doctrine. Although parallels to the *Theogony* of Hesiod are apparent, there are meaningful differences and variations. The major stages in the Orphic theogony run as follows, although divergent statements in the tradition are many.

The first principle was Chronus (Time), sometimes described as a monstrous serpent having the heads of a bull and a lion with a god's face between; Chronus was accompanied by brooding Adrasteia (Necessity), and from Chronus came Aether, Chaos, and Erebus. In Aether, Chronus fashioned an egg that split in two; and from this appeared the firstborn of all the gods, Phanes, the creator of everything, called by many names, among them Eros.[10] He was a bisexual deity, with gleaming golden wings and four eyes, described as possessing the appearance of various animals. Phanes bore a daughter, Night, who became his partner in creation and eventually his successor in power. Night then bore Gaea (Earth) and Uranus (Heaven), and they produced the Titans. Next Cronus succeeded to the rule of Night and subsequently (as in the Hesiodic account) Zeus wrested power from his father, Cronus.

Then Zeus swallowed Phanes, and with him all previous creation (including a special race of human beings of a golden age); Zeus now created everything anew, with the help of Night. As second creator, Zeus became the beginning and middle and end of all things. Eventually Zeus mated with Kore (Persephone), and Dionysus was born. This myth of the birth of Dionysus is most potent for the dogma it provides, but we have related it in connection with the study of Dionysus himself. Its essential features are that the infant god is killed and devoured by the monstrous Titans, who are struck down in punishment by the thunderbolt of Zeus. From the ashes of the Titans came mortals; thus humans are partly evil and mortal but also partly pure and divine, since the wicked Titans had consumed the god, although not completely. The heart of Dionysus was saved, and he was born again.

In this way, the Orphic bible provided the divine authority for belief in an immortal soul; the necessity for keeping this soul pure despite the contamination and degradation of the body; the concept of a kind of original sin; the transmigration of the soul to an afterlife of reward or punishment; and finally, after various stages of purification, an apotheosis, a union with the divine spirit in the realms of the upper aether. The seeds of everything came from Phanes or Zeus; out of the One, all things come to be and into the One they are once again resolved.

Plato's myth of Er and Vergil's vision of the afterlife are, as far as we can tell, strongly influenced by Orphic concepts; a reading of both, translated in Chapter 13, conveys most simply and directly a feeling for the basic tenets of Orphism. The ritual purification and catharsis of the great god Apollo are mingled with the Dionysiac belief in the ultimate immortality of the human soul to provide a discipline and control of the ecstatic passion of his Bacchic mysteries.

Mystery religions have been a persistent theme; their spiritual ethos has been associated with Eros, Rhea, Cybele and Attis, Aphrodite and Adonis, Dionysus, Demeter, and Orpheus. We cannot distinguish with clear precision among the many different mystery religions and philosophies of the ancient world. It is possible, for example, to argue that the mysteries of Demeter, with their emphasis on participation in certain dramatic rites, lacked the spiritual depth of Orphism, with its insistence on the good life as well as mere initiation and ritual. In any comparison or contrast for the greater glory or detriment of one god or goddess and one religion as opposed to another, it must be remembered that we know practically nothing about the Greek and Roman mysteries. In contrast, our knowledge, say, of Christianity, particularly in its full development, is infinitely greater.

The correspondences between Christianity and the other mystery religions of antiquity are perhaps more startling than the differences. Orpheus and Christ share attributes in the early centuries of our era;[11] and of all the ancient deities, Dionysus has most in common with the figure of Christ.

Mystery Religions in Roman Times

Indeed, the association of Christ with the vine frequently led to the use of the myths and attributes of Dionysus in early Christian iconography. We discuss below (p. 584) the third-century A.D. wall mosaic in the cemetery beneath St. Peter's basilica in the Vatican and the fourth-century vault mosaics in the church of Santa Costanza in Rome (see Color Plate 5). In both cases, the vine of Dionysus, the symbol of new life after release from the old life, is associated with the Christian resurrection and the words of Christ in John 15. 1, "I am the true vine." In the same cemetery there is a tomb containing both pagan and Christian burials, one of which is a third-century sarcophagus decorated with a relief showing Dionysus finding Ariadne. Whether the occupant of the sarcophagus was Christian or not, the finding of Ariadne as she wakes from sleep, by the god of life renewed, is an allegory of the soul waking from death equally applicable to the Christian doctrine of the resurrection or to pagan beliefs in an afterlife. The mysteries of Dionysus were widely practiced, and the similarities between them and the Christian *mythoi* made the process of *syncretism* inevitable. This term literally means "growing together," and in the context of religion and mythology it describes the harmonizing of different cults and their myths into some sort of unity. We give a famous example of the process in our discussion of Isis below.

Mystery religions were widely practiced in the Roman Empire during the first four centuries of the Christian era.[12] Like Christianity, they gave the individual worshiper hope for a better life in an uncertain world and frequently the expectation of a new life after death. Since mystery religions involved initiation into secret knowledge, our information about them is at best partial and generally inadequate. We can say with certainty that the mysteries involved a sense of belonging to a group and that initiation preceded some sort of revelation, which resulted in a sense of release and joy, with hope for a better future in this life and in the life after death. Often the initiate submitted to the discipline of a rule of life, so that morality and religion were closely associated.

The mysteries of Demeter at Eleusis (discussed at length in Chapter 12) attracted initiates from all classes all over the empire and continued to be practiced down into late antiquity.[13] The sanctuary was destroyed by the Huns in A.D. 395, and the Christians saw to it that it was never rebuilt.

Other Greek mystery cults continued to flourish in the Roman Empire. The mysteries of Cybele and Attis continued to be important throughout the Roman world, but their violent elements, especially the self-mutilation of the *Galli* (i.e., priests), made the cult less attractive than other cults with central resurrection myths (see p. 536). Shedding the blood of a bull came to be a spectacular feature of the rite of initiation into these mysteries. It was called the *taurobolium,* and the initiate stood in a pit under the bull, so that its blood poured down upon him.[14] This baptism symbolized purification, the washing away of the old life, and resurrection to a new one; and the rebirth was further symbolized by the drinking of milk, the drink of a newborn child, while the ancient musical instruments of Cybele's worship became part of a kind of communion: "I have eaten from the tambourine, I have drunk from the cymbal, I have become a mystic of Attis," are the words of one hymn. Like the Eleusinian mysteries, the mysteries of Cybele ceased to be practiced after the fourth century.

Three Eastern mystery religions widely practiced in the Roman Empire were sometimes assimilated to Greek and Roman mythology. From Persia came the mysteries of Mithras (or Mithra), the god of light and truth and righteous champion of good against evil. His myth included a miraculous birth from a rock and the slaying of a bull, from whose blood sprang the fertility of the earth. Mithraism was practiced in underground chapels or *Mithraea.* More than four hundred of these have been found all over the Roman world, wherever Roman soldiers and merchants traveled. Basic to the iconography of a Mithraeum was a *tauroctony,* a scene depicting Mithras, amidst other figures, killing a bull, presumably a ritualistic sacrifice by which the god assured beneficence and rebirth for his initiates.[15] The cult appealed especially to officers, soldiers, and sailors; and only men could be initiated. We do not know the details of the initiation rituals, but we do know that there were seven grades of initiation and that the cult demanded a high level of self-discipline from its initiates. Its ceremonies also involved a communal meal. Mithraism was a major rival to Christianity; and, like the other mystery religions we have mentioned, it continued to be practiced widely until the end of the fourth century.

The second Eastern religion, which was not strictly a mystery religion with the usual elements of secrecy and revelation, was the worship of Atargatis, known to the Romans simply as *Dea Syria*, the Syrian goddess. She was originally an earth-mother, like Cybele and Demeter, whose cult was spread through the Roman world especially by soldiers. Shrines have been found at Rome itself and as far away as Hadrian's Wall, which the Romans built in northern England. Her consort was variously called Tammuz or Dushara, but her sacred marriage to the Semitic god of the thunder, Hadad, led to her association with the other sky-gods, the Syrian Baal, the Greek Zeus, and the Roman Jupiter. She was worshiped in wild rituals with self-flagellation by ecstatic priests.[16] Amongst Romans her consort was usually called Jupiter Dolichenus, who was portrayed holding an axe and a thunderbolt and standing upon the back of a bull.[17]

The one mystery religion for which we have a full account of an initiate's conversion is the worship of the Egyptian goddess Isis.[18] Like Demeter and Cybele, she was a goddess of fertility, bringer of new life and hope. Her myth involved a search, in this case for her husband and brother, Osiris (dismembered by the evil power, Seth), and for a child, Horus (also known as Harpocrates). Her attributes included a musical instrument (the *sistrum,* a kind of rattle), a breast-shaped container (the *situla*) for milk, and a jug for the holy water of the Nile. Her cult was associated with the god Serapis, whose origin is quite obscure; temples to Isis and Serapis are found all over the Roman world. Isis herself, however, as mother and nurturer, appealed to multitudes of men and women, who found in her a less terrible presence than that of Cybele or the Syrian goddess. Lucius, the hero of Apuleius' novel *Metamorphoses* (or *The Golden Ass*) appealed to her for help in becoming a human being again and shedding his form as a donkey. She appeared to him in a dream and instructed him to take the garland of roses from the hand of a priest, who would be taking part in the procession in her honor the next day. When Lucius did this, he resumed his human form, and the miracle was greeted with the praise of the crowd (*Metamorphoses* 11. 16):

> The august divinity of the all-powerful goddess today has restored this man to human form. Fortunate indeed and thrice blessed is he who has deserved such glorious protection from heaven because of the innocence of his earlier life and faith.

When Isis first appeared to Lucius in answer to his prayer, she described herself in terms that perfectly illustrate the meaning of syncretism, expressed with a power and enthusiasm that even translation cannot totally obliterate (*Metamorphoses* 11. 5):

> Behold, Lucius, I have come, moved by your prayers. I am the mother of things in nature, the mistress of all the elements, the firstborn of the ages, the sum of the divine powers, queen of the souls of the dead, first of the heavenly powers, the single form of the gods and goddesses, who by my nod control the bright heights of heaven, the health-bringing winds of the sea, the grievous silence of the gods of the Underworld. My name, one with many forms, varied rituals, and many names, is revered by the whole world. Thus the firstborn Phrygians call me Pessinuntia, the Mother of the Gods; the autochthonous people of Attica call me Cecropian Minerva; the Cyprians, tossed by the waves, call me Paphian Venus; the archer Cretans call me Dictynna Diana; the Sicilians of three languages call me Stygian Proserpina; the Eleusinians the ancient goddess Ceres; some call me Juno, others Bellona, some Hecate, others Rhamnusia [i.e., Nemesis]; the . . . Ethiopians . . . and the . . . Egyptians, who worship me with proper ceremonies, call me by my true name, Queen Isis.

Cybele, Athena, Aphrodite, Artemis, Demeter, Persephone, Hera—the ancient Queens of Heaven and Earth—are here, through the process of syncretism, included in the great Egyptian goddess, Isis. Apuleius, whose evidence is almost certainly reliable, shows us how in the second century (he was born about A.D. 120) the figures of Greek and Roman mythology had given way to the idea of a single divine power. Her devotees experienced a sense of liberation, of hope and joy. Lucius (through whom Apuleius is evidently describing his own experience) was initiated three times into the mysteries of Isis and Serapis; and his life was consecrated to Isis. In this experience we can see how the mythology of the gods of the Greek city-state became incorporated in the mysteries that brought hope of salvation to the individual worshiper. The power of that experience is revealed in Lucius' description, with which we end our survey of the mystery religions (*Metamorphoses* 11. 23):

Perhaps you may ask, studious reader, what then was said, what was done. I would tell you, if it were lawful to speak; and you would know, if it were lawful to hear. . . . I do not wish to torture you . . . with the pain of long suspense. Therefore hear, but believe, because these things are true. I approached the boundaries of death; I trod the entrance of Proserpina and, carried through all the elements, I returned. At midnight I saw the sun shining with brilliant light, I came into the presence of the gods below and the gods above, and close by I worshiped them. Behold, I have told you that about which, although you have heard, you must remain ignorant.

SELECT BIBLIOGRAPHY

Orpheus

Alderink, Larry J. *Creation and Salvation in Ancient Orphism.* American Classical Studies 8. Atlanta, Ga.: Scholars Press, 1981.

Athanassakis, Apostolos N. *The Orphic Hymns.* Text, translation, and notes. Atlanta, Ga.: Scholars Press, 1977.

Friedman, John Block. *Orpheus in the Middle Ages.* Cambridge: Harvard University Press, 1970.

Guthrie, W. K. C. *Orpheus and Greek Religion: A Study in the Orphic Movement.* New York: Norton, 1966. The best introductory survey.

Segal, Charles. *Orpheus: The Myth of the Poet.* Baltimore and London: Johns Hopkins University Press, 1989. Chapters deal with various aspects of the subject. Vergil, Ovid, Seneca, H. D., Rukeyser, Rich, Ashbery, and Rilke are among the authors treated. A concluding chapter is called "Orpheus from Antiquity to Today."

Warden, J., ed. *Orpheus: The Metamorphoses of a Myth.* Toronto: University of Toronto Press, 1985.

Mystery Religions

Burkert, Walter. *Ancient Mystery Cults.* Cambridge: Harvard University Press, 1987.

Cole, Susan. *Theoi Megaloi: The Cult of the Great Gods of Samothrace.* Leiden: Brill, 1984.

Cumont, Franz. *The Mysteries of Mithra.* New York: Dover, 1956 [1903].

———. *Oriental Religions in Roman Paganism.* New York: Dover, 1956 [1911].

Reprint of English translation (London: Routledge, 1911) of *Les religions orientales dans le paganisme romain* (Paris, 1906).

Ferguson, John. *The Religions of the Roman Empire.* Ithaca, N.Y.: Cornell University Press, 1970. See especially Chapter 7.

Godwin, Joscelyn. *Mystery Religions in the Ancient World.* Ithaca, N.Y.: Cornell University Press, 1971.

Meyer, Marvin W., ed. *Sacred Texts of the Mystery Religions, A Sourcebook.* San Francisco: Harper & Row, 1987. The translated texts relate to the following mysteries: of the Grain Mother and Daughter; of Andania in Messenia; of Dionysus; of the Great Mother and her Lover and the Syrian Goddess; of Isis and Osiris; of Mithras; and those within Judaism and Christianity.

Mylonas, George E. *Eleusis and the Eleusinian Mysteries.* Princeton: Princeton University Press, 1961.

Nock, Arthur Darby. *Conversion: The Old and the New in Religion from Alexander the Great to Augustine of Hippo.* New York: Oxford University Press, 1961 [1933]. The classic account of the effect of the mysteries on the individual worshiper.

Rahner, Hugo. *Greek Myths and Christian Mystery.* Foreword by E. O. James. New York: Harper & Row, 1963.

Teeple, H. M., ed. Mystery Religions Lecture Series. Ten parts with slides and commentary: 1. H. M. Teeple, *The Mystery Religions: An Overview;* 2. D. E. Aune, *The Eleusinian Mysteries;* 3. S. G. Cole, *The Dionysus Cult;* 4. S. G. Cole, *The Samothracian Mysteries;* 5. L. M. Hoppe, *The Cult of Mithra;* 6. R. A. Wild, *The Isis-Serapis Cult;* 7. L. J. Alderink, *Orphism;* 8. P. F. Gehl, *Cybele and Attis;* 9. R. A. Oden, *The Syrian Goddess;* 10. H. M. Teeple, *The Mystery Religions and Christianity.* Evanston, 1976. Available from Scholars Press, Atlanta, Ga.

Ulansey, David. *The Origins of the Mithraic Mysteries: Cosmology and Salvation in the Ancient World.* New York: Oxford University Press, 1989.

Vermaseren, Maarten J. *Cybele and Attis: The Myth and the Cult.* London: Thames & Hudson, 1977.

PART TWO

THE GREEK SAGAS:

GREEK LOCAL LEGENDS

THE THEBAN SAGA

U niversal themes are persistent in the myths of Greek gods, who present archetypal images of fundamental human traits—the passions, psychology, and mores of mortal men and women writ large—and basic familial relationships, social ties, and political aspirations. Variations of these recurring themes are equally prominent in saga (or legend) and folktale. These classes of myth have been discussed in the introductory chapter (pp. 1–18), and saga will be the principal focus of the following chapters. Although saga has a relationship (however tenuous) to history, it often includes elements of folktale that are common to other legends, and its heroes are descended from gods and often associate with divine beings. A defining feature of saga is the focus upon the deeds of one or more heroes.

The Hero in Saga and Folktale

We have seen (pp. 11–13) how the Russian scholar Vladimir Propp has shown how one particular kind of folktale (the Quest) has a universal structure, in which the elements always appear in the same sequence. In Greek saga, as in folktales, we find many recurring motifs, though not always as predictably as in Propp's structural theory. Nine motifs frequently appear: (1) the hero usually has elements of the extraordinary linked to his birth and his childhood. (2) He inevitably faces opposition of one sort or another from the beginning, and as a result he must prove his inherent worth by surmounting challenges of every kind. (3) His enemy or enemies usually instigate his achievement, and (4) he is helped by at least one ally, divine or human. (5) He faces apparently insuperable obstacles, often labors that must be accomplished or a quest that must be completed. (6) Adventurous conflicts with divine, human, or monstrous opponents present him with physical, sexual, and spiritual challenges. (7) He may also have to observe taboos—he must not, for example, look back, eat of a forbidden fruit, or be too inquisitive. (8) Death itself is the ultimate conquest, usually achieved by going to and returning from the Underworld. (9) The hero's success may be rewarded with marriage, political security, or wealth and power. (10) But knowledge through suffering and more lasting spiritual enlightenment (literal or symbolic)—entailing purification, rebirth, redemption, and even deification—are also part of a hero's attainment. These and other motifs recur with seemingly infinite variation, and they will continue to do so as long as human nature remains the same. Refined by artistic experience, they delight and inform, while they touch the very depths of the human spirit.

The Mycenaean World and Greek Saga

The cycles of Greek saga are for the most part connected with cities and areas that were important in the later Bronze Age—that is, from about 1600 to 1100 B.C. The richest of these cities, Mycenae, gave its name to the period, and it was the king of Mycenae who led the Greeks on the greatest of their expeditions, the war against Troy. There are three major geographical groups in the cycles of saga: first, cities of the Peloponnese—Mycenae, Tiryns, Argos, and Sparta, and the rural area of Arcadia; second, cities of the rest of the Greek mainland and their surrounding areas—Athens in Attica, Thebes and Orchomenus in Boeotia, and Iolcus in Thessaly; third, Troy in Asia Minor, whose relations with the Mycenaean cities may have been extensive. Beyond these groups there are legends connected with Crete, whose Minoan civilization preceded Mycenae as the dominant power in the Aegean world, before its collapse at the end of the fifteenth century B.C. Finally, the story of Odysseus, although based in the Mycenaean world, extends far beyond it and incorporates many folktales.

While there is a historical dimension to Greek saga that archaeological discoveries have confirmed, it cannot be confused with history. Saga concentrates on a few personages (divine or heroic) and their deeds, and is not concerned with geographical and economic facts or the lives of ordinary people.

THE FOUNDING
OF THEBES

The historical Thebes was the leading city of Boeotia, the plainland area of central Greece, ringed by the mountain ranges of Parnes, Cithaeron, Helicon, and Parnassus, and on the east bounded by the Straits of Euboea. Thebes was situated on the low ridge that separates the two chief plains of Boeotia; its citadel was called the Cadmeia, preserving the name of Cadmus, legendary founder of the city. Cadmus was son of Agenor, king of Tyre, and brother of Europa. Agenor sent him to find Europa, whose abduction from Tyre is one of several myths in which a woman was taken against her will from Asia to Europe or vice versa. Herodotus narrates these legends at the beginning of his History in order to underline the difference between mythology and history. In these myths the opposition of the Greek and Asiatic worlds, which came to a historical climax in the Persian Wars of 494–479 B.C., began when Phoenician traders kidnapped the Argive princess Io and took her to Egypt. The Greeks (whom Herodotus calls "Cretans") in return seized the Phoenician princess Europa and took her to Crete. The pattern was then reversed: the Greeks took Medea from Colchis and in return the Trojan Alexander (Paris) took Helen from Sparta. Herodotus explained that the Persians, reasoning from these myths, believed that Europe and Asia were permanently divided and hostile. As a historian he was skeptical about these tales, for he could not vouch for their truth, whereas he could report things of which he had knowledge: "About these things I am not going to come and say that they happened in this way or in another, but the man who I myself know was the beginner of unjust works against the Greeks, this man I will point out and advance with my story . . ." (1.5). So for the Greek historian of the Persian Wars the distinction between myth and history was evident.

Europa

The story of Europa is the first in which the Asiatic figure makes her way to the Greek world. In the usual version of the myth (which is different from the skeptical account of Herodotus) Zeus, disguised as a bull, took her to Crete. Here is Ovid's description of the abduction (*Metamorphoses* 2. 846–3. 2), which should be compared with the illustrations on pages 318 and 319:

 Majesty and love are not well joined, nor do they sit well together. Abandoning the dignity of his royal office, the father and ruler of the gods took on the appearance of a bull, and as a beautiful

The Rape of Europa. Limestone metope from Selinus, ca. 540 B.C.; height 58 in. Europa rides over the sea, represented by the dolphins, upon the bull, which looks frontally at the viewer. The formality and restraint of the relief contrast with the swirling motion of Titian's painting. *(Museo Nazionale, Palermo. Photograph courtesy of Hirmer Verlag, München.)*

animal shambled over the tender grass. Agenor's daughter [Europa] wondered at the bull's beauty, amazed that he did not threaten to attack, yet, gentle as he seemed, she at first was afraid to touch him. After a while she came up close and offered flowers to his white face. The young princess even dared to sit upon the bull's back. Then the god little by little began to take his deceptive steps further from the dry land into the sea, then he went further and carried his prey across the central waters of the sea. At length

The Rape of Europa, by Titian (ca. 1488–1576). Oil on canvas, 1559–1562; 73 × 81 in. Titian relies upon Ovid's narratives (*Fasti* 5. 605–614 and *Metamorphoses* 2. 843–875). As in the Selinus metope, dolphins swim near the bull (one in the right foreground and one supporting a cupid), and Europa grasps the bull's horn. Her windblown drapery and desperate gestures, and the cupids flying through the air, impart an air of agitated movement in keeping with the mixed emotions, fear and anticipation, of the principal figures. In the distant background Europa's companions vainly call her back to the shore. *(Isabella Stewart Gardner Museum, Boston. Reproduced by permission.)*

he laid aside the disguise of the deceiving bull and revealed who he was and reached the shores of Crete.

In Crete Europa became the mother of Minos by Zeus.

Cadmus, Founder of Thebes

Meanwhile Cadmus, Europa's brother, set out to find her and came to Delphi, where he asked the oracle for advice. Apollo told him not to worry about Europa any more but to follow a certain cow until she lay down out of weariness and there to found a city. Cadmus found the cow in Phocis (the district of Greece in which Delphi is situated), and she led him to Boeotia, where he founded his city, Cadmeia, later called Thebes. As for the divinely sent cow, it was Cadmus' duty to sacrifice her; to perform the ceremony, he needed water, which he sent his companions to draw from the nearby spring sacred to Ares. A serpent, a child of Ares, guarded the spring; it killed most of Cadmus' men, and in return was itself killed by Cadmus. Ovid relates that Cadmus then heard a voice saying: "Why, son of Agenor, do you look at the dead serpent? You too will be looked at as a serpent." Thus the final episode in the life of Cadmus was prophesied.

Athena, to whom Cadmus had been sacrificing the cow, now advised Cadmus to take the serpent's teeth and sow them; from the ground sprang up armed men, who fought and killed each other until only five were left. From these five survivors, who were called Spartoi (i.e., "sown men"), descended the noble families of Thebes.

Euripides' recounts Cadmus' achievement as follows (*Phoenissae [The Phoenician Women] 639-675*):

> Tyrian Cadmus came to this land where the cow fell down on all fours, providing irrevocable fulfillment of the oracle by which god had ordained that he was to make his home amid the fertile plains—here where the beautiful stream of Dirce waters the rich and green fields. In this place the bloodthirsty serpent of Ares kept his savage guard over the freshly flowing waters, looking far and wide with his swiftly darting glances. Cadmus came for sacrificial water and destroyed him, wielding a stone by the might of his arm and showering deadly blows upon the monster's head. At the bidding of Pallas Athena he sowed its teeth in the bountiful ground; and in their place Earth sent up onto its surface the spectacle of armored men. Iron-willed Slaughter sent them back to Mother Earth; and she who had presented them to the bright breezes of the upper air was steeped in their blood.

Now Cadmus had to appease Ares for the death of the serpent; he therefore became his slave for a year (which was the equivalent of eight of our years). At the end of this time he was freed and given Harmonia, daughter of Ares and Aphrodite, as his wife. The marriage was celebrated on the Cadmeia, and all the gods came as guests. Among the gifts for the bride were a robe and a necklace from her husband; the necklace was made by Hephaestus and given by him to Cadmus; it came to play an important part in the Theban saga.

Cadmus and Harmonia had four daughters—Ino, Semele, Autonoë, and Agave—whose stories, with those of their husbands and sons, are told in Chapters 8 and 11.

Despite the misfortunes of their daughters, Cadmus and Harmonia reigned a long time, civilizing their people and introducing knowledge of writing. Eventually they went away to northwest Greece where Cadmus became king of the Illyrians; at the end of their lives, they both were turned into great harmless serpents (according to Euripides and Ovid; Apollodorus says that Zeus sent them to Elysium). They were worshiped by their descendants, and their departure from Cadmeia was not the outcome of any misdeed or grief, but a symbol of their change from mortal to heroic or divine status.

THE FAMILIES OF LABDACUS AND LYCUS

Lycus and Antiope

Cadmus' successor as king was his grandson Pentheus, son of Agave, whose misfortunes are dealt with in Chapter 11. After his death, a new dynasty was founded by Labdacus, possibly a grandson of Cadmus. He is said to have perished while pursuing the same policy as Pentheus, leaving as his successor an infant son, Laius. Lycus, a great-great-uncle of Laius, first assumed the regency and then made himself king, reigning for twenty years. He was the son of Chthonius, one of the five Spartoi, and his family has an important legend. His brother's daughter Antiope was loved by Zeus; while she was pregnant, she fled to Sicyon (a city in the northern Peloponnese) to escape from the anger of her

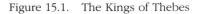

1. Cadmus	6. Laius
2. Pentheus	7. Oedipus (regency of Creon)
3. Labdacus	8. Eteocles
4. Lycus	9. Creon
5. Zethus and Amphion	10. Laodamas

Figure 15.1.   The Kings of Thebes

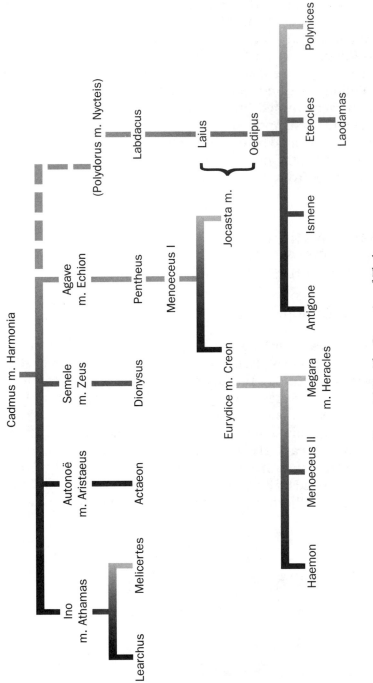

Figure 15.2. The Dynasties of Thebes

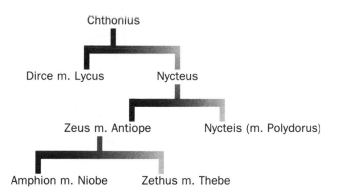

Figure 15.3. The Descendants of Chthonius

father, Nycteus. In despair Nycteus killed himself, and his brother (Lycus) then attacked Sicyon and recovered Antiope.

Somewhere in Boeotia, Antiope gave birth to twin sons, who were left to die. A shepherd found them and named them Amphion and Zethus. Zethus became a skilled herdsman, Amphion a musician, playing on a lyre given him by the god Hermes. Many years later, Amphion and Zethus met and recognized their mother, who had escaped from the imprisonment in which she was kept by Lycus and his wife, Dirce. They avenged Antiope by killing Lycus and tying Dirce to the horns of a bull that dragged her to her death. From her blood sprang the fountain at Thebes that is called by her name.

Amphion and Zethus now became rulers of Cadmeia and drove Laius into exile. They built walls for the city, whose stones were moved into place by the music of Amphion's lyre. Amphion married Niobe (whose story is told above, pp. 159–160), and Zethus married Thebe, in whose honor the newly walled city was renamed Thebes.

The story of the family of Lycus repeats motifs from the story of Cadmus. The walling of Cadmeia and its renaming is a doublet of the founding of the city by Cadmus, and just as Cadmus and Harmonia civilized their people, so Amphion's music demonstrated the power of harmony and beauty over the disunited and inanimate stones.

Laius

After a reign of many years Amphion and Zethus died, and Laius returned from exile and resumed the kingship of which he had been deprived as an infant. In exile, he had been hospitably received by

Pelops, king of Elis. The ties of guest and host were among the most sacred of human relationships, and Laius brought upon himself and his descendants a curse by abducting Chrysippus, the son of Pelops, with whom he had fallen in love. Apollo foretold the working out of the curse in the first generation when Laius (now king of Thebes) consulted the Delphic oracle about the children who should be born to him and his wife, Jocasta. This is the reply of the oracle (Sophocles, Argument to *Oedipus Tyrannus*):

> I will give you a son, but you are destined to die at his hands. This is the decision of Zeus, in answer to the bitter curses of Pelops, whose son you abducted; all this did Pelops call down upon you.

Oedipus, Son of Laius and Jocasta

When a son was born, Laius attempted to avoid the fate foretold by the oracle by ordering the infant to be exposed upon Mt. Cithaeron, with a spike driven through his ankles. The servant entrusted with the task pitied the baby, and instead gave him to a Corinthian shepherd (for the Theban and Corinthian summer pastures were adjacent on Cithaeron). The shepherd in turn brought the infant to his master, Polybus, king of Corinth. The child was brought up as the son of Polybus and his queen, Merope, and was called Oedipus (which means "swellfoot") from the injury to his ankles.

Years later, a drunken companion jeered at Oedipus during a feast at Corinth and said that he was not Polybus' natural son. In alarm and shame at the taunt (which soon spread through the city), Oedipus left Corinth to ask the oracle at Delphi who his parents were. The oracle warned him in reply to avoid his homeland, since he must murder his father and marry his mother. So he determined not to return to Corinth and took the road from Delphi that led to Thebes. What happened then, Oedipus himself relates to Jocasta (Sophocles, *Oedipus Tyrannus* 800–813):

> As I came on my journey to this junction of three roads, a herald and a man (like him whom you described) riding in a horse-drawn chariot blocked my way; they violently drove me off the road. In anger I struck the driver, who was pushing me aside; and when the old man saw me passing by him, he took aim at the middle of my head and struck me with the two-pronged goad. But he paid for this with interest; struck promptly by the staff in this hand of mine, he quickly tumbled out of the chariot. I killed them all.[1]

The old man, whom Oedipus did not recognize, was Laius. The curse of Pelops was being fulfilled.

Oedipus and the Sphinx

So Oedipus came to Thebes, a city in distress; not only was the king dead, but also the city was plagued by a monster sent by Hera, called Sphinx (which means "strangler"). This creature had the face of a woman, the body of a lion, and the wings of a bird. It had learned a riddle from the Muses, which it asked the Thebans. Those who could not answer the riddle, it ate; and it was prophesied that Thebes would be free of the Sphinx only when the riddle was answered. The riddle was: "What is it that has one name that is four-footed, two-footed, and three-footed?"[2] No Theban had been able to find the answer; and in despair, the regent Creon (son of Menoeceus and brother of Jocasta) offered both the throne and his sister as wife to anyone who could do so. Oedipus succeeded. "Man," said he, "is the answer: for as an infant he goes upon four feet; in his prime upon two; and in old age he takes a stick as a third foot." And so the Sphinx threw itself off the Theban acropolis; Oedipus became king of Thebes and husband of the widowed queen, his mother.

The Recognition of Oedipus

Thus the prophecy of Apollo was fulfilled; what remained was for the truth to be discovered. There are three versions, two Homeric and one Sophoclean, of Oedipus' fate. According to Homer, Epicasta (Homer's name for Jocasta) married her own son "and the gods speedily made it known to mortals. Unhappily he reigned on at Thebes, but she went down to the house of Hades, fastening a noose to the roof of the lofty hall" (*Odyssey* 11. 271). In the *Iliad,* Oedipus is spoken of as having fallen in battle. In this version, another wife is the mother of the children of Oedipus.

The most widely accepted story, however, is the later version, that of Sophocles. Oedipus and Jocasta lived happily together, and she bore him two sons, Polynices and Eteocles, and two daughters, Antigone and Ismene. After many years, a plague afflicted Thebes, and the oracle of Apollo advised the Thebans that it was the result of a pollution on their state, for the murderer of Laius was in their midst. At this point, Polybus died, and the messenger who brought the news also brought the invitation to Oedipus from the people of Corinth to become their king. Oedipus, still thinking that Merope was his mother, refused to return to Corinth; but the messenger—who was the same shepherd to whom the infant exposed on Cithaeron had been given—tried to reassure him by telling him that he was not in fact the son of Merope and Polybus. Oedipus then sent for the servant to whom Laius had given his infant son to be exposed on Mt. Cithaeron. This man was also the sole survivor of the incident in which Laius died. Now the truth came out. This is how Sophocles describes the moment of Oedipus' discovery. He is questioning the servant (who already knows the truth) in the presence of the messenger (*Oedipus Tyrannus* 1164–1185):

OEDIPUS: Which of these citizens [gave you the baby] and from what house [did it come]?

SERVANT: Do not, I beg you by the gods, master, do not question me any more.

OEDIPUS: You will be killed if I have to ask you this question again.

SERVANT: Well, it was one of the children of Laius.

OEDIPUS: A slave? Or one of his own children?

SERVANT: Alas! I am on the point of revealing a terrible secret!

OEDIPUS: And I of hearing it. Yet hear it I must.

SERVANT: Well, it was called the son of Laius. The woman inside the palace best would tell—your wife—the facts.

OEDIPUS: So she it was who gave you the baby?

SERVANT: Yes, my lord.

OEDIPUS: For what purpose?

SERVANT: That I might kill him.

OEDIPUS: Was she his mother, unhappy woman?

SERVANT: Yes, and she was afraid of the harm that had been foretold by the oracle.

OEDIPUS: And what was that?

SERVANT: The prophecy was that he would kill his parents.

OEDIPUS: How then did you give him up to this old man, how did *you?*

SERVANT: I was sorry for him, master, and I thought this man would carry him to another country, from which he came himself. But he saved him for evils much worse. For if *you* are the person this man says you are, then, I tell you, you were born to a wretched destiny.

OEDIPUS: Alas! Alas! All is revealed! O light, may this be the last time I look upon you, I who have been shown to be born from those from whom I should not have been born, to be living with those with whom I should not live, and to have killed those whom I should not have killed!

The horror of Oedipus' predicament is powerfully expressed in the stark dialogue, and it is no wonder that Sophocles' version of the myth has swept aside all other versions.[3] While Oedipus was questioning the servant, Jocasta, who already knew the truth, had gone into the palace and hanged herself. Oedipus rushed into the palace and, when he saw her corpse, blinded himself with the brooches from her robe. Creon became regent again, and Oedipus was banished, in accordance with a curse he himself earlier pronounced on the (as yet unknown) killer of Laius and in obedience to an oracle of Apollo.

The Exile of Oedipus and the End of His Life

Oedipus wandered for years, accompanied by his daughter Antigone, until he finally came to Colonus in Attica. There he was received with kindness by the king of Athens, Theseus, who did not allow the Thebans to force him to return (for it had been prophesied that the land in which he was buried would prosper); shortly afterward he disappeared from the earth.

Sophocles describes the end of Oedipus' life at Colonus. We give the passage in full here, since it clearly tells us how Sophocles viewed the relationship of Oedipus the man to Oedipus the hero. The poet carefully describes the place, for a hero is associated with a particular locality. He connects Oedipus' passing with the powers beneath the earth (Zeus is called by his title Chthonius, that is, "Zeus of the Earth"); yet Theseus rightly worships the powers of both earth and heaven after the miracle, for the hero is part of the array of Greek divinities, those of heaven as well as the chthonic powers. And Oedipus' passing is miraculous and without grief, in this symbolizing his benign influence upon the place where he passed from mortal sight and his power as a hero to perform miracles for those who worship him. Here then is Sophocles' description, spoken by a messenger (*Oedipus Coloneus* 1587–1665):

You know how he left this place without any of his friends to guide him, himself the leader of us all. When he came to the edge of the ravine, which is rooted in the earth by the brazen stairs, he stood in one of the paths which meet there—the place is by the hollow basin where the pact of Theseus and Pirithoüs was forever made. Around him were the rock of Thoricus, the hollow wild pear tree, and the stone tomb. Here he sat and loosened his dust-stained garments. Then he called his daughters and bade them bring him water from the running stream to wash with and make libations. So they went to the hill of Demeter, bringer of green freshness, which overlooks the place, and soon returned bringing what their father had asked for. Thus they washed and clothed him as custom demands. When he was satisfied with all that they were doing and none of his commands had gone unfulfilled, then Zeus of the Earth thundered, and the girls shuddered as they heard. They clasped their father's knees and wept; continuously they beat their breasts and wailed. But he immediately answered their unhappy cry, clasped his arms around them, and said: "My children, today your father ceases to be. All that is mine has come to an end; no more need you labor to support me. Hard was that task, I know, my daughters; yet one word alone relieves all that toil—for of *Love* you never will have more from any man than me. And now you will pass your lives bereft of me."

In this way they all sobbed and wept, embracing each other. When they came to an end of weeping and were silent, a sudden voice called him and all were afraid and their hair stood on end. It was God who called him repeatedly. "Oedipus, Oedipus," he called, "why wait we to go? Too long have you delayed." Then Oedipus, knowing that God was calling him, called King Theseus to him, and when he drew near said: "Dear friend, give your hand to my children as a solemn pledge, and you, my children, give yours to him. And do you, Theseus, swear never knowingly to betray these girls and always to act for their good." And Theseus, without complaint, swore on his oath that he would do as his friend asked, for he was a man of generous nature.

When this was done, Oedipus straightway felt his children with unseeing hands and said: "My daughters, you must resolutely leave this place; you may not ask to see what is not right for you to see, nor hear words that you should not hear. Go then; let only King Theseus stay and behold what will be done."

All of us heard his words, and with groans and tears went with the girls. As we began to leave, we turned and saw Oedipus no longer there; the king we saw, shielding his eyes with his hand, as if some dread sight had appeared which he could not bear to look upon. Yet soon after we saw him worship Earth and Olympus, the gods' home above, with the same words.

How Oedipus died no man can tell except Theseus. No fiery thunderbolt from God consumed him, no whirlwind from the sea. Some divine messenger came for him, or the deep foundations of the earth parted to receive him, kindly and without pain. Without grief he passed from us, without the agony of sickness; his going was more than mortal, a miracle.

So Oedipus became a hero, bringing good to the country in which he lay.

Sophocles developed this version of the story to do honor to Attica and to his own deme of Colonus. Outside Athens, the story was different. According to this version, Oedipus shut himself up in the palace and lived there while Creon was regent. One day his sons put before him a less honorable portion of meat than was his due; he cursed them, praying that they might fight to divide their kingdom. After his death the curse was fulfilled.[4]

The story of Oedipus is among the best-known classical legends, largely because of the use made of it by psychologists ever since Freud's identification of the "Oedipus complex" in 1910. Sophocles was aware of the Oedipus complex, in part, at any rate: "Many men," says Jocasta (*Oedipus Tyrannus* 981), "have in dreams lain with their mothers," and we have already noted how Greek myths of creation are permeated with the concepts of the mother-son relationship and of conflict between father and son. We should be skeptical of attempts to interpret the legend in purely psychological terms, for Sophocles and his predecessors were concerned with the historical, theological and other aspects of the myth.

THE SEVEN AGAINST THEBES

The Preliminaries to the Expedition

Eteocles and Polynices, the two sons of Oedipus, quarreled over the kingship at Thebes. They agreed that each should rule in alternate years, while the other went into exile. Eteocles ruled for the first year, while Polynices went to Argos, taking with him the necklace and robe of Harmonia. At Argos Polynices and another exile, Tydeus of Arcadia, married the daughters of the king, Adrastus, who promised to restore them to their lands, and decided to attack Thebes first. This war and its consequences are the subject of the saga of the Seven against Thebes, which is the title of one of the tragedies of Aeschylus.

Several other dramas deal with the saga, including two with the title *Phoenician Women,* one by Euripides and the other by the Roman author Seneca. The consequences of the war are the subject of *The Suppliant Women* by Euripides and of *Antigone* by Sophocles. The saga is most fully narrated by the Roman poet Statius, whose epic, *Thebaid,* written in about A.D. 90, was widely read in medieval and Renaissance Europe.

The Argive army had seven leaders: besides Adrastus, Polynices, and Tydeus, there were Capaneus, Hippomedon, Parthenopaeus, and Amphiaraüs. Amphiaraüs, who had the gift of prophecy, knew that except for Adrastus all seven would be killed, and therefore opposed the expedition. But Polynices bribed Amphiaraüs' wife, Eriphyle, with the necklace of Harmonia, to persuade her husband to change his mind. As he set out, he ordered his sons to avenge his death on their mother, and themselves to make an expedition against Thebes when that of the Seven had failed.

Incidents on the Journey from Argos to Thebes

Before the army reached Thebes, two episodes intervened. At Nemea (not far from the Isthmus of Corinth) they were led to a spring of water by Hypsipyle, nurse of Opheltes, the infant son of the local king. She left the baby lying on the ground while she showed the way, and he was killed by a serpent. The Seven killed the serpent and celebrated in honor of the dead child the athletic contests that became the Nemean Games. His name was changed by Amphiaraüs from Opheltes (Snake Child) to Archemorus (Beginner of Death), as an omen of what was yet to come.

In the second episode Tydeus was sent to Thebes as an ambassador to demand the abdication of Eteocles in accordance with his agreement with Polynices. While at Thebes, he took part in an athletic contest and by winning humiliated the Thebans, who ambushed him as he returned to the army. He killed all fifty of his attackers, except for one man who took the news to Thebes.

The Failure of the Attack on Thebes

When the army reached Thebes each leader attacked one of the city's seven gates. The central part of Aeschylus' tragedy *Seven against Thebes,* consists of matched speeches in which the herald describes each of the Seven and is answered by Eteocles, who stations a Theban hero at each gate of the city. The herald's speeches give a vivid idea of the qualities of each of the Argive heroes (selections from Aeschylus, *Seven against Thebes* 375–685):[5]

Tydeus raging . . . shouts out with midday cries like a dragon. . . . Upon his shield he has this proud sign embossed, the heaven blazing beneath the stars. The bright full moon, the oldest of the stars, the eye of night, shines brightly in the middle of the shield. . . .

Capaneus . . . is another giant, greater than the one already named. . . . He threatens to sack the city, whether the god is willing or not. . . . His device is a naked man carrying fire, and the torch with which his hand is equipped blazes, and in golden letters he says, "I will burn the city."

Hippomedon with a war-cry stands before the gates of Athena. . . . It was no mean craftsman who placed this work upon his shield, Typhon, belching fiery smoke through his mouth, and the encircling hollow of the shield is covered with wreathed serpents. . . .

[Parthenopaeus the Arcadian] swears . . . that he will violently sack the city of Cadmeia. . . . Upon his bronze shield he wields the flesh-eating Sphinx, the reproach of the city. . . .

The sixth I would say is the most virtuous man, the prophet best in might, strong Amphiaraüs. . . . Upon his shield was no sign, for he did not wish to seem, but to be, the best. . . . Against him I advise setting wise and virtuous defenders, for terrible are those whom the gods revere.

Finally the herald describes Polynices, whose threats against his brother are the most terrible of all. Upon his shield is a double device, a woman leading an armed man:

She says she is Justice, as the inscription says: "I will bring this man back, and he shall possess his father's city and go about its houses."

In these descriptions, Aeschylus has given an impressive picture of the heroic stature of the Seven, whose individual characters are delineated through the devices on their shields. Eteocles refuses to be intimidated and arms himself for battle, denying that Justice is on Polynices' side. He knows that he must kill his brother, and he knows that in so doing he will be the instrument fulfilling the curse of Oedipus. When the chorus ask him if he wishes to kill his own brother, he replies, "When the gods give evil, you cannot escape their gift."

These were the final words of Eteocles before the Seven attacked the city, and they express the inevitability of the curse on the sons of Oedipus. The failure of the Seven was foretold by the Theban prophet Tiresias, who prophesied that if one of the Spartoi sacrificed himself, the city would have atoned fully for the blood-guilt incurred by the killing of Ares' sacred serpent and so be saved. Here is part of the prophecy of Tiresias, as given by Euripides (*Phoenissae* 931–941):

This man [i.e., Menoeceus] must be killed at the lair of the earthborn serpent, the guardian of Dirce's fountain, and he must pay the earth with his blood for the water drawn by Cadmus. This is the result of the ancient anger of Ares, who will avenge the death of the earthborn serpent. If you [i.e., Creon and the Thebans] do this, you will have Ares as your ally. If the earth takes your fruit for hers, and for her blood the blood of mortals, she will favor you—she who once put forth the gold-helmeted crop of Sown Men [*Spartoi*]. Of their descendants, one must die, one who is descended from the serpent.

Menoeceus, son of Creon and a descendant of the Spartoi, willingly died for the city: "Dying for the city," says the messenger in Euripides' play (*Phoenissae* 1090–1092), "he plunged the black-bound sword through his throat to save this land, upon the top of the city-walls," and so he fell into the serpent's lair. In the ensuing fight, only Capaneus succeeded in scaling the wall. As he reached the top, he boasted that not even Zeus could keep him out, and for his blasphemy "Zeus," says Sophocles (*Antigone* 131–137), "hurled him with brandished fire as he stood upon the parapet eager to raise the victory cry. Down he fell to the hard earth, hurled through the air, as he breathed out rage and madness in his frenzied assault."

Eteocles and Polynices killed each other in single combat, which Statius describes at great length in Book 11 of his epic, *Thebaid*. Even after death their enmity continued. Statius imagines Antigone, after the battle, trying to burn the corpse of Polynices on the very place where Eteocles had been cremated. She cries out in horror as the flames split in two with divided tongues, symbols of the brothers' eternal hatred.

Of the other heroes, Hippomedon, Parthenopaeus, and Tydeus fell in battle. (Tydeus, indeed, could have been made immortal by Athena, whose favorite he was, but she revoked her gift when she saw him eating the brains of the man who had fatally wounded him.)

Amphiaraüs

Only Amphiaraüs and Adrastus escaped; Adrastus was saved by the speed of his divine horse Arion and returned to Argos; Amphiaraüs was swallowed up in the earth, with his chariot and driver, as he fled along the banks of the river Ismenus, one of the rivers of Thebes. The scene is vividly described by Statius (*Thebaid* 7. 816–820):

 The earth parted with a deep, steep-sided chasm, and the stars above and the dead below were both struck with fear. The huge abyss swallowed Amphiaraüs and enveloped the horses as they began to cross. He did not relax his hold on his arms or the reins: just as he was, he drove the chariot straight into Tartarus.

Amphiaraüs became an important hero, and chthonic cults (i.e., cults whose ritual was directed towards the earth and the Under-world) were established in his honor in several places. He was worshiped at the place beside the river Ismenus where he was said to have descended into the earth. His most famous cult was at Oropus (a city in northeastern Attica near the border with Boeotia), where an elaborate shrine, the Amphiaraüm, was developed in the fifth century B.C. He exemplifies the hero who is associated with the place (or places) where his life was said to have ended. Like Oedipus at Colonus, he experienced a mysterious death and made the place where he disappeared holy.

Antigone

The deaths of Eteocles and Polynices posed difficult religious and political dilemmas, which are presented in Sophocles' tragedy *Antigone*. The four children of Oedipus and Jocasta were Antigone, Ismene, Eteocles, and Polynices. Creon, Antigone's uncle, became king of Thebes again on the death of Eteocles. He gave orders that Polynices was not to be buried, on the grounds that he was a traitor who had attacked his own city. To leave the dead unburied was an offense against the gods, for it was the religious duty of the relatives of the dead to give them a pious burial. Antigone, as the sister of both Eteocles and Polynices, owed such a burial to both brothers, even though she would be breaking Creon's edict by burying Polynices. Alone (for Ismene refused to join in her defiance) she gave him a symbolic burial by throwing three handfuls of dust over his corpse. For this Creon condemned her to be buried alive. Antigone expresses her defiance of Creon in words of unforgettable power (Sophocles, *Antigone* 441–455):

CREON: Do you admit that you did this or deny it?

ANTIGONE: I admit it and I do not deny it.

CREON: Did you know that this was forbidden by my decree?

ANTIGONE: I knew it for it was clear to all.

CREON: And yet you dared to break these laws?

ANTIGONE: Yes, for it was not Zeus who gave me this decree, nor did Justice, the companion of the gods below, define such laws for human beings. Nor did I think that your decrees were so strong that you, a mortal man, could overrule the unwritten and unshaken laws of the gods.

Antigone was right. Creon's order defied the law of the gods, and he was soon punished. His son Haemon attempted to save Antigone (to whom he was engaged to be married) and, finding she had hanged herself in her tomb, killed himself with his sword. Creon's wife, Eurydice, killed herself when she heard the news of her son's death. Warned by Tiresias, Creon himself relented too late.

The *Antigone* of Sophocles, like his *Oedipus Tyrannus*, shows how human beings cannot ignore the demands of the gods. Antigone is a heroine who is willing to incur a lonely death rather than dishonor the gods by obeying the king's command.[6]

The Burial of the Seven against Thebes

According to Euripides (in his tragedy *The Suppliant Women*), Adrastus and the mothers of the Seven went to Eleusis (in Attica) as suppliants. Helped by Aethra, mother of Theseus, they persuaded Theseus to attack Thebes and obtain an honorable burial for the dead Argives. Theseus returned victorious with the corpses of the heroes (other than Polynices, Amphiaraüs, and Adrastus himself), and conducted their funeral rites. Capaneus was granted a separate pyre, and his widow, Evadne, threw herself into its flames.

THE EPIGONI,
SONS OF THE
SEVEN AGAINST THEBES

Alcmaeon, Son of Amphiaraüs

Amphiaraüs had ordered his sons to attack Thebes and to punish their mother, Eriphyle, for her treachery in accepting the necklace of Harmonia from Polynices as a bribe. Alcmaeon, one of his sons, carried out these commands ten years later. He and the sons of the Seven (they are known as the Epigoni, "the later generation") made a successful expedition against Thebes and destroyed the city, which the Thebans had abandoned on the advice of Tiresias. At this point saga touches on history, for the war of the Epigoni took place, it was said, not long before the Trojan War. In the catalogue of ships in the *Iliad,* which is certainly historical, only Hypothebae (Lower Thebes) is mentioned, implying that the ancient town and its citadel had been abandoned.

Alcmaeon, Eriphyle, and the Necklace of Harmonia

Alcmaeon, encouraged by an oracle of Apollo, avenged his father by killing Eriphyle. The Furies pursued him as a matricide until he found temporary shelter in Arcadia, where he married the daughter of King Phegeus, giving her the necklace of Harmonia. But the land was soon afflicted with famine, the result of the pollution caused by the presence of the matricide Alcmaeon. Obedient to another oracle, he searched for a land on which the sun had not shone when he killed his mother. In western Greece he found land at the mouth of the river Achelous recently formed by the river's silt. Settling here, he was purified of his guilt by the river-god, whose daughter Callirhoë he married. But he soon was killed by the sons of Phegeus for the crime of stealing the necklace of Harmonia in order to give it to Callirhoë. The necklace eventually was dedicated by the sons of Callirhoë and Alcmaeon at Delphi. Alcmaeon's sons became the founders of Acarnania, a district of western Greece.

Tiresias

A recurring figure in the Theban saga is the blind prophet Tiresias. Descended from one of the Spartoi, he was the son of a nymph, Chariclo, a follower of Athena. He lived for seven generations, says Hesiod, and continued to have the gift of prophecy after his death, for in the Underworld, where the souls of the dead are insubstantial and futile, he alone retained his full mental faculties. Accordingly Homer makes him Odysseus' informant when he consults with the dead, and he foretells the end of Odysseus' wanderings and the manner of his death.

There are different stories about his blindness, an affliction shared by many prophets and poets in Greek literature. Ovid tells the story in full (*Metamorphoses* 3. 318–338):

They say that Jupiter once had driven away his serious worries with nectar and was joking with Juno, saying, "You women have more pleasure than men, I am sure." She disagreed, and they decided to ask the experienced Tiresias for his opinion, since he had known the act of love both as man and as woman. For once he had struck with his staff the bodies of two large serpents copulating in the green forest, and he miraculously passed seven autumn seasons turned from man into woman. In the eighth, he saw the same serpents and said, "If striking you has the power to change the striker to the other sex, then I will strike you again now." He struck the serpents, and his former body returned with his native physique. So, being made the judge of the lighthearted quarrel, he agreed with Jupiter. Juno, they say, was more angry than was just and condcmned the arbiter [Tiresias] to eternal blindness. But the all-powerful father [Jupiter] granted him in return for the loss of his sight knowledge of the future.

In another version he was blinded by Athena after he saw her naked. Chariclo, his mother, was unable to prevent this punishment, but she made it possible for him to understand the speech of birds. He was the honored prophet at Thebes. In the story of Oedipus, he revealed the truth before Oedipus or the Thebans were ready to understand it (Sophocles, *Oedipus Tyrannus* 350-367):

TIRESIAS: I bid you obey your own decree, and on this day speak neither to these men here nor to me, for you are the unholy pollution on this land.

OEDIPUS: Tell me again, that I may better learn.

TIRESIAS: I say that you are the murderer of Laius. Unwittingly you live most shamefully with those who are dearest to you, and you do not see how far gone you are in evil.

Oedipus still cannot believe Tiresias and goads him into telling him the truth even more terribly (412-419):

TIRESIAS: These are my words, since you have reproached me with being blind: you see, and you do not see the evil in which you are, nor where you live, nor with whom you dwell. Do you know from whom you are sprung? You do not know that you are hateful to your family below and above upon the earth, and that the double curse from your mother and your father will track you down and drive you from this land, now seeing clear, but then in darkness.

The words of Tiresias powerfully express the horror of Oedipus' crimes. Through the images of seeing and blindness, they bring before us the inevitability of the justice of the gods.

Tiresias, in Sophocles' *Antigone,* also warned Creon of the disastrous mistakes he was making, only to be understood too late. Finally, before the attack of the Epigoni, he advised the Thebans to abandon the city and migrate to found the city of Hestiaea. Tiresias never reached the new city; on the way he drank from the spring called Telphusa and died on the spot.

THE MYCENAEAN SAGA

16

The legends of Mycenae are particularly concerned with the House of Atreus and the greatest of its princes, Agamemnon, leader of the Achaeans against Troy. We consider the Trojan War later; in the present chapter we discuss the fortunes of the house as they developed in Greece itself.

Pelops and Tantalus

The ancestor of the family of Atreus was Pelops, son of Tantalus, who came from Asia Minor as a suitor for the hand of Hippodamia, daughter of Oenomaüs, king of Pisa, whose territory included Olympia. This fact accounts for the importance of Pelops in the religious cults at Olympia. From the end of the Mycenaean Age, Pisa and Olympia were for most of the time controlled by Elis.

In the time of Tantalus and Pelops there was easy intercourse between gods and mortals, and in some way Tantalus abused the privilege of eating with the gods. In the best-known version of the myth, he invited the gods to dine with him and cut up his son Pelops, boiled the parts in a cauldron, and served them at the feast. Pindar is reluctant to believe the story, but he told it nevertheless (Pindar, *Olympian Ode* 1. 46–58):

One of the envious neighbors secretly told the tale that they cut your limbs up with a knife and [put them] into the water boiling over the fire, and at the second course of the meat at the tables they divided you and ate. I cannot say that any of the blessed gods

Figure 16.1. Map of the Peloponnese and Central Greece. *(© Laszlo Kubinyi, 1994.)*

was gluttonous—I stand aside. . . . But if the guardians of Olympus honored a mortal man, that man was this Tantalus. Yet he could not digest great fortune, and in his fullness he brought on himself great madness. Thus the Father [Zeus] balanced above him a mighty rock, and longing always to throw it away from his head, he is an exile from good cheer.

The usual punishment of Tantalus is that he was condemned to suffer everlasting thirst and hunger in the Underworld. We have given Homer's account (*Odyssey* 11. 582–592) in Chapter 13. There are two other Greek myths that involve cannibalism, both from places connected with Elis. The one is the story of Lycaon, king of Arcadia, told by Ovid (*Metamorphoses* 1. 211–243: see above, pp. 70–71), and the other is the banquet of Thyestes, which we discuss later in this chapter. The existence of these myths is evidence enough that in the distant past some form of cannibalism once underlay the sacrificial rituals.[1]

In the usual version of the myth, the gods recognized the deception of Tantalus, and all, except for Demeter, refused to eat. She, it was said, ate the flesh from Pelops' shoulder, so that when he was restored to life and wholeness by the gods, an ivory shoulder had to be substituted. Pindar gives a different explanation of the temporary disappearance of Pelops, saying that Poseidon fell in love with him and took him up to Olympus, as Zeus had done with Ganymede. In any case, says Pindar, "the immortal gods sent back the son [of Tantalus] to be among the short-lived race of mortals." It was after this that Pelops traveled to Greece as the suitor of Hippodamia.

Pelops became an important hero with a cult at Olympia, where his shrine, the Pelopion, was next to the temple of Zeus. Pindar says (*Olympian Ode* 1. 90–93):

> Now he lies by the crossing of the Alpheus and is present at the blood-drenched festival. He has a busy tomb, close by the altar [of Zeus] visited by multitudes.

Indeed, sacrifices to Zeus and Pelops were central to the ritual of the Olympic festival, and Pelops received a sacrifice (usually a black ram) before each sacrifice to Zeus. Not only did he give his name to the southern part of the Greek mainland, the Peloponnese (Pelops' Island), but he received honors at the center of the greatest of the Panhellenic festivals. When the great temple of Zeus was built around 460 b.c. to house Pheidias' gold and ivory statue of Zeus seated upon his throne, the sculptures of the west pediment showed the moment before the start of the race between Pelops and Oenomaüs (we have described the temple in Chapter 3).

This race was the origin of the curse on the descendants of Pelops. To win Hippodamia, a suitor had first to win a chariot race against Oenomaüs from Pisa to the Isthmus of Corinth. He would have a short start and take Hippodamia in his chariot with him; Oenomaüs would follow, and if he caught up, he would kill the suitor. Thirteen suitors had failed before Pelops came, and their heads decorated Oenomaüs' palace.

Acording to Pindar, Pelops prayed to his lover, Poseidon, before the race. His words give a sense of the heroic stature of Pelops (*Olympian Ode* 1. 75–89):

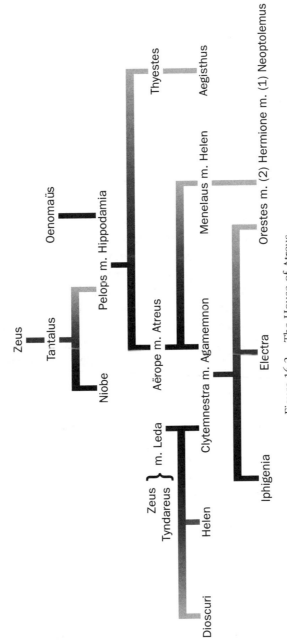

Figure 16.2. The House of Atreus

[Pelops said] "If the dear gifts of Love, Poseidon, can be turned to good, shackle the brazen spear of Oenomaüs and bring me upon the swiftest chariot to Elis and set me near to power. For he has killed thirteen suitors and puts off his daughter's marriage. Great danger, however, does not take hold of the coward. Among those who must die, why should a man sitting in darkness pursue old age without glory, to no purpose? Before me, however, lies this contest. May you give me the action dear to me." Thus he spoke, and his words were not without success. Honoring him, the god gave him a golden chariot and tireless winged horses. He overcame the violence of Oenomaüs and took the girl as wife. And she bore him six princes, sons eager in virtue.

This version is simpler and probably older than the better-known one, according to which Pelops bribed Oenomaüs' charioteer, Myrtilus (son of the god Hermes), to remove the linchpins from Oenomaüs' chariot so that it crashed during the pursuit, killing Oenomaüs.

So Pelops won Hippodamia and drove away with her, accompanied by Myrtilus. Now Myrtilus expected that Pelops would reward him by allowing him to enjoy Hippodamia on the first night. At a resting place on the journey, he attempted to violate her, and when Pelops discovered this, he threw Myrtilus from a cliff into the sea. As Myrtilus fell, he cursed Pelops and his descendants. This curse, and the blood-guilt of the murder of Myrtilus, led to the misfortunes of the House of Atreus. Seneca, however, whose tragedy *Thyestes* is the only classical drama on this theme to survive, connects the murder with the crime of Tantalus (*Thyestes* 138–148):

Neither right nor shared crimes have prevailed. Betrayed, the master [Oenomaüs] of Myrtilus has perished, and he, meeting with the same loyalty [from Pelops] as he had shown [to Oenomaüs] has given his name to the noble sea [the Myrtoan Sea]. . . . The child Pelops, running to kiss his father, was met with the impious sword and fell, a young victim at the hearth. He was cut up by your hand, Tantalus, so that you might make a feast for your guests, the gods.

Atreus and Thyestes

Pelops returned to Pisa and became king in place of Oenomaüs. His children, Thyestes and Atreus, quarreled over the kingdom of Mycenae, which had been offered to "a son of Pelops" in obedience to an oracle. It was agreed that the possessor of a golden-fleeced ram should become king. According to Euripides (*Electra* 698–725), Pan brought the golden-fleeced ram to Atreus, and the people of Mycenae were celebrating his succession to the throne:

 The golden censers were set out, and throughout the city the altar-fires blazed. The flute, the Muses' servant, sounded its music, most beautiful. The lovely dances spread, honoring the golden ram—of Thyestes. For he had persuaded Atreus' own wife [Aërope] with secret love and took the talisman to his house. Then he came to the assembly-place and cried out that he had the horned sheep in his house, the golden-fleeced one.

Euripides further says that Zeus, in anger at Thyestes' deception, caused the sun to travel in the opposite direction. So Thyestes for a time enjoyed the reward of his adultery, and Atreus was banished. Later, Atreus returned and became king, exiling Thyestes in his turn, only to recall him and avenge himself for Aërope's seduction. He pretended to be reconciled with Thyestes and invited him to a banquet to celebrate the reconciliation. He killed Thyestes' sons and gave them to him to eat (the banquet is described in the fifth act of Seneca's *Thyestes* in a scene of overpowering horror). Too late, Thyestes realized what he had eaten. As the heavens darkened and the sun hid from sight of the crime, Thyestes cursed Atreus and went into exile.

Agamemnon, Clytemnestra, and Aegisthus

Thus the curse of Myrtilus affected the first generation of Pelops' descendants. The quarrel of Thyestes and Atreus was continued by their sons. In his second exile, Thyestes lay with his daughter Pelopia, as he had been advised to do by an oracle, and became the father of Aegisthus, who continued the vendetta in the next generation. The son of Atreus, Agamemnon, succeeded his father as king of Mycenae, and in his turn committed an unspeakable crime against one of his children. He sacrificed his daughter Iphigenia at the start of the Trojan expedition, in order to appease Artemis and gain favorable winds to sail from Greece. This is one of the most powerful and pervasive of all Greek myths and was frequently represented in literature and art. It is the central myth with which Aeschylus sets forth the background to the action of his tragedy *Agamemnon* (lines 184–249), and it is the theme of Euripides' final tragedy, *Iphigenia in Aulis*. It was narrated by the Roman poet Lucretius in a moving passage that we translate below on pp. 369–370.

Agamemnon's crime earned the implacable hatred of his wife, Clytemnestra. During his absence at Troy she committed adultery with

Aegisthus, who had his own reasons to join her in plotting vengeance against Agamemnon. On his return from Troy with his prisoner, the Trojan princess Cassandra, Agamemnon was enticed into the palace and murdered by Clytemnestra and Aegisthus. This is the central event (although it takes place off stage) of the *Agamemnon* of Aeschylus. After the murder, Clytemnestra comes out and justifies the deed in a speech which we translate below (Aeschylus, *Agamemnon* 1372–1398). Aegisthus also took full responsibility for the deed, which he welcomed as a just vengeance upon the son of Atreus, the enemy of his father, Thyestes.

In the *Odyssey,* Agamemnon's ghost tells Odysseus how he and Cassandra were murdered (Homer, *Odyssey* 11. 408–426):

It was not brigands who murdered me on land, but Aegisthus, with my cursed wife, who killed me, arranging my death and fate, having called me into the house and given me a feast—killing me like an ox at the manger. Thus I died a most pitiable death, and around me my other companions were being ruthlessly killed, like tusked boars. . . . You have in the past experienced the death of many men, but if you had seen those deaths you would have most of all been grieved to see us lying in the hall amid the wine-bowls and tables full with food, and the whole floor flowing with blood. Most pitiable was the voice of the daughter of Priam that I heard, of Cassandra, whom treacherous Clytemnestra killed with me. But I, lifting my hands [in supplication] let them fall to the earth as I died by the sword, and my shameless wife turned away, nor did she dare, even though I was going down to the House of Hades, to close my eyes or mouth with her hands.

In this version Agamemnon was killed by Aegisthus and Clytemnestra at the banquet celebrating his homecoming. The more widely accepted version is that of Aeschylus, in which Clytemnestra kills him in his bath, trapping him in a robe while she stabs him. Aeschylus has Cassandra foresee the murder and her own death in a dramatic prophecy before she enters the palace. She links Agamemnon's murder to the banquet of Thyestes, which she describes as if it were before her eyes (*Agamemnon* 1095–1125):

Yes, I am persuaded by the evidence I see, as I weep for these children murdered, for the cooked flesh eaten by their father. . . . What now is this new sorrow? Great is the evil being plotted in this palace, intolerable to its friends, hard to atone for, and one where defense is far away. . . . Oh, wretched woman, is this your purpose? As you wash your husband, who shares your bed, . . . how shall I describe the end? . . . What is this I see? Some net, the net of Hades? But the net is she who shares the guilt for the murder. . . . Ah! Ah! Keep the bull from the cow! She takes him in the robes and strikes him with the black-horned weapon.[2] He falls in the bath full of water. It is the fate brought by the bath, contriver of treacherous murder, that I describe to you.

The prophetic cries of the inspired victim describe as vividly as any objective report the death of Agamemnon, which she shortly is to share. With the corpses of Agamemnon and Cassandra at her feet, Clytemnestra defends the justice of her actions. Her speech ends with the terrifying image of Clytemnestra as the earth-mother being renewed by the rain of the sky-god—in this case the blood of her murdered husband. The archetypal Sacred Marriage has never been used with greater poetic effect (Aeschylus, *Agamemnon* 1372–1398):

> I have said many things previously to serve my purpose, all of which I shall now contradict, without any shame. For how else could anyone fulfill hatred for an enemy who pretends to be a friend and string up nets of woe too high for him to overleap? For me this contest in this ancient quarrel has come after long planning—in the fullness of time, I say. I stand here where I struck him, over my deeds. Thus did I act, I shall not deny it, so that he could not escape or ward off his doom. I entrapped him in the fatal richness of the robe, encircling him with the huge net, like fishes. I struck him twice, and with two cries he let his limbs go slack; a third blow did I add as a thank offering to Zeus below the earth, keeper of the dead. Thus fallen he gasped out his life, and at his dying breath he spattered me with rapid spurts, a dark-red rain of blood, and I rejoiced no less than the sown Earth rejoices in the glory of the rain that Zeus sends for the birth of the swelling buds. Thus my case rests, elders of Argos assembled, and may you too rejoice, if you would like to rejoice. As for me, I exult in my imprecations. If I had poured a libation for the corpse as would be fitting, it would have been of wine and curses—with justice, yes, with more than justice. So great were the accursed evils with which he filled our cup in the house, and now by his homecoming he drinks it to the dregs.

It is notable that of the sons of Atreus only Agamemnon was affected by the curse of Myrtilus. Menelaus had his own sorrows in the adultery and flight of his wife, Helen, the cause of the Trojan War. Euripides portrays him in a contemptible light in his tragedy *Orestes*, the action of which takes place soon after Orestes has murdered Clytemnestra. He is hardly any more attractive in the *Andromache* (whose action we describe below) or in the *Trojan Women,* whose action takes place immediately after the sack of Troy. All the literary versions of the myth portray the working out of the curse on the House of Atreus exclusively in the family of Agamemnon, whose son, Orestes, inherits its consequences.

Orestes and Electra

According to Aeschylus, Orestes was away from Mycenae at the time of Agamemnon's murder. While Clytemnestra and Aegisthus usurped the throne, he grew to manhood in exile at the court of Strophius, king of Phocis. It was now his duty to avenge the murder of his father, even though one of the murderers happened to be his own mother; and Apollo commanded him to carry out his duty. He returned to Mycenae, and with the encouragement of his sister Electra, murdered Clytemnestra and Aegisthus. In the *Odyssey,* Homer makes Zeus praise Orestes for his piety toward his dead father; and Sophocles, of the three Athenian tragedians (each of whom wrote a tragedy on the murder of Clytemnestra), is the most neutral. In both Aeschylus and Euripides, however, the feeling of revulsion at the matricide predominates. In this tradition Orestes was pursued by the Erinyes, the Furies, the ancient divinities who avenge the victims of murder. At the end of Euripides' *Electra,* the Dioscuri prophesy that Orestes must go into exile, pursued by the Furies. Eventually, they promise, he will appeal to Athena and be acquitted of the charge of matricide by the court of the Areopagus at Athens.

These events are the subject of the *Eumenides,* the third drama in Aeschylus' trilogy *Oresteia.* The play begins at Delphi, where Orestes has come pursued by the Furies. There Apollo orders him to go to Athens, promising to protect him. At Athens he pleads his case before the court of the Areopagus, whose members, citizens of Athens, are the jury.[3] Apollo defends him, and Athena presides, while the Erinyes claim the justice of their punishment. The jury's votes are tied, and Athena gives her casting vote in favor of Orestes' acquittal, on the grounds that the killing of a mother does not outweigh the murder of a husband and father and that the son's duty toward a father outweighs all other relationships. Thus the curse on the House of Atreus comes to an end; the Erinyes are appeased and given a new name, the Eumenides (Kindly Ones), and worshiped thereafter at Athens.

This version of the myth focuses on the development of law as the vehicle for justice, as against the ancient system (represented by the Erinyes) of blood-guilt and vengeance. But the arguments of Athena are hardly persuasive, and we are left in some doubt as to whether Aeschylus himself believed in their validity. Nor is this as important as the fact that it was the will of Zeus that had already determined that Orestes would be acquitted. Indeed, to Aeschylus, as to many poets since his time (including Eugene O'Neill and T. S. Eliot in this century), the legend of Orestes is important because of the new moral and religious principles that it introduces. In its original form, the story of the House of Atreus is one of blood-guilt descending from one generation to another. The murder of Agamemnon is an act of vengeance, which is more fundamental to the myth than the tragic pride *(hubris)* that precedes the fall of Agamemnon, or the jealousy of Clytemnestra against Cassandra. Similarly Orestes acted with piety in avenging his father's death; his "guilt" is a later—if more humane—interpretation. Indeed, it is illogical, for it ignores the fact that Apollo had ordered him to murder Clytemnestra. It was the genius of Aeschylus that transformed the primitive legend and in place of the ancient doctrine of blood-guilt and vengeance substituted the rule of reason and law.

Aeschylus presents his monumental tragic version in his trilogy *Oresteia*, consisting of *Agamemnon, Libation Bearers (Choephori)*, and *Eumenides*. We are fortunate to have dramas of all three tragedians—Aeschylus, Sophocles, and Euripides—that deal with the events of the saga that concern Electra, the return of Orestes, and the murder of Clytemnestra and Aegisthus. These are the subjects of the second play *(Libation Bearers)* in Aeschylus' trilogy, and of the *Electra* of Sophocles and the *Electra* of Euripides. Thus we are in the unique position of being able to compare the three great dramatists in their manipulation of the same plot. Each has produced a masterpiece, stamped with an individual conception of motivation, character, and religion. These three plays on an identical theme could not be more different in their personal statement and universal implications.

Electra is the focal point of Sophocles' play. Even while Orestes is killing their mother, it is Electra whom we see outside the palace with her cry, "Strike her once again!" And it is Electra who, with exquisite Sophoclean irony, taunts and lures Aegisthus to his death at the hands of Orestes. Sophocles accepts the fact that Orestes has acted justly in his obedience to Apollo's command, and he presents us with a compelling portrait of Electra, passionate in her devotion to her murdered father, consumed by hatred for her mother, Clytemnestra, and her mother's lover, Aegisthus, and kept alive by the hope that Orestes will return to mete out retribution and justice. Among the glories of Sophocles' version are a dramatic confrontation between mother and daughter and a recognition scene between brother and sister of great emotional intensity. Sophocles shows us what anger, frustration, and longing can do to the psyche of a young woman.

Even more brutal, Euripides' portrayal of Electra affords its own kind of pity and fear, tinged as it is by the sordid, realistic, and mundane. Electra and Orestes act at times as little more than neurotic thugs: Electra's revenge, in particular, is motivated as much by sexual jealousy as by any sublime sense of absolute justice. Her monologue to the head of Aegisthus is a study in horror, and brother and sister join side by side in butchering their mother. Castor, the deus ex machina, with typically Euripidean philosophical ambiguity, tells us that Apollo is wise but that his orders to Orestes were not wise.

It is not surprising that there are other versions of Orestes' story, which allow him to be purified from the blood-guilt either by some ritual or by performing an expiatory deed, without undergoing trial and acquittal. In Euripides' play *Iphigenia in Tauris* not all the Erinyes have accepted the judgment of Athena, and some still pursue Orestes. Once again he comes to Delphi where he is told by Apollo to go to the land of the Tauri (the modern Crimea) and fetch a wooden statue of Artemis. It was the custom of the Tauri to sacrifice strangers to Artemis in her temple, and Orestes and his companion Pylades (now the husband of Electra) are handed over to the priestess of Artemis, none other than Orestes' sister Iphigenia. She questions the Greek strangers about events at Argos and Mycenae and then reveals to Orestes who she is and how she has been miraculously saved at Aulis by Artemis and transported to the land of the Tauri. Once she recognizes Orestes, they deceive Thoas, king of the Tauri, into letting them take the statue of Artemis to the sea, to be cleansed of the pollution caused by Orestes, the matricide. They board Orestes' ship and set sail, but adverse wind and waves drive them back towards the land. Before Thoas can seize them, Athena appears and instructs him to let them go. So Orestes and Iphigenia return to Greece. They dedicate the statue of Taurian Artemis at Halae in Attica. Orestes returns to Mycenae, while Iphigenia stays in Attica as the priestess of Artemis at Brauron for the rest of her life.

Thus Orestes recovered his sanity and reigned at Mycenae. Later, he is said to have married his cousin Hermione (daughter of Helen and Menelaus), and by her to have been the father of Tisamenus. Before his madness, he was betrothed to her, but she married Neoptolemus, son of Achilles, and accompanied him to the land of the Molossi in Epirus. According to Euripides, however, in his tragedy *Andromache,* Neoptolemus lived in Phthia (the home of his grandfather Peleus) with Hermione and Andromache, widow of the Trojan hero, Hector, and now given to Neoptolemus as the spoils of war. Hermione, who is barren (while Andromache bears a child), plots to escape with Orestes, who has unexpectedly appeared while journeying to the oracle of Zeus at Dodona. This all takes place while Neoptolemus is away at Delphi on a mission to appease Apollo for his anger with him after the death of his father, Achilles, at Troy. Orestes himself goes to Delphi, and there Neoptolemus is brutally murdered by the Delphians in the sanctuary of Apollo. Orestes organizes the attack, but it is not clear if he actually takes part in the murder. Neoptolemus is buried in the sanctuary of Apollo, thus gaining the status of a hero with a cult. Pindar twice tells the story of his death, each time without mentioning the name of Orestes (*Nemean Ode* 7. 33–47: cf. *Paean* 6. 98–120):

> Neoptolemus came as a defender to the great navel of the broad-bosomed earth, when he had sacked the city of Priam, where the Danaans had labored. He sailed from Troy past Scyros, and wandering they came to Ephyra [Corinth]. And for a short time he ruled over Molossia, and his descendants always have this honor. But he went to the god [Apollo], bringing the first fruits of the spoils from Troy. And there a man killed him with a dagger fighting over the [sacrificial] meat.

As for Orestes, he married Hermione and came to rule over Argos and Sparta, as well as Mycenae. After his death (from a snake bite) he was buried at Tegea, which in historical times was the rival of Sparta. According to Herodotus, the Spartans got possession of his bones, on the advice of the Delphic oracle, and afterwards always were victorious over the Tegeans. Tisamenus was the Achaean leader against the Heraclidae, at whose hands he perished. Electra, as has already been mentioned, married Orestes' constant friend and companion, Pylades, son of Strophius, and by him bore two sons, Strophius and Medon. Thereafter she disappears from the legend.[4]

THE TROJAN SAGA

THE CHILDREN OF LEDA

Leda, wife of Tyndareus, king of Sparta, bore four children to Zeus, who visited her in the shape of a swan; the four were born from two eggs—from the one sprang Polydeuces and Helen, from the other Castor and Clytemnestra.

The Dioscuri

The legends of the Dioscuri (Sons of Zeus), Castor and Polydeuces (his Roman name is Pollux), are not part of the saga of the Trojan War. Castor was renowned as a tamer of horses and Polydeuces for his skill in boxing. Polydeuces was the immortal son of Zeus, whereas Castor was the mortal son of Tyndareus, who eventually shared in the immortality of his brother. They were perhaps originally mortal heroes, later worshiped as gods.

According to Pindar the Dioscuri quarreled with the two sons of Aphareus, Idas and Lynceus, over the division of some cattle that the four of them had taken in a raid. In the quarrel Lynceus and Castor were killed, and Idas was destroyed by Zeus's thunderbolt. As Castor lay dying, Polydeuces prayed to Zeus that he might die with him. Zeus gave him the choice either of immortality for himself and death for Castor or of living with Castor but spending alternate days on Olympus and in Hades. Polydeuces chose the latter, and so the Dioscuri shared both immortality and death.[1]

As gods Castor and Polydeuces were especially connected with

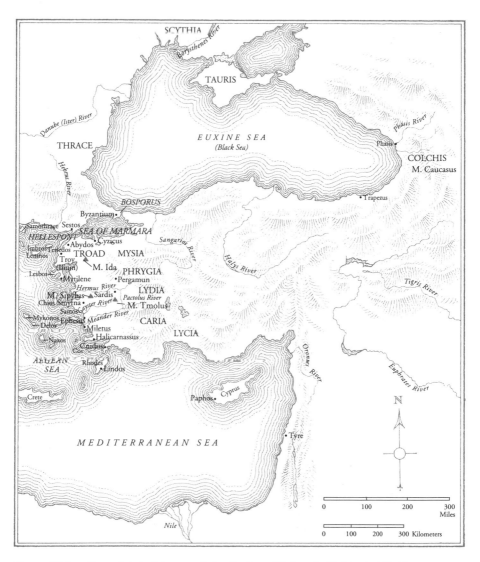

Figure 17.1.   Map of Asia Minor and the Euxine. *(© Laszlo Kubinyi, 1994.)*

seafarers, to whom they appear as St. Elmo's fire.[2] They were particularly honored at Sparta, and in the early fifth century B.C. their cult spread to Rome.[3] One of the most prominent buildings in the Forum at Rome was the temple of Castor.

In the two *Homeric Hymns to the Dioscuri* they are addressed as the Tyndaridae because their mother, Leda, was the daughter of Tyndareus. Hymn 17 is short and focuses on their conception and birth:

About Castor and Polydeuces sing, clear-voiced Muse, the Tyndaridae, who are sprung from Olympian Zeus. Beneath the peaks of Mt. Taÿgetus lady Leda bore them, after she had been stealthily seduced by the dark-clouded son of Cronus.

Hymn 33 depicts the Dioscuri in their important role as patron deities of sailors and seafarers:

O bright-eyed Muses, tell about the sons of Zeus, the Tyndaridae, splendid children of lovely-ankled Leda—Castor, the horse-tamer, and faultless Polydeuces. Leda joined in love with Zeus, the dark-clouded son of Cronus, and she gave birth beneath the summit of thc great mountain, Taÿgetus, to these children, saviors of people on earth and of swift-moving ships, when wintry winds rage over a savage sea. Those on the ship go to the highest part of the stern and call on great Zeus with promises of white lambs. The strong wind and swell of the sea put the ship under water, but suddenly the two brothers appear, darting on tawny wings through the air. At once they calm the blasts of the harsh winds and quell the waves on the expanse of the whitecapped sea. Those who have been freed from pain and toil rejoice, since they have seen these two fair signs of deliverance from distress. Hail, Tyndaridae, riders of swift horses! Yet I shall remember you and another song too.

Helen

The daughters of Zeus and Leda were Clytemnestra and Helen. Clytemnestra became the wife of Agamemnon, and we have discussed her part in the Mycenaean saga (Chapter 16). Helen grew up to be the most beautiful of women, and from the many Greek princes (including Theseus and Odysseus) who were her suitors she chose Menelaus, who became king of Sparta. The rejected suitors swore to respect her choice and help Menelaus in time of need.

Helen lived for some years at Sparta and bore a daughter, Hermione, to Menelaus. In time, however, the Trojan prince Paris (also called Alexander), the son of Priam and Hecuba, visited Sparta while Menelaus was away in Crete. There he seduced Helen and took her back to Troy with him. To recover her and vindicate the rights of Menelaus, the Achaean (Mycenaean Greek) expedition, led by Agamemnon, brother of Menelaus, was raised against Troy.

Another version of Helen's story was invented by the seventh-century poet Stesichorus, who says in his *Palinode:*

That story is not true; you did not go in the well-benched ships, nor did you go to the towers of Troy.

In Stesichorus' version Helen got only as far as Egypt, where King Proteus detained her until Menelaus took her back to Sparta after the Trojan War. It was merely a phantom of Helen that accompanied Paris to Troy, and this was sufficient pretext for the war, which Zeus had determined should occur to reduce the population of the earth.[4]

The Judgment of Paris

The Olympian gods were guests at the wedding feast of Peleus and Thetis. During the feast, Eris, goddess of Discord (who was not a guest), threw onto the table an apple inscribed with the words "For the most beautiful." Hera, Athena, and Aphrodite each claimed it, and Zeus decided that the argument should be settled by Paris.

Now Paris had been exposed as an infant because of a dream that came to his mother Hecuba (the Greek form of her name is Hekabe) before his birth. She dreamed that she had given birth to a firebrand that consumed the whole of Troy, and a soothsayer[5] foretold that her baby would be the destruction of the city. The infant was exposed on Mt. Ida, and suckled by a bear. He was found and brought up by a shepherd. Hermes led the three goddesses to him, and each offered the best gift she could provide in return for his favorable decision. Hera promised him royal power and Athena, victory in war, while Aphrodite promised Helen as his wife (see Color Plate 7). He chose Aphrodite, and so the train of events that led to the Trojan War was set in motion, in which Hera and Athena were hostile to the Trojans.

Lucian (*Dialogues of the Gods* 20) offers a satiric version of the judgment of Paris, in tone not unlike Cranach's painting reproduced on p. 354. The sardonic wit and irony of his portrayal illuminate the bitter rivalry, ruthless ambition, and irresponsible passion of the characters, and in so doing they intensify the horror of the tragic events to follow. The satire begins as Zeus gives the golden apple to Hermes with directions to take it and the three goddesses to Paris, who is tending his flocks on Mt. Ida. Hermes is to tell Paris that he has been chosen to make the decision because he is so handsome and knowledgeable in matters of love. Zeus disqualifies himself as judge by saying that he loves all three equally and that if he gives the apple to one he will incur the anger of the others. The goddesses agree to Zeus' scheme and fly away to Ida with Hermes as their guide.

The Judgment of Paris, by Lucas Cranach the Elder (1472–1553). Oil on panel, 1530; $13\frac{1}{2} \times 8\frac{3}{4}$ in. This tiny painting wittily exploits the incongruities of a tale where great goddesses appear naked before a shepherd. Paris is a corpulent Renaissance knight in armor and foppish hat, while Hermes is an aged warrior (barefoot, as befits a god) whose decrepit appearance sets off the sensuality of the goddesses. Aphrodite looks fully at the viewer, while Athena rests her arm on Hermes. In the background the towers and spires of Troy can be seen. Cupid draws his bow above, and to the left the horse seems to add his own view of the contest. *(Staatliche Kunsthalle, Karlsruhe, Germany. Reproduced by permission of Staatliche Kunsthalle.)*

In the course of the journey, each goddess asks for pertinent information about their judge, Paris. As they approach Mt. Ida, Hermes decides that they had better make a landing and walk up to Paris amiably, rather than frighten him by swooping down from the sky. Hermes explains everything to the bewildered Paris and hands him the golden apple with its inscription:

PARIS: Well then, look at what it says: "Let the beautiful one take me." Now, lord Hermes, I am a mere mortal and from the country; how am I to become the judge of this marvelous spectacle, too great for a herdsman to handle? To make a decision such as this is a job for a city sophisticate. I could probably judge which is the more beautiful in a contest between two she-goats or two cows, but all these goddesses are equally beautiful. Their beauty surrounds and engulfs me completely. My only regret is that I am not Argus, and so I cannot look at them with eyes all over my body. It seems to me that my best judgment would be to give the apple to all three. For, besides everything else, this one happens to be the sister and wife of Zeus, and these two are his daughters. Doesn't all this make the decision extremely difficult?

HERMES: I don't know. Yet it is impossible to avoid an order given by Zeus.

PARIS: Just this one request, Hermes. Convince them—I mean the two who lose—not to hold their defeat against me and to realize that the fault was in my eyes.

HERMES: They agree that they will not blame you; but now the time has come to go through with the contest.

PARIS: I'll try. What else can a man do? Still, first I want to know if it will be enough to look at them as they are, or will it be necessary for them to undress for a proper examination?

HERMES: This would be up to you as the judge. Conduct the proceedings as you desire.

PARIS: As I desire; I'd like to see them naked.

HERMES: You goddesses there, undress! And you, Paris, look them over. I have already turned my back.

The goddesses proceed to undress, and Paris is overwhelmed.

PARIS: O Zeus, god of marvels! What a sight, what beauty, what ecstasy! The virgin Athena is such a vision! How regal and august is the radiance of Hera, truly a wife worthy of Zeus! The gaze of Aphrodite is so sweet and lovely, and she gave me such a seductive smile. Already this rapture is too much, but if it is all right with you, I'd like to see each one separately, since at this moment I am overwhelmed.

APHRODITE: Let's do what he wants.

PARIS: Then the two of you go away, but, Hera, you stay here.

HERA: Here I stay, and after you have looked me over carefully, the time will be right for you to think about whether other considerations are beautiful too—I mean, the gifts that you will get in return for your vote for me. Paris, if you judge me to be the beautiful one, you will be master of all Asia.

PARIS: My vote is not determined by gifts: go on now. Athena, you step forward.

ATHENA: I am right beside you, and if you judge me the beautiful one, Paris, you will never leave a battle in defeat but always victorious. I shall turn you into a warrior and a conquering hero.

PARIS: War and battles serve absolutely no purpose for me. As you see, there is peace throughout Phrygia and Lydia and the entire kingdom of my father. But cheer up! You will not be at a disadvantage, even if my judgment is not to be made on the basis of gifts. Get dressed now and put on your helmet, for I have seen enough. It's time for Aphrodite to step forward.

APHRODITE: No rush! Here I am, right beside you. Look at every detail scrupulously. Take your time over every inch of my body, and as you examine me, my beautiful lad, listen to what I have to say. I noticed the moment I saw you how young and handsome you are—I doubt if there is any other fellow in the whole of Troy who is better looking. I congratulate you on your beauty, but it pains me that you do not leave these stony crags for a life in the city. Instead, you are letting your beauty go to waste amidst this isolation. What fun do you get out of these mountains? What good is your beauty to the cows? By now you should be married, not to some country bumpkin like the women from Mt. Ida but to someone from Greece—from Argos or Corinth—or to a Spartan like Helen, young and beautiful as I am and, above all, amorous. If she only got a look at you, I know very well that she would leave everything behind, succumb to you completely, follow you home in surrender to live with you as your wife. Of course, you have heard at least something about her?

PARIS: Not a thing, Aphrodite, but it would be my pleasure to hear you tell me everything about her.

APHRODITE: She is actually the daughter of beautiful Leda, whom Zeus seduced after flying down to her in the form of a swan.

PARIS: What does she look like?

APHRODITE: As fair as you would expect the daughter of a swan to be, and soft and delicate, since she was hatched from an eggshell, but yet very athletic too—so sought-after, in fact, that even a war has already been waged over her, because Theseus carried her off when she was still quite young. Furthermore, when she reached the peak of her present perfection, all the best of the Achaeans gathered to seek her hand in marriage. Menelaus, of the family of Pelops, was the one chosen. If you'd like, I'll arrange her marriage to you.

PARIS: What are you saying? Me with a married woman?

APHRODITE: You are young and naive, but I know how this kind of thing must be managed.

PARIS: How? I want to know too.

APHRODITE: You will take a trip, ostensibly a tour of Greece, and when you come to Sparta, Helen will see you. From then on, it will be up to me to manage how she will fall in love and follow you home.

PARIS: This is the very thing that seems so incredible to me, that she would want to leave her husband and sail away with a foreigner she doesn't know.

APHRODITE: Don't fret about it, for I have two beautiful children, Desire *(Himeros)* and Love *(Eros)*. I shall give them to you as guides for your journey. Love will insinuate himself completely into her very being and compel the woman to love you. Desire will make you desirable and irresistible by suffusing you with the very essence of his being. I'll be there myself, too, and I'll ask the Graces to accompany me. In this way, all of us together will persuade her to submit.

PARIS: It is not in the least clear to me how this will all turn out, Aphrodite. But I am already in love with Helen. I seem to see her now—I'm sailing straight for Greece—I'm visiting Sparta—I'm returning home holding the woman in my arms! I am very upset that I am not doing all this right now.

APHRODITE: Hold on, Paris! Don't fall in love until you have rewarded me with your decision—me, the one who is fixing the marriage and giving away the bride. It would be only fitting that I, your helper, be the winner of the prize, and that we celebrate at the same time both your marriage and my victory. For it is up to you. You can buy everything—love, beauty, marriage—the cost is this apple.

PARIS: I am afraid that you will forget about me after my decision.

APHRODITE: And so you want me to swear an oath?

PARIS: Not at all, only promise me again.

APHRODITE: I promise to give you Helen as your wife and that she herself will follow and come with you to your family in Troy. I shall be at your side myself, and I shall help accomplish everything.

PARIS: And you will bring Love, Desire, and the Graces?

APHRODITE: Never fear, I shall even bring along Passionate Longing and Hymen, the god of Marriage.

Homer never mentions this story; according to him Paris once insulted Hera and Athena when they visited him but praised Aphrodite, who gave him the power to attract women irresistibly. This simpler version is certainly older than the more famous literary account of the judgment, but it is the latter that has dominated the tradition and fascinated an endless line of poets and artists.

TROY AND ITS LEADERS

Laomedon

Apollo and Poseidon (disguised as mortals) built the walls of Troy for its king Laomedon, who then cheated them of their pay.[6] In punishment, Apollo sent a plague and Poseidon a sea monster to harass the Trojans. The oracles advised that the only way to get rid of the monster was to expose Laomedon's daughter Hesione and let it devour her. When Heracles came to Troy (see p. 428) he agreed to kill the monster and save Hesione in return for Laomedon's immortal horses, which were the gift of Zeus.[7] Once again Laomedon cheated his benefactor; Heracles therefore returned with an army, captured Troy, and gave Hesione as wife to his companion, Telamon, by whom she became the mother of Teucer. Heracles killed Laomedon but spared his young son Podarces, who became king of the ruined city, changing his name to Priam.

Priam and Hecuba

King Priam was father of fifty sons and twelve (or fifty) daughters, of whom nineteen were children of his second wife, Hecuba (Arisba, his first wife, is not significant in the legend). In the *Iliad* Hecuba appears as a tragic figure whose sons and husband are doomed; her most famous legend takes place after the fall of Troy (p. 388).

Paris (Alexander)

The most important sons of Priam and Hecuba were Paris and Hector. While Paris was a shepherd on Mt. Ida (see p. 353) he fell in love with a nymph, Oenone, who had the gift of healing. He left her for Helen. Years later, when he was wounded by Philoctetes, she refused to heal him, but when he died she killed herself in remorse. As a young man, Paris had returned to the royal palace and had been

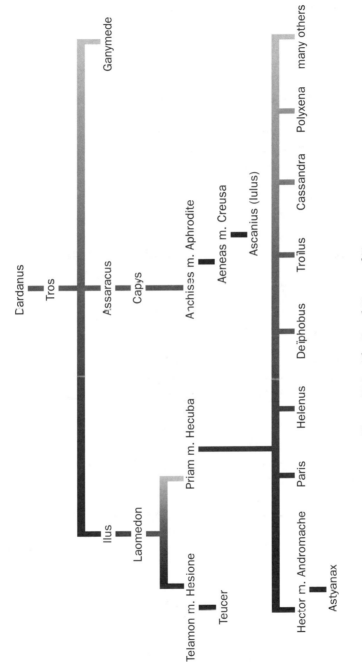

Figure 17.2. The Royal House of Troy

recognized by Priam as his son. As we have seen, his actions led to the Trojan War, in which he appears as a brave warrior if somewhat uxorious. He was the favorite of Aphrodite, who saved him from being killed in combat by Menelaus. His vanity and sensuality contrasted with the dignity and courage of Hector. Paris shot the arrow that fatally wounded Achilles.

Hector, Andromache, and Astyanax

Hector, brother of Paris, was the champion of the Trojans, brave and honorable, and as a warrior excelled only by Achilles, by whom he was killed in single combat. As long as Achilles took no part in the fighting, Hector carried all before him. When he was killed, the Trojans knew they were doomed. His wife was Andromache, daughter of Eëtion (an ally of the Trojans killed by Achilles), and their child was Astyanax. In the *Iliad* Homer draws unforgettable portraits of Paris and Helen and of Hector and Andromache, as he juxtaposes their characters and their relationships in moving scenes of universal power (pp. 374–376).

Helenus, Deïphobus, and Troïlus

Priam's son Helenus had the gift of prophecy, for when he was a child serpents had licked his ears. In the last year of the war the prophet Calchas (pp. 385–386) advised the Greeks to capture him, since he alone could tell what must be done to end the war. He was caught by Odysseus and honorably treated, so that he alone of Priam's sons survived the war. He eventually married Andromache and became a ruler in Epirus. As a prophet he appears for the last time in the *Aeneid*, where he foretells the course of Aeneas' future wanderings (p. 539).

Of Priam's many other sons, Deïphobus married Helen after the death of Paris; his ghost spoke with Aeneas in the Underworld; and Troïlus, who was killed by Achilles, became more significant in later times.[8]

Cassandra and Polyxena

Cassandra and Polyxena are the most important of the daughters of Priam. Cassandra had been loved by Apollo, who gave her the gift of prophecy. When she rejected him, he added to the gift the fate that she should never be believed (p. 179). Thus she foretold the fall of Troy and warned the Trojans against the Trojan horse all in vain. Her fate in the the sack of Troy is described below (p. 388); as we have seen, she died in Mycenae, murdered by Clytemnestra (p. 344).

Polyxena was sacrificed on the tomb of Achilles as his share of the spoils after the sack of Troy, as we describe below (p. 384).

Aeneas

Of the Trojan leaders outside Priam's immediate family, the most prominent is Aeneas, who belonged to another branch of the royal family. Although he was the son of Anchises and Aphrodite (pp. 136–140), he was not the equal of Priam in prestige or of Hector as a warrior. In the *Iliad* he fights in single combat with Achilles and is saved from death by Poseidon, who transports him miraculously from the fight. Poseidon prophesies that Aeneas and his descendants, now that Zeus has withdrawn his favor from Priam's family, will be the future rulers of Troy. We consider his later prominence, as depicted by Vergil, in Chapter 24.

Antenor

Antenor, brother of Hecuba, was conspicuous among those who did not want the war, and he advised returning Helen to the Greeks. When the Greeks first landed, he saved their ambassadors from being treacherously killed by the Trojans. In the last year of the war, he protested the breaking of a truce by the Trojans and still proposed the voluntary return of Helen. The Greeks spared him at the sack, and he and his wife, Theano, the priestess of Athena, were allowed to sail away. They reached Italy where they founded the city of Patavium (Padua).

Glaucus and Sarpedon

Of the allies of Troy, the most prominent in the *Iliad* were the Lycians, led by Glaucus and Sarpedon. When Glaucus and Diomedes were about to fight, they discovered that they were hereditary guest-friends (i.e., their ancestors had entertained one another and exchanged gifts). They exchanged armor instead of fighting and parted amicably. Since Glaucus' armor was made of gold and that of Diomedes of bronze, Diomedes had the better of the exchange, as Homer says (*Iliad* 6. 234–236):

Zeus took away Glaucus' wits, for he exchanged golden armor with Diomedes for bronze, armor worth a hundred oxen for that worth nine.

Glaucus eventually was killed by Ajax (son of Telamon) in the fight over the corpse of Achilles.

Sarpedon was the son of Zeus and the Lycian princess Laodamia, daughter of Bellerophon. Zeus foresaw Sarpedon's death but could not change his destiny *(moira)* without upsetting the established order. He therefore had to be content with raining drops of blood on the earth to honor his son before the catastrophe and with saving his body after it. Here is Homer's description of the scene (*Iliad* 16. 676–683), after Sarpedon has been killed by Patroclus and Zeus has instructed Apollo to save his body (see Color Plate 3):

Thus [Zeus] spoke, and Apollo did not disobey his father. He went down from the peaks of Ida into the terrible din of battle and straightway lifted godlike Sarpedon out of the way of the missiles and carried him far off. He washed him in the flowing waters of the river and anointed him with ambrosia and clothed him with immortal garments. And he sent him to be carried by two swift escorts, the twins Sleep and Death, who quickly set him down in the fertile land of broad Lycia.

After Hector, Sarpedon is the most noble of the heroes on the Trojan side. In Book 12 of the *Iliad,* when the Trojans are attacking the wall of the Greek camp, he addresses Glaucus in words expressing heroic *arete* (excellence) and nobility as memorable as those of Achilles in Book 9 (translated below, pp. 377–378). Unlike Achilles, he speaks as the leader of a community (*Iliad* 12. 310–328):

Glaucus, why are we specially honored in Lycia with seats of honor, with meat and more cups of wine, and all people look upon us like gods, and we have been allotted a great domain beside the banks of the Xanthus, fine for the planting of vineyards and for grain-bearing tillage? Therefore now must we stand in the front rank of the Lycians and face the raging battle, so that one of the well-armored Lycians may say: "Indeed not without glory do our kings rule over Lycia and eat the fat lambs and drink choice honey-sweet wine. Noble also is their strength, since they fight among the leaders of the Lycians." My friend, if we were to avoid this war and were to live out our lives ever ageless and deathless, then neither would I myself fight among the leaders nor would I station you in the battle that destroys men. Now, as it is, let us go, for ten thousand death-bringing fates are close upon us.

Rhesus

Other allied contingents who appeared at Troy were those of the Amazons and the Ethiopians (mentioned later, p. 384), and the

Thracians led by Rhesus. Their arrival coincided with a night patrol by Diomedes and Odysseus, during which they caught and killed a Trojan spy, Dolon, who first told them of the Thracians. They went on to kill Rhesus and twelve of his men and to capture his white horses. Rhesus, who was a son of one of the Muses, was worshiped as a hero in Thrace.

THE ACHAEAN LEADERS

The organization of the Greek army was different from that of the Trojans, for Troy was a great city led by a powerful king and helped in war by independent allies. We have seen that Helen's suitors had sworn to help Menelaus if he called on them, and they assembled for war under the leadership of Agamemnon, king of Mycenae. While Agamemnon's position as leader was unquestioned, each of the Greek princes led his contingent independently and could at any time withdraw, as Achilles did.

Agamemnon

Agamemnon was the "lord of men," greatest in prestige among the Greeks, although neither the greatest warrior nor the wisest in council. His stature is shown in the scene in Book 3 of the *Iliad* when Helen names the Greek warrior whom Priam points out to her from their viewpoint on the wall (hence the scene is known as the "viewing from the wall," or *teichoskopia*). Priam begins (*Iliad* 3. 166–190):

"Tell me the name of this mighty man, whoever he is of the Greeks, a man valiant and great." Then Helen answered in words, goddess-like among women: "This is the son of Atreus, Agamemnon, ruler of a broad kingdom, both a noble king and a strong warrior. He was my husband's brother." Thus she spoke, and the old man was filled with wonder and said: "O happy son of Atreus, favored by Destiny, blest by fortune, many sons of the Achaeans are your subjects. Long ago I went to Phrygia rich in vineyards, and there I saw great numbers of Phrygian warriors on their swift horses. But not even they were as great as are the quick-eyed Achaeans."

In Book 11 (36–40) the terror inspired by Agamemnon as a warrior is shown in the devices on his shield and shield-strap, "The grim-looking Gorgon with her terrifying gaze, and around the shield Terror and Fear. And on the strap coiled a dark serpent, and it had three heads turning all ways, growing from one neck.'' Yet great warrior as Agamemnon was, he was a lesser hero than Achilles.

Menelaus

We have seen how Menelaus, king of Sparta, and his wife Helen were involved in the origin of the war. In the war itself he fought Paris in single combat. Aphrodite saved Paris just as Menelaus was on the point of killing him (p. 373).

Diomedes

Diomedes, king of Argos, was a much greater warrior than Menelaus. He was the son of Tydeus, and second only to Agamemnon in power and prestige. He was also a wise counselor. He was a favorite of Athena and with her help could oppose even the gods in battle. He wounded both Ares and Aphrodite. He was especially associated with Odysseus, with whom he fetched Achilles from Scyros and later Philoctetes from Lemnos. Odysseus was also his companion in the night patrol where Dolon and Rhesus were killed and in the theft of the Palladium from Troy. This Palladium (the statue of Pallas, which Athena had made and Zeus cast down from heaven into Troy), was worshiped and looked upon as a talisman for the city's survival. When Odysseus and Diomedes stole it, Troy was doomed. Diomedes' meeting with Glaucus has already been described (p. 361); his adventures after the war are discussed in Chapter 18 (p. 392).

Nestor

Nestor, son of Neleus and king of Pylos, was the oldest and wisest of the Greek leaders. Like Priam, he had become king after Heracles sacked his city. In the sack Neleus and all his sons except Nestor were killed. At Troy Nestor was a respected counselor, and his speeches, full of reminiscences, contrast with the impetuosity of the younger princes. He himself survived the war, although his son Antilochus was killed by Memnon. There is no tradition of his death.

Ajax the Greater of Salamis, the Son of Telamon

Ajax, son of Telamon, was second only to Achilles as a warrior.[9] He is called the Great (or Greater) to distinguish him from Ajax the Less (or Lesser), son of Oileus. In the fighting before the Greek ships

(Books 13–15) he was the most stalwart defender, always courageous and the last to give ground to the enemy. Again he was the Greek champion in the fight over the body of Patroclus in Book 17, providing the cover while Menelaus and Meriones retreated with the body. At the climax of that battle, he prayed to Zeus to dispel the mist of battle and let him die in the clear sunlight, a striking scene in which the sudden appearance of the sun and clear vision seems especially appropriate for this straightforward warrior. In the *teichoskopia* Priam asks Helen (*Iliad* 3. 226–229):

"Who is this other Achaean warrior, valiant and great, who stands out from the Achaeans with his head and broad shoulders?" [Helen replies] "This is Ajax, of huge size, the bulwark of the Achaeans."

Ajax is both the foil to and the rival of Odysseus. His gruff and laconic speech in the embassy to Achilles (Book 9), which we discuss later, contrasts with the smooth words of the diplomatic Odysseus. In Book 23 they compete in the footrace in the funeral games, and Ajax' defeat there foreshadows his far more tragic defeat in the contest with Odysseus for the armor of Achilles, discussed below (pp. 384–385).

Ajax the Less (or Lesser)

Ajax the Less (as Homer calls him), prince of the Locrians and son of Oileus, is a less attractive character than his namesake. Although he figured prominently in the fighting and was the leader of a large contingent, his sacrilegious violation of Cassandra during the sack of Troy diminished his stature and led to his death on the voyage back to Greece (p. 391).

Idomeneus

Another important fighter with a large contingent was Idomeneus, son of Deucalion and leader of the Cretans. He stood in a different relationship to Agamemnon from most of the other leaders in that he came as a voluntary ally. He had long been a friend of Menelaus, and Agamemnon showed him great respect. In Book 13 of the *Iliad* he defends the Greek camp bravely and kills a number of leading Trojan warriors. Good as he was, however, as fighter and counselor at Troy, his most important legend is concerned with his return (p. 392).[10]

Odysseus

When Menelaus and Agamemnon sent heralds throughout Greece and the islands to summon the Greek leaders and their contingents to the war, not all the Greek heroes came willingly; two of the most important, Odysseus and Achilles, attempted to avoid the war by subterfuge.

Odysseus, king of Ithaca, pretended to be mad. When Agamemnon's envoys came, he yoked an ox and an ass and plowed a field, sowing salt in the furrows. One of the envoys, Palamedes, took Odysseus' infant son Telemachus from his mother, Penelope, and put him in the path of the plow. Odysseus was sane enough to avoid him; his pretense was uncovered, and he joined the expedition.[11]

Odysseus was the craftiest and wisest of the Greeks, as well as a brave warrior. He was the best in council, and his powerful speech in Book 2 (284–332) decided the debate in favor of staying before Troy to finish the war. He attacked the unattractive and sardonic Thersites for intervening in the debate, when only princes should speak, and for this he was greatly honored by the Greeks. He was the principal speaker in the embassy to Achilles in Book 9, and he undertook the dangerous night mission with Diomedes as well as other missions mentioned earlier. Above all Odysseus was a skilled speaker, and this is brought out in the *teichoskopia* (*Iliad* 3. 191–224):

Next the old man [Priam] asked about Odysseus. "Come, tell me also about this man, dear child, who he is. He is shorter by a head than Agamemnon, son of Atreus, but I see that he is broader in the shoulders and chest. His arms lie on the fruitful earth, and he like a ram is going up and down the ranks of warriors. I liken him to a thick-fleeced ram which goes through the flocks of white-fleeced sheep." Then Helen, daughter of Zeus, answered: "This is crafty Odysseus, son of Laertes, who was raised in the land of Ithaca, rocky though it is. He knows all kinds of deceit and clever plans."

Then wise Antenor spoke to her and said: "Lady, true indeed are your words. Godlike Odysseus came here once before with Menelaus, dear to Ares, for news of you. I was their host and welcomed them in my home, and I knew their stature and their wise intelligence. But when they joined in the assembly of the Trojans, Menelaus was taller when they stood by his [head and] broad shoulders; yet when they both were seated Odysseus was the more noble. But when they began to weave their speeches and proposals before all, then indeed Menelaus spoke glibly, a few words in a clear voice, since he was not long-winded or irrelevant, and he was younger also. But whenever wise Odysseus rose to speak he would stand and look down and fix his eyes on the ground, and he would not gesture with the sceptre before or behind him, but held it stiffly, like some unskilled man. You would say that he was angry and unintelligent too. But when he sent forth the great voice from his chest and the words that were like falling winter snows, then no other mortal could compete with Odysseus. Indeed then we were not amazed as we looked at the appearance of Odysseus.''

The double portrait of the wise orator and the glib young king vividly puts before us two sides of the heroic ethos, and it prepares us for the complexity of Odysseus' character in the saga of his return from Troy.

Achilles and His Son Neoptolemus (Pyrrhus)

The second chieftain who attempted to avoid the war was the mighty Achilles, prince of the Myrmidons (a tribe of Phthia, in central Greece) and the greatest of the Greek warriors, as well as the swiftest and most handsome. He was the son of Peleus and Thetis; Thetis was a sea-goddess, daughter of Nereus, who was avoided by Zeus when the secret was revealed hitherto known only to Prometheus and Themis—that Thetis' son would be greater than his father.[12]

Accordingly, Thetis was married to a mortal, Peleus, king of the Phthians. Peleus took part in the Argonauts' expedition and the Calydonian boar hunt (pp. 475 and 496–500), but as a mere mortal he was hardly a match for Thetis. It was with difficulty that he married her, for she was able to turn herself into various shapes in attempting to escape from him. Although the gods attended their wedding feast, Thetis left Peleus not long after the birth of Achilles. She tried to make Achilles immortal, either by roasting him in the fire by night and anointing him with ambrosia by day[13] or by dipping him in the waters of the Styx. In the latter story, all parts of Achilles' body that had been submerged were invulnerable. Only his heel, by which Thetis held him, remained vulnerable. It was here that he received the fatal arrow wound.

Once Thetis left Peleus, Achilles was sent to the centaur Chiron for his education. From him he learned the art of music and other skills. While Achilles was with Chiron, Thetis learned that Troy could not be taken without Achilles; she also knew that he could live long and die ingloriously or go to Troy and die young and glorious. To circumvent his early death, she tried to prevent his going by disguising him as a girl and taking him to the island of Scyros, where he was brought up with the daughters of Lycomedes, king of the island. One of them was Deïdamia, with whom Achilles fell in love; their child, born after Achilles left Scyros, was Neoptolemus (also called Pyrrhus, which means "redhead"), who took part in the capture of Troy after his father's death. Odysseus and Diomedes exposed Achilles' disguise at Scyros. They took gifts for the daughters of Lycomedes, among them weapons and armor, in which Achilles alone showed any interest. As the women were looking at the gifts, Odysseus arranged for a trumpet to sound; the women all ran away, thinking it was a battle signal, but Achilles took off his disguise and put on the armor. Here is the description of the scene by the Roman poet Statius (*Achilleid* 1. 852–884), after the gifts have been set out by Diomedes:

The daughters of Lycomedes see the arms and assume that they are a present for their mighty father. But when fierce Achilles saw the shining shield close by, chased with scenes of war and lying next to the spear, he grew violent . . . and Troy filled his heart. . . . When he saw his reflection in the golden shield he shuddered and blushed. Then observant Odysseus stood close to him and whispered: "Why do you hesitate? We know. You are the pupil of the centaur, Chiron, you are the descendant of [the gods of] sky and sea. The Greek fleet is waiting for you, the Greek army is waiting for you before raising its standards, the walls of Troy itself are ready to fall before you. Hurry, no more delaying!" . . . Already Achilles was beginning to take off his woman's dress when Agyrtes sounded a loud blast on the trumpet, as he had been ordered to do [by Odysseus]. The girls began to run away, scattering the gifts. . . . Achilles' clothing of itself fell from his chest, and he quickly seized the shield and short spear and, miraculously, he seemed to be taller by head and shoulders than Odysseus and Diomedes. . . . Stepping like a hero he stood forth.

So Achilles was discovered and joined the expedition. At Troy, he proved to be the mightiest of the champions on either side and a hero of enormous passions.

Phoenix and Patroclus

Two of Achilles' associates, Phoenix and Patroclus, are important. Phoenix, at the instigation of his mother, lay with his father's mistress. His father cursed him with childlessness, and Phoenix sought refuge from his father's wrath with Peleus, who made him the tutor and companion of Achilles both in Phthia and at Troy.

Patroclus was a great warrior. When very young, he had killed a rival in anger over a dice game. Peleus took him in and brought him up to be the companion of Achilles. Achilles and Patroclus become beloved friends and their relationship provides a major theme for the *Iliad*.[14]

THE GATHERING OF THE EXPEDITION AT AULIS

Menelaus and Agamemnon sent heralds throughout Greece and the islands to summon the Greek leaders and contingents to the war; the expedition gathered at Aulis (on the coast of Boeotia, opposite Euboea) numbering nearly twelve hundred ships with their crews and fighting men.[15]

The Sacrifice of Iphigenia

There were delays before the fleet could sail; for a long time contrary winds blew, and in despair Agamemnon consulted the prophet Calchas. He knew that Artemis had caused the unfavorable weather because Agamemnon had offended her,[16] and that she could only be appeased by the sacrifice of Agamemnon's daughter Iphigenia, who therefore was fetched from Mycenae (on the pretext that she was to be married to Achilles) and sacrificed. In another version, however, Artemis saved her at the last moment, substituted a stag as the victim, and took Iphigenia to the land of the Tauri (the modern Crimea) to be her priestess.[17]

Lucretius, the Roman poet (ca. 55 B.C.), tells the story of Iphigenia with bitter pathos in order to show to what lengths men will go in the name of religion (*De Rerum Natura* 1. 84–101):

> Look how the chosen leaders of the Greeks, the foremost of men, foully defiled the altar of virgin Artemis at Aulis with the blood of Iphigenia. As they placed around her maiden's hair the headband which hung down evenly by her cheeks, she suddenly caught sight of her father standing sadly before the altar and at his side his ministers hiding the knife, while the people shed tears at the sight of her. Dumb with fear she fell to the ground on her knees. At such a moment little help to her in her misery was it that she had been his first child, that she had first bestowed upon the king the name of father. The hands of men brought her trembling to the altar, not that she might perform the customary ritual of marriage to the clear-

ringing songs of Hymen, but that at the very time for her wedding she might fall a sad and sinless victim, sinfully butchered by her own father, all for the happy and auspicious departure of the fleet. Such are the monstrous evils to which religion could lead.

Calchas' Prophecy

Calchas the prophet was an important figure in the Greek expedition, especially in times of doubt or perplexity. At Troy, as we shall see below, he gave the reason for Apollo's anger and advised the return of Chryseïs to her father. At Aulis he interpreted a famous omen. A snake was seen to climb up a tree and devour eight chicks from a nest high in its branches; it then ate the mother, and was itself turned into stone by Zeus. Calchas correctly interpreted this to mean that the Greeks would fight unsuccessfully at Troy for nine years before capturing the city in the tenth.[18]

THE ARRIVAL AT TROY

Philoctetes

The expedition finally sailed from Aulis, but did not go straight to Troy. On the way the Greeks were guided by Philoctetes, son of Poeas, to the island of Chryse to sacrifice to its goddess. There Philoctetes was bitten in the foot by a snake; and as the fleet sailed on, the stench from his wound became so noisome that the Greeks abandoned him on the island of Lemnos, where he remained alone and in agony for nearly ten years. Now Philoctetes' father, Poeas, had lit the funeral pyre of Heracles and had in return been given Heracles' bow and arrows, which Philoctetes later inherited. In the last year of the war, the Greeks captured Priam's son Helenus, who prophesied that only with the aid of Heracles' bow and arrows could Troy be captured. Accordingly, Odysseus and Diomedes fetched Philoctetes from Lemnos. The sons of Asclepius, Podalirius and Machaon, healed his wound, and with the arrows he shot Paris, thus removing the most formidable of the surviving Trojan champions.[19]

Achilles Heals Telephus

On the way to Troy the Greeks landed in Mysia, a district of Asia Minor. In the battle against the Mysians, Achilles wounded the Mysian Telephus, a son of Heracles. When the wound would not heal, Telephus despairingly asked the Delphic oracle for advice. Learning that "he that wounded shall heal," he went to the Greek army disguised as a beggar and asked Achilles to cure his wound. Achilles said he could not, for he was not a doctor, but Odysseus pointed out that it was Achilles' spear that had caused the wound. Scrapings from it were applied, and Telephus was healed.

Protesilaüs and Laodamia

When the Greeks reached Troy the first to leap ashore was Protesilaüs, who was immediately killed by Hector. His wife, Laodamia, could not be comforted in her grief. Pitying her, Hermes brought back her husband from Hades for a few hours, and when he was taken away again, she killed herself. Another person to die in the first skirmish was a Trojan, Cycnus, son of Poseidon, who was turned into a swan. The Greeks successfully established a beachhead, made a permanent camp with their ships drawn up on shore, and settled down to besiege Troy.

THE *ILIAD*

While the events of the first nine years of the war are obscure (since the epic poems in which they were described survive only in prose summaries), those of the tenth are in part brilliantly illuminated by the *Iliad.* The poem, however, deals only with events from the outbreak of the quarrel between Achilles and Agamemnon to the ransoming and burial of Hector.

Nine years were spent in a fruitless siege of Troy, varied only by abortive diplomatic exchanges and raids against cities allied with Troy. The division of the spoil from these cities led to the quarrel between Agamemnon and Achilles. Agamemnon was given in his share Chryseïs, daughter of Chryses, priest of Apollo—but (as we shall see) he had to send her back. Therefore he took Briseïs, who had been given to Achilles and whom Achilles had come to love greatly. The wrath of Achilles, the principal theme of the *Iliad,* is characterized in the poem's opening lines (1. 1–7):

The wrath of Achilles, Peleus' son, sing, O goddess, a ruinous wrath, which put countless woes upon the Achaeans and hurled many mighty souls of heroes to Hades, and made them a feast for dogs and a banquet for birds, and the will of Zeus was being accomplished, from the time when first Agamemnon and Achilles stood opposed in strife.

The passionate theme of "wrath," the very word with which the poem begins, determines the intensity of emotion and the scope and form of its action. In verses of visual and auditory clarity as deceptively simple as they are profound, the story unfolds through scenes of great dramatic power. With Chryseïs in his possession, Agamemnon refused to allow Chryses to ransom his daughter, and Chryses therefore prayed to Apollo to punish the Greeks. Apollo's answer to the prayer is described in these vivid lines (*Iliad* 1. 43–52):

So Chryses prayed, and Phoebus Apollo heard him. Angry at heart, he strode down from the peaks of Olympus, having his bow slung from his shoulder and his hollow quiver. The arrows clashed loudly upon his shoulders as he strode in his anger, and like night did he go. Then he sat apart from the ships and shot an arrow; terrible was the twang of his silver bow. First he shot the mules and the swift dogs, and next he shot his sharp arrow at the men. Constantly were the funeral pyres burning in great numbers.

This is the first appearance of a god in the *Iliad*, and it shows how the gods are participants in the saga of Troy, with Apollo constantly favoring the Trojans. Calchas advised that the evil could be ended only by the return, without ransom, of Chryseïs. Accordingly she was sent back, but this left Agamemnon without his share of the spoils, a humiliating situation for the greatest of the Greek kings. He therefore took Briseïs from Achilles, and Achilles repaid the dishonor by withdrawing his contingent, the Myrmidons, from the war.

Achilles is the embodiment of heroic *arete* (excellence). Important in the concept of *arete* is one's standing in the eyes of others, which is gained not only by words and deeds but also by gifts and spoils relative to those of others. Therefore Achilles' honor was slighted when Agamemnon took away Briseïs, and he had good cause to withdraw from the fighting, even though the Greeks suffered terribly as a result. Homer describes the mighty quarrel, in the course of which Athena restrains Achilles from attacking Agamemnon, and he describes the prophecy of Achilles as he withdraws from the war (1. 234–246):[20]

"By this sceptre, which will never grow leaves or roots, since it was cut in the mountains, and now the sons of the Achaeans bear it in their hands when they administer justice, for they defend Justice in the name of Zeus—and this will be a great oath: In time all the sons of the Achaeans will long for Achilles. Then you [Agamemnon] will not be able to do anything, grieved though you be, while many men fall in death before Hector, slayer of men. And you will tear your heart, angry that you did not honor the best of the Achaeans." So spoke the son of Peleus, and he cast the golden-studded sceptre upon the ground, and down he sat.

Angry, hurt, and resentful, Achilles finds comfort and support from his mother, Thetis. Theirs is a sad and touching relationship, tragic in the knowledge that Achilles has chosen to come to Troy to die young and gloriously rather than stay at home to live a long but mundane existence. Thetis agrees to go to Zeus for help, and she obtains from the supreme god an oath that he will honor her son, whom Agamemnon has dishonored, and grant success to the Trojans in his absence, so that the Greeks will come to regret Agamemnon's actions and increase the glory of Achilles.

At the end of Book 1, it is difficult not to condemn Agamemnon as a guilty, arrogant sinner, first against Apollo and his priest and then against Achilles. Achilles' tragic withdrawal, like Apollo's arrows, will cause the deaths of countless of his Greek companions, and he will be condemned for his selfish, cruel, and pitiless behavior. Yet the wrath of Apollo, until properly appeased, has been just as devastating, heartless, and indiscriminate, causing innumerable deaths, in this case, too, because of the arrogance of Agamemnon. Homer juxtaposes the wrath of Achilles and that of Apollo at the beginning of his epic. Are we to judge the actions of the god and those of the mortal demigod by two different standards?

In Book 3 a truce is agreed upon to allow Menelaus and Paris to fight in individual combat, in order to decide the issues and the fate of Helen. In the duel, Menelaus gets the better of Paris. He takes hold of Paris by the helmet and swings him around so that he is choked by the neck-strap. When Aphrodite notices that Paris is lost, she quickly snatches up her favorite with the ease of a goddess and transports him to his fragrant bedchamber. She goes to summon Helen, who has already witnessed the humiliation of her husband from a high tower of Troy. Although Aphrodite is disguised as an old woman, Helen recognizes the beautiful breasts and flashing eyes of her mirror image, and with this recognition of herself she rebels.

As the scene proceeds, through the literal depiction of the goddess Aphrodite, the inner soul (the psyche) of Helen is laid bare. Helen wonders where in the world beauty and passion—Aphrodite—will lead her next, and in indignation she demands that the goddess abandon Olympus and go herself to Paris until he makes her his wife or his slave. Helen is too ashamed before the eyes of the Trojan women to return to his bed. At this Aphrodite becomes enraged and threatens to turn against Helen. Helen submissively returns to her bedchamber and to Paris, whom Aphrodite has restored from a bedraggled loser into a beautiful dandy. Yet a disillusioned Helen greets her beloved with these demeaning words (3. 428–436):

> You have come out of battle? You ought to have died there, beaten by a stronger man, who was my former husband. To be sure you boasted before that you were mightier than warlike Menelaus in the might of your hands and your sword. So then go now and challenge warlike Menelaus again to face you in battle. No, I bid you hold on and do not fight in combat against blond Menelaus in your rashness, lest somehow you will quickly be subdued by his spear.

Paris responds with characteristic nonchalance, and Aphrodite is victorious once again (3. 438–447):

> "My wife, do not rebuke me with harsh words; now Menelaus has won with the help of Athena. At another time I will beat him, for the gods are on our side too. Come on now, let us go to bed and make love. Never at any time has desire so clouded my senses, not even when we first consummated our love on the island of Cranaë, after I had carried you out of lovely Sparta and we sailed away. This is how I love you now and how sweet desire takes hold of me." He spoke, and led her to bed, and his wife followed along.

In Book 6, Hector, the valiant brother of Paris, seeks out his wife, Andromache, to bid her farewell before returning to the battlefield. On his way he looks in on Paris, who is still dallying with Helen in their home. After his defeat by Menelaus and his lovemaking with Helen, Paris is sullenly polishing his armor. Hector has obviously inter-rupted another of their quarrels. Paris tells his brother how Helen has just now been urging him to go out to battle, and he agrees with them both that it is time for him to return. Helen speaks to Hector in words fraught with misery and self-reproach (6. 344–358):

> My brother-in-law, how I wish that I—cold, evil-scheming bitch that I am—had died on the day when first I was born before all this had happened—that a terrible blast of wind had hurled me into the side of a mountain or into a wave of the resounding sea to be swept away. But since the gods have so ordained these evils, I wish that I were the wife of a better man, who felt a sense of guilt

and shame before the eyes of society. But his character is not rooted in such values and he will never change, and so I think that he will reap the rewards. Now come here and sit down in this chair, brother-in-law, since the battle toil has crushed you the most, all on account of me, a bitch, and retribution for Paris' guilt. Upon us both has Zeus imposed an evil fate, so that we might become for future generations the subjects for poetic songs.

Hector tells Helen that he must be on his way. He finds that his wife, their son Astyanax, and the boy's nurse are not at home; they have been anxiously watching from the battlements in concern for his fate. In the sad farewell between husband and wife, Andromache implores Hector not to go to battle and leave her a widow and their child an orphan (see Color Plate 21). Achilles has already killed her father and seven brothers; he captured their mother, and although he accepted a ransom for her return, she has died too. So Hector is father, mother, and brother to her, as well as dear husband. Hector responds with loving conviction (6. 441–485):

"To be sure, all these things are of deep concern to me too, but I should feel terrible shame before the Trojan women with their long robes if like a coward I were to shrink from battle. Nor would my spirit allow me to, since I have learned to be brave always and to fight amidst the first of the Trojans, winning great glory for myself and for my father. For I know this well in my heart and in my soul. The day will come when Troy will be destroyed and Priam and the people of Priam of the fine ashen spear. The suffering that will follow for the Trojans—for Hecuba herself and king Priam and my many brave brothers who will fall in the dust under the hands of their enemies—is not so much a grief for me as is the pain that you will endure when one of the bronze-clad Achaeans leads you away weeping and takes from you the day of your liberty. In Greece at another's bidding you will work the loom and draw water from a spring in Laconia or Thessaly, much against your will, but heavy necessity will lie upon you. Then someone, seeing you in tears, will say, 'This is the wife of Hector, who was by far the best fighter when the horse-taming Trojans did battle for Ilium.' Thus at some time will someone speak, and your grief will be awakened anew because you are without such a husband to ward off the day of your slavery. But may I die with the earth heaped up over my grave before I hear your cries of anguish as you are dragged away a captive."

Thus radiant Hector spoke and reached out for his son, but the child clung to the bosom of the fair-girdled nurse, screaming in dismay at the sight of his father, startled as he saw the bronze crest of his helmet and the horsehair plume nodding dreadful from its peak. His dear father laughed aloud and his lady mother, and immediately Hector took the helmet from his head and placed it all-shining on the ground. Then he kissed his dear son and fondled him in his arms and spoke in prayer to Zeus and the other gods:

"Zeus and you other gods, grant that this son of mine become outstanding among the Trojans, just as I am, excellent in his might and a strong ruler over Ilium. Some day let someone say that this boy has turned out to be far better than his father, as he comes out of the battle, and when he has killed his enemy may he bring home the gory spoils and may his mother rejoice in her heart." Thus speaking he placed his son in the hands of his dear wife. She took him to her fragrant bosom, laughing amidst her tears.

On two other occasions, Andromache prophesies her fate and that of her son and of the city, each time addressing Hector's corpse. Here is how she takes her farewell of him (24. 725–738):

My husband, you were young when you were taken from life, and you leave me a widow in the palace. The boy is still just a baby, who is our child, yours and mine, ill-fated that we are. I do not think that he will grow to manhood, for the city will first be utterly sacked now that you, its guardian, are dead, who defended the city, the chaste wives, and the little children. They will soon go away in the hollow ships, and I with them. And you, my child, either will go with me, where you will perform demeaning tasks, laboring for a harsh master; or else one of the Achaeans will take you by the hand and hurl you in anger from the tower—a grim death—because Hector once killed his brother or father or son.

Indeed, Andromache became the slave of Neoptolemus after the fall of Troy, and her infant son Astyanax was thrown from the city walls.

A major development in the theme of Achilles' wrath occurs in the ninth book. Should Achilles have relented when Agamemnon offered to restore Briseïs with many valuable gifts? It is a measure of his sensitive and passionate nature that he refused the offer, presented by three envoys, Odysseus, Phoenix, and Ajax, son of Telamon.

Odysseus' speech to Achilles echoes for the most part the directions given by Agamemnon, but it begins and ends with more tactful and artful persuasion. In describing the successes of the Trojans, Odysseus emphasizes the danger to Achilles and the opportunity to destroy Hector. The fury of Hector cannot wait to come down to destroy their ships. Then he lists the gifts to be given to Achilles immediately upon his return: seven tripods, ten talents of gold, twenty shining cauldrons, twelve prize-winning horses, seven women from Lesbos, particularly beautiful and skilled (whom Achilles had picked out for himself when he took Lesbos!), and Briseïs, with a solemn oath that Agamemnon had never slept with her. In addition, if the gods were to grant that Priam's city be sacked, Achilles might heap up his ship with gold and bronze and choose twenty Trojan women for himself, the most beautiful after Helen. Beyond this, if they return safely to Greece, Agamemnon promises to make Achilles his son-in-law, with a dowry larger than any ever given before and a kingdom of seven rich cities over which he might rule like a god.

At the conclusion of his speech, Odysseus is careful not to repeat Agamemnon's final instructions: "Let him be subdued—Hades is the most hateful of gods and mortals because he is inexorable and inflexible. Let him submit to me, inasmuch as I am more royal and assert that I am the elder" (9. 158–161). Instead Odysseus begs that Achilles, even if his anger and hatred of Agamemnon are too great for forgiveness, should at least have pity on the other Greeks, who are worn out in battle and will upon his return honor him like a god. In conclusion Odysseus tries to win Achilles over by playing upon his jealousy of Hector's arrogant success, implying that now is his chance to achieve his desire for glory through the defeat of Hector, who thinks that no Greek is his match. By questioning some of these values in his reply, Achilles reveals a sensitivity and introspection that make him unique (9. 308–345):

I must give a direct answer to your speech, telling you honestly what I think and what I will do, so that you ambassadors may not try to wheedle me one after the other. For I hate the man who hides one thing in his heart and says something else as much as I hate Hades and his realm. I will say outright what seems to me best. I do not believe that the son of Atreus, Agamemnon, will persuade me, nor will the other Greeks, since it was no pleasure for me always to fight against the enemy relentlessly. The coward is held in equal honor with the brave man who endures and fights hard, and equal is his fate. The one who does nothing and the one who does much find a similar end in death. It was no advantage to me when I suffered deeply, continually risking my life in battle. As a bird brings food to her unfledged nestlings, after she has won it with much distress, so I used to spend many sleepless nights and endure days of blood in fighting against enemies belligerent in the defense of their wives.

Indeed, I say to you, I plundered twelve populated cities by ship and attacked another eleven by land; from all these I took many splendid treasures and brought them back to give to Agamemnon, the son of Atreus. He who had remained behind by his swift ships took them, distributing a few things but keeping much for himself. All that he gave as prizes to the nobles and kings they keep secure; it was from me alone of the Achaeans that he stole. He has a dear wife, let him sleep with her for his pleasure. Why must the Greeks fight with the Trojans? Why did the son of Atreus gather an army to bring here? Was it not on account of Helen with her beautiful hair? Are the sons of Atreus the only ones among mortals who love their wives? To be sure, any decent and responsible man loves and cares for his own, just as I loved Briseïs from the depths of my heart, even though she was won by my spear. As it is now, since he took my prize out of my hands and deceived me, let him not try me, since I know him too well—he will not persuade me.

Achilles' response continues at some length. He makes it clear that he despises gifts from Agamemnon, however grand they may be, and he has no need or desire to be chosen as his son-in-law. Surely Agamemnon could find someone more royal and worthy of respect! The shameless Agamemnon, "dog that he is, would not dare to look me in the face!" The gifts are excessively generous, but Achilles sees through Agamemnon's façade. This is not reconciliation but bribery. Many critics have said, with some justice, that Achilles by his rejection of these gifts has gone too far in his pride and that he is guilty of the sin of hubris. He should understand, they say, that Agamemnon cannot humiliate himself by coming to Achilles with apologies, as if to a god. Is it really too much, however, to ask a good king to admit his error in person? Agamemnon by his royal arrogance may be as guilty as Achilles, if not more so, because he, the commander in chief, is ultimately responsible for all the slaughter and suffering that might have been avoided.

So Agamemnon's attempt to win Achilles back has failed. After Achilles' old tutor, Phoenix, also tries to persuade Achilles, the third envoy, the warrior Ajax, son of Telamon, bluntly concludes the embassy (9. 628–638):

Achilles has put a savage and proud spirit within his breast. Obdurate, he does not care for the love of his friends, with which we honored him above all men beside the ships, unpitying as he is. Yet others have accepted payment for the death of a brother or a son. But the gods have put in your breast a spirit unforgiving and harsh, because of one girl.

Without Achilles, the Greeks were driven back by the Trojans until Hector began to set fire to the ships. All this was done, says Homer, in fulfillment of the will of Zeus (1 5), for Zeus had agreed to honor Achilles in this way after Thetis had prayed to him to avenge the wrong done by Agamemnon.

When Hector broke through to the Greek ships, Achilles finally allowed his friend and companion, Patroclus, to take his armor and fight Hector and the Trojans. For a while, Patroclus carried all before him, even killing Sarpedon, son of Zeus (see Color Plate 3). But he went too far in his fury. Homer describes (16. 786–867) how Apollo opposed him in the battle and struck him across the back with his hand. Patroclus was dazed by the blow, and the Trojan Euphorbus wounded him with a spear. It was left for Hector to deal the death-blow to the enfeebled and stunned Patroclus.

The death of Patroclus is the turning point of the epic. Achilles is overcome by grief, guilt, and remorse. His anguish is so terrifying that his comrades fear he may take his own life. Yet his mother, Thetis, provides comfort once again as Achilles steadfastly makes the tragic decision to return to battle to avenge Patroclus and so, assuredly, to fix the seal upon his own fate. Grief over the death of Patroclus drove Achilles to end his quarrel with Agamemnon and to return to the fighting with one goal, to kill Hector. So Briseïs was returned with costly gifts, and upon her return she lamented over the corpse of Patroclus (19. 287–300):

> Patroclus, most dear to my unhappy heart, I left you alive when I was taken from the hut and, now upon my return I find you, leader of the host, dead. Thus for me evil follows upon evil. I saw my husband, to whom my father and lady mother gave me, transfixed by a sharp spear in front of his city, and my dear brothers, all three born to our mother, on that day found their way to ruinous death. You would not let me cry when swift Achilles killed my husband and sacked the city of godlike Mynes, but you said that I would be made the wedded wife of godlike Achilles and that I would be taken back in his ship to Phthia to celebrate our marriage among the Myrmidons. So I lament for you unceasingly, you who were always gentle.

Thetis brought new armor, made by Hephaestus, to her son. Homer describes the shield of Achilles in detail, with its portrayal of the human world of the Mycenaeans—cities at war and at peace, scenes of farming and other peaceful activities (a lawsuit, for example, marriage, dancing, and music).

Meanwhile Hector has spoiled Patroclus' corpse of the armor of Achilles, which he himself put on. As he changes his armor, Zeus watches and foretells his doom (17. 194–208):

He put on the immortal armor of Achilles, son of Peleus, which the gods had given to his father and he in turn in his old age gave to Achilles his son. But the son did not grow old in the armor. And when Zeus the cloud-gatherer saw Hector from afar arming himself with the arms of the godlike son of Peleus, he moved his head and spoke to his own heart: "Ah, wretched man! You do not now think of death that will come close to you. You are putting on the immortal arms of the best of men, before whom others also tremble. That man's friend you have killed, gentle and strong, and you have taken the arms from his head and shoulders, as you should not have done. For now I will give you great strength. In return, Andromache will never take the noble arms of the son of Peleus from you when you return from battle."

Achilles returned to the battle and drove the Trojans back to the city, in his rage fighting even the river-god Scamander and filling the river with Trojan corpses. Eventually the Trojans were driven into the city, and only Hector remained outside the wall. The single combat between Hector and Achilles is the climax of the *Iliad*. Hector is chased by Achilles three times around the walls, "as in a dream the pursuer cannot catch him who is running away, nor can he who runs escape nor the other catch him" (22. 199–200). Finally Zeus agrees to the death of Hector (Iliad, 22. 209–213):

 Then indeed the Father held up the golden scales, and in them he put two lots of grievous death, the one for Achilles, and the other for Hector, tamer of horses, and he held the scales by the middle. And the fatal day of Hector sank down toward the house of Hades. Then Phoebus Apollo left Hector, and Athena, the grey-eyed goddess, came to the son of Peleus.

Athena helps Achilles by leading Hector to his death through treachery. She takes the form of his brother, Deïphobus, in whom Hector, now rendered defenseless, puts his final trust (22. 295–301):

 He called with a great shout to white-shielded Deïphobus and asked for a long spear, but Deïphobus was nowhere near him. And Hector knew the truth in his heart and said, "Alas! Now for sure the gods have summoned me deathward. For I thought that the hero Deïphobus was beside me, but he is inside the walls and Athena has deceived me. Now indeed evil death is not far away but very near, and I have no way out."

Deserted by the gods and deceived by Athena, Hector died at the hands of Achilles, who refused to show any mercy and dragged the

Hector and Achilles, by Eunice Pinney (1770–1849). Watercolor on paper, 1809–1826; 16 × 20 in. Eunice Pinney was a member of a prominent Connecticut family, who took up painting when she was thirty-nine years old. Her work has more vigor and originality than that of less mature artists in the early Republic. Here Achilles thrusts his spear into Hector's neck (*Iliad* 22. 326–329), while Athena encourages him from above. In the background are the walls and people of Troy and, to the left, the springs of the river Scamander "where the wives and daughters of the Trojans used to wash their clothes" (*Iliad* 22. 154–155). Note the elaborate clothing of the warriors, the miniature Gorgon's head on Athena's robe, and the owl that accompanies her. All three of the major figures are left-handed, as sometimes happens with designs for engravings or tapestries, for which the final product would be reversed. A copy of such a design may have been the basis of this painting. (*Abby Aldrich Rockefeller Folk Art Collection, Williamsburg, Virginia. Reproduced by permission.*)

corpse back to his hut behind his chariot. Next Achilles celebrated the funeral of Patroclus, on whose pyre he sacrificed twelve Trojan prisoners. He also held athletic games in honor of Patroclus, at which he presided and gave valuable prizes for the winners. Yet his anger against Hector was still unassuaged, and daily for twelve days he dragged Hector's body round the tomb of Patroclus behind his chariot; the mutilated corpse was refreshed and restored by Apollo each day. Only when Thetis brought him the message of Zeus was Achilles ready to relent. Priam himself, with the help of Hermes, came to Achilles' hut and ransomed the corpse of his son. The scene where the old man kneels before the killer of so many of his sons is one of the most moving in all Greek saga (24. 477–484):

Great Priam entered, unseen by Achilles' companions, and stood near Achilles. With his hands he took hold of Achilles' knees and kissed his hands, hands terrible and man-killing, which had killed many of Priam's sons. Achilles was full of wonder as he looked at godlike Priam, and the others also wondered and they looked at each other.

When Priam has made his appeal to Achilles and they both have had their fill of lamentation, each remembering his sorrows, Achilles explains the ultimate reason for human misery (24. 524–533):

No [human] action is without chilling grief. For thus the gods have spun out for wretched mortals the fate of living in distress, while they live without care. Two jars sit on the doorsill of Zeus, filled with gifts that he bestows, one jar of evils, the other of blessings. When Zeus, who delights in thunder, takes from both and mixes the bad with the good, a human being at one time encounters evil, and at another good. But the one to whom Zeus gives only troubles from the jar of sorrows, this one he makes an object of abuse, to be driven by cruel misery over the divine earth.

Achilles has finally learned through suffering true compassion. His pessimistic view of human existence lies at the core of the Greek tragic view of life. It is a view mirrored with sad beauty by Herodotus, as we have seen in Chapter 4, and echoed again and again by the dramatists, who delight in the splendid fall of those who were once great and blessed. "Never count a person happy until dead."

So Priam ransomed Hector and returned to Troy with the corpse. The *Iliad* ends with the funeral of Hector, over whose body Andromache, Hecuba, and finally Helen had poured out their lamentations. For nine days the people of Troy mourned for Hector, whose death had made inevitable their own fate.

Achilles is not only subject to vehement passions. Alone of the Greek heroes he knows his destiny clearly: to Odysseus' speech in the embassy he replies (9. 410–416):

> My mother, Thetis of the silver feet, has told me that two fates are carrying me to the goal of my death. If I stay here and fight before the city of the Trojans, then I lose my homecoming, but my glory will never fade. But if I return home to my own dear land, then gone is my noble glory, and my life will be long.

The character of Achilles is perfectly expressed in these words. When his horse, Xanthus, prophesies his death (19. 404–417), Achilles replies:

> Well do I know that my destiny is to die here, far from my dear father and mother. Even so, I shall keep on. I shall not stop until I have harried the Trojans enough with my warfare.

Again, when the dying Hector foretells Achilles' death, Achilles resolutely accepts his fate. Nor is Achilles always violent. At the funeral games for Patroclus, he presides with princely dignity and even makes peace between the hot-tempered competitors. We have also seen how he gave up his anger against Hector and treated Priam with dignity and generosity. Achilles is a splendid and complex hero, incomparably the greatest figure in the Trojan saga.

THE FALL OF TROY

The brilliance of the *Iliad* makes the rest of the saga of the Trojan War pale by comparison. Episodes are recorded in summaries of lost epics, in drama, in many vase-paintings, and in Vergil's *Aeneid,* so that we can tell the story of the rest of the war.

Achilles and Penthesilea

After the funeral of Hector the fighting resumed, and Achilles killed the leaders of two contingents that came from the ends of the earth to help the Trojans. From the north came the Amazons—the legendary warrior women—led by Penthesilea. Achilles killed her; in some versions, just as Achilles was about to deal the fatal thrust, their eyes met and he fell in love with her. Achilles mourned over her death and her beauty and killed Thersites, who taunted him.[21] For this murder Achilles had to withdraw for a time to Lesbos, where he was purified by Odysseus.

Achilles and Memnon

A second foreign contingent was that of the Ethiopians, from the south. They were led by Memnon, son of Eos (Aurora), goddess of the dawn, and of Tithonus (a brother of Priam). After Memnon's death, his followers were turned into birds that fought around his tomb. Achilles did not long survive these victories.

The Death of Achilles

As he pursued the Trojans toward the city, Achilles was fatally wounded in the heel by an arrow shot by Paris with the help of Apollo. After a fierce fight, his corpse was recovered by Ajax, son of Telamon, and buried at Sigeum, the promontory near Troy. The funeral was a magnificent affair, and among the mourners were his mother, Thetis, and the sea-nymphs; Thetis is said to have removed the corpse to the island of Leuce (in the Black Sea) where she restored it to life and immortality. Homer sends Achilles to the Underworld, where his ghost later met Odysseus and complained bitterly of his fate.

Achilles' ghost demanded that Polyxena, the daughter of Priam and Hecuba, be sacrificed at his tomb. The sacrifice of Polyxena is one of the principal themes of Euripides' tragedy *Hecuba,* in which the dignity and virtue of Polyxena are a striking contrast to the violence of the young Greeks and their leaders. Thus the aftermath of the war involved the sacrifice of a maiden before the Greek army just as it had been preceded by the sacrifice of Iphigenia. In a version especially popular in medieval legend, Polyxena had been loved by Achilles, and it was while he was meeting her that he had been ambushed and killed by Paris.

Odysseus and Ajax Compete for the Armor of Achilles

Achilles' armor was claimed by both Odysseus and Ajax, son of Telamon, as the leading warriors surviving on the Greek side. Each made a speech before an assembly of the Greeks, presided over by Athena. Trojan prisoners gave evidence that Odysseus had done them more harm than Ajax, and the arms were awarded to Odysseus. The disgrace of losing sent Ajax mad; he slaughtered a flock of sheep (which he believed were his enemies) and on becoming sane again killed himself for shame by falling on his sword. From his blood sprang a flower (perhaps a type of hyacinth) with the initials of his name (AI-AI) on its petals.[22]

This legend is the subject of Sophocles' tragedy *Ajax*, in which the hostility of Athena to Ajax contrasts with Odysseus' appreciation of the human predicament. Athena asks Odysseus if he knows of a hero who was greater than Ajax, and his reply is a final commentary on the heroic tragedy of the *Iliad* (Sophocles, *Ajax* 121–133):

ODYSSEUS: I do not know [of a greater hero]. I pity him in his misery, nevertheless, although he is my enemy. Because he is yoked to evil madness *(ate)* I look at this man's troubles no more than at my own. For I see that we who live are nothing more than ghosts and weightless shadow.

ATHENA: Therefore when you see such things, say nothing yourself against the gods and swear no boastful oath if your hand is heavy [with success] or with deep and enduring wealth. For time lays low and brings back again all human things. The gods love those who are moderate *(sophrones)* and hate those who are evil.

We can hardly find a better expression of the way in which the Greeks used mythology to express their deepest understanding of human life.

The Roman poet Ovid tells the story of Ajax and the armor of Achilles at length. Here is how he describes its end (*Metamorphoses* 13. 382–398):

The Greek leaders were impressed [i.e., by the speech of Odysseus], and the power of eloquence was made clear in the consequences. The eloquent man took away the armor of the brave warrior. Ajax, who alone so many times had resisted Hector, who had opposed iron missiles and fire and the will of Jupiter, could not resist one thing, anger. Shame conquered the unconquered hero. He seized the sword and thrust the lethal blade into his breast, never before wounded. The ground reddened with his blood and put forth a purple flower from the green grass, the flower which earlier had sprung from the wound of Hyacinthus. The same letters were written on the petals for hero and youth, for the one signifying his name, for the other the mourning cry.

The Wooden Horse

After Achilles' death, Odysseus captured Helenus, who told the Greeks of a number of conditions that must be fulfilled before they could capture the city. Among these was the summoning of two absent heroes, Neoptolemus (Pyrrhus) and Philoctetes. As we have mentioned, Philoctetes was brought from Lemnos, cured of his snake-bite, and with his indispensable bow and arrows shot Paris. Neopto-lemus (his name means "new recruit"), the son of Achilles, proved himself to be a brutal warrior and his butchering of Priam at the altar during the sack of Troy is one of the most moving scenes in the *Aeneid*. Vergil's description of Priam's remains echoes a familiar theme: the once mighty king now "lies, a great and mutilated body, head torn from the shoulders, a nameless corpse on the seashore" (2. 557–558).

The Greeks finally took the city by deception. One of them, Epeus, built an enormous hollow wooden horse, in which the leading war-riors were concealed.[23] The horse was then left outside the city walls, while the other Greeks sailed off to the island of Tenedos, leaving behind one man, Sinon. The Trojans, thinking that their troubles were over, came out of the city and captured Sinon, who pretended to be the bitter enemy of Odysseus and the other Greeks. He told the Tro-jans that the horse was an offering to Athena, purposely made too big to pass through the city walls; if it were brought inside, the city would never be captured. Not all the Trojans believed him; Cassandra, the prophetic daughter of Priam, foretold the truth, and Laocoön, son of Antenor and priest of Apollo, hurled his spear into the horse's flank and said that it should be destroyed. Yet the Trojans ignored Cassandra and failed to hear the clash of armor as Laocoön's spear struck the horse. Their judgment appeared to be vindicated when two huge serpents swam over the sea from Tenedos as Laocoön was sacrificing to Apollo and throttled him and his two sons.

The Sack of Troy

The Trojans pulled down part of the city walls and dragged the horse in. Helen walked round it calling to the Greek leaders, imitating the voice of each one's wife, but they were restrained from answering by Odysseus. So the horse achieved its purpose; that night, as the Trojans slept after celebrating the end of the war, Sinon opened the horse and released the Greeks. The other Greeks sailed back from Tenedos and entered the city; the Trojans were put to the sword and the city burned.

Antenor was spared, and of the other Trojan leaders only Aeneas escaped, along with his son, Ascanius, and his father, Anchises. Priam and the others were killed; Hector's infant son, Astyanax, was thrown from the walls, and his widow, Andromache, along with Hecuba and the other Trojan women, were made slaves of the Greek leaders. Neoptolemus' share of the spoil included Andromache, but eventually

The Building of the Trojan Horse by Giovann Domenico Tiepolo (1727–1804). Oil on canvas, 1773; 15 × 26 in. This is part of a series of oil sketches on the fall of Troy by the younger Tiepolo (formerly ascribed to his more famous father). The massive horse dwarfs the workmen, while the walls of the doomed city brood in the background. The final painting, nearly six times the size of the sketch, hangs in the Wadsworth Atheneum in Hartford, Connecticut. *(National Gallery, London. Reproduced by courtesy of the Trustees.)*

she married Helenus and founded the dynasty of the Molossian kings. In Book 3 of the *Aeneid,* she and Helenus figure prominently. She is the only one of the Trojan women to regain some sort of independent status after the fall of Troy.

During the sack of the city, Cassandra took refuge in the temple of Athena. She was dragged from this asylum by Ajax the Locrian, son of Oileus, and for this he was killed by the gods on his way home.[24] Cassandra became the slave and concubine of Agamemnon who took her back to Mycenae, where she was murdered with him by Clytemnestra. In Aeschylus' play *Agamemnon* she foresees her own death in a moving scene (see pp. 344–345); yet her audience, the chorus in the play, does not believe her. The curse of Apollo remained with her to the end.

As Hecuba sailed back to Greece with Odysseus (to whom she had been given as part of the spoils), she landed in Thrace and there recognized the corpse of her son Polydorus when it was washed up on the seashore. He had been murdered by the local king Polymestor (to whom he had been sent for safety during the war), because of the treasure that had been sent with him. Taking advantage of Polymestor's avarice, Hecuba enticed him and his children into her tent, pretending that she knew the whereabouts in Troy of some hidden treasure, while she appeared to know nothing of the murder of Polydorus. Once they were in the tent, Hecuba's women murdered the children before Polymestor's eyes, then blinded him with their brooches. After this, Hecuba was turned into a bitch; when she died, the place of her burial (in Thrace) was called Cynossema, which means the "dog's tomb."

The *Trojan Women* of Euripides

In Euripides' tragedy the *Trojan Women,* the results of the fall are seen through the eyes of Hecuba, Cassandra, and Andromache. The death of Astyanax is a central part of the tragedy, in which he is torn from his mother's embrace to be hurled from the walls. Later his body is brought back on stage and placed by Hecuba on the shield of Hector, a symbol of the defenselessness of Troy once her champion had been killed. The chorus of Trojan captives recalls the entry of the wooden horse (*Trojan Women* 515–540):

 Now I shall sing of Troy, how I was destroyed by the four-wheeled contrivance of the Greeks and made their prisoner, when they left the horse at the gates, echoing to the skies with the clash of armor and caparisoned with gold. And the Trojan people shouted as it stood on the rock of Troy: "Come, the labor of war is over! Bring in this wooden horse as a holy offering to the daughter of Zeus, guardian of Troy!" Who of the young women did not go, who of the old men stayed at home? Charmed by music, they took hold of the treacherous means of their destruction. All the Phrygian people gathered at the gates, and with ropes of flax they dragged it, like the dark hull of a ship, to the stone temple's floor, bringing death to their city—the temple of the goddess Pallas.

The Sack of Troy in the *Aeneid*

The principal source for the fall of Troy is the second book of the *Aeneid*. Here is how Vergil describes the horror of the end of a city deserted by its divine protectors in Aeneas' vision at the climactic moment of the sack, as his mother Venus allows him a moment of divine insight (*Aeneid* 2. 602–603, 610–625):[25]

[Aeneas recalls the words of Venus:] "It is the pitiless gods, the gods who are destroying the wealth of Troy and laying the city low from top to bottom. Look—for I will remove the cloud that now dulls your mortal sight. Here, where you see the shattered towers and huge stones torn up, where dust and smoke are billowing, Neptune is convulsing the walls, shaking the foundations with his trident as he uproots the city. Here Juno, most cruel, leads the others in seizing the Scaean gates: raging and clad in iron armor she calls the Greeks from the ships. Look over here—even now Tritonian Pallas has taken up her place upon the height of Troy's citadel: see how she is lit with the lurid storm-cloud and the ferocious Gorgon! The Father of the gods himself renews the courage and violence of the Greeks, himself he urges them on to fight."

I saw the fatal vision and the mighty power of the gods hostile to Troy. Then, indeed, I saw all Ilium collapse into the flames and Troy, built by Neptune, overturned from its foundations.

Yet Aeneas escaped, taking with him his father, Anchises (who carried the images of the city's gods in his hands), and his son, Ascanius (also called Iulus). His wife, Creusa, started with him and was lost to Aeneas' sight. Only her ghost appeared to him, foretelling his destiny and encouraging him to travel to a new world. The scene of Aeneas leaving Troy is heavy with symbolism, and it is with hope for the future that Aeneas, burdened with the past, leaves the doomed city (*Aeneid* 2. 707–711, 721–725):

Study for "Aeneas' Flight from Troy," by Federico Barocci (ca. 1535–1612). Pen and brown ink, brown wash, opaque watercolor, over black chalk on paper; ca. 1587–1588; 11 × 16¾ in. The tightly structured group of Aeneas, Anchises, and Ascanius are separated from Creusa. In the background are the burning buildings of Troy (the circular temple, like a Roman church of Barocci's time, is prominent) and confused forms of Trojans and Greeks are sketched on the right. To the left a dog adds a poignant touch to the departure. With great economy the artist faithfully represents Vergil's narrative. *(Italian. © The Cleveland Museum of Art, L. E. Holden Fund, 60.26.)*

"Then come, dear father, sit on my shoulders; I will carry you, the load will not weigh me down. Whatever chance may fall, we will share a common danger and a common salvation. Let little Iulus walk beside me and let my wife follow." With these words I spread my cloak and the skin of a tawny lion across my shoulders and neck and lifted the burden. Little Iulus took my right hand and, hardly able to keep up, walked beside his father.

THE RETURNS

18

T he returns of the Greek leaders from Troy were narrated in an epic called *Nostoi* (Returns), of which only a brief prose summary and three lines of verse are extant.[1] It omits the return of Odysseus, which is the subject of Homer's *Odyssey*.

Agamemnon, Menelaus, and Nestor

Agamemnon and Menelaus quarreled over the departure and so parted company. Agamemnon sailed for Greece with part of the fleet, including the contingent of the Locrians. Near the island of Mykonos, Athena, in her anger at the sacrilege committed at Troy by the Locrian leader Ajax (p. 388), caused a storm to wreck many of the ships. Ajax swam to a nearby rock, where he boasted that not even the gods could prevent his escape from the dangers of the sea. For this Poseidon struck the rock with his trident, and Ajax was hurled into the sea and drowned.

During a second storm, which struck Agamemnon's fleet at Cape Caphareus in Euboea, Nauplius avenged the death of his son Palamedes by luring many ships onto the rocks with a false beacon. Agamemnon finally reached Mycenae, only to be murdered by Aegisthus and Clytemnestra.

Meanwhile Menelaus, Nestor, and Diomedes set sail together from Troy. Nestor returned to Pylos safely. In the *Odyssey* he tells Telemachus how Menelaus lost all his fleet except for five ships in a storm off Crete and eventually reached Egypt. On the advice of the seanymph Eidothea, he forced her father, Nereus, to tell him how to appease the gods and secure a safe voyage home. Thus after seven years he and Helen returned to Sparta, where they resumed their rule.[2] At the end of his life he was transported to the Elysian Fields, avoiding the usual fate of going to Hades, because he was the husband of Helen and the son-in-law of Zeus.

Diomedes

Diomedes reached Argos quickly, but there he found that his wife, Aegialia (daughter of Adrastus) had been unfaithful. Her adulteries were caused by Aphrodite, angry because Diomedes had wounded her at Troy. Diomedes left Argos and came to Italy, where the Apulian king, Daunus, gave him land. Diomedes founded several cities in Italy, but he declined to help King Latinus against Aeneas. After his death he was worshiped as a hero in many places in Italy, and in one story Athena made him an immortal god.[3] His followers were turned into birds.[4]

Idomeneus

Idomeneus returned to Crete to find that his wife, Meda, had committed adultery with Leucus, who had then murdered her and her daughter and made himself king over ten of the cities of Crete. Idomeneus was driven out by Leucus and came to Calabria in southern Italy, where he was worshiped as a hero after his death.[5]

Servius, the ancient commentator on Vergil, tells a legend which is similar to the biblical story of Jephthah's vow (Judges 11. 30–40). Idomeneus was caught in a storm during the voyage home and vowed, if he were saved, to sacrifice to Poseidon the first thing that met him. When he returned home, his son came out first to meet him. After Idomeneus had fulfilled his vow, a pestilence attacked the Cretans, who took it to be a divine punishment for Idomeneus' act and drove him into exile.

Philoctetes

Philoctetes returned to Thessaly but was driven out by his people. He came to southern Italy and there he founded a number of cities and after his death was worshiped as a hero.

The stories of Diomedes, Idomeneus, and Philoctetes seem to reflect the founding of Greek colonies in southern Italy from the eighth century onwards. All three were worshiped as heroes after their death.

Neoptolemus

Achilles' son, Neoptolemus, warned by Thetis not to return by sea, took the land route back to Greece, accompanied by Helenus and Andromache (pp. 386–387). With them and his wife, Hermione (daughter of Menelaus), he left his home in Phthia and came to Molossia in Epirus, where he ruled over the Molossi. He was killed at Delphi and there became a hero with his own cult.

ODYSSEUS

The return of Odysseus forms a saga in itself, to which many folktale elements have accrued. Here is the summary of the *Odyssey* given by Aristotle in his *Poetics* (17):

> The story of the *Odyssey* is not long; a man is away from home for many years; Poseidon constantly is on the watch to destroy him, and he is alone, at home his property is being wasted by suitors, and his son is the intended victim of a plot. He reaches home, tempest-tossed; he makes himself known, attacks his enemies and destroys them, and is himself saved. This is the heart of the matter: the rest is episodes.

The adventures of Odysseus have been taken as symbolic (e.g., Odysseus conquers death in his visit to the Underworld) or as connected with real places that had become known to the Greeks as their trade and colonization expanded. For the most part, however, they are romantic legends and folktales set in imaginary places and grafted onto the saga of a historical prince's return from a long absence.[6]

During the Trojan War, Odysseus was the wisest of the Greek heroes and a brave warrior. After the death of Achilles he inherited the divine armor of Achilles. In the *Odyssey* he experiences many adventures, usually escaping from danger through his intelligence and courage. He meets with many men and women, with goddesses and monsters, and he remains faithful to Penelope, the wife whom he left in Ithaca with his son, Telemachus.[7]

The Story of the *Odyssey*

The poem begins in the middle of Odysseus' adventures, with the hero detained on Ogygia, the island of the goddess Calypso. After he has sailed away from this island and his raft has been wrecked, Odysseus relates to his rescuers the events previous to his arrival on Ogygia. The poem then continues with the arrival of Odysseus on Ithaca, his revenge on the suitors for the hand of Penelope, and his eventual recognition by and reunion with Penelope.

The resourceful character of Odysseus dominates the story, but the gods also play a significant part, especially Poseidon, who is hostile to the hero, and Athena, who protects him. Homer introduces Odysseus in the opening lines (1–21) of the *Odyssey:*

Of the man tell me, O Muse, the man of many ways,[8] who traveled afar after he had sacked the holy city of Troy. He experienced the cities and the thoughts of many men, and his spirit suffered many sorrows on the sea, as he labored for his own life and for the homecoming of his companions. Yet even so he could not protect his companions, much though he wished it, for they perished by their own folly, when thoughtlessly they had eaten the cattle of Helios, Hyperion the sun-god. And the god took away the day of their homecoming. From some point in these things, O goddess, daughter of Zeus, begin to tell me also the tale.

Then all the others, who had escaped sheer destruction, were at home, safe from the sea and the war. But this man alone, longing for his homecoming and his wife, did the nymph, the lady Calypso, keep in her hollow cave, desiring him as her husband. But when, as the years rolled round, that year came in which the gods had destined his return home to Ithaca, not even then did he escape from his labors nor was he with his friends. Yet the gods pitied him, all except Poseidon, and he unrelentingly was hostile to godlike Odysseus, until he returned to his own land.

The Cicones and the Lotus Eaters

It took Odysseus ten years to reach home. When he and his contingent left Troy, they came to the Thracian city of Ismarus, home of the Cicones, which they sacked before being driven off. They had spared Maron, priest of Apollo, in their attack, and he in return gave them twelve jars of fragrant red wine, which was to prove its value later. They were driven southward by a storm to the land of the lotus eaters. Here their reception was friendly but no less dangerous, for whoever ate of the fruit of the lotus forgot everything and wanted only to stay where he was, eating lotus fruit. Odysseus got his men away, even those who had tasted the fruit, and sailed to the land of the Cyclopes.

The Cyclopes

The Cyclopes were one-eyed giants, herdsmen, living each in his own cave. One of them was Polyphemus, son of Poseidon, whose cave Odysseus and twelve picked companions entered. In the cave were sheep and lambs, cheeses, and other provisions, to which they helped themselves while waiting for the return of the cave's owner. When Polyphemus returned with his flocks, he shut the entrance of the cave with a huge stone, and then caught sight of the visitors, two of whom he ate for his supper. He breakfasted on two more the next day and another two when he returned the second evening.

Now Odysseus had with him some of the wine of Maron, and with this he made Polyphemus drunk; he told him his name was Nobody *(Outis)* and the giant, in return for the excellent wine, promised that he would reward Nobody by eating him last. He then fell asleep. Odysseus sharpened a wooden stake and heated it in the fire; then he and his surviving men drove it into the solitary eye of the sleeping giant. As he cried out in agony the other Cyclopes came running to the cave's entrance, only to hear the cry "Nobody is killing me," so that they assumed that not much was wrong and left Polyphemus alone.

Next morning Polyphemus, now blind, removed the stone at the entrance and let his flocks out, feeling each animal as it passed. But Odysseus had tied his men each to the undersides of three sheep, and himself clung to the belly of the biggest ram; so he and his men escaped. As Odysseus sailed away, he shouted his real name to the Cyclops, who hurled the top of a mountain at him and nearly wrecked the ship. Polyphemus had long before been warned of Odysseus, and as he recognized the name he prayed to his father Poseidon (*Odyssey* 9. 530–535):

> Grant that Odysseus may not return home, but if it is fated for him once more to see those he loves and reach his home and country, then let him arrive after many years, in distress, without his companions, upon another's ship, and may he find trouble in his house.

The prayer was heard.

Aeolus and the Laestrygonians

Odysseus, reunited with the rest of his fleet, next reached the floating island of Aeolus, keeper of the winds, who lived with his six sons, who were married to his six daughters. After he had entertained

The Blinding of Polyphemus. Proto-Attic vase from Eleusis, mid-seventh century B.C.; height of vase 56 in., of neck 15 in. Odysseus (painted in white) and his companions drive a long pole into the eye of the Cyclops, who holds the cup of wine that has made him drunk. This brutal scene is one of the earliest "free" vase-paintings after the Geometric period. *(Eleusis, Museum. Photograph courtesy of Hirmer Verlag, München.)*

Odysseus, Aeolus gave him as a parting gift a leather bag containing all the winds and showed him which one to release so as to reach home. Thus he sailed back to Ithaca and was within reach of land when he fell asleep. His men, believing that the bag contained gold that Odysseus was keeping for himself, opened it, and all the winds rushed out and blew the ships back to Aeolus' island. Aeolus refused to help them any more, reasoning that they must be hated by the gods.

Odysseus and his men sailed on to the land of the Laestrygonians. They sank all Odysseus' ships except his own and ate up the crews. So Polyphemus' curse was already working, and Odysseus sailed away with his solitary ship.

Circe

He reached the island of Aeaea, the home of the witch Circe, daughter of the Sun. Odysseus divided his men into two groups; he stayed behind with the one while the other, twenty-three men in all, went to visit the ruler of the island. They found Circe with various animals around her, and they themselves (except for Eurylochus, who

Circe and Her Lovers in a Landscape, by Dosso Dossi (ca. 1479–1542). Oil on canvas, ca. 1525; $39\frac{1}{2} \times 53\frac{1}{2}$ in. Dossi was court painter to the dukes of Ferrara, where Ariosto composed his poem *Orlando Furioso,* whose Alcina is probably the origin of Dossi's Circe. She points to an inscribed tablet, and on the ground lies an open book of magic, whereas Homer's Circe used a wand and drugs to transform her victims. The exquisite landscape is populated by peaceful animals and birds, far different from Homer's wolves and lions and the swine into which she turned Odysseus' men. *(Samuel H. Kress Collection, © 1993 National Gallery of Art, Washington, D.C.)*

brought the news back to Odysseus) became pigs when they ate her food, swine in appearance and sound, but still having human minds.[9] As Odysseus went to rescue his men, he encountered the god Hermes, who told him how to counter Circe's charms and gave him as an antidote the magic herb *moly,* whose "root is black and flower as white as milk." So he ate Circe's food unharmed and threatened her with his sword when she tried to turn him into a pig. She recognized him and instead made love to him. She then set a feast before him, which he would not touch before he had made her change his men back into their human shape. Odysseus lived with Circe for a year and by her begot a son, Telegonus.

At the end of a year Odysseus, urged on by his men, asked Circe to send him on his way home. She agreed, but told him that he first had to go to the Underworld and there learn the way home from the prophet Tiresias.

The *Nekuia*

Book 11 of the *Odyssey,* which tells of Odysseus' experiences in the Underworld, is generally referred to as the Book of the Dead or the *Nekuia,* the name of the rite by which ghosts were summoned and questioned. Odysseus' visit to the Underworld is a conquest of death, the most formidable struggle a hero has to face. The hero who can return from the house of Hades alive has achieved all that a mortal can achieve. The *Nekuia* of Odysseus is different in one important respect from its most famous imitation: in the *Aeneid* Aeneas actually descends to the Underworld and himself passes through it (see pp. 284–294), whereas Odysseus goes to the entrance and there performs the ritual sacrifice that summons up the spirits of the dead. Passages that tell of Odysseus' journey from Aeaea to the Underworld, his performance of the rite, and his conversations with a number of the ghosts are translated at length in Chapter 13; here we provide a summary of his visit.

Following Circe's directions, Odysseus sailed with his men to the western limit of the world. As he performed the ritual sacrifice at the entrance to the world of the dead, many ghosts came, among them Tiresias, who foretold the disasters that yet awaited Odysseus on his journey. He would reach home, but alone and after many years. At Ithaca he would find the arrogant suitors pressing Penelope hard and wasting his substance. But he would kill them all, and he would have still more travels ahead of him before death came.

From Tiresias, Odysseus also learned that the spirits with whom he wished to speak must be allowed to drink the blood of the sacrificial victim; the others he kept away by threatening them with his sword. Among the ghosts who appeared and spoke were those of Odysseus' mother, Anticlea, and of Agamemnon, Achilles, and Ajax, son of Telamon. Achilles said that "he would rather be a slave to a poor man on earth than be king over all the souls of the dead." Ajax would not answer Odysseus a word, for he still was grieved by his loss in the contest for Achilles' arms.

Eventually Odysseus left the house of Hades for fear that the Gorgon's head (which turns all whom it beholds to stone) might appear. He rejoined his men and sailed back to Aeaea.

The Sirens, the Planctae, Charybdis, and Scylla

Circe sent him on his way after warning him of the dangers that lay ahead. First were the Sirens (said by Homer to be two in number, but by other authors to be more). To Homer they were human in

Odysseus and the Sirens. Athenian red-figure stamnos, ca. 450 B.C.; height $13\frac{3}{4}$ in. Odysseus, lashed to the mast, safely hears the song of the sirens as his men row by, their ears plugged with wax. Two sirens (winged creatures with human heads) stand on cliffs, while a third plunges headlong into the sea. The artist, by the dramatic angle of Odysseus' head, expresses the hero's longing to be free of his bonds, and the turned head of the oarsman on the right and the helmsman's gesture add further tension to the scene. *(British Museum, London. Reproduced by courtesy of the Trustees.)*

form, but in popular tradition they were birdlike, with women's heads. From their island meadow they would lure passing sailors onto the rocks; all around them were the whitened bones of their victims. Odysseus sailed by them unharmed, stopping his men's ears with wax, while he had himself bound to the ship's mast so that he could not yield to the irresistible beauty of the Sirens' song.

The next danger was the two wandering rocks *(Planctae)* between which one ship only, the *Argo,* had ever safely passed. Odysseus avoided them by sailing close to two high cliffs; in the lower of these lived Charybdis (she is not described by Homer), who three times a day sucked in the water of the strait and spouted it upward again. To sail near that cliff was certain destruction, and Odysseus chose as the lesser evil the higher cliff where was the cave of Scylla, daughter of the sea deity Phorcys. Originally a sea-nymph, she had been changed through the jealousy of Poseidon's wife Amphitrite into a monster with a girdle of six dogs' heads and with twelve feet, by means of which she would snatch sailors from passing ships. From Odysseus' ship she snatched six men, whom she ate in her cave. Odysseus and the rest of the crew were unharmed.

The Cattle of the Sun

Last, Circe told Odysseus of the island of Thrinacia, where Helius (the Sun) pastured his herds of cattle and sheep; she strictly warned Odysseus not to touch a single one of the animals if he and his men wished ever to return to Ithaca. But Odysseus' men could not show such restraint after weeks of being detained by adverse winds, and while he was sleeping they killed some of the cattle for food. Helius complained to Zeus, and as a punishment for the sacrilege of killing the god's cattle Zeus raised a storm when the ship set sail and hurled a thunderbolt at it. The ship sank, and all the men were drowned except for Odysseus, who escaped, floating on the mast and part of the keel.

After the wreck, Odysseus drifted back to Charybdis, where he avoided death by clinging to a tree growing on the cliff until the whirlpool propelled his mast to the surface after sucking it down.

Calypso

Odysseus drifted over the sea to Ogygia, the island home of Calypso, daughter of Atlas, with whom he lived for seven years. Although she loved him and offered to make him immortal, he could not forget

Hermes Ordering Calypso to Release Odysseus, by Gerard de Lairesse (1641–1711). Oil on canvas, 1670; 36 × 45 in. Odysseus, loosely garbed in a scarlet robe, and Calypso embrace on a voluptuous bed. Above, Zeus addresses the council of the gods (Apollo is behind him), from which Hermes descends to bring the commands of Zeus. To the left a child plays with the armor of Odysseus, and to the right in the background servants prepare a feast in a columned banqueting hall. At the right is a clothed statue of a woman holding a basket in which is a bird, perhaps Aphrodite and her dove. De Lairesse has changed Calypso's cave into a luxurious palace, and there is no hint of the longing of Odysseus for Ithaca and Penelope in his splendid reinterpretation of Homer's text. *(Dutch. © The Cleveland Museum of Art, Mr. and Mrs. William H. Marlatt Fund, 92.2.)*

Penelope. Finally, after Hermes brought her the express orders of Zeus, Calypso helped Odysseus build a raft and sail away.

The Phaeacians

Even now Odysseus was not free from disaster; Poseidon saw him as he approached Scheria (the island of the Phaeacians) and shattered the raft with a storm. After two days and two nights, helped

Calypso and Ulysses, by Emily Marshall. Watercolor on paper, 1820–1835; 19 × 24 in. Calypso, in the dress of a woman of the early nineteenth century, tries to comfort Odysseus as he looks over the ocean and thinks of Penelope. Her left hand rests on his shoulder and behind is a river landscape with a palm tree to give a suitably exotic air. Nothing is known of the artist, whose deceptively naive style has caught the pathos of the situation in which the goddess and the hero find themselves. *(Abby Aldrich Rockefeller Folk Art Collection, Williamsburg, Virginia. Reproduced by permission.)*

by the sea-goddess Leucothea (formerly the mortal Ino, daughter of Cadmus) and by Athena, he reached land, naked, exhausted, and alone.

The king of the Phaeacians was Alcinoüs, and his daughter was Nausicaä. The day after Odysseus' landing Nausicaä went to wash clothes near the seashore and came face to face with Odysseus. She gave him her protection and brought him back to the palace. Here he was warmly entertained by Alcinoüs and his queen, Arete, and related the story of his adventures to them. The Phaeacians gave him rich gifts, and a day later they brought him back to

Ithaca on one of their ships, in a deep sleep. So Odysseus reached Ithaca ten years after the fall of Troy, alone and on another's ship, as Polyphemus had prayed. Yet even now Poseidon did not relax his hostility; as the Phaeacians' ship was entering the harbor of Scheria on its return, he turned the ship and its crew to stone as a punishment upon the Phaeacians for conveying strangers over the seas, especially those who were the objects of Poseidon's hatred.

Ithaca

In Ithaca more than one hundred suitors (young noblemen from Ithaca and the nearby islands) were courting Penelope in the hope of taking Odysseus' place as her husband and as king of Ithaca (for Telemachus, Odysseus' son by Penelope, was considered still too young to succeed). They spent their days feasting at Odysseus' palace, wasting his possessions. Penelope, however, remained faithful to Odysseus, even though he seemed to be dead. She put the suitors off by promising to choose one of them when she should have finished weaving a magnificent cloak to be a burial garment for Odysseus' father, Laertes. For three years she wove the robe by day and undid her work by night, but in the fourth year her deception was uncovered, and a decision was now unavoidable.

At this stage Odysseus returned (see Color Plate 8). Helped by Athena, he gained entrance at the palace disguised as a beggar, after being recognized by his faithful old swineherd, Eumaeus, and by Telemachus. Telemachus had been on a journey to Pylos and Sparta and had learned from Nestor and Menelaus that his father was still alive. Outside the palace Odysseus' old hound, Argus, recognized his master after nineteen years' absence, and died.

At the palace Odysseus was insulted by the suitors and by another beggar, Irus, whom he knocked out in a fight. Still in disguise, he gave to Penelope an exact description of Odysseus and of a curious brooch he had worn. As a result, she confided in him her plan to give herself next day to the suitor who succeeded in stringing Odysseus' great bow and shooting an arrow straight through a row of twelve ax heads. Also at this time Odysseus was recognized by his old nurse, Euryclea, who knew him from a scar on his thigh, which he had received when hunting a boar with his grandfather, Autolycus. Thus the scene was set for Odysseus' triumphant return; his son and his faithful retainers knew the truth, and Penelope had fresh encouragement to prepare her for the eventual recognition.

The Bow and the Killing of the Suitors

The trial of the bow took place next day. When none of the suitors could even so much as string it, Odysseus asked to be allowed to try. Effortlessly he achieved the task and shot the arrow through the axes. Next he shot the leading suitor, Antinoüs, and in the ensuing fight he and Telemachus and their two faithful servants killed all the other suitors. The scene where Odysseus strings the bow and reveals himself to the suitors is one of the most dramatic in all epic poetry (*Odyssey* 21. 404–423; 22. 1–8):

> But crafty Odysseus straightway took the great bow in his hands and looked at it on all sides, just as a man who is skilled at the lyre and at song easily stretches a string round a new peg, fitting the well-turned sheep's gut around the peg—even so without effort did he string the great bow, did Odysseus. He took it in his right hand and made trial of the string, and it sang sweetly under his hand, in sound like a swallow. Then great sorrow seized the suitors, and in all of them their skin changed color. Zeus, giving a sign, thundered loudly. Then godlike, patient Odysseus rejoiced that the wily son of Cronus had sent him a sign. Then he chose a swift arrow, one that lay on the table beside him uncovered, while the others lay in the hollow quiver—and these the Achaeans would soon feel. This arrow, then, he took, and he drew back the string and the notched arrow, sitting where he was on his stool. And he shot the arrow aiming straight ahead, and of the hafted axes he missed none from the first to the last, and the arrow weighted with bronze sped straight through to the end. . . .
>
> Then wily Odysseus stripped off his rags, and he leaped to the great threshold holding the bow and the quiver full of arrows, and he poured out the arrows in front of his feet. Then he spoke to the suitors: "This my labor inexorable has been completed. Now I shall aim at another target which no man has yet struck, if I can hit it and Apollo grants my prayer." He spoke and shot a death-dealing arrow straight at Antinoüs.

The Reunion of Penelope and Odysseus

After the suitors had all been killed, Odysseus cleansed the hall and hanged the twelve maidservants who had allowed themselves to be seduced by the suitors. Even so, Penelope could not believe it really was Odysseus who was there, and only when he showed knowledge of the secret construction of their bed (a symbol of the physical and spiritual strength of their devotion) did she relent and end their twenty years' separation.

The poet describes the end of Odysseus' labors with tact and delicacy. At the same time he allows Odysseus to recall his adventures (*Odyssey* 23. 300–343):

So when they (Odysseus and Penelope) had taken their delight in the joys of love, they took delight in words and spoke to each other. She, goddess-like among women, told of all she had endured in the hall as she watched the unseemly mob of suitors, who to win her slaughtered many oxen and fine sheep and drank many casks of wine. In his turn godlike Odysseus told all, the cares he had brought upon men and the grievous sufferings that he had endured. She delighted in his tale, and sleep did not fall upon her eyes until he had finished his tale.

He told first how he had subdued the Cicones and how he had come to the fertile land of the lotus-eating men. He told of the Cyclops' deeds and how he avenged his valiant companions, whom the Cyclops had pitilessly devoured. He told how he came to Aeolus, who received him kindly and sent him onward, yet it was not yet destined for him to come to his own dear land, for a storm again snatched him and bore him over the fish-full sea, groaning deeply. He told how he came to Telepolus and the Laestrygonians, who destroyed his ships and his well-greaved companions. He told of the deceit and wiles of Circe, and he told how he came to the dank house of Hades to consult the soul of Theban Tiresias, sailing on his well-benched ship. There he saw his companions and his mother, who bore him and nourished him when he was a baby.

He told how he heard the song of the clear-voiced Sirens, and how he came to the wandering rocks of the Planctae, and to terrible Charybdis and Scylla, whom no man before had escaped alive. He told how his companions had slain the cattle of Helius, and how Zeus, who thunders in the high heavens, had struck his swift ship with a smoky thunderbolt and killed all his companions, and only he escaped evil death. He told how he came to the island Ogygia and the nymph Calypso, who kept him there in her hollow cave, desiring him to be her husband. She fed him and promised to make him immortal and ageless all his days, yet she did not persuade the heart in his breast. He told how, after many sufferings, he reached the Phaeacians, who honored him like a god and sent him with a ship to his own dear homeland with ample gifts of bronze and gold and clothing.

This was the last tale he told, when sweet sleep came upon him, sleep that relaxes the limbs and releases the cares of the spirit.

The next day Odysseus made himself known to his father, Laertes;

the *Odyssey* ends with Athena intervening between Odysseus and the relatives of the dead suitors (who demanded vengeance, blood for blood) and making peace between them.

Odysseus and Athena

Odysseus was especially helped by the goddess Athena, whose own attributes of wisdom and courage complement his gifts. The relationship of goddess and hero is brilliantly depicted by the poet in a scene after Odysseus, asleep, has been put ashore on Ithaca by the Phaeacians and wakes up, not knowing where he is. Athena, disguised as a young shepherd, has told him that he is on Ithaca (*Odyssey* 13. 250–255, 287–301):

Thus she spoke, and patient godlike Odysseus was glad, rejoicing in his own fatherland, as Pallas Athena had told him, the daughter of Zeus, bearer of the aegis. And he replied to her with winged words. He did not tell her the truth, but he held it back, always directing his mind in his breast for every advantage. [Odysseus then makes up a story which, however, does not fool the goddess.]

Thus he spoke, and the goddess, grey-eyed Athena, smiled and stroked him with her hand. In form she was like to a beautiful and tall woman, one who is expert in fine handiwork. She addressed him with these winged words:

"Crafty and wily would he be who could surpass you in every trick, even if a god were to compete with you. You rogue, deviser of tricks, never satisfied with deceit, even in your own land you were not going to abandon your deceit and your deceiving words, which are dear to you from your inmost heart. Still, come now, let us no longer talk like this, since we both know how to get the advantage. For you are by far the best of all mortals in counsel and in words, and I am famous among all the gods for wisdom and cunning. Yet you did not recognize Pallas Athena, daughter of Zeus, who stands beside you in every labor and protects you."

The End of Odysseus' Life

Homer tells the subsequent history of Odysseus in the words of Tiresias' prophecy (*Odyssey* 11. 119–137):

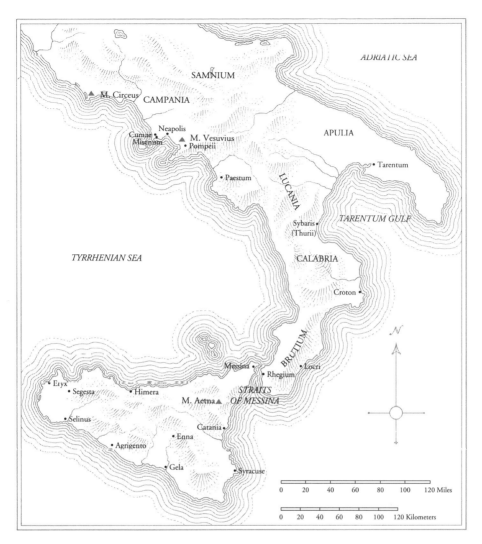

Figure 18.1.   Map of Southern Italy and Sicily. (© *Laszlo Kubinyi, 1994.*)

When you have killed the suitors in your palace, then you must
go, carrying a well-made oar, until you come to men who know
not the sea nor eat food flavored with salt; nor know they of red-
painted ships nor of shapely oars, which are the wings of ships.
This shall be a clear sign that you shall not miss: when another
traveler meets you and says that you have a winnowing-fan upon
your fine shoulder, then plant the well-turned oar in the ground
and sacrifice to Poseidon and to all the immortal gods. And death
shall come to you easily, from the sea, such as will end your life
when you are weary after a comfortable old age, and around you
shall be a prosperous people.

Odysseus appeased Poseidon in the manner foretold by Tiresias, founding a shrine to Poseidon where he planted the oar. He returned to Ithaca. Years later Telegonus, who had grown up on his mother Circe's island, sailed to Ithaca in search of his father. He was plundering the island and killed Odysseus, who was defending his possessions, not knowing who he was.[10]

PERSEUS AND THE LEGENDS OF ARGOS

19

Hera and Phoroneus

Argos was connected in history and in legend with Corinth and Thebes, and the Argive sagas demonstrate the many contacts of Argos with the eastern Mediterranean, notably the Levant and Egypt. While some of the legendary heroes are associated with a particular city of the Mycenaean Argolid (e.g., Heracles with Tiryns, Diomedes with Argos, and Perseus with Mycenae), it is often hard to distinguish between the separate cities. We shall generally use "Argos" to cover the whole Argolid and its cities.

Argos was the greatest center in Greece for the worship of Hera, and the Heraeum, the hill where Hera's sanctuary stood, was the religious center of the whole area. In the Argive saga, the first of men was Phoroneus, who established the kingdom of Argos and decided in favor of Hera in the contest for the land between Poseidon and Hera. In anger Poseidon dried up the Argive rivers, one of which, Inachus, was the father of Phoroneus. Ever after, the Argive rivers have been short of water.

The richness of Argive saga can be seen from the opening lines of Pindar's tenth *Nemean Ode:*

Sing, O Graces, of the city of Danaüs and his fifty daughters on their shining thrones, of Argos, dwelling of Hera, a home fit for the gods; bright is the flame of her brave deeds unnumbered in their excellence. Long is the tale of Perseus and the Gorgon, Medusa; many are the cities of Egypt founded by the wisdom of Epaphus; Hypermnestra kept to the path of virtue and alone did not draw the dagger from its sheath. Fair Athena once made Diomedes divine; in Thebes the earth, struck by Zeus'

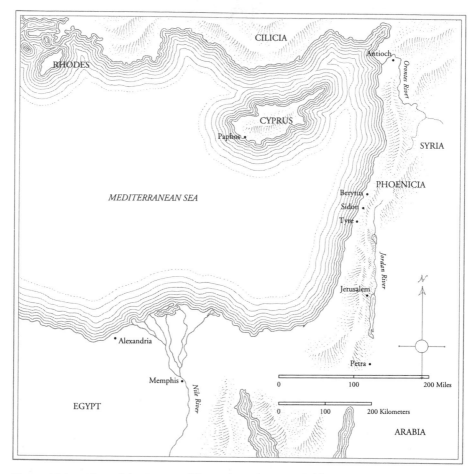

Figure 19.1. Map of the Levant. *(© Laszlo Kubinyi, 1994.)*

thunderbolts, received the seer Amphiaraüs, the storm cloud of
war. Ancient is Argos' excellence in beautiful women; Zeus
revealed this truth when he came to Alcmena and to Danaë.

PERSEUS

Danaë and Acrisius

Of the heroes of Argos, first in importance, though not in time, is
Perseus. His great-grandfather Abas had twin sons, Proetus and Acrisius, who quarreled even before their birth.[1] Acrisius, who became
king of Argos itself while Proetus ruled Tiryns, had no sons and only

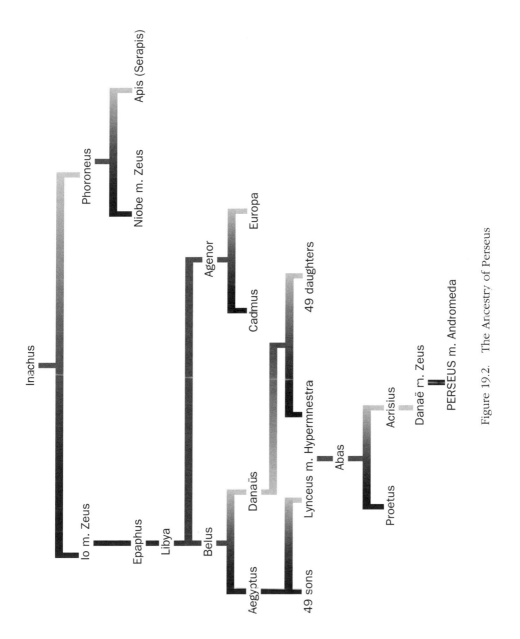

Figure 19.2. The Ancestry of Perseus

one daughter, Danaë; an oracle foretold that her son would kill Acrisius. To keep her from having children, Acrisius shut Danaë up in a brazen underground chamber in his palace, but Zeus loved her and entered the chamber in the form of a shower of gold and lay with her.[2] Their child was Perseus, and Danaë kept him in the chamber for four years, unknown to Acrisius, until he was discovered from the noise he made while playing. Acrisius refused to believe that Zeus was the child's father and put mother and child into a chest which he set afloat on the sea. The chest floated to the island of Seriphos, where the fisherman Dictys (whose name means "net") found it and rescued Danaë and Perseus, giving them shelter in his own home.

Polydectes

Now Polydectes, brother of Dictys, was king of Seriphos, and as Perseus grew to manhood, he fell in love with Danaë, who refused him. He then summoned the leading men of the island to a banquet at which each man had to present him with the gift of a horse. Perseus boasted that he could just as easily give Polydectes the Gorgon's head. Polydectes, eager to get Perseus out of the way, took him at his word and ordered him to perform the task. In despair Perseus wandered to a lonely part of Seriphos, where Hermes and Athena came to his help with advice. That two gods should assist him is remarkable; Hermes belongs more to the Peloponnese than Athena, and it is very likely he was originally the hero's only supernatural helper. Since the Gorgon's head was an attribute of Athena's aegis, she may very early have been associated with the saga, for much of the literary tradition was in the hands of Athenians.[3] Pindar, writing in the first half of the fifth century B.C., makes Athena the sole helper: "Breathing courage, Danaë's son joined the company of blessed men, and Athena was his guide" (*Pythian Odes* 10. 44–46).

The Graeae

Advised by Hermes and Athena, Perseus made his way to the three daughters of Phorcys, sisters of the Gorgons and old women (in Greek, the *Graiai*) from their birth. They alone could tell Perseus the way to some nymphs who possessed certain magic objects he would need for his task, but would part with their information only under duress. Among them they had one eye and one tooth, which they passed to one another in turn. Perseus got hold of these and gave them back only when the Graeae had told him the way to the nymphs. From the nymphs he received three objects: a Cap of Invisibility, a pair of winged sandals, and a wallet or *kibisis*.[4] From Hermes he received a scimitar, the only object given directly by Hermes.[5]

The Gorgons

Perseus now flew to the Gorgons, whose home was somewhere on the edge of the world, usually situated in North Africa.[6] Pindar, who makes Perseus go to the far north gives a beautiful description of the perfect life lived by the Hyperboreans, and his account is one of the few continuous passages in extant classical Greek literature that deals with the legend of Perseus (*Pythian Odes* 10. 29–48):

> Not with ships nor on foot would you find the marvelous road to the assembly of the Hyperboreans. Once did Prince Perseus feast among them when he entered their palace; he found them solemnly sacrificing one hundred donkeys to their god. In their feasts continually and in their hymns Apollo especially takes delight, and he laughs as he sees the pride of the animals rearing up. The Muse is always with them and is a part of their customs: everywhere are the maidens' dances, the music of lyres and of the deep-sounding flutes. They bind their hair with golden laurel-wreaths, feasting with joy. Neither disease nor wasting old age has any part in their holy nation. Without labor, without battles, they live, escaping the severe justice of Nemesis. Breathing courage, Danaë's son joined the company of blessed men, and Athena was his guide. And he slew the Gorgon and came bearing the head with hair of writhing snakes, for the islanders a stony death.

The three Gorgons, of whom only Medusa was mortal, were of terrifying aspect, and those who looked upon their faces were turned to stone.[7] They were asleep when Perseus came; guided by Athena and looking only at the Gorgon's reflection in his brazen shield he beheaded Medusa and put the head in the *kibisis*. As she was beheaded, Chrysaor (He of the Golden Sword) and Pegasus, the winged horse, sprang from her body. Their father was Poseidon; Chrysaor became father of the monster Geryon, and Pegasus was prominent in the legend of Bellerophon. According to Ovid, his hoof struck Mt. Helicon and caused the fountain Hippocrene (Horse's Fountain) to gush forth, which from then on was loved by the Muses and associated with poetic inspiration.

This is not the only association of the legend of Medusa with music and poetry. Pindar, praising Midas of Akragas, winner in the competition for flute-playing at the Pythian games, tells how the music of the

Medusa, by Harriet Hosmer (1830–1908). Marble, 1854; height 27 in. Hosmer emphasizes the beauty and pathos of Medusa, whereas most artists, ancient and modern, have preferred to focus on the horror of the Gorgon's head. A visitor to her studio said "To fulfill the true idea of the old myth, Medusa should be wonderfully beautiful, but I never saw her so represented before." *(© The Detroit Institute of Arts, Founders' Society Purchase, Robert H. Tannahill Foundation Fund.)*

flute was invented by Athena in imitation of the Gorgons' lament for the death of Medusa (*Pythian Odes* 12. 5–23):

Receive this garland from Delphi for glorious Midas who is the best in Greece in the art that Pallas Athena wove from the deadly lament of the impetuous Gorgons, which Perseus heard pouring from the snaky heads that could not be approached. Grievously he labored when he killed the third part of the sisters, bringing death to sea-girt Seriphos and its people. Indeed he brought the darkness of death to the Gorgons, god-born children of Phorcys; and grievous did the son of Danaë make the banquet of Polydectes, and the long servitude of his mother and her forced love. His spoil was the head of fair-cheeked Medusa. And he, we say, was born from the shower of gold. But when the virgin Athena had delivered the hero dear to her from these labors, she made the music of the flutes with its many notes, so that with instruments she might imitate the loud-sounding lamentation that was forced from the hungry jaws of Euryale.[8] This was the goddess' invention, but she gave it to mortals and called it "the music of many heads."

Perseus was able to fly away from Medusa's sisters unharmed, since he was wearing the Cap of Invisibility. In the original version of the saga, he probably returned directly to Seriphos and dealt with Polydectes.

Andromeda

At a very early stage the legend of Andromeda was added to the story of Perseus' return. Andromeda was daughter of King Cepheus and his queen, Cassiepea. Their kingdom is variously placed in Ethiopia or in the Levant.[9]

Cassiepea boasted that she was more beautiful than the Nereids. As a punishment Poseidon flooded Cepheus' kingdom and sent a sea monster to ravage the land. Cepheus consulted the oracle of Zeus Ammon and learned that the monster could be appeased only if Andromeda were offered to it, chained to a rock. Cepheus obeyed; but at this point, Perseus came on the scene and undertook to kill the monster if he could marry Andromeda. Making use of his sandals and cap, Perseus killed the beast with Hermes' scimitar and released Andromeda, whom he married, using the Gorgon's head to deal with the opposition of Cepheus' brother Phineus, to whom Andromeda had previously been betrothed. After their son Perses was born, Perseus and Andromeda flew back to Seriphos, leaving Perses behind as heir to Cepheus' kingdom.

The Origin of Libyan Snakes, the Atlas Range, and Coral

A number of other details have been added to the original account of Perseus' flight with the Gorgon's head. The Gorgon's blood is said to have dripped through the *kibisis* as Perseus flew over Libya, and from the drops sprang the infinite number of poisonous snakes that (according to the belief of the ancients) infested the Libyan desert. The giant Atlas, supporter of the heavens, refused to show Perseus any hospitality, and Perseus turned him into stone with the Gorgon's head. His head and body became a mountain range, his hair the forests upon the mountains. As an example of these ingenious additions to the legend we give Ovid's description of the creation of coral (*Meta-morphoses* 4. 740–752):

 Perseus washed his hands, bloody from his victory over the monster, in the sea. So that the hard sand should not damage the snake-bearing head, he made the ground soft with leaves and branches that grow beneath the sea's surface, and on these he placed the head of Medusa, daughter of Phorcys. The branch that a few moments before had been fresh and filled with living pith absorbed the monster's power; and touched by the head, its leaves and stems took on a new hardness. But the sea-nymphs tested the miraculous change on other branches and rejoiced to see the same thing happen. Now coral still retains its same nature: it grows hard in contact with air, and what in the sea was flexible becomes stone out of the water.

Polydectes and Perseus' Return to Argos

When Perseus and Andromeda reached Seriphos, they found that Danaë and Dictys had taken refuge at an altar from the violence of Polydectes. Perseus displayed the Gorgon's head before Polydectes and his assembled followers, who were all turned to stone. Thus Danaë was released and returned to Argos with Perseus and Andromeda. Perseus made Dictys king of Seriphos and returned the magic objects to the gods—the sandals, *kibisis,* and cap to Hermes (who returned them to the nymphs) and the Gorgon's head to Athena, who set it in the middle of her shield (see illustration on pp. 121 and 122).

The Death of Acrisius

When Acrisius heard that Danaë's son was indeed alive and returning to Argos, he left the city and went to the city of Larissa, in Thessaly, where Perseus followed him. Here Acrisius met his long-foretold death. Competing in the athletic games the king of Larissa was celebrating in honor of his dead father, Perseus threw a discus that accidentally killed Acrisius. He was buried outside Larissa and honored there as a hero. Perseus, having shed kindred blood, returned not to Argos but to Tiryns, whose king Megapenthes, son of Proetus, exchanged kingdoms with him. As king of Tiryns, Perseus founded Mycenae, where in historical times he was honored as a hero. The children of Perseus and Andromeda became kings of Mycenae, and from them descended Heracles and Eurystheus.

Saga and Folktale

An interesting feature of the saga of Perseus is the number of folktale motifs, more so than in any other Greek saga. These include the magic conception of the hero by the princess his mother; the discovery of the hero as a child by the noise of his playing; the villainous king and his good and humble brother; the rash promise of the hero, which he performs with the aid of supernatural helpers and magic objects; the three old women from whom advice must be sought; the Gorgons, imaginary monsters of ferocious ugliness; and finally the vindication of the hero and the punishment of the villain.

OTHER LEGENDS OF ARGOS

The Family of Inachus

Among the earliest legends of Argos are those of the family of Inachus. The daughter of Inachus was Io, much of whose story is told on pp. 68–70 in connection with Aeschylus' *Prometheus Bound.* Beloved by Zeus, Io was changed into a white cow by jealous Hera and guarded by all-seeing Argus until Hermes, sent by Zeus to rescue her, cut off Argus' head. Next Hera sent a gadfly to madden her; but after wandering the earth, Io came at last to Egypt, where Zeus restored her human form. There she gave birth to a son, Epaphus, destined to be the ancester of the hero Heracles.

From other sources we learn the Egyptians identified Epaphus with Apis, the sacred bull. And his birth did not bring an end to Io's wanderings. Hera had Epaphus kidnapped, and Io set out in search of him, eventually finding him in Syria. She now returned to Egypt where eventually she was worshiped as Isis.

The story of Io has many confusing elements. An Apis was said to have been a son of Phoroneus and to have given the Peloponnese its ancient name of Apia; after his death he was identified with Serapis, who is the same as the Egyptian bull-god Apis. Io was originally a goddess; she may have been a form of Hera herself. Herodotus, who himself visited Egypt, said that Isis was identified there with Demeter, whose image Io had first brought there, and that Isis was always represented as a woman with cow's horns (in this being similar to the great Phoenician moon-goddess, Astarte). The versions of Io's legend vary considerably, and Aeschylus gives different reasons for her departure from home and her transformation in his two plays, the *Supplices* and *Prometheus Bound*. She was originally a divine being rather than a human heroine and through Greek contacts with the East (especially Egypt), she was assimilated into Egyptian mythology.

The Descendants of Io

Through Epaphus, Io was the founder of the royal families of Egypt and Argos, as well as those of Phoenicia, Thebes, and Crete. Epaphus himself was said to have founded many cities in Egypt, including the royal city of Memphis. His daughter was Libya, who gave her name to part of North Africa; he also had twin sons, Agenor and Belus. The former became the Phoenician king, father of Cadmus (founder of Thebes) and Europa (mother of the Cretan king Minos). Belus stayed in Egypt and also became the father of twin sons, Aegyptus and Danaüs, who like their descendants Proetus and Acrisius were bitter enemies.

The Daughters of Danaüs

Aegyptus and Danaüs quarreled over the kingdom, so that Danaüs was compelled to leave Egypt. Sailing with his fifty daughters (the Danaids) via Rhodes, he came to Argos, where he peaceably established himself as king. (His subjects were called after him *Danaï*—the term by which Homer generally refers to the Greeks.) Now Aegyptus had fifty sons, who claimed as next of kin the right to marry their cousins and pursued them to Argos. Danaüs gave his daughters in marriage, but to each he gave a dagger with orders to kill her husband that night. All obeyed, save one only, Hypermnestra, who spared her husband, Lynceus, and hid him. As to the sequel, accounts vary; according to the most popular version, the forty-nine Danaids who obeyed their father were punished in the Underworld by eternally having to fill water jars, through which the water leaked away. According to Pindar, however, Danaüs gave them as wives to the winners of an athletic contest. After a period of imprisonment by Danaüs, Hypermnestra was reunited with Lynceus and became the mother of

Abas, father of Proetus and Acrisius. Thus the line of descent of the Argive kings from Inachus to Heracles remained unbroken.

Amymone

The Danaid Amymone was sent by her father to search for water and came upon a satyr who attempted to seduce her. She was saved by Poseidon, who then himself lay with her and as a reward caused a spring to burst from a rock with a stroke of his trident. In historical times, the spring Amymone was still shown near Argos.

Other Argive Heroes

Important Argive heroes were the seer Melampus and the heroes who took part in the expedition of the Seven against Thebes. Among these was Tydeus, whose son Diomedes, a leading Greek hero in the Trojan War and the last great mythical prince of Argos, was widely worshiped as a hero after his death. Pindar says that Athena gave him the immortality that she denied Tydeus.[10]

HERACLES

20

H eracles is the most popular of the Greek heroes and his legends include elements of saga and folktale.[1] His status as man, hero, and god is controversial, and continues to be a source of debate. He is particularly associated with the area around Argos and with Thebes, where his birth is traditionally placed. The two areas are connected in the account of his parents' adventures.

Amphitryon and Alcmena

Electryon, king of Mycenae, and his sons fought at Mycenae against the sons of Pterelaüs, king of the Teleboans (a people of western Greece). Only one son from each family survived.[2] The Teleboans then retreated, taking with them Electryon's cattle. Electryon planned to attack the Teleboans and made Amphitryon (son of his brother, Alcaeus) king in his place, betrothing him to his daughter Alcmena on the condition that Amphitryon leave her a virgin until after his return from the Teleboans. Now Amphitryon had already recovered the stolen cattle, and while he was herding them, he threw his club at one of them and accidentally killed Electryon. For his homicide, he was exiled from Mycenae, while his uncle Sthenelus became king.

Taking Alcmena, Amphitryon went to Thebes, where Creon purified him. Alcmena, nevertheless, refused to lie with Amphitryon until he had avenged the death of her brothers by punishing the Teleboans.[3] Amphitryon's expedition was successful through the treachery of Comaetho, daughter of the Teleboan king Pterelaüs. Out of love for Amphitryon she pulled from Pterelaüs' head the golden hair that guaranteed him immortality and made the Teleboans invincible.

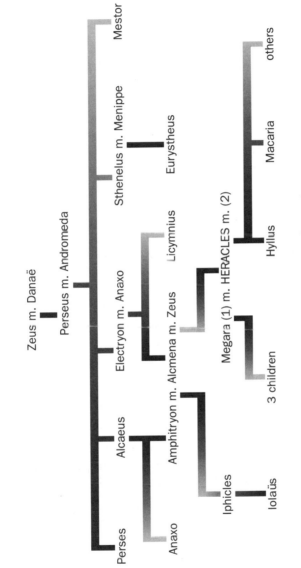

Figure 20.1.   The Family of Heracles

Thus Pterelaüs died and Amphitryon was victorious. Amphitryon killed Comaetho and returned to Thebes.

Amphitryon expected to lie with Alcmena, and he did not know that Zeus, disguised as Amphitryon, had visited her the previous night, which he extended to three times its proper length, and had told her the full story of the Teleboan expedition. Alcmena only accepted Amphitryon after Tiresias had revealed the truth. Thus she conceived twins (it was said); the elder by one night was Heracles, son of Zeus, and the younger was Iphicles, son of Amphitryon.

There are several variants of this story. According to Hesiod, Amphitryon killed Electryon in a fit of anger and for this reason left Argos with Alcmena and came to Thebes. There he lived with Alcmena, but he did not consummate their marriage until he had returned victorious over the Teleboans. Meanwhile Zeus had lain with Alcmena that same night; yet Amphitryon was able to lie "all night long with his chaste wife, delighting in the gifts of golden Aphrodite."

Another variant is the plot of the "tragicomedy" (as the playwright himself called it) by Plautus, *Amphitruo*. In this version, Jupiter (Zeus) and Mercury (Hermes) disguise themselves respectively as Amphitryon and Amphitryon's servant Sosia. Amphitryon returns just after Jupiter has left Alcmena, who is thoroughly confused. She gives birth to twins, one of whom is stronger than the other and immediately strangles two serpents sent by Juno (Hera) to kill him. Just as Alcmena's servant Bromia is describing the scene, Jupiter himself appears and reveals the truth to Amphitryon. This is the only one of the surviving plays of Plautus whose plot is taken from mythology.

The Birth of Heracles and His Early Exploits

The birth of Heracles introduces a constant feature of his story, the hostility of Hera. Zeus had boasted on Olympus on the day when Heracles was to be born (Homer, *Iliad* 19. 102–105):

> Today Eileithyia, helper in childbirth, will bring to the light a man who shall rule over all that dwell around him; he shall be of the race that is of my blood.

Hera deceived Zeus by hastening the birth of the child of Sthenelus (king of Mycenae), whose wife was seven months pregnant, and sending Eileithyia to delay the birth of Alcmena's sons.[4] Sthenelus was the grandson of Zeus, and so his son rather than Alcmena's fulfilled the terms of Zeus' boast. He was Eurystheus, for whom Heracles performed the Labors.

Pindar tells the story (mentioned above in connection with the *Amphitruo* of Plautus) that Hera also sent a pair of snakes to kill the infant Heracles, whose birth she had not been able to prevent. The passage ends with the prophet Tiresias foretelling the hero's part in the battle of the gods against the Giants and his eventual deification (*Nemean Odes* 1. 33–72):

Willingly do I take hold of Heracles upon the high peaks of Virtue as I retell an ancient tale. When the son of Zeus had escaped from the birth pangs with his twin and had come into the bright light, he was wrapped in the yellow swaddling bands, and Hera of the golden throne saw him. Straightway in hasty anger, the queen of the gods sent snakes, which passed through the open doors into the farthest part of the wide room, eager to coil their quick jaws around the children. But Heracles lifted up his head and for the first time made trial of battle; with his two hands, from which there was no escape, he seized by their necks the two serpents, and his grip squeezed the life out of the huge monsters, strangling them.

Then fear unbearable struck the women who were helping Alcmena at the birth. Alcmena, too, leaped to her feet from the bedclothes, unclothed as she was, as if to protect her babies from the attack of the beasts. Then the Theban leaders quickly ran and assembled with their bronze weapons, and Amphitryon came, smitten with the bitter pangs of anxiety and brandishing his sword unsheathed. . . . He stood with amazement hard to bear mixed with joy, for he saw the immeasurable spirit and power of his son. The immortals indeed had made the words of the messengers untrue. Then he summoned Tiresias, his neighbor, excellent mouthpiece of Zeus the most high. To Amphitryon and to all his armed men he foretold with what fortunes Heracles would meet, how many lawless wild beasts he would kill on the sea, how many on land. He foretold how Heracles would give to his fate the man who walks with crooked insolence, most hateful of men. For, he foretold, when the gods should do battle with the giants on the plain of Phlegra, beneath the onrush of his missiles, bright hair would be soiled in the dust. But Heracles himself, in peace for all time without end, would win rest as the choice reward for his great labors, and in the palaces of the blessed he would take Hebe to be his youthful bride. Feasting at his wedding beside Zeus, son of Cronus, he would praise the holy customs of the gods.

Thus Heracles survived. In his education he was taught chariot driving by Amphitryon, wrestling by Autolycus, archery by Eurytus, and music by Linus.[5] Heracles killed Linus, who was a son of Apollo, by striking him with his lyre, and for this was sent away to the Theban pastures on Mt. Cithaeron, where he performed a number of exploits. He killed a lion that was preying on the cattle of Amphitryon and of Thespius, king of the Boeotian town of Thespiae. During the hunt for the lion, Heracles was entertained for fifty days by Thespius and lay with one of his fifty daughters each night (or with all fifty in the same night). He also freed the Thebans from paying tribute to the Minyans of Orchomenus, leading the Theban army himself into battle. In gratitude Creon gave him his daughter Megara as wife, and by her he had three children.

The Madness of Heracles

Some time later, Hera brought about a fit of madness in which Heracles killed Megara and her children. When he recovered his sanity, he left Thebes and went first to Thespiae, where Thespius purified him, and then to Delphi, where he sought further advice. Here the priestess of Apollo called him Heracles for the first time (until then he had been known as Alcides) and told him to go to Tiryns and there for twelve years serve Eurystheus, performing the labors that he would impose. If he did them, she said, he would become immortal.

This is the simplest story of the origin of the Labors; there is, however, great confusion over the chronology of Heracles' legends. Euripides in his *Heracles* puts the murder of Megara and her children after the Labors. Sophocles in his *Trachiniae* has Heracles marry his second wife Deïanira before the Labors, whereas Apollodorus places the marriage after them. All are agreed that for a number of years Heracles served Eurystheus. Heracles' ghost says to Odysseus: "I was a son of Zeus, but infinite was my suffering; for I was slave to a far inferior mortal, and heavy were the labors he laid upon me." (Homer, *Odyssey* 11. 620–633).

THE
TWELVE LABORS

The Greek word for labors is *athloi,* which really means contests undertaken for a prize. In Heracles' case the prize was immortality, and at least three of his Labors are really conquests of death.[6] Heracles did not always perform the Labors unaided; sometimes Athena helped him, sometimes his nephew, Iolaüs. The first six Labors all take place in the Peloponnese, and the remaining six in different parts of the world. In these Heracles has changed from a local hero into the benefactor of all humankind. The list of the labors varies, but the twelve given are traditional and were represented on the metopes of the temple of Zeus at Olympia (see pp. 80–81).

The Peloponnesian Labors

1. The Nemean Lion   Heracles was required to bring the skin of this beast to Eurystheus. He killed it with a club that he had himself cut. Theocritus (in his twenty-fifth *Idyll*) makes the lion invulnerable, and Heracles has to strangle it and then flay it by using its own claws to cut its hide. The club and lionskin henceforth were Heracles' weapon and clothing and are his attributes in art and literature.

2. The Lernaean Hydra   This serpent lived in the swamps of Lerna, near Argos. It had nine heads, of which eight were mortal and the ninth immortal. Each time Heracles clubbed a head off, two grew in its place. The labor was made the harder by a huge crab, which Hera sent to aid the Hydra. First Heracles killed this monster, and then killed the Hydra, helped by his nephew, Iolaüs, son of Iphicles. Each time he removed one of the heads, Iolaüs cauterized the stump with a burning brand so that another could not grow. Heracles buried the immortal head under a huge rock. He then dipped his arrows in the Hydra's poison. As for the crab, Hera took it and made it into the constellation Cancer.

3. The Cerynean Hind   The hind had golden horns and was sacred to Artemis; it took its name from Mt. Cerynea in Arcadia.[7] It was harmless nor might it be harmed without incurring Artemis' wrath. After pursuing it for a year Heracles caught it by the river Ladon, and carried it back to Eurystheus. On the way Artemis met him and claimed her sacred animal, but she was appeased when Heracles laid the blame on Eurystheus.

This version of the story is entirely set in the Peloponnese. A different account, however, is given by Pindar in his beautiful third *Olympian Ode*. In it Heracles went to the land of the Hyperboreans in the far north in search of the hind, on whose golden horns the nymph

Taÿgete, a daughter of Atlas, had stamped the name of Artemis.[8] Pindar's narrative allows us to connect this labor with that of the Apples of the Hesperides, for in the latter story Heracles goes to the limits of the world in search of a miraculous golden object, and again Ladon (in the form of a dragon) and Atlas appear.[9] The labor of the Apples of the Hesperides is a conquest of death, and it seems that the story of the Cerynean stag is another version of the same theme.

4. The Erymanthian Boar This destructive animal had to be brought back alive from Mt. Erymanthus. Heracles chased the boar into deep snow and there trapped it with nets. He brought it back to Eurystheus, who cowered in terror in a large jar.

This labor resulted in a side adventure (or *parergon*).[10] On his way to the chase, Heracles was entertained by the centaur Pholus, who set before him a jar of wine that belonged to all the centaurs in common. When it was opened, the other centaurs, attracted by its fragrance, attacked Heracles, who repelled and pursued them. Most of them were scattered all over Greece, but Chiron was wounded by one of Heracles' poisoned arrows. Since he was immortal and could not die, he suffered incurable agonies until Prometheus interceded with Zeus and took upon himself the immortality of Chiron. Pholus also met his death when he accidentally dropped a poisoned arrow on his foot.

5. The Augean Stables Augeas, son of Helius (the Sun) and king of Elis, owned vast herds of cattle whose stables had never been cleaned out. Heracles was commanded by Eurystheus to perform the task, and successfully achieved it within one day by diverting the rivers Alpheus and Peneus so that they flowed through the stables. Augeas agreed to give Heracles one-tenth of his herds as a reward, but refused to keep his promise and expelled both Heracles and his own son Phyleus (who had taken Heracles' part in the quarrel). Heracles was received by a nearby prince, Dexamenus (whose name, indeed, means "the receiver"), whose daughter he saved from the centaur Eurytion. After he had finished the Labors Heracles returned to Elis at the head of an army, took the city, and killed Augeas, making Phyleus king in his place.

It was after this expedition that Heracles was said to have instituted the Olympic Games, the greatest of Greek festivals, held every four years in honor of Zeus. He marked out the stadium by pacing it out himself, and he fetched an olive tree from the land of the Hyperboreans to be, as Pindar described it, "a shade for the sacred precinct and a crown of glory for men" (*Olympian Odes* 3. 16–18), for at that

Heracles, Assisted by Athena, Cleans the Augean Stables. Marble metope over the east porch of the temple of Zeus at Olympia, ca. 460 B.C.; height 63 in. This local legend is given the place of honor as the final one of the series of the Labors of Heracles in the metopes of the temple of Zeus (see pp. 80–81). Athena is helmeted and clothed in the Doric *peplos,* her left hand resting on her shield. With her spear (now missing) she directs Heracles as he labors to open (with a crowbar) the stables so that the river Alpheus can flush them clean. *(From metope no. 12 of the Temple of Zeus at Olympia. Courtesy of Alinari/Art Resource, New York.)*

time there were no trees at Olympia, and at the games the victors were awarded a garland of olive leaves.[11]

6. The Stymphalian Birds Heracles was required to shoot these creatures, which flocked together in a wood by the Arcadian lake Stymphalus. He flushed them by clashing brazen castanets given him by Athena and then shot them.[12]

7. The Cretan Bull   This bull was one that Minos had refused to sacrifice to Poseidon. Heracles caught it and brought it back alive to Eurystheus. It was then turned loose and eventually came to Marathon, where in time Theseus caught and sacrificed it.

8. The Mares of Diomedes   Diomedes, son of Ares, was a Thracian king who owned a herd of mares that were fed on human flesh. Heracles, either alone or with an army got possession of them and tamed them by feeding them Diomedes himself. He took them back to Argos, where Eurystheus set them free and dedicated them to Hera.

On his way to Thrace Heracles was entertained by Admetus, king of Pherae, who disguised his grief at the recent death of his wife, Alcestis. Heracles discovered the truth and himself wrestled with Thanatos (Death), forcing him to give up Alcestis, whom he restored to her husband.

9. The Girdle of Hippolyta   Hippolyta was queen of the Amazons, the warrior women at the northern limits of the world. Heracles was sent to fetch her girdle, which had magic powers. He killed Hippolyta in battle and took the girdle. It was displayed at Argos in historical times.

While returning from this labor, Heracles came to Troy and there rescued Hesione from the sea monster (see p. 358). Cheated by King Laomedon of his reward, he returned later (after his time as the servant of Omphale) with an armed force and sacked the city, giving Hesione to his ally Telamon, and leaving Podarces (Priam) on the throne of the ruined city.

10. The Cattle of Geryon   The last three labors are most clearly conquests of death, with the abduction of Cerberus as their climax. Geryon lived in the island of Erythia, far away to the west. Geryon was a three-bodied monster, offspring of the Oceanid Callirhoë and Chrysaor; he tended a herd of cattle, helped by a giant herdsman, Eurytion, and a two-headed hound, Orthus (or Orthrus). Heracles' labor was to bring the cattle back to Eurystheus. To reach Erythia, Heracles was helped by Helius (the Sun), who gave him a golden cup in which to sail upon the River of Ocean, which girdles the world. He killed Orthus, Eurytion, and Geryon, and then sailed back in the cup to Tartessus (i.e., Spain) with the cattle. He returned the cup to Helius and then began to drive the cattle back to Greece.

As a monument of his journey to the western edge of the world, he set up the Pillars of Heracles at the Atlantic entrance to the Mediterranean. They are sometimes identified with the rocks of Calpe (Gibraltar) and Abyla (Ceuta), which flank the Straits of Gibraltar.

Heracles' journey back to Greece has many *parerga*. While crossing the south of France, he was attacked by the tribe of the Ligurians and exhausted his supply of arrows defending himself. He prayed for help from Zeus, who sent a rain of stones that gave Heracles the ammunition he needed to drive off the attackers. He then crossed the Alps and traversed Italy, where he was said to have founded several cities.[13]

Heracles' wanderings in Italy also took him across the strait to Sicily. Here he wrestled with Eryx (king of the mountain of the same name at the western end of the island), whom he killed. He returned to Greece by traveling around the head of the Adriatic and through Dalmatia. At the Isthmus of Corinth he killed the giant and brigand, Alcyoneus. As for the cattle, Eurystheus sacrificed them to Hera.

Quite a different version of the legend of Geryon is told by Herodotus. In this, Heracles journeyed to the cold lands beyond the Danube and there lay with Echidna (Snake Woman), a monster who was half woman and half serpent, who bore him three sons, Agathyrsus, Gelonus, and Scythes. When the three grew up, only Scythes was able to draw a bow and put on a belt that Heracles had left behind. The other two were driven away by Echidna, and Scythes became king and ancestor of the Scythians.[14]

11. The Apples of the Hesperides The Hesperides were the three daughters of Night, living far away to the west; they guarded a tree upon which grew golden apples. They were helped by the serpent Ladon, who was coiled around the tree. The apples had originally been a wedding gift from Ge to Hera when she married Zeus, and Ge put them in the garden of the Hesperides. Heracles first had to find the sea-god Nereus and learn from him the whereabouts of the garden. Nereus would tell him only after he had turned himself into many different shapes, being held all the while by Heracles. At the garden, in Euripides' version, he killed Ladon and plucked the apples himself. In the tradition represented by the metopes at Olympia, however, he got the help of the Titan Atlas, who held up the heavens. Heracles, helped by Athena, took the heavens on his own shoulders while Atlas fetched the apples. He then returned the load to Atlas' shoulders and brought the apples back to Eurystheus. Athena is then said to have taken the apples back to the garden of the Hesperides.

This labor is a conquest of death. The apples are symbols of immortality, and the tree in the garden of the Hesperides is a kind of Tree of Life. As in the labor of Geryon, the journey to a mysterious place in the far west is really a journey to the realm of death.

On his journey to the garden of the Hesperides, Heracles killed the king of Egypt, Busiris, who would sacrifice all strangers to Zeus.[15] In Libya he conquered the giant Antaeus, son of Ge and Poseidon, who would wrestle with those who came to his kingdom. He was invincible, since every time an opponent threw him he came in contact with his mother (Earth) and rose with renewed strength. Thus he had killed all comers and used their skulls in building a temple to his father, Poseidon. Heracles held him aloft and crushed him to death.

Some versions of this story take Heracles to the Caucasus Mountains. Here he found Prometheus chained to his rock and released him after killing the eagle that tormented him. Prometheus advised him to use Atlas in getting the apples and foretold the battle against the Ligurians. On this occasion, too, Prometheus took over the immortality of Chiron and satisfied Zeus by letting Chiron die in his place.

12. Cerberus The final labor was to fetch Cerberus, the three-headed hound of Hades. This labor is most clearly a conquest of death, and Heracles himself (in the *Odyssey*) said that it was the hardest of the Labors and that he could not have achieved it without the aid of Hermes and Athena. In the Underworld he wrestled with Cerberus, brought him back to Eurystheus, and then returned him to Hades.

In Hades, Heracles saw Theseus and Pirithoüs, chained fast because of their attempt to carry off Persephone. He was able to release Theseus, who out of gratitude sheltered him after his madness and the murder of Megara. He also saw the ghost of Meleager, whose sister, if he still had one living, he offered to marry. Meleager named Deïanira, "upon whose neck was still the green of youth, nor did she know yet of the ways of Aphrodite, charmer of men" (Bacchylides, *Epinician Ode* 5. 172–175). Thus the train of events was set in motion that led eventually to the death of Heracles.

In conclusion we translate a chorus from Euripides' *Heracles,* which tells of the great hero's Labors. This choral ode also reveals the nature of our sources for Greek legends, where the dry facts are enlivened by poetic expression (Euripides, *Heracles* 352–427):

I wish to offer a glorious crown for labors done, by singing the praises of him who descended into the darkness of earth's realm of shades—whether I am to call him the son of Zeus or of Amphitryon. For the renown of noble deeds is a joy to those who have died. First he cleared Zeus' grove of the lion; and he wore its

Heracles Shows Cerberus to Eurystheus. Etruscan hydria from Caere, ca. 530 B.C.; height 17 in. The terrified Eurystheus leaps into a storage jar to escape from the Hound of Hades, which bares its three sets of teeth while its snakes furiously hiss at him. Heracles, with club and lionskin, strides forward confidently, guiding Cerberus with a leash. The humor in this splendid vase is remarkable. *(Musée du Louvre, Paris. © Réunion des Musées Nationaux.)*

tawny skin upon his back, with the fearful jaws of the beast framing his fair head.

He laid low the mountain race of savage Centaurs with his deadly arrows, slaughtering them with his winged shafts. The beautiful stream of Peneus was a witness and the vast extent of the plains without crops and the vales of Mt. Pelion and the places on the green glens of Homole—all haunts where they filled their hands with weapons of pine and, galloping as horses, brought fear to the land of the Thessalians.

He slew the dappled hind with golden horns and dedicated this ravaging plunderer to the huntress Artemis of Oenoe.

He mounted the chariot of Diomedes and mastered with the bit the four mares, who ranged wild in stables drenched in blood and reveled in their horrid feasts of human flesh with ravenous jaws.

In his labors for the king of Mycenae, he crossed over the banks of the silver-flowing Hebrus; and along the sea-cliff of Pelion, by the waters of the Amaurus, he killed with his bow Cycnus, the guest-murderer who lived alone near Amphanaea.

He came to the western home of the singing maidens, to pluck from amid the golden leaves the fruit of the apple, and the fiery dragon who kept guard coiled around the tree, hard even to approach, him he killed.

He made his way into the farthest corners of the sea and made them safe for men who ply the oar.

Having come to the abode of Atlas, he extended his hand to support the vault of heaven in its midst, and by his manly strength held up the starry homes of the gods.

He crossed the swell of the Euxine Sea to the land of the Amazons, who rode in force where many rivers flow into Lake Maeotis. Mustering a band of friends from Hellas, he sought to win the gold-encrusted adornment of the warrior maid—the deadly booty of her girdle—and Hellas captured the renowned prize of the foreign queen, which is kept safe in Mycenae.

He seared the many heads of the deadly monster, the Lernaean Hydra, and dipped his arrows in its venom; with that he killed three-bodied Geryon, the herdsman of Erythia.

He won the glorious crown for these and other labors; and he sailed to the tearful realm of Hades—the final task of all.

OTHER DEEDS OF HERACLES

Cycnus, Syleus, and the Cercopes

Heracles fought and killed a number of harmful beings. Cycnus, son of Ares, used to rob men passing on their way through Thessaly to Delphi. Heracles, helped by Athena and with Iolaüs as charioteer, killed Cycnus (who was helped by Ares) in single combat.[16] Another robber was Syleus, who lived by the Straits of Euboea. Heracles destroyed his vineyard, in which Syleus compelled passers by to work, and then killed Syleus himself.

Heracles and the Cercopes. Limestone metope from Selinus, ca. 540 B.C.; height 58 in. Heracles looks straight at the viewer, like the bull in the metope from the same group (p. 318), and the faces of the Cercopes are also shown frontally. Despite the archaic formality of the composition the hero's power is forcefully expressed. *(Museo Nazionale, Palermo, Italy. Courtesy of Alinari/Art Resource, New York.)*

Closer to folktale is Heraclcs' encounter with the Cercopes, whose home is placed in various parts of Greece or Asia Minor. They were a pair of dwarfs who spent their time playing tricks on people. They had been warned by their mother "to beware of the black-bottomed man." Now as Heracles was asleep under a tree, they attempted to steal his weapons, but he caught them and slung them from a pole across his shoulders upside down. They thus had an uninterrupted view of his backside which, since the lionskin did not cover it, had been burned black by the sun. They joked about the sight so much that Heracles, himself amused, let them go. Later they tried to trick Zeus and were punished by being turned into either apes or stones.

Hylas

Heracles was among the heroes who sailed on the *Argo*. But he was too important to be subordinate to other heroes in the saga, and so he soon dropped out of the expedition. In one version he went looking for the boy Hylas, whom he loved. When the *Argo* put in at Cios (in Asia Minor), Hylas went to a nearby spring to draw water, and the water-nymphs were so entranced by his beauty that they pulled him into the water, to remain with them forever. Heracles spent so long searching for him that the rest of the Argonauts sailed away without him and he returned on his own to Argos. A cult of Hylas was established at Cios by Heracles. In late antiquity the people still searched for him annually, calling out his name.[17]

Military Expeditions

Heracles took part in Zeus' battle against the giants, during which he slew the terrible Alcyoneus. He attacked Laomedon, king of Troy, and Augeas, king of Elis, who had both cheated him. He made an expedition against Neleus, king of Pylos, who had refused to purify Heracles after the murder of Iphitus. He killed eleven of the twelve sons of Neleus and the twelfth, Nestor, eventually became king of Pylos and took part in the Trojan War. According to Hesiod, one of the sons of Neleus was Periclymenus, to whom Poseidon had given the ability to transform himself into every sort of bird, beast, or insect. With the help of Athena, Heracles recognized him in the form of a bee settled upon the yoke of his horse-drawn chariot and shot him with an arrow.

In this expedition also, says Homer, Heracles wounded the god Hades, "in Pylos among the corpses" (*Iliad* 5. 395–397), as if the expedition were another conquest of death. Homer also mentions that Heracles wounded Hera, and says that this was another example of Heracles' violence—"brutal and violent man, who did not scruple to do evil and wounded the Olympian gods with his arrows" (*Iliad* 5. 403–404). This is an older view of Heracles, and is more likely to represent the character of the original mythical hero than that of Pindar, who makes the following protest (*Olympian Odes* 9. 29–36):

How would Heracles have brandished his club with his hands against the trident, when, in defense of Pylos Poseidon pushed him back, and Apollo shook him and drove him back with his silver bow, nor did Hades keep his staff unmoved, with which he drives mortal bodies to the hollow ways of the dead? Hurl this story, my mouth, far away!

We can see that by Pindar's time (the first half of the fifth century B.C.) the transformation of Heracles was already well advanced, from the primitive strongman into a paragon of virtue. Heracles also made an expedition against Hippocoön, king of Sparta, and his sons, who had given assistance to Neleus. Iphicles was killed in this campaign. While returning home from Sparta Heracles lay at Tegea with Auge, whose father, fearing an oracle that Auge's son would kill her brothers, had made her priestess of Athena. The son she conceived was Telephus, and mother and baby crossed the sea to Asia Minor floating in a chest. There Telephus eventually became king of the Mysians.[18]

In Thessaly, Heracles appeared as an ally of Aegimius, king of the Dorians, against the attacks of his neighbors, the Lapiths and the Dryopes. This legend brings Heracles back to central Greece, where the legends of the last part of his life are placed.

HERACLES, DEÏANIRA, AND IOLE

Marriage to Deïanira

Some time after the completion of the Labors, Heracles fulfilled the promise he had made to the soul of Meleager, to marry his sister Deïanira, daughter of Oeneus, king of Calydon. To win her Heracles had to wrestle with the river-god Acheloüs, who was horned like a bull and had the power of changing himself into different shapes. This is how Sophocles describes the scene (*Trachiniae* 513–525):

They came together desiring marriage; alone between them as umpire was Aphrodite, maker of marriages. Then was there confusion of sounds, the beating of fists, the twang of bow, the clash of bull's horns. There were the wrestling holds, the painful collision of heads, and the groans of both. But she, the prize, fair and delicate, sat afar upon a hill, waiting for him who was to be her husband.

In the struggle Heracles broke off one of Acheloüs' horns; and after his victory, he gave it back, receiving in return the miraculous horn of Amalthea, which could supply its owner with as much food and drink as he wished.[19]

Heracles returned with Deïanira to Tiryns. On the way the centaur Nessus carried Deïanira across the river Evenus. He attempted to violate her, but Heracles shot him with his bow. As he was dying he advised Deïanira to gather some of the blood that flowed from his wound, which had been caused by an arrow that had been dipped in the Hydra's poison. It would, he said, prevent Heracles from loving any other woman more than he loved Deïanira. She therefore kept the blood, and for a number of years she and Heracles lived at Tiryns, where she bore him children, including a son, Hyllus, and a daughter, Macaria.

The Death of Nessus. Detail of an Attic black-figure amphora, ca. 620 B.C.; height of vase 48 in., of painting 14 in. The scene is painted on the neck of the vase, with owls, a swan, and a pigeon on the handles. The names of Heracles (written right to left) and Nessus (spelled "Netos") are given. Heracles finishes Nessus off with a sword, grasping his hair and violently thrusting his left foot into the Centaur's back. He ignores the pleas of Nessus for mercy, shown by the gesture of touching the chin. The hero does not wear the lionskin, nor does he carry his club and bow. *(National Museum, Athens, Greece. Courtesy of Foto Marburg/Art Resource, New York.)*

Iole

But Heracles fell in love with Iole, daughter of Eurytus, king of Oechalia, who had once taught Heracles archery. Eurytus refused to let him have Iole, even though he won an archery contest that was to decide whose wife (or concubine) Iole should be. Heracles returned to Tiryns, bitter at the insult, and when Iphitus, brother of Iole, came to Tiryns in search of some lost mares Heracles threw him from the citadel to his death. For this murder, he had to leave Tiryns, going first to Pylos, where Neleus refused to purify him. Having obtained purification at Amyclae, he went to Delphi to find out what more he should do to be cured of the madness that had caused him to kill Iphitus. When the Pythia would not reply he attempted to carry off the sacred tripod, intending to establish an oracle of his own. Apollo himself wrestled with him to prevent this, and their fight ended when Zeus threw a thunderbolt between them. Finally Heracles obtained the advice he had asked for, which was that he must be sold as a slave and serve for one year.

Omphale

Accordingly Hermes auctioned Heracles, and he was bought by Omphale, queen of the Lydians; he served her for a year and performed various tasks for her in keeping with his heroic character. Later versions, however, make Heracles perform women's work for the queen and picture him dressed as a woman and spinning wool. At the end of his year, he mounted the expedition against Troy and then returned to Greece, determined to punish Eurytus and to win Iole.

The Death of Heracles

Deïanira, meanwhile, was living in Trachis, where King Ceyx had received her and Heracles after they left the Peloponnese. According to Sophocles, whose *Trachiniae* is the most important source for the last part of Heracles' life, she knew nothing of Oechalia and Iole until the herald Lichas brought news of the sack of the city. She had not seen Heracles for fifteen months, before his servitude to Omphale. In this account Heracles killed Eurytus and sacked Oechalia on his way back from Asia, sending Iole and the other captive women back to Trachis with Lichas. When she realized that Heracles' loved Iole, Deïanira, hoping to win him back, dipped a robe in the blood of Nessus and sent it to Heracles by Lichas' hand for him to wear at his thanksgiving sacrifice to Zeus.

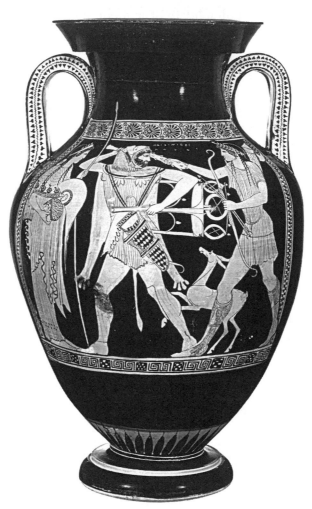

Heracles and Apollo Struggle for the Pythian Tripod. Attic red-figure amphora attributed to the Geras Painter, ca. 480 B.C; height 22 in. Heracles rushes off holding the tripod and threatening Apollo with his club. He wears the lionskin and a bow and quiver are slung in front of him. On the left stands Athena, wearing the aegis and holding a crested helmet and spear. Apollo grasps the tripod with his left hand (which also holds his bow and arrows; the quiver is on his back) and with his right restrains Heracles' club. He wears the laurel wreath and hunter's clothing and boots, appropriate for the god who has slain Python with his arrows. The deer is also a lively hunting motif. *(Collection of the J. Paul Getty Museum, Malibu, California.)*

As the flames of the sacrificial fire warmed the poisoned blood, the robe clung to Heracles and burned him with unendurable torment. In his agony, he hurled Lichas to his death in the sea and had himself carried back to Trachis, where a huge funeral pyre was made for him upon Mt. Oeta. Deïanira killed herself with a sword when she realized what she had done, while Hyllus went with his father to Oeta. There Heracles instructed Hyllus to marry Iole after his death and gave his bow to the shepherd Poeas (father of Philoctetes), since he alone had dared to light the pyre. So the mortal part of Heracles was burned away and he gained immortality, ascending to Olympus, there to be reconciled with Hera and to marry her daughter Hebe. This is Pindar's version (*Isthmian Odes* 4. 61–67):

> To Olympus went Alcmena's son, when he had explored every land and the cliff-girt levels of the foaming sea, to tame the straits for seafarers. Now beside Zeus he enjoys a perfect happiness; he is loved and honored by the immortals; Hebe is his wife, and he is lord of a golden palace, the husband of Hera's daughter.

Sophocles' *Trachiniae* ends with Heracles, in torment, being carried from his palace to the pyre on Mt. Oeta. In this scene, Hyllus says: "No one foresees what is to come" (line 1270), thus leaving the destiny of Heracles shrouded in ambiguity. Ovid's description is explicit (*Metamorphoses* 9. 134–272):

> And now . . . the flames were attacking the limbs that did not fear them and him who despised them. The gods were anxious for earth's champion [Hercules] and them did Jupiter . . . in happiness thus address: "Your fear is my joy, O gods . . . let not your hearts tremble with empty fear, despite Oeta's flames! He who conquered all will conquer the flames which you see, and only his mother's part will feel the power of Vulcan [i.e., fire]. That part which he inherited from me is immortal, immune to death, impervious to fire, and it will I receive in the heavens when its time on earth is done. . . ." The gods approved. Meanwhile Vulcan had consumed all that fire could consume, and the recognizable form of Hercules was no longer to be seen. He kept no part of himself that came from his mother, and he kept only the features drawn from Jupiter. . . . So, when the hero of Tiryns had put off his mortal body, his better part kept its vigor. He began to seem greater in size and awe-inspiring with august dignity. The almighty Father received him as he ascended into the surrounding clouds in a four-horse chariot, and placed him among the shining constellations.

The Apotheosis of Hercules, by Peter Paul Rubens (1577–1640). Oil on panel, 1636; 11 × 12¾ in. In this oil sketch for Philip IV's hunting lodge near Madrid Rubens represents Ovid's narrative at the moment when Hercules ascends from the pyre to Olympus. The flames can be seen at the bottom left and the bulky hero (Ovid says that "he began to seem greater in size") climbs on the chariot provided by Jupiter. A flying putto puts the victor's wreath on his head, and a second guides the chariot. Rubens does not show Jupiter, so as not to detract from the focus on the triumphant hero. *(Musées Royaux des Beaux-Arts de Belgique, Brussels.)*

HERACLES: MAN, HERO, AND GOD

Odysseus describes his meeting with the ghost of Heracles in this way (Homer, *Odyssey* 11. 601–603):

 Then saw I mighty Heracles—his ghost, but he himself delights in feasting among the immortal gods, with fair-ankled Hebe for his wife.

In this very early passage, the ambiguity of Heracles' status as man and god is evident. That he was a man before he became a god is shown by his name (which means "glory of Hera"), since Greek gods do not form their names from compounds of other gods' names.

Since his legend is particularly associated with Argos, Mycenae, and Tiryns, his saga may have had its origin in a prince of Tiryns who was vassal to the lord of Mycenae. This fits with the theme of subservience to Eurystheus. But other areas with which he is especially associated are Boeotia (the traditional setting of his birth and of a group of his exploits) and Trachis, scene of his final exploits and death.

This leads to one of two possibilities: either legends of the hero of Tiryns spread to Boeotia and other parts of Greece, where his fame attracted local legends, or else he was brought into Greece by early settlers from the north and his fame spread all over Greece. The latter explanation seems the more acceptable, but it has led many people to believe wrongly that Heracles was a Dorian hero, brought in by invaders who entered Greece at the end of the Mycenaean Age. It is better to suppose that Heracles is an older hero common to all the Greek peoples but associated more with certain areas (Argos, Thebes, Trachis) than with others. Thus we find his exploits covering the whole of the Greek world and his legends and cult flourishing in areas of Greek colonization, such as Asia Minor and Italy (where as Hercules he passed into the Roman state religion).

Many people have thought of him primarily as a god. Herodotus believed that Heracles the god was quite distinct from Heracles the man and that the god was one of the twelve ancient gods of Egypt. He himself even traveled to the Phoenician city of Tyre, whose chief god, Melkart, was identified with Heracles, to find support for his theory. Since the mythology of Melkart is virtually unknown, the similarities between him and Heracles remain unclear; nor can we establish the exact relationship between Heracles and other Oriental figures with whom he shares many similarities, for example, the Israelite hero Samson, the Mesopotamian Gilgamesh, and the Cilician god Sandas. These figures may have contributed elements toward the Greek hero's legend. In general, it is safe to reject Herodotus' theory and accept the nearly unanimous view of the ancients that Heracles the man became a god.

Still, the origins of Heracles are a subject of great interest. The similarities to the Eastern figures mentioned above are undeniable, as are similarities to the Indian hero Indra who killed the three-headed monster Visvarupa and released the cattle penned in his cave. The monsters that Heracles overcame, such as the lion and the many-headed Hydra, belong more to Eastern mythology, yet Heracles is very definitely a *Greek* hero, and his myths are Greek traditional tales. Many different tales, then, have become attached to the hero called Heracles. The process can be seen in the large number of *parerga* that cluster around several of the Labors. Some of the myths have a structure consistent with Propp's Quest (see pp. 11–12), and in these the basic structure of the myth remains, despite its varied appearances. The primitive origins of much of Heracles' mythology are apparent from his violence and brutality. His association with many different types of animals has led some scholars to see in him a kind of "Master of Animals," not least because of his association with cattle, the chief source of food in a pastoral society. There is much that is persuasive in Walter Burkert's conclusion:

 Heracles is, basically, not a heroic figure in the Homeric sense: he is not a warrior fighting warriors, he is mainly concerned with animals, just as he is a savage clad in a skin; and his main job is to tame and bring back the animals which are eaten by man.[20]

The Greek hero, son of Zeus and exemplar of strength and patience, is also the man wielding the primitive weapon of the club and wearing the lion's skin, whose origins lie perhaps far from Greece and certainly in a time long before the development even of Mycenaean culture.

So diverse a character attracted a variety of interpretations and uses. Indeed, as Aristotle pointed out in the *Poetics* (chap. 8), his very diversity made it impossible for a unified epic or tragedy to be written about him. Only three extant Greek tragedies deal with his legend—Sophocles' *Trachiniae* and Euripides' *Heracles* and *Alcestis* (the latter almost incidentally). To the comic poets like Aristophanes, he is good material for slapstick; in the *Frogs,* for example, he is largely motivated by gluttony and lust.

More significant was the use made of his virtues by the moralists and philosophers, to whom he became a model of unselfish fortitude, laboring for the good of humankind and achieving immortality by his virtue. This process is best typified by the famous parable told by Prodicus of Ceos:[21] As a young man, Heracles was faced with the choice between two women, representing Vice (with ease) and Virtue (with hardship), and chose the latter. Heracles was especially important as a paradigm of virtue in Roman Stoicism, whose doctrines set high value on the Heraclean qualities of endurance and self-reliance. In a modern setting, the character of Harcourt-Reilly in T. S.

The Farnese Hercules. Marble copy by Glycon, early third century A.D., of an original by Lysippus, mid-fourth century B.C.; height 125 in. This huge statue was found in the Baths of Caracalla at Rome, for which it had been specially copied. The weary hero leans on his club, which rests on a stump over which the lionskin is draped. His vast body is bursting with mountainous muscles. It has been suggested (by M. Robertson) that he is "an athlete in decay"; more likely his stance is one of weariness after his labors. *(Museo Nazionale, Naples. Courtesy of Alinari/Art Resource, New York.)*

Eliot's *The Cocktail Party* (1949) combines the Heracles of the myth of Alcestis with the virtues of a Christlike hero.

Perhaps we would do better to leave Heracles by returning to the ancient invocation to him in the *Homeric Hymn to Heracles, the Lion-Hearted* (15); here we may focus on the man who after a lifetime of toil became a hero and a god:

CAPTIONS FOR COLOR PLATES 12–22

12. *Cephalus and Aurora,* by Nicolas Poussin (1594–1665). Oil on canvas, ca. 1630; 38 × 51½ in. Cephalus gazes at a portrait of Procris, held up to him by a cupid, as he resists the advances of Aurora. In the background Pegasus waits to pull the chariot of the Dawn. The sleeping god with the urn is a river-god used by Poussin to signify a mythological landscape.

13. *The Forge of Vulcan,* by Diego Velázquez (1599–1660). Oil on canvas, 1630; 88 × 114 in. Velázquez has painted the moment when Helius tells Hephaestus that his wife, Aphrodite, is making love to Ares (Homer, *Odyssey* 8. 270–271). At the appearance of Helius in the forge Hephaestus and his four assistants stop their work on a suit of armor (perhaps for Ares himself), stunned by the news. Helius, whose white flesh, blue-thonged sandals, and orange robe contrast with the burly torsos of the blacksmiths, is both sun-god and Apollo, god of poetry (as his laurel wreath indicates). The rays from his head illuminate the dark forge, while the exquisite white jug on the mantelpiece provides another focus of light on the opposite side of the painting. Velázquez catches the intersection of divine omniscience and the blacksmith's toil without diminishing the wit and pathos of Homer's tale. The great anvil in the left foreground, we know, waits for Hephaestus to forge on it the inescapable metal net that will trap the lovers.

14. *The Triumph of Neptune and Amphitrite,* by Nicolas Poussin (1594–1665). Oil on canvas, ca. 1637; 45 × 58 in. Amphitrite is at the center, accompanied by Nereids and Tritons as she rides over the sea in her shell drawn by four dolphins. Neptune comes alongside his bride in a chariot drawn by four sea-horses. Above, winged cupids (one with butterfly's wings and one with a wedding torch) strew flowers, and in the background to the left ride two cupids, above whom fly the swans of Venus. Poussin exuberantly reinterprets a theme found in Roman floor mosaics and in Raphael's fresco *Galatea* (ca. 1512) in the Villa Farnesina at Rome.

15. *Pilgrimage to the Island of Cythera,* by Antoine Watteau (1684–1721). Oil on canvas, 1717; 51 × 76 in. To the right, three pairs of lovers prepare to embark for Cythera (or, perhaps, to sail from the island), while below five other couples approach the richly ornamented galley, whose shell motifs recall the birth of Venus. An armless herm of Venus looks down on the lovers from the wood on the right. It is garlanded with flowers and Cupid's bow and arrows are tied to it by a ribbon. A half-naked cupid, seated on his quiver, tugs at the skirt of one of the lovers, and other cupids fly through the air (one with a torch) and around the galley. The spirit of love fills Watteau's exquisite landscape, in which eighteenth-century lovers find joy in the timeless mythological setting. Watteau submitted this painting to the French Academy as his "reception piece," and he painted a second version (now in Berlin) in 1718. The Academy gave it the title *Une fête galante* (A courtly celebration), but Watteau's title more accurately expresses the power of the goddess who rules the island of Cythera.

16. *Earth: Vertumnus and Pomona,* by François Boucher (1703–1770). Oil on canvas, 1749; 34½ × 53½ in. *Earth* is one of a planned series representing the Four Elements by means of classical myths. The legend of Pomona and Vertumnus illustrates the fertility and variety of Earth. Pomona is shown as a beauty at the court of Louis XV in a pastoral scene such as was produced in the court ballets and operas at Versailles. The deception of Vertumnus is indicated by the mask held up by the cupid, and his intentions are made clear by the lascivious head of Pan on the urn at the right and by the fountain on the left with Cupid riding a dolphin.

PLATE 14   *The Triumph of Neptune and Amphitrite*, by Nicolas Poussin.
(Philadelphia, Philadelphia Museum of Art, The George W. Elkins Collection.)

PLATE 12   *Cephalus and Aurora,* by Nicolas Poussin. *(London, National Gallery. Reproduced by courtesy of the Trustees.)*

PLATE 13   *The Forge of Vulcan,* by Diego Velázquez. *([Madrid, Museo del Prado] Scala/Art Resource, NY.*

Captions to color plates precede and follow this insert.

PLATE 15 *Pilgrimage to the Island of Cythera.*, by Antoine Watteau. *(Paris, France: Musée du Louvre] Giraudon/Art Resource, NY)*

PLATE 16 *Earth: Vertumnus and Pomona*, by François Boucher. (*Columbus Museum of Art, Obio: Museum Purchase, Derby Fund.*)

PLATE 17 *Ariadne Asleep on the Island of Naxos*, by John Vanderlyn. *(Philadelphia, Pennsylvania Academy of the Fine Arts. Courtesy of the Pennsylvania Academy of the Fine Arts. Gift of Mrs. Sarah Harrison [The Joseph Harrison, Jr. Collection.])*

PLATE 18 *Pandora,* by Odilon Redon. (*New York, Metropolitan Museum of Art, Bequest of Alexander M. Bing, 1959.*)

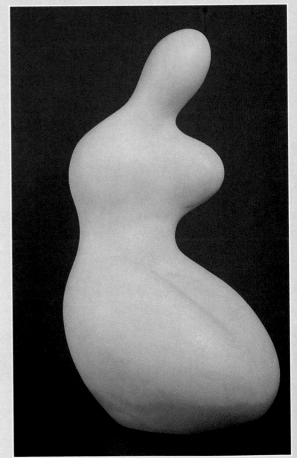

PLATE 19 *Demeter,* by Jean Arp. (*New York, Art Resource, ©1994 Artists Rights Society (ARS), New York/VG Bild-Kunst, Bonn.*)

un moment
si libres.
Ne devrait-on
pas faire ac-
complir un
grand voyage
en avion aux
jeunes gens
ayant terminé
leurs études.

PLATE 20   *Icarus,* by Henri Matisse. (New York, Museum of Modern Art. The Louis E. Stern Collection. Photograph © 1994 The Museum of Modern Art, New York. © 1994 Succession H. Matisse, Paris/Artists Society [ARS], New York.)

PLATE 21 *Hector and Andromache,* by Giorgio de Chirico. (*Milan, Italy: Fondazione Gianni Mattioli. © Foundation Giorgio de Chirico/ VAGA, New York 1994. Photograph courtesy of Scala/Art Resource, NY*).

PLATE 22 *Landscape for Philemon and Baucis,* by David Ligare. (*Hartford, Connecticut, Wadsworth Atheneum. Courtesy of the Wadsworth Atheneum, Ella Gallup Sumner and Mary Catlin Sumner Collection. Photo by Joseph Szaszfai.*)

17. *Ariadne Asleep on the Island of Naxos,* by John Vanderlyn (1775–1852). Oil on canvas, 1814; 68 × 87 in. Ariadne lies asleep, unaware that Theseus (who can be seen in the background at the right) is setting sail. Painted in Paris, this is one of the earliest nudes by an American painter to have been exhibited in America. Vanderlyn hoped that his masterpiece "while not chaste enough . . . to be displayed in the house of any private individual . . . [would] attract a great crowd if exhibited publickly."

18. *Pandora,* by Odilon Redon (1840–1916). Oil on canvas, ca. 1910; $56\frac{1}{2}$ × $24\frac{1}{2}$ in. Pandora, holding her box, is framed by jewellike flowers, but above her is a leafless tree. Redon used symbols "to clothe ideas in a sensuous form" (in the words of the *Symbolist Manifesto* of 1886). This painting is nearly contemporary with Freud's *Interpretation of Dreams* (1909). Like Freud, Redon used the symbols of mythology to express his innermost ideas and emotions.

19. *Demeter,* by Jean Arp (1887–1966). Marble, 1960; 26 × 11 in. At the age of seventy-three Arp returned to the ancient and abstract form of the earth-mother, whose swelling curves and strong thighs presage the fertility of nature that is described at the end of the *Homeric Hymn to Demeter.*

20. *Icarus,* by Henri Matisse (1869–1954). Stencil print of a paper cutout, 1947; $16\frac{1}{2}$ × $25\frac{1}{2}$ in. This is Plate 8 (p. 54) in Matisse's *Jazz* (Paris: Tériade, 1947). The plates were printed from paper cutouts pasted on and painted through stencils. He wrote the text in his own firm handwriting, and opposite *Icarus* is the last of seven pages titled *L'Avion* (The Airplane). Matisse reflects on the freedom in space experienced by air travelers, then he concludes "Ought one not to make young people who have finished their studies take a long journey in an airplane." The red heart of Icarus—symbol of his courage and creativity—stands out in the black silhouette against the sky and stars that he tried, and failed, to reach.

21. *Hector and Andromache,* by Giorgio de Chirico (1888–1978). Oil on canvas, 1917; $35\frac{1}{2}$ × $23\frac{1}{2}$ in. Husband and wife, mannequins backed by receding frames, part at the Scaean Gate in an austere, stagelike setting with receding perspective. They are sheathed in geometrically shaped metallic plates, and the baby Astyanax is reduced to a steel wedge with a black disk for his head. De Chirico's images of the intersection of war and the family are a disturbing interpretation of Homer's moving scene.

22. *Landscape for Philemon and Baucis,* by David Ligare (b. 1945). Oil on canvas, 1984; 32 × 48 in. The cottage of Baucis and Philemon has become a temple, while they have been transformed into the intertwined trees on the right. The lake conceals the homes of the villagers who were so inhospitable to Zeus and Hermes. The size of the trees and the ruinous state of the temple indicate that the metamorphosis took place long ago.

Hercules Victor (The Farnese Hercules), by Hendrik Goltzius (1558–1617). Engraving 1589; published 1617. Goltzius' engraving shows the overmuscled body of the hero from the rear, clutching the Apples of the Hesperides in his right hand. The two contemporary observers emphasize the vastness of his body silhouetted against the sky. The Latin iambic lines (to the left and right of the caption) say: "I, Hercules, terror of the world, rest, weary after subduing the three-formed king [Geryon] of further Spain and after taking the apples from the turning-point of Hesperus, where the never-sleeping serpent had guarded them in gardens of gold." *(The Metropolitan Museum of Art, New York, Gift of Henry Walters, 1917.)*

 Of Heracles will I sing, son of Zeus, whom Alcmena bore in Thebes, city of delightful dances, when she had lain with the son of Cronus, lord of the dark clouds, to be by far the greatest of men on earth. He traversed long ago vast distances of land and sea at the order of King Eurystheus; many were the bold deeds he did, many were the things he endured. Now he dwells in joy in the

Hercules Prodicius. Engraving by T. van Thulden after a design by Peter Paul Rubens, from C. Gevartius, *Pompa Introitus Ferdinandi*, Antwerp, 1642. The virtuous hero of Prodicus' parable of the Choice of Heracles is at the center of baroque political allegory. The victorious Archduke Ferdinand, wearing Heracles' lionskin and holding his club, refuses the temptations of women representing Love and Pleasure (a cupid tugs at the lionskin), as he prepares to ascend the rocky path of Virtue pointed out to him by Athena, towards the temple of Virtue and Honor. The allegory is set in a triumphal arch erected over the processional way along which Ferdinand made his "Joyful Entry" into Antwerp in 1635 after his victory at Nördlingen, to which the cannon at the lower right of the panel alludes. *(The Library of Congress, Washington, D.C.)*

beautiful palace of snowy Olympus and has for wife slender-ankled Hebe. Hail, lord, son of Zeus. Grant [me] both excellence and wealth.[22]

THE HERACLIDAE

Alcmena, Eurystheus, and the Children of Heracles

After the death of Heracles, his mother Alcmena and his children were persecuted by Eurystheus. King Ceyx was unable to protect them and they fled to Athens. The Athenians fought Eurystheus, who died in battle with his five sons. His head was brought to Alcmena, who gouged out the eyes with brooches.

According to Euripides, however, in his drama *Heraclidae,* Alcmena and her grandchildren were received at Athens by King Demophon, son of Theseus. Demophon was ordered "by all the oracles to sacrifice a virgin, daughter of a noble father, to the daughter of Demeter [Persephone], to be the defeat of our enemies and the salvation of the city" (*Heraclidae* 407–409, 402). Macaria, daughter of Heracles, voluntarily offered herself for the sacrifice and so brought victory to the Athenians. In the battle, Iolaüs, the nephew of Heracles, was miraculously rejuvenated by Heracles and Hebe and pursued Eurystheus, whom he captured and brought back to Alcmena. The play ends with Alcmena gloating over her prisoner and ordering him off to be executed. With his last words Eurystheus prophesies that his body, if it were buried in Attica, would protect the land from invaders.

Yet another version was given by Pindar (*Pythian Odes* 9. 79–84):

Seven-gated Thebes knew that the Right Time *(Kairos)* favored Iolaüs. Him they buried, after he had cut off the head of Eurystheus with his sword, deep in the earth in the tomb of Amphitryon the charioteer. His grandfather [Amphitryon] lay there, guest of the Spartoi, who lived as a foreigner in Cadmeia, city of white horses.

In this version, Iolaüs killed Eurystheus, and his body, rather than that of Eurystheus, protected the foreign land that had welcomed him—in this case Thebes (which was Pindar's own city).

Alcmena herself also became associated with a cult. In one version, she died in Thebes and was transported by Hermes to the Elysian

Fields, where she married Rhadamanthys, brother of Minos. In the version of Apollodorus, she married Rhadamanthys in Thebes after the death of Amphitryon and was reunited with him in the Underworld. As she was being carried out to burial in a coffin Hermes, at the command of Zeus, substituted for her body a large stone, which the sons of Heracles discovered (for the coffin had suddenly become very heavy) and set up in a shrine sacred to her.[23]

The Return of the Heraclidae

The saga of the descendants of Heracles (the Heraclidae) explains the occupation of a large part of the Peloponnese by Dorian tribes in the period after the end of the Mycenaean Age. Hyllus married Iole as his father had commanded and consulted Delphi about his return to the Peloponnese. He was advised to wait "until the third fruit" and that victory would come "from the Narrows." After waiting two more years, he attacked by way of the Isthmus of Corinth. He himself was killed in single combat by Echemus, king of Tegea; his army withdrew, and a truce of one hundred years was agreed upon. At the end of that time, the Heraclid Temenus again consulted the oracle, who told him that the "third fruit" meant not the third harvest but the third generation, and that "the Narrows" meant the entrance to the Gulf of Corinth. Temenus therefore invaded the northwest Peloponnese, crossing over near Patrae and taking as a guide a "three-eyed man" in accordance with the advice of the oracle; this was an Aetolian exile named Oxylus, whom he found riding a one-eyed horse. With his help, the Heraclids defeated the Peloponnesian defenders, who were led by Tisamenus, son of Orestes. Thucydides (1. 12) relates these events to the disruptions in Greece that followed the Trojan War and the return of the Greek leaders. He says that "the Dorians with the Heraclidae took possession of the Peloponnese in the eightieth year [after the fall of Troy]."

Thus the "Return of the Heraclidae" took place. The leaders divided up the three principal areas which they had conquered. Lacedaemon (Sparta) was given to Procles and Eurysthenes, sons of the lately dead leader Aristodemus, and they became founders of the two royal houses of Sparta. Argos fell to Temenus, and Messene to Cresphontes. Temenus was killed by his sons, whom he had passed over in the succession to his throne; Cresphontes was also murdered, along with two of his sons, by a rival Heraclid, Polyphontes. His widow, Merope, was forced to become Polyphontes' queen, but she succeeded in getting her surviving son Aepytus out of the kingdom to Aetolia, where he grew up. Later he secretly returned to Messene and was recognized by Merope, with whose connivance he killed Polyphontes and recovered his father's throne. Of the three Dorian kingdoms, Sparta and Argos flourished for many centuries, but Messene was subjugated by the Spartans within a comparatively short time.

THESEUS AND THE
LEGENDS OF ATTICA

21

THE EARLY KINGS
AND THEIR LEGENDS

Cecrops, Erichthonius, and Erechtheus

The Athenians boasted that they were autochthonous (literally, "sprung from the earth"), that is, that they were not descended from any invaders of Attica. They said that Cecrops, their earliest king, had sprung from the earth and was serpent-shaped in the lower half of his body. He has little importance in legend except as the founder of Attica, which he called Cecropia after himself. It was in his time that the contest between Poseidon and Athena for the possession of Attica took place (see p. 119). Poseidon continued to be an important divinity at Athens, and his worship on the Acropolis was closely connected with that of Athena.

Another early figure in Attic mythology is Erichthonius, who was also partly serpent-shaped and (as the element *-chthon-* in his name implies) sprung from the earth. When Hephaestus attempted to violate Athena, his semen fell on the ground, and from it sprang Erichthonius. Athena took him up and put him in a chest, which she gave to the daughters of Cecrops, forbidding them to look inside. The sisters disobeyed: driven mad by what they saw, they hurled themselves off the Acropolis.[1] . After this Athena took Erichthonius back and brought him up herself. As king of Athens he was credited with instituting the great annual festival of the Panathenaea and setting up the wooden statue of Athena on the Acropolis.

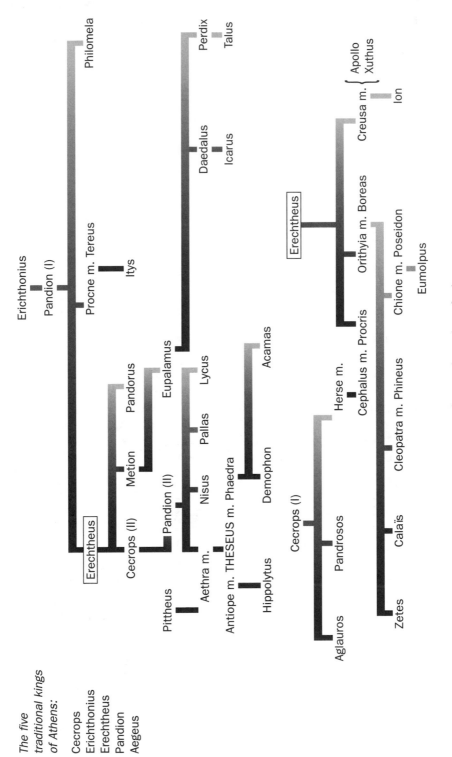

The five
traditional kings
of Athens:

Cecrops
Erichthonius
Erechtheus
Pandion
Aegeus

Figure 21.1. The Royal Families of Athens

Erichthonius' myth focuses upon his birth, whose most important feature is that he was "sprung from the earth." He is to some extent confused with his grandson and successor as king of Athens, Erechtheus. Both are in fact forms of Poseidon. Athena prophesied that after his death Erechtheus would be worshiped at Athens with his own cult-site, "ringed around with stones," and that under the title of "Poseidon-Erechtheus he will be offered sacrifices of bulls."[2]

Towards the end of the fifth century, the beautiful temple on the Acropolis known as the Erechtheum was dedicated jointly to Athena Polias (i.e., Athena as Guardian of the City) and Erechtheus. In it were sacred objects associated with the earliest stages of Athenian religion, including the wooden statue of Athena, the tomb of Erechtheus, and the salt spring produced by the blow of Poseidon's trident in his contest with Athena, which was known as "the sea of Erechtheus." In this "sea" were the marks of Poseidon's trident where he struck the earth, and linked to the sanctuary was the olive-tree produced by Athena. The temple took the name by which it is generally known, Erechtheum, from Erechtheus-Poseidon; but in antiquity it was known officially as "the temple in which is the ancient statue."

Thus the Erechtheum and its neighboring shrines were closely bound up with the most ancient myths of Athens. It was built upon

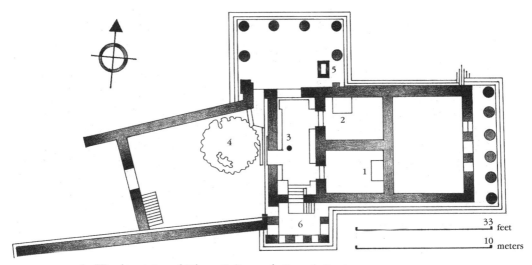

1. Wooden statue of Athena Polias   4. Sacred olive tree
2. Tomb of Erechtheus   5. Zeus' thunderbolt
3. Salt Spring   6. Porch of the maidens (caryatids)

Figure 21.2. Plan of the Erechtheum. *(After W. B. Dinsmoore.)*

the Acropolis, the site of the Mycenaean fortress of Athens, and so it linked Athenians to the earliest stages of their city's history. Athena, the great Olympian protectress of the city, here was associated with both her rival Poseidon and her predecessor, the chthonic divinity Erechtheus. Her triumph in the struggle for the honor of protecting the city was visible nearby in the sculptures of the west pediment of the Parthenon.

Erechtheus was important in the mythology of Athens. He successfully defended Athens in her earliest war, the attack of the Eleusinians led by the Thracian Eumolpus, who was a son of Poseidon and ancestor of the hereditary priests of Eleusis. With the approval of his wife, Praxithea, Erechtheus sacrificed one of his daughters to secure the victory for Athens.[3] In the battle he killed Eumolpus, and for this was himself killed by Poseidon, who thrust him into the earth with his trident. The sacrifice of the daughter was a central theme in Euripides' tragedy *Erechtheus,* in which Praxithea played a prominent part.[4]

In Euripides' tragedy *Ion,* Ion's mother, Creusa, one of Erechtheus' daughters, gives a different version, in which all the daughters of Erechtheus were sacrificed except for herself (*Ion* 277–282):

ION: Did your father Erechtheus sacrifice your sisters?

CREUSA: He hardened himself to kill the maidens as a sacrificial offering for the earth.

ION: How then were you saved alone amongst your sisters?

CREUSA: I was a newborn baby in my mother's arms.

ION: And does a chasm in the earth truly hide your father?

CREUSA: Yes—blows from the ocean-god's trident killed him.

As a final reminder of the importance of Erechtheus in Athenian mythology and the pride of the Athenians in being autochthonous, we quote from the opening lines (824–830) of the beautiful chorus in praise of Athens that Euripides composed for his tragedy *Medea:*[5]

The descendants of Erechtheus are fortunate from of old and children of the blessed gods, [dwelling in] a holy land that has never been conquered, feeding on most famous wisdom and walking lightly through the shining air.

We have earlier mentioned the daughters of Cecrops to whom Athena entrusted the infant Erichthonius (see Color Plate 11). They were three in number, Aglauros, Herse, and Pandrosos, whose names, meaning "bright," "dew," and "all-dew," show that they are truly mythological beings, in origin fertility goddesses.[6]

Ovid tells how Herse was loved by Hermes, who was first noticed by Aglauros as he flew down to the Acropolis. Aglauros asked Hermes for gold as a reward for her help in bringing him to Herse. For this she further angered Athena, who was already angry because of her disobedience in looking inside the chest of Erichthonius. Athena therefore filled Aglauros with envy so that she tried to prevent Hermes from going in to Herse and he turned her into a rock. He then lay with Herse, and their son was Cephalus.

Cephalus and Procris

Cephalus was loved by Eos (Dawn) and was an ally of Amphitryon. In later legend he is the husband of Procris, daughter of Erechtheus. In Ovid's story, he was tempted by Aurora (the Latin form of Eos), who also loved him, to make trial of Procris' faithfulness (see Color Plate 12). In disguise he attempted to seduce her, and when he was on the point of succeeding, revealed himself. In shame Procris fled and joined Artemis, who gave her a hound, Laelaps, that always caught its quarry, and a javelin that never missed its mark. Later she was reconciled to Cephalus and returned home, bringing with her the magic gifts. According to Ovid, the hound was turned into marble, along with its prey, when Cephalus was hunting near Thebes. The javelin had a longer and more tragic history. Here is part of Ovid's story (*Metamorphoses* 7. 804–859; Cephalus is the speaker):

When the sun's first rays had just begun to touch the topmost peaks, I used to go, like the young man I was, to the forest to hunt. No servants went with me, nor horses, nor keen-scented dogs trained to follow the knotted hunting nets—all I relied upon was the javelin. When my right hand had had enough of killing wild beasts, I would look for the cool shade and the breeze *(aura)* that came from the cold valleys. The gentle breeze would I call for in the midday heat; the breeze would I wait for, refreshment after my labors. "Come, aura" (for I remember my words), would I sing, "assist me and most pleasing, enter my bosom; be willing to relieve as you do, the heat with which I burn."[7] Perhaps I would add (for this way tended my fate) more endearments and would say, "You are my great pleasure; you restore and refresh me, you make me love the forest and solitary places; may your breath always be caught by my mouth."

Someone listening to my words with their double meaning was deceived; thinking the name of *aura* that I called upon so often was the name of a nymph, she believed that it was a nymph I loved. Soon a rash informer falsely charged me before Procris and repeated the murmurings she had heard. Love is credulous, yet often Procris hesitated and refused to believe the informer; she would not condemn her husband's crime unless she saw it herself.

The next dawn's light had driven the night away: I went to the forest and, successful in the hunt, lay on the grass and said, "Come, Aura, and give relief to my labor." Suddenly I thought I heard a sob as I spoke, yet still as I was saying, "Come, most excellent Aura," a fallen leaf rustled; and, thinking it was a wild animal, I hurled my javelin through the air. It was Procris; and as she held her wounded breast, she groaned "Ah, me." When I recognized the voice of my faithful wife, headlong I ran to her in dismay. I found her half dead, her blood staining her torn clothes, and plucking her own gift, alas, from the wound. Gently I lifted her body, dearer to me than my own . . . and implored her not to leave me, guilty of her death.

Weakened and on the point of death, with an effort she said these few words: "By our marriage vows . . . and by my love that still endures, the cause, even as I am dying, of my death, do not let Aura take my place as your wife."

Those were her words, then finally I realized how she had mistaken the name, and told her of the mistake. Yet what use was it to tell her? She fainted away, and her feeble strength failed as her blood flowed out.[8]

Philomela, Procne, and Tereus

The successor of Erichthonius was Pandion, who is famous in legend chiefly for his daughters Philomela and Procne. The Thracian king Tereus came to help Pandion in a war against Thebes and was rewarded with the hand of Procne. He took her back to Thrace and by her became the father of Itys. Later Philomela came to visit her sister and was attacked by Tereus, who violated her, cut out her tongue, and shut her up in a remote building deep in the forest. Here is how Ovid continues the story (*Metamorphoses* 6. 572–600):

What could Philomela do? Her prison, with its walls of unyielding stone, kept her from flight. Her mouth, dumb, could not tell of the crime. Yet sorrow is inventive, and cunning is an ally in distress. Skillfully she hung the threads from the barbarian loom and interwove purple scenes with the white threads, telling of the crime. She gave the finished embroidery to a servant and by signs asked her to take it to her mistress. The servant, not knowing what she was bringing, obeyed and took the embroidery to Procne. The cruel tyrant's wife unrolled the tapestry and read the unhappy saga of her own misfortunes. She held her peace (a miracle that she could!); sorrow restrained her words.

Now came the time when the Thracian matrons celebrated Bacchus' triennial feast; Night accompanied their rites. Queen Procne left her palace, garbed in the god's ritual dress and holding the instruments of his ecstasy. In a frenzy, with threatening looks, Procne rushed through the forest with a crowd of followers; driven by the madness of sorrow she pretended, Bacchus, that it was your madness. At length she reached the lonely prison and raised the Bacchic cry, *Evoe;* she broke down the doors, seized her sister, and put on her the Bacchic vestments, veiling her face with leaves of ivy. Dragging the stunned Philomela, Procne brought her sister to the palace.

Ovid then tells how Procne decides to revenge herself upon Tereus by murdering their son Itys (636–645):

Without delay, Procne seized Itys. . . . In a distant part of the lofty palace, as he stretched out his hands (for he saw his fate before him) and cried, "Mother, mother," trying to embrace her, she struck him with a sword, where the chest meets the body's flank, and she did not look away. One wound was enough to kill him, but Philomela cut his throat with a knife. They tore apart his body, while it still retained vestiges of life.

Ovid describes, in considerable detail, how the sisters cooked Itys and served him up to Tereus, who recognized too late what he had eaten. The tale continues (666–674):

Now Tereus drew his sword and pursued the daughters of Pandion: you would think that their bodies were clothed with feathers, and indeed they were. One flew to the forest; the other to the roof, and still the murder marked her breast and her feathers were stained with blood. Tereus, rushing swiftly in sorrow and in eagerness for revenge, turned into a bird with crested head; a long beak projects in place of his sword; the bird's name is Epops (Hoopoe), and its face seems armed.

In the Greek version of the story it is the nightingale (Procne) that mourns for her dead son, while the tongueless swallow (Philomela) tries to tell her story by her incoherent chatter. The Latin authors, however, changed the names, making Philomela the nightingale and Procne the swallow.

The *Ion* of Euripides

Pandion was said to have been succeeded as king by Erechtheus, whose myths we have discussed above. Among his daughters was Creusa, the heroine of Euripides' play *Ion*. Creusa was the only one of the daughters not to have been sacrificed by her father before the battle against Eumolpus. She was loved by Apollo and bore him a son, Ion, whom she exposed out of fear of her father. Ion was saved by Hermes at Apollo's request and taken by him to Delphi, where he was brought up as a temple servant and became treasurer of the sanctuary. Creusa, meanwhile, was given as wife to Xuthus as a reward for aiding Erechtheus in defeating the Chalcodontids of Euboea. After years of childlessness, Xuthus and Creusa consulted the Delphic oracle as to how they might have children; Xuthus was told to greet as his son the first person he met on going out of the temple.[9] This person was Ion but Creusa, who did not know that he was her own son, took him for a bastard son of Xuthus and attempted to kill him. The attempt miscarried, and with the intervention of Athena mother and son recognized each other. Xuthus, Creusa, and Ion returned together to Athens, where Ion became the ancestor of the four Ionic tribes (which were the main units of the early Athenian political structure). His descendants colonized part of the coast of Asia Minor and the islands, thereafter called Ionia.[10]

Orithyia and Boreas and Their Children

Another daughter of Erechtheus, Orithyia, was loved by the North Wind, Boreas. He carried her off to Thrace as she was playing by the river Ilissus.[11] In Thrace she became the mother of the winged heroes Zetes and Calaïs, and of two daughters, Cleopatra and Chione. Zetes and Calaïs were prominent in the Argonauts' expedition (see p. 478). Phineus himself was married to Cleopatra, who was said to have caused the blindness of her stepsons (born to Phineus from another woman) by falsely accusing them of attempting to seduce her. Chione became the mother, by Poseidon, of Eumolpus, whose expedition against Athens we have discussed above.

The Confused Genealogy of the Kings of Athens

According to Apollodorus, Erechtheus was succeeded by his son Cecrops, and Cecrops by his son Pandion; Cecrops and Pandion thus repeat the names of earlier kings. Pandion was driven out of Attica by his uncle Metion and fled to Megara, where he became the father of four sons, Aegeus, Pallas, Nisus, and Lycus. After Pandion's death, the four brothers recovered the throne at Athens and shared the power; Aegeus, however, as the oldest, was in effect the sovereign, while Nisus returned to Megara as its king.

THESEUS

Aegeus, like Erechtheus, is another form of the god Poseidon. This is indicated by his connection with the Aegean Sea and by the tradition that Poseidon was Theseus' father rather than Aegeus.[12] As king of Athens he was threatened by the opposition of his brother Pallas. Being childless, he was told by the Delphic oracle "not to undo the wineskin's mouth" until he had returned home. Perplexed by this riddle, he asked the advice of Pittheus, king of Troezen, his host on the journey. Pittheus, who understood the oracle, made Aegeus drunk and gave him his daughter Aethra to lie with.[13] When Aegeus left Troezen, he told Aethra that if their child were a boy she must bring him up without saying who his father was. She was to send him to Athens when he was old enough to lift a rock by himself, under which Aegeus would leave a sword and a pair of sandals as tokens by which he could recognize his son. In due time Aethra bore a son, Theseus, who grew up and set out for Athens after securing the tokens.

Theseus is the great national hero of Attica, and Athens came to be the focal point of his legends. His earlier links with Marathon and Troezen were weakened. He is associated with Heracles in some of his adventures, and his deeds are similar to those of Heracles—for example, his ridding the land of brigands and monsters and his expedition against the Amazons. Some of the characters in his saga were themselves heroes with cults of their own, for example, Sciron and Hippolytus. The legends of Theseus have become famous largely through the genius of Athenian writers.[14]

Theseus' Six Labors on His Journey from Troezen to Athens

The adventures of Theseus fall into fairly well defined groups,[15] of which the first contains six deeds he performed while traveling to Athens from Troezen. Theseus chose the land route so as to expose himself to the challenge of more dangerous adventures.

At Epidaurus he killed the brigand Periphetes, a son of Hephaestus,

The Labors of Theseus. Attic red-figure kylix, ca. 475 B.C.; height of kylix 5 in.; diameter 12¾ in. The cycle of Theseus' labors was often painted on Athenian vases, especially drinking cups (*kylikes*), in the fifth century. This cup is unusual in that the cycle is painted (almost identically, except for the Minotaur) on both the exterior and interior. The interior, with the Minotaur at the center, is shown here. Starting at the top and going in a clockwise direction the labors are: (1) Cercyon; (2) Procrustes; (3) Sciron (note the turtle); (4) the Bull of Marathon; (5) Sinis (Pityocamptes); (6) the Sow of Crommyon. At the center Theseus drags the dying Minotaur out of the Labyrinth to dispatch him with his sword. Periphetes does not appear, since this labor does not enter the cycle until after 475 B.C. *(British Museum, London. Reproduced by permission of the Trustees.)*

who was armed with a club and generally called Corynetes (Club Man). Theseus took the club for himself, and it plays no further part in his legend (except in artistic representations).

At the Isthmus of Corinth, he killed the robber Sinis, called Pityocamptes (Pine Bender) from the way in which he killed his victims. He would bend two pine tree saplings to the ground, tie one end of his victim to each of the two trees, and then release the trees. Theseus killed him in this way.

On the border of the Isthmus and the Megarid he killed a monstrous sow near the village of Crommyon. Next he found the brigand Sciron barring his way at the so-called Cliffs of Sciron. Sciron, originally a local hero of neighboring areas,[16] blocked the path along which travelers through the Megarid must go to pass the cliffs and compelled all comers to stoop and wash his feet. He would then kick his victims into the sea, where a gigantic turtle ate them up. Theseus killed him by his own methods.

Drawing closer to Athens, Theseus met Cercyon at Eleusis. Like Sciron, Cercyon was also originally a local hero. He compelled travelers to wrestle with him to the death. Theseus defeated him in wrestling, held him high in the air, and then dashed him to his death upon the ground.

Finally, between Eleusis and Athens, Theseus met the brigand Procrustes (his name means "the stretcher"),[17] who possessed a hammer, a saw, and a bed. He compelled travelers to lie on the bed, and those who were too long for it he would cut down to size; those who were too short he would hammer out until they fit it exactly. He too perished at Theseus' hands in the way in which he had killed his victims.

Theseus Is Recognized by Aegeus

Theseus' arrival at Athens is dramatically described by the lyric poet Bacchylides of Ceos. In reply to the citizens' questions, Aegeus speaks (Bacchylides, *Dithyramb* 18. 16–60):

"A messenger has come, traversing the long road from the Isthmus; incredible are the deeds of a mighty man that he relates. This man killed violent Sinis, strongest of mortals. He killed the man-slaying sow in the glens of Cremmyon and killed the cruel Sciron. The wrestling ring of Cercyon has he suppressed; Procoptes has dropped the mighty hammer of Polypemon, for he has met a more valiant man. I fear what this news portends."
"Who is this man?" [ask the citizens, and Aegeus continues]:
"Two companions only come with him, says the messenger; upon his shoulders he wears an ivory-hilted sword and in his hand he carries two polished spears; upon his red-haired head is set a Spartan cap, well-made; around his body he has cast a purple tunic and over it a woolen cloak from Thessaly. From his eyes darts blood-red flame, as from Lemnos' volcano. Yet he is but a youth in his first prime, whose skill is in the delight of war and the brazen blows of battle. In quest of shining Athens does he come."

Theseus' arrival was hedged with further danger. Aegeus was married to Medea, who expected their son Medus to succeed as king of Athens. Medea immediately recognized Theseus as Aegeus' son and a rival to Medus, and attempted to have Theseus poisoned before Aegeus could recognize him. She advised Aegeus that the newcomer would be a threat to his power. He should entertain Theseus at a banquet where he would drink poisoned wine, for which Medea would provide the poison. Theseus at the banquet carved his meat with the sword that he had recovered from under the rock at Troezen; Aegeus recognized the sword, dashed the cup of poison out of Theseus' hand, and publicly recognized him as his son and successor.

Pallas, brother of Acgeus, and his sons had hoped and plotted to take over Aegeus' power and resorted to violence upon Theseus' recognition. Theseus killed all the members of one of the two groups into which they had divided, and Pallas himself and his surviving sons ceased to be a threat.

The Bull of Marathon

Theseus' next labor was to catch the bull of Marathon, said to have been the one that Heracles had brought from Crete. He mastered the bull and drove it back to Athens, where he sacrificed it to Apollo Delphinius. On his way to Marathon an old woman, Hecale, entertained Theseus. She promised she would sacrifice to Zeus if Theseus returned successful, but on his return he found her already dead and ordered that she share the honors henceforth paid to Zeus Hecalus at an annual festival by the people of that locality.

The Minotaur

Androgeos, son of the Cretan king Minos, had been killed in Attica because of the jealousy he aroused by winning all the contests at the Panathenaic games. In revenge Minos mounted an expedition against Athens and her ally, Megara, where Nisus, brother of Aegeus, was king. Megara was attacked first, and some time after its fall Athens made a treaty with Minos, with the provision that at intervals (of one or nine years) seven Athenian youths and seven girls, children of noble families, should be sent to Crete as tribute, there to be shut up in the Labyrinth and devoured by the Minotaur. The victims were chosen by lot and Theseus volunteered to go.[18]

On the voyage to Crete, Minos attacked one of the maidens, Eriboea, who called on Theseus for help. When Theseus intervened,

Minos prayed to Zeus for a sign that he was indeed Minos' father (and therefore that his son need be under no restraint in dealing with other men). Zeus sent lightning, and Minos then challenged Theseus' claim to be the son of Poseidon by throwing a ring overboard which Theseus was to recover. A beautiful poem by Bacchylides describes the sequel (*Dithyramb* 17. 92-116):

> The Athenian youths trembled as the hero leaped into the sea, and tears poured from their lilylike eyes as they awaited the sorrow of what had to be. Yet the dolphins, dwellers in the sea, swiftly brought great Theseus to the palace of his father, the ruler of horses. There with awe he saw the noble daughters of rich Nereus, and in the lovely palace he saw his father's own wife, the beauteous Amphitrite, in all her majesty. Round him she cast a purple robe, and upon his thick hair the unwithered wreath, dark with roses, which subtle Aphrodite had given her at her own marriage.

With these gifts (the poet does not mention the ring) Theseus returned miraculously to the ship and so came to Crete. Here the daughter of Minos, Ariadne, fell in love with him and gave him a thread with which he could trace his way back out of the Labyrinth. With this aid he entered the Labyrinth, killed the Minotaur, and emerged unharmed. He then sailed from Crete with his thirteen Athenian companions, taking Ariadne with him.

Ariadne on Naxos

Another tradition, however, makes Ariadne give Theseus a wreath that lights up the darkness of the Labryrinth and so helps him escape. In the poem of Bacchylides, this wreath is made the gift not of Ariadne but of Amphitrite, so that Theseus himself brings it to Crete. Ariadne wore the wreath on her flight with Theseus until he deserted her on Naxos and she was found by Dionysus. The god took the wreath and set it in the heavens, where it became the constellation Corona.

Here is Ovid's version of the metamorphosis (*Metamorphoses* 8. 174-181):

> Quickly the son of Aegeus sailed to Dia after seizing Minos' daughter, and cruelly left his companion deserted upon that shore. Alone and bitterly complaining, Ariadne found comfort in the embraces of Bacchus, who took the wreath from her brow and placed it in the heavens so that Ariadne might be made famous by a constellation. The wreath flies through the thin air, and as it flies

Death of a Monster, by Pablo Picasso (1881–1973). Pencil on paper, 1937; 15 × 22¼ in. The contorted and dying Minotaur sees himself in a mirror held up by a sea-goddess, perhaps Amphitrite herself. Picasso used the violence and horror of the Minotaur to express his anger at the atrocities of the Spanish Civil War; this drawing is dated December 6, 1937, eight months after the bombing of Guernica. *(Photograph courtesy of Lee Miller Archives, Chiddingly, England. All rights reserved. © 1994 Artists Rights Society [ARS], New York/SPADEM, Paris.)*

> its jewels are turned into fires and become fixed in their place,
> still with the appearance of a wreath *(corona)*.

Ariadne is originally a divine person, perhaps another form of Aphrodite. Hesiod *(Theogony* 947–949) describes her as the "wife of Dionysus, whom Zeus made immortal." Later versions of the Theseus legend make her a forlorn heroine, deserted by her lover Theseus upon the island of Dia (the early name for Naxos) during the voyage back to Athens (see Color Plate 17). Here is the narrative of Catullus (64. 52–59):

> Ariadne, with uncontrolled passion in her heart, looking out from
> the shore of Dia with its sounding waves, saw Theseus receding
> into the distance with his fleet at full speed. Not yet could she
> believe her eyes, for she had only just been wakened from
> deceitful sleep and saw that she was alone, unhappy, upon the

shore. But the young man, forgetful, parted the waves with his
oars in flight, leaving his promises unfulfilled to the gusts of wind.

Ovid, who related this legend three times,[19] describes the arrival
of Dionysus and his companions (*Ars Amatoria* 1. 535–564):

 And now Ariadne beat her soft breast again and again: "My
faithless lover has gone," cried she. "What will become of me?"
"What will become of me?" she cried; the shore reechoed to the
sound of cymbals and the frenzied beating of drums. She swooned
in fear, and her words trailed away; no blood remained in her
fainting body. Look! here are the maenads, their hair streaming
down their backs. Look! here come the dancing satyrs, forerunners
of the god. Look! here is old Silenus, hardly able to keep his seat
upon the swaybacked donkey. And now came the god in his
chariot decked to the top with vines, driving yoked tigers with
golden reins. Ariadne lost her color, her voice, her thoughts of
Theseus; twice she tried to run away, and twice fear held her
rooted. Then said the god: "Behold I am here, a more faithful
object of your love. Away with fear! You shall be the Cretan wife
of Bacchus. Take the heavens as my gift; you shall be observed in
the heavens as a constellation. Often as the Cretan Crown
(Corona) will you guide lost sailors." So he spoke and jumped
down from the chariot, lest she be alarmed by the tigers, and took
her up in his arms, for she could not resist; all things are easy for a
god. Some of his followers chant the marriage cry, "O Hymen,"
and others cry, *"Evoe, evoe";* so the god and his bride lay together
in the sacred bed.

Homer says that Ariadne was killed by Artemis upon Naxos as a
punishment for eloping with Theseus when she was already betrothed to Dionysus. Yet another story has her die in Cyprus in giving
birth to Theseus' child. When Theseus returned, he instituted a ritual
in her honor, and in historical times she was honored under the title
of Ariadne Aphrodite, part of the ritual being for a young man to lie
down and imitate a woman in childbirth. In all these conflicting stories it is clear that Ariadne is no ordinary mortal and that her partner
was not a man, Theseus, but a god (see Color Plate 4).

Theseus Becomes King of Athens

After leaving Dia (Naxos), Theseus went to Delos, where he sacrificed
to Apollo and danced the Crane dance (in Greek, *geranos*) with his
companions. The dance became traditional at Delos, and its intricate

Dionysus and Ariadne. Marble sarcophagus, ca. 180 A.D.; width 77 in., height (without lid) $20\frac{1}{2}$ in., height of lid 11 in. Dionysus approaches from the left riding on a chariot drawn by a lyre-playing centaur, behind and to the right of whom a centauress blows on a kind of flute. Before him go Pan and a silenus, and a silenus mask lies on the ground in the left center. A cupid hovers near the god. In the center the god stands, now clothed in a long robe, holding a reversed thyrsus in his left hand, his right hand resting on the leading silenus. He looks towards the sleeping Ariadne, whose robe is being drawn aside by a cupid, while two maenads look back at the god. To the right two maenads are about to attack Pentheus. On the lid are reliefs of the god's thiasos, and a deer is being sacrificed to the right. The waking of Ariadne to the coming of the god of new life was popular in the funerary art of late antiquity as a parable of the waking of the soul to eternal life after death. This sarcophagus is in a tomb in the cemetery under St. Peter's basilica in the Vatican. It is not known whether its occupant was pagan or Christian. (*Photo courtesy of the Foto Fabbrica di San Pietro.*)

movements were said to imitate the windings of the Labyrinth.[20] From Delos he sailed home to Athens. Now he had arranged with Aegeus that he should change the black sail of his ship for white if he had been successful. This he forgot to do, and as Aegeus saw the black-sailed ship approaching, he threw himself from a cliff into the sea, which thereafter was called the Aegean Sea.

So Theseus became king of Athens. He was credited with a number of historical reforms and institutions, including the synoecism of Attica (i.e., the union of the different villages into one political unit with Athens as its center) and the refounding of the Isthmian Games (see p. 501).

The Amazons

Theseus joined with Heracles in his expedition against the Amazons, and as his share of the spoil received the Amazon Antiope, by whom he became the father of Hippolytus. The Amazons in revenge invaded Attica and were defeated by Theseus. During the Amazon attack Antiope died. The battle between Theseus and the Amazons became a favorite theme in Athenian art after the Persian Wars, when the Amazons were seen as symbols of the barbarians, who, like the Persians, had been defeated by the Greeks.[21]

Theseus and Pirithoüs

Pirithoüs, king of the Thessalian tribe of the Lapiths and son of Ixion, was Theseus' friend. Theseus was among the guests at the marriage of Pirithoüs and took part in the fight against the Centaurs, which became an important theme in Greek art (see pp. 80 and 119).

Theseus and Pirithoüs vowed to help each other in securing a wife. Theseus attempted to take Helen, and Pirithoüs, Persephone. Helen, who at the time was only a child, was kidnapped from Sparta and brought back to Attica, where she was put in the care of Theseus' mother, Aethra, in the Attic village of Aphidnae. While Theseus and Pirithoüs were away on their attempt against Persephone, the Dioscuri invaded Attica and recovered their sister. The Dioscuri were favorably received in Athens itself, where the regent Menestheus instituted a cult in their honor.[22] Aethra was taken back to Sparta as Helen's servant and went with her to Troy.

Pirithoüs met his end in attempting to abduct Persephone. He and Theseus descended to the Underworld where they were held fast in magic chairs. In the Athenian tradition, Heracles interceded for

Theseus' release, while Pirithoüs stayed forever in Hades. Thus the Athenian hero was again associated with Heracles, in this case in his last and greatest labor, the conquest of death.

Theseus, Phaedra, and Hippolytus

Theseus was also married to Phaedra, another daughter of Minos, and by her was the father of two sons, Demophon and Acamas. Phaedra (whose name means "bright") may originally have been a Cretan goddess like Ariadne. As we learned in Chapter 8, she fell passionately in love with Hippolytus, Theseus' son by Antiope, but did not tell him of her desire. During an absence of Theseus, her old nurse found out the secret and told Hippolytus. In shame at the discovery of her secret, Phaedra hanged herself and left behind a letter falsely accusing Hippolytus of attempting to seduce her. When Theseus returned, saw Phaedra's corpse, and read the letter, he banished Hippolytus and called on Poseidon to destroy him.[23] As Hippolytus was driving his chariot along the seashore on his way into exile, Poseidon sent a bull from the sea, which so frightened the horses that they bolted, threw Hippolytus from the chariot, and dragged him almost to his death. He was carried back to Theseus and died after a reconciliation with his father, assured by Artemis of his future honor as a hero with a cult.

The legend of Hippolytus owes its fame largely to Euripides who wrote two tragedies on the subject (one of which is extant), and to Seneca, whose *Phaedra* was the model for Racine's *Phèdre.*[24] In Euripides' *Hippolytus,* the drama is set at Troezen; but most other authors make Athens the scene. Hippolytus himself was honored with a cult at Troezen and was closely connected with Artemis, in whose honor he avoided all women. At Athens he was connected with Aphrodite, whose temple on the south side of the Acropolis was called "Aphrodite by Hippolytus." He himself was said to have been brought to life by Asclepius, and in his resurrected form he was absorbed by the Italians with the name of Virbius. His legend is of the greatest literary importance and it connects Attica and Troezen and links Theseus to the great goddesses worshiped in Crete, Troezen, and Athens.

Theseus as Champion of the Oppressed

In the fifth century, a number of legends were developed in which kings of Athens were portrayed as protectors of victims of tyranny who had been driven from their homes. In Euripides' *Medea,* Aegeus, father of Theseus, promises to protect Medea, who has been exiled from Corinth. Theseus was especially popular in these legends. He generously gave refuge to the exiled Oedipus (see p. 327), and in the *Suppliant Women* of Euripides he champions the mothers of the dead heroes of the Seven against Thebes. Led by Adrastus, the sole survivor of the expedition, they come to Eleusis, where Aethra has come to sacrifice to Demeter. She takes pity on the women and appeals to Theseus to protect them and help them persuade the Theban king Creon to allow them to bury the dead Argive princes. Theseus is at first unpersuaded by her pleas and those of Adrastus, but eventually he relents and attacks Thebes with an Athenian army. He returns victorious, bringing the bodies of the dead Argive leaders, over whom Adrastus makes a funeral oration. The bodies are then cremated, although the pyre of Capaneus is separate from the others because he was killed by the thunderbolt of Zeus and therefore sacred to the god. In the climactic scene of the tragedy, Evadne, the widow of Capaneus, hurls herself into the flames of his pyre (see p. 334).

The figure of Theseus as the noble king has frequently been portrayed in later literature.[25] He is the compassionate champion of the Argive women in the twelfth book of Statius' *Thebaid,* in which he actually kills Creon. In Chaucer's *Canterbury Tales* he is, in "The Knight's Tale," the protector of the Argive women and the wise king. He is "Duke Theseus" rather less loftily in Shakespeare's *Midsummer Night's Dream.*

Other Adventures of Theseus

Theseus was not originally a member of the great expeditions of saga, but so important a national hero naturally came to be included in the roster of heroic adventurers, so that he was said to have been an Argonaut and one of those present on the Calydonian boar hunt. Indeed, "not without Theseus" became an Athenian proverb, and he was called "a second Heracles." His life was said to have ended in failure. He was driven out of Athens, his power usurped by Menestheus, who is mentioned in the *Iliad*'s catalogue of ships as the Athenian leader at Troy. Theseus went to the island of Scyros, and was there killed by Lycomedes, the local king. Menestheus continued to reign at Athens but died at Troy. The sons of Theseus then recovered their father's throne. After the Persian Wars, the Greek allies, led by the Athenian Cimon, captured Scyros in the years 476-475. There Cimon, obedient to a command of the Delphic oracle, searched for the bones of Theseus. He found the bones of a very large man with a bronze spearhead and sword and brought them back to Athens. So

Theseus returned, a symbol of Athens' connection with the heroic age and of her claim to lead the Ionian Greeks.

Demophon

Theseus' son Demophon helped the children of Heracles (see p. 446) and he has a number of other legends.[26] He loved the Thracian princess Phyllis, and on leaving her in Thrace, he swore to return soon. When he never came back, she hanged herself and became an almond tree. Too late he returned and embraced the tree, which burst into leaf.

Codrus

The last king of Athens was Codrus, who sacrificed himself for his city. The Peloponnesians invaded Attica, assured by the Delphic oracle that the side would win whose king was killed. When Codrus learned of the oracle he disguised himself as a peasant and provoked a quarrel with some enemy soldiers, who killed him; the Peloponnesians were defeated.

MINOS

Daedalus and Minos

Daedalus was son or grandson of Metion, younger brother of Cecrops, and therefore a member of the Athenian royal house. Daedalus was a skilled craftsman and inventor; his assistant was his nephew Perdix.[27] One day Perdix invented the saw, getting the idea from a fish's backbone. In a fit of jealousy, Daedalus hurled him from a rock. As he fell, he was turned into a partridge, which still bears the name *perdix.* Being now guilty of homicide, Daedalus had to leave Athens. He went to Crete, where his skill was employed by Minos and Pasiphaë.

Now Minos had prayed to Poseidon to send him a bull from the sea for sacrifice; when Poseidon answered his prayer, Minos was so covetous that he sacrificed another, less beautiful bull, keeping Poseidon's animal for himself. As a punishment, Poseidon caused his wife, Pasiphaë, to fall in love with the bull. To satisfy her passion, Daedalus constructed a lifelike hollow cow in which Pasiphaë was shut up to mate with the bull. Her offspring was the Minotaur. It had a man's body and the head of a bull, and was kept shut up in the Labyrinth, a mazelike prison of Daedalus' devising. We have already seen how Theseus destroyed it (p. 461). The famous discoveries at Cnossus in Crete (p. 20) have shown that the bull played a significant part in Cretan ritual, and that a common sacred object was the *labrys,* or double-headed axe, which is certainly to be connected with the word *labyrinth.* The idea of the maze has plausibly been thought to have its origin in the huge and complex palace of Cnossus, with its many passageways and endless series of rooms. Minos and Pasiphaë, like their daughters Ariadne and Phaedra, are probably divine figures; Minos was son and friend of Zeus,[28] while Pasiphaë (All Shining) was the daughter of Helius.

The Flight of Icarus

Daedalus eventually tired of his life in Crete, but Minos would not let him go. He therefore contrived feathered wings, held together by wax, by means of which he and his son Icarus could escape. As they flew high above the sea, Icarus ignored his father's warning not to fly too close to the sun, and as the wax on his wings melted he fell into the sea, which thereafter was called *Mare Icarium* (see Color Plate 20). The story is told by Ovid *(Metamorphoses* 8. 200–230):

 When Daedalus the craftsman had finished [making the wings], he balanced his body between the twin wings and by moving them hung suspended in air. He also gave instructions to his son, saying: "Icarus, I advise you to take a middle course. If you fly too low, the sea will soak the wings; if you fly too high, the sun's heat will burn them. Fly between sea and sun! Take the course along which I shall lead you."

As he gave the instructions for flying, he fitted the novel wings to Icarus' shoulders. While he worked and gave his advice, the old man's face was wet with tears, and his hands trembled with a father's anxiety. For the last time, he kissed his son and rose into the air upon his wings. He led the way in flight and was anxious for his companion, like a bird that leads its young from the nest into the air. He encouraged Icarus to follow and showed him the skills that were to destroy him; he moved his wings and looked back at those of his son. Some fisherman with trembling rod, or shepherd leaning on his crook, or farmer resting on his plow saw them and was amazed, and believed that those who could travel through the air were gods.

Now Juno's Samos was on the left (they had already passed Delos and Paros), and Lebinthos and Calymne, rich in honey, were on the right, when the boy began to exult in his bold flight. He left his guide and, drawn by a desire to reach the heavens, took his course too high. The burning heat of the nearby sun softened the scented wax that fastened the wings. The wax melted; Icarus moved his arms, now uncovered, and without the wings to drive him on, vainly beat the air. Even as he called upon his father's name the sea received him and from him took its name.

Daedalus himself reached Sicily, where Cocalus, king of the city of Camicus, received him.[29] Here he was pursued by Minos, who discovered him by the ruse of carrying round a spiral shell, which he asked Cocalus to have threaded. Cocalus gave the shell to Daedalus, who alone of men was ingenious enough to succeed. Minos knew that Daedalus was there when Cocalus gave him back the threaded shell. However, Daedalus still stayed out of Minos' reach, for the daughters of Cocalus drowned Minos in boiling water. There is no reliable legend about the further history or death of Daedalus.

The Family of Minos

Several of the children of Minos and Pasiphaë have their own legends; there were four sons—Catreus, Deucalion, Glaucus, and Androgeos—and four daughters, of whom only Ariadne and Phaedra have important legends.

Catreus, who became the Cretan king, had a son Althaemenes, of whom an oracle foretold that he would kill his father. Althaemenes tried to avoid his fate by leaving Crete and going to Rhodes with his sister Apemosyne.[30] She was seduced by Hermes and killed by Althaemenes as a punishment for her apparent unchastity. Catreus later came to Rhodes in search of his son; he and his party were taken for pirates, and in the ensuing skirmish he was killed by his son. When Althaemenes learned how the oracle had been fulfilled, he avoided the company of other men and was eventually swallowed up by the earth. The Rhodians honored him as a hero.

Of the other sons of Minos, Deucalion (not to be confused with Deucalion of the flood legend) became the father of Idomeneus, the Cretan leader at Troy. Glaucus as a boy fell into a vat of honey and drowned. Minos could not find him and was told by the oracle that that person who could find an exact simile for a magic calf in the herds of Minos would be able both to find Glaucus and to restore him to life. This calf changed color every four hours, from white to red to black; but the seer Polyidus most fittingly likened it to a mulberry, which changes from white to red to black as it ripens. With the help of various birds, Polyidus found Glaucus' corpse in the vat. It was placed in a tomb, and Polyidus was then shut up in the tomb and ordered to bring Glaucus back to life. While he was wondering what to do, a snake came. Polyidus killed it with his sword, where-upon another snake came, looked at the dead snake, and went away, returning with a herb which it put on the dead snake's body. The dead snake then came to life again, and Polyidus took the herb and used it on Glaucus, who likewise came to life. Even now, Minos was not satisfied; he compelled Polyidus to teach Glaucus the seer's art before he would let him return home to Argos. Polyidus obeyed, but as he left, he told Glaucus to spit into his mouth, whereupon Glaucus forgot all that he had learned.[31]

Androgeos was killed in Attica, and his death led to Minos' expedi-tion and the attack on Megara. The king of Megara, Nisus, had a purple lock of hair, which was the city's talisman, for the city would fall if the lock were cut off. Now Scylla, daughter of Nisus, fell in love with Minos (whom she could see from the city walls). To please him she cut off her father's purple lock and brought it to Minos. When the city fell, Minos rejected Scylla and sailed away; she clung to the stern of his ship and was turned into a sea bird called *ciris*,[32] while Nisus turned into a sea eagle, forever pursuing her.

THE ARGONAUTS

Introduction: The Minyae

The saga of the Argonauts covers much of the Greek world in its geographical scope and includes many of the leading Greek heroes of the age before the Trojan War. The crew of the *Argo* included the flower of Greece, descendants of gods and ancestors of Greek nobles. They are often referred to as Minyae, and among cities that claimed Minyan descent were Iolcus in Thessaly and Miletus in Ionia. Jason belonged to the ruling family of Iolcus, and the Euxine Sea (i.e., the Black Sea), where the main part of the saga takes place, was an area particularly colonized by the Milesians.

The name *Minyae* therefore tells us something about the origin of the saga. Homer calls the *Argo* "all men's concern," reflecting the adventures of the seamen of Mycenaean Greece. Later additions reflect the expansion of the Greeks into the Black Sea area from the eighth century onward. Folktale elements can be seen in the name *Aea* (which means no more than "land") that Homer uses for the country to which the *Argo* sailed, and its king, Aeëtes (Man of the Land). It is a mysterious land on the edge of the world, a suitable setting for a story in which magic and miracle play a big part. The folktale element can further be distinguished in the formal outline of the legend, where a hero is set a number of impossible tasks that he performs unscathed, helped by the local princess, whom he then marries.[1]

THE GOLDEN
FLEECE

The saga concerns the quest for the Golden Fleece by Jason and the crew of the *Argo*. The Boeotian king Athamas took as his first wife Nephele, whose name means "cloud." After bearing Athamas two children, Phrixus and Helle, she returned to the sky. Athamas then married Ino, one of the daughters of Cadmus, who attempted to destroy her stepchildren. She also persuaded the Boeotian women to parch the seed grain so that when it was sown nothing grew.

In the ensuing famine, Athamas sent to Delphi for advice, but Ino suborned the envoys to report that the god advised Athamas to sacrifice Phrixus if he wanted the famine to end. As he was about to perform the sacrifice, Nephele caught Phrixus and Helle up to the sky and set them on a golden-fleeced ram that Hermes had given her. The ram carried them eastward through the heavens. Above the straits between Europe and Asia (the Dardanelles), Helle fell off and drowned, and the straits were called the Hellespont after her. Phrixus continued his flight and came to Colchis, at the eastern end of the Black Sea, where King Aeëtes (son of Helius and brother of Circe and Pasiphaë) received him with kindness and gave him his elder daughter, Chalciope, as wife. Phrixus sacrificed the ram to Zeus Phyxius (i.e., Zeus as god of escape) and gave the Golden Fleece to Aeëtes, who hung it up on an oak tree in a grove sacred to Ares, where it was guarded by a never-sleeping serpent. Phrixus himself lived on at Colchis, where he finally died; his four sons by Chalciope—Argus, Melas, Phrontis, and Cytisorus—play a minor part in the Argonauts' saga. The fleece, a golden treasure guarded by a dragon, became a goal for a hero's quest.

Jason and Pelias

Cretheus, brother of Athamas, was king of Iolcus. At his death his stepson Pelias (son of Poseidon and Tyro, wife of Cretheus) usurped the throne and deposed the rightful heir, Aeson, son of Cretheus and Tyro and father of Jason. Jason's mother, Polymede,[2] sent the boy away to the hills to be educated by the centaur Chiron and cared for by Chiron's mother, Philyra. After twenty years Jason returned to Iolcus to claim the throne that rightly belonged to his family. Pelias knew that he was fated to be killed by a descendant of Aeolus, and the Delphic oracle had warned him to "beware of the man with one sandal." He therefore realized that his fate was approaching when Jason appeared wearing one sandal.

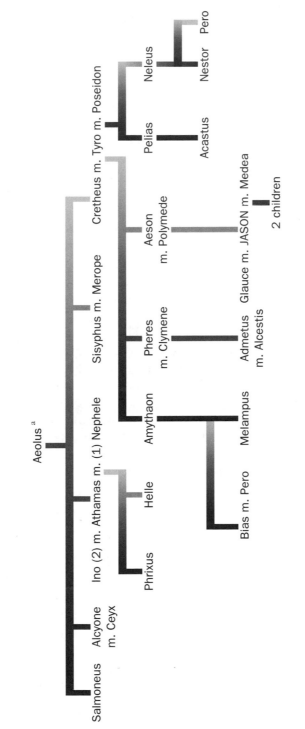

[a] This Aeolus was the son of Hellen and is to be distinguished from Aeolus, the king of the winds.

Figure 22.1. The Family of Jason

On the way down from the hills, Jason had carried an old woman across the river Anaurus in full spate, losing one sandal as he tried to get a foothold in the mud. The old woman was the goddess Hera, who thereafter favored him, just as she remained hostile to Pelias, who had neglected to sacrifice to her. Pelias promised to yield the throne as soon as Jason brought him the Golden Fleece, which Phrixus, appearing to him in a dream, had ordered him to obtain. Whether for this reason or for some other, Jason readily undertook the task.

The Argonauts

In preparation for the expedition, the *Argo* was built, "which . . . first through the Euxine seas bore all the flower of Greece" (Spenser, *Faerie Queen* 2. 12. 44). Its name means "swift," and it was built by Argus, son of Arestor, with the help of Athena. In its bows she put a piece of wood made from an oak of Dodona (where there was an oracle of Zeus), which had the power of speech.

The crew came from all over Greece, motivated by the heroic quality of *arete* (Pindar, *Pythian Odes* 4. 185–188):

Hera kindled all-persuading sweet desire in the sons of gods for the ship *Argo,* so that none should be left behind to nurse a life without danger at his mother's side, but rather that he should find even against death the fairest antidote in his own courage along with others of his age.

Lists of the names of the Argonauts vary, since the Greeks of later ages were eager to claim an Argonaut for an ancestor. Two heroes who figure prominently in all the lists, Orpheus and Heracles, have no place in the original story. The former is a post-Homeric figure, and the latter as the most important of the Greek heroes, could hardly be left out of a saga that occurred in his own lifetime. He refused to accept the leadership, in favor of Jason, and he disappeared from the expedition before the *Argo* had even reached the Black Sea.

Of the fifty or so names included among the Argonauts certain groups stand out. These are the heroes from Thessaly, such as Jason, and those from the Peloponnese, such as Augeas, king of Elis; a third group consists of Meleager and other heroes who took part in the Calydonian boar hunt; a fourth includes the parents of Trojan War heroes, such as Peleus (father of Achilles), Telamon (father of Ajax Telamonius), Oileus (father of Ajax the Less), and Nauplius (father of Palamedes).

Some of the Argonauts had special gifts. These were the seers Idmon and Mopsus; Castor and Polydeuces, excellent respectively as horseman and boxer, with their later enemies, Idas and Lynceus, the latter of whom had such keen sight that he could see even beneath the earth; Periclymenus, son of Neleus, who could take whatever shape he liked in battle (this was Poseidon's gift); Euphemus, son of Poseidon, who could run so fast over the waves of the sea that his feet stayed dry; Zetes and Calaïs, the winged sons of Boreas; Argus, the skilled shipwright; finally, the helmsman, Tiphys. Of these, only Polydeuces, Zetes, Calaïs, Argus, and Tiphys have any significant part in the legend as we now have it. Originally the individual Argonauts must have used their gifts to help Jason perform his otherwise impossible tasks.

THE VOYAGE TO COLCHIS

Hypsipyle and the Lemnian Women

After leaving Iolcus, the Argonauts sailed to the island of Lemnos, where they found only women, led by their queen, Hypsipyle. Aphrodite had punished them for neglecting her worship and had made them unattractive to their husbands. The men therefore had taken Thracian concubines whom they had captured in war. In revenge, the Lemnian women murdered every male on the island, with the exception of the king, Thoas, who was son of Dionysus and father of Hypsipyle. Hypsipyle first hid him in the temple of Dionysus and then put him in a chest in which he floated to the land of the Tauri (i.e., southern Russia) and there became a priest of Artemis. Meanwhile the Lemnian women received the Argonauts, who stayed on the island for a year. Among the many children born as a result of their stay were the twin sons of Jason and Hypsipyle, Euneos and Thoas (or Nebrophonus). After the departure of Jason, Hypsipyle's deception in saving Thoas was discovered and she was driven from the island. Eventually she was captured by pirates and sold into slavery, becoming the servant of Lycurgus, king of Nemea.

In Greece, Hypsipyle became the nurse of the child of Lycurgus, Opheltes (see p. 330). She was eventually brought back to Lemnos by her sons. As a mythological figure Hypsipyle is significant as the queen of a society from which males have been driven out and because of her connection with the founding of the Nemean Games in honor of Opheltes. The Roman epic poet Statius devoted a long episode of his *Thebaid* to her story, as did his contemporary Valerius Flaccus, in his epic *Argonautica*. Ovid made her a romantically deserted heroine in his *Heroides*.

Cyzicus and Cios

After touching at Samothrace, where they were initiated into the mysteries, the Argonauts sailed on to the Propontis and put in at Cyzicus, where the Doliones lived under King Cyzicus, who received them well. In return for this hospitality, Heracles killed the earthborn giants who lived nearby. The Argonauts were driven back to Cyzicus

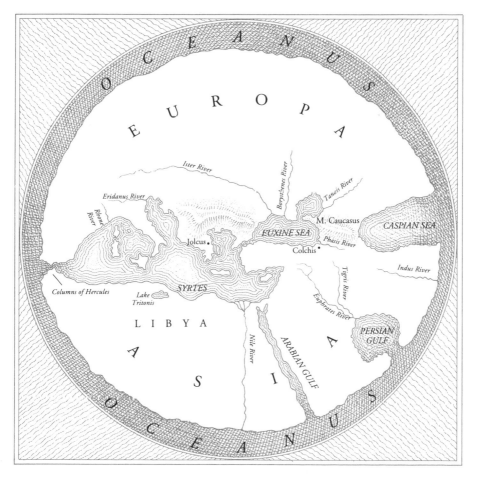

Figure 22.2. Map of the World According to the Ideas of Hecataeus of Miletus (ca. 500 B.C.). The River of Ocean is assumed to run around the edge of the inhabited world, which is divided into Europe and Asia. (© *Laszlo Kubinyi, 1994.*)

by contrary winds, and in a night battle (for the Doliones took them for night raiders) they killed the king. Next day they helped bury Cyzicus before sailing off again.

Their next port of call was Cios, farther eastward along the Asiatic shore of the Propontis, where they landed so that Heracles could replace his broken oar. Here Hylas was lost and Heracles left the expedition (see p. 434).

Amycus

Next the Argonauts passed into the Euxine (the Black Sea) and came to the land of the Bebryces, a Bithynian tribe whose custom was to compel strangers to box with their king, Amycus, a son of Poseidon, who had never lost a boxing match. Polydeuces fought Amycus and killed him.

Phineus and the Harpies and the Symplegades

Next they came to Salmydessus on the Euxine shore of Thrace, where they were received by King Phineus, a blind prophet.[3] He was tormented by the Harpies, two winged monsters (their name means "the snatchers") who, every time a meal was set before him, swooped down upon it, snatched away most of the food, and fouled the rest. When the Harpies next appeared, Zetes and Calaïs, the winged sons of Boreas, pursued them with drawn swords to the Strophades Islands, where Iris put an end to the chase by making the sons of Boreas return and the Harpies swear never to go near Phineus again. Phineus foretold the rest of the voyage to the Argonauts and forewarned them of its dangers. He told them of the the Symplegades (Clashing Rocks), two huge rocks near the western end of the Black Sea that clashed together driven by the force of the winds. Nothing had ever yet passed between them, and it was fated that they should remain fixed once a ship had made the passage. Phineus advised the Argonauts to release a dove, and if it succeeded in flying between the rocks, then they themselves were to row hard between them as they recoiled. If it failed, they were to turn back. In the event, the dove was successful and the Argonauts, with the help of Athena (or Hera), got through before the rocks clashed for the last time, losing part of the ship's stern ornament. The Symplegades remained fixed, never to threaten seafarers again.[4]

The Voyage through the Euxine Sea

Not far along the Asiatic coast of the Euxine lived the Mariandyni, whose king, Lycus, received the Argonauts hospitably. Here Idmon was killed by a boar, and the helmsman, Tiphys, died. Nevertheless, with the Arcadian hero Ancaeus, son of Lycurgus, as the new helmsman, they sailed on past the land of the Amazons and that of the iron-working Chalybes and came to the Island of Ares, where the Stymphalian Birds (frightened away from Greece by Heracles in his sixth labor) now lived. These they kept at bay by clashing their shields together. Here they also found Phrixus' four sons, shipwrecked during an attempted voyage from Colchis to Boeotia. They took them on board the *Argo* and found them of no little help when they reached Colchis. Finally, they sailed up the river Phasis to Colchis.

JASON
AT COLCHIS

Jason's Tasks

At Colchis, Aeëtes was prepared to let Jason take the fleece only if he first performed a series of impossible tasks. These were to yoke a pair of brazen-footed, fire breathing bulls, the gift of Hephaestus to Aeëtes, and with them plow a large field and sow it with dragon's teeth, from which would spring up armed men, whom he would then have to kill.[5]

Medea's Role

Medea, Aeëtes' younger daughter, now enters the saga, and brings to it elements of magic and folktale. Through the agency of Hera and Aphrodite, she fell in love with Jason and agreed to help him at the request of Chalciope, mother of Argus (who had returned to Colchis with the Argonauts). She was herself priestess of Hecate, as skilled in magic as her aunt Circe. She gave Jason a magic ointment that would protect him from harm by fire or iron for the space of a day. So he plowed the field with the fire-breathing bulls, and he threw a stone among the armed men who sprang from the dragon's teeth to set them fighting one another. Then he took the fleece, with Medea's help, drugging the serpent with herbs that she had provided.

Euripides, however, in his tragedy *Medea,* gives Medea a larger part in performing the tasks and gaining the fleece. She, rather than Jason, is the dragonslayer, as she reminds Jason (*Medea* 476–482):

> I saved you, as all the Greeks know who embarked with you on the ship *Argo*, when you were sent to master the fire-breathing bulls with yokes and sow the death-bringing field. I killed the serpent, which unsleeping guarded the golden fleece, twining its many coils around it, and I brought you the light of salvation.

In the vase-painting reproduced on p. 481 Jason's part is even less heroic, as he hangs limply from the jaws of the serpent while Athena (not Medea) stands before him.

Ovid's Narrative

Ovid's account restores Jason's heroic stature. It begins the day after Medea's meeting with Jason at the shrine of Hecate (*Metamorphoses* 7. 100–158):

> The next dawn had put to flight the gleaming stars when the people assembled in Mars' sacred field and took their place on the higher ground. The king himself sat enthroned among his army, conspicuous by his purple robe and ivory scepter. The brazen-footed bulls puffed forth fire from their adamantine nostrils, and the grass burned at the touch of their breath. . . . Yet Jason faced them; with threatening look, they turned their awesome faces toward him as he came, their horns tipped with iron; with their cloven hooves they pounded the dusty earth and filled the place with their bellowing and clouds of smoke. The Argonauts were petrified with fear. On came Jason and felt not their fiery breath, so great was the power of [Medea's] drugs. He stroked their deep dewlaps with fearless hand and compelled them, driven beneath the yoke, to draw the plow's heavy weight and tear open the soil as yet unplowed. The Colchians were amazed, while the Argonauts shouted encouragement and strengthened Jason's spirits.
>
> Next he took the serpent's teeth in a bronze helmet and sowed them in the plowed field. The soil softened the seed, which had been smeared with strong poison, and the teeth grew and became new bodies. Just as a baby takes on human form in its mother's womb and inside its whole body grows in due proportion, only to issue into the outside world when it is fully formed, so, when the forms of men had been made in the womb of the pregnant earth, they rose from the mother-furrows, and, yet more miraculously, at their birth clashed their weapons.

Jason Is Disgorged by the Dragon That Guards the Golden Fleece. Athenian red-figure cup by Douris, ca. 470 B.C.; diameter $11\frac{3}{4}$ in. Athena (not Medea) watches the bearded dragon disgorge Jason. She holds an owl and wears the aegis. The fleece hangs on the tree in the background. There are no literary sources for this version of the myth. *(Museo di Villa Giulia, Rome, Italy. Courtesy of Alinari/Art Resource, New York.)*

When the Greeks saw these warriors preparing to hurl their sharp spears at the head of the young Thessalian, their eyes and spirits were lowered by fear. Medea, too, who had made him safe from attack, grew pale when she saw so many enemies attacking the solitary young hero. . . . Jason threw a heavy rock into the middle of the enemy and turned their attack from himself to them: the earthborn brothers killed each other and fell in civil war. The Greeks applauded and eagerly embraced the victor.

It remained yet to put to sleep with drugs the wakeful serpent. It was the fearsome guardian of the golden tree, a monster with a crest, three tongues, and curved teeth. This serpent Aeson's heroic son fed with a soporific herb and repeated thrice a charm that brought peaceful sleep. When sleep came upon those eyes that it had not visited before, Jason took the gold, and in the pride of his spoils, took her who had made possible his success, a second prize. Victorious he returned to the harbor of Iolcus with his wife.

THE RETURN
OF THE ARGONAUTS

Pindar's Narrative

Ovid's narrative focuses upon Jason the hero, winner not only of the fleece, the prize of his quest, but also of the princess Medea. He set sail with her, pursued by the Colchians under the leadership of Medea's brother, Apsyrtus, whom he killed in an ambush near the mouth of the Danube.[6] Pindar gives the earliest continuous account of the capture of the fleece and the return journey. The poem is addressed to Arcesilas, king of Cyrene and winner of the chariot race at Delphi in 462.[7] Pindar's narrative begins after Jason has successfully completed plowing with the fire-breathing bulls (*Pythian Odes* 4. 239–254):

 His companions stretched out their welcoming hands to the valiant hero, and they crowned him with garlands of grass and congratulated him with honeyed words. Then [Aeëtes] the wonderful child of the Sun told him of the shining fleece, where the knives of Phrixus had stretched it out. And he did not expect that Jason would complete that labor. For the fleece lay in a thicket, the lair of a serpent, held in its fearsome jaws, and the serpent in thickness and length was greater than a fifty-oared ship which the blows of iron have built.

He killed the grey-eyed spotted serpent, O Arcesilas, and he stole Medea with her connivance, and she caused the death of Pelias.

> And they came to the waves of Oceanus and the Red Sea and the
> nation of the women of Lemnos, who had killed their men. And
> there they showed their strength in physical contests with
> clothing for the prize, and there they lay together.

Pindar's narrative is brief and clear. Jason, as befits the hero of the quest, himself performed the final labor, took the prize, and returned home with the princess. Their journey took them to the ends of the earth (for the River of Ocean encircles the earth; see Figure 22.2) and to the mysterious but unspecified "Red Sea," which in Pindar's time usually meant the Indian Ocean. Earlier in the poem, Medea had referred to the journey during which "relying on my counsel we carried the sea-ship on our shoulders for twelve days, hauling it up from Ocean, across the desert lands" (4. 26–28). Although the twelve-day portage appears to have taken place in Africa, Pindar seems rather to be describing a voyage whose details are set in a mythological landscape (indicated by the River of Ocean beyond the boundaries of the world) than in any particular lands. Lemnos is a recognizable place in the Greek world, and Pindar places the Lemnian episode during the return. He adds the celebration of the Lemnian Games, which evidently were part of the funerary ritual in honor of the dead men of Lemnos, with a cloak as the appropriate prize for a festival that marked also the resumption of marriage.

Apollonius' Narrative and the Marriage of Jason and Medea

Apollonius of Rhodes takes the Argonauts up the Danube, across to the head of the Adriatic, then up the mythical Eridanus River and across to the Rhone, down which they sailed to the Mediterranean Sea. Here they sailed to the western coast of Italy, where they visited Circe (the aunt of Medea), who purified Jason and Medea from the pollution caused by Jason's murder of Apsyrtus. After this, they encountered many of the same dangers described by Odysseus—the Planctae, Scylla and Charybdis, and the Sirens.

Next they came to the land of the Phaeacians, still pursued by the Colchians. Medea appealed to Queen Arete for protection, and she and the king, Alcinoüs, agreed not to give Medea up if she were already married to Jason. That night they celebrated the marriage, and the Colchians gave up their pursuit. Resuming their journey, the Argonauts sailed to Libya, where they were stranded on the shoals of the Syrtes. They carried the *Argo* on their shoulders to Lake Tritonis (a twelve-day journey), past the garden of the Hesperides. On the way Mopsus was killed by a snake. From the lake, they made their way back to the Mediterranean, guided by the sea-god Triton.[8]

Talus

Another adventure took place off the coast of Crete. The island was guarded by the bronze giant Talus, who walked around it three times a day and kept strangers from landing by throwing rocks at them. His life depended on a membrane (or bronze nail) that closed the entrance to a vein above one ankle. If this were opened, the ichor (the divine equivalent of human blood) would flow out and he would die. The Argonauts caused this to happen and thus Talus perished.[9]

The End of the Journey

Finally the Argonauts reached Iolcus and there the saga (like the epic of Apollonius) ends. Jason handed the fleece over to Pelias, and he dedicated the *Argo* to Poseidon at the Isthmus of Corinth. Years later, he was struck on the head and killed by a piece of timber from its stern that fell upon him.

The geographical details of the return of the Argonauts are confused and largely fanciful. The time when the saga was taking its final form (i.e., in the archaic period, before the sixth century) was one of expansion and discovery in the Greek world, when Greeks traveled far to the east and west for trade and colonization, venturing as far as Russia and North Africa. The voyage of the *Argo* perhaps recalls actual voyages, but it is impossible to attempt to match details from Pindar and Apollonius with actual places.[10]

JASON AND MEDEA IN GREECE

Iolcus

At Iolcus, Pelias refused to honor his pact with Jason, and Medea therefore contrived to cause his death. Making a display of her magic arts she rejuvenated Jason's father, Aeson, by cutting him up and boiling him in a cauldron along with magic herbs, and then rejuvenated an old ram as well. Persuaded by these examples, the daughters of Pelias tried to rejuvenate their father in the same way. But Medea did not give them the magic herbs, and their attempt led only to his death.

Corinth

Thus Jason was revenged on Pelias, but he did not gain the throne of Iolcus, for, being defiled by the murder of Pelias, he and Medea were driven out of the city by Acastus, son of Pelias. They went to Corinth, the setting for Euripides' tragedy *Medea*. The connection between Medea and Corinth was made as early as the eighth century by the Corinthian poet Eumelos. In his version, Aeëtes and his brother Aloeus were the sons of Helius and Antiope. Helius divided his lands between the brothers, so that Aloeus inherited Arcadia and Aeëtes received "Ephyra," which Eumelos identified with Corinth. Aeëtes then went to Colchis, leaving Corinth in the hands of a regent. Later the Corinthians summoned Medea from Iolcus to be their queen. Thus Jason became king of Corinth through his marriage with Medea, who meanwhile had resisted the advances of Zeus out of respect for Hera (who was especially worshiped at Corinth). As a reward, Hera promised to make Medea's children immortal. Medea therefore concealed her children in the sanctuary of Hera, believing that in this way she would make them immortal, but they died and were honored with a cult. Medea refers to this in her final speech to Jason in Euripides' tragedy (*Medea* 1378–1383):

 I shall bury them with my hand, carrying them into the sanctuary of Hera Akraia [Hera of the Acropolis], so that none of my enemies can violate them by digging up their graves. And I shall impose upon this land of Sisyphus [Corinth] a solemn feast and ritual for the future, in return for this impious murder.

The death of the children of Jason and Medea therefore was a central feature in the original myth.

Another variant, however, named Creon as king of Corinth and the enemy of Medea, who killed him and left her children in the sanctuary of Hera when she fled to Athens. They were killed by Creon's family, who said that Medea had killed them. This version was the foundation of Euripides' powerful drama, in which Jason and Medea lived in Corinth as exiles from Iolcus. Jason divorced Medea to marry Glauce (also called Creusa), the daughter of King Creon. In revenge, Medea sent her two children with a robe and a crown as wedding gifts to Glauce. The magic ointment with which Medea had smeared the gifts burned Glauce and Creon to death. After this Medea killed her children as a final act of vengeance against Jason and escaped to Athens in a chariot drawn by winged dragons provided by her grandfather Helius. In the final scene of the drama, Medea appears in the chariot

Medea, by Eduardo Paolozzi (b. 1924). Welded aluminum, 1964; height 81 in. The machine parts threateningly imply the destructive power of the barbarian princess. The mythological title suggests an allegorical meaning for the work without precise narrative content. *(Courtesy of Rijksmuseum Kröller-Müller, Otterlo, Netherlands.)*

high above the stage holding the bodies of her murdered children, triumphing over Jason and foretelling his miserable end. Jason lived on at Corinth, and Medea was given asylum at Athens by King Aegeus.

Athens

While at Athens, Medea was said to have become the mother of Medus by Aegeus. Later she nearly caused Aegeus to poison his son Theseus (see p. 460). Failing in this, she fled from Athens to Persia, where

Medea Leaves Corinth in a Chariot Drawn by Dragons. South Italian Krater, attributed to the Policoro Painter, ca. 400 B.C.; height 20¼ in. Medea, wearing oriental cap and dress drives a chariot sent by the Sun, whose rays encircle her. Winged Furies look down on the human figures below—on the left, Jason railing at Medea, and on the right the children's tutor and Medea's nurse mourning over the bodies of the two children, which are draped across an altar. A spotted feline reacts energetically to the dragons. The painting represents the final scene of Euripides' *Medea. (The Medea Krater. Earthenware with slip decoration and added red, white, and yellow, late 5th–early 4th century B.C. © The Cleveland Museum of Art, Leonard C. Hanna Jr. Fund, 91.1.)*

Medus established the kingdom of Media. Medea herself eventually returned to Colchis, and the rest of her legend is lost in the ingenious fancies of individual authors.

INTERPRETATIONS OF THE SAGA

The Argonauts in Later Literature

The saga of Jason and the Argonauts has been filtered through literary interpretations as much as any other Greek saga. It was known to Homer (who does not mention Medea) and it formed part of the epics of the eighth-century Corinthian poet Eumelos. In the third century B.C. it was the subject of the epic *Argonautica* of Apollonius of Rhodes, and this was translated or adapted by more than one Roman epic poet. The unfinished *Argonautica* of Valerius Flaccus, dating from the second half of the first century A.D., includes much of Apollonius' narrative, to which Valerius added episodes of his own, including the rescue of Hesione by Hercules and Telamon (see pp. 358 and 428). Statius, as we noted above, included a lengthy account of the legend of Hypsipyle in his *Thebaid*.

In drama, the *Medea* of Euripides has been a powerful influence, inspiring tragedies by Ovid (now lost) and Seneca (which survives), and in our own century, by Robinson Jeffers (*Medea*, 1946), to say nothing of many versions by French and German playwrights. The saga appealed especially to the Victorians. William Morris's long narrative poem, *The Life and Death of Jason*, was published in 1867 and soon became popular. Its seventeen books cover the whole of Jason's saga, including the events in Corinth and his death. It owes as much, however, to Morris's feeling for medieval chivalry as to the classical epics, and Jason is a less ambiguous hero than he is in Apollonius or Euripides. Episodes from the saga were brilliantly narrated in Nathaniel Hawthorne's *Tanglewood Tales* (1853) and Charles Kingsley's *The Heroes* (1855). These versions were written with a strong moral bias toward courage and adventure, and they are, as Michael Grant has happily described them, "brisk, antiseptic narratives . . . jolly good hero-worshipping yarns, without esoteric overtones or significances."[11]

The Hero's Quest

Jason's legend is better seen as a quest, on Propp's model. This view makes many of the folktale elements fall into a coherent structure. At the same time, much of the saga goes back to the earliest stages of Greek mythology, not excepting Medea, whose status as the grand-daughter of the Sun must once have been more important than her functions as a magician. By far the most powerful interpretation of her part in the saga is the tragedy of Euripides, produced at Athens in 431 B.C. While Euripides concentrates upon the psychology of Medea and explores the tensions in her relations with Jason, he also makes Medea into a quasi-divine being in the final scene, as she leaves in the chariot of the Sun. Medea is older (in terms of the development of the myth) and grander than the romantic heroine of Apollonius and Valerius Flaccus, and more formal than the driven, deserted, and clever heroine of Euripides. She and many of the other leading characters in the saga have attributes that point to elements in the myth that are both earlier and more significant than the quasi-historical tale of adventure that it has become.

MYTHS OF LOCAL HEROES AND HEROINES

23

Every district in the Greek world had its local heroes and heroines, whose legends were often associated with local cults. Some of these became famous throughout Greece, for example, Theseus of Athens and Bellerophon of Corinth. Some were important local heroes who are known for their spectacular punishments, like Ixion of Thessaly and Sisyphus of Corinth. Some, like Melampus of Thessaly, attracted folktales and cult practices that spread their fame to other areas. Some, like Ovid's Pyramus and Thisbe, have become famous because their legend has been preserved by a master storyteller like Ovid. In this chapter we discuss some of the legends that are associated with particular localities.

THESSALY

Ixion

Pindar tells the myth of Ixion, king of the Lapiths, son of Phlegyas (*Pythian Odes* 2. 21–48):

 They say that Ixion, upon the winged wheel that rolls in every direction, by the orders of the gods says this to mortals: "pay back the one who does you good with gentle recompense." He learned this clearly. For he obtained a sweet life among the children of Cronus, yet he did not long enjoy happiness. For with mad thoughts he loved Hera, whom the bed of Zeus with its many pleasures had as his portion. But Pride urged him on to overbearing folly, and soon the man obtained a special woe, suffering what was reasonable. Two crimes bring him lasting labor:

the first, because he was the first hero to shed kindred blood amongst mortals, not without clever planning; the second, that he made trial of the wife of Zeus in the deeply hidden marriage chamber. But his unlawful passion cast him into overwhelming evil when he approached the bed, since he lay beside a cloud, ignorant man, a sweet deception. For in appearance it was like the daughter of Cronus, the greatest of the daughters of the son of Uranus. The hands of Zeus put it there to deceive him, a beautiful cause of suffering. And he accomplished his own destruction, bound to the four spokes. Cast down in ineluctable fetters he proclaims his message to all. To him she [i.e., the cloud, *Nephele*] bore a monstrous child, alone, without the Graces, a solitary child that had no honor amongst human beings nor in the homes of the gods. This she nursed and named it Centaurus. And it mated with the mares in Magnesia, in the foothills of Pelion, and from them sprung a wondrous host, like both parents, below like their mother, above like their father.

We have already encountered Ixion as a sinner being punished in the Underworld (p. 290). Originally his punishment was in the sky. He was the first to shed kindred blood. He invited his father-in-law Eïoneus to come and collect the price that Ixion was to pay for his bride, Dia. Eïoneus came, but fell into a pit of burning coals that Ixion had dug and camouflaged. Since this was a new crime, no mortal was able to purify Ixion, and Zeus himself purified him, receiving him as a guest at his own hearth. Yet Ixion repaid him with a second crime, the attempt on Hera. Pindar describes the deception practiced by Zeus and the punishment of Ixion, bound to the wheel.

Centaurs and Lapiths

The cloud (Nephele) that Ixion had impregnated gave birth to the monster Centaurus, which mated with the mares that grazed the slopes of Mt. Pelion and became the father of the Centaurs, creatures with a human head and torso and the legs and body of a horse. The most famous centaur was Chiron, who differs from the others in that he was wise and gentle, skilled in medicine and music.[1] Pindar calls him the son of Cronus and the nymph Philyra. The other centaurs are generally portrayed as violent beings, and their best-known legend is that of their fight with the Thessalian tribe of the Lapiths.

The Lapith chieftain Pirithoüs was the son of Ixion, and the centaurs were invited to his wedding to Hippodamia. At the feast they got drunk and attempted to carry off the bride and the other Lapith women. The violent scene was frequently represented in Greek art, for example in the west pediment of the temple of Zeus at Olympia and in the metopes of the Parthenon at Athens. The battle is described at length in the twelfth book of Ovid's *Metamorphoses.*

Another Lapith was Caeneus. Born a girl, Caenis, she was seduced by Poseidon, who then granted her anything she wanted. She asked to be turned into a man and to become invulnerable. As a man, Caeneus set up his spear and ordered people to worship it. This impiety led Zeus to bring about his death. During the battle at the wedding of Pirithoüs and Hippodamia he was attacked by the centaurs, who buried him under the enormous pile of tree trunks that they hurled at him. Either his body was driven down into the Underworld by their weight or else a yellow-winged bird emerged from the pile, which the seer Mopsus announced to be Caeneus transformed.

Peleus

On the southern border of Thessaly lies Phthia. Its prince was Peleus, the father of Achilles. He was the son of Aeacus, king of Aegina, and brother of Telamon. For killing his half-brother Phocus he had to leave Aegina and came to Eurytion of Phthia, who purified him and gave him part of his kingdom. Peleus accompanied Eurytion on the Calydonian boar hunt (see pp. 496–497) and accidentally killed him with a javelin intended for the boar. He went into exile again, and was purified by Acastus, son of Pelias and king of Iolcus.

Now the wife of Acastus, Astydamia, fell in love with Peleus; and when he refused her advances, she accused him before her husband of trying to seduce her.[2] Rather than kill his guest, Acastus took him hunting on Mt. Pelion, where he left him asleep, but not before hiding his sword (a gift from Hephaestus) in a pile of dung. Peleus awoke to find himself surrounded by wild animals and centaurs, who would have killed him had not Chiron protected him and given him back his sword.[3]

When Zeus avoided a union with Thetis, whose son was destined to be greater than his father (see p. 108), she was given to Peleus because of his virtue. The wedding feast was celebrated on Mt. Pelion, and all the gods and goddesses came as guests. With them came Eris (Discord) as an uninvited guest, bringing the apple that eventually led to the judgment of Paris and the Trojan War. Peleus returned to Phthia where he became the father of Achilles. Thetis soon left Peleus, angry because he interrupted her while she was making Achilles immortal.[4]

After the death of Achilles, Peleus defended Andromache at Delphi against Orestes and Hermione, who had killed his grandson Neoptolemus, the son of Achilles. At the end of Euripides' tragedy *Andromache*, Thetis reappears and promises Peleus immortality and eternal reunion with her in her ocean dwelling.

Salmoneus

A group of Thessalian stories is associated with the family of Aeolus (see Figure 22.1, p. 474). Salmoneus, a son of Aeolus, left Thessaly and founded Salmone in Elis. He dressed himself as Zeus and imitated the god's thunder and lightning by driving in a chariot with brazen vessels attached to it and hurling lighted torches, until Zeus killed him with his thunderbolt. Vergil describes his crime and fate (*Aeneid* 6. 585–594):

 I saw Salmoneus also being cruelly punished, who imitated the flames of Jupiter and the thunder of Olympus. He drove arrogantly through the Greek states and the city in the middle of Elis, riding in a chariot drawn by four horses, and he demanded that he be honored like a god. He was mad, because he tried to imitate the storm-clouds and the lightning that cannot be imitated with bronze and the clatter of horses' hooves. But Jupiter, all-powerful, hurled his thunderbolt through the thick clouds and cast him headlong down with a violent whirlwind.

Ceyx and Alcyone

Ceyx, king of Trachis and son of Eosphoros (Lucifer, the Morning Star), and his wife Alcyone, daughter of Aeolus, called themselves Zeus and Hera. There were punished by being turned into seabirds. In Ovid, however, they are romantic lovers. Ceyx left Trachis on a sea voyage and drowned during a storm. Alcyone, who had been left in Trachis, learned of her husband's death in a dream. She found his corpse washed up on the shore and in her grief she became a seabird. As she flew by the corpse and touched it, it came to life and became a bird. For seven days each winter Aeolus forbids the winds to blow while the halcyon (*alcyone*) sits on the eggs in her nest as it floats upon the waves.

Tyro

Tyro, daughter of Salmoneus, was loved by Poseidon, who disguised himself as the Thessalian river Enipeus (Homer, *Odyssey* 11. 245):

In the form of Enipeus did the Earthshaker lie by her at the mouth of the eddying river. About them rose a crested wave, mountainous in size, which hid both god and mortal woman.

The children born of this union were twins, Neleus and Pelias. Pelias became king of Iolcus, while Neleus founded Pylos (in Messene), which was sacked by Heracles. Neleus and all his sons, save only Nestor, were killed.[5]

Tyro later married her uncle Cretheus, the founder and king of Iolcus, and by him she became the mother of Aeson, Pheres, and Amythaon. Aeson was the father of Jason and Pheres, founder of Pherae, was the father of Admetus, husband of Alcestis. In order to marry Alcestis Admetus had to perform the task of harnessing a lion and a boar together to a chariot.[6]

Bias and Melampus

The children of Amythaon were Bias and Melampus (see Figure 22.1, p. 474). Melampus was a seer with the power of understanding the speech of animals. He had honored a pair of snakes killed by his servants by burning their bodies and rearing their young, who later licked his ears and so enabled him to understand the tongues of animals and birds, and from them know what was going to happen.

Bias was a suitor for the hand of Pero, daughter of Neleus, for whom the bride-price was the cattle of Phylacus, the king of Phylace (in Phthia). He appealed to Melampus for help, and Melampus agreed to get the cattle, even though he knew he would have to spend a year in prison at Phylace. The cattle were guarded by a monstrous dog, and Melampus was caught in the act of stealing them and imprisoned. After nearly a year, he heard two woodworms saying to each other that they had very nearly finished gnawing through the roof-beams of the cell. He insisted on being moved to another cell, and shortly afterward the first cell collapsed. Phylacus then set Melampus free and asked him how to cure the impotence of his son Iphiclus. Melampus agreed to tell him on condition that he be given the cattle. He sacrificed a pair of bulls, and from a vulture that was feeding on their flesh he learned that Iphiclus' debility was the result of being frightened as a child while watching his father gelding some rams. On that occasion, Phylacus had stuck the knife, still bloody, into an oak tree, and the tree's bark by now covered it over. If it could be found and the rust from its blade scraped off and put in Iphiclus' drink for ten days, his impotence would cease. All this came to pass and Iphiclus became the father of two sons, Podarces and Protesilaüs.

Melampus was given the cattle, which he drove back to Pylos and handed over to Neleus. In return he got Pero and gave her to Bias.

The myth of Melampus is like the tenth labor of Heracles. He must bring back cattle from a distant place guarded, like Geryon's Erythia or Hades itself, by a dog. Like Heracles, Melampus is the bringer of cattle and even the conqueror of death itself.[7]

Other legends of Melampus are located in the Peloponnese. According to Herodotus (2. 49), he introduced the rituals of Dionysus to Greece. At Tiryns the daughters of King Proetus resisted Dionysus, who caused them to rush over the countryside, leaving their homes and killing their children. In return for half of the kingdom, Melampus cured the madness of the daughters of Proetus by joining a group of strong young men in performing a kind of war dance although one daughter, Iphinoë, died during the pursuit. This myth was connected with the festival of the Agriania, which involved a ritual pursuit of women by night and a return the next day to the normal order of society. It was celebrated at Orchomenus and at many other places in Greece.

Amphiaraüs, a seer and one of the Seven against Thebes, was a descendant of Melampus. The wife of Proetus, Stheneboea, is prominent in the myth of Bellerophon (see pp. 503-504)

BOEOTIA

The principal myths of Boeotia are those of Thebes, involving the families of Cadmus and Laius (see Chapter 15). At Orchomenus, the daughters of Minyas resisted Dionysus and were driven mad, tearing apart one of their children, chosen by lot, and rushing out of the city. Unlike the daughters of Proetus, the Minyads did not return to normal life; they became winged creatures of the night, either owls or bats. Clymene, however, one of the daughters of Minyas, appears as the wife of five different husbands and thus becomes both the aunt of Jason (through her marriage to Pheres) and the mother (by Iasus) of Atalanta.

The Loves of Helius

As wife of Helius (the Sun), Clymene became the mother of Phaëthon (see pp. 44-45). Helius also loved the eastern princess Leucothoë, daughter of the Persian king Orchamus. Disguising himself as Eurynome, her mother, he seduced her. Another of the lovers of Helius, the Oceanid Clytië, jealous because Helius preferred Leucothoë to her, told Leucothoë's father. He buried Leucothoë and Helius was too late to save her. He shed drops of nectar on her corpse, which grew into a frankincense tree. Clytië could not persuade Helius to forgive her nor could she recover his love. She sat, following the Sun's progress with her eyes until she turned into a sunflower, which forever turns its face toward the sun.

Trophonius

The famous oracle of Trophonius was situated at Lebadeia in northern Boeotia. He is a chthonic hero (his name means "he who fosters growth") and he was therefore consulted in a subterranean setting with an awesome ritual. His legend is similar to the story of the Egyptian Pharaoh Rhampsinitus (Rameses), which Herodotus tells (2. 121). Trophonius and his brother Agamedes were skilled builders, sons of Erginus of Orchomenus. They built for King Augeas of Elis (or, as some say, the Boeotian king Hyrieus) a treasury with a moveable stone, which they used to steal the king's treasure. In time the king set a trap for the unknown thief, and Agamedes was caught. At his own suggestion his head was cut off by Trophonius, who then escaped carrying the head. He fled to Lebadeia, where he was swallowed up by the earth and thereafter worshiped as a god.

Pindar (frags. 2–3), however, has a different story of the brothers' death, one very similar to Herodotus' story of the Argives Cleobis and Biton (see pp. 99–100). In this version, Trophonius and Agamedes built the temple of Apollo at Delphi.[8] When they asked the god for their wages, he said he would pay them on the seventh day. On that day they fell asleep, never to wake.

AETOLIA

The Calydonian Boar Hunt

Among the descendants of Aeolus was Oeneus, king of Calydon and father of Heracles' wife Deïanira; his son was Meleager. Shortly after the birth of Meleager, the Fates (Moirai) appeared before his mother, Althaea, and told her that Meleager would die when a log, which was burning on the hearth, had burned out. Althaea snatched up the log, extinguished it, and kept it in a chest. Years later, when Meleager was a young man, Oeneus offended Artemis by failing to sacrifice her share of the first fruits, and she sent a huge boar to ravage Calydon.

Meleager gathered many of the noblest Greek heroes to hunt the boar, and with them came Atalanta, daughter of the Boeotian king

Schoeneus. In the hunt, after several heroes had been killed, Atalanta was the first to wound the boar. Meleager gave it the *coup de grâce* and therefore received the boar's skin, which he presented to Atalanta. His uncles, the brothers of Althaea, were insulted at being given less honor than Atalanta, and in the ensuing quarrel Meleager killed them. In grief and anger at their deaths Althaea took the unburned log from its chest and cast it on the fire. As it burned to ashes, Meleager's life ebbed away. Both Althaea and Meleager's wife Cleopatra hanged themselves, while the women who mourned for him at his funeral became guinea fowl, which the Greeks called *meleagrides*.

This is Ovid's version of the Calydonian boar hunt. Homer, however, says that Artemis sent the boar to ravage the land during a war between the Calydonians and the Curetes. Meleager killed it and led the Calydonians in the battle against the Curetes over the boar's body. But his mother Althaea cursed him "because of the murder of her brother" and called on Hades to kill him (*Iliad* 9. 553–572). Meleager withdrew in anger. Then he relented, went back into battle and saved Calydon. Homer says that the Calydonians did not reward him as they had promised, and he implies that Meleager died as a result of Althaea's curse.

In the Underworld, Meleager's ghost talked with Heracles, and in Bacchylides' fifth *Epinician Ode* (93–154) he tells Heracles his story,

The François Vase. (Overleaf). Attic black-figure krater by the potter Ergotimos and the painter Kletias, ca. 575 B.C.; height 30 in. There are four bands of mythological scenes, a fifth band with plants and animals, a battle of pygmies and cranes on the foot, and more figures, including Ajax carrying the corpse of Achilles, on the handles. *(Detail 1)* The first detail shows the top bands on one side: Meleager and Peleus thrust at the Calydonian boar with their spears, with Atalanta and Milanion behind them. A dead hound and hunter lie on the ground, and other hunters (all named) attack or prepare to attack the beast. The band below shows the chariot race from the funeral games for Patroclus: Diomedes leads Damasippus, and the prize, a tripod, is shown below to the left. *(Detail 2)* The second detail shows the top bands on the other side: Theseus and the Athenian boys and girls (thirteen in the complete band) begin the Crane dance (see p. 463) that celebrates their release, as the sailors in the Athenian ship that will take them from Crete cheer. One sailor swims eagerly to land. In the band immediately below is the battle of Centaurs and Lapiths. *(Detail 3)* In the third detail, the band below the chariot race shows the wedding procession of Peleus and Thetis, who are on the chariot to the left. The lower band shows Achilles pursuing Troilus: on the left is the fountain-house where Polyxena (sister of Troilus) had been drawing water. To its right a Trojan woman gesticulates in alarm, and next to her (in order) are Thetis, Hermes, and Athena, the latter urging on Achilles (the top half of whose body is missing). Troilus rides a horse beside a second riderless horse, and beneath lies Polyxena's amphora, which she has dropped in her flight. She runs in front of Troilus (her top half is missing) toward the walls of Troy, from which two armed warriors, Hector and Polites, are emerging. In front of Troy sits Priam, who is receiving a report from Antenor about the danger to Troilus. *(Museo Archeologico, Florence. Photograph courtesy of Hirmer Verlag, München)*.

Detail 1

Detail 2

Detail 3

in which the Homeric details of the boar and the battle with the Curetes are combined with the burning log:

 There [i.e., in the battle with the Curetes] I killed with many others Iphiclus and Aphares, my mother's swift brothers; for bold Ares does not distinguish a friend in war, but blind are the weapons hurled from one's hands. My mother, ill-fated and unfearing woman, planned my death. She burned the log that brought me a speedy death, taking it from the cunningly made chest. It had the *Moira* [i.e., allotted portion] fated to be the limit of my life. And my sweet life ebbed, and I knew that I was losing my strength—alas!—and unhappily I wept as I breathed my last, leaving lovely youth.

In this version, although Meleager accidentally kills his uncles in battle, their sister still avenges their death, her ties to her father's family being even stronger than those to her son. As Bacchylides also tells us, Heracles responded to Meleager's story with a promise to marry Deïanira, Meleager's sister, when he returned to the world of the living (see p. 430).

Nowhere in Homer or Bacchylides is there any mention of Atalanta, nor is there any complete account of her part in the legend earlier than Ovid. She appears in the François Vase, which was made in about 575 B.C., a century before Bacchylides' poem. About 165 years later, in 411–410, Euripides says in his play *Phoenissae* (1104–1109) that Atalanta's son, Parthenopaeus, one of the seven heroes who attacked Thebes, had the device on his shield of "Atalanta subduing the Aetolian boar with her arrows shot from afar," whereas in the François Vase she brandishes a hunting spear and marches in the second rank, behind Meleager and Peleus. Finally, her companion on the vase is named Milanion, who wins the Boeotian Atalanta as his bride in yet another tale.

From all this we can conclude that several legends have been conflated around Meleager and Atalanta, whose myths were originally separate. Ovid created a unified narrative from these different elements.

The Boeotian Atalanta

Atalanta, daughter of the Boeotian Schoeneus, is easily confused with Atalanta, daughter of the Arcadian Iasus. She also is a virgin huntress who joins in the Calydonian boar hunt and the Argonauts' expedition. As a baby she was exposed by her father and nurtured by a bear that suckled her until some hunters found her and brought her up. Grown up, she was recognized by her father, but she refused to let him give her in marriage unless her suitor could beat her in a footrace. Those who lost were executed. After many young men had died in the attempt, Milanion (also called Hippomenes) raced her. He had three golden apples given him by Aphrodite. These he dropped one by one during the race so as to delay Atalanta. So he won the race and his wife, but in their impatience to lie together they made love in a sacred place (a precinct of either Zeus or Cybele), and for this sacrilege they were turned into a lion and lioness.

CORINTH

The Corinthian poet Eumelos identified the Homeric "Ephyra" with Corinth. Homer (*Iliad* 6. 152–159) says:

> There is a city, Ephyra, in a corner of horse-rearing Argos, and there lived Sisyphus, who was the most cunning of men, Sisyphus, son of Aeolus. He was father to Glaucus, and Glaucus was father to virtuous Bellerophon, to whom the gods gave beauty and lovely manliness. But Proetus devised evil against him in his heart and drove him out from the people of Argos, since Bellerophon was a better man than he. For Zeus had made him subject to Proetus.

Originally Ephyra was no more than a minor city in the kingdom of Argos (which includes Tiryns, normally given as the city ruled by Proetus), and its rulers, Sisyphus and his grandson Bellerophon, were minor chieftains subject to the king of Argos. By identifying Ephyra with Corinth, Eumelos magnified the status of the city and of its rulers. According to him, Sisyphus became the king of Corinth (which had been founded by the son of Helius, Aeëtes) after Medea left. Others make Sisyphus the founder of Corinth.

Sisyphus

Sisyphus, a son of Aeolus and brother of Salmoneus, Cretheus, and Athamas, came from Thessaly to Ephyra. Ino, the wife of his brother Athamas, leaped into the sea with her child Melicertes and became the sea-goddess Leucothea, while her child became the god Palaemon (see note 3 on p. 630). Melicertes' body was brought ashore on the Isthmus of Corinth by a dolphin. Sisyphus found and buried it, instituting the Isthmian Games in the child's honor. At first the games were mainly religious and ritualistic; Theseus is said to have founded them a second time and thus given them the athletic character that they acquired in historical times.

The legends of Sisyphus are less concerned with him as king than as the craftiest of men. One story makes him the father of Odysseus, whose mother, Anticlea, he seduced before she married Laertes. Anticlea's father was the master-thief Autolycus, son of Hermes, who gave him the power to steal whatever he wished undetected. For a long time he was in the habit of stealing Sisyphus' cattle until Sisyphus branded the animals on their hooves and so easily recognized and recovered those that Autolycus had stolen. The two heroes became friends, and Autolycus allowed Sisyphus to lie with Anticlea. Thus (in this version) Sisyphus, not Laertes, was really the father of Odysseus.

Sisyphus' greatest exploit was outwitting Death (Thanatos) himself. In its simplest form it is alluded to by the seventh-century poet Alcaeus of Lesbos (frag. 110. 5–10):

> For Sisyphus also, the son of Aeolus, thought that he was the cleverest of men to overpower Death. Yet, although he was crafty and crossed swirling Acheron twice (avoiding his destiny), the King [Zeus], son of Cronus, devised labor for him beneath the black earth.

Sisyphus aroused the anger of Zeus by telling the river-god Asopus that Zeus had carried off his daughter Aegina, and Zeus sent Death to carry Sisyphus off. Sisyphus chained Death, and so long as he was bound, no mortals could die. Eventually Ares freed Death and handed Sisyphus over to him, but before he went down to the Underworld, Sisyphus left instructions with his wife, Merope, not to make the customary sacrifices after his death. When Hades found that no sacrifices were being made, he sent Sisyphus back to remonstrate with Merope. So he returned to Corinth and stayed there until he died in advanced old age. It was for his revelation of Zeus' secret that he was punished in the Underworld by having to roll a huge rock uphill only to have it roll down again (see p. 276).

Sisyphus, therefore, combines a number of heroic and folktale elements in his legend. He is the founder of a city and of games and rituals in honor of a god. But he is also the trickster, peer of the master-thief Autolycus, and deceiver of Death itself.

Bellerophon

The greatest of Corinthian heroes was Bellerophon, grandson of Sisyphus. His legend is told in Homer by the Lycian leader Glaucus, when he meets Diomedes in battle. It is set both in the Argolid and in Asia Minor. Bellerophon may even have been introduced into Greek legend from the East.

Born in Corinth, he left home, perhaps because of blood-guilt after unintentionally killing a brother, and went to the court of Proetus, king of Tiryns, who purified him. There Proetus' wife Stheneboea (or Antea, as Homer calls her) fell in love with him. When he rejected her, she accused him before Proetus of trying to seduce her. Proetus therefore sent Bellerophon to his wife's father, Iobates, king of Lycia, with a sealed letter that told of Stheneboea's accusation and asked Iobates to destroy Bellerophon. Accordingly Iobates sent the hero on a number of dangerous expeditions (Homer, *Iliad* 6. 179-193):

First he bid him kill the fearsome Chimaera, which was of divine, not mortal, breed—a lion in its forepart with a serpent's tail and in the middle a goat, and it breathed fire. He killed it, trusting in the gods' signs. Next he fought the mighty Solymi, and this was his most violent battle with men. Third, he slew the warrior Amazons. And as he returned the king devised another plot against him; he chose the most valiant men in all Lycia and set them in ambush. Not one of them returned home, for gallant Bellerophon killed them all.

So when the king realized that he was truly of divine descent, he kept him there in Lycia and gave him his daughter and the half of his kingdom.

Bellerophon became the father of Hippolochus (Glaucus' father) and of Isandrus, who was killed fighting the Solymi, and of a daughter, Laodamia. She was loved by Zeus and by him became the mother of Sarpedon, whom Patroclus killed at Troy. Laodamia was "killed by Artemis in anger," and Bellerophon ended his days in sorrow; "hated by the gods he wandered over the Alean plain alone, eating out his heart and avoiding the paths of men." (Homer, *Iliad* 6. 200-202).

In Homer Bellerophon is the hero who performs certain tasks and wins the prize of a kingdom and a princess. His tragic end, to which Homer refers in vague terms, is the theme of Euripides' tragedy *Bellerophon*, in which Bellerophon tries to mount to heaven itself and fails.

Both Euripides and Pindar introduce the winged horse Pegasus into the myth of Bellerophon. Poseidon gave it to him, but he could not master it, as it stood by the Corinthian spring Pirene, until Athena appeared to him in a dream and gave him a magic bridle with golden trappings (Pindar, *Olympian Odes* 13. 63-92):

Much did he labor beside the spring in his desire to harness the offspring of the snake-girdled Gorgon, until the maiden Pallas brought him the gold-accoutred bridle, and quickly his dream became reality. "Are you sleeping," said she, "King, descendant of Aeolus? Come, take this charm to soothe the horse and sacrifice a white bull to your forefather Poseidon, the Tamer of Horses."

These were the words which the maiden with the dark aegis seemed to speak as he slept; he leaped to his feet and took the divine object that lay beside him. And strong Bellerophon, after all his efforts, caught the winged horse by putting the gentle charm around its mouth. Mounting it straightway, he brandished his arms, himself in armor of bronze. With it he slew the archer army of women, the Amazons, shooting them from the unpeopled bosom of the cold upper air, and he slew the fire-breathing Chimaera and the Solymi. His fate I shall not mention; the ancient stalls of Zeus' stable in Olympus shelter the horse.

Bellerophon, then, met his end in attempting to rise too high. This theme of Euripides' *Bellerophon* is also expressed in Pindar's words (*Isthmian Odes* 7. 60–68):

If any man sets his eye on a distant target, he is too short to reach the brass-paved home of the gods. For winged Pegasus hurled his rider Bellerophon, who wished to enter the palaces of Heaven and join Zeus' company.

Euripides also wrote a tragedy, *Stheneboea,* in which Bellerophon returned to Tiryns after his labors in Lycia and killed Stheneboea by luring her onto Pegasus and throwing her down as they flew high over the sea. For Euripides, Bellerophon's end is that of a human being who fails in a high endeavor, but originally he must have been punished, like Tantalus and Ixion, because he abused the friendship of the gods.

Arion of Lesbos

Herodotus (1. 23–24) tells the story of the musician, Arion of Lesbos. He had traveled round Greece and the Greek cities of Italy teaching the ritual of Dionysus, particularly the singing of the *dithyramb*, the sacred choral song performed in honor of the god. He was particularly favored by Periander, tyrant of Corinth, and he decided to return to Greece from Italy in a Corinthian ship. Plotting to steal the money Arion had gained from his performances in Italy, the sailors threw him overboard, allowing him first to give a final performance standing on the stern of the ship. When he jumped into the sea, a dolphin saved him and carried him on its back to the sanctuary of Poseidon at Cape Taenarum (the southern cape of the Peloponnese). From there he made his way back to Corinth, where he told Periander what had happened and appeared at Periander's behest to confound the sailors when they told him that Arion was safe in Italy.

Periander was a historical figure who ruled over Corinth around 600 B.C., and Arion was perhaps also historical. He was credited with the invention of the dithyramb. Dionysus is associated with dolphins in the myth of the sailors narrated in the seventh *Homeric Hymn* (see pp. 242–244), and Herodotus tells how there was a statue of a man on a dolphin (said to have been dedicated by Arion himself) in the temple of Poseidon at Taenarum. Thus the story of Arion is undoubtedly connected with the worship of Poseidon and Dionysus.

OTHER PELOPONNESIAN LEGENDS

Arethusa

The river-god Alpheus loved the nymph Arethusa, a follower of Artemis.[9] As he pursued her along the river bank, she prayed to Artemis, who covered her with a cloud; as the god watched the cloud, both it and the nymph melted into a stream for which Artemis cleft the earth. Flowing underground (where it was united with the waters of Alpheus) and under the sea, it emerged at Syracuse in Sicily, where it is still called by the same name, the fountain Arethusa.

Iamus

A daughter of Poseidon, Evadne, left her newborn son Iamus, whose father was Apollo, on the banks of the Alpheus. Evadne's foster father Aepytus, aware of her condition, inquired about the child at Delphi and learned that he would be the greatest of human seers. He returned, found the child (who had been miraculously fed on honey by two serpents), and brought him up. When he grew up, Poseidon and Apollo brought Iamus to Olympia, where he received the gift of prophecy. His oracle, says Pindar, was established by Heracles upon the altar of Zeus at Olympia.[10]

The Aegean islands with the most important religious cults were Delos and Samothrace. At Delos Apollo was honored, and in the mysteries on Samothrace the Cabiri were worshiped as "the great gods" (*theoi megaloi*).

Delos

Delos was the home of Anius, son of Apollo, who was both his father's priest and king of the island at the time of the Trojan War. He had three daughters, Elaïs (Olive Girl), Spermo (Seed Girl), and Oeno (Wine Girl), who received from Dionysus the power of producing, respectively, oil, grain, and wine. Agamemnon attempted to compel them to go to Troy with the Greeks to supply the army with these provisions. As they resisted and tried to escape, Dionysus turned them into white doves; ever after, doves were sacrosanct at Delos.

Ceos

Ceos was the home of Cyparissus, a boy loved by Apollo. On the island was a beautiful stag, a favorite of Cyparissus, which he accidentally killed with his javelin. As he grieved he became a tree, the cypress, ever after called by his name and associated with mourning.

A Cean girl, Cydippe, was loved by Acontius, a youth who was not her social equal. He left in her path an apple on which were inscribed the words, "I swear before Artemis to marry only Acontius." She picked it up and read the words out loud, thus binding herself by the vow. Each time her parents found a suitable husband for her, she fell so ill that she could not be married; eventually the truth was revealed, and she and Acontius were united.

Rhodes

The island of Rhodes was sacred to Helius, the Sun. When Zeus was dividing up the lands of the world among the gods, Rhodes had not yet appeared above the surface of the sea. Helius was accidentally not given a share, but he refused Zeus' offer of a redivision, for he could see the future island below the sea, and he took it as his possession when it appeared. There he loved the island's nymph Rhode, and one of her seven sons became the father of the heroes of the three principal cities of Rhodes, Camirus, Ialysus, and Lindos. Even late in historical times, the people of Rhodes threw a chariot and four horses into the sea every October, as a replacement for the old chariot and horses of the Sun that would be worn out after the labors of the summer.

Rhodes was associated with several figures of saga. From Egypt came Danaüs, who visited the island on his journey to Argos and there founded the great temple of Athena at Lindos. A son of Heracles, Tlepolemus, murdered his uncle Licymnius at Tiryns, and on the advice of Apollo fled to Rhodes. He later led the Rhodian contingent in the Trojan War. Rhodes was also the home of the Telchines, who were skilled craftsmen and metalworkers. They were also credited with having the evil eye; and for this reason (says Ovid), Zeus drowned them in the sea.

Lesbos

On the island of Lesbos lived Macareus, a son of Aeolus, whose story was told by Euripides in his lost play *Aeolus*. He fell in love with his sister Canace and by her became father of a child. When Aeolus discovered the truth, he sent Canace a sword with which to kill herself, and Macareus also committed suicide.

Cyprus

The island of Cyprus is especially associated with Aphrodite (Venus), who was worshiped particularly at Paphos. For the story of Pygmalion and Galatea, parents of Paphos, who gave his name to the city, see pp. 130–132.

In the Cypriot city of Salamis lived Anaxarete, who scorned her lover, Iphis. In despair, he hanged himself at the door of her house, yet she still showed no pity. As she was watching his funeral procession pass her house, she was turned into stone. Ovid says that her stone figure became the cult statue of Venus at Salamis, with the title of Venus the Beholder *(Venus Prospiciens)*.

Crete

Crete is the setting for Ovid's legend of Iphis, daughter of Ligdus (different from the boy Iphis who loved Anaxarete). Her mother Telethusa, when pregnant, was ordered by Ligdus to expose the baby if it proved to be a girl. Encouraged by a vision of the Egyptian goddess Isis, Telethusa kept the baby girl, giving her a name suitable for a either boy or a girl and dressing her like a boy. Thus deceived, Ligdus betrothed Iphis to another girl, Ianthe, whom Iphis did indeed come to love. On the night before they were to be married, Telethusa prayed to Isis to pity Iphis and Ianthe (for Ianthe was ignorant as yet of the real sex of her lover). The goddess heard her prayer: Iphis became a boy and next day married his Ianthe.

ASIA MINOR

Dardanus

Electra, daughter of Atlas, had two sons by Zeus, Iasion and Dardanus. On the death of Iasion in Samothrace, Dardanus sailed to the Troad, where Teucer, son of the river-god Scamander, was king. There Dardanus married the king's daughter and built a city called by his name. On the death of Teucer, the land was called Dardania and its inhabitants (as in Homer) Dardani. From Dardanus was descended the Trojan royal house.

Hero and Leander

Leander, a young man from the city of Abydos on the Asiatic shore of the Hellespont, loved Hero, priestess of Aphrodite in Sestos, on the European shore. He swam the Hellespont each night to visit her, guided by a light that she placed in a tower on the shore. One stormy night the lamp was extinguished, and Leander, bereft of its guidance, drowned. Next day his body was washed up on the shore near the tower, and Hero in grief threw herself from the tower to join her lover in death.

Baucis and Philemon

This chapter ends with three stories related by Ovid that are almost certainly not Greek in origin, although the names of the principal characters are Greek. From Phrygia comes the legend of Baucis and Philemon, a poor and pious old couple who unwittingly entertained Zeus and Hermes in their cottage. The gods, who had not been received kindly by anyone else on their visit to the earth, saved Baucis and Philemon from the flood with which they punished the rest of Phrygia, and their cottage became the gods' temple (see Color Plate 22). Being granted a wish each, they prayed that they might together

Pyramus and Thisbe, by Hans Wechtlin (ca. 1480–ca. 1526). Chiaroscuro woodcut, ca. 1515; $10\frac{1}{2} \times 7$ in. Ovid's tale is set in a German Renaissance landscape. Thisbe comes upon Pyramus dying beneath the mulberry tree. The Latin inscription means: "The lover Pyramus at this death of Thisbe shows the power that raging Love has in his veins, clinging to his bones." (The death of Thisbe here is her supposed death.) The blindfolded Cupid on the fountain further alludes to Pyramus' love, which so blinded him to rational thought that he rashly took his own life. *(German. © The Cleveland Museum of Art, John L. Severance Fund, 50.396.)*

be priest and priestess of the shrine and die together. And so it happened; full of years, they simultaneously turned into trees, an oak and a linden.

Byblis and Caunus

Byblis, daughter of Miletus, fell in love with her brother, Caunus. Unable either to forget her love or to declare it, she wrote a letter to Caunus confessing it. In horror he left Miletus (the city named after his father), and Byblis followed him. Still unable to achieve her desire, she sank down to the ground in exhaustion and became a fountain that was called by her name.

Pyramus and Thisbe

Ovid's setting for the story of Pyramus and Thisbe is Babylon. Perhaps Cilicia in southern Asia Minor is the home of the legend, for the river Pyramus was there, and the name Thisbe was variously associated with springs in Cilicia or Cyprus.

Pyramus and Thisbe were next-door neighbors in Babylon, forbidden by their parents to marry or even to meet each other. They conversed through a crack in the common wall of their houses and arranged to meet at the tomb of Ninus outside the city. Thisbe arrived first only to be frightened by a lioness that had come to drink in a nearby fountain. As she fled, she dropped her veil, which the lioness mangled with her jaws, bloodstained from a recent kill. Pyramus came and found the footprints of the lioness and the bloodstained veil. He concluded that the lioness had eaten Thisbe and fell on his sword; as he lay dying, Thisbe returned and in grief killed herself with the same sword. They lay together in death beneath a mulberry tree, whose fruit, which before had been white, henceforward was black, in answer to Thisbe's dying prayer that it be a memorial of the tragedy.

This is one of Ovid's most beautifully told stories (*Metamorphoses* 4. 55–166), of which a paraphrase is at best a pale reflection. The structure of the tale was used by Shakespeare for the main plot of *A Midsummer Night's Dream,* with its meetings outside the city and lovers' errors, while countless people have enjoyed Shakespeare's hilarious yet pathetic burlesque of the tale presented by the "rude mechanicals" in the last act of the play.

THE

SURVIVAL OF

CLASSICAL MYTHOLOGY

THE NATURE OF
ROMAN MYTHOLOGY

24

T he fundamental differences between Greek and Roman mythology account for the dominant influence of Greek myths
over native Italian myths and Roman legends. The Italian gods
were not as generally anthropomorphic as the Olympian gods, about
whom the Greeks developed legends which they expressed in poetry
and art of great power. The Roman gods were originally associated
more with cult than with myth, and such traditional tales as were
told about them did not have the power of Greek legends. In the
third century B.C., when the first historians and epic poets began to
write in Latin, the influence of Greek literature was already dominant.
Many of the early authors were themselves Greeks, and were familiar
with Greek mythology. Thus many Roman legends are adaptations
of Greek legends, and to a varying extent they owe their present form
to sophisticated authors such as Vergil or Ovid.

Roman mythology nevertheless had an independent existence in
the cults of Roman religion and the legends of early Roman history.
The roots of Roman religion lay in the traditions of pre-Roman Italic
peoples such as the Sabines and in the Etruscans. The native Italian
gods, however, became identified with Greek gods—Saturnus with
Cronus, Jupiter with Zeus, and so on. The poet Ennius (239-169),
came from southern Italy and spoke Greek, Oscan, and Latin. He
equated the twelve principal Roman gods with the twelve Olympians
as follows:[1]

 Iuno (Hera), Vesta (Hestia), Minerva (Athena), Ceres (Demeter),
Diana (Artemis), Venus (Aphrodite), Mars (Ares), Mercurius
(Hermes), Iovis (Zeus), Neptunus (Poseidon), Vulcanus
(Hephaestus), Apollo.

Of these only Apollo is identical with his Greek counterpart. Of the others, the Italian fertility spirit, Venus, becomes the great goddess underlying the fertility of nature and human love. In contrast, the great Italian agricultural and war deity, Mars, is identified with Ares, one of the less important Olympians. The others more or less retain their relative importance.

As a result of these identifications Greek myths were transferred to Roman gods. In Ovid's *Metamorphoses*, for example, most of the myths of the Olympians are Greek, although the names of the gods are Roman. Some genuinely Roman or Italic legends, however, have been preserved in the poetry of Ovid, Vergil, and Propertius (to name the three most important poets in this respect), and in the prose writers Cicero, Varro (a polymath and antiquarian who died at the age of 89 in 27 B.C.), and Livy. The outline of other legends can be recovered from what is known of the cults and rituals of Roman divinities. Especially important in this respect is Ovid's *Fasti*, in which he describes the festivals of the first six months of the Roman calendar. He tells many legends of the gods, while describing their cults and explaining the origins of their rituals.

Legends attached to the early history of Rome are the Roman equivalent of saga. A few of these are associated with specific local heroes, of whom the most important are Aeneas and Romulus. A large group of legends associated with the early history of Rome idealized the past, and their central figures exemplify Roman virtues. Such idealizing was especially practiced in the time of Augustus (who reigned from 27 B.C. to A.D. 14), a period of reconstruction and revival of the supposed principles of the early Romans. All the authors named above as sources for Roman mythology were contemporaries of Augustus, and of them, only Varro (fifty-three years older than Augustus) and Cicero (forty-three years older) died before the Augustan reconstruction had begun.

Thus the definition of myth as a "traditional tale" has a special coloring in Roman mythology. Livy justifies the process of idealization in the "Preface" to his history (sects. 6–10):

 I do not intend to accept or deny the truth of traditional legends about events before and during the founding of the city. These are more suitable for poetic fables than for reliable historical records. But one can excuse ancient legends because they make the origins of the city more august by uniting human and divine actions. If any nation has the right to consider its origins sacred and to ascribe them to the gods, it is the Roman people, for they claim that Mars is their ancestor and the father of the founder [Romulus].

Janus, Mars, and Bellona

Among the gods of the Roman state, Janus takes first place; in formal prayers to the gods he was named first. He is a very ancient deity, and there is no equivalent for him in other mythologies. He is the god who presides over beginnings, and in this connection we preserve his name in the month that begins our year. It is likely, however, that in his earliest form he was connected with water, especially with crossing places and bridges. Thus in the city of Rome there were five shrines to Janus, all placed near crossings over the river or watercourses, and he was intimately connected with the boundaries of the earliest settlements at Rome, the approaches to which required crossing the Tiber or one of its tributary brooks. As the city expanded, these early crossing-places lost their importance, and Janus' original functions were obscured. Yet they can be detected in later times; the gates of his shrine near the Argiletum entrance to the Forum were open in time of war and closed in time of peace. They were closed by Augustus with great ceremony, for example, to mark the end of the protracted civil wars that brought him to power. In the early days of Rome, the bridges would have been broken when the city was threatened by an enemy; an analogy for opening the gates of Janus in time of war would be raising a drawbridge over a moat.

In later times, "Janus" was used not only as the name of a deity but also as a common noun (a janus), which Cicero (*De Natura Deorum* 2. 67) defined as "a crossing-place with a roadway," in this recalling the god's early functions. While Janus' significance as a god of bridges waned, he attracted to himself other functions; he was the god of going in and coming out, and therefore of doors, entrances, and archways, as well as of beginnings. In another form, as the youthful god Portunus, he was god of harbors (which are the entrances to lands from overseas) and ferries. Portunus helped the winners of the boat race in the *Aeneid*.

There are few legends of Janus; it was said that after the Sabines, under Titus Tatius, had captured the Capitol they were kept from entering the Forum by jets of boiling water that Janus caused to gush forth. The only ancient statues of Janus surviving are two four-faced marble "herms" upon the parapet of the Pons Fabricius in Rome; on coins he is portrayed with two faces, for as a god of entrances and exits he could look both before and behind.

Mars (or Mavors) was much more important as an Italian deity than Ares, his Greek equivalent. In origin he was an agricultural deity worshiped by many Italian tribes. His association with spring, the time of regeneration and growth, is shown by the use of his name for the month of March, which began the Roman year in the pre-Julian calendar. As an agricultural god, he is associated with a number of rural deities like Silvanus and Flora; the latter supposedly provided Juno with a magical flower whose touch enabled her to conceive Mars without any father. Mars sometimes has as his consort the Sabine fertility goddess Nerio, who is often identified with Minerva. Ovid tells how Mars asked Anna Perenna (the ancient goddess of the year) to act as his go-between with Nerio. After he had made love to Nerio, he found on unveiling her that his bride was none other than Anna, who was old and wrinkled and thoroughly enjoyed her deception. This, says Ovid, was the origin of jokes and obscenities at marriage parties.

Just as the Roman people turned from farming to war, so Mars became a war god, and this aspect became more important than his agricultural character. Sacrifices were offered to him before and after a battle, and a portion of the spoils was dedicated to him. The most famous of his temples at Rome was that of Mars Ultor (Mars the Avenger) vowed by Augustus at the battle of Philippi (42 B.C.) and dedicated forty years later. The Campus Martius (Field of Mars) was the open space outside the gates of the ancient city where the people assembled under arms and practiced their military skills. As the god of war, Mars often had the title Gradivus (perhaps meaning "the marcher"); he was also closely associated with the Sabine war deity Quirinus, with whom Romulus was later identified. In battle, Mars was generally accompanied by a number of lesser deities and personifications, of whom the war goddess Bellona is the best known. Bellona herself was often identified with the Greek personification of war, Enyo (connected with the title of Ares, *Enyalios*), and a temple was first dedicated to her in Rome in 296 B.C.

Mars is particularly associated with two animals, the wolf and the woodpecker. A she-wolf suckled his sons, the infants Romulus and Remus. The woodpecker, *picus*, was said in one legend to have been a Latin king Picus, whose wife was the nymph Canens (Singer). Circe, the magician, tried to seduce him, and when he rejected her, she turned him into a woodpecker. After searching in vain for him for six days and six nights, Canens wasted away into nothing more than a voice.

Jupiter

The great Italian sky-god was Jupiter, the forms of whose name are etymologically connected with those of other Indo-European sky-gods, including Zeus. At the end of the regal period (509 B.C.) the

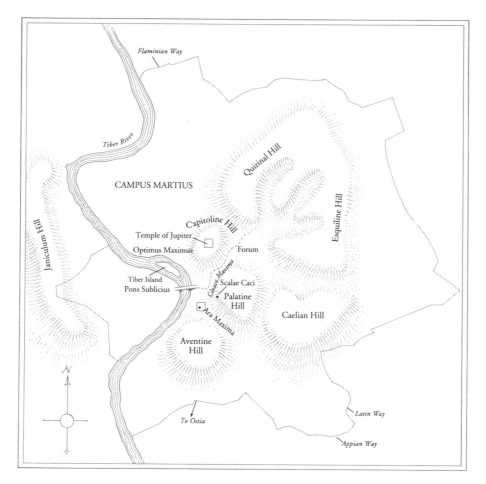

Figure 24.1. Map of Early Rome. (© *Laszlo Kubinyi, 1994.*)

temple of Jupiter Optimus Maximus was built on the Capitoline Hill and the great sky-god became localized in a temple with a statue like a Greek city god. He shared the temple with Juno, the chief Italian goddess of women, and Minerva, an Italian fertility and war goddess who at Rome was worshiped principally as the patroness of handicrafts and wisdom. These three deities formed the "Capitoline triad."

Jupiter was called by many titles. In his temple on the Capitol he was worshiped as Jupiter Optimus Maximus (Best and Greatest). The great ceremonial procession of the *Triumph* wound its way through the Forum up to this temple. The triumphing general was robed as if he were a god, proceeding in his chariot amid the cheering crowds, with his soldiers around him and his prisoners before him. On the Capitoline Hill he sacrificed to Jupiter, acknowledging by this ritual that Jupiter was the source of Roman greatness and military might.

As sky-god, Jupiter directly influenced Roman public life, in which the weather omens of thunder and lightning, his special weapons, played an important role. After lightning had struck, a ritual purification or expiatory rite was required, and Jupiter himself was said to have given King Numa the original instructions for the sacrifice. Advised by the nymph Egeria, Numa captured the two forest divinities, Picus and Faunus, on the Aventine Hill and compelled them to tell him how to summon Jupiter. When Jupiter himself came, Numa asked what objects were necessary for the expiatory rite. "A head," the god replied, and Numa interrupted with "of an onion." "Of a man," Jupiter went on, and Numa added "a hair"; finally Jupiter demanded "a life." "Of a fish," said Numa, and Jupiter good-naturedly agreed to accept these objects (the head of an onion, a human hair, and a fish) as part of the expiatory ritual. Ovid's narrative (*Fasti* 3. 285-346), which is summarized here, explains why these objects were offered instead of a human sacrifice, almost certainly the original form of expiation.

Jupiter also promised to give Numa a sign to support Rome's claim to exercise power over other communities. In full view of the people of Rome, he caused a shield (*ancile*) to fall miraculously from heaven. This *ancile* was of the archaic figure-eight shape; since it was a talisman of Roman power, Numa had eleven others made exactly like it, so that it would hard to steal the genuine *ancile*. The twelve *ancilia* were kept in the Regia (the office of the Pontifex Maximus, the official head of the hierarchy of the state religion),[2] and were used by the priests of Mars, the Salii, in the sacred war dance which they performed each spring. As they danced, they sang an ancient hymn containing the words *mamuri veturi*, whose meaning had long since been forgotten. According to tradition, the craftsman who made the eleven false *ancilia* was named Mamurius, who asked for his name to be included in the hymn as a reward.

The many titles of Jupiter indicate his supreme importance in all matters of the state's life in war and peace. As Jupiter Latiaris, he was the chief god of the Latins, worshiped by the Romans in an annual ceremony upon the Mons Albanus (the modern Monte Cavo) twenty miles from Rome. As the god before whom the most solemn oaths were sworn, he was closely associated with the goddess Fides (Good Faith) and identified with the old Sabine god Dius Fidius. Oaths sworn by Dius Fidius had to be sworn under the open sky (Jupiter's realm). The Latin deity Semo Sancus (the name comes from the same root as *sancire*, the Latin word for ratifying an oath) is also identified with Dius Fidius and Jupiter.

Another title of Jupiter is Indiges, by which he was worshiped near the river Numicus. The word *Indiges* has never been explained. It evidently refers to a state god, and the Di Indigetes were a well-known group of gods whose exact role remains unknown. Livy believed that Aeneas was worshiped as Jupiter Indiges after his death beside the river Numicus. Ovid tells the story (*Metamorphoses* 14. 598–608):

> [Venus] came to the shore at Laurentum, where the waters of the river Numicus, concealed by reeds, wind into the nearby sea. She commanded the river to wash away from Aeneas all that was mortal and to carry it away silently into the sea. The horned river-god performed the commands of Venus and purified all that was mortal of Aeneas and cleansed it with his waters. The best part of Aeneas remained. His mother [Venus] anointed the purified body with divine perfume; she touched his face with ambrosia and sweet nectar and made him a god. Him the people of Quirinus [i.e., the Romans] hailed as "Indiges," and received him with a temple and altars.

Juno

Juno, the second member of the Capitoline triad, was originally an independent Italian deity, who presided over every aspect of the life of women. She was especially associated with marriage and (as Juno Lucina) childbirth. The festival of Juno Lucina, the Matronalia, was celebrated in March as a spring festival, when all nature was being renewed. Juno was also worshiped as Juno Moneta on the Arx (Citadel), the northern peak of the Capitoline Hill. Moneta means "adviser" (from the same root as the Latin word *monere*), but the word survives in the English word "mint," for Juno's temple on the Arx was next to the Roman Mint, which was known as *ad Monetam*.

Another title of Juno was Juno Regina (Queen Juno). Livy (5. 21) describes how Juno was invited by the Romans to leave the Etruscan city of Veii after its defeat in 396 B.C. At Rome Camillus dedicated a temple in her honor on the Aventine Hill. The ritual of persuading an enemy's gods to leave their city was called *evocatio* (calling out). By accepting the invitation the goddess was believed to have come willingly to her new home in Rome, while the Etruscans were deprived of her protection.

Under the influence of Greek literature Juno, the great Italian goddess of the life of women, became the wife and sister of Jupiter. In the *Aeneid* she has a prominent role in opposing the fated success of Aeneas, but eventually Jupiter and Fate are superior and she accepts the union of the Trojan newcomers and the indigenous Italian tribes.

Minerva

Minerva, the third member of the Capitoline triad, was also an Italian deity, introduced to Rome by the Etruscans. She became identified with Athena and Athena's legends, so that it is hard to distinguish her original functions. She may have been a war goddess, for she shared her great festival, the Quinquatrus, with Mars, whose consort, the Sabine goddess Nerio, was often identified with her. Her chief importance for the Romans, however, was as the goddess of all activities involving mental skill. She was the patroness of craftspeople and skilled workers, among whom Ovid (in his invocation to Minerva in the *Fasti*) includes authors and painters.[3] She was also the goddess of schoolchildren, and the Quinquatrus was the time both of school holidays and the payment of school fees.

Divinities of Fire: Vesta, Vulcan, and Cacus

The most important of the other Roman state gods who were of Italian origin were the two concerned with fire, Vesta and Vulcan (Volcanus). Vesta (whose name is etymologically identical with the Greek Hestia) was the goddess of the hearth, the center of family life. Since the state was a community of families, it had a hearth with an ever-burning fire as the symbolic center of its life. The fire was kept alight in the round temple of Vesta in the Roman Forum and tended by the six Vestal Virgins. These were daughters of noble families, who entered the service of Vesta before their tenth birthday and remained until their fortieth year or even longer. Their life was hedged with many taboos and rituals, and their vow of chastity was strictly observed. The Vestals were treated with the highest honor and were some of the most important persons in the hierarchy of Roman state religion. Their offices and living quarters were in the Forum, next to the Regia.

The second Roman king, Numa, was said to have founded the cult of Vesta. The myths of Vesta are few and uninteresting. Ovid (*Fasti* 6. 319–338) tells how the fertility god Priapus tried to seduce her and was prevented by the braying of a donkey. He gives another version of the story (see below, pp. 527–528), in which the nymph Lotis is the intended victim of Priapus.

Closely associated with Vesta were the household spirits of the Romans, the Penates, whose name derives from the *penus*, or store cupboard, source of food and therefore symbol of the continuing life of the family. Originally the spirits on whom the life and food of the individual family depended, they became an essential part of the life of the state. The Romans were vague about their number or identity, and a useful definition is that of Servius (fourth century A.D.), "all the gods who are worshiped in the home." The Penates were originally Italian, and were especially worshiped at the Latin town of Lavinium. It was said that, when an attempt was made to remove them from Lavinium to Alba Longa, they miraculously returned to their original home. At Rome they became identified with the Trojan gods entrusted by Hector to Aeneas on the night of Troy's destruction and brought by him to Italy. Among the sacred objects kept in the *penus Vestae* (i.e., the sacred repository in the temple of Vesta) was the Palladium, the statue of the Trojan Athena given by Diomedes to one of Aeneas' followers (see the illustration on p. 547). When the temple of Vesta was burned in 241 B.C., the consul L. Caecilius Metellus earned great glory by saving the Palladium with his own hands, yet he was blinded for the act because he had looked upon a sacred object that it was not lawful for a man to see.

Vulcan (Volcanus) was the chief Italian fire-god, more important than his Greek equivalent, Hephaestus. The Greek god was the god of industrial, creative fire, while Vulcan was the god of destructive fire and a potent power to be worshiped in a city frequently ravaged by conflagrations.[4] Through his identification with Hephaestus Vulcan acquired creative attributes, shown by his other name, Mulciber (He Who Tempers). Vergil has a fine description of Vulcan's smithy deep below the Mt. Actna (*Aeneid* 8. 424–438):

The Cyclopes were working the iron in the vast cave, Brontes and Steropes and naked Pyracmon. In their hands was a thunderbolt, partly finished and partly yet to be finished, one of very many which the Father (i.e., Jupiter) hurls to the earth from all over the sky. They had put onto it three rays of twisted rainstorms, three of watery clouds, three of red fire and the winged south wind. Just then they were adding the terrifying lightning to the weapon and the penetrating flames of [Jupiter's] anger. In another part they were working on the chariot of Mars and its winged wheels, with which he stirs up men and cities. They were busily polishing the fearsome aegis, the weapon of aroused Minerva, with serpents' scales and gold. It had entwined snakes and the Gorgon's head itself turning its gaze.

The Italian fire-god, Cacus, was associated with Vulcan. Vergil narrates how he was killed by Hercules (*Aeneid* 190–267). Cacus had stolen the Cattle of Geryon from Hercules and had hidden them in his cave on the Aventine Hill. Here is the climax of the fight, when Hercules has broken open the cave of Cacus (*Aeneid* 8. 247–261):

Hercules overwhelmed Cacus from above with missiles, Cacus who had been suddenly trapped by the unexpected daylight, shut in his rocky cave and bellowing as he was not used to do. Hercules summoned up all his weapons and attacked him with branches and huge boulders. But Cacus (who had no escape from the danger) belched forth (a miracle to narrate) clouds of smoke, enveloping his cave in blind darkness and taking away the sight from Hercules' eyes. He filled the cave with the smoky blackness of night and darkness mixed with fire. Brave Hercules did not put up with this: he leaped headlong through the fire, where the waves of smoke were the thickest and the black clouds billowed through the cave. Here he held Cacus knotted in his grip, as he vainly belched forth fire in the darkness. Clinging tight he throttled him, so that his eyes burst out and no blood was left in his throat. Then the doors of the black cave were wrenched off and it was suddenly thrown open. Displayed to the sky were the stolen cattle and the theft that Cacus had denied, and the monstrous corpse was dragged out by its feet. The people could not have enough of gazing on the terrible eyes of the monster, on the face and the chest with its bristling hair and the throat with fire extinct.

Vergil's narrative ostensibly explains the origin of the worship of Hercules at the Ara Maxima, an ancient cult-site in the low-lying ground (called the Forum Boarium) between the Aventine and the Tiber. But he makes a monster of the ancient Italian fire-god, whose name survived in the *Scalae Caci* (Steps of Cacus), a pathway leading up onto the corner of the Palatine Hill that was associated with the earliest settlement on the site of Rome.

AGRICULTURAL AND FERTILITY DIVINITIES

Saturn, Ceres, and Their Associates

Saturn was an ancient god, perhaps of Etruscan origin. His temple dated from the early days of the Republic, and beneath it was the state treasury. His origins are obscure; he was an agricultural deity, and his festival, the Saturnalia, celebrated on December 17, was perhaps originally connected with the winter grain sowing. Like many other country festivals, it was accompanied by a relaxation of the normal social inhibitions. This was a prominent feature of the Saturnalia in historical times, when slaves were allowed freedom of speech. The Saturnalia came to be linked with the festival of Ops, which was celebrated two days later, and eventually the festival period lasted for a week.

Saturn was very soon identified with the Greek Cronus, and like him was believed to have ruled over a golden age. Rhea, the Greek consort of Cronus, was likewise identified with Ops, the Italian goddess of plenty, who was the partner of Saturn in popular mythology. His partner in cult, however, was the obscure Italian deity Lua. In the cult of Ops, her partner was Consus, an Italian harvest deity, whose festival, the Consualia, was celebrated in both August and December. Livy tells us that the seizure of the Sabine women took place at the games held during the Consualia.

Agricultural deities were very prominent in early Roman religion, and others besides Mars, Saturn, and their associates, were connected with the fertility of the land. The cult of Ceres at Rome went back to the earliest days of the Roman Republic, when in 493 B.C. a temple on the Aventine was dedicated to Ceres, Liber, and Libera. Ceres was identified with Demeter, Liber with Dionysus, and Libera with Kore (i.e., Persephone, Demeter's daughter). Thus the Eleusinian triad of Demeter, Kore, and Iacchus/Bacchus had its exact counterpart at Rome. The mythology of Ceres and Liber is entirely Hellenized, and the ritual of worship in their temple was Greek, even the prayers being spoken in Greek. The wine-god Liber, however, did not share in the ecstatic aspects of Dionysus.

The Aventine temple of Ceres, Liber, and Libera was also important as a political and commercial center. It was a center of plebeian activity, and was especially connected with the plebeian aediles and tribunes. In front of it was the headquarters of the state-subsidized grain supply *(statio annonae)*.

Also associated with Ceres was the Italian earth-goddess Tellus Mater, with whom she shared the festival of the sowing of the seed *(feriae sementivae)* in January. Thus the grain was watched over from seed to granary by three divinities—Ceres before it was sown, Tellus Mater when it was put in the earth, Consus when it was harvested and stored.

Two minor fertility goddesses were Flora and Pomona. The former was the goddess of flowering, especially of grain and the vine. In Ovid she is the consort of the West Wind, Zephyrus, who gave her a garden filled with flowers. Here is how she describes it (Ovid, *Fasti* 5. 209–230):

I have a fertile garden in the lands that are my wedding gift, filled with noble flowers by my husband, who said, "Be ruler, O goddess, over flowers." As soon as the dewy frost is shaken from the leaves . . . the Hours come together clothed in many colors and gather my flowers in lightly woven baskets. Then come the Graces, twining flowers into garlands. . . . I was the first to make a flower from the blood of the boy from Therapnae [Hyacinthus]. . . . You too, Narcissus, keep your name in my well-tended garden. . . . And need I tell of Crocus and Attis and Adonis, the son of Cinyras, from whose wounds I caused the flowers to spring that honor them?

In this passage Ovid uses Greek mythology to give substance to the Italian fertility goddess. The Greek figures of Zephyrus, the Seasons (in Latin, *Horae*) and Charites (Latin, *Gratiae* or Graces), and the youths who were changed into flowers, give a narrative element to Flora, who otherwise has no myths. Ovid has created a Roman mythology from the Greek stories. His description of the garden of Flora, moreover, was the inspiration for Nicolas Poussin's famous painting with this title, now in Dresden. In this work Poussin has gathered six of the young men and women who were changed into flowers and were celebrated as the subjects of Ovid's stories.

Even with divinities for whom there was no Greek equivalent, Ovid created stories in the Greek manner that gave them character and substance. Pomona, goddess of fruit that can be picked from trees, was linked by Ovid with an Etruscan deity, Vertumnus, whose name appears to be connected with the Latin word *vortere,* which means "to turn" or "to change." An old statue of Vertumnus stood not far from the Forum in Rome, the subject of a poem by Propertius, who was a contemporary of Ovid.

In Ovid's story, Pomona had a garden from which she excluded her lovers, among them Vertumnus, who could change himself into different shapes. Disguised as an old woman, he approached Pomona and advised her to marry Vertumnus. This he did so successfully (his advice included the cautionary tale of Iphis and Anaxarete, narrated earlier, p. 507) that he resumed his natural appearance as a young man and won Pomona's love. The legend of Pomona and Vertumnus has been one of the most popular of Ovid's stories and has been the subject of innumerable paintings and musical works (see Color Plate 16).

The deities who presided over the livestock of the farm were called Pales. Originally a pair, their name was later used for one deity, either male or female. The festival of Pales, the Parilia (or

Palilia), was celebrated in April and was also considered to be the anniversary of the founding of Rome.

Forest Divinities: Silvanus and Faunus

Silvanus (Forester) and Faunus (Favorer) were gods of the woods and forests. Silvanus had to be propitiated when a forest was being cleared or trees felled. In the *Aeneid* Faunus is the son of Picus and grandson of Saturn, and the father of Latinus by an Italian birth-goddess, Marica. Originally he was a woodland spirit, occasionally mischievous but generally favorable to the farmer who worshiped him. His consort (or daughter) was Fauna, who was identified with the Bona Dea (Good Goddess), a divinity worshiped only by women. Both Faunus and Silvanus were identified with the Arcadian pastoral god Pan. Faunus and Fauna were further identified with minor gods of woodland sounds because they were considered responsible for strange and sudden forest noises. Thus, in Livy, the night after a closely fought battle against the Etruscans, the Romans heard Silvanus (whom Livy here confuses with Faunus) cry out from a nearby forest that they had won the victory, with the result that the Etruscans acknowledged defeat and returned home. Faunus also had oracular powers; Latinus consulted him about the prodigies that accompanied the arrival of Aeneas in Italy, and Numa received advice from him in a time of famine.

Faunus was officially worshiped at Rome, and had a temple on the Tiber island. His festival was in December, but he was closely connected with the more famous festival of the Lupercalia, which took place in February. The Arcadian king Evander was said to have come to Rome and there to have founded the first settlement upon the Palatine Hill. On the side of the hill is a cave, the Lupercal, where the she-wolf (*lupa*) was later believed to have suckled Romulus and Remus. Here Evander worshiped his Arcadian god Pan, who was the equivalent of Faunus. Thus Faunus was connected with the Lupercalia, whose central ritual was a sacrifice in the Lupercal, at which two young noblemen were smeared with the victims' blood. They were called the *Luperci,* and after the sacrifice they ran nearly naked around the boundary of the Palatine, striking the women they met with leather straps. Barren women, it was believed, became fertile by this act.

Ovid relates a folktale explaining the nudity of the Luperci. Hercules and the Lydian queen Omphale came once to a cave where they exchanged clothes while supper was being prepared. After the meal they went to sleep, still each in the other's clothes. Meanwhile,

Faunus had determined to seduce Omphale. He entered the cave and lay with the person dressed as a girl. His reception was far from warm, and ever after he ordered his followers (i.e., the Luperci) to be naked at his cult, to prevent the repetition of so painful a mistake.

Garden Divinities: Venus and Priapus

Venus was an Italian fertility goddess, whose original functions are not known. She was worshiped in a number of places under titles that indicate that she had as much to do with luck and the favor of the gods as with beauty and fertility, and she was apparently particularly the protectress of gardens. A temple to her was dedicated at Rome in 295 B.C. with the title *Venus Obsequens* (Venus Who Is Favorable), which is also her title in Plautus' comedy *Rudens,* which takes place in front of her temple by the seashore in Libya. During the fourth century, contact with the Greek world led to identification of Venus with the Greek goddess of love, Aphrodite.

In 217, after the Roman defeat at the battle of Lake Trasimene, the dictator Quintus Fabius Maximus Cunctator consulted the Sibylline books, which ordered him to dedicate a temple on the Capitoline Hill to Venus Erycina. Eryx, at the western end of Sicily, was the site of a great temple to the Phoenician fertility goddess Astarte, who later became identified with Aphrodite and then with Venus. The dedication of the temple of Venus Erycina in 215 was significant in the development of the worship of Venus at Rome. In that year a *lectisternium* was also conducted, a festival at which the statues of the gods were laid out on couches, two to a couch, and offered a banquet while supplication was made to them. The ceremony had first been conducted at Rome in 399 for six gods. The ceremony of 215 was the first in which the twelve great gods were so honored, and Ennius' lines naming them (see p. 513) described this event. In the *lectisternium* Venus was paired with Mars. Thus she gained in status, since Mars was acknowledged as the ancestor of the Romans.

In about 55 B.C. Lucretius began his poem with an eloquent invocation to Venus as the creative principle of life. The opening lines of the poem transfer the majesty and creative power of the Greek Aphrodite to a Roman context (*De Rerum Natura* 1. 1–13):

> Mother of the descendants of Aeneas, bringer of pleasure to gods and men, nurturing Venus, beneath the gliding constellations of heaven you fill the ship-bearing sea and the fruitful lands. Through you all living things are conceived and at birth see the light of the sun. Before you, O goddess, the winds withdraw; and at your

coming, the clouds in heaven retreat. For you the variegated earth puts forth her lovely flowers, for you the waters of the sea laugh and the sky at peace shines, overspread with light. For you the West Wind, creator of life, is unbarred. You first, O goddess, and your coming do the birds of the air salute, their hearts struck by your power.

At about the time that Lucretius was writing his poem, the Roman general Pompey dedicated a temple in his theater (the first permanent stone theater at Rome) to Venus Victrix (Bringer of Victory). The family of Julius Caesar traced its ancestry back to her, and he dedicated a temple to her in his forum (which was completed by Augustus). Her connection with Troy led to her importance in the *Aeneid* as the mother of Aeneas. More than a century later, Hadrian dedicated one of Rome's most magnificent temples to the two goddesses, Venus Felix (Bringer of Success) and Roma Aeterna, thus uniting the personification of the city with its divine ancestress.

The shrine of Venus Cloacina stood in the Forum Romanum. Cloacina was presumably the goddess of the Cloaca, the Etruscan drainage system that drained the Forum area and allowed the city of Rome to develop in the low-lying ground from the sixth century onwards. How this goddess was identified with Venus is unknown. Among Italian divinities connected with the success of agriculture was Robigo, the goddess of blight, whose festival, the Robigalia, was celebrated in April. She was offered the gruesome sacrifice of a dog and a sheep so that the growing crops would not be attacked by mildew. Naming a divinity after a natural feature (good or ill) is typical of Roman religion.

The protector of gardens, Priapus, was orginally Greek. He was represented by a wooden statue, painted red, with an enormous erect phallus. His principal cult in the Greek world was at Lampsacus (a city overlooking the Hellespont), where he was offered the sacrifice of a donkey (see Color Plate 9). Ovid explains the choice of this victim in this story (*Fasti* 1. 415–440):[5]

 Red Priapus, the ornament and guardian of gardens, loved Lotis, above all the Naiads. She laughed at him scornfully. It was night, and [the Naiads], made drowsy by wine, lay in different places overcome with sleep. Lotis, just as she was, tired by play, slept farthest away on the grassy ground beneath the branches of a maple. Up rose her lover, and holding his breath he silently made his way on tiptoe to the nymph's resting place. Even now he was balancing [on tiptoe] on the distant grass, yet she still was sleeping soundly. He rejoiced; and lifting her dress from her feet, he had

happily begun to reach his longed-for goal. But look! The donkey, Silenus' mount, began ill-timed braying. Up leaped the terrified nymph and pushed Priapus away, arousing the whole wood as she fled. But the god, all too ready with his obscene member, was an object of ridicule to all by the light of the moon. The source of the noise paid the penalty with his life, and this is the victim that is pleasing to the god of the Hellespont.

Water Gods: Portunus and the Gods of Rivers and Springs

Water gods were important to the Italian farmer. Each river and spring had its deity, who needed to be propitiated by offerings. Tiberinus, god of the river Tiber, was propitiated each May when twenty-seven straw dummies, called *Argei*, were thrown into the river from the Pons Sublicius, the wooden bridge of the early city. This ceremony was attended by the *pontifices* (priests of the state religion) and the Vestal Virgins, but even the Romans did not know its origin. Propitiation of a potentially damaging god by means of dummies (substitutes for human sacrifice) is as likely an explanation as any.

Neptunus, later identified with Poseidon, was originally a freshwater divinity whose festival occurred in July, when the hot Italian summer was at its driest. Portunus also was an old Italian god, originally the god of gates *(portae)*, but later the god of harbors *(portus)*, whose temple was near the Aemilian bridge in Rome. Vergil makes him help Cloanthus to victory in the boat race in the *Aeneid* (5. 241–243). He was also identified with the Greek sea-god Palaemon, originally Melicertes (see p. 630, note 3). Both of the Roman sea-gods, therefore, were originally freshwater divinities, who acquired their attributes as sea-gods from Greek mythology.

Of the river-gods, the most important was Tiberinus, and bridging his river was a significant religious matter. The Pons Sublicius (mentioned above) was administered by the *pontifices* (whose title may originally have meant "bridge builders"), and there were various religious taboos involved in its construction and administration. Tiberinus himself plays an important role in Book 8 of the *Aeneid* when he appears to Aeneas in a dream and tells him that he has arrived at his final home. He shows him the sign of the sow and her thirty piglets, and he calms his waters so that the boat of Aeneas can move smoothly upstream to Pallanteum (*Aeneid* 8. 31–96).

Springs of running water were under the protection of the nymphs. In the Forum at Rome was the spring of Juturna, who in Vergil appears as the sister of Turnus and the victim of Jupiter's lust. She was wor-

shiped in the Forum and the Campus Martius, and the headquarters of the city's water administration lay in her precinct. Her festival was the Juturnalia. After the battle of Lake Regillus in 496 B.C. the Dioscuri (Castor and Pollux) watered their horses at her spring in the Forum. Their temple was next to her precinct.

Outside the Porta Capena at Rome were a spring and a small park dedicated to the Camenae, water-nymphs of great antiquity but unknown origin. Later they were identified with the Greek Muses. The Vestals drew water from the fountain of the Camenae for the purification of the temple of Vesta. Closely associated with the spring of the Camenae was the nymph Egeria, said to have been the counselor and consort of Numa, to whom so much of Roman religious custom was ascribed. Egeria is also found in the precinct of Diana at Aricia, and her spring was one of those that fed Lake Nemi. She was the helper of pregnant women and may indeed have once been a birth-goddess. Another nymph associated with the Camenae is Carmentis (or Carmenta), who also has the double association with water and with birth. As a water-nymph she shared the festival of Juturna, and she is sometimes named as the mother of Evander, the king of Pallanteum, an earlier city on the site of Rome. Like the Parcae (the Roman birth-goddesses identified with the three Fates) she had prophetic powers, as is indicated by her name, for *carmen* means a song or prophetic utterance.

Diana

The Italian goddess Diana was worshiped at Aricia with a cult that was established by members of the Latin League. Aricia is near Lake Nemi, which was known as "Diana's mirror," perhaps indicating her association with the moon, reflected in the waters of the lake. This cult was the starting point for Sir James Frazer's *The Golden Bough*. The priest of Diana at Aricia was a fugitive slave, who had the title of "King of the Grove" (*rex nemorensis*). He became priest by killing his predecessor in single combat, having challenged him by plucking a bough from a sacred tree. As priest he always went armed, watching for the successor who would kill him. It is likely that the sacred grove was originally an asylum for runaway slaves and the sacred bough was the branch carried by suppliants at an altar.

Diana was concerned with the life of women (especially in childbirth). She was often identified with the Italian goddess Lucina, who brought babies into the light (Latin, *lux, lucis*), although Lucina was more commonly a title of Juno.

Diana was also worshiped at Mt. Tifata near Capua. It is possible this is where she began to be identified with Artemis. Through Artemis she acquired her powers as goddess of the hunt and (as Hecate) her association with the Underworld. At Rome she was worshiped upon the Aventine Hill, and her cult was established by Servius Tullius. Like her cult at Aricia, it was originally shared by members of the Latin League, being situated outside the early city's walls. Under Augustus her status as sister of Apollo was emphasized and was dramatically expressed in Horace's *Carmen Saeculare,* sung at the celebration of the Secular Games in 17 B.C. by antiphonal choirs of boys and girls, standing respectively upon the Palatine and Aventine hills.

Horace embodies the triple functions of Diana (as Artemis, mistress of animals; Lucina, goddess of childbirth; and Hecate, goddess of the Underworld) in the following hymn, in which he dedicates a pine tree to her (*Odes* 3. 22):

 Guardian of mountains and woods, virgin, you who, when called upon three times, hear women laboring in childbirth, three-formed goddess, let the pine that overshadows my villa be yours, to which I will gladly sacrifice at the end of each year the blood of a boar as it prepares the sideways slash [of its tusk].

At Aricia the resurrected Hippolytus was identified with the minor Italian divinity, Virbius, and associated with Diana. Both Vergil and Ovid tell his story, in which he is put under the protection of the nymph Egeria, and Vergil suggests that it was because of his violent death in a chariot crash that horses were excluded from Diana's shrine.

Mercury

The god Mercury (Mercurius) was early worshiped at Rome as a god of trading and profit (the Latin word *merces* means "merchandise"), and his temple stood by the Circus Maximus in the busiest commercial center of Rome. As a character in Plautus' play *Amphitruo,* he describes himself still as the god of commerce and gain. As he came to be identificd with the Greek Hermes, however, he acquired Hermes' other functions—musician, messenger of Jupiter, and escorter of the dead. Horace, who elsewhere called himself *mercurialis,* that is, a lyric poet under the special protection of Mercury, inventor of the lyre, addressed a hymn to Mercury that elegantly combines his functions (*Odes* 1. 10):

Mercury, eloquent grandson of Atlas, who with language and the rules of the well-mannered gymnasium cleverly fashioned the crude manners of new-made humankind, of you shall I sing, messenger of great Jupiter and the gods, inventor of the curved lyre, clever at concealing with light-hearted theft whatever you like. Apollo laughed at you when he found his quiver missing as he threatened you, a child, unless you returned his stolen cattle. Indeed, with you as guide rich Priam left Troy and unnoticed passed by the proud sons of Atreus, the watch-fires of the Thessalians, and the enemy camp. You bring back the souls of the good to the blessed fields; and with your golden wand you restrain the weightless crowd [of ghosts of the dead], welcome to the gods on high and in the Underworld.

Thus the Roman Mercury adopts the functions that were described in the *Homeric Hymn to Hermes* (see Chapter 10), in Priam's journey to the tent of Achilles in Book 24 of the *Iliad,* and in escorting the dead suitors to the Underworld in the opening lines of Book 24 of the *Odyssey* (where the "golden wand" of Hermes is described).

Divinities of Death and the Underworld

We have already seen (in Chapter 13) something of the Roman idea of the Underworld and its system of rewards and punishments. This conception, which is found principally in Vergil, is literary and sophisticated, derived from different philosophical, religious, and literary sources, most of them Greek. The native Italian ideas of the Underworld and its spirits originated in the simple religion of the early agricultural communities. The spirits of dead ancestors were propitiated at the festival of the Parentalia that took place from February 13 to 21 (which in the old Roman calendar was the last month of the year). During this period, no one got married, the temples were closed, and offerings were made to the spirits by the head of the family as a guarantee of their friendliness to the family in the ensuing year. The Parentalia was a family celebration. Its gods were simply "gods of the ancestors" (*divi parentum*), without names and without mythology.

The festival of the Lemuria was celebrated in May. The head of the family would propitiate the Lemures, spirits who could do great harm to the household. The ceremony was conducted by night with a magic ritual—the *paterfamilias* was barefoot, his fingers and thumb forming an "O," his hands ritually washed before he threw behind him black beans for the Lemures to pick up, while uttering nine times a formula intended to drive the spirits from the house.

Ovid identifies the Lemures with the Manes, who were synonymous with the dead. Each person has his or her Manes, and epitaphs conventionally began with *Dis Manibus Sacrum*, "sacred to the divine Manes of . . . ," followed by the person's name.

The Manes, the Parentalia, and the Lemuria, which involve no mythology or legend, are far removed from Vergil's elaborate Underworld, which was derived mostly from Greek sources. From the Etruscans the Romans learned to propitiate the dead by offering human blood spilled on the earth. This is the origin of the gladiatorial games, which were first celebrated at Rome in 264 B.C. at the funeral games for Decimus Junius Brutus. The Etruscans shared with the Greeks many Underworld divinities, such as Charon and Persephone, and added some of their own, such as the demon Tuculcha. The Underworld itself in Roman literature is commonly called Orcus (sometimes personalized as a god) and its ruler was Dis Pater, whose name (Dis = *dives*, "wealth") is the equivalent of the Greek Pluto. The worship of Dis Pater was established at Rome in 249, although he was certainly known there long before. He and Proserpine shared a cult at an underground altar in the Campus Martius, whose precinct was called Tarentum (the etymology of the name is still unexplained), and its cult was associated with the festival of the Secular Games.

The burial goddess, Libitina, was Italian; but her name, origin, and associations have never been satisfactorily explained. Her name was used by the later poets as synonymous with Death, and undertakers were known as *libitinarii*.

Lares and Genius

The Lares were divinities often linked with the Penates. The origin and etymology of their name are unknown. Although they have been identified with spirits of the dead, particularly of ancestors, the Lares were probably household spirits in origin who could bring prosperity and happiness to the farmer and his farm.

This agricultural origin survived in the Compitalia (crossroads festival), a winter feast celebrated when work on the farm had been completed. A crossroads in primitive communities was regularly the meeting point of the boundaries of four farms, and the Lares honored at the Compitalia were the protecting spirits of the farms. At each crossroads was a shrine, with one opening for each of the four properties. The farmer would hang a doll in the shrine for each free member of his household and a ball of wool for each slave. This seems to have been a purification ritual at the end of the farmer's labor, when substitutes for the human beings were hung up to be purified by the air.

The Lares are basically kindly spirits, protecting the household. Transferred from farm to city, they kept this function, and each house had its *Lar familiaris* to whom offerings of incense, wine, and garlands were made. In Plautus' play *Aulularia*, the *Lar familiaris* speaks the prologue and describes how he can bring happiness and prosperity if he is duly worshiped; if he is neglected, the household will not prosper. Just as each household had its Lar, so the city had its Lares (called the *Lares praestites* or "guardian Lares"), who were worshiped on May 1. Augustus revived the celebration of the Compitalia in the city by instituting shrines of the Lares Compitales in each of the 265 *vici* or subdivisions of the city. In this function, according to Ovid, the Lares "protect the crossroads and are constantly on guard in our city" (*Fasti* 2. 616). At the city Compitalia, the Lares were worshiped together with the Genius of Augustus himself.

The Lares were also protectors of travelers by land *(Lares viales)* and by sea *(Lares permarini)*. In 179 B.C. a temple was dedicated to the Lares Permarini to commemorate a naval victory over King Antiochus eleven years earlier.

The Genius represented the creative power of a man, seen most especially in the *lectus genialis,* or marriage bed, symbol of the continuing life of the family. It was associated more generally with the continued well-being of the family. Slaves swore oaths by the Genius of the head of the family, and offerings were made to it on his birthday. For women, the equivalent of the male Genius was her Juno.

NON-ITALIAN GODS

Hercules

Several foreign deities had an important place in Roman religion. In most cases, they came from Greece or the East, and their arrival can often be dated.

The earliest newcomer was the Greek Heracles, called Hercules at Rome. Livy says that when Romulus founded the city the cult of Hercules was the only foreign one that he accepted. We have seen how Hercules visited Rome with the Cattle of Geryon and there killed the monster Cacus (pp. 521–522). To commemorate the event, his cult was established, either by Hercules himself or by Evander, in the Forum Boarium (the cattle market between the Circus Maximus and the Tiber). His precinct there was the Ara Maxima (Greatest Altar), and the cult was in the hands of two noble families until 312, when it was taken over by the state. The Forum Boarium area was a natural landing place on the Tiber, and it was among the earliest commercial quarters of the city. Since Hercules was the patron of traders, this area was appropriate for his worship. Like Mercury, Hercules brought luck (including chance finds) and profit, and successful traders dedicated a tithe of their profits to him. Besides the Ara Maxima there were at least twelve shrines or temples dedicated to him in the city.

The Dioscuri

The Dioscuri, Castor and Pollux, were worshiped from the time of the early Republic. After they appeared at the battle of Lake Regillus (probably in 496) a temple in the Forum was dedicated to them both, although its official name was the temple of Castor. In the battle the Romans were being hard pressed by the Latins, when the Dioscuri appeared before them on horseback and led them to victory. They then appeared in the Roman Forum and announced the victory. After watering their horses at the fountain of Juturna they vanished. The appearance of the Dioscuri in battle is fairly common in ancient legend, and they were said to have appeared at other battles in later Roman history. They came to Rome from the Greek cities of southern Italy (perhaps from Tarentum) after a period as important deities at Tusculum, a Latin city near Lake Regillus. At Rome they were especially the patrons of horsemen and of the knights (i.e., the economic and social class below the senators). Only women swore by them, using the oath *ecastor*.

The Sibylline Oracles

An even older arrival in Rome than the Dioscuri were the Sibylline oracles, which were traditionally associated with the Greek colony of Cumae. Collections of oracles written in Greek hexameters were common throughout the Greek world; they were especially associated with the Sibyls, prophetesses said to be inspired by Apollo. The Cumaean Sibyl was said to have been granted a life of one thousand years by Apollo, who withheld the compensation of eternal youth (see pp. 178–179). She was Aeneas' guide in the Underworld.

A well-known legend tells how the Sibylline books came to Rome. The Sibyl mysteriously appeared before the last Roman king, Tarquinius Superbus, and offered to sell him nine books of oracles for a high price; when he refused, she burned three of the books and offered the remaining six at the same price. Again he refused, and again she burned three books and offered the last three at the same price. This time acting on the advice of the augurs (an important group of priests) Tarquin bought the books. The Sibyl handed them over and promptly disappeared. The books were stored in the Capitoline temple of Jupiter, to be consulted only on the orders of the senate—for guidance in times of calamity and perplexity or during a pestilence or after the appearance of disturbing prodigies. The priests who had charge of them were prominent citizens. The books were considered so important that after they were destroyed in the Capitoline fire of 83 B.C., a new collection was made, which Augustus later deposited in the base of the statue of Apollo in his new temple on the Palatine Hill. The Sibylline books are an example of early Greek influence at Rome. They also were influential in bringing new cults to Rome. For example, they advised the introduction of the cults of Ceres, Liber, and Libera in 496 B.C. and of Apollo in 433.

Apollo and Aesculapius

Apollo—the only one of the great Greek gods not to change his name at Rome—arrived as the result of a pestilence, and his temple was dedicated in 431, two years after the Sibylline books had been consulted. Until the time of Augustus, this remained his only temple at Rome. Except for his cult under Augustus and, to a lesser extent, under Nero, he was never as prominent at Rome as he was in the Greek world. He was worshiped originally as Apollo Medicus (corresponding to his Greek title of Paean, the Healer). Later his other attributes and interests were introduced, and in 212 the Ludi Apollinares (Games of Apollo, an annual festival), were instituted. Augustus had a special regard for Apollo, and in 28 B.C. he dedicated a magnificent new temple to him on the Palatine Hill.

In 293 B.C., during an epidemic, the Sibylline books counseled bringing Asclepius, the Greek god of healing, to Rome from Epidaurus. He came in the form of a sacred serpent; when the ship bringing him came up the Tiber to Rome, the serpent slipped onto the island that is in the middle of the present-day city and there made its home. A temple to Aesculapius (his Latin name) was built on the island and his cult was established.

Cybele

In 205, during another period of public distress, the Sibylline books advised the Romans to bring in the Phrygian mother-goddess Cybele, known also at Rome as the Magna Mater (Great Mother). After a visit to Delphi, a solemn embassy went to the city of Pessinus in Phrygia, where it received a black stone which was said to be the goddess. It was brought to Rome with much ceremony; a temple was built on the Palatine Hill, and the festival of the Megalensia was instituted in honor of Cybele. The ecstatic nature of her worship was exceptional at Rome. Her priests (known as *Galli*) practiced self-castration and until the reign of Claudius Roman citizens were forbidden to become Galli. The Megalensia, however, and its processions, celebrated in April, were a colorful and popular feature of the Roman religious calendar. Lucretius (2. 614–624) and Ovid (*Fasti* 4. 181–186) have left vivid descriptions of the Galli with their wild music, and Catullus (Poem 63) has brilliantly told the myth of Attis (see above, pp. 135–136).

Other Eastern gods made their way to Rome, especially in the time of the Empire. The Egyptian Isis, the Asiatic Ma, the Syrian Baal, the Persian Mithras, were widely worshiped. (The mysteries of Isis and Mithras are discussed in Chapter 14, pp. 308–311.)

LEGENDS OF THE FOUNDING OF ROME

Aeneas and Romulus

The origins of Rome traditionally went back to Aeneas, whose son Iulus (also called Ascanius) was ancestor of the *gens Iulia,* the family of Augustus. But Aeneas left Troy some 475 years before the traditional date for the founding of Rome in 753. The gap between the two dates was filled by a line of kings at the Latin city of Alba Longa. Aeneas succeeded in establishing a foothold in Latium but died soon after. Iulus then founded Alba Longa, and from there Romulus came eventually to found Rome itself. The earliest settlement at Rome may indeed date from the eighth century, and it is also known that early Rome was an alliance of villages on the different hills by the Tiber, which in time were unified. As Rome became a city, it was sometimes under the control of neighboring peoples (the Tarquins, the fifth and seventh kings of Rome, were Etruscans), but by the early part of the fifth century, the city was strong enough to assert its independence. Then it extended its control over the Etruscan cities and the Sabine and Latin tribes, whose customs and gods it often absorbed. The legendary connection between Rome and Alba Longa is historically likely. That between Rome and Troy is more doubtful.

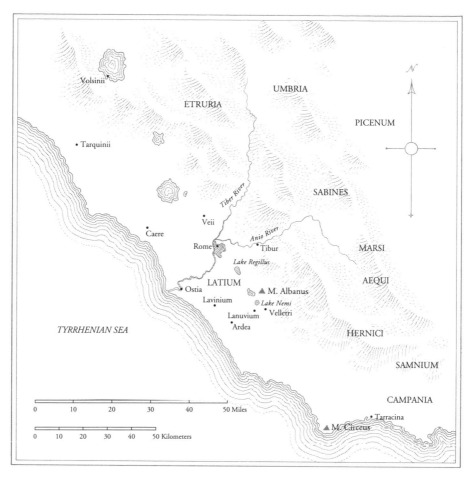

Figure 24.2.   Map of Central Italy. *(© Laszlo Kubinyi, 1994.)*

Aeneas: The Tradition before Vergil

In the foundation myth that connects Rome with Troy, the central figure is Aeneas, son of Aphrodite and Anchises (see Figure 17.2, p. 539). In the *Iliad* he was an important warrior but inferior to the Trojan champion Hector. When he meets Achilles in single combat (*Iliad* 20. 158–352), he is saved from death by Poseidon, who makes this prophecy (*Iliad* 20. 300–308):

Come, let us lead him away from imminent death, lest Zeus be angry if Achilles kill him. For he is fated to escape, so that the race of Dardanus may not perish without seed and invisible. For Zeus loved Dardanus most of all his children whom mortal women bare to him. Already Zeus is angry with the family of Priam. Now indeed strong Aeneas and his children's children will rule over the Trojans.

Thus there was Homeric authority for the development of Aeneas' saga after the fall of Troy. There are many irreconcilable variations in his legend before Vergil, but his wanderings over the Aegean and Mediterranean and his arrival in Italy seem to have become traditional quite early, and he was associated with a number of shrines of Aphrodite in the areas to which he was said to have traveled. The fifth-century Greek historian Hellanicus recorded his arrival in Italy, and he was well known to the Etruscans. At Veii, for example, a number of statuettes have been found, dating from about 500 B.C., showing Aeneas carrying Anchises from Troy, and the same scene appears on seventeen Greek vases from the same period found in Etruria. His travels were narrated in the epics on the Punic Wars by Naevius (who died shortly before 200) and Ennius, and it is possible that Naevius introduced his meeting with Dido into the tradition.

The early Roman historians also developed the legend of Aeneas. Around 200 Fabius Pictor, who wrote in Greek, described his arrival in Italy and the founding of Alba Longa by Ascanius (Iulus) thirty years later. In his *Origines,* the founder of Latin historiography, Cato the Elder (who died in 149), brought Aeneas to Italy, where he married Lavinia and founded the city of Laurolavinium (which is evidently the same as Lavinium) in an area called the *ager Laurens.* In this version, Latinus fought against Aeneas, while both Turnus and Aeneas perished in a later battle, and the Etruscan warrior Mezentius was killed by Ascanius in a third battle. Ascanius then left Laurolavinium to found Alba. Finally, Cato calculated that there were 432 years between the fall of Troy and the founding of Rome by Romulus.

This is the basic version of Aeneas' myth, which is also told with some variations by Livy, Vergil's contemporary. All these stories make Aeneas fight with the indigenous inhabitants (called *Aborigines* by Cato and Livy), marry a local princess (Lavinia), found a city (Lavinium), die, become a god, and leave Ascanius, now called Iulus, as his successor. Ascanius then founds Alba; and some four hundred years later Romulus founds Rome itself from Alba.

Vergil's *Aeneid*

This was the material from which Vergil created his epic, the great national poem of Rome, combining Homeric conventions, Greek mythology, and Roman ethical and historical insights. It records the events of a distant mythological past, yet it has reference to the events and hopes of Vergil's own day, when Augustus was rebuilding the Roman state after decades of civil war and instability. In the prologue Vergil links Roman history to the mythological tradition and focuses on the hero Aeneas, survivor of the fall of Troy and ancestor of Rome's leaders (*Aeneid* 1. 1–7):

> Of war and a man I sing, who first from Troy's shores, an exile by the decree of fate, came to Italy and Lavinium's shores. Much was he tossed on sea and land by the violence of the gods, because of cruel Juno's unforgetting anger. Much, too, did he endure in war as he sought to found a city and bring his gods to Latium. From him are descended the Latin people, the elders of Alba, and the walls of lofty Rome.

According to Vergil, Aeneas sailed by way of Thrace and Delos to Crete, where he stayed a year, believing that this was the place from which Dardanus came and that therefore it was the future home foretold him by the oracle at Delos. But a pestilence and a vision of the Penates led him to sail in search of Italy, which proved to be Dardanus' original home. He sailed to Epirus, where Helenus and Andromache had settled. Here Helenus foretold some of his future wanderings, and in particular told of their ending, which Aeneas would know had come when he saw a white sow with thirty piglets on a river bank in Italy. This prophecy complemented one that Aeneas received from the Harpy Celaeno, who foretold that he would reach Italy and would only found his new city when hunger had compelled the Trojans to eat the tables upon which their food lay.

Leaving Helenus, Aeneas reached Sicily, sailing past the shore of southern Italy and avoiding the perils of Charybdis. A direct link with Odysseus was provided by the appearance of one of his men, Achaemenides, a survivor of the adventure with the Cyclopes, who warned Aeneas of Polyphemus and other dangers. It was in Sicily, too, that Anchises died and was buried.

The fall of Troy and Aeneas' wanderings to this point are narrated by him to Dido in Books 2 and 3 of the *Aeneid*. The poem begins with a storm that scatters Aeneas' fleet after setting sail from Sicily. The survivors were reunited in northern Africa, where Dido, queen of Carthage, hospitably received them. She fell deeply in love with Aeneas, who would himself have been content to stay with her had not Mercury appeared to him and ordered him sail away to fulfill his destiny in Italy. As he left, Dido laid a curse on Aeneas and his descendants that they should always be the enemies of Carthage, and then killed herself with the sword that Aeneas had given her.

Aeneas sailed back to Sicily and was welcomed by the king of Egesta, the Trojan Acestes. Here he celebrated funeral games in honor of Anchises, during which the Trojan women, incited by Juno, set fire to some of the ships, the rest being saved by Jupiter in a miraculous rainstorm.[6] Aeneas left some of his followers behind in Sicily and now sailed on to Italy where he reached Cumae. Here the Sibyl foretold the wars he must fight in the new land and escorted him to the Underworld, where he talked with many of the dead whom he had known in his past life. The climax of his visit to the Underworld was his meeting with Anchises, who foretold the greatness of Rome and showed him a pageant of future Romans. The visit to the Underworld is the turning point in Aeneas' saga; after it, he is sure of his destiny and determined to settle in Italy, whatever obstacles have to be surmounted.

From Cumae, Aeneas sailed to the mouth of the Tiber, where the prophecy of Celaeno was fulfilled; as the Trojans ate the flat cakes upon which their food was placed, Iulus said, "Why, we are even eating our tables!" In Latium, King Latinus had betrothed his daughter Lavinia to the prince of the tribe of the Rutuli, Turnus. Worried by prodigies, Latinus consulted the oracle of Faunus, who advised him to give Lavinia to a foreigner instead. Latinus attempted to obey this advice by giving Lavinia to Aeneas, but Juno sent the Fury Allecto to madden Turnus and Lavinia's mother Amata, so that they violently opposed Aeneas.

War became inevitable, and Latinus was powerless to prevent it. Turnus and the Latins, with other Italian leaders (notably the Etruscan exile Mezentius), opposed the Trojans, who had for allies the Etruscans under Tarchon and the men of Pallanteum, Evander's city on the future site of Rome. Aeneas' visit to Evander had been preceded by the vision of the river-god Tiberinus (see p. 528). Evander himself showed Aeneas the city that was to become Rome and sent back with him his own son, Pallas, who later was killed by Turnus. After ferocious battles between the Latin allies and the Trojans Aeneas killed Turnus in single combat. At this point the *Aeneid* ends.

This bald outline hardly reveals the extraordinary power of Vergil's poem. Writing in the epic tradition of Homer, he created a new kind of Roman epic. We illustrate three of his innovations—his use of Jupiter and prophecy to combine myth and Roman history; his creation of a different kind of hero, in some ways like Achilles and Odysseus, but differing completely in the Roman nature of his *pietas* (a virtue that includes a sense of duty and service); finally the prominent role he gives to Dido.

Jupiter in the *Aeneid*

In the *Aeneid* the traditional Olympian figure of Zeus-Jupiter becomes identified with destiny or fate. Therefore his prophecies are especially important, and through them Vergil links mythology and Roman history to make the destiny of Rome both noble and inevitable.

In Book 1, Aeneas is driven to land near Carthage by a storm raised by Juno and Aeolus, and Venus complains to Jupiter of the sufferings of her son. In reply Jupiter foretells his glorious destiny and that of his Roman descendants. Here are a few lines from this prophecy (*Aeneid* 1. 267–279):

> But young Ascanius, who now has assumed the additional name of Iulus . . . will complete thirty mighty cycles of the rolling months as king, and he will transfer his kingdom from its place at Lavinium and will found with much force Alba Longa. Here the family of Hector will rule for three hundred whole years, until the royal priestess Ilia, pregnant by Mars, will bear twin children. Then Romulus, rejoicing in the tawny covering of the skin of the wolf (his nurse) will succeed as ruler of the race and will found the city of Mars and call its people Romans after his own name. For them I give no limits of events or time: I have given them empire without end.

This sense of high destiny, in which the traditional myths serve a historical purpose, is repeatedly emphasized by Vergil, in Aeneas' visit to the Underworld in Book 6 (see Chapter 13), in the description of his shield at the end of Book 8, and in the final prophecy of Jupiter in Book 12 (830–840). By these means Vergil preserves the Homeric figures of the Olympian gods, but Jupiter is a more powerful figure than Zeus, while the other gods play their traditional roles, favoring one side or the other. Juno is hostile to Aeneas and favors those who would divert him from his destiny, notably Dido and Turnus, while Venus consistently favors her son and intercedes with Jupiter for him.

Aeneas: A New Epic Hero

Aeneas is motivated by *pietas,* which leads him to leave ease and comfort to pursue a destiny of which he does not become fully aware until after his visit to the Underworld. He is a wanderer, like Odysseus, in search of a home; and he is the son of a goddess, like Achilles, terrible in single combat. But he is also an exile, who has been defeated in a great war and has seen his city destroyed. His character is epitomized in the scene where he leaves Troy with Anchises, symbol of the past, on his shoulders, while holding the hand of Ascanius, hope of the future. When we first meet Aeneas in the storm in Book 1, he wishes he were dead and his "limbs were loosened with cold fear" (1. 92–96), yet on coming to land he speaks to his followers words that show his patience, courage, and hope (*Aeneid* 1. 198–207):

> My companions—for we are not inexperienced in adversity—O friends who have suffered worse, the god will bring an end to these things also. You came to the fury of Scylla and the sounding rocks, you experienced the cave of the Cyclops. Recall your courage and dismiss dejected fear. Perhaps we shall be glad to remember these things also in the future. Through varied fortunes, through so many dangers, we go to Latium, where fate shows us a peaceful home. There the kingdom of Troy is destined to rise again. Endure, and keep yourselves for prosperous times!

Yet Aeneas' path is never simple. In Carthage he loves and is loved by Dido, and in a last interview with her he tells her that he must obey Jupiter, whose messenger Mercury has appeared to him, however unwillingly (4. 356–361):

> Now also the messenger of the gods sent from Jupiter himself has brought his orders flying swiftly through the air. I myself saw the god in the clear light entering the city and with my own ears I heard him speak. Do not inflame me and yourself with your complaints. I go to Italy not of my own will.

In the last part of the poem, Aeneas must fight a terrible war against the Rutulians, led by Turnus, and their allies. In the final scene of the poem, Aeneas and Turnus meet in single combat, and the poem ends with the death of Turnus, who has pleaded with Aeneas for his life. Turnus had earlier killed Pallas, son of Evander, Aeneas' host at Pallanteum, and put on his victim's sword-belt. Here are the last fifteen lines of the poem (12. 938–952):

> Aeneas stood armed eager to attack, surveying [Turnus], and he kept his hand from striking. Even now more and more Turnus' appeal had begun to deflect him as he hesitated, while the ill-starred belt came into his view high on [Turnus'] shoulder and the well-known studs glittered on the boy Pallas' strap. Turnus had felled him with a [fatal] wound and wore his enemy's fittings on his shoulders. Aeneas gazed profoundly at the reminder of his savage grief and at the spoils; and on fire with rage and terrible in

his anger, he spoke: "Will you, wearing the spoils taken from my friends, be snatched from me? Pallas with this blow sacrifices you and exacts payment from your sinful blood."

With these words in hot anger he sank the sword in Turnus' chest. His limbs collapsed in the coldness [of death] and his life fled with a groan complaining to the Underworld.

Thus at the end Aeneas is overcome by anger mixed with devotion to his dead friend. Vergil leaves us in doubt—is the *pietas* of Aeneas weaker than his passion? Is he after all a hero motivated by passion like Achilles, rather than the Roman hero inspired by *pietas*? Vergil leaves his readers to decide.

Dido

The greatest obstacle to Aeneas' success is Dido, queen of Carthage and favorite of Juno. She welcomed the Trojan survivors of the storm, and Aeneas is moved as he sees the history of his own sufferings at Troy portrayed on the city's temple. When Dido first appears, she is likened to Diana herself, all is light and activity. She graciously invites the Trojans to her palace, for, she says, "I also was tossed about with many sufferings and Fortune finally wished me to settle in this land. Not without experience of evil, I know how to help the unfortunate" (*Aeneid* 1. 628–630).

But destiny is against Dido; Venus and Juno conspire to make her fall in love with Aeneas; and after he has recounted to her the fall of Troy and his wanderings, she is stricken with love, likened by Vergil to a wounded deer. Her passion is described in Book 4, along with the hunt and her union with Aeneas, the complaint of her rejected suitor Iarbas to his father, Jupiter (who had seduced Iarbas' mother), the appearances of Mercury urging Aeneas to leave, the final confrontation of Dido and Aeneas, Aeneas' departure, and Dido's decision to die. Before she dies Dido utters a curse on Aeneas and his descendants (4. 607–629):

 O Sun, you who traverse all earth's works with your flames, and you, O Juno, mediator in these troubles and witness, and Hecate, called on with weird cries by night at the crossways in the cities, and dire avenging goddesses *(Dirae)*, and gods of dying Elissa [i.e., Dido], accept my words and hear my prayer! If it is necessary for his cursed head to reach harbor and come to land, and if Jupiter's fate so demands and this ending is fixed, then let him beg for help, harried by war with a brave and well-armed people, an exile

Dido and Anna, by Washington Allston (1779–1843). Oil on millboard, 1809(?); 24 × 18 in. Anna comforts her sister, while Aeneas stealthily slips away from the palace to the waiting fleet in the background. In this unfinished painting Allston's focus is the closeness of the sisters rather than the solitary tragedy of Dido. *(Lowe Art Museum, University of Miami, Miami, Florida, Gift of the Washington Allston Trust. Courtesy of Lowe Art Museum.)*

with no home, torn from the embrace of Iulus, and let him see the untimely death of his companions. And when he has yielded himself to the terms of an unfair peace then may he not enjoy his kingdom nor the light he longed for. Let him fall before his time and lie unburied on the shore. This is my prayer, this is my final word as I shed my blood. Then may you, O my Tyrians, harass his family and all his future descendants with hatred and send this offering to my ashes. Let there be no love, no treaty between our peoples. May you arise, some avenger, from my bones, and may you pursue the Trojan settlers with fire and sword, now, in the future, whenever time gives you strength. This is my curse—shore with opposing shore, sea with sea, arms with arms, let them and their descendants fight!

Vergil has again united myth and history, for Dido's curse vividly reminds the reader of Rome's times of greatest danger, the wars against Carthage. But in Dido Vergil also created a character who has always aroused the sympathy of his readers—we are reminded of Augustine, who confessed that he shed tears for Dido before he did for Christ. As with Aeneas and his legend, Vergil took the traditional story of the founding of Carthage by the Phoenician queen Elissa and transformed the saga into profoundly moving tragedy.

Other Characters in the *Aeneid*

The *Aeneid* is full of characters and scenes that have become part of traditional Roman legend. Besides the fall of Troy, Vergil takes Aeneas to the future site of Rome, where he is welcomed by the Arcadian king Evander and hears the story of Hercules and Cacus (see pp. 521–522). We have seen in Chapter 13 how Aeneas visits the Underworld. In Book 7 we see how Juno rouses the malevolent powers of the Underworld in her attempt to thwart the fulfillment of destiny. Aeneas' enemy Turnus is, like Dido, a victim of destiny, both a cruel warrior and a gallant champion of his people. Mythical Italian characters are vividly portrayed, Nisus and and his lover, Euryalus, who died tragically during a nocturnal patrol; the warrior maiden Camilla, leader of the Volscians, who could run over the fields of ripe grain without bruising the crops and over the waves of the sea without her feet touching the water (7. 808–811); Mezentius, "despiser of the gods," the Etruscan leader who in other versions of the saga survived the war and was later killed by Ascanius. In the *Aeneid,* both he and his son, Lausus, are killed by Aeneas. Camilla is killed by the Etruscan Arruns, who is himself killed by Diana's follower Opis in punishment for killing her favorite.

The Death of Aeneas

The *Aeneid* ends with the death of Turnus. The saga continues with Aeneas' marriage to Lavinia and his founding of Lavinium. He died in battle after only three more years and became a god, being worshiped with the divine title *Indiges.*[7]

Anna and Anna Perenna

The myth of Anna, Dido's sister, is related by Ovid (*Fasti* 3. 523–656) in connection with the New Year's festival (celebrated in March, originally the first month of the Roman calendar) in honor of Anna Perenna. Anna fled from Carthage, which had been occupied by Iarbas, and came to Melita (Malta). Here her brother Pygmalion, who had killed Dido's husband Sychaeus and driven her from Tyre, found her and demanded that she be handed over. Fleeing again, she was shipwrecked off the coast of Latium, reaching land in Aeneas' territory in the *ager Laurens*. Aeneas found her and gave her a refuge in his palace, but Lavinia out of jealousy plotted to kill her. Warned by Dido in a dream, Anna fled once more and came to the bank of the river Numicus, where Aeneas' followers searched for her. Here is how the story ends (*Fasti* 3. 651–656):

They came to the banks [of the Numicus], where her footsteps were. The river, which knew [what had happened], stopped the flow of his silent waters. Anna herself seemed to speak: "I am a nymph of the peaceful Numicus. I hide in the river that flows year round (*perenne*) and my name is Anna Perenna." Immediately they feasted in the meadows where they had wandered in their search and celebrated the day and themselves with copious wine.

Thus Ovid identified Anna, sister of Dido, with Anna Perenna, the Italian goddess of the New Year, whose festival was marked by feasting in the open air, drinking, and lovemaking.

ROMULUS AND THE EARLIEST LEGENDS OF ROME

Romulus and Remus

The last of the kings of Alba Longa was Amulius, who had usurped the throne from his brother Numitor. Numitor's daughter was Rhea Silvia, also called Ilia, whom Amulius attempted to keep from marriage by making her a Vestal Virgin. Mars loved her, however, and she bore him twin sons, Romulus and Remus, whom Amulius ordered to be thrown into the Tiber. But the servants pitied them and left them by the edge of the river, which was in flood. As the waters receded, they were safe on dry ground, where they were found by a she-wolf, who suckled them. The place was marked by the Ficus (fig tree)

Mars and Rhea Silvia, by Peter Paul Rubens (1577–1640), Oil sketch on canvas, 1616–1617; $21\frac{1}{2} \times 29\frac{1}{4}$ in. Mars, in armor, rushes impetuously towards the Vestal Virgin. Already a cupid has removed his helmet, and another (with a quiver of arrows) is unbuckling his breastplate. Rhea looks at him with mixed emotions, including fear and love. The setting is the temple of Vesta, whose sacred fire burns on the altar in front of the Palladium. The sketch may have been intended for a tapestry, since Athena's spear and shield are reversed (her shield would normally be on the left arm) and Mars' sword is on his right side. *(Courtesy of the Collections of the Prince of Liechtenstein, Vaduz Castle.)*

Ruminalis, a name that is related either to the word *ruma*, a teat, or to the word *rumon*, a river. It grew near the Lupercal cave below the Palatine Hill, which was the site of Evander's city, Pallanteum.

The babies were found by one of Amulius' shepherds, Faustulus, who brought them to his home, where he and his wife Acca Larentia brought them up. When they were grown up, they made their living, it was said, by attacking brigands and relieving them of their spoils. Eventually Remus was arrested and brought before Numitor, but his punishment was prevented by the appearance of Romulus, who related the story told to him by Faustulus of the twins' rescue. So grandfather and grandsons recognized each other, and together they brought about the death of Amulius and the restoration of Numitor to the throne of Alba. Romulus and Remus

Romulus and Remus, by Alexander Calder (1898–1976). Wire sculpture, 1928; 31 × 112 in. This large construction is a witty reinterpretation of the famous Etruscan bronze "Capitoline Wolf" in Rome suckling the mythical founders of Rome. *(Gift of the Artist, 1965. © Solomon R. Guggenheim Foundation, New York. Photograph by Robert E. Mates. © 1994 Artists Rights Society [ARS], New York/ADAGP, Paris.)*

then left Alba and founded their own city at the site of their miraculous rescue from the Tiber.

The theme of fraternal rivalry now appears in the story of Romulus and Remus, and it led to the death of Remus. To decide which should give his name to the city, Romulus and Remus resorted to augury, that is, taking omens from the flight of birds. Here is how Ennius describes the scene (*Annales* 1, frag. 47):

Then caring with great care and desiring to rule they give their attention to auspices and augury. Remus takes his place on the hill and alone watches for a favorable bird. But handsome Romulus watches from the heights of the Aventine, observing the race of high-flying birds. Their contest was whether to name the city Roma or Remora. All [the people] were in suspense as to who would be their leader. Straightway the bright light came forth, struck by the rays [of the sun], and at the same time high up a bird flew on the left, by far the most beautiful bird of augury. At the same time the golden sun rose, and thrice four sacred bodies of birds flew from the heavens and settled in the lucky places of good omen. Then Romulus saw that the throne and land of the kingdom had been given to him as his own by augury.

In Ennius' account, Romulus and Remus watch from different parts of the Aventine and the birds appear only to Romulus. In later versions, Romulus watched from the Palatine Hill, Remus from the Aventine. The first omen, six vultures, appeared to Remus, and then twelve appeared to Romulus. In the ensuing quarrel as to whether the winner was he who saw more birds or he who saw the omen first, Remus was killed. Romulus gave his name to the new city of Rome and became its king.

Ennius, however, gave a different version of Remus' death, which was followed by Livy and Ovid. Romulus began to build his city on the Palatine, and when the walls had risen a little way, Remus scornfully leaped over them and was killed by his brother because he had acted as an enemy, for a friend enters a city by the gate.

Romulus and the Sabines

Romulus now set about establishing his kingdom and laying the foundations of Rome's political structure. In order to increase the population, he declared the area between the two parts of the Capitoline Hill an *asylum* (i.e., a sanctuary where any man could be assured of freedom from violence or prosecution). To this place men came from many directions to become Rome's future citizens. There was a shortage of women, however, and attempts to remedy this situation led to a long series of incidents involving the Romans and the Sabines.

In the first place, the surrounding tribes refused requests from Roman embassies for young women to be wives for Roman men. Romulus decided therefore to use deceit and force. Men and women from the Sabine tribes were invited to attend the festival games of the Consualia. At a given signal, the Roman men seized the young Sabine women, whose relatives fled. Such an act could not go unavenged, and the Sabines, under the leadership of Titus Tatius, organized themselves for war on the Romans. In the first encounter, Romulus killed the king of the Sabine town of Caenina and dedicated his armor to Jupiter Feretrius (perhaps Jupiter "to whom one brings"). This was the first of only three occasions in the history of the Roman Republic that a Roman commander dedicated the armor of an enemy commander whom he had personally slain; such dedications were known as the *spolia opima* (the finest trophy). In the second battle, when Romulus was again victorious, Hersilia, the wife of Romulus, acted as conciliator and persuaded her husband to accept the defeated Sabines as Roman citizens.

Finally the Sabines attacked Rome itself and through the treachery of Tarpeia captured the Capitoline Hill. In the legend Tarpeia was the daughter of the Roman commander upon the Capitol; greedy for gold, she agreed to let the Sabines in if they would give her "what they had upon their left arms''—meaning their gold bracelets. After the capture, they crushed her to death under their shields, for the left arm is the shield arm. Although they were masters of the citadel, the Sabines could not capture the Forum—its entrance was barred by miraculous jets of boiling water emitted by Janus. In the low ground where the Forum lay, fierce fighting took place, and the Sabines were successful until Romulus turned the tide of battle by vowing a temple to Jupiter Stator (Jupiter the Stayer).

The next stage of the battle is associated with a cavity in the Roman Forum called the Lacus Curtius. The fiercest of the Sabine soldiers was Mettus Curtius, who rode on his horse into the marshy ground and miraculously escaped from his pursuers. The low-lying depression was named after him. Livy also gives another (more patriotic) account of the Lacus Curtius which has proved more popular. In 362 a chasm mysteriously opened up in the Forum, and the soothsayers announced that it could be closed only by putting into it that which was most valuable to Rome; if it were so filled, the Roman state would endure forever. A young Roman, Marcus Curtius, realized that military courage was Rome's greatest treasure, and in full panoply and before the assembled people he prayed to the gods and rode into the chasm. Thus it was closed, and the place took its name from the hero who had been swallowed up by the earth.

The battle between Romulus and the Sabines was brought to an end by the Sabine women themselves, wives (and now mothers) of Romans and daughters of Sabines. They ran into the middle of the battle and by their direct appeals brought about a truce. Peace was made, and the Sabines and Romans agreed to live together at Rome, with Titus Tatius becoming Romulus' colleague in the kingship, while the Sabines provided the name by which the Roman citizens were addressed, *Quirites.*[8]

Thus the unification of the two peoples was achieved. Titus Tatius was killed some years later by the people of Lavinium. Romulus himself, after a long reign, disappeared while reviewing his army in the Campus Martius, amid thunder and lightning. He became the god Quirinus, and appeared to a farmer, Proculus Julius, who reported his final words. They eloquently embody the ideals that later Romans attributed to the founder of their state (Livy 1. 16):

 "Go," said he, "and tell the Romans that it is the gods' will that my city of Rome should be the capital of the world. Let them exercise their military skill and let them know—and let them tell their descendants—that no mortal power can resist the Romans."

Some of the saga of Romulus is rooted in fact, as has been proved by recent archaeological discoveries. Much of his legend, however, is literary invention. Romulus himself is the eponym of Rome, to whom many features of the Roman constitution are ascribed. His deification is problematic, since Quirinus was a Sabine god with whom Mars was associated. Sometimes his name stands by itself; sometimes it is attached to Mars (Mars Quirinus) or to Janus, Jupiter, or even Hercules. One ancient Roman scholar (Servius on *Aeneid* 1. 292) described Quirinus as "Mars when he presides in peacetime." The idea of a god of a military state when it is not at war is particularly suitable for Romulus, organizer of the peaceful state and successful leader in its first wars. Quirinus, moreover, being Sabine, is suitably fused with the Roman Romulus; there were separate communities with different cultures upon the Palatine, Oppian, and Quirinal hills in the eighth century, and the legend of a fusion, symbolized by the god Romulus-Quirinus, is supported by archaeological evidence.

Other Characters in the Legend of Romulus

Several other characters in the Romulus legend are divine. Faustulus, the shepherd who reared the twins, may have some connection with Faunus, since the root of his name is the same and has the connotation of "favoring" or "bringing increase." Cato and Varro, followed by Ovid, connected Acca Larentia, Faustulus' wife, with the festival of the Larentalia on December 23, at which offerings were made to the dead, but her exact divine function is unknown. It has been suggested that her name, Acca, is the same as the Sanskrit word for "mother," and that she was therefore the *mater Larum*, mother of the Lares (although the *a* of *Larentia* is long and that of *Larum* is short). All that can be said with certainty is that both Acca and Faustulus are old divinities whose precise attributes and functions had been forgotten by the time of the early Roman writers.

Hersilia, the wife of Romulus, became Hora Quirini, the consort of the deified Romulus. Almost certainly her name, Hora, meant "the power" or "the will" of Quirinus, and this was her original function, before the myth made her the wife of the mortal Romulus.

The treacherous Tarpeia gave her name to the Tarpeian Rock, from which criminals were thrown to their death. She too was divine, for libations were offered at her tomb. Although Livy makes her a Sabine, her name is Etruscan.

Some of the elements in the legend explain features of the Roman constitution. The dual kingship of Romulus and the colorless Titus

Tatius foreshadows the collegiate principle of Republican magistracies, in particular the dual consulship.

LEGENDS OF THE REGAL PERIOD

The period of the kings (which traditionally ended in 509 B.C.) and of the early Republic is full of stories that are more myth than history. We give a few examples here.

The Horatii

In the reign of the third king, Tullus Hostilius, there was war between Rome and Alba Longa, which ended in the destruction of Alba. At an earlier stage, the two sides agreed to decide the issue by a battle between champions, three brothers on each side; the Alban champions were the Curiatii, the Romans were the Horatii. Two Romans were quickly killed, but the third, who was unwounded, separated and dispatched singly his wounded opponents. Now his sister had been betrothed to one of the Curiatii; and as her brother was triumphantly entering Rome, bearing the spoils of the dead Curiatii, she cried out in grief. Horatius killed her immediately for her inopportune and unpatriotic gesture. As a murderer, he was condemned to death, but on appeal to the people, he gained a reversal of the verdict because of his popularity as a courageous soldier. He underwent a ritual purification by offering a sacrifice and passing with veiled head beneath a kind of yoke or crossbar (i.e., a horizontal beam supported by two upright poles). The crossbar was called the *tigillum sororium* and was flanked by two altars, one dedicated to Janus Curiatius, the other to Juno Sororia.

The association of Horatius with the *tigillum sororium* was the result of confusing the archaic title of Juno Sororia with the Latin word *soror*, a sister. Passing under the yoke was indeed a ceremony of purification, but, as the titles of the two divinities prove, the purification in this case was of boys and girls reaching the age of puberty. The boys, initiated at the altar of Janus Curiatius, went out to their first battle, and on their return they were purified from blood-guilt by passing beneath the *tigillum*. Juno Sororia likewise presided over the initiation of girls into adult life.

Other details of the legend are etiological. The appeal of Horatius explains the Roman citizen's right of appeal to the people. The legend of the Horatii and Curiatii may have derived from five ancient mound tombs, in two groups of two and three, respectively, outside Rome in the direction of Alba. Another ancient stone tomb stood near the place where Horatia was said to have been killed by her brother.

The Tarquins and Servius Tullius

The last three kings of Rome were Tarquinius Priscus, Servius Tullius, and Tarquinius Superbus. The two Tarquins were Etruscans, while Servius, whose name is Latin, probably was not. Servius was a founder and organizer of Roman institutions second only to Romulus, and a number of legends gathered round him. His mother, Ocrisia, was a slave who had been captured in war and assigned to the household of Tarquinius Priscus. She was of the royal house at Corniculum. According to the legend, Servius' father was the son of Vulcan, who miraculously appeared in phallic form to Ocrisia as she was sitting by the fire in the palace. When Servius was a baby Vulcan showed his favor by causing a miraculous flame to play around the child's head without harming him. Favored by such portents, Servius was assured of special treatment in the palace; he was brought up in the king's family and married to his daughter. When Tarquin was murdered his widow, Tanaquil, skillfully arranged for the transfer of power to Servius.

Apart from his political and military reforms, Servius is credited with introducing the cult of Diana to Rome. Like King Numa he is said to have had a divine counselor and consort, in this case the goddess Fortuna. His death was said to have been caused by his daughter Tullia, who was married to Arruns, the son of Tarquinius Priscus, while her sister (also called Tullia) was married to his brother Tarquinius. She had her husband and her sister murdered and then married Tarquinius, whom she urged to usurp the throne and murder Servius. The corpse of Servius lay in the street called the Clivus Urbius; Tullia drove her coach over her father's body; and because of the crime, the name of the street was changed to Vicus Sceleratus (Crime Street).

Lucretia and the End of the Monarchy

Thus Tarquinius Superbus (the proud) became king; in the historical tradition he is a tyrant, and his expulsion led to the establishment of the Roman Republic. The crime that caused his removal became one of the most famous of Roman legends. In the Roman army besieging the Rutulian capital of Ardea were a number of young nobles, includ-

Rape of Lucrece, by Reuben Nakian (1897–1986). Steel, 1953–1958; height 144 in. Nakian has transformed conventional representations of the scene into a violent confrontation of abstract forms constructed from steel plates and pipes. The intimidating figure on the left, topped by a helmetlike shape, threatens the slighter figure on the right, who starts back from the attacker, while she leaps (we can imagine) to the ground from her bed. Nakian's disjointed shapes starkly express the breakdown of moral and social order represented by the crime of Tarquinius. *(Hirshhorn Museum and Sculpture Garden, Smithsonian Institution, Washington, D.C. Gift of Joseph H. Hirshhorn, 1974. Photograph by Lee Stalsworth.)*

ing Tarquinius Collatinus and Sextus Tarquinius, the son of the Roman king. Full of wine one evening, they rode off to pay surprise visits to their wives in order to see who was the most virtuous and faithful. Alone of all whom they visited, the wife of Collatinus, Lucretia, was acting in a chaste and matronly way; they all judged her to be the best and returned to camp. Now Sextus Tarquinius was so taken by Lucretia's beauty that he returned alone to Collatia some nights later and surprised and violated her. Next day she sent for both her father and her husband, who came together with Lucius Junius Brutus. She told them what had happened and made them promise to avenge themselves on her attacker. Then she plunged a dagger into her heart.

Lucretia's martyrdom led to the end of the monarchy. Tarquinius Superbus was driven into exile with two of his sons. Sextus Tarquinius went to the Latin town of Gabii, where he was murdered. Rome became a republic, the chief power being exercised by two praetors elected annually (the title was changed to "consuls" some sixty years later), one of whom was Brutus.

The early centuries of the Roman Republic were idealized by historians and poets. As early as the fourth century, legends were created about Roman leaders which expressed heroic and moral ideals. It is doubtful whether these stories can truly be said to be a part of mythology.

In the view of Georges Dumézil, the legends of the monarchy and early Republic reflect the tripartite organization of Indo-European society (for there were three tribes in early Rome), which he classifies by function, that is, priest-kings, warriors, and food producers. He believes that the traditional tales enshrined in the historians (most notably the early books of Livy) were the genuine myths of this society. This view is controversial, but it does recognize the peculiar ability of the Romans to make national heroes of their historical figures, as Livy saw. Nevertheless, the stories of these early Roman heroes belong more to the realm of history than to that of pure myth, and we end our survey of Roman mythology with the end of the Roman monarchy.[9]

THE SURVIVAL OF CLASSICAL MYTHOLOGY IN LITERATURE AND ART

The Decline of the Gods of the Greek City-State

The connection between religion and the state in classical Greece is evident in Greek drama and in the sculpture of the great temples. The gods and their myths were central in the life of the city-state, which reached its climax in many parts of the Greek world during the fifth century B.C. In the following century the self-confidence of many city-states was weakened in part by political strife and warfare, in part by the need for alliances with other Greek cities or with non-Greek peoples. Citizens were less motivated by patriotism to make great sacrifices on behalf of their city, whose gods were no longer ubiquitous in its life. They were less relevant to a world where citizens sought from religion comfort for their individual concerns.

The process of undermining Homeric religion had begun centuries earlier, when the Ionian philosophers began to explain the place of human beings in the macrocosm in nontheological terms. A whole world separates Hesiod's cosmogony and theogony from the Ionians' theories about the universe. Anaximenes of Miletus (ca. 545), for example, said that air was the elemental substance of the universe (including the gods) and did not hesitate to refer to it as *theos* (God). Heraclitus of Ephesus (ca. 500) taught that fire was the prime element and further criticized the rituals of Homeric religion, in particular its central feature, the animal sacrifice; purifying oneself with blood, he said, was like washing in mud. The most outspoken of these early critics was Xenophanes of Colophon (ca. 525), who attacked Homeric anthropomorphism: "Homer and Hesiod," he said, "have attributed to the gods everything that is shameful and a reproach among mortals: theft, adultery, and deceit" (Fragment 11 [Diels]). Toward the end of the fifth century, the criticisms of the philosophers were widely accepted among thoughtful people, whose confidence in the old order and established religion was shaken by the political, moral, and intellectual upheavals that surrounded them. In the period of the Peloponnesian War (431–404), the Sophists, professional philosophers, were to be found lecturing in many Greek cities. Their skepticism about traditional religion caused a strong conservative reaction, which finds its expression in Aristophanes' play *The Clouds* (423), and in the condemnation and execution of Socrates (who was not a Sophist) in 399. The charges against Socrates show how serious was the debate about the gods of the state (Xenophon, *Memorabilia* 1. 1):

> Socrates is guilty of refusing to recognize the gods recognized by the state and introducing other, new gods. He is also guilty of corrupting the young.

About twenty-five years later Plato banished Homer from the educational curriculum of his ideal state because he believed the Homeric gods and their myths set a bad moral example for the young. People turned more and more to philosophy for assurance, and the great philosophical schools—such as the Academy of Plato—were founded during the fourth century.

Alexandrianism

The conquests of Alexander the Great renewed the influence of Oriental ideas and religions in the Greek world. He and his father, Philip II of Macedon, further weakened the independence of Greek city-states and loosened the hold of traditional religion. The period after Alexander's death in 323 is called the Hellenistic Age, which continued until the final absorption of Greece into the Roman Empire in 146 B.C. The intellectual center of the Greek world in the Hellenistic Age was the Egyptian city of Alexandria, and its library was the greatest of the Greek centers of scholarship. Here in the third century scholars were interested in traditional mythology, which they explained and classified or used as a source of learned allusions. Callimachus (ca. 265) was the most distinguished of the Alexandrian scholar-poets. Amongst his works was the *Aetia*

(Causes), a poem more than four thousand lines in length, of which only about four hundred survive, containing many myths and legends about the origins of customs, institutions, and historical events. He also wrote six hymns modeled on the *Homeric Hymns.* Among his contemporaries were Apollonius of Rhodes, who wrote an epic on the Argonauts, and Theocritus of Cos, whose poems included episodes from the sagas of Heracles and the Argonauts. Often, however, the Alexandrians used mythology as a source for literary ornamentation or learned allusion.

One of Callimachus' *Aetia* was adapted by Catullus in his sixty-sixth poem, "Berenice's Lock," and we give here a few lines whose ingenuity is typical of the Alexandrian use of mythological allusion. Berenice was queen of Egypt, wife of Ptolemy III, who vowed to dedicate a lock of her hair if her husband returned safe from a campaign in Syria. After the lock disappeared from the temple where it was dedicated, it was identified with a newly discovered constellation, *coma Berenices.* The lock of hair is the speaker (Catullus 66. 51–56):

> The sisters of the lock that had just been cut off were mourning my fate, when the twin of Ethiopian Memnon arrived on hovering wings, the horse that belongs to Locrian Arsinoë, and he lifting me up flew off through the dark upper air and placed me in the chaste lap of Venus.

It would take a learned reader to understand that the "twin of Memnon" is the West Wind, here identified with the winged horse Pegasus. Pegasus is made the servant of Arsinoë, wife of king Ptolemy II, who after her death was deified as Aphrodite Zephyritis (her title coming from the place, Zephyrium, but punningly interpreted to mean "having power over Zephyrus," that is, able to send the West Wind on errands).

The Alexandrians and their Roman followers were not always so ingenious in their allusions. Catullus himself created the finest narrative of the myth of Ariadne and Theseus in his sixty-fourth poem, and the Alexandrian taste for romantic detail was brilliantly united with mythological narrative in the *Metamorphoses* of Ovid, the master storyteller.

Thus the myths enjoyed a revival in the Alexandrian tradition, which at its best led to entertaining and often moving narratives, and at its worst to a paralyzing use of ingenious allusion. In art also, the search for ingenious expression of a particular emotion, or for a particular effect on the viewer, led to works such as the *Hermes* of Praxiteles, whose technical brilliance should be compared with the dignity of the Apollo of the temple of Zeus at Olympia. The *Demeter* of Cnidus, however, dating from the later part of the fourth century, showed that artists could still represent the majesty of the Olympian gods (see p. 252).

In the thousand years between the rise of Alexandrianism and the early Middle Ages (i.e., ca. 300 B.C. to 700 A.D.) the survival of classical mythology was ensured both by the uses to which it was put and by its critics. We discuss four of these modes of survival: (1) Euhemerism; (2) mythographers and handbooks; (3) astronomy and astrology; and (4) pagan and Christian critics.

Euhemerism

The work of Euhemerus of Messene (ca. 300 B.C.), which achieved an influence out of all proportion to its merits, took a different approach to the traditional myths. The theory of *Euhemerism* states that the gods were originally men who had been kings or otherwise distinguished men. Euhemerus claimed in his book *The Sacred Scripture* to have journeyed to the Indian Ocean and, on an island there, to have seen a golden column in the temple of Zeus upon which were inscribed the deeds of Uranus, Cronus, and Zeus. From this he discovered that the gods were human beings deified for their great deeds. Euhemerus' book was translated into Latin by Ennius (ca. 180) and summarized in Greek by the historian Diodorus Siculus (ca. 30); Ennius' version was summarized by the Christian writer Lactantius (ca. A.D. 300).

Euhemerism owed its importance in the Christian era to the fact that it provided pagan material with which to attack the pagan gods. St. Augustine, writing around A.D. 415, could explain the errors of pagan religion "most reasonably," he said, "by the belief that the pagan gods were once men" (*De Civitate Dei* 7. 18). The seventh-century bishop Isidore of Seville began his chapters on the pagan gods with the Euhemeristic statement: "Those whom the pagans call gods are said to have once been men" (*Etymologiae* 8. 11). Isidore tried to give historical dates for the men who became gods, and his summary of world history (*Etymologiae* 5. 39) did not distinguish between myth and history. Thus he dated as "historical facts" the invention of the lyre by Hermes and Heracles' self-immolation. Euhemerism survived throughout the Middle Ages, and it was an important element in the survival of the gods of Greek mythology.

Mythographers and Handbooks of Classical Mythology

Mythographers, who summarized and classified Greek mythology, demonstrate another aspect of scholarly interest in mythology. The Alexandrian polymath Eratosthenes (ca. 225 B.C.) and the Athenian scholar Apollodorus (ca. 145) are known to have written handbooks on mythology, now lost, and their names are attached to two surviving mythological compendia. That of "Apollodorus" (perhaps ca. A.D. 120) is the most complete and contains versions of many of the legends that are still useful. The shorter work of pseudo-Eratosthenes, called *Catasterisms,* deals exclusively with metamorphoses of people into stars. Astral legends are an aspect of Alexandrianism, and genuinely early Greek astral myths are rare (the myth of Orion is one example). The *Catasterisms*, however, include forty-four such legends, for example, the origins of the Great Bear (Callisto), the signs of the Zodiac, and the Milky Way. These legends are not myths in the strict sense, but they are a significant element in the survival of some of the persons named in classical mythology.

We give two examples of these catasterisms. In the tenth, the constellation Gemini (the Twins) was formerly the Dioscuri (Castor and Pollux):

> They exceeded all men in brotherly love, for they never quarreled about power or about anything else. So Zeus, wishing to make a memorial of their unanimity, called them, "the Twins" and placed them together among the stars.

In Catasterism 44, the origin of the Milky Way is given thus:

> The sons of Zeus might only share in divine honors if Hera had suckled them. Hermes, therefore (so they say), brought Heracles at his birth to Hera and held him to Hera's breast and she suckled him. But when she realized it was Heracles, she shook him off and the excess milk spurted out to form the Galaxy.[1]

A few other mythological handbooks still survive. In the first century B.C. Parthenius compiled a collection of love stories for the use of the Roman poet Gallus. A Latin compendium was made in about A.D. 160 by an author who called himself Hyginus (the name of the librarian of the Emperor Augustus around 10 B.C.), containing summaries of more than 250 legends. The *Mitologiae* of the African bishop Fulgentius (late fifth century A.D.) summarized and explained the pagan myths. These works, whatever their literary worth, at least helped keep the myths alive through the early Middle Ages.

Astronomy and Astrology

The names of mythology often survived through astronomy and astrology. We have already mentioned the interest of the Alexandrians in astral legends. The astronomical poem *Phaenomena*, by Aratus (a Greek from Asia Minor, ca. 275 B.C.), was one of the most popular of all Hellenistic works. It was translated into Latin by several authors (including Cicero), and more than two dozen ancient commentaries are known. Astrology, however, was more significant in the survival of the pagan gods. It had been important in the East since the time of the Sumerians and became popular in the Greek world after the conquests of Alexander. Before the Hellenistic Age the Greeks had been skeptical about astrology, but after the fourth century B.C. the influence of the stars on human life was widely studied and feared.

Astrology was not confined to the uneducated or the superstitious; it was encouraged by the Stoic philosophers, and among the Romans even so rational a man as Cicero admitted that there was "divinity in the stars." Astrologers believed in the sympathy of the heavenly bodies and human beings. Human life, they said, was bound up with the movements of the heavenly bodies, so that the stars came to have the power formerly held by the gods. It was an easy step then to give them the names of gods and to link these names with existing legends. Moreover, as countless peoples and religions were included in the Roman Empire, a host of foreign gods joined the classical pantheon, and they transformed the images of the classical gods. This process is especially clear in the influence of Egyptian religion and its mother-goddess, Isis, and in the representations of gods in the religions of the Near East such as Mithraism.

One great Roman poem on astrology survives, the *Astronomica* of Manilius, written early in the first century A.D. Manilius recognized the authority of Homer and other Greek poets, but he found traditional mythology to be too restrictive. In Book 2, he recalls the *Iliad* and the *Odyssey* (*Astronomica* 2. 1–7):

> The greatest of poets with his sacred mouth sang of the struggles of the Trojan people, of the king and father of fifty princes [Priam], of Hector conquered by Achilles and Troy conquered after Hector, and the wanderings of the leader [Odysseus] . . . and his final battle in his own land and in a home taken captive [i.e., by the suitors].

Manilius goes on to praise Hesiod and other poets, showing that Greek mythology still exerted a strong influence on even the most rational of poets. In Book 3, however, he shows how he needed to go beyond the traditional themes of mythology and epic (*Astronomica* 3. 1-13):

Lead me on, O Muses, as I rise to new themes and dare things greater than my strength, not afraid to enter woods not yet visited. I try to extend your bounds and to bring new treasure to poetry. I shall not tell of the war coming into being to destroy the heaven [i.e., the war of the giants], nor of the unborn baby [Dionysus] buried by the flames of the thunderbolt in its mother, nor of the kings [i.e., Agamemnon and the Greek leaders] bound by their oath, nor of Hector ransomed for his cremation as Troy was falling, and Priam bringing him [back to Troy]. I shall not tell of the Colchian woman selling the kingdom of her father and dismembering her brother for love, nor of the crop of warriors and the cruel flames of the bulls and the watchful dragon, nor of the years restored [i.e., to Aeson], nor the fire lit by gold [i.e., the killing of Glauce and Creon], nor [Medea's] children sinfully conceived and more sinfully murdered.

In the next century (ca. A.D. 140) the Greek-Egyptian astronomer and mathematician Ptolemy (Claudius Ptolemaeus) published his astrological treatise, the *Tetrabiblos,* which explained the heavenly bodies and the nature of their influence upon human character and action.

Christianity was unable to resist the popularity of astrology. St. Augustine vigorously attacked it in his *City of God* (especially in Book 5), yet even he believed that the stars did have an influence, to which God and human free will were nevertheless superior. In any case, astrology was too much a part of late classical and early medieval culture to be extirpated. It therefore survived the coming of Christianity and with it the classical gods prolonged their existence, often, it is true, in scarcely recognizable forms.

Pagan and Christian Critics

Even the critics of mythology acknowledged its uses. As early as 55 B.C. the Roman poet Lucretius found the names of the gods useful as symbols (*De Rerum Natura* 2. 655-660):

Let us allow a man to use "Neptune" and "Ceres" for "sea" and "grain," "Bacchus" for the proper word "wine," "mother of the gods" for "earth," provided that he does not in fact allow his mind to be touched by base superstition.

Elsewhere in *De Rerum Natura* (3. 978–1023) Lucretius interprets myths allegorically, so that the sinners in the Underworld (Tantalus, Tityus, Sisyphus) become allegories of human passions. He comments on Tityus as follows (3. 992-994):

 Tityus is in us here, whom the birds tear as he lies in the throes of love and as painful anxiety eats him up or as the cares of some other desire consume him.

By rationalizing the myths writers such as Lucretius were also ensuring their survival. This also was the case when they were attacked by the Christian Fathers. Augustine's goal in writing his *City of God* (ca. A.D. 420) was, in his words, "to defend the City of God against those who prefer their gods to its founder," that is, preferring the gods of classical mythology to Christianity. Yet Augustine, Jerome, and other Christian Fathers actually helped to prolong the life of the classical legends. The myths survived not only in classical literary texts but also in Christian literature and works of art. The process of absorption and mingling during late antiquity and the Middle Ages reached its climax in the work of Dante, who used, criticized, and, in the process, vindicated the classical myths.

The mythological figures, then, did indeed survive, despite the passing of the religion that created them. In Western literature they were used as symbols or as allegories; they became vehicles for romantic storytelling or were identified with constellations. They traveled to the East, to be depicted in Arab manuscripts in forms very different from their Greek originals. However changed they were, the important fact is that they survived, and at the end of the Middle Ages they took out a new lease on life that still endures.

LITERARY USES OF THE MYTHS

Ovid in the Later Middle Ages

A new age in European literature, beginning toward the end of the eleventh century, has rightly been called an Ovidian Age, since Ovid's *Metamorphoses* were supremely important in bringing about the revival of classical mythology that reached its climax in Renaissance literature and art. In the Middle Ages classical and biblical history and mythology were mingled without distinction between history and legend. In the period of the eleventh to the thirteenth century Ovid's tales were retold not merely for their own sake, but also as vehicles for moralizing allegory. The goddesses and heroines of the *Metamorphoses* even appear as nuns in one work, and a whole series of poems and prose works explain the *Metamorphoses* in Christian terms.

This process reached its zenith with the enormous *Ovide Moralisé* of the early fourteenth century, a French reworking of the *Metamorphoses* in which the legends were interpreted as moral allegories. As an example we give a translation (from a fifteenth-century French prose summary of the poem) of one of several interpretations of the legend of (Apollo and Daphne):

> Here we may suppose that by the maiden Daphne is meant the glorious Virgin Mary, who was so lowly, pure, and beautiful that God the Father chose her to conceive his only Son by the work of the Holy Spirit. She carried him for nine months and then bore him, virgin before the birth and at the birth; virgin after the birth she remained without ever losing her virginity. This sovereign Virgin is the laurel, always green in virtue, which God planted in the garden of his paradise.

A similar approach is to be found in the translation (from the French of Raoul le Fèvre) of the *Metamorphoses* by William Caxton *(Ovyde Hys Booke of Methamorphose,* 1480):

> Another sentence may be had for the storye of Daphne which was a ryght fayre damoysel. . . . On a tyme he [Apollo] fonde her alone and anone beganne to renne after her. And she for to kepe her maydenhode and for to eschewe the voice of Phebus fledde so faste and asprely [roughly] that al a swoun she fel down dede under a laurel tree. In which place she was entered [interred] and buryed without deflourynge or towchynge of her vyrgynyte. And therefore fayneth the fable that she was chaunged and transformed into a laurel tree, whiche is contynuelly grene. Which sygnefyeth the vertu of chastete.[2]

Quaint as the medieval uses of Ovid may seem, they show a lively interest in classical mythology. Ovid's legends were to return in their full glory in the art and poetry of the Renaissance, and his poem still remains the single most fruitful ancient source of classical legend.

Medieval use of classical mythology was not limited to allegory. The romantic side of Ovid's legends was often preserved. The "most lamentable comedy and most cruel death of Pyramus and Thisby" presented by the "rude mechanicals" in Shakespeare's *A Midsummer*

Night's Dream has several predecessors in French, Italian, and English. They appear in Chaucer and Boccaccio, in the songs of the medieval troubadours, and in the twelfth-century *Piramus et Tisbé*. All go back finally to Ovid.

The Trojan Legend in the Middle Ages

A different romantic tradition is embraced by the medieval versions of the Trojan legend. During the twelfth and thirteenth centuries, a number of epic *romances* were composed with classical themes. The most influential of these was the *Roman de Troie* by Benoît de Ste. Maure, a thirty-thousand-line romance written around 1160. In scope it extends from the Argonautic expedition through the founding and destruction of Troy to the death of Odysseus. Benoît was using two Latin prose versions of the Trojan legend as his sources. The first, by Dictys Cretensis, describes the war and the returns from the Greek point of view. It is a forgery of uncertain date (second to fourth century A.D.), purporting to be a translation from the Greek version of a diary written on bark in Phoenician script by Dictys of Crete during the Trojan War. The second of Benoît's sources, the *De Excidio Troiae* of Dares Phrygius, is likewise a late Latin forgery (perhaps of the sixth century A.D.), purporting also to be a translation from the Greek, this time of the eyewitness diary of the war from the Trojan point of view kept by the Phrygian Dares. These works were thought to be better sources than Homer because they were apparently written by eyewitnesses. They also had realistic details about the war and its participants and romantic elements. They appealed to medieval tastes and they are, through Benoît, the ancestors of much writing on the Trojan legend. Joseph of Exeter, for example, wrote a Latin verse paraphrase of Dares, which Chaucer used as a source for his *Troilus and Criseyde* (ca. 1380). The legend of Troilus and Cressida, indeed, which was first elaborated by Benoît, went through several stages of transformation. Benoît's narrative was paraphrased in Latin by an Italian, Guido delle Colonne (ca. 1275), and Guido was put into French by Raoul le Fèvre (1464). The French version was used by Chaucer and Caxton, who were the principal sources for Shakespeare's play *Troilus and Cressida*. Here are a few lines from Caxton's *Recuyell of the Historye of Troye*:

Whan Troylus knewe certaynly that Breseyda [Cressida] shold be sente to her fader he made grete sorowe. For she was his soverain lady of love, and in semblable wyse Breseyda lovyd strongly Troylus. And she made also the grettest sorowe of the world for to leve her soverayn lord in love. There was never seen so much sorowe made betwene two lovers at their departyng. Who that lyste to here of alle theyr love, late [let] hym rede the booke of Troyllus that Chawcer made wherein he shall fynde the storye hooll [whole] whiche were to longe to wryte here.[3]

Dante

Dante (1265–1321), the last of the great medieval writers and the forerunner of the Italian Renaissance, took Vergil as his guide in the *Inferno,* and named Homer and Ovid among the "great shades" of classical authors inhabiting the Inferno. Thus the importance of three of the principal sources for classical legends (Homer, Vergil, and Ovid) was confirmed.

THE ITALIAN RENAISSANCE

The figures of classical mythology first returned to their classical forms in Italy, after the centuries of metamorphosis. Their revival was part of the Renaissance ("rebirth") of classical Greek.[4] During the fourteenth century scholars journeyed to Byzantium, where they learned Greek. If they were lucky or persistent, they also acquired manuscripts of classical Greek authors, which they brought back to Italy. Thus the study of classical Greek (which had been limited during the preceding centuries) was expanded. Petrarch (1304–1374) and Boccaccio (1313–1375) learned classical Greek, and the latter's teacher translated Homer and some Euripides into Latin. The most powerful impetus to the revival of Greek studies came from the capture of Byzantium by the Turks in 1453, for many Greek scholars fled to Italy bringing with them manuscripts of classical authors. They taught Greek to Italian humanists, although it is hard to say how many of these learned enough to be able to read a Greek text with ease.

In the fourteenth and fifteenth centuries Italian scholars hunted for classical manuscripts, which they copied in the libraries of monasteries, and even stole. Petrarch, for example, possessed and copied a manuscript of Livy. Boccaccio possessed copies of Varro and Apuleius, while others—of whom Coluccio, Poggio, and Politian are the most distinguished—formed extensive classical libraries and commented upon the classical works. Thus by the time classical authors began to be printed (Cicero *De Oratore* was printed at Subiaco in 1465) there was a large corpus of fairly reliable texts.

Another aspect of the Italian Renaissance was the publication of mythological handbooks, often illustrated with woodcuts.[5] The earliest was Boccaccio's *De Genealogia Deorum* (1371), which was first printed in 1472 at Venice. Giraldi's *De Deis Gentium* was published in 1548, and the *Mythologiae* of Conti (Natalis Comes) in 1551. These were written in Latin, while in Italian Vincenzo Cartari published his *Le Imagini degli Dei Antichi* at Venice in 1556. These handbooks gave basic narratives for writers and artists to draw on, and their woodcuts provided basic iconographies for artists to copy or elaborate. They were a significant element in the recovery of the classical forms of the gods.

Petrarch, Boccaccio, and Chaucer's "Knight's Tale"

Petrarch and Boccaccio used classical mythology in their poems—Petrarch in his Latin epic, *Africa*, and Boccaccio in his Italian epic *Teseida (Theseid)*. Chaucer used the *Teseida* as his principal source for "The Knight's Tale" (ca. 1387), the first of his *Canterbury Tales*. The tale begins at the point in the Theban legend when the Seven have failed and their widows come to Attica and ask Theseus for help. Chaucer's Theseus is a Duke of Athens, whose virtues are more typical of the ideal medieval leader than of the classical epic hero. In telling of the theater in which the jousting is to take place, Chaucer describes three "oratories" of Mars, Venus, and Diana. We give part of the description of Diana's oratory, which combines Ovidian mythology and medieval allegory ("The Knight's Tale" 2051–2072):

> Now to the temple of Diane the chaste
> As shortly as I can I wol me haste,
> To telle yow al the descripcioun.
> Depeynted been the walles up and doun
> Of hunting and of shamfast chastitee.
> Ther saugh I how woful Calistopee [Callisto],
> Whan that Diane agreved was with here,
> Was turned from a womman til a bere,
> And after was she maad the lode-sterre [star];
> Thus was it peynt, I can say yow no ferre [further];
> Hir sone is eek [also] a sterre, as men may see.
> Ther saugh I Dane [Daphne], y-turned til a tree,
> I mene nat the goddesse Diane,
> But Penneus doughter, which that highte [was called] Dane.
> Ther saugh I Attheon [Acteon] an hert [stag] y-maked,

For vengeaunce that he saugh Diane al naked;
I saugh how that his houndes have him caught,
And freten [eaten] him, for that they knewe him naught.
Yet peynted was a litel further-moor,
How Atthalante hunted the wilde boor,
And Meleagre, and many another mo,
For which Diane wroghte him care and wo.

Thus Chaucer, drawing on Boccaccio, embellished his tale with legends drawn from Ovid's *Metamorphoses*.

Pastoral

In Italy pastoral Latin poetry, modeled on the *Eclogues* of Vergil, was composed during the Renaissance. In these poems, the form and language are Vergilian, while the characters have classical names with figures from classical mythology used for ornament and allusion. The setting is Renaissance Italy; for example, in the *Eclogues* of Sannazaro (1458–1530), Vergilian shepherds have become Neapolitan fishermen, who on one occasion meet with Proteus and a band of Tritons as they are sailing back from Capri. The classical conventions of pastoral were widely used in the sixteenth and seventeenth centuries in England and France, and influenced the development of opera and masque, especially in France.

ENGLAND IN THE SIXTEENTH AND SEVENTEENTH CENTURIES

Translations of Ovid

In England classical mythology was widely used. Ovid was the most popular source and the *Metamorphoses* were known to educated people, in Latin, French, or English versions. The English version by Arthur Golding (1567), preeminent in the latter part of the sixteenth century, was used by Shakespeare. Although it was clear and faithful to the text of Ovid, its fourteen-syllable lines hardly did justice to Ovid's swift-moving energy. The translation of George Sandys (1626) largely took its place, and was in part successful because of the tighter rhythm of its ten-syllable heroic couplets. Here are the opening two lines of the poem in Golding's version, then in Sandys':

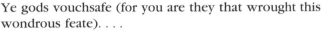

(G) Of shapes transformde to bodies straunge, I purpose to
entreate;
Ye gods vouchsafe (for you are they that wrought this
wondrous feate). . . .
(S) Of bodies chang'd to other shapes I sing.
Assist you gods (from you these changes spring). . . .

Sandys (1578–1644) worked on his translation during the voyage
from England to Virginia, where he was treasurer of the Virginia Company, and he completed it during his time in Jamestown. He probably
returned to England in 1626 to see to its publication. *Ovid's Metamorphosis Englished* is therefore the first verse work in English (other
than a ballad, *Good Newes from Virginia*, about the vengeance taken
by the settlers for the Indian massacre of 1622) completed in America.
Its importance was assured by the second edition, published at Oxford in 1632, which included an allegorical commentary and a full-
page woodcut to illustrate each of the fifteen books.[6] The commentary interpreted the legends in moralizing or Christian terms, but
Sandys excelled his predecessors in the breadth of his learning and
the incisiveness of his prose. Here are some of his comments on the
transformation of Arachne (for her story see pp. 123–125 above):

These personages, with the places, being woven to the life by
Arachne, she incloseth the web with a traile of Ivy; well suting
with the wanton argument and her owne ambition. Worne in
garlands at lascivious meetings; and climing as ambitious men, to
compasse their owne ends with the ruin of their supporters.
Minerva tears in peeces what envy could not but commend,
because it published the vices of great ones; and beats her with
the shuttle to chastise her presumption: who not induring the
indignity hangs her selfe; and is by the Goddesse converted into a
Spider: that she might still retain the art which she had taught her,
but toile without profit. For uselesse and worthlesse labors are
expressed by the spiders web: by which the Psalmist presents the
infirmity of man, and vanity of his actions.

Shakespeare, Marlowe, and Spenser

English authors in the sixteenth and seventeenth centuries made extensive use of classical mythology, in drama and narrative poems, as
ornaments in lyric poetry, and by means of mythological allusion in
prose and verse works. Allusions were not always explicit. For example, when Ben Jonson addresses the moon as "Queen and huntress,
chaste and fair," he is alluding to Artemis (Diana). In Shakespeare's
Twelfth Night, the Duke imagines himself to be Actaeon as he recalls
his first sight of Olivia (1. 1. 19–23):

O! When mine eyes did see Olivia first,
Methought she purg'd the air of pestilence.
That instant was I turn'd into a hart,
And my desires, like fell and cruel hounds,
E'er since pursue me.

Marlowe's *Hero and Leander* (1598, completed by Chapman) and Shakespeare's *Venus and Adonis* (1593) are outstanding examples of narrative poems drawn from Ovid's legends. In drama, history rather than mythology more commonly provided Renaissance authors with material, but one distinguished exception is Marlowe's *Doctor Faustus*, published in 1604 and, in a revised version, in 1616. Marlowe makes the mythological Helen a symbol of surpassing sensual beauty, an object of Faustus' desire. Here are the famous lines in which Faustus embraces Helen (*Doctor Faustus* 1328–1334):

Was this the face that launch'd a thousand ships
And burn't the topless towers of Ilium?
Sweet Helen, make me immortal with a kiss!
Her lips suck forth my soul. See where it flies!
Come, Helen, come give me my soul again.
Here will I dwell, for heaven be in these lips,
And all is dross that is not Helena.

Masques were dramatic productions, usually allegorical in nature, in which the characters were drawn from classical mythology. The most distinguished example of the genre is Milton's *Comus* (1634), which combines a pastoral setting with classical allegory. Another example is the masque in Shakespeare's *The Tempest* (act 4, scene 1). The custom of having aristocrats dress up as classical gods and goddesses survived in France and England well into the eighteenth century.

More important was the use of mythology for didactic purposes, as allegory, or as symbolic of universal truths, especially in the works of Spenser and Milton. In the second book of Spenser's *Faerie Queen,* Guyon journeys with the good Palmer and destroys the evil Bower of Bliss. On the way he is tempted by the Sirens and he is only saved from destruction by the "temperate advice" of the Palmer. In this episode the classical Sirens are symbolic of evil, and Homer's Odysseus has become a Christian holy man. In Book 2, Canto 12, Spenser's alludes to Homer's tale of Ares and Aphrodite when the enchantress throws "a subtle net" over Guyon and the Palmer, and he alludes to Ovid's Arachne in the description of her delicate silk dress ("More subtile web Arachne cannot spin"). The enchantress herself, with her bewitched animals is the Homeric Circe. Thus Spenser uses several classical legends in his allegory of Temperance.

Milton

Milton of all English writers displays the deepest knowledge and most controlled use of classical mythology. In an allusion to the Adonis legend, he describes the Garden of Eden as a "spot more delicious than those gardens feigned or of revived Adonis," combining ornamental simile and adverse judgment. In *Paradise Lost* his classical allusions are especially associated with Satan and his followers, and Hell is peopled with the full complement of the classical Underworld. The violence of the fallen angels is described in a simile drawn from Heracles' death *(Paradise Lost* 2. 542-546):

As when Alcides, from Oechalia crowned
With conquest, felt th'envenomed robe, and tore
Through pain up by the roots Thessalian pines,
And Lichas from the top of Oeta threw
Into th' Euboic sea.

This passage is followed by another describing the more peaceful fallen angels in terms of Vergil's Elysian Fields. Throughout Milton's poetry, classical mythology is intertwined with biblical and contemporary learning. Like the Christian Fathers, Milton knew classical mythology so well that he felt it necessary to appeal to the superiority of Christian doctrine. In the invocation to his Muse, Urania, he follows his description of the fate of Orpheus (whose mother, the Muse Calliope, could not save him), with these words *(Paradise Lost* 7. 1-39):

So fail not thou, who thee implores
For thou are heav'nlie, shee an empty dreame.

The tension between classical paganism and puritan Christianity is yet more explicitly put by Milton's contemporary, Abraham Cowley:

Still the old heathen gods in numbers (i.e., poetry) dwell.
The heav'nliest thing on earth still keeps up hell.

FRANCE IN THE SEVENTEENTH AND EIGHTEENTH CENTURIES

The great dramas of the French Renaissance were founded on classical sources, although their themes were more often taken from Roman history than from mythology. Thus Garnier (1534–1590) wrote tragedies on the themes of Phaedra (*Hippolyte*) and Antigone (*Antigone*). The first tragedy of Corneille (1606–1684) was *Médée* (1635), and Racine (1639–1699) likewise wrote his first tragedy, *La Thébaïde* (1664) on a theme drawn from classical mythology, the legend of the Seven against Thebes. His *Andromaque* (1667) deals with the legend of Andromache and Pyrrhus, with the significant variation that Astyanax is supposed to have survived the fall of Troy. By far the greatest of Racine's mythological tragedies is *Phèdre* (1677), based largely on the *Hippolytus* of Euripides and the *Phaedra* of Seneca.

Classical mythology was the principal source for court entertainments under Louis XIV and Louis XV, whose reigns spanned the period from 1643 to 1774. In these productions members of the court appeared as mythological beings or as characters from classical pastoral poetry. They included music and dancing as well as words, and they were performed in elaborate settings, often designed by the most prominent artists of the day. They were operas, in which the singing predominated, or court ballets, in which dancing was more prominent. The earliest French opera was *Pomone,* by Robert Cambert, produced in 1671. Ovid's legend of Pomona and Vertumnus was one of many classical tales used by court composers (including the great French masters, Lully and Rameau) for their operas and court ballets. Toward the end of the long reign of Louis XV, critics such as Denis Diderot attacked the frivolity of such artificial productions and related works of art such as the mythological paintings of François Boucher (see Color Plate 16). Their opinions helped turn contemporary taste toward the high seriousness of historical subjects (drawn especially from Roman Republican history as portrayed by Livy and Plutarch) and away from mythology.

The burlesques of Paul Scarron (1610–1660) comically deflated the pretentions of classical epic and mythology. The best known of these was his unfinished parody of the *Aeneid, Virgile Travesti.* Scarron was a serious writer, and he was most unfortunately imitated in a host of tasteless and less skillful travesties in England.

Classical mythology was also the basis of important French prose works, of which the most significant was the *Télémaque* of François

Fénelon (1651–1715), a didactic romance published in 1699. The basis of this work is the first four books of the *Odyssey,* in which Telemachus, accompanied by Minerva, travels from Ithaca in search of Ulysses. Into these adventures were worked Fénelon's moral and political precepts.

Classical mythology, therefore, had been an inseparable part of French literary and artistic life in the two centuries before the French Revolution. By then it had lost its freshness, and its use eventually became too formal for it to continue to be inspiring. Voltaire (1694–1778) ironically views the rise and fall of the influence of classical mythology in France in his late poem addressed to Pindar:

Sors du tombeau, divin Pindare,
Toi qui célébras autrefois
Les chevaux de quelques bourgeois
Ou de Corinthe ou de Mégare;
Toi qui possédas le talent
De parler beaucoup sans rien dire;
Toi qui modulas savamment
Des vers qui personne n'entend,
Et qu'il faut toujours qu'on admire.

[Come out of your grave, divine Pindar, you who in other times used to celebrate the horses of some rich citizens, whether from Corinth or Megara; you who possessed the gift of speaking much without saying anything; you who skillfully modulated lyrics that no one listens to and everyone must always admire.]

GERMANY IN THE EIGHTEENTH AND NINETEENTH CENTURIES

The renaissance of classical studies took place later in Germany than in Italy, France, Spain, Austria, the Netherlands, and England. Although there had been fine classical scholars in German universities and princely courts since the sixteenth century, the classical renaissance did not reach its full vigor until well on into the eighteenth century. It differed also from the classical renaissance elsewhere in that the Greeks were admired more than the Romans, and Homer and the Greek gods reigned supreme. A short work by J. J. Winckelmann (1717–1768) led to revived interest in Greek sculpture and its ideals. This was *Thoughts on the Imitation of Greek Works in Painting* and Sculpture (Gedanken über die Nachahmung der griechischen Werke in der Malerei und Bildhauerkunst), published in 1755. Its influence grew with the publication in England of Stuart and Revett's *The Antiquities of Athens Measured and Delineated* (1762), which directed attention to Greek buildings and the sculpture that decorated them. Winckelmann's ideas spread with the publication in 1766 of Lessing's *Laocoon*, which encouraged viewers to admire and become emotionally involved in works of Greek sculpture.

Thus Germany was prepared for the emergence of a group of great poets whose inspiration was drawn from Greece, and through them Greek mythology enjoyed a new life. The first of these were Goethe (1749-1832) and Schiller (1759-1805). Schiller's poem *The Gods of Greece (Die Götter Griechenlands)*, which appeared in 1788, laments the passing of the world of Greek mythology and contrasts it with the materialism that the poet perceived in the Christian world around him.

Goethe was constantly inspired by the classical myths. He wrote a drama on *Iphigenie auf Tauris* (first in prose, 1779, then in verse, 1788) and a long succession of lyric poems evoking Greek mythology. Sometimes the Greek myths symbolized freedom and clarity (as in his *Ganymed*, where Ganymede expresses his joy at union with Zeus), sometimes they are the vehicle for expression of human independence and dignity, as in his *Prometheus*:

Hier sitz ich, forme Menschen
Nach meinem Bilde,
Ein Geschlecht, das mir gleich sei,
Zu leiden, zu weinen,
Zu geniessen und zu freuen sich,
Und dein nicht zu achten,
Wie ich!

[Here I sit, I make human beings in my image, a race that will be like me, to suffer, to weep, to enjoy and to be glad, and to pay no attention to you, as I do!]

Goethe's most powerful evocation of Greek mythology is his use of Helen in *Faust*, Part 2, completed in 1832, the year of his death. Helen, whom Faust loves and loses, symbolizes all that is beautiful in classical antiquity, most specifically the beauty of Greek art. Goethe's Helen is more complex than Marlowe's (discussed above), for she represents the power and beauty of classical humanism. Here are

Faust's words when he first sees the phantom of Helen, the ideal of classical beauty (*Faust* 2. 1. 6487–6500):

Have I still eyes? Is the spring of beauty most richly poured deep into my soul? My fearsome journey has brought a blessed prize. How empty was the world to me and closed! What is it now since my Priesthood? For the first time worth wishing for, firm-founded, everlasting! Let my life's breath die if ever I go back from you! The beauty that once enchanted me, that in the magic glass delighted me, was only a foam-born image of such beauty! You are she, to whom I give the rule of all my strength, the embodiment of my passion, to you I give longing, love, worship, madness!

Later Faust travels to Greece and there is united with Helen. Here are his words of happiness as he looks forward to "years of happiness" with Helen in Arcadia, the pastoral landscape of perfect bliss (2. 3. 9562–9569):

So has success come to me and you; let the past be behind us! O feel yourself sprung from the highest god! You belong solely to the first [the ancient] world. No strong fortress should enclose you! Eternally young, Arcadia, Sparta's neighbor, surrounds us, there to stay in full happiness!

The third of the great German poets inspired by Greek antiquity was Hölderlin (1770–1843), whose work was most deeply infused with longing for the world of Greek mythology and with regret for its passing. "We have come too late," he says (*Brot und Wein* 7): "the gods still live, but above our heads in another world." In the same poem he evokes the landscape of Greek mythology:

Come to the Isthmus! There, where the open sea roars by Parnassus and the snow shines on the Delphic cliffs! There, to the land of Olympus, there on the heights of Cithaeron! There, under the pine trees, under the clusters of grapes, whence Thebe and Ismenus [flow and] roar in the land of Cadmus below, whence comes the god and where he points back as he comes.

Hölderlin evokes the places associated with the great Olympian gods, Poseidon, Apollo, Zeus, and Dionysus, but "gone are the thrones and the temples," and Delphi is silent. Yet Greece still was a source of inspiration, and throughout his work, Hölderlin used Greek mythology to contrast the excitement and purity of its world with the harsher reality of his own day. This kind of escapism was a positive influence on the romantic poets in Germany and England.

ENGLAND IN THE EIGHTEENTH AND NINETEENTH CENTURIES

Dryden and Pope

During the eighteenth century, classical influences reached their zenith in English literary circles. Unlike the fashionable writers who inhabited court circles in France, the English authors succeeded in keeping the classical tradition alive and vigorous over a longer period. There were, of course, many jejune uses of classical myths as ornament or mere allusion. The lack of patronage comparable to that of the courts of Louis XIV and XV meant less brilliant achievements in painting and music, but the independence of British authors led to a vigorous use of classical literature. English taste inclined more to Roman models than to Greek, and to history and satire rather than to epic and tragedy. Of authors after Milton, Dryden and Pope were especially important influences for the survival of classical mythology.

John Dryden (1631–1700), although a seventeenth-century figure, exercised such influence as critic, translator, and poet that he established criteria for poetry for the first half of the eighteenth century as well. For our survey, his importance lies especially in his monumental achievements as a translator, mostly from Latin authors, including much of Ovid's *Metamorphoses*. His translation of Vergil, in which other translators collaborated, was published in 1693. Dryden successfully employed the heroic couplet as the proper meter for the translation of epic, and the style of his translation certainly affected the way in which his readers approached classical mythology. Pope described it as follows (*Imitations of Horace: The First Epistle of the Second Book of Horace* 267–269):

> . . . Dryden taught to join
> The varying verse, the full-resounding line,
> The long majestic march and energy divine.

The dignity and energy of Dryden's heroic couplets were also attributes of the classical figures who appeared in them. As an example of Dryden's style, we quote his translation of Ovid's description of Triton blowing his horn (*Metamorphoses* 1. 447–461):

> The billows fall, while Neptune lays his mace
> On the rough sea, and smooths its furrow'd face.
> Already Triton at his call appears
> Above the waves; a Tyrian robe he wears,

And in his hand a crooked trumpet bears.
The sovereign bids him peaceful sounds inspire,
And give the waves the signal to retire.
His writhen shell he takes, whose narrow vent
Grows by degrees into a large extent;
Then gives it breath; the blast, with doubling sound,
Runs the wide circuit of the world around . . .
The waters, list'ning to the trumpet's roar,
Obey the summons and forsake the shore.

A greater poet was Alexander Pope (1688-1744), whose translation of the *Iliad*, published in 1720, was for many decades the way by which readers in Britain and America became familiar with Homer and the world of Greek mythology. Pope succeeded in his "first grand duty" as a translator, which was "to give his author entire . . . [and] above all things to keep alive the spirit and fire which make his chief character" (from the preface to the *Iliad*). The translation, however, is as much a creation of Pope's time and taste as it is Homeric, and many would agree with Thomas Jefferson who said: "I enjoyed Homer in his own language infinitely beyond Pope's translation of him." Like Dryden's translations, however, Pope's *Iliad* created a certain view of the Greek gods and their myths, which not only spread knowledge of them but also established the criteria by which they were valued. Here are a few lines from Pope's translation, in which Achilles swears his great the oath at the height of his quarrel with Agamemnon (*Iliad* 1. 233-247):

"Now by this sacred sceptre hear me swear,
Which never more shall leaves or blossoms bear,
Which sever'd from the trunk (as I from thee)
On the bare mountains left its parent tree:
This sceptre, form'd by temper'd steel to prove
An ensign of the delegates of Jove,
From whom the power of laws and justice springs
(Tremendous oath! inviolate to kings);
By this I swear—when bleeding Greece again
Shall call Achilles, she shall call in vain.
When, flush'd with slaughter, Hector comes to spread
The purpl'd shore with mountains of the dead,
Then shalt thou mourn the affront thy madness gave,
Forced to deplore when impotent to save:
Then rage in bitterness of soul to know
This act has made the bravest Greek thy foe."
He spoke; and furious hurl'd against the ground
His sceptre starr'd with golden studs around:
Then sternly silent sat.

Romantics and Victorians

By the end of the eighteenth century, Pope's heroic couplets were no longer considered the appropriate vehicle for classical myths. Like the German romantic poets mentioned earlier, English poets used the myths to express the effect of classical literature and art on their own emotions. John Keats (1795–1821) was inspired by the Greeks, although he knew no Greek, and expressed his admiration and enthusiasm in the sonnet "On First Looking into Chapman's Homer" and the "Ode on a Grecian Urn." He used the myth of Diana and Endymion as the basis of his long poem *Endymion*, in which other myths (Venus and Adonis, Glaucus and Scylla, Arethusa) were included.

His slightly older contemporary and friend, Percy Bysshe Shelley (1792–1822), was very widely read in the classics and translated many Greek and Roman works. His drama *Prometheus Unbound* used the Aeschylean hero to express his views on tyranny and liberty. Prometheus is the unconquered champion of humanity, who is released from his agony while Jupiter is overthrown. "I was averse," said Shelley, "from a catastrophe so feeble as that of reconciling the Champion with the Oppressor of mankind." Thus, in the tradition of Aeschylus and Euripides, Shelley changed the myth for his own moral and political purposes. His poems are full of allusions to classical mythology. One of the greatest, *Adonais*, is his lament for the death of Keats, whom he portrays as the dead Adonis. Aphrodite (Urania) mourns for him, as do a succession of personifications, including Spring and Autumn (*Adonais* 16):

> Grief made the young Spring wild, and she threw down
> Her kindling [growing] buds, as if she Autumn were,
> Or they dead leaves; since her delight is flown,
> For whom should she have waked the sullen year?
> To Phoebus was not Hyacinth so dear
> Nor to himself Narcissus, as to both
> Thou, Adonais.

Shelley and the Romantics anticipate the uses of classical myths in nineteenth-century literature, art, and education.[7] In England the classics remained the foundation of formal schooling, and the knowledge of classical mythology was widespread if not very deeply understood. Increasingly the learning of classical literature was linked to morality, a process that was furthered by the doctrines of Matthew Arnold (1822–1888), who in *Culture and Anarchy* (1869) saw "Hebraism" and "Hellenism" as the inspiration of modern ideals. The latter, he said, aimed at seeing "things as they really are." Nevertheless, there were many creative uses of the classical myths. Arnold himself was a very good classicist and translator and a gifted critic and poet, who looked back to the classical world for the "moral grandeur" that he found to be missing in his own age.

Many other poets used the classical myths for their own purposes; in *Ulysses* (1833, published in 1842) Alfred Tennyson used the hero setting forth once more "to strive, to seek, to find, and not to yield," as an example for the poet who must continue "going forward and braving the struggle of life." The epic *Life and Death of Jason* (1867) by William Morris was unusual in scale, since most authors, poets, and novelists (of whom George Eliot was perhaps the most imbued with knowledge of the classics) preferred to use themes from classical literature for shorter poems, allegory, or allusion. The influence of Homer was especially strong in the ideals of English education, where the *arete* of Achilles was thought to inspire physical courage and manly vigor. At the same time, the aristocratic milieu of Homeric action appealed to the sentiment of educated Victorians, who had little sympathy for the Homeric Thersites. Nevertheless, it was not so much the individualism of Achilles as the group discipline of Sparta that proved to be a more important influence, and lessons were learned more from classical history than from mythology.

Classical mythology also became the object of serious study by linguists and anthropologists, of whom Max Müller (1823–1900), professor of comparative philology at Oxford, was the earliest and in some ways the most influential and most misleading (see p. 6). Once scholars began to develop unitary theories of mythology, the creative use of classical mythology was threatened. Yet, as we have seen in our own century, the myths have refused to die, and they still inspire writers, artists, and musicians.

CLASSICAL MYTHOLOGY IN AMERICA

The Seventeenth through the Nineteenth Centuries

The hard life and grinding work ethic in colonial America left little opportunity for the study of classical mythology, even though Sandys' translation of Ovid was largely written in Virginia. Americans in colonial times read Homer (in Pope's translation), Vergil (more in Dryden's translation than in Latin), and Ovid (both in Latin and in Sandys' translation and in the literal prose translation of John Clarke, published in London in 1742) and included Vergil and Ovid in the school curriculum, not always with approval. Cotton Mather believed that classical poetry was frivolous and dangerous for the soul: "Preserve the chastity of your soul from the dangers you may incur, by a conversation with the Muses, that are no better than harlots," he said in 1726. The great Boston teacher, Ezekiel Cheever, warned his pupils not to be charmed by Ovid's *Metamorphoses* and reminded them of the example of "young Austin" (St. Augustine), who wept for Dido when he should have shed tears for Christ.[8]

More powerful voices attacked the primacy of the classics in education on utilitarian grounds or because they were thought to be a sign of the subservience of America to the Old World. Emerson in 1837 spoke for the intellectual independence of America: "We have listened too long to the courtly muses of Europe." Noah Webster in 1783, Francis Hopkinson in 1784, Benjamin Rush in 1789, Thomas Paine in 1795, all spoke eloquently for broadening the base of American education. Although the classical languages remained an essential part of college entrance requirements (and therefore of the school curriculum) until the twentieth century, the arguments of Webster and Rush were effective and the moral arguments that supported the classics in Europe (especially in Britain) were less widely heard in America. Nevertheless, the study of mythology was still thought to have some value, and Thomas Bulfinch, whose *Age of Fable* was published in 1855, believed that it could promote virtue and happiness even if it was not useful knowledge.

Nathaniel Hawthorne quite purposefully pursued a moral goal in retelling the myths in his *Wonder Book* (1851) and *Tanglewood Tales* (1853). In the preface to the former, he said that the myths were "legitimate subjects for every age to clothe with its own garniture of manners and sentiment, and to imbue with its own morality." Thus in the story of the Apples of the Hesperides ("The Three Golden Apples") Hercules is imagined to feel regret that he had spent so long talking to the Graeae, and Hawthorne comments:

 But thus it always is with persons who are destined to perform great things. What they have already done seems less than nothing. What they have taken in hand to do seems worth toil, danger, and life itself.

It is difficult to combine this attitude with Ovid's stories of the gods in love or with the shameful acts of many heroes. Hawthorne simply left out Theseus' desertion of Ariadne and Jason's of Medea. "The objectionable characteristics seem to be a parasitical growth, having no essential connection with the original fable" (from "The

Wayside," in *Tanglewood Tales*). Jupiter becomes consistently digni-fied: in the tale of Baucis and Philemon ("The Miraculous Pitcher"), Philemon is impressed by the disguised god:

> Here was the grandest figure that ever sat so humbly beside a
> cottage door. When the stranger conversed it was with gravity,
> and in such a way that Philemon felt irresistibly moved to tell him
> everything which he had most at heart. This is always the feeling
> that people have, when they meet with anyone wise enough to
> comprehend all their good and evil, and to despise not a tittle
> of it.

Indeed the bowdlerization of Ovid was both a feature of school texts in the nineteenth century and a reason for his decline. George Stuart (1882), in his widely used text, omitted all the love stories (even Daphne!), except for those involving boys (Hyacinthus was included), and chose to emphasize manly courage and violence, along with the most desiccated grammar. This approach could, and did, lead only to the death of mythology as a living subject of study and pleasure.

The Twentieth Century

In the twentieth century, the traditional tales have taken on vigorous new life. In part this is the result of studies in comparative anthropol-ogy and psychology, which have led to new versions of the old leg-ends. We can only mention here a few examples from a vast number. Isamu Noguchi's sets for the ballet *Orpheus* (1948) are one example (see p. 303), John Cheever's story "The Swimmer," a retelling of the saga of Odysseus with a sardonic ending, is another. Several films described in Chapter 26 are clearly indebted to the theories of Jung and Freud. Among poets, Ezra Pound (1885–1972) used classical mythological allusions throughout his poems.

Like Pound, T. S. Eliot (1888–1965) spent his creative years in Europe, having gained a classical education in America. His poetry and plays are full of allusions to classical mythology, and his play *The Family Reunion* (1939) is based on the saga of the House of Atreus. So also is the trilogy by Eugene O'Neill, *Mourning Becomes Electra* (1931), where the saga is set in nineteenth-century New England. O'Neill's *Desire Under the Elms* (1924) sets the myth of Phaedra and Hippolytus in New England in 1850. Robinson Jeffers (1887-1962) adapted Euripides' *Medea* in 1947 and *Hippolytus,* entitled *The Cretan Woman,* in 1954.

More recently feminist theories and interpretations (discussed on pp. 14–15) have given new life to many classical myths, particularly those involving the tragic heroines (e.g., Clytemnestra, Antigone, Medea, Phaedra), who stand as universal examples of leaders, victims, destroyers, mothers, daughters, wives, or lovers. The feminist approach has led also to a deeper understanding of Ovid's *Metamorphoses*, in which young women so often are portrayed as victims.

OTHER TWENTIETH-CENTURY USES OF CLASSICAL MYTHOLOGY

In Europe and elsewhere, classical myths have been a rich source of inspiration in the twentieth century. Among the most famous and complex works is *Ulysses* (1922), by James Joyce (1882–1941), in which the events of Bloomsday (June 16, 1904) are narrated in chapters that roughly correspond to episodes in the *Odyssey*. The hero, as is often the case in modern adaptations of classical saga, is antiheroic; but the transformation of the world of Odysseus into Dublin in 1904 is both faithful to Homer and original. The work owes much to psychological discoveries, especially those of Freud; yet in the Circe episode (set in a Dublin brothel with Bella as Circe), the substance of the allegory is also close both to Homer and to Spenser (discussed above).

Metamorphosis itself is the theme of *The Metamorphosis (Die Verwandlung,* 1915) by Franz Kafka (1883–1924), in which again Freudian psychology enriches the theme of human transformation into a "monstrous bug" (or "vermin"). While there is no direct derivation from Ovid's *Metamorphoses,* the theme itself is common to Ovid and Kafka. To give one example from many, Ovid's Io (Book 1) is alienated, like Kafka's Gregor Samsa, from her family by her metamorphosis, and we observe her tragedy, like his, through the medium of her human mind.

In French literature, the Theban saga and the myth of Orpheus have both been especially popular. The dramas of Jean Anouilh (1910–1987) include *Eurydice* and *Antigone* (as well as *Médée*). In the first named, Orpheus is a café violinist, Eurydice an actress, and Death a commercial traveler. Jean Cocteau (1889–1963) wrote *Orphée* (1927), *Antigone* (1928), and *La machine infernale* (1934), on the Oedipus theme. André Gide (1869–1951), turned to the myths of Philoctetes (1897) and Narcissus (1899) to discuss moral questions;

and his play *Oedipe* (1926) discusses the "the quarrel between individualism and submission to religious authority." Finally, *Amphitryon 38* (1929), by Jean Giraudoux (1882–1944), owes its serial number, according to the author, to the thirty-seven previous dramatizations of the myth that he had identified. Giraudoux also wrote a one-act play, *The Apollo of Bellac,* in which the god appears as a nondescript inventor. Better known is his play *La Guerre de Troie n'aura pas lieu* (The Trojan War Will Not Take Place, 1935), translated by Christopher Fry with the title *Tiger at the Gates.* In this play, Hector and Ulysses agree that Helen will be returned to Menelaus and so the war will be avoided. But a drunken incident nevertheless precipitates the fated hostilities, and Cassandra at the end prophesies the inevitable action of Homer's *Iliad*—"and now the Grecian poet will have his word."

In literature in Spanish, the Argentinian Jorge Luis Borges (1899–1986) was especially provocative in his use of classical mythology, whose importance to him is indicated by the title of his best-known collection of short stories, *Labyrinths* (1953, translated into English, 1962). "The Immortal" begins with the antique dealer Joseph Cartaphilus of Smyrna offering the Princess of Lucinge a six-volume set of Pope's *Iliad.* A little later he dies during a voyage to Smyrna on the ship *Zeus,* but he leaves in one of the volumes a manuscript relating his experiences in many ages as a kind of Odysseus. His account ends:

 "I have been Homer; shortly I shall be No One, like Ulysses; shortly I shall be all men; I shall be dead."

On quite a different scale, the enormous *Odyssey, A Modern Sequel* of the Greek author Nikos Kazantzakis (1938, translated into English, 1958) also takes Odysseus beyond the limitations of place. He travels through the world until his search for a perfect society is transformed into a search for himself, ending with his isolation in the Antarctic, where death comes gently to him, as Tiresias had foretold in the *Odyssey.*

It is not surprising that our survey ends with Homer, the first and greatest creator of the literature of classical mythology. The myths and sagas, like the great mythical figures of the gods and heroes, have proved indestructible because of their universal quality, expressed in the words of Borges quoted above, and interpreted in countless works of poets, dramatists, and other writers for the greater part of three thousand years.

CLASSICAL MYTHOLOGY IN ART

CLASSICAL MYTHOLOGY IN THE ART OF LATE ANTIQUITY

Despite the decline of the influence of the gods in the life of the cities and individuals, they continued to be a source of allegory, especially in funerary art. With the spread of inhumation (from about A.D. 140), wealthy patrons commissioned reliefs on sarcophagi (i.e., marble or stone coffins), whose mythological subjects were allegories of the resurrection of the soul (the finding of Ariadne by Dionysus, illustrated on p. 464, was especially popular in this connection), of the triumph of virtue over evil (e.g., the Labors of Heracles or scenes of battles with the Amazons), or of hope for everlasting life (symbolized especially by Dionysus and the vine). These subjects were equally appropriate for pagan and Christian patrons, and so classical mythology continued to provide material for artistic representations even after the triumph of Christianity.

Here are a few examples from the third and fourth centuries. In the cemetery beneath St. Peter's basilica in the Vatican is a third-century wall mosaic showing Christ with the attributes of Apollo as sun-god (Color Plate 5). He ascends in the chariot of the sun, whose rays, as well as the cross, emanate from his head, while in the background the vine of Dionysus is both a decorative and a symbolic feature. Also in the third century, Christ appears as Orpheus in a fresco in a Christian catacomb in Rome, and a century later Hercules is shown killing the Hydra in another Christian catacomb fresco. In the fourth century, a Christian woman, Projecta, had her splendid silver-gilt wedding casket decorated with figures of the Muses and of sea-gods and goddesses attended by mythological monsters. The Muses and sea divinities appear in mosaics from the provinces, including Britain and Germany, and the myth of Actaeon is the subject of a third-century mosaic from Cirencester (the Roman Corinium) in Britain.

Of all mythological figures Dionysus proved the most durable, in part because the vine was a powerful symbol in Christian allegory, in part because Dionysus and his myths were associated with mysteries that gave hope of salvation to individuals. The myth of Ariadne (mentioned above) often appears for this reason. In the Church of Sta. Costanza at Rome, built in the fourth century to house the sarcophagi of members of the Christian Emperor Constantine's family, the vault mosaics show Dionysus and the vintage in a Christian context. The vintage is again the subject of the reliefs on the sarcophagus of Constantine's daughter. In contexts that may be Christian or pagan, Dionysus and his maenads, along with Hercules and his lion, appear on the silver dishes from the fourth century that were found at Mildenhall in Britain. An opponent of Dionysus, the Thracian king Lycurgus, is the subject of a floor mosaic now in Vienna and of a famous glass cup (Color Plate 6), both showing Lycurgus trapped in the god's vine.

Scenes from classical mythology continued to inspire painters of manuscript illuminations. For example, the "Vatican Vergil" manuscript of about A.D. 400 has forty-one miniatures, and there are ten in the so-called *Vergilius Romanus* manuscript, which dates from about 500. Mythological figures maintained their classical forms better in the Byzantine East than in the West. They appear in manuscripts, on ivory plaques and boxes, and in many other media, including silver work, pottery, and textiles.

Mythological Representations and the Stars

We have seen above how the mythological figures survived in astronomy and astrology, and they were frequently depicted in astronomical and astrological manuscripts. The ninth-century manuscripts of Aratus (in Cicero's Latin translation) show Perseus still in recognizable classical form, with cap, sword, winged sandals, and Gorgon's head, and ancient classical forms still appear in a few manuscripts as late as the eleventh century.

Two other traditions, however, combined to change the classical gods beyond recognition, the one Western and the other Eastern. In the West the artist would plot the position of a constellation and then link up the individual stars in the form of the mythological figure whose name the constellation bore. Since the artists were more interested in the pictorial qualities of the subject, the illustrations were usually astronomically inaccurate. In the East, however, the approach was scientifically more accurate, since the Arabs used Ptolemy's astronomical work, which (by a corruption of the word *megiste* in the Greek title) they called *Almagest*. The Arab artists therefore plotted the constellations accurately, while the mythological figures took on new forms. Hercules appeared as an Arab, with scimitar, turban, and Oriental trousers; Perseus carried, in place of the Gorgon's head, a bearded demon's head, which gave its name *Algol* (Arabic for "demon") to one of the stars in the constellation of Perseus. (See the sky-map illustrated on p. 589.)

Some of these changes went back to Babylonian religion. In the Arab manuscripts Mercury is a scribe and Jupiter a judge, just as in Babylonian mythology the god Nebo had been a scribe and Marduk a judge. Even in the West, in thirteenth-century Italian sculpture, Mercury appears as a scribe or teacher, Jupiter as a monk or bishop, and other classical gods take on similar guises.

Mythological Handbooks and Their Iconography

We have already mentioned the importance of handbooks in the survival of classical mythology. In the later Middle Ages handbooks appeared giving detailed instructions for the appearance of the gods, for it was important in astrology and magic to have an accurate image of the divinity whose favor was needed. One Arab handbook appeared in a Latin translation in the West after the tenth century with the title *Picatrix,* and contained, besides magic rituals and prayers, fifty detailed descriptions of gods. Some, like Saturn with "a crow's head and the feet of a camel," were changed into Oriental monsters; but in some, for example, Jupiter, who "sits on a throne and he is made of gold and ivory," the classical form remains.

An important iconography in this period was the *Liber Ymaginum Deorum* of "Albricus" (perhaps Alexander Neckham, who died in 1217), which was certainly used by Petrarch in his description of the Olympian gods (*Africa* 3. 140–262), from which we give a short extract (140–146):

> First is Jupiter, sitting in state upon his throne, holding scepter and thunderbolt. Before him his armor bearer [the eagle] lifts the Trojan boy [i.e., Ganymede] above the stars. Next with more stately gait, weighed down with gloomy age, is Saturn; with veiled head and a gray cloak, holding a rake and sickle, a farmer in aspect, he devours his sons.

A third type of handbook is represented by the *Emblemata* of Andrea Alciati (1531), in which woodcuts of gods, virtues and vices, proverbs and aphorisms, and many other subjects were depicted, each with a few lines of Latin elegiac couplets, usually containing a moral lesson. Friendship, for example was represented by a vine with clusters of grapes entwined round the trunk of a leafless elm. Alciati concluded: "[The vine] warns us by its example to choose friends whom the final day with its laws may not part from us." In 1571 a Latin commentary was added to the *Emblemata* by the French jurist Claude Mignault, which was extensive and important in its own right.

The expanded work was frequently reprinted, including duodecimo editions small enough to be carried in the pocket or saddlebag of an artist or sightseer. Alciati's *Emblemata* was one of the most important sources for the "correct" use of mythological figures as symbols or allegories, and his emblems can often be found in paintings of the later Renaissance and Baroque periods.

Two other handbooks were equally important. The *Iconologia* of Cesare Ripa was published in 1593 and reissued with woodcuts in 1603. Ripa's commentary, which was in Italian, separated the mythological figures from their narrative contexts, so that they often became abstractions with a moral meaning. This approach was valuable for artists who wished to employ allegory; and the book was translated and reissued frequently until the end of the eighteenth century.

The other important iconography was the *Imagines* of Philostratus, a Greek work of the third century A.D. describing an art collection in Naples. It was translated into French by Blaise de Vigenère in 1578 and reissued in a splendidly illustrated version in 1614, with woodcuts, explanatory poems, and commentary containing a very wide range of classical myths.

CLASSICAL MYTHOLOGY IN RENAISSANCE ART

The classical gods had survived in late antiquity and the Middle Ages, but in many disguises. Renaissance artists gave them back their classical forms. In Florence, Botticelli (1444-1510) combined medieval allegory with classical mythology in his allegorical masterpieces, *The Birth of Venus, Primavera, Venus and Mars*, and *Pallas and the Centaur*. In Venice, Giovanni Bellini (1430-1516), Giorgione (1478-1510), and his pupil Titian (1487-1576) also drew on a variety of traditions while representing the myths more or less in agreement with the handbooks. Great artists, of course, like the four named here were hardly limited by these criteria, as can be seen in Bellini's *Feast of the Gods* (see Color Plate 9).

Besides the painters already mentioned, Michelangelo at Florence and Rome, Correggio at Ferrara, and Paolo Veronese and Tintoretto at Venice were sixteenth-century masters who found inspiration in classical mythology. One of the most extensive mythological programs is the great series of paintings by the Carracci brothers in the Gallery of the Farnese Palace at Rome (1597-1604) depicting the triumph of Love by means of one classical legend after another.

Two other Renaissance works show how the classical gods recovered their antique forms. One is the map of the sky published in 1515 by the German Albrecht Dürer (see p. 589), in which the classical forms of the Western astronomical tradition combine with the scientific accuracy of the Arabs. Dürer gave the mythological figures their ancient forms; Hercules is a Greek once more and recovers his club and lionskin.

The second work is the decoration of the Vatican Stanza della Segnatura by Raphael after 1508. Here the classical, allegorical, and Christian traditions combined to exalt the glory of the Church and its doctrine. In the place of honor (though not supreme) was Apollo, surrounded by the Muses, the poets of antiquity, and Renaissance humanists. Classical mythology and Renaissance humanism had achieved the perfect synthesis.

ILLUSTRATED EDITIONS OF OVID

In the sixteenth and seventeenth centuries Ovid's works were repeatedly issued in illustrated editions, which were frequently used as sources by artists. The series began with a prose translation of the *Metamorphoses* known as the *Grande Olympe,* published at Paris in 1539. The most important of the early editions was that of Bernard Salomon, *La Métamorphose d'Ovide Figurée,* published at Lyons in 1557 and reissued at Lyons in 1559 (in Italian) and at Antwerp in 1591. A German translation of the *Metamorphoses* was issued by Virgilio Solis at Frankfurt in 1563, and another at Leipzig in 1582, while an Italian translation by Andrea d'Anguillara was published at Venice in 1584.

The most influential editions were those of Antonio Tempestà and George Sandys. Tempestà published *Metamorphoseon sive Transformationum Ovidianarum Libri Quindecim* at Amsterdam in 1606. His book consists of engravings of 150 scenes from the *Metamorphoses* without text, and it became an important sourcebook of classical stories for painters. The importance of Sandys lay rather in his connection of pictures with the text and commentary, which we have mentioned above (pp. 568–569). In his preface to the 1632 edition he says:

    And for thy farther delight I have contracted the substance of every Booke into as many Figures . . . since there is betweene Poetry and Picture so great a congruitie; the one . . . a speaking Picture, and the other a silent Poesie: Both Daughters of the Imagination.

Sky-Map of the Northern Hemisphere, by Albrecht Dürer (1471–1528). Woodcut, 1515; $16\frac{3}{4} \times 16\frac{3}{4}$ in. The Latin title means "Figures of the northern sky with the twelve signs of the Zodiac." Dürer's sky-maps are patterned on Arab celestial maps, but this is one of the earliest Renaissance works in which the classical figures resume their classical forms. Hercules (seen just below and to the right of center) has his club and lionskin; Perseus (just above and to the left of center) holds the Gorgon's head *(caput Meduse)* instead of the Arabic monster, Algol. Individual stars are indicated by numbers corresponding to Books 8 and 9 of Ptolemy's *Almagest*. The signs of the Zodiac encircle the map, and in the corners are three ancient writers on astronomy and one medieval scholar: Aratus of Cilicia (third century B.C.); Ptolemy of Egypt (second century A.D.); Al Sufi, written here as Azophi (Abdul Rahman, Arab astronomer of the tenth century A.D.); Manilius of Rome (early first century A.D.). Dürer made the original version of this map in 1503, showing the heavens as they were in 1499–1500. *(The Metropolitan Museum of Art, New York, Harris Brisbane Dick Fund, 1951.)*

Sandys was helped by the outstanding quality of his artist, Francis Clein, and his engraver, Salomon Savery. They engraved a full-page illustration for each book of the poem, in which the stories of the book were represented, choosing more often the moment of greatest drama rather than the moment of metamorphosis. In addition Clein designed a splendid title page and a portrait of Ovid, each decorated with allegorical figures from classical mythology.

The principle of the interaction of words and pictures has remained a regular feature of the influence of Ovid since the publication of Sandys' 1632 edition. Ovid is the most visual of poets, and his landscapes and narrative invite pictorial representation, as can be seen in a large number of school editions of the *Metamorphoses*.

EUROPEAN ART OF THE SEVENTEENTH THROUGH THE NINETEENTH CENTURIES

Rubens

Peter Paul Rubens (1577-1640) found in classical mythology a constant source of inspiration throughout his career. During his years in Italy, between 1600 and 1608, he studied and copied classical works of art and became thoroughly familiar with the representations of classical mythology. He already had a good knowledge of Latin literature, and through his brother, Philip (an excellent classicist), he had access to the brilliant circle of humanists that centered on his fellow countryman, Justus Lipsius. Rubens painted great numbers of scenes in which he showed with energy and brilliance his understanding of classical mythology.

In his last years Rubens was commissioned to decorate the hunting lodge of King Philip IV in Madrid with a series of paintings illustrating the legends in Ovid's *Metamorphoses*. Rubens, who began the commission in his sixtieth year, completed no less than 112 oil sketches, of which about 45 survive (see p. 440 for *The Apotheosis of Hercules*). Only a handful of the final full-size paintings survive, still to be seen together in Madrid. This series is perhaps the most ambitious of all the illustrated Ovids, and the oil sketches are among the most beautiful of all the Baroque representations of classical myths. Rubens also turned to Homer and Statius for inspiration for his designs for the tapestries portraying the life of Achilles. Most of these oil sketches can still be seen together in Rotterdam.

Poussin

Nicolas Poussin (1594–1665), although French by birth, spent nearly all his productive life in Rome, and, like Rubens, he never ceased to draw inspiration from the classical legends and to meditate on their deeper meaning beyond the narrative. Among painters he is the most intellectual interpreter of the classical myths, and those who wish to understand best what "classicism" means in the centuries following the Renaissance should study the long series of drawings and paintings done by Poussin on mythological themes (see Color Plates 12 and 14).

Other Painters

From the time of Poussin to our own day, artists have returned again and again to the classical myths, and the ancient gods and heroes have survived in art as in literature. We cannot here satisfactorily survey even a corner of this vast field of study, but we can refer to some important stages in the use of classical myths by artists.

Painters in France and Italy in the seventeenth and eighteenth centuries used classical myths for narrative paintings on a heroic scale, for these were considered to belong to history painting, the most highly esteemed genre. The leading painter at the court of Louis XV, François Boucher (1703–1770), produced a long series of classical scenes, often pastoral and usually erotic. In the last third of the eighteenth century, this somewhat sentimental approach to classical mythology gave way to a sterner view of the classical past, which placed a high value on the moral lessons to be drawn from history. In the nineteenth century, therefore, when painters in England and France returned to subjects taken from classical mythology, their approach tended to be moralistic, paralleling (as far as art can parallel literature) the approach typified by Hawthorne and Kingsley, discussed earlier.

CLASSICAL MYTHOLOGY IN AMERICAN ART

During the first century of the Republic, mythological subjects were often copied by schoolgirls from engravings (the illustrations for Pope's translation of the *Iliad* were a favorite source), or were imaginatively treated by women in their spare time at home (the illustration on the cover of this book is an example). Artists who studied in Europe copied paintings of classical subjects and exhibited them when they returned. The earliest such exhibition, given in Boston in 1730 by John Smibert (1688-1751), aroused great public interest. Ten years earlier, a Swedish immigrant, Gustavus Hesselius (1682-1755), painted the earliest known American mythological works, *Bacchus and Ariadne* (now in Detroit) and *Bacchanal* (now in Philadelphia).

While the leading American painters (such as Copley, West, Allston, and Vanderlyn) sometimes painted mythological subjects, American taste soon turned to historical themes and to the dramatic potential of the American landscape. One of the best American mythological paintings is John Vanderlyn's *Ariadne,* painted in 1811 and now in Philadelphia (see Color Plate 17). It depicts the scene described in Ovid's *Heroides* 10. 7-10, as Ariadne wakes to find herself deserted. When it was first exhibited it aroused interest and controversy. But by Vanderlyn's time it was already clear that American painters would find material in sources other than classical mythology.

In sculpture, however, the classical influence continued to be strong. Horatio Greenough (1805-1852) used Pheidias' statue of Zeus at Olympia as the basis for his seated statue (1832-1839) of George Washington, now in the National Museum of American History but planned originally for the Rotunda of the Capitol. On the sides of Washington's throne are mythological reliefs, on one side Apollo as the sun-god rising into the sky with his chariot and on the other the infants Heracles and Iphicles with the serpents sent by Hera. Greenough wanted Heracles to be an allegory of North America which "struggles successfully with the obstacles and dangers of an incipient political existence."

There was a group of expatriate American artists living in Rome, who are described in Hawthorne's *The Marble Faun* (1859). Among these was Harriet Hosmer (1820-1908), whose busts of *Medusa* (illustrated on p. 414), and *Daphne* (both completed in 1854) were meant to express her views on celibacy and beauty. Her *Oenone* was based on Tennyson's poem *Oenone* rather than directly on Ovid's *Heroides*.

CLASSICAL MYTHOLOGY IN TWENTIETH-CENTURY ART

Classical mythology has continued to be a vigorous source of inspiration for artists in our own century. In France and Spain especially, Georges Braque (1882-1963) and Pablo Picasso (1881-1973) returned frequently to classical themes. Perhaps the most famous example of such inspiration is Picasso's long series of works involving the legend of the Minotaur, which he used (especially in the period of the Spanish Civil War) to comment on the horror and violence of much of modern life as he observed it. (See the illustration on p. 462.)

In recent decades, artists have interpreted the classical myths allegorically, as we have seen with Noguchi's use of the myth of Orpheus. Many artists have been influenced by psychological theories, especially those of Freud, and the series of works by Reuben Nakian on *Leda and the Swan* is an outstanding example. Many artists have returned to fairly literal representations of the myths, including David Ligare, whose *Landscape for Philemon and Baucis* we reproduce as Color Plate 22, and Milet Andrejevic, whose *Apollo and Daphne* is set in a city park. A group of Italian neoclassicsts has revived the mythological tradition in Italy, of whom Carlo Maria Mariani is the best known. All in all, it can be said the the classical tradition in mythology will continue to inspire all who care for the creative use of the imagination.

BIBLIOGRAPHY

Allen, Don Cameron. *Mysteriously Meant*. Baltimore: Johns Hopkins University Press, 1970. Deals with the rediscovery of pagan symbolism and the uses of allegory in the Renaissance.

Bush, Douglas. *Mythology and the Renaissance Tradition in English Poetry*. Minneapolis: University of Minnesota Press, 1932; New York: Norton, 1963. Includes a chronological list of poems on mythological subjects.

————. *Mythology and the Romantic Tradition in English Poetry*. Cambridge: Harvard University Press, 1937; New York: Norton, 1963.

Cumont, Franz. *Oriental Religions in Roman Paganism*. New York: Dover, 1956 [1911]. Reprint of English translation (London: Routledge, 1911) of *Les religions orientales dans le paganisme romain* (Paris, 1906). Chapter 7 is an good introduction to ancient astrology.

Galinsky, G. Karl. *The Herakles Theme*. Oxford: Basil Blackwell, 1972.

————. *Ovid's Metamorphoses: An Introduction to the Basic Aspects*. Berkeley: University of California Press, 1975.

Gilbert, Stuart. *James Joyce's Ulysses*. London: Faber & Faber, 1930.

Highet, Gilbert. *The Classical Tradition*. New York: Oxford University Press, 1939; Harper & Row, 1962. Covers an enormous range superficially, but is useful for its references.

Mayerson, Philip. *Classical Mythology in Literature, Art, and Music*. Waltham, Mass.: Xerox College Publishing, 1971. An exceptionally well-written survey designed to increase understanding of works of literature, art, and music inspired by classical mythology.

Pearcy, Lee. *The Mediated Muse: English Translations of Ovid, 1560–1700.* Hamden, Conn.: Archon Press, 1984.

Reid, Jane Davidson. *The Oxford Guide to Classical Mythology in the Arts 1300–1900s.* 2 vols. Oxford: Oxford University Press, 1993. The most comprehensive reference work listing works of art, music, and literature, with a bibliography.

Scherer, Margaret R. *The Legends of Troy in Art and Literature.* 2d ed. New York: Phaidon, 1964

Seznec, J. *The Survival of the Pagan Gods.* New York: Pantheon Books, 1953. First published in French as *La Survivance des dieux antiques.* Studies of the Warburg Institute. 11. London, 1940.

Stanford, W. B. *The Ulysses Theme.* Oxford: Blackwell, 1963; Ann Arbor: University of Michigan Press, 1968.

Starnes, DeWitt T., and **Talbert, Ernest W.** *Classical Myth and Legend in Renaissance Dictionaries.* Chapel Hill: University of North Carolina Press, 1955.

Van Keuren, Frances. *Guide to Research in Classical Art and Mythology.* Chicago: American Library Association, 1991. A bibliographical reference book, clearly arranged by topic and period.

Weitzmann, Kurt. *Age of Spirituality.* New York: Metropolitan Museum of Art; Princeton: Princeton University Press, 1979. This catalogue of the art of the late antique and early Christian worlds contains an authoritative account of the uses of classical mythology in the art of late antiquity.

Wilkinson, L. P. *Ovid Recalled.* New York: Cambridge University Press, 1955.

The principal Renaissance mythographies, iconologies, and iconographies have been reissued in a fifty-five volume facsimile series edited by Stephen Orgel, *The Renaissance and the Gods* (New York and London: Garland Press, 1976).

CLASSICAL MYTHOLOGY IN MUSIC AND FILM

26

MYTHOLOGY IN MUSIC

The topic of classical mythology in music is vast, rich, and important; we can only attempt to suggest the significance and vitality of Greek and Roman inspiration in this fascinating and rewarding area. The genre of opera provides the most obvious and significant focal point for such a cursory discussion, with an emphasis upon works that may be seen or heard in contemporary performances. Fortunately, the ever-expanding repertoires of the recording companies are making even the more esoteric works accessible. To derive the most value from this section, a recent complete catalogue of compact discs and cassette tapes will be a great asset; we may be hopeful that *all* the many important compositions once issued on 78s and LPs will be reissued as compact discs.

Music was inherent in the culture of ancient Greece and Rome. Drama, for example, was rooted in music and the dance, and its origins were religious. Music was also linked with drama in the Middle Ages, in the liturgical mystery and miracle plays, and again the impetus was religious. During the Renaissance, with its veneration of antiquity, tragedy and comedy were often inspired by Greek and Roman originals, and quite elaborate musical choruses and interludes were sometimes added. The years ushering in the Baroque period (ca. 1600–1750), however, provide the real beginning for our survey.

In 1581, Vincenzo Galilei (father of the renowned astronomer), spokesman for a literary and artistic society of Florence called the Camerata, published *Dialogo della Musica Antica e della Moderna.*

The revolutionary goals of the Camerata were inspired by a reaction against the prevailing polyphonic style of music—intricate and multi-textured in its counterpoint, with words sung by several voices to create a tapestry of sound. Texts set to music in this way could not be understood; Galilei suggested a return to the simplicity of ancient Greek music and drama. Now Galilei and company knew very little about the actual musical setting of a Greek play by Aeschylus, Sophocles, or Euripides (for that matter, we do not know much more), but they believed that ancient drama was sung in its entirety, not realizing fully the distinction between the episodes and the choral interludes. We can agree, however, that Greek musical settings must have been simple in terms of instrumentation and melodic harmony. Choral music was generally accompanied by the *aulos,* or *auloi* (double pipe)—often translated as "flute" but actually more akin to a modern oboe.

The Camerata argued that words should be clearly heard and understood and the melodic line should reflect and underscore the meaning and emotion of the text. Their new style was appropriately labeled *monodic* (as opposed to polyphonic); it represents in large part the declamatory element that survived in opera as *recitativo,* or recitative—spoken dialogue lightly accompanied by music (of various kinds depending on period and composer), to be distinguished from set melodic pieces—arias, duets, trios, and so on.

In 1594 or 1597, members of the Camerata produced what may be called the first opera; its title *Dafne* and its theme reflect the spell cast by the ancient world. Ottavio Rinuccini wrote the text (which is still extant); Jacopo Peri composed the music, with the help of Jacopo Corsi (some of whose music is all that survives); and Giulio Caccini may have contributed as well. A second opera followed, *Euridice,* which has survived and on occasion receives scholarly revivals. Peri again wrote most of the score, but apparently Caccini added some music and then composed another *Euridice* of his own.

The first genius in the history of this new form was Claudio Monteverdi (1567–1643); his first opera, *Orfeo* (1607), lifts the musical and dramatic potential initiated by his predecessors to the level of great art appreciated in performance to this day. The subjects of some of his subsequent works reveal the power and impetus provided by Greece and Rome: *Arianna* (her "Lament," which is all that survives, is still popular today), *Tirse e Clori, Il Matrimonio d'Alceste con Admeto, Adone, Le Nozze d'Enea con Lavinia, Il Ritorno d'Ulisse in Patria,* and finally *L'Incoronazione di Poppea,* which is based upon Roman history.

Monteverdi's pupil, Cavalli, wrote more than forty operas. Among his best known are *Giasone (Jason,* 1649) and *Ercole Amante* (1662). His contemporary, Marc Antonio Cesti, is said to have composed more than one hundred operas; of the eleven surviving (all from the years 1649–1669), *Il Pomo d'Oro (The Golden Apple),* which deals with the contest for the Apple of Discord, was the most famous—a super-spectacle in five acts and sixty-six scenes, including several ballets in each act and requiring twenty-four separate stage sets. And thus opera developed in Italy. The list of composers is long and the bibliography of their many works inspired by classical antiquity impressive; particularly startling is the number of repetitions of favorite subjects.

Many of the operatic composers of the early period wrote cantatas as well. As examples of this musical form, we shall mention two works by Johann Sebastian Bach (1685–1750) in the catalogue of his secular cantatas. Some of these he himself entitled *dramma per musica,* and modern critics have gone so far as to label them "operettas." In Cantata 201 *(Der Streit zwischen Phoebus und Pan),* Bach presents the contest between Phoebus and Pan as a musical satire against a hostile critic of his works, Johann Adolph Scheibe. The text is derived from Ovid's version. Mt. Tmolus and Momus, god of mirth, award the victory to Pan, while Midas is punished with a pair of ass's ears. Cantata 213 *(Hercules auf dem Scheidewege)* depicts Hercules at the crossroads; he rejects the blandishments of Pleasure in favor of the hardship, virtue, and renown promised to him by Virtue. The more familiar *Christmas Oratorio* uses the musical themes of this cantata.

In England during the Baroque period, plays with incidental music and ballet became very much the fashion; these led eventually to the evolution of opera in a more traditional sense. John Blow wrote (ca. 1684) a musical-dramatic composition, *Venus and Adonis.* Although the work bears the subtitle "A masque for the entertainment of the king," it is in reality a pastoral opera constructed along the most simple lines. But it was Blow's pupil, Henry Purcell, who created a masterpiece that has become one of the landmarks in the history of opera, *Dido and Aeneas* (ca. 1689). The work was composed for Josias Priest's Boarding School for Girls, in Chelsea; the libretto by Nahum Tate comes from Book 4 of Vergil's *Aeneid.*[1] The artful economy and tasteful blending of the various elements in Purcell's score have often been admired. Dido's lament ("When I am laid in Earth") as she breathes her last is surely one of the most noble and touching of arias.

In France, Jean-Baptiste Lully (1632–1687), a giant in the development of opera, produced *Cadmus et Hermione* (1673) in collaboration with the poet Philippe Quinault; this was the first of a series of fifteen such tragic operas (twelve of them to texts by Quinault). Some of the other titles confirm the extent of the debt to Greece and Rome: *Alceste, Thesée, Atys, Proserpine, Persée, Phaéton, Acis et Galatée*. Jean-Philippe Rameau (1683–1764) was the most significant heir to the mantle of Lully. He too created many operas and opera-ballets on Greek and Roman themes, for example, *Hippolyte et Aricie, Castor et Pollux, Dardanus,* and *Les Fêtes d'Hébé.*

George Frideric Handel (1685–1759) was one of the greatest composers of the first half of the eighteenth century. He was a prolific musician, and although the general public knows him primarily for his oratorios, he was very much concerned with the composition of operas. In fact many of his oratorios on secular themes are operatic in nature and, although intended for the concert hall, are much closer to the theater than to the church; and some deal with mythology, for example, *Semele* and *Hercules.* Handel wrote forty operas and fortunately revivals and recordings have become more frequent in recent years to reveal their abundant riches. Many of Handel's operas are based on history, for example, *Attone, Agrippina, Giulio Cesare,* and *Serse;* some are more strictly mythological—*Acis and Galatea* (a pastorale), *Admeto,* and *Deidamia.*

Christoph Willibald Gluck (1714–1787) is the composer of the earliest opera to maintain any kind of position in the standard repertoire, *Orfeo ed Euridice* (first version 1762). This beautiful work, restrained in its passion and exquisite in its melody, remains one of the most artistically rewarding settings of the myth. The libretto, by Raniero Calzabigi, proved a great help to Gluck, whose avowed purpose was to compose music that would best serve the poetry and the plot. Musical extravaganzas with artificial and even absurd plots and the immoderate intrusion of ballet and spectacle had become too fashionable. As a result Gluck and Calzabigi desperately felt a need for reform. It was appropriate that Gluck should resort to the same theme as that of his idealistic predecessors. Orpheus' arias expressing his anguish at the loss of his wife, *"Che puro ciel"* and *"Che farò senza Euridice,"* well illustrate the highest embodiment of these ideals. In the first version of Gluck's opera, the role Orfeo was written for a castrato—a male who had been castrated and therefore sang soprano and who undertook both male and female roles. When Gluck wrote a second version of his opera for production in Paris in 1774, he reworked the role for a tenor. It is now usually sung by a mezzo-soprano or contralto; but performances and recordings may be found sung by both male and female voices.

Gluck again worked with Calzabigi for *Alceste* (first version 1767). Derived from Euripides' play, it is another impressive achievement more monumental in character than *Orfeo,* but nevertheless equally touching in its nobility and sentiment. Their third collaboration, *Paride ed Elena* (1770), although originally a failure, sounds most enjoyable today. Subsequent operas by Gluck, *Iphigénie en Aulide, Iphigénie en Tauride,* and *Écho et Narcisse,* are all beautiful works. Richard Wagner admired and reworked the score of *Iphigénie en Aulide* to create the version that is usually performed. Niccolò (or Nicola) Piccinni, a rival of Gluck (they were both commissioned by the French Opéra to write an *Orfeo*), composed more than one hundred operas, many of them on classical subjects.

There are many other important composers of the eighteenth century who were classically inspired. Antonio Sacchini wrote *Dardanus* (1784) and a popular masterwork, *Oedipe à Colone* (1786). Luigi Cherubini (1760–1842) deserves special mention for his excellent *Médée* (1797), an opera on occasion revived for a prima donna of the caliber of Magda Olivero or Maria Callas, who can meet the technical and histrionic demands of the title role. Franz Joseph Haydn (1732–1809) composed an *Orfeo ed Euridice* (1791), which is considered by many to be the finest of his many operas.

Wolfgang Amadeus Mozart (1756–1791) had some interest in mythological themes. His *Idomeneo, Rè di Creta* (1781) is a fascinating, although imperfect, masterpiece, well worth investigation, as is his "theater serenade," *Ascanio in Alba* (1771). Other youthful works by Mozart deal with Roman history as legend: *Mitridate, Rè di Ponto* (1770), based upon Racine's play about King Mithridates, and *Il Sogno di Scipione* (1772). The latter, a serenata, has a text by Metastasio, derived from Cicero's *Somnium Scipionis (Dream of Scipio),* wherein Scipio Aemilianus has a vision of an Elysium that is Platonic to be sure but also, in its chauvinism and substance, very much like the Elysium of Vergil. Also by Mozart (when only eleven years old) is a short opera *Apollo et Hyacinthus* (1767). The Latin text by Father Rufinus Widl transforms this famous tale of homosexual passion into a romantic, heterosexual triangle: Zephyrus (West Wind) falls in love with Hyacinthus' sister, who also happens to be the beloved of Apollo. Mozart's much loved and admired opera, *The Magic Flute* (1791), is significant for the mythographer because of its Masonic symbolism and motifs. The matriarchal Queen of the Night, the ritual worship of Isis and Osiris, and the ordeals that the hero Tamino must endure for the revelation of the Mysteries all represent universal, thematic patterns. Mozart's last opera, *La Clemenza di Tito* (1791) is based on Roman history.

Ludwig van Beethoven (1770–1827) found some direct influence from Greece and Rome. His *Coriolanus* Overture (1807), inspired by the legendary Roman hero, might be mentioned; more to the point is his ballet music *The Creatures of Prometheus* (1801). The thematic material of this work seems in a special way to epitomize the indomitable spirit of the composer. He arranged it as a set of variations for piano; and it appears again in the final movement of his great Third Symphony (the *Eroica*). The whole aura of defiance conjured up by the romantic image of the life and music of Beethoven is strikingly parallel to that evoked by the Titan Prometheus. At any rate, Beethoven's career provides the chronological and spiritual link between eighteenth-century classicism and nineteenth-century romanticism.

The German *Lied* of the nineteenth century embodies much of the passion and longing that are the exquisite torture and delight of the romantic soul. The musical mood runs parallel to that of the *Sturm und Drang* movement in literature as typified by the works of Goethe. Several of the songs of Franz Schubert (1797–1828), for example, are set to poems on ancient themes: *Der Atlas, Fahrt zum Hades, Orest auf Tauris, Der zürnenden Diana, Fragment aus dem Aeschylus* (a chorus from the *Eumenides*), *Memnon, Philoktet,* and *Orpheus.* Also by Schubert are two lovely duets *Hektors Abschied* and *Antigone und Oedip.*

Two songs by a later romantic composer, Hugo Wolf (1860–1903), *Prometheus* and *Ganymed,* are staples of the lieder repertoire. On the other hand, his one symphonic work, a tone poem entitled *Penthesilea,* is an interesting piece of program music that is not so well known. Other interesting examples of the genre of the symphonic poem are offered by Franz Liszt (1811–1886), *Orpheus* and *Prometheus,* and by César Franck (1822–1890), *Psyché.*

The operatic achievements of the nineteenth century are among its most conspicuous glories, but by then Greek and Roman themes were no longer generally in vogue. Yet *Der Ring des Nibelungen* by Richard Wagner (1813–1883) offers exciting parallels for the study of classical mythology, particularly since he was so profoundly influenced by the *Oresteia* of Aeschylus.[2] Operas like Bellini's *Norma* (the tragic story of a Druid priestess) are, it is true, built upon Roman legendary themes, but such an exception only brings home to us more forcefully the changes being wrought in subject matter and style. It is nevertheless rash to generalize. Charles Gounod (1818–1893) wrote the opera *Philémon et Baucis* (1860), and Hector Berlioz (1803–1863) created a monumental work with *Les Troyens* (1856–1858), one of the most important masterpieces ever created on an ancient mythological subject. The work, which draws heavily upon Vergil, consists of two parts: *La Prise de Troie* (based upon Book 2 of the *Aeneid*) and *Troyens à Carthage* (the Dido and Aeneas episode from Book 4).

Toward the end of the nineteenth century, the Russian composer Sergei Ivanovich Taneiev (1856–1915), a pupil of Tchaikovsky, completed his impressive *Oresteia* (1894), based on Aeschylus. Jules Massenet (1842–1912) composed the opera *Bacchus* (1909), and Gabriel Fauré (1845–1924) wrote *Prométhée* (1900) and *Pénélope* (1913). Verismo opera, which became the rage at the turn of the century because of the genius of composers like Giacomo Puccini, turned away from classical themes in favor of the realistic and shocking or the Oriental and exotic; yet the realistic Ruggiero Leoncavallo (1858–1919) wrote an *Edipo Rè* (posthumously produced in 1920). This is in keeping with the trend in the twentieth century of returning to classical subjects. Gian Francesco Malipiero (1882–1973) used the Orpheus theme for a trilogy, *L'Orfeide* (1925), and his *Ecuba* (1941) is modeled on Euripides.

The operas of Richard Strauss (1864–1949) are among the greatest of the twentieth century. His reworkings of Greek myth in terms of modern psychology and philosophy are among the most rewarding artistic products of this or any other age. Strauss was fortunate in having as his librettist for most of these the brilliant dramatist Hugo von Hofmannsthal (1874–1929). Their collaboration for *Elektra* (1909), a work based upon Sophocles but startling in the originality of its conception, is a brilliant and profound tour de force. Strauss and Hofmannsthal again worked together to create the charming and sublime *Ariadne auf Naxos* (original version of 1912, redone in 1916); this opera-within-an-opera focuses upon the desolate and abandoned Ariadne, who longs for death but finds instead an apotheosis through the love of Bacchus.

The last three mythological operas of Strauss do not deserve the relative neglect they have suffered. *Die Aegyptische Helena* (1929, again Hofmannsthal is the librettist) plays upon the ancient version of the myth that distinguishes between the phantom Helen who went to Troy with Paris and the real Helen who remained faithful to Menelaus in Egypt. *Daphne* (1938, text by Joseph Gregor) is a most touching treatment of the same subject as that of the very first opera; its final scene (for soprano and orchestra) depicts a magical and evocative transformation that soars with typical Straussian majesty and power. Gregor was also the librettist for *Die Liebe der Danae* (1940), although he drew upon a sketch left by Hofmannsthal. The plot evolved from an ingenious amalgamation of two originally separate tales concerning Midas and his golden touch and the wooing of Danaë by Zeus in the form of a shower of gold.

A supreme operatic masterpiece is the *Oedipe* (1936) of the Romanian composer Georges Enesco (1881–1955); the brilliant score is set to a libretto by Edmond Fleg, which embraces the whole legend of Oedipus. Other works of the twentieth-century should be mentioned. Among the operas of Darius Milhaud (1892–1974) are *Oreste* (a trilogy comprising *Agamemnon, Les Choéphores,* and *Les Euménides,* 1913–1924), composed to a translation of Aeschylus by Paul Claudel; *Les Malheurs d'Orphée* (1924); and *Médée* (1938). In 1927 he wrote three short operas (each only about ten minutes long): *L'Enlèvement d'Europe, L'Abandon d'Ariane,* and *La Délivrance de Thésée.* The Swiss composer Arthur Honegger (1892–1955) wrote an impressive opera, *Antigone* (1927), set to a libretto by Jean Cocteau based upon Sophocles.

Among English composers, Benjamin Britten (1913–1976) deserves special mention for his chamber opera *The Rape of Lucretia* (1946), a beautifully taut and concise rendition of the Roman legend; the libretto by Ronald Duncan is derived from the play by André Obey, *Le Viol de Lucrèce.* Another work by Britten, *Young Apollo* (1939), a youthful "fanfare" for piano solo, string quartet, and string orchestra, depicts in sound the sun-god as a new and radiant epitome of ideal beauty. Britten's last opera, *Death in Venice* (1973), based upon the celebrated novella by Thomas Mann, also treats the idea of beauty through important archetypal images. This story about a famous writer, Aschenbach, who becomes enamored of the beautiful boy Tadzio, is framed in terms of concepts of love and beauty that are familiar from Plato's *Symposium*; the structure is also mythological because of the Nietzschean conflict between a restrained Apollo and a passionate Dionysus for the soul of the creative artist. Interwoven as well are the allegorical themes of disease, plague, and death, which go as far back as the *Iliad* and gain a specially potent classic expression in Sophocles' *Oedipus.* Also among Britten's last compositions is *Phaedra* (1975), a cantata to a text from Racine's play (in a verse translation by Robert Lowell), written expressly for the mezzo-soprano Janet Baker. Finally, among Britten's mature works is an affecting composition, *Six Metamorphoses after Ovid* for oboe solo *(Pan, Phaethon, Niobe, Bacchus, Narcissus,* and *Arethusa).*

Another English composer, William Walton (1902–1983), wrote a striking operatic version of an episode in the Trojan War, *Troilus and Cressida* (1954), based upon the medieval romance. The text of a scene from Euripides' *The Trojan Women* (in a special translation by the poet John Patrick Creagh) was scored for soprano and orchestra by the American composer Samuel Barber (1910–1981) under the title *Andromache's Farewell* (1963); a messenger has come to tell Andromache that she must relinquish her son Astyanax to the Greeks, who have decided to hurl the boy to his death from the walls of Troy. Andromache begins with the words, "So you must die, my son."

Igor Stravinsky (1882–1971) was also drawn to classical subjects. His ballet score for string orchestra, *Apollon Musagète* (1928), takes for its subject Apollo and his association with three of the Muses—Calliope, Polyhymnia, and Terpsichore (i.e., Poetry, Mime, and Dance).[3] Stravinsky also composed a melodrama entitled *Perséphone* (1934), a work utilizing orchestra, narrator, tenor soloist, mixed chorus, and children's chorus, which was inspired by the *Homeric Hymn to Demeter*. But his *Oedipus Rex* was his most significant achievement on a classical theme—a highly stylized opera-oratorio, liturgical, ritualistic, and statuesque, composed to a Latin text provided by Jean Cocteau, who condensed Sophocles' play into six episodes (Stravinsky gave Cocteau's French version to Jean Danielou, to translate into Church Latin). This ecclesiastical work, in spirit more akin to a Christian morality play than to ancient Greek drama, is scored for six solo voices, a narrator, a male chorus, and orchestra; suprisingly enough many of its musical themes are adapted from Verdi's *Aida*.

The twelve-tone (or "atonal") school of musical composition founded by Arnold Schönberg has produced some works on classical themes, for example, Egon Wellesz (1885–1974) wrote *Alkestis* (1924, libretto by Hofmannsthal) and *Die Bakchantinnen*, both from Euripides. Ernst Krenck (b. 1900), who has adopted various styles in his career (jazz idiom, romanticism, and atonality), treated the Orestes myth in *Leben des Orest* (1929). His other operas include *Orpheus und Eurydike* (1923), *Cefalo e Procri* (1933), *Tarquin* (1941), and *Pallas Athena Weint* (1952).

Peggy Glanville-Hicks (b. 1912) has composed an opera, *Nausicaa* (1961), to a text based upon the novel *Homer's Daughter* by Robert Graves; and Elizabeth Maconchy's dramatic monologue *Ariadne* (1954) offers a musical setting for a poem by Cecil Day Lewis.

Arthur Bliss (1891–1975) turned to Greek themes with his cantata, *Hymn to Apollo* (1926); an opera, *The Olympians* (1949); and a symphony for orator, chorus, and orchestra entitled *Morning Heroes*—the latter written as a tribute to his brother and his comrades who died in the Great War of 1914–1918; among the texts used are Hector's Farewell to Andromache (*Iliad* 6) and Achilles Goes Forth to Battle (*Iliad* 19).

Michael Tippett (b. 1905) has written both the text and the music for an imaginative operatic treatment of the Trojan War (largely inspired by the *Iliad*), *King Priam*. From this work, he extracted one of Achilles' songs (with guitar accompaniment) and added two others, all focusing upon the relationship between Achilles and Patroclus, to create an effectively terse and tragic cycle (1961), *Songs for Achilles* ("In the Tent," "Across the Plain," and "By the Sea"). Also inspired by the Trojan Cycle is an opera in one act by Othmar Schoeck (1886–1957), *Penthesilea* (1925, after Kleist), which may be compared, not unfavorably, to Strauss's *Electra* for dramatic impact and musical idiom.

The British composer Harrison Birtwistle (b. 1934) has provided (to a text by Peter Zinovieff) a lament upon the sorrow and death of Orpheus, for soprano soloist, *Nenia, the Death of Orpheus,* which relies upon startlingly gymnastic effects both instrumental and vocal. Nenia is a funeral dirge or the Roman goddess thereof. Birtwistle has since expanded this work into a larger-scaled composition.

Carl Orff (1895–1982) won considerable renown with his operatic treatment of mythological subjects. In 1925 he adapted Monteverdi's *Orfeo;* he wrote an *Antigonae* (1949) and subsequently *Oedipus der Tyrann,* both of which follow Sophocles closely. His late opera, *Prometheus* (1966), is actually set to the classical Greek text of Aeschylus.

Ned Rorem (b. 1923), author and musician, who is particularly acclaimed as an American composer of songs, has written a cantata for voices and piano on ten poems by Howard Moss, entitled *King Midas* (of the golden touch). Another American, Marvin David Levy (b. 1932) has given us an operatic version of O'Neill's *Mourning Becomes Electra,* which had its premiere at the Metropolitan Opera in 1967. One of the most original of American composers is Harry Partch (1901–1976). His *Revelation in the Courthouse Park* is based on Euripides' *Bacchae*, and the plot juxtaposes a Rock star in America (modeled on Elvis Presley) and his frenzied worshipers against the Dionysus of Euripides. He created his own instruments for his special music, which uses a scale with forty-three notes. He also composed an *Oedipus Rex* and a work for dance-theater, *Castor and Pollux.*

Among iconoclastic avant-garde composers, Yannis Xenakis (b. 1922), a political exile from Greece and now a French citizen living in Paris, is representative of modern attitudes, innovations, and techniques. A mathematician and architect, as well as a musician, Xenakis is a champion of mathematical and automatic music; in theory and in practice he attempts to unite (in the ancient tradition of Pythagoras) numbers and harmonies, with the help of modern electronic equipment. Among Xenakis' compositions are an *Oresteia* and a *Medea,* which employ orchestra and chorus.

The revolution in music caused by the development of electronic instruments (particularly the guitar) has led to the evolution of the musical idiom and style called Rock. It is refreshing (but perhaps not surprising) to find that in Rock, too, there exists a repertoire inspired by classical themes. The legend of Icarus appears to be a favorite: for example, "Icarus Ascending" by Steve Hackett, "Flight of Icarus" by the heavy metal group Iron Maiden, "Icarus" by Paul Winter, and "Icarus, Borne on Wings of Steel" by Kansas. A song, "The Fountain of Salmacis," is the work of Genesis; and an instrumental piece, "The Waters of Lethe," was composed by Tony Banks, the keyboard player in Genesis. Others worth singling out are "The Three Fates" by Emerson, "Pegasus" by the Allman Brothers, "Jason and the Argonauts" by English Settlement, and "Daphne" by Kayak. Odysseus and the *Odyssey* in particular have inspired more lengthy and ambitious works. Examples include "Tales of Brave Ulysses" by Cream; David Bedford's *The Odyssey,* an entire album that musically presents major episodes in the story; and Bob Freedman's *The Journeys of Odysseus,* a jazz suite for chamber orchestra. Particularly appealing in its melodies and imaginative in its lyrics is *Ulysses,* the *Greek Suite* by Michael Rapp. In the category of more traditional popular music, there are songs associated with particular singers that have become perennial favorites, e.g., "Stupid Cupid" sung by Connie Francis and "Venus," by Frankie Avalon.

Other musical genres have inevitably been influenced by classical mythology and legend. The boisterous, satiric, and melodic works of Jacques Offenbach (1819–1880) provide splendid introductions to the world of light opera and operetta. His opera bouffe, *Orphée aux Enfers (Orpheus in the Underworld,* 1858) is a delight; surely everyone has heard from this score some version of the can-can, which Offenbach immortalized. Equally witty and entertaining is his later *La Belle Hélène (The Beautiful Helen,* 1865). Amid its tuneful arias is the famous "Judgment of Paris."

Another charming operetta is by Franz von Suppé (1819–1895), *Die Schöne Galathée (The Beautiful Galatea,* 1865). In this musical treatment of the story of Pygmalion, the sculptor despairs of the woman whom he has brought to life; she is so flirtatious and troublesome that, to his relief, Venus grants his request that Galatea be changed back into a statue once again. In the same spirit is an operetta by Henri Christine, *Phi-Phi* (1918). Phi-Phi is the nickname of the famous sculptor Pheidias; but this treatment of the historical Pheidias, Pericles, and Aspasia belongs to the realm of legend.

Operetta has had an important history. For the classicist, we may isolate from the brilliant works of Gilbert and Sullivan the obscure *Thespis,* which is on a Greek and Roman theme. Yet, in this genre, Americans have made their own striking contribution to musical theater; and in its brashness or in its earnestness the American musical has developed a characteristic style and coloring all its own. Among the classics, we must certainly place *My Fair Lady* (1956) by Alan Jay Lerner and Frederick Loewe, another adaptation of the legend of Pygmalion via Bernard Shaw. Some other Broadway musicals that may delight the heart of the classicist perhaps are not so widely known.

Richard Rogers and Lorenz Hart wrote *By Jupiter* (1942), derived from Julian Thompson's play *The Warrior's Husband,* which starred Katharine Hepburn. The story is based on Hercules' ninth labor, his quest for the magical girdle of Hippolyta, queen of the Amazons. On this expedition, as we know, Theseus joins Hercules and receives the Amazon Antiope as his share of the spoils. In *By Jupiter,* we are given a light-hearted picture of Hippolyta's queendom, where the women are rulers and warriors and the men take care of domestic duties. Among other things, the Greeks conquer the Amazons through the invincible power of love, and Sapiens (known as Sappy), the timid husband of Hippolyta, becomes the rightful king. Rogers and Hart felt that this amusing treatment of the conflict between the Greeks and the Amazons had serious and timely things to say about relationships between men and women.

The musical *Out of This World* (1950) is a witty satire on the amatory pursuits of Jupiter, by the master, Cole Porter. The plot bears some resemblance to the legend of Amphitryon, revolving as it does upon Jupiter's infatuation for a lovely American mortal. During previews in Boston, there was trouble with the censor because of the lyrics thought to be too risqué, the scanty dress of the performers, and an evocative ballet sequence directed by Agnes de Mille. Despite striking visual effects and an excellent cast, *Out of This World* did not have a long run on Broadway. Nevertheless both the score and the lyrics are vintage Cole Porter.

The Happiest Girl in the World (1961) is based very loosely upon Aristophanes' *Lysistrata.* The musical comedy becomes mythological indeed as a result of the inclusion of the deities Diana and Pluto Although the essential idea concerning Lysistrata's scheme for ending the war by abstaining from sexual relations with the men remains firmly intact, this Lysistrata is no longer truly Aristophanic but merely naughty but nice, in the spirit of the operettas of Offenbach; in fact a potpourri of Offenbach's tunes has been adapted to provide the musical score. The clever lyrics are by E. L. Harburg, famous for other musicals and, in particular, the Academy Award-winning song "Over the Rainbow" from *The Wizard of Oz.*

One of the most creative of modern musical adaptations is *The*

Golden Apple, designated significantly as a musical play. The text by John Latouche and music by Jerome Moross received great acclaim and indeed won the Drama Critics Award for the best musical of the 1953–1954 season. This colorful retelling of the legend of the Trojan War is set in the United States at the turn of the century and is both serious and comic—all in all, pure Americana. The scene is the small town of Angels' Roost (in the state of Washington, famous both for Mt. Olympus and for apples), where the rich old sheriff Menelaus has married Helen, a sexy and bored farmer's daughter. The local heroes have returned from the Spanish-American War; and Ulysses, in particular, is happily reunited with his faithful wife, Penelope. A county fair and a church social are organized to celebrate the homecoming, and the women bring their cakes and pies to be judged in a contest. Jealous old Mother Hare contributes the golden apple ("symbol of our proud state of Washington"). Just in time, a young and attractive traveling salesman named Paris descends in a balloon to act as "impartial" judge and award the apple to Lovey Mars, wife of a military man and vehement about utilizing her flair for matchmaking.

Paris runs off with Helen to nearby Rhododendron, but Ulysses and his men track her down and send her home in disgrace. They themselves dally in the big city to face numerous temptations, among them Madame Calypso, a most scandalous hostess, and Circe, the woman without mercy who turns water into gin and men into swine. Of course, Ulysses realizes the folly of his ways and, like the good American that he is, returns home a second time to his beloved Penelope, whom he surprises as she is busily at work in the company of her sewing bee.

In a different vein and musical style is another startlingly original conception, *The Gospel at Colonus* (1983), wherein Sophocles' play *Oedipus at Colonus* is successfully reinterpreted in the contemporary setting of an American gospel service. The text (often a close adaptation of the original) by Lee Breuer works in beautiful collaboration with the idiomatic score by Bob Telson. The agonized spirituality of the Greek play becomes transformed into a biblical parable of human fate and divine redemption that finds natural expression in the ecstatic intensity of black religious fervor. Among the many highlights is the incorporation of the most famous choral ode from Sophocles' *Antigone,* extolling the wondrous nature of man.

Olympus on My Mind (1986) is an entertaining, lightweight musical comedy of no great consequence; the book and lyrics by Barry Harman were "suggested by" the *Amphitryon* of Heinrich von Kleist; music is by Grant Sturiale. Jupiter, Alcmena, Mercury, a slave Sosia, and his wife Charis offer plenty of humorous antics revolving around mistaken identities; they are assisted by an amusing chorus made up of Tom, Dick, Horace, and Delores.

MYTHOLOGY IN FILM

This brief survey concentrates on movies that seem to be available, particularly on videotape or video disc, which may be judged of some interest and significance. Even the most casual perusal of films that deal with the ancient world reveals an impressive number of treatments.[4] We omit with regret the many adaptations of Greek and Roman history, legendary or otherwise; but begin by mentioning one in this genre because of its mythological and musical interest: *Seven Brides for Seven Brothers* (1954), a gem of a Hollywood musical, based very loosely upon the accounts by Plutarch and Livy of the rape of the Sabine women in the early saga of Rome (reset in the American West by Stephen Vincent Benet). The dances are choreographed by Michael Kidd.

Lerner and Loewe's *My Fair Lady* (1964) is also a musical delight, particularly for Rex Harrison's Professor Henry Higgins. The play upon which it is based, Shaw's *Pygmalion*, may also be enjoyed in its classic movie version (1938), starring Leslie Howard and Wendy Hiller. The Broadway musical by Kurt Weill, *One Touch of Venus* (1948), has been considerably modified for the screen; yet it remains amusing enough as it tells about a statue of Venus (Ava Gardner) in a department store that comes to life and falls in love with a window dresser (Robert Walker). The powerful *Gospel at Colonus* (discussed in the previous section) is another musical now available for viewing; this is a piece that definitely should be seen and not just heard.

As far as dance is concerned, the following may be found on video: three of Martha Graham's works: *Night Journey*, a recreation of the Oedipus legend at the moment of Jocasta's final nightmare and suicide (music by William Schuman); *Errand into the Maze*, the story of the Minotaur (music by Gian Carlo Menotti); and *Cave of the Heart*, the tragedy of Medea (music by Samuel Barber). Another *Medea*, a ballet from the Soviet Union, choreographed by Georgiy Aleksize (music by Revaz Gabichvadze) offers a more traditional version danced by a Russian cast. *Daphnis and Chloe*, choreographed by Graeme Murphy (The Sydney Dance Company), is provocative and daring, not least of all because of its frank sensuality. The scenario is based on the novel by Longus, and the famous score is by Maurice Ravel.

Operatic performances are also available on film. Of note are Tippett's *King Priam* (Kent Opera), and two Glyndebourne Festival Opera productions, Gluck's *Orfeo ed Euridice* (with Janet Baker) and Monteverdi's *Il Ritorno d'Ulisse in Patria*. Two versions of Strauss's *Electra* have been filmed, one from the Metropolitan Opera with Birgit Nilsson in the title role and Leonie Rysanek as Chrysothemis, and the other (directed by Götz Friedrich and shot on the outskirts of Vienna amidst filth and rain) with Leonie Rysanek as Electra and Karl Böhm conducting the Vienna Philharmonic. We also have a choice of two performances of Mozart's *Idomeneo*, one from Glynde-bourne and one from the Metropolitan Opera, the latter starring Luciano Pavarotti, in a production by the controversial Jean-Pierre Ponnelle. *Ariadne auf Naxos* from the Metropolitan Opera stars Jessye Norman. Norman also appears as Cassandra in the Metropolitan's production of Berlioz' *Les Troyens,* in a cast that includes Placido Domingo as Aeneas.

It may surprise all but the die-hard movie buff that many films inspired by Greece and Rome were made between the years 1888 and 1918. We shall begin, however, with *Helen of Troy,* produced by Warner Brothers in 1955, with a musical score by Max Steiner. This epic is lavish in its production but, alas, weak in its script. *Ulysses* (1954), an Italian film with English dialogue, has rightly received critical acclaim for its cinematic techniques and performances by Kirk Douglas (as Ulysses) and Silvana Mangano, who offers haunting portrayals of both Penelope and Circe.

There are several movies about the hero Hercules; some freely manipulate legendary material, while others (e.g., *Hercules and the Moon Men)* make little or no attempt to remain faithful to antiquity. Although these films are of dubious quality, two are worth mentioning: *Hercules* (1959) and *Hercules Unchained* (1959), both starring bodybuilder Steve Reeves, attempt to recapture aspects of the original legend and offer a modicum of entertainment, if one is not too discriminating. *The Three Stooges Meet Hercules* is a very funny screwball comedy for those who dare to admit that they like this sort of thing.

Colossus and the Amazon Queen (1964), with Rod Taylor, Dorian Gray, and Ed Fury, is a tale about two veterans of the Trojan War and their encounter with the Amazons; the main virtue of this romantic comedy is that its humor is intentional. An important mythical adaptation, *Jason and the Argonauts* (1963), is especially noteworthy for its exciting special effects by Ray Harryhausen and a musical score by Mario Nascimbene, conducted by Bernard Herrmann.

Artful and compelling is the controversial Italian film *Medea* (1970), directed by Pier Paolo Pasolini. Bold in its depiction of the bloodier and more brutal elements, and fraught with interpretive insight, it is by no means confined to the events of Euripides' play but includes the essential episodes in the entire tragedy of Medea and Jason. Particularly astonishing is the depiction of the archetypal, ritualistic sacrifice of the young male to ensure mother earth's fertility and the renewal of the crops. For many, the major asset of this movie is opera star Maria Callas, who offers her only nonsinging cinematic appearance as Medea.

Another adaptation of the Medea story, *A Dream of Passion* (1978), directed by Jules Dassin, presents the tragic and harrowing study of a modern-day Medea in Greece, played most realistically by Ellen Burstyn. In addition, Melina Mercouri convincingly portrays an aging actress who is engaged in a performance of the *Medea* of Euripides. Thus this gripping film also offers, among its many riches, scenes from the play, in both Modern Greek and English. The American poet Robinson Jeffers wrote an artful adaptation of Euripides' *Medea* in 1947; Judith Anderson created the title role, and her striking performance is preserved.[5] A revival of Jeffers' play starring Zoe Caldwell, also a fine Medea (with Judith Anderson as the nurse), is also available in its Kennedy Center production (1983).[6] Startling, to say the least, is a production of *Medea* by the New York Greek Drama Company in the original Greek of Euripides, with English subtitles; the actors wear masks, and William Arrowsmith provides introductory comments that tell us why we should appreciate this strange attempt at authenticity.[7]

Sophocles' *Oedipus the King* is presented in the ancient Greek theater of Amphiaraion, with the actors wearing masks. James Mason plays Oedipus; Claire Bloom, Jocasta; and Ian Richardson, Tiresias. This abridged performance includes narration by Anthony Quayle. Among other performances of *Oedipus the King,* a version directed by Tyrone Guthrie (1957) should be singled out. This film of a performance of the Stratford Shakespearean Festival Players of Canada employs William Butler Yeats's translation. Although not entirely a cinematic success, its professionalism and its use of striking masks are of great interest. A strong British version (1967), starring Christopher Plummer, Orson Welles, and Lilli Palmer, makes more of an attempt to transform the play into a movie.

The film by the Italian director Pier Paolo Pasolini, *Oedipus Rex* (1967), includes many unforgettable episodes from the saga, for example, the brutal exposure of the infant Oedipus and later his youthful and bloody encounter with his father; such amplifications reveal psychoanalytic insight and a personal and modern vision. One of the finest productions of all three Theban plays of Sophocles *(Oedipus the King, Oedipus at Colonus,* and *Antigone*) was done for BBC Television, in a new translation by the director Don Taylor, with a cast that includes John Gielgud, Claire Bloom, and Anthony Quayle, all of whom are superb. A movie version of *Antigone*, written and directed by George Tzavellas, in Greek with English subtitles, has the incomparable Irene Pappas in the title role as its greatest strength.

The highest standard for the filming of Euripidean plays has been set by the Greek director Michael Cacoyannis: his *Electra* (1962), with Irene Pappas; *The Trojan Women* (1971), with Katharine Hepburn, Vanessa Redgrave, and Irene Pappas; and *Iphigenia* (1977), with Irene Pappas, should not be missed. Each of these movies is a masterpiece in its own way. The genius of Cacoyannis becomes all the more evident in comparison with a movie like *Bacchantes*, directed by George Ferroni—an embarrassing travesty of Euripides to be avoided by all but the insatiably curious.

An unusual production of Aeschylus' *Oresteia*, by the National Theatre of Great Britain, directed by Peter Hall, employs both a new rhyming translation by Tony Harrison and the stylized use of masks; although in many ways dramatically intense and well worth seeing, the overall conception verges at times on the monotonous. Of historic and histrionic importance is the movie version (1947) of Eugene O'Neill's American Oresteia, *Mourning Becomes Electra,* particularly for the performances (very much in the grand manner) of Katina Paxinou and Michael Redgrave. The Italian director Pier Paolo Pasolini recounts his preparations for a film made in Africa of a modern version of the *Oresteia* (which he never lived to complete) in *Notes for an African Orestes*; he documented local rituals and searched local villages in Uganda and Tanzania for likely candidates and situations for the filming. This is a study of specialized interest, to be sure, even though it attempts, not always successfully, to illuminate many parallels between the political and social issues in the ancient trilogy and those of Africa in the twentieth century.

Of great interest is the movie of Eugene O'Neill's *Desire Under the Elms* (1958); this version of the Hippolytus legend, set in New England, also combines thematic elements from the legends of Oedipus and Medea; Anthony Perkins, Sophia Loren, and Burl Ives give strong performances. Anthony Perkins is also the Hippolytus figure in a modern adaptation of *Phaedra* (1962), directed by Jules Dassin and also starring Melina Mercouri. Although heavy-handed and at times absurd, this movie has some power.

The legend of Perseus has received imaginative and entertaining treatment in *Clash of the Titans* (1981), with a star-studded cast including Harry Hamlin, Laurence Olivier, and Maggie Smith. Despite its misleading title, this movie has many strengths that have not always been justly appreciated, among them a chilling decapitation of Medusa (imaginatively set in the Underworld),[8] an exhilarating depiction of the flying horse Pegasus, and the addition of Bubo, a mechanical owl straight out of science fiction. Special effects are by Ray Harryhausen (who surpasses his splendid work for *Jason and the Argonauts*), and the stirring music is by Laurence Rosenthal. Not in the same class is *The Gorgon*, a horror vehicle for Peter Cushing and Christopher Lee.

In *Seven Faces of Dr. Lao* (1964), an elderly Chinese in a circus (Tony Randall) is a master of disguises who gives us a vision of Medusa and Pan. *Time Bandits* (1981) has as one of its sequences an episode with Sean Connery playing Agamemnon. The episode "Who Mourns for Adonais" from the television series *Star Trek* presents Apollo, as the last of the Olympian gods, who demands to be worshiped.

Among the more significant treatments of ancient mythology are modern retellings of the Orpheus legend. The problematic but arresting play *Orpheus Descending*, by Tennessee Williams, has become a noteworthy film (under the title *The Fugitive Kind*), thanks to its stars, Marlon Brando, Anna Magnani, Joanne Woodward, Maureen Stapleton, and Victor Jory. The Brazilian *Black Orpheus* (1959), directed by Marcel Camus, with a relentless but compelling musical score by A. C. Jobim and Luis Bonfa, which sets the myth in Rio at carnival time, has deservedly won critical acclaim and popularity. Also, everyone should experience more than once the exciting and evocative *Orphée* (1949) of Cocteau, a landmark in the history of the cinema. Cocteau's obsession with the Orphic archetype appears in his last movie, *Le Testament d'Orphée* (1959), which offers plenty of mythological allusion.

We are all enriched by meaningful and stimulating cinematic treatments of mythology and legend; and in our search for movies on Greek and Roman themes, those that deal with comparative thematic material should not be forgotten. The film *Dragonslayer*, for example, which is based on Anglo-Saxon myth, exploits one of the most dominant themes in all mythology. *The Wicker Man* presents with chilling insight an archetypal pattern of daemonic ritual and human sacrifice. The popular movies about Superman and Tarzan certainly can be related to the archetypes of classical saga. *Superman* (the first of the series with Christopher Reeve) presents a disarming variation of the patterns in the birth, childhood, and adventures of a hero; and the version of the Tarzan legend called *Greystoke* is of particularly high caliber and worth mentioning not only for its own sake but also for the opportunity to point out that Tarzan has been identified as an Odyssean type of hero.[9] There is something of the *Iliad* (not literally of course) in the heroic sadness and epic devotion of *The Deer Hunter*; the protagonist of *Angel Heart* suffers in his ignorant guilt like an Oedipus; *Pretty Woman* is yet another metamorphosis of Pygmalion's Galatea; and so it goes.

This highly selective review is intended only as a mere sampling of the richness and variety in the treatment of Greek and Roman themes readily to be found in works by artists of every sort. Nevertheless, even the briefest account cannot help but forcefully remind us once again of the potent inspiration that classical mythology provides for all facets of creative artistic expression.

BIBLIOGRAPHY

Brockway, Wallace, and Weinstock, Herbert. *The World of Opera.* New York: Random House, 1941.

Constantine, James S. "Vergil in Opera." *Classical Outlook* 46 (1969): 49, 63-65, 77-78, 87-89.

Dickinson, A. E. F. "Music for the Aeneid." *Greece & Rome* 6 (1959): 129-147.

Evans, Arthur B. *Jean Cocteau and His Films of Orphic Identity.* Philadelphia: Art Alliance Press, 1977.

Ewen, David. *The New Encyclopedia of the Opera.* New York: Hill & Wang, 1971.

Grout, Donald Jay. *A Short History of Opera.* 2 vols. New York: Columbia University Press, 1947.

Lang, Paul Henry. *Music in Western Civilization.* New York: Norton, 1941.

Levine, Robert. *Guide to Opera & Dance on Videocassette.* Mount Vernon, N.Y.: Consumers Union, Consumer Reports Books, 1989.

McDonald, Marianne. *Euripides in Cinema: The Heart Made Visible.* Philadelphia: Centrum, 1983.

Mackinnon, Kenneth. *Greek Tragedy into Film.* London and Sydney: Croom Helm, 1986.

Martin, George. *The Opera Companion to Twentieth Century Opera.* New York: Dodd, Mead, 1979.

Sadie, Stanley. *The New Grove Dictionary of Music and Musicians.* 20 vols. London: Macmillan; New York: Grove's Dictionaries of Music, 1980.

————. *The New Grove Dictionary of Opera.* 4 vols. London: Macmillan. New York: Grove's Dictionaries of Music, 1992.

Solomon, Jon. *The Ancient World in the Cinema.* New York: Barnes, 1978.

Traubner, Richard. *Operetta: A Theatrical History.* New York: Doubleday, 1983.

Winkler, Martin M., ed. *Classics and Cinema.* Lewisburg: Bucknell University Press, 1991 (Bucknell Review 35, no. 1).

NOTES

Notes to the Introduction

1. G. S. Kirk, *The Nature of Greek Myths* (Harmondsworth and Baltimore: Penguin Books, 1974), p. 27. Kirk identifies a "traditional tale" as a myth that has "*succeeded* in becoming traditional . . . important enough to be passed from generation to generation."

2. See especially H. J. Rose, *A Handbook of Classical Mythology*, 6th ed. (London: Methuen, 1958), pp. 12–14, for his designations of myth, saga, and folktale.

3. *Legend* may be used as a general term like *myth* in its broadest sense. Often, however, it is defined as equivalent to *saga* and made to refer to stories inspired by actual persons and events. Thus for us legend and saga are one and the same. Rose prefers the German word *Marchen* for the designation of folktales (fairy tales, of course, belong in this category).

4. Sometimes *fable* is also applied as a general term, but it is better to restrict its meaning to designate a story in which the characters are animals endowed with human traits, the primary purpose being moral and didactic.

5. See the bibliography on pp. 30–34.

6. The original version of a myth (usually hypothetical) is designated as the Ur-myth.

7. This was the attitude, for example, of L. Lévy-Bruhl, *Primitive Mentality* (New York: Macmillan, 1923 [1922]).

8. Cf. Mircea Eliade, *Myth and Reality* (New York: Harper & Row, 1963). Also Paul Veyne, *Did the Greeks Believe in Their Myths? An Essay on the Constitutive Imagination* (Chicago: University of Chicago Press, 1988 [1983]) on the creation of truth and history.

9. This has become a commonplace explanation of the human need for mythology; it has been formulated with particular conviction by Leszek Kolakowski in his *The Presence of Myth* (Chicago: University of Chicago Press, 1989 [1972]). Kolakowski frames his discussion in terms of a contrast between myth and science; for him science in its technological aspect represents the truth that is to be distinguished from myth.

10. A case for discussion is presented by the excerpts from the historical myth of Herodotus, translated in Chapter 4.

11. Martha Graham, *Blood Memory* (New York: Doubleday, 1991), p. 4.

12. Bronislav Malinowski, "Myth in Primitive Psychology" (1926); reprinted in *Magic, Science and Religion* (New York: Doubleday, 1955).

13. Robert Graves, *The Greek Myths* (Baltimore: Penguin Books, 1955), 1:10. His interpretation of Greek mythology is based on the assumption that permeates his writing: an early matriarchal society once existed in Europe with the worship of a great mother deity, and subsequently there was an invasion of a patriarchal society from the north and east.

14. E. R. Leach, *Political Systems of Highland Burma* (Cambridge: Harvard University Press, 1954), p. 13; quoted in Kirk, *Nature of Greek Myths,* pp. 67 and 226. The best short expositions of the ritualist theory are the essays by Lord Raglan, "Myth and Ritual," and S. E. Hyman, "The Ritual View of Myth and the Mythic," in T. A. Sebeok, ed., *Myth: A Symposium* (Bloomington: Indiana University Press, 1971), pp. 122–135 and 136–153.

15. See Chapter 25, esp. p. 559.

16. For Ixion and the Centaurs, see pp. 490–491.

17. See Friedrich Max Müller, *Comparative Mythology: An Essay* (1856; reprint of rev. ed. of 1909, Salem, N.H.: Ayer Company Publishers, 1977), which includes an "Introductory Preface on Solar Mythology" by Abram Smythe Palmer and a parody by R. F. Littledale, "The Oxford Solar Myth," i.e., Müller himself. For an assessment of Müller's theories, see the essay by R. M. Dorson, "The Eclipse of Solar Mythology," in Sebeok, *Myth,* pp. 25–63.

18. Also "contextualism" or "situationism" and "behaviorism" are to be found in Aristotle's writings, "the first scientific work on bio-social psychology . . . practically unknown to students of human nature today." For these and other observations explaining the profound debt of modern psychology to the perceptions of Greek dramatists and philosophers, see Patrick Mullahy, *Oedipus Myth and Complex, A Review of Psychoanalytic Theory* (New York: Grove Press, 1955), pp. 335–337.

19. "The Interpretation of Dreams" in *The Basic Writings of Sigmund Freud,* ed. A. A. Brill (New York: Random House, Modern Library, 1938), p. 308, quoted at greater length by Mullahy as an introduction to Chapter 1 of *Oedipus Myth.* Plato in his *Republic* (571C) has a famous description of the unbridled nature of dreams that includes the mention of intercourse with one's mother.

20. We do not attempt to summarize a complex and fruitful subject; see Mullahy, *Oedipus Myth,* pp. 102–113. For the beginner, Richard Wollheim, *Freud* (Glasgow: William Collins, 1971), provides a concise introduction to Freudian thought; similarly, one might consult Frieda Fordham, *An Introduction to Jung's Psychology,* 3d ed. (Baltimore: Penguin Books, 1966), with a foreword by Jung. The bibliography for both Freud and Jung is, not surprisingly, voluminous and accessible.

21. Cf. Xenophanes, translated on p. 96.

22. Richard I. Evans, *Dialogue with C. G. Jung,* 2d ed. (New York: Praeger, 1981), p. 67.

23. Cf. Joseph Campbell, *Myths to Live By* (New York: Viking Press, 1972). Typically and unfortunately, Campbell does not pay enough attention to the Greeks and the Romans.

24. The best introduction to Lévi-Strauss is the "Overture" to *The Raw and the Cooked,* and classicists should read his article, "The Structural Study of Myth" (which includes his interpretation of the Oedipus myth), to be found in Sebeok, *Myth,* pp. 81–106.

25. Lévi-Strauss, quoted in G. S. Kirk, *Myth: Its Meaning and Function in Ancient and Other Cultures* (Berkeley: University of California Press, 1971), p. 44.

26. Vladimir Propp, *Morphology of the Folktale,* 2d ed., rev. (Austin: University of Texas Press, 1968 [1928]). Chapter 2 (pp. 19–24) is the essential statement of Propp's methodology.

27. Propp's thirty-one functions are set out in his third chapter, pp. 25–65. The term *motifeme* was coined by the anthropologist Alan Dundes.

28. This sequence of five functions is worked out by Walter Burkert, *Structure and History in Greek Mythology and Ritual* (Berkeley: University of California Press, 1979), n. 22, pp. 6–7. He points out that the metamorphosis of the mother (e.g., Callisto into a bear, Io into a cow) is not part of a fixed sequence of functions.

29. See Burkert, *Structure and History.*

30. Numbers 1 and 16 in D. A. Campbell's *Greek Lyric* (New York: St. Martin's Press, 1967), vol. 1.

31. Marilyn Katz, *Penelope's Renown. Meaning and Indeterminacy in the Odyssey* (Princeton: Princeton University Press, 1991), p. 13. A starting point for the study of feminism and mythology is Mary R. Lefkowitz, *Women in Greek Myth* (Baltimore: Johns Hopkins University Press, 1986). The "moderate" approach of the author, however, is vigorously criticized by some feminists.

32. For comparative study see James B. Pritchard, *Ancient Near Eastern Texts Relating to the Old Testament,* 3d ed. (Princeton: Princeton University Press, 1969). Usually abbreviated in references as *ANET,* this is the most authoritative collection of texts for Near Eastern mythology, in readable English translation. A selection of texts, mostly taken from *ANET,* is available in paperback in the same editor's *The Ancient Near East,* 2 vols. (Princeton: Princeton University Press, 1958–1975).

33. The bibliography for Joseph Campbell is considerable. See, for example, *The Hero with a Thousand Faces,* 2d ed., Bollingen Series 17 (New York: Princeton University Press, 1968); *The Masks of God,* 4 vols. (New York: Viking Press, 1959–1968). These are preferable to his works for a more general audience of television viewers, for whom his approach is exceedingly attractive, but disappointing to the serious classicist who expects a deeper appreciation of Greek and Roman mythology; see *The Power of Myth,* with Bill Moyers (New York: Doubleday, 1988).

34. A realization forcefully brought home after a reading of George Steiner, *Antigones* (New York: Oxford University Press, 1984), which discusses treatments of the Antigone theme in European literature; also Ian Donaldson, *The Rapes of Lucretia: A Myth and Its Transformations* (New York: Oxford University Press, 1982). Cf. Käte Hamburger, *From Sophocles to Sartre: Figures from Greek Tragedy Classical and Modern* (New York: Frederick Unger, 1969); ten major characters from Greek tragedy are discussed with reference to treatments by twenty-eight modern playwrights.

35. Lowell Edmunds, *Oedipus, The Ancient Legend and Its Later Analogues*

(Baltimore: Johns Hopkins University Press, 1985), a survey of the many variations in ancient, medieval, and modern versions of this eternal myth.

36. See the bibliography on Orpheus at the end of Chapter 14; and we should not forget the Orpheus of music, theater, and the dance.

37. Emily Vermeule, *Greece in the Bronze Age* (Chicago: University of Chicago Press, 1964), offers a survey and contains an important bibliography.

38. Schliemann's life and career are the material for a bizarre and exciting success story. He amassed a fortune so that he could prove the validity of his convictions, which he pursued with passion. Several biographies are available: Emil Ludwig, *Schliemann, the Story of a Gold-Seeker* (Boston: Little, Brown, 1931); Robert Payne, *The Gold of Troy* (New York: Funk and Wagnalls, 1959); Lynn and Gray Poole, *One Passion, Two Loves* (New York: Thomas Y. Crowell, 1966); and Irving Stone, *The Greek Treasure* (New York: Doubleday, 1975).

39. See the bibliography for Iconography and Religion, p. 34.

40. The dates for these periods are serviceable. It is rash to insist on greater precision for this early period, the evidence for which fluctuates daily. The chronology of the Bronze Age is a subject of passionate dispute. Thus, attempts at a more precise chronology with further subdivisions within the periods are not reproduced here. For a scholarly treatment consult pertinent chapters and charts in *The Cambridge Ancient History*, 3d ed., vol. 2, pt. 1, *The Middle East and the Aegean Region 1800–1380 B.C.,* ed. L. E. S. Edwards, N. G. L. Hammond and E. Sollberger (New York: Cambridge University Press, 1973); and pt. 2, *The Middle East and the Aegean Region c. 1380–1000 B.C.* (1975).

41. For a more detailed interpretation of the evidence in terms of Minoan-Mycenaean religion, see W. K. C. Guthrie, "The Religion and Mythology of the Greeks," in *The Cambridge Ancient History,* vol. 2, pt. 2, chap. 40.

42. For a survey of the excavations at Thera, its relationship to Crete, and theories about Atlantis, see Christos G. Doumas, *Thera, Pompeii of the Ancient Aegean* (London: Thames & Hudson, 1983).

43. Some believe that a later wave of invaders (ca. 1600) is to be specifically identified as the Achaeans in Homer; it is better to consider Achaeans virtually an equivalent term for the Mycenaean Greeks.

44. Linear A tablets (Linear B is derived from the Linear A script), found on Crete, have not yet been deciphered; apparently Minoan Linear A is not Greek. Linear B tablets (written in an early form of Greek) have also been found at Cnossus with provocative implications for historical reconstruction. Hostile criticism of Evans is offered by Leonard R. Palmer, *Mycenaeans and Minoans,* 2d ed. (New York: Alfred A. Knopf, 1965).

45. John Chadwick, *The Decipherment of Linear B,* 2d ed. (New York: Cambridge University Press, 1958).

46. Blegen's results have been published in a series of highly technical volumes. Like the reports of his excavations at Pylos, they are a monumental testimony to the scientific precision of modern archaeological procedures. Blegen has provided a survey of the excavations at Troy for the general reader: Carl W. Blegen, *Troy and the Trojans* (New York: Praeger, 1963). We are grateful to C. Brian Rose and Getzel Cohen for preliminary information about the new excavations of Troy.

47. A sensible and readable survey of the problems is given by Michael Wood, *In Search of the Trojan War* (New York: Facts on File Publications, 1984). Some historians are now rash enough to assign the destruction of Troy to invaders from the east and entirely dissociate Troy from the history of Mycenaean Greece; M. I. Finley, *Early Greece,* rev. ed. (New York: Norton, 1981), discusses the fall of Troy and associated problems in "The End of the Bronze Age," pp. 56-66.

48. Invaluable is the Greek edition by T. W. Allen, W. R. Halliday, and E. E. Sikes (New York: Oxford University Press, 1963 [1934]).

49. Published by Bantam Books (New York, 1960); also in their catalogue is *The Complete Plays of Sophocles* in the stately translation of R. C. Jebb, revised by Hadas.

Notes to Chapter 1

1. Dates for Homer and Hesiod are tentative and controversial.

2. Since the Muses are the daughters of Zeus, their revelation comes from the infallible knowledge of the supreme god.

3. Perhaps Hesiod may anticipate the pre-Socratic philosophers who sought a primal world substance or substances. Thales (ca. 540) seems to provide a startling break with mythological and theological concepts when he claims water to be the source of everything, with shattering implications for both science and philosophy.

4. We shall use the names Gaia, Gaea, and Ge, which mean "earth," interchangeably.

5. For the Orphic myth of creation in particular, see pp. 305-307.

6. The concept of god creating something out of nothing is not found in the Greek and Roman tradition.

7. These Cyclopes are distinct from the Cyclops Polyphemus and his fellows.

8. See the bibliography for Iconography and Religion, p. 34.

9. Cf. Erich Neumann, *The Great Mother: An Analysis of the Archetype,* 2d ed. (Princeton: Princeton University Press, 1963).

10. Indeed some scholars are ready to find Ge's presence in every goddess and are deeply suspicious of even the most circumspect virgin deities.

11. Included are many important rivers such as the Nile, Alpheus, and Scamander, to mention only three in this world, and the Styx, an imaginary one in the realm of Hades. The patronymic Oceanid regularly refers to a daughter of Oceanus and not a son.

12. When a Roman version of a myth is recounted, the Roman names of the original text will be used. Vulcan is Hephaestus, Jupiter is Zeus, etc. For the Roman names of the major Greek deities, see the beginning of Chapter 3, p. 76.

13. His sisters (daughters of the Sun) in their mourning for Phaëthon are turned into trees, from whose bark tears flow, which are hardened into amber by the sun and dropped into the river. Away in Liguria his cousin, Cycnus, mourns for him, and he too changes and becomes a swan.

14. Artemis, like Selene, as a moon-goddess is associated with magic, since the

link between magic and the worship of the moon is close. Apollo and Artemis themselves have a close link with the Titans. The Titan Coeus mated with his sister Phoebe, and their daughter Leto bore Artemis and Apollo to Zeus. Coeus and Phoebe are little more than names to us, but Phoebe is the feminine form of Phoebus, and she herself may very well be another moon-goddess. Hecate, goddess of the moon, ghosts, and black magic, is but another aspect of both Selene and Artemis (see p. 466).

15. Orion, Cleitus, and Cephalus were also all beloved by Eos.

16. Perhaps an intentional play upon the word *philommeides*, "laughter-loving," a standard epithet of Aphrodite.

17. There is trouble in the text concerning Hesiod's identification of the mountain as Dicte or Aegeum.

18. Another version places the birth on the mainland of Greece in Arcadia.

19. W. K. C. Guthrie, *The Greeks and Their Gods* (Boston: Beacon Press, 1955), p. 31.

Notes to Chapter 2

1. This very stone was exhibited at Delphi in ancient times; it was not large, and oil was poured over it every day. On festival days, unspun wool was placed upon it.

2. Ten years is the traditional length for a serious war, be it this one or the famous conflict of the Greeks against the Trojans.

3. Notus is the South Wind; Boreas, the North Wind; and Zephyr, the West Wind.

4. Later versions have it that Heracles was an ally of Zeus in the battle; the giants could be defeated only if the gods had a mortal as their ally. In addition Earth produced a magic plant that would make the giants invincible; Zeus by a clever stratagem plucked it for himself.

5. A fragment attributed to Hesiod (no. 268 Rzach; 382 Merkelbach and West) adds that Athena breathed life into the clay. At Panopea in Boeotia, stones were identified in historical times as solidified remains of the clay used by Prometheus.

6. Aidos is a sense of modesty and shame; Nemesis, righteous indignation against evil.

7. In his fourth eclogue, Vergil celebrates gloriously the return of a new golden age ushered in by the birth of a child. The identity of this child has long been in dispute, but the poem itself was labeled Messianic because of the sublime and solemn nature of its tone, reminiscent of the prophet Isaiah.

8. A similar but more sober and scientific statement of human development, made by some of the Greek philosophers and by Lucretius, the Roman poet of Epicureanism, provides a penetrating account of human evolution that in many of its details is astoundingly modern (*De Rerum Natura* 5. 783-1457).

9. Aeschylus has Themis as the mother of Prometheus, sometimes identified as Ge-Themis, to show that she is a goddess of earth, who possesses oracular power and is associated with justice. The name Prometheus means "forethinker," or, "the one who plans ahead"; Epimetheus means

"afterthinker," or, "the one who plans too late." Prometheus is often called merely "the Titan," since he is the son of the Titan Iapetus.

10. An early name of Sicyon.

11. The name suggests a link with the typical conception of the fertility mother-goddess.

12. He was worshiped by the potters in Athens alongside Hephaestus, with whom he has several attributes in common.

13. For a comparison of Eve with Pandora and female deities throughout the ages, see John A. Phillips, *Eve: The History of an Idea* (New York: Harper & Row, 1984).

14. Aeschylus even manages to characterize the brutish Kratos, the unreasonable and monstrous henchman of a tyrannical Zeus. Kratos is the willing and anxious supporter of a new regime rooted in force, the one thing he can understand; to him forceful power is the key to all: "Everything is hard except to rule the gods. For no one except Zeus is free."

15. Any interpretation of Aeschylus' tragedy is difficult since precise details in the outcome as conceived by Aeschylus are unknown. We have the titles and fragments of three additional plays on the Prometheus legend attributed to Aeschylus: *Prometheus the Fire-Bearer, Prometheus Unbound,* and *Prometheus the Fire-Kindler.* This last may be merely another title for *Prometheus the Fire-Bearer,* or possibly it was a satyr play belonging either to the Prometheus trilogy itself or to another trilogy on a different theme. We cannot even be sure of the position of the extant *Prometheus Bound* in the sequence.

16. Io is the daughter of Inachus, whose family appears in the legends of Argos; see pp. 417–418.

17. Versions other than that of Aeschylus have Zeus attempt to deceive Hera by transforming Io into a cow, which Hera asked to have for herself.

18. The Egyptians identified Epaphus with Apis, the sacred bull, and Io with their goddess Isis. See pp. 417–418.

19. Chiron possibly dies for Prometheus and bestows his immortality upon Heracles.

20. This is Ovid's version of a tale about a werewolf that appears elsewhere in the Greek and Roman tradition. The name Lycaon was taken to be derived from the Greek word for wolf. The story may reflect primitive rites in honor of Lycaean Zeus performed on Mt. Lycaeus.

21. In addition to the Bible, the Babylonian epic of Gilgamesh offers interesting parallels to the flood story. See *The Epic of Gilgamesh,* an English translation with an introduction by N. K. Sandars (New York: Penguin Books, 1960), pp. 105–110; cf. also Alexander Heidel, *The Gilgamesh Epic and Old Testament Parallels,* 2d ed. (Chicago: University of Chicago Press, 1949). *The Flood Myth,* edited by Alan Dundes (Berkeley: University of California Press, 1988) provides a fascinating collection of writings by authors in a variety of disciplines who analyze the motif of the flood throughout the world.

22. That is, nymphs of the Corycian cave on Mt. Parnassus.

23. Hellen had three sons: Dorus, Aeolus, and Xuthus. Xuthus in turn had two sons: Ion and Achaeus. Thus eponyms were provided for the four major divisions of the Greeks on the basis of dialect and geography: Dorians,

Aeolians, Ionians, and Achaeans. The names *Greeks* and *Greece* came through the Romans, who first met a group of Hellenes called the *Graioi,* participants in the colonization of Cumae just north of Naples.

24. See Samuel Noah Kramer, *Sumerian Mythology,* rev. ed. (New York: Harper & Row, 1961); S. H. Hooke, *Middle Eastern Mythology* (New York: Penguin Books, 1963); and *The Poems of Hesiod,* trans. with introduction and comments by R. M. Frazer (Norman: University of Oklahoma Press, 1983). The Eastern texts are taken from J. B. Pritchard, trans. and ed., *Ancient Near Eastern Texts,* 3d ed. (Princeton: Princeton University Press, 1969). Cf. p. 16, above.

Notes to Chapter 3

1. The Roman gods are discussed on pp. 515–536.

2. See the lines about Hestia in the *Homeric Hymn to Aphrodite,* translated in Chapter 7, p. 137. Sometimes Hestia does not seem to be conceived fully as an anthropomorphic deity.

3. Pytho is Delphi, the site of Apollo's great temple; oil was used as an ointment for hair and in religious rites it was poured over the heads of statues.

4. The warrior-goddess Athena will also carry the aegis, on which may be depicted the head of the Gorgon Medusa whom she helped Perseus slay. Athena's aegis may be her own or lent by Zeus to his favorite daughter.

5. Zeus and Hera find their archetypal counterparts in the Wotan and Fricka of Nordic mythology.

6. These games were celebrated every four years after 776; an important system of dating for the Greeks was by Olympiads.

7. Long before 776, the pre-Olympian deities Cronus and Gaia were worshiped at Olympia. For Heracles at Olympia, see pp. 426–427.

8. The temple was completed in 456; the statue, ca. 430.

9. It was described in detail by the traveler, Pausanias (5. 11), in the second century A.D.; the Roman Quintilian wrote, "its beauty added something even to the traditional religion."

10. Olympia was not as famous for its oracles as was the sanctuary of Apollo at Delphi, another famous Panhellenic festival (i.e., one to which "all Hellenes" came). Delphi was similar to Olympia and is described in Chapter 9 in some detail as representative of this facet of Hellenic worship and life. See pp. 173–177.

11. In the *Iliad* (5. 905) Hebe bathes and clothes Ares after he has been healed of the wounds inflicted by the hero Diomedes.

12. Cf. Apollo and Hyacinthus (pp. 184–185) and Narcissus (pp. 245–250) among others; for the theme, see B. Sergent, *Homosexuality in Greek Myth,* with a preface by G. Dumézil (London: Athlone Press, 1987). See also p. 143 and n.11 on pp. 625–626.

13. Homer (*Iliad* 18) presents a splendid picture of his house on Olympus when Thetis appeals to Hephaestus to forge new armor for her son Achilles. Vergil (*Aeneid* 8) locates Vulcan's workshop in a cave on the island of Vulcania near Sicily. There he fashions magnificent armor for Aeneas, the son of Venus.

14. For this version, see the *Homeric Hymn to Apollo* in the appendix to Chapter 9, p. 195. Hera also claimed that Hephaestus was her son alone without Zeus; thus Hera has her own favorite child, born from herself, just as Zeus has his special daughter, Athena, who was born from his head.

15. Pheidias' majestic statue of the seated figure of Zeus in the temple at Olympia (described above) was supposedly inspired by these lines from Homer describing Zeus as he nods.

16. Sometimes Hephaestus' mate is one of the Graces, either the youngest, Aglaea, or Grace herself (Charis), which actually may be but another designation for Aphrodite.

17. This hymn probably belongs to Hellenistic times or even later; some, not very convincingly, associate it with the corpus of Orphic hymns. The richer connotations given to Ares' character and the emphasis upon strength in peace as well as war look to Mars, the Roman counterpart of Ares; see pp. 515-516.

18. Ares is in the third planetary zone, if you count from the one that is farthest from Earth.

19. The Muses are sometimes called the Pierides, but Ovid (*Metamorphoses* 5. 205-678) tells a story of nine daughters of Pierus of Pella in Macedonia who were also called Pierides. They challenged the Muses to a musical contest, lost, and were changed into magpies, birds that imitate sounds and clatter incessantly.

20. The Romans developed this same tragic view of human existence. For them Fate is personified by the Parcae, or more abstractly conceived as Fatum (Fate).

21. The Horae, Hours, become the Seasons, goddesses who are two, three, or four in number and closely connected with vegetation. They attend the greater deities and provide attractive decoration in literature and art. Zeus and Themis as sky-god and earth-goddess enact once again the ritual of the sacred marriage.

Notes to Chapter 4

1. Nymphs are sometimes classified as follows: the spirits of water, springs, lakes, and rivers are called Naiads; Potamiads are specifically the nymphs of rivers; tree-nymphs are generally called Dryads or Hamadryads, although their name means "spirits of oak trees" in particular; Meliae are the nymphs of the ash tree.

2. The mortal parent may bask in the grand aura of the great mythological age of saga and boast of a genealogy that in the not too distant past included at least one divine ancestor.

3. Her name was Cydippe and she was a priestess of Hera, hence the necessity for her presence at the festival. The temple would be the Argive Heraeum.

4. Herodotus here uses the masculine article with the word for god; he is thinking specifically of one supreme god or generically of the divine power of deity. Significantly he does not refer to Hera specifically, although subsequently it is to the goddess Hera that the mother prays on behalf of her sons.

5. These statues have been excavated and do much to tantalize in the quest for precise distinctions between myth and history in Herodotus' account.

6. That is, human beings are entirely at the mercy of what befalls them.

7. The ritual consisted at least in part of slaying a suckling pig and pouring the blood over the hands of the guilty murderer, who sat in silence at the hearth while Zeus was invoked as the Purifier.

8. These words of Croesus at first strike the modern reader as extremely cruel, but he means only that he cannot consider the other boy as his son in the same way. Since the boy is deaf and dumb, Croesus' hopes, both domestic and political, must rest in his other son, Atys. We are told elsewhere that Croesus did everything for the unfortunate boy.

9. Solon held office in Athens as archon extraordinary in 594 B.C., and his travels took place at some time after that date; his death may be placed in the years following 560. Croesus did not become king of Sardis until around 560, and his defeat by Cyrus occurred in 546.

Notes to Chapter 5

1. Ovid provides a typical description in his version of the flood (see pp. 71–73); it includes a vivid characterization of Poseidon under his Roman name of Neptune.

2. There are two classic accounts of Proteus' nature and his powers: those of Homer (*Odyssey* 4. 363–570) and Vergil (*Georgics* 4. 386–528). In Homer, Menelaus, on his way home from Troy was unduly detained off the coast of Egypt; he consulted Proteus, the old man of the sea, with the help of Proteus' daughter Eidothea. Menelaus explains: "We rushed upon him with a shout and threw our arms about him; but the old man did not forget his devious arts. First off he became a thickly maned lion, and then a serpent, a leopard, and a great boar. And he became liquid water and a tree with lofty branches. But we held on to him firmly with steadfast spirits." Finally the devious Proteus grew weary and answered Menelaus' questions about his return home.

3. Poseidon Heliconius was worshiped by Ionian Greeks, especially at Mycale in Asia Minor. It is uncertain whether the reference in the hymn to Helicon (from which Heliconius is derived) means Mt. Helicon (in Boeotia) or the town of Helice; Helice and Aegae were both on the Corinthian gulf.

4. The result is the birth both of a daughter and of the wonderful horse Arion, which belonged to Adrastus. Similarly Poseidon united with Ge to produce Antaeus, a giant encountered by Heracles.

5. Ovid (*Metamorphoses* 13. 917–968; 14. 1–71) tells this same story about Glaucus, a mortal who was transformed into a sea-god. It was he who fell in love with Scylla; when he was rejected, he turned to the sorceress Circe for help. But Circe fell in love with him and, in her jealousy, poisoned the waters of Scylla's bathing place.

6. The Harpies are not unlike the Sirens, who lure human beings to destruction and death by the enticement of their song.

Notes to Chapter 6

1. Sometimes Prometheus or even Hermes are helpers.

2. Or Poseidon produced the first horse; Athena may plant an olive tree or, more dramatically, as on this pediment, bring one forth by the touch of her spear.

The contest took place on the Acropolis with Athena judged the victor by the gods, or the Athenians, or their king Cecrops. The importance of the olive in Athenian life is symbolized by Athena's victory.

3. Angry at losing, Poseidon flooded the Thriasian plain but he was appeased. The Athenians were seafarers and Poseidon remained important to them.

4. Games and contests were also a part of the festivities; the prize awarded was an amphora filled with oil. On it was depicted Athena in her war gear with an inscription identifying the vase as Panathenaic.

5. The *peplos* was dedicated to the ancient wooden statue of Athena Polias (i.e., "guardian of the city") in the nearby sanctuary of Erechtheus. The old temple was destroyed by the Persians, and the new Erectheum was completed some thirty years after the Parthenon. For its religious significance, see Chapter 21, pp. 451–452.

6. Some parts of the friezes are still in situ, but the major fragments of the pediments and the friezes are in the British Museum in London and known as the Elgin marbles.

7. The are a number of ancient, miniature replicas and a description by Pausanias (1. 24). Copyright permission cannot be obtained to reproduce the most recent full-scale reconstruction in the Parthenon at Nashville.

Notes to Chapter 7

1. In the speech of Pausanias.

2. His mistress, the courtesan Phryne, was said to be his model, and some claim that Aphrodite herself asked: "Where did Praxiteles see me naked?"

3. Aphrodite's union with Hermes produced Hermaphroditus, whose story is told at the end of Chapter 10.

4. Many of Aphrodite's characteristics are Oriental in tone, and specific links can be found that are clearly Phrygian, Syrian, and Semitic in origin.

5. Cf. the Assyro-Babylonian myth of Ishtar and Tammuz.

6. Catullus (63) makes the anguish, love, and remorse of Attis the stuff of great poetry.

7. Her worship was introduced into Rome in 204. Lucretius (*De Rerum Natura* 2. 600–651) presents a hostile but vivid account of its orgiastic nature. For Lucretius the very nature of deity is that it exists forever tranquil and aloof, untouched by the human condition and immune to human prayers. See pp. 535–536.

8. *The New Golden Bough, a New Abridgement of the Classic Work* (by James G. Frazer), ed. Theodor H. Gaster, pp. 313–314. Copyright © 1959 by S. G. Phillips, Inc.

9. Hestia, the first-born of Cronus, was the first to be swallowed and the last to be brought up.

10. The name *Aeneas* is here derived from the Greek *ainos*, which means "dread."

11. There has been much discussion about the *Symposium* as a reflection of Athenian views generally about homosexuality. One wonders how typical of the mores of Victorian England would have been the speeches (however profound) of a select group of friends at a dinner party given by Oscar Wilde.

For some contemporary thinking on sexual matters, see David M. Halperin, *One Hundred Years of Homosexuality, and Other Essays on Greek Love* (New York: Routledge, 1989), who argues that modern attitudes towards homosexuality are inadequate for an understanding of sexual mores in the ancient world: of particular interest here is "Why Is Diotima a Woman," pp. 113–151. Cf. John J. Winkler, *Constraints of Desire, The Anthropology of Sex and Gender in Ancient Greece* (New York: Routledge, 1990), a study of the sexuality of women (e.g., Penelope and Sappho) and the interpretation of rituals (e.g., in honor of Demeter, Aphrodite, and Adonis).

12. This reference to the dispersion of the inhabitants of Mantinea (an Arcadian city) by the Spartans in 385 B.C. is an anachronism since the dramatic date of the speech is purportedly 416.

13. Literature, great and not so great, is permeated by this concept; particularly affecting in American literature is Carson McCullers's *Member of the Wedding*.

14. It is difficult to find one word that expresses adequately the abstract conceptions personified. The name *Poros* also suggests contrivance; *Metis*, wisdom or invention; and *Penia*, need.

Notes to Chapter 8

1. Sometimes the place of birth is called Ortygia (the name means "quail island"), which cannot be identified with certainty. In some accounts, it is clearly not merely another name for Delos; in others, it is.

2. Niobe was the wife of Amphion, ruling by his side in the royal palace of Cadmus. As the daughter of Tantalus and the granddaughter of Atlas, her lineage was much more splendid than that of Leto, the daughter of an obscure Titan, Coeus.

3. A rock on Mt. Sipylus in Asia Minor was identified in antiquity as the figure of Niobe.

4. Actaeon was the son of Aristaeus and Autonoë.

5. The nymphs' names, which are omitted in the translation, are Greek words suggestive of cool, crystal-clear water.

6. A stag was commonly believed to live nine times as long as a man.

7. Still Ovid goes on to give thirty-one more names, which are omitted in the translation.

8. Orion sometimes appears as the son of Earth; in other accounts his father is Poseidon.

9. Or Orion was run through by Artemis' arrows. Orion also attempted to rape Opis, a follower of Artemis, if indeed she is not the goddess herself.

10. Several of the nymphs associated with her (e.g., Callisto and Opis) were probably once goddesses in their own right and may actually represent various manifestations of Artemis' own complex nature. One of them, Britomartis, is closely linked to Crete, and perhaps was once a traditional mother-goddess.

11. Hecate's mother, Asterie, is Leto's sister; her father is Perses.

12. For more on the legend of Hippolytus and his cult-sites, see p. 530.

13. The attempted seduction of a holy man and its dire consequences represent familiar motifs in literature; cf. the Biblical stories of Joseph and Potiphar's wife and of John the Baptist and Salome.

Notes to Chapter 9

1. Many had cults of Apollo. Leto's wanderings are at times geographically erratic. Most of the places mentioned are familiar enough, but some names are problematical. Any attempt to trace Leto's wanderings precisely should begin with the notes in *The Homeric Hymns,* ed. T. W. Allen, W. R. Halliday, and E. E. Sikes, 2d ed. (New York: Oxford University Press, 1963).

2. In later accounts, Hera employs various schemes to prevent Leto from finding a place to bear her children, and through fear of Hera the whole earth rejects Leto's pleas. Hera also is said to have decreed that Leto's children could not be born in any place where the sun shone, so Poseidon kept the island of Delos (which in this early time was afloat) covered by his waves from the sun's rays during the birth of the twins.

3. These lines were thought to refer to Homer who, among the many traditions, becomes a blind bard from the island of Chios. It is extremely unlikely that the Homer associated with the *Iliad* and *Odyssey* wrote this hymn or any of the others. Bards are archetypically blind as opposed to the hale and hearty politicians and warriors; in terms of another fundamental motif, blind poets see the Muses' truth.

4. It is not difficult to imagine a fluid bardic tradition in which hymns could vary in length and be presented in diverse combinations.

5. In later accounts, the dragon or serpent is sometimes masculine with the name Python (as in Ovid's story of Apollo and Daphne, translated later in this chapter). It may also be described as the hostile opponent of Leto before the birth of her children. Some versions stress the great prowess of Apollo early in his life and career (as in the case of the wondrous childhood of Hermes and Heracles) to the extent of having him kill the dragon while still a child.

6. Aeschylus in the prologue to his *Eumenides* and Euripides in a chorus from his *Iphigenia in Tauris.* A scholarly survey of the problems, with a reconstruction of the origins and procedures of the oracle, is provided by H. W. Parke and D. E. W. Wormell, *The Delphic Oracle,* 2 vols. (Oxford: Basil Blackwell, 1956).

7. A festival (called the Stepteria) was celebrated every ninth year at Delphi to commemorate these events in the early history of the sanctuary.

8. The omphalos found in the excavations and originally identified as the archaic sacred stone has subsequently been labeled a fraud.

9. The other major Panhellenic festivals were those at Olympia and Nemea, both in honor of Zeus, and the Isthmian Games at Corinth, dedicated to Poseidon.

10. For the oracular Apollo elsewhere, see H. W. Parke, *The Oracles of Apollo in Asia Minor* (London: Croom Helm, 1985); also Joseph Fontenrose, *Didyma, Apollo's Oracle, Cult and Companions* (Berkeley: University of California Press, 1988), who is overly skeptical in his scholarly treatment of evidence.

11. One could inquire on one's own behalf or on the behalf of someone else. Inquiries often came from state representatives. Both the question and the answer were usually set down in writing. See Joseph Fontenrose, *The Delphic Oracle: Its Responses and Operations* (Berkeley: University of California Press, 1978).

12. Among the religious objects that decked the temple was the tomb of Dionysus. The god Dionysus was worshiped alongside Apollo in the sanctuary

(perhaps as early as the sixth century). The prophetic madness of the Pythia has much in common with Dionysiac frenzy. Some believe such frenzy was induced by drugs of one sort or another. See Walter Burkert, *Ancient Mystery Cults* (Cambridge: Harvard University Press, 1987), p. 108.

13. The first Pythia, who is named Phemonoë (Prophetic Mind), is a poetic figure; we have from Herodotus the names of later ones (Aristonice and Perallus), historically much more real.

14. See H. W. Parke, *Sibyls and Sibylline Prophecy in Classical Antiquity,* ed. Brian C. McGing, Croom Helm Classical Studies (New York: Routledge, 1988).

15. This Sibyl is Deïphobe, daughter of Glaucus, priestess of the temple of Phoebus Apollo and Diana.

16. Vergil's works themselves were consulted as oracles in later times as the *sortes Vergilianae.*

17. A total of one thousand years, counting the generations *(saecula)* as one hundred years each.

18. Petronius, *Satyricon* 48. 8. The Sibyl's story appears to be late in its reminiscences of Cassandra and Tithonus.

19. This is the Aristaeus who will become the husband of Autonoë and father of Actaeon; he too is the one who made advances to Eurydice. He is particularly linked with agricultural pursuits, especially beekeeping.

20. Cf. the stories of Zeus and Ganymede (p. 141) and Narcissus (pp. 245–250), among others. See also the sections on Plato's *Symposium* (pp. 143–151 and related references in n. 11, p. 625). For more on the theme, see B. Sergent, *Homosexuality in Greek Myth,* with a preface by G. Dumézil (London: Athlone Press, 1987).

21. Ovid puts the story in the mouth of Orpheus. Other accounts have Zephyrus (the West Wind) deliberately divert the course of the discus because of his jealous love for Hyacinthus.

22. These marks not only reproduce Apollo's moans of grief, they are also the initial letters of the name of the hero of the Trojan saga, the great Ajax (Greek *Aias*), son of Telamon, as Apollo indicates in his prophetic words. When Ajax committed suicide, the same flower, the hyacinth, sprang from his blood (Ovid, *Metamorphoses* 13. 391–398).

23. This is the famous Midas of the golden touch (Ovid's version of his story, *Metamorphoses* 11. 85–145, is well known). His story is told in Chapter 11, p. 242.

24. Elements of folktale appear dominant in this story, particularly in the traditional depiction of the garrulous barber. In some versions, Midas plays this same role in the contest between Apollo and Marsyas. Thus he favors the satyr against Apollo and suffers the same humiliation.

25. Apollo's epithet Lykios was believed by the Greeks to refer to him as a "wolf-god," whatever this may mean—that he was hunter like a wolf? that he was the protector against the wolf? Perhaps Lykios is to be derived from Lycia, a district in southwestern Asia Minor.

26. These lines about Apollo as a suitor are full of problems; the text seems to be corrupt. Ischys and Apollo vied for Coronis, and Leucippus and Apollo vied for Daphne (in a version given by Pausanias, 8. 20. 3). Nothing much can be made of the other rivals.

27. Apollo's itinerary offers some geographical problems, but in general he goes from Olympus through Larissa (the home of the Perrhaebi) to Iolchus and eventually crosses to the Lelantine plain (between Chalcis and Eretria) on the island of Euboea, and then back again to the mainland and Onchestus, Thebes, Lake Copais, and the Cephisus River—all in Boeotia. Next, continuing westward, Apollo comes to the spring Telphusa in the region of Mt. Helicon, and from there finally to Crisa, the site of his Delphi.

28. This is our only evidence for this ritual in honor of Poseidon at his famous precinct in Onchestus, and the numerous conjectures made by scholars about its meaning and purpose are not at all convincing.

29. Some etymologists do not agree with the ancients, who thought this name was derived from the cry *Ie* and *Paean,* meaning "healer." Later in this hymn, it is the name of a song.

30. *Typhaon* is also the name of the monster killed by Zeus, i.e., Typhoeus or Typhaon or Typhon; see pp. 55–56.

31. The ship sails along the south coast of the Peloponnesus, then up the north coast until it turns into the Corinthian gulf and makes for Crisa.

32. The Greek word translated as "overlooking" is *epopsios* and may refer to another epithet of Apollo (and Zeus) as "overseers" of everything; or the adjective may only mean that the altar is "conspicuous."

Notes to Chapter 10

1. The live tortoise was believed to be a taboo against harm and sorcery.

2. This is probably the well-known Pieria near Mt. Olympus in northern Thessaly. On his journey from Pieria, Hermes passes through Onchestus, situated between Thebes and Orchomenus, and brings the cattle to the river Alpheus, which flows near Olympia in the western Peloponnesus.

3. As he walks along (we learn below, pp. 205 and 208), Hermes makes the cattle walk backward. Thus the hoofprints of the cattle will seem to be going toward the meadow and not out of it. Hermes' own tracks will be obscured by his sandals.

4. As we have seen, according to Hesiod (*Theogony* 387) Selene is the daughter of Hyperion and Theia; Pallas (*Theogony* 375, 377, 409) was the son of the Titan Crius; and his brother Perses was the father of Hecate. Megamedes is not found elsewhere.

5. The text is corrupt at this point; apparently Hermes used the laurel branch to rub against a piece of wood grasped in the palm of his hand, thus creating the friction to produce fire.

6. Hermes offers a portion to each of the twelve gods. According to sacrificial ritual, he (as one of them) must not eat his portion or those of the other gods but merely savor the aroma.

7. Presumably Apollo intends to bind either Hermes or the cows.

8. The lyre is mentioned as a beloved companion, that is, a girlfriend, and in the next few lines Hermes sustains the metaphor, which reads naturally in Greek but is difficult to render in English. Thus she will accompany Apollo to the feast and the dance and she will behave and respond as a beloved should, if only she is treated in the right way.

9. These are shepherds' pipes of reed, also called panpipes since they are often said to be the invention of the god Pan. Hermes sometimes is named as the father of Pan, whom he resembles in certain respects.

10. These are identified as the Thriae; their name means "pebbles"; thus they are the eponymous nymphs of divining pebbles, i.e., pebbles used for divination. They appear to be women with wings; probably their hair is literally powdered with white flour; some suggest that they are meant to be white-haired and old or that the image intended is that of bees covered with pollen.

11. In tone and mood this story is not unlike that of Aphrodite, Ares, and Hephaestus in Homer (*Odyssey* 8. 266-366, translated in Chapter 3, pp. 87-89).

12. A historical incident concerning herms warns us to be wary of facile generalizations about Greek religious attitudes. In 415 B.C., on the eve of the great Athenian expedition against Sicily, the herms in the city of Athens were mutilated during the night. The religious scandal that ensued became a political football; the general Alcibiades was charged and the consequences were serious—quite a fuss over phallic statues of a god in a period fraught with sophistic skepticism, agnosticism, and atheism. Alcibiades was also charged with the parody and desecration of the Eleusinian mysteries of Demeter in a private home; he called himself Hierophant and wore a robe like that of the high priest when he shows the holy secrets to the initiates (Plutarch, *Alcibiades* 22. 3).

13. In context, Alcithoë is telling the story to her sisters. The spring Salmacis was located at Halicarnassus.

14. See Marie Delcourt, *Hermaphrodite: Myths and Rites of the Bisexual Figure in Classical Antiquity* (London: Studio Books, 1961).

Notes to Chapter 11

1. Bacchus, the name for the god preferred by the Romans, is often used by the Greeks as well.

2. The word *dithyrambos,* an epithet of Dionysus and the name of a type of choral poetry that included hymns sung in the god's honor, was in ancient times believed to refer etymologically to his double birth.

3. The career of Ino is extremely confusing because of the multiple versions of her story. She was the second wife of Athamas (whom we shall meet again in the Argonautic saga), and they had two sons, Learchus and Melicertes. Angry with Ino because of her care for Dionysus, Hera drove both Ino and her husband mad. Athamas killed his son Learchus and pursued Ino, who escaped with Melicertes in her arms. She leaped from a cliff into the sea and was transformed into the sea-goddess Leucothea; Melicertes also became deified under the new name of Palaemon.

4. Note the Dionysiac aspects of Orpheus' missionary zeal in Thrace. The date for the introduction of the worship of the god into Hellas is difficult to establish; it probably belongs to the obscure period of transition after the fall of Mycenae (ca. 1100). But it is foolhardy to be dogmatic, especially if the decipherment of a Linear B tablet is correct and the name Dionysus (whether that of the god or not) can be identified as belonging to the Mycenaean Age.

5. The Curetes, as we have seen, are the attendants of Rhea, who hid the cries of the infant Zeus from his father Cronus. In this passage, Euripides associates them with the Corybantes, the ministers of Cybele.

6. We have translated only the beginning and end of Tiresias' lengthy and learned sermon on the great power of Dionysus.

7. Other less famous stories of opposition to Dionysus convey the same terrifying message. In Argos, the daughters of Proetus, king of Tiryns, refused to accept the god and were driven mad; but the famous seer Melampus knew of certain therapeutic dances or herbs to cure them.

    In Orchomenus, a city of Boeotia, the daughters of Minyas refused to participate in Bacchic worship but remained at home to weave. Dionysus, in the guise of a girl, warned them of their folly to no avail, and they were driven mad; one of them, Leucippe, bore a son named Hippasus, who (like Pentheus) was torn to pieces. The women eventually were turned into bats.

    Lycurgus of Thrace (Homer, *Iliad* 6. 130–140) pursued the nurses of Dionysus with an ox goad, and Dionysus himself in terror jumped into the sea and was rescued and comforted by Thetis. The gods became angry with Lycurgus, and Zeus struck him with blindness and he died soon afterwards.

8. The initial nine lines, quoted by Diodorus Siculus (3. 66. 3), are probably not a separate hymn but should in some way be joined to the fragmentary last section of this first hymn, which is found in manuscript.

9. The epithet *eiraphiotes* is of uncertain derivation. It may mean "insewn," but it may instead refer to Dionysus' connection with the ivy plant or the goat or the bull.

10. Dracanum is a cape on the island of Cos; Icarus and Naxos are islands, and the Alpheus is a river in Elis.

11. There must be a lacuna after these lines from Diodorus and before the next section from the manuscript text.

12. The reference to three things is unclear; it may refer to the ritual of dismemberment.

13. E. R. Dodds's helpful edition of the Greek text of the *Bacchae,* 2d ed. (New York: Oxford University Press, 1960), includes an enlightening introduction; he notes that Dionysiac religion shares a belief, found universally, that musical rhythms and ritual dances lead to the most satisfying and highest religious experiences. See also Walter F. Otto, *Dionysus: Myth and Cult* (Bloomington: Indiana University Press, 1965 [1933]); M. Detienne, *Dionysos at Large* (Cambridge: Harvard University Press, 1989 [1986]).

14. A famous adaptation of this legend was made by Vergil in his sixth *Eclogue,* in which the utterance of the silenus is cosmogonical and mythological.

15. Variations in the story are obviously etiological attempts to account for elements of Bacchic ritual. Later ceremonies enacted the passion, death, and resurrection of the god in all its details.

16. Friedrich Nietzsche has provided the most imaginative and influential modern analysis of the Dionysiac experience, particularly in enunciating its antithetical relationship to the Apollonian. See M. S. Silk and J. P. Stern, *Nietzsche on Tragedy* (New York: Cambridge University Press, 1981), a study of Nietzsche's first book, *The Birth of Tragedy.*

17. Ovid's version of Midas' story (*Metamorphoses* 11. 85–145), is well known.

This is the same Midas whose ears were turned into those of an ass as a result of his preference for the music of Pan over that of Apollo; see pp. 188–189.

18. The same story is told by Ovid (*Metamorphoses* 3. 597–691), who provides an interesting comparison in artistic method and purpose.

19. See Philippe Borgeaud, *The Cult of Pan in Ancient Greece* (Chicago: University of Chicago Press, 1988) for a study of changing representations of Pan. Also Patricia Merivale, *Pan the Goat-God, His Myth in Modern Times* (Cambridge: Harvard University Press, 1969).

20. According to Herodotus (6. 106), Pan was encountered by the runner Phidippides, who had been sent to Sparta by the Athenians to ask for help when they were about to fight the Persians at Marathon in 490. Phidippides claimed that Pan called him by name and asked why the Athenians ignored him although he was a deity friendly to them. The Athenians believed Phidippides and later built a shrine to Pan and honored him with annual sacrifices and torch races.

21. Another nymph he pursued was turned into a tree that bore her name, Pitys (the Greek word for "pine").

22. This is Dryope; Ovid (*Metamorphoses* 9. 325 ff.) has a different version.

23. The Greek word *pan* means "all."

24. See Louise Vinge, *The Narcissus Theme in Western European Literature up to the Early 19th Century* (Lund, Sweden: Gleerups, 1967); also Gerasimos Santas, *Plato and Freud: Two Theories of Love* (Oxford: Basil Blackwell, 1988): Freud believed that an individual's sexual development as an infant may determine his or her choices as an adult concerning the object and nature of love; thus the theory of narcissism had a great impact on his conviction that, for some, relationships in love may stem not from their primal attachment to their mothers but from infantile self-love.

Notes to Chapter 12

1. That is, "to initiate and observe the holy rite or sacrament." There appears to be a lacuna after this sentence. The words translated "for the sake of the holy rite" are difficult, and their precise meaning is disputed. The reference must be to an important part of the ceremony of the Eleusinian mysteries, namely the partaking of a drink called the *Kykeon*. But the nature and significance of the ritual are unknown: was this in any real sense the sharing of a sacrament, an act of communion fraught with mystic significance, or was it merely a token remembrance of these hallowed actions of the goddess?

2. Sixteen of these names are listed among the daughters of Oceanus and Tethys by Hesiod, *Theogony* 346–361; and Melite is a Nereid (246). The poet adds Leucippe, Phaeno, Iache, and Rhodope.

3. The charges against Alcibiades mentioned in Chapter 10 (note 12, p. 630), are indicative of the seriousness of the consequences if the sacred ceremonies were divulged or desecrated in any way.

4. See in particular George E. Mylonas, *Eleusis and the Eleusinian Mysteries* (Princeton: Princeton University Press, 1961); this provides the best general survey of all the evidence and the inherent archaeological, historical, religious, and philosophical problems.

5. As a place for the celebration of the mysteries (the Greek word is *teletai*), the temple of Demeter is called a *telesterion*.

6. Known as the *Epopteia*.

7. The Eumolpids (whose ancestor Eumolpus, according to the hymn, received the mysteries from Demeter herself) and the Kerykes.

8. The initiate was the *mystes* and his patron the *mystagogos*.

9. Aristophanes' *Frogs,* 340 ff., gives us some idea of this procession.

10. Herodotus (8. 65) tells a tale about a mysterious cloud (arising from Eleusis amidst the strains of the mystic hymn to Iacchus) that provided a true omen of future events; in the context, the worship of the mother and the maiden is mentioned. This miracle sets the right tone for elements common to the worship and myths of both Demeter and Dionysus. It is not impossible that the passion of this resurrection-god played some role in the mysteries; Dionysus too is close to drama, and drama lies at the essence of the emotional aspects of Eleusinian ritual.

11. Mylonas, *Eleusis and the Eleusinian Mysteries,* pp. 284–285; footnotes are omitted.

12. For a survey of festivals, including the important *Thesmophoria,* in honor of Demeter, see H. W. Parke, *Festivals of the Athenians* (Ithaca, N.Y.: Cornell University Press, 1977); also, Erika Simon, *Festivals of Attica, An Archaeological Commentary* (Madison: University of Wisconsin Press, 1983). For Ovid's treatment of the rape of Persephone in the *Metamorphoses* 5 and *Fasti* 4, see Stephen Hinds, *The Metamorphosis of Persephone: Ovid and the Self-conscious Muse* (New York: Cambridge University Press, 1987).

Notes to Chapter 13

1. Tiresias is the famous seer of the Theban cycle, who holds special prerogatives in the world of the dead; his wits are intact, and to him alone in death Persephone has left a mind for reasoning; all others are mere shadows *(Odyssey* 10. 492–495).

2. Another name for Hades' realm or part of it.

3. Elpenor can address Odysseus first without drinking the blood because his corpse has not yet been cremated.

4. As we learn in Book 10 (551–560), Elpenor got drunk and, wanting fresh air, left his companions in Circe's palace. He fell asleep on the roof; in the morning he was awakened suddenly and forgot where he was.

5. Tiresias does not have to drink the blood before he can speak, but he needs to drink it in order to express his prophetic powers to the full. He may also be drinking it as a mortal would drink wine, for refreshment, and thus he establishes ties of hospitality and friendship with Odysseus.

6. An early name of Delphi.

7. Tantalus' crime is variously described by later writers; whatever its specific nature, it is a crime against the gods, often identified as some abuse of their trust or hospitality. The verb *tantalize* comes from his name and his punishment. For Pindar's version, see pp. 338–339.

8. Sisyphus' crimes are recounted on pp. 501–502.

9. Plato's image is of a spindle with its shaft at one end and a fly or whorl at the other. We may liken this to an open umbrella held upside down and filled with eight concentric circular rings, which revolve and carry with them the stars and the planets.

10. This divinity *(daimon)* is the destiny that accompanies each soul through its life on earth, its good or bad *genius*.

11. In Hesiod *(Theogony* 713–814) Tartarus is a dark place in the depths of the earth into which Zeus hurled the Titans after he defeated them. It is surrounded by a fortification of bronze, and inside dwell Night and her children Sleep and Death. The house of Hades and Persephone is guarded by a terrifying hound. The river of Tartarus is the Styx, by whose water the gods swear dread oaths; if they break these oaths, they must suffer terrible penalties for a full nine years.

12. In graves in southern Italy and Crete have been found thin plates of gold inscribed with religious verses that were presumably intended to help the mystic believer in the afterlife; some of the sentiments reflect the eschatology found in Plato, especially concerning the drinking of the waters of Lethe.

13. Vergil's conception of the rivers of the Underworld is far from clear. Charon seems to ferry the souls across Acheron, although Cocytus is mentioned in the immediate context; the Styx is identified by Vergil later. Tradition often has Charon cross the river Styx.

14. By poor, Vergil probably means that they do not have the fare to pay Charon. A coin was traditionally placed between the lips of the dead for passage to the Underworld.

15. The mother of the Aloadae was Iphimedeia, who said that their real father was Poseidon, according to the Greek version. These twins grew to be giants, and their attack on Zeus was made by piling Mt. Ossa upon Olympus and then Mt. Pelion upon Ossa. For this presumption, they were both while still young killed by Apollo.

16. In some accounts Phlegyas is the father of Ixion; he burned the temple of Apollo at Delphi because of Apollo's affair with his daughter Coronis.

17. Sometimes the wheel is on fire. For Ixion's crime, see pp. 490–491.

18. Near its source, the Po River flowed for some distance underground, and the legendary river of the Underworld, Eridanus, was identified with it.

19. Vergil echoes Homer's lines about Odysseus trying to embrace the shade of his mother.

20. That is, each of us has a soul that must bear the consequences of its life on earth.

21. The Danaids, the forty-nine daughters of Danaüs who killed their husbands on their wedding night, are frequently added to the group in Tartarus; their punishment is that they must attempt in vain to carry water in containers that have no real bottoms.

22. Thus, for example, Tityus has his liver devoured because he attempted to violate Leto, since the liver was believed to be the seat of the passions.

23. For Charon in the western tradition, see R. H. Terpenig, *Charon and the Crossing: Ancient, Medieval and Renaissance Transformations of a Myth* (Lewisburg, Pa.: Bucknell University Press, 1985).

24. Tantalus' misery is vividly described in Seneca's play *Thyestes* (152-175).

25. The Furies also may be called the Eumenides in an attempt to ward off their hostility by a euphemistic appellation, as in the case of Hades.

26. Zeus and the gods may destroy human beings and punish evil in this life, at times in opposition to one another. And the justice of the moral order of the Olympian gods and the Fates is the same as that of the realm of Hades. It is Prometheus who champions the human race as a whole against the antagonism of Zeus, but this is a quite different story.

27. Also the brilliant, satiric *Dialogues of the Dead* (e.g., nos. 18 and 22) by Lucian illustrate the varied moods of the Greek and Roman portrayal of the Underworld.

Notes to Chapter 14

1. One of the many places identified as an entrance to the Underworld was a cave near Taenarus, a town in Laconia.

2. *Georgics* 4. 452–526.

3. Aristaeus, the son of Apollo and Cyrene, is the traditional hero or deity of rustic pursuits, especially beekeeping. When Eurydice died, her sister Dryads in their grief and anger caused all the bees of Aristaeus to die. Perplexed at this, he eventually consulted the wise old man of the sea, Proteus. Aristaeus appeased the nymphs, and a new swarm of bees was created. Through the role of Aristaeus, Vergil artfully introduces the touching account of Orpheus and Eurydice in the last book of his didactic poem on farming.

4. An important survey offers the general reader a scholarly examination of the whole question: W. K. C. Guthrie, *Orpheus and Greek Religion: A Study of the Orphic Movement* (New York: Norton, 1966).

5. He does not seem really to belong, but the gentle bard was placed among the brawny heroes because of his prestige and the magical powers of his song, which saved them all in more than one crisis; Orpheus appropriately was the leader in religious matters. The chronology also seems wrong for our historical Orpheus, if we must put him back in the heroic age in the generation before the Trojan War.

6. The chronological tradition for Orpheus is equally muddled. Those who connect his dates with Homer's deserve the most credibility. Thus either he was the inventor of writing and his works immediately preceded the Homeric epics, or Homer was the first poet and Orpheus followed shortly after.

7. This link with Dionysus may mean that Orpheus is yet another god (however faded) of the death and rebirth of vegetation; Eurydice, too, has some of the chthonian characteristics of Semele and Persephone. These parallels could likewise have been added to the legend that grew up about a historical prophet. Some of the themes also look like motifs common to folktale: conjugal devotion, the journey to Hades' realm, the taboo of looking back.

8. The date and authorship of these hymns are not securely established; perhaps at least some of them are earlier. See Apostolos N. Athanassakis, *The Orphic*

Hymns, text, translation, and notes (Atlanta, Ga.: Scholars Press, 1977); Athanassakis (pp. viii–ix) inclines to accept the theories of Otto Kern that the hymns belong to the city of Pergamum for use in the celebration of the mysteries of Dionysus, third century A.D.

9. An attractive thesis claims that the religion attributed to the legendary musician was formulated in large part by philosophers in southern Italy and Sicily (although not necessarily confined to this region) in the sixth century B.C. Thus we can explain the elements identified as Orphic in the philosophy of Empedocles and in the religious sect of Pythagoras and thereby account for the Orphic-Pythagorean thought transmitted by Plato.

10. See Aristophanes' parody translated on p. 39.

11. For the archetypal Orpheus and subsequent motifs, including that of the Good Shepherd, see John Block Friedman, *Orpheus in the Middle Ages* (Cambridge: Harvard University Press, 1970).

12. The Roman emperor Augustus himself was initiated, while Nero, according to his biographer Suetonius, did not dare to become a candidate because of his guilty conscience. In the third century, Gallienus (253–268) commemorated his initiation by issuing a coin with his name and title in the feminine gender (*Galliena Augusta*) in honor of the goddess.

13. The oldest of the Greek mysteries after those of Demeter were those of the Cabiri, whose cult center was associated with the island of Samothrace and the city of Pergamum. The Cabiri themselves were usually referred to as *theoi megaloi,* the "great gods." Sometimes they were identified with the Dioscuri, Castor and Pollux, and thus offered protection from the dangers of seafaring. The Argonauts were said to have been initiated, and there are innumerable records of actual initiations right down until the end of the fourth century. See Susan Cole, *Theoi Megaloi: The Cult of the Great Gods of Samothrace* (Leiden: Brill, 1984).

14. The *taurobolium* is described in detail by the fourth-century Christian poet Prudentius in the tenth of his hymns about martyrs, *Peri Stephanon* (On Crowns). The most vivid details are translated in John Ferguson, *Religions of the Roman Empire* (Ithaca, N.Y.: Cornell University Press, 1970), pp. 104–105. The *taurobolium,* which is recorded in many inscriptions, the first being in A.D. 105, was practiced by initiates of Mithraism and even of Demeter; for a description by Frazer in connection with the worship of Attis see above pp. 135–136.

15. This interpretation, advocated by Franz Cumont, *The Mysteries of Mithra* (New York: Dover, 1956 [1903]), has been challenged; David Ulansey, *The Origins of the Mithraic Mysteries* (New York: Oxford University Press, 1989), follows those scholars who believe the tauroctony represents a series of stars and constellations, and in this kind of star map, the figure of Mithras is to be equated with the Greek and Roman Perseus.

16. Vividly described by Apuleius, *Metamorphoses* 8. 27–29.

17. To this Jupiter the Romans assimilated the dedications of the great temples of Baal at Baalbek (in modern Lebanon), usually referred to as the temple of Jupiter, and of Bel at Palmyra.

18. See R. E. Witt, *Isis in the Greek and Roman World* (Ithaca, N.Y.: Cornell University Press, 1971). For Io, who came to be worshiped as Isis, see pp. 68–69 and 417–418.

Notes to Chapter 15

1. One of Laius' retainers escaped: in Sophocles' play he is the very servant who originally failed to expose Oedipus, and his story brings about the final discovery of Oedipus' identity.
2. There are several variants of the riddle and its answer. The shortest (Apollodorus 3. 5. 8) is given here.
3. Cf. Lowell Edmunds, *Oedipus: The Ancient Legend and Its Later Analogues* (Baltimore: Johns Hopkins University Press, 1985), a survey of the many versions of the myth.
4. In Euripides' play *Phoenissae* Jocasta kills herself during the attack of the Seven against Thebes, and then Oedipus is exiled.
5. The herald's description of Eteoclus (son of Iphis), whom Aeschylus names as the third hero in place of Adrastus, is omitted.
6. Antigone, as the symbol of individual conscience against the unjust laws of the state, has inspired many literary and musical works. See George Steiner, *Antigones* (Oxford: Oxford University Press, 1984).

Notes to Chapter 16

1. These tales are brilliantly discussed by Walter Burkert, *Homo Necans* (Berkeley: University of California Press, 1983), pp. 83–109, part of his chapter entitled "Werewolves around the Tripod Kettle."
2. The Greek phrase is obscure. Cassandra refers to the instrument of the murder, either a sword or an axe, one or the other of which appears in different poetic accounts and vase paintings of the murder.
3. The Areopagus was the court at Athens that heard homicide cases; its members were former archons, that is, state officials. The court had been a center of political controversy shortly before Aeschylus produced his play.
4. A third daughter of Agamemnon, Chrysothemis, has no independent legend of her own. She appears as a foil for Electra in Sophocles.

Notes to Chapter 17

1. Pindar, *Nemean Ode* 10. In Theocritus, *Idyll* 22), the quarrel begins when the Dioscuri carry off the daughters of Leucippus from their intended husbands, Idas and Lynceus. The "Rape of the Leucippides" was a common subject in ancient art. Another version has one of the divine twins in heaven and the other in Hades on alternate days.
2. Euripides brings them on dramatically at the end of his *Electra,* not only as the protectors of sailors but also as champions of a better morality than that represented by Apollo.
3. Their appearance as horsemen on white steeds at the battle of Lake Regillus in 496 led to a great Roman victory.
4. Aphrodite is said (also by Stesichorus) to have made Helen unfaithful as punishment for Helen's father, Tyndareus, who had once omitted to sacrifice to the goddess.

5. Hecuba's stepson, Aesacus.

6. For the historical facts about Troy and the Trojan War, see pp. 23-24.

7. Laomedon was a nephew of Ganymede, whom Zeus had snatched up to Olympus to become the cupbearer of the gods (p. 141). In compensation, Zeus gave Tros (father of Ganymede) the divine horses that Laomedon inherited and failed to give to Heracles.

8. The story of Troïlus' love for Cressida (daughter, in this version, of Calchas) is an invention of the Middle Ages; Boccaccio and Chaucer took the story from the *Roman de Troie* of Benôit de Ste. Maure. Shakespeare's play is a further variation.

9. Although the contingents supplied by Odysseus, king of Ithaca, and Ajax, prince of Salamis, were among the smallest (only twelve ships each), their personal prowess gave them preeminence.

10. The comparative importance of the Greek leaders may be gauged from the size of their contingents in the *Catalogue* in Book 2 of the *Iliad:* Agamemnon, 100 ships; Nestor, 90; Diomedes and Idomeneus, 80 each; Menelaus, 60; Achilles, 60; Ajax the Less, 40; Ajax, son of Telamon, and Odysseus, 12 each.

11. Palamedes, son of Nauplius, was, after Odysseus, the cleverest of the Greeks; he was credited with a number of inventions. His unmasking of the ''madness'' earned him the hostility of Odysseus, who eventually contrived his death.

12. For the role of this secret in the story of Prometheus, see pp. 66 and 108; for Thetis' supplication to Zeus on behalf of Achilles, see p. 84.

13. Similar magic was practiced by Demeter at Eleusis on the child Demophoön.

14. Nowhere does Homer mention a physical relationship between Achilles and Patroclus. In Plato's *Symposium,* Pausanias, probably not speaking in purely spiritual terms, identifies Patroclus as older and less beautiful than Achilles and his lover, contradicting Aeschylus, who (in a play no longer extant) made Achilles the lover rather than the beloved of Patroclus.

15. The figure is given in the *Catalogue* in Book 2 of the *Iliad.* Ancient as this document is and historically of the greatest importance, its numbers are inflated.

16. The commonest version of his offense is that he had killed a stag sacred to the goddess. Some say that Artemis caused no winds to blow at all.

17. This version underlies Euripides' tragedy *Iphigenia in Tauris.* See p. 348.

18. After the Trojan War, Calchas challenged the seer Mopsus to a contest by asking him how many unripe figs there were on a nearby tree. When Mopsus gave the correct answer, Calchas died, for he was fated to do so if he met a cleverer prophet than himself.

19. Some versions have Calchas make the prophecy, and Neoptolemus accompany Odysseus to Lemnos. Sophocles and Aeschylus both wrote tragedies on Philoctetes; that of Sophocles is extant.

20. Pope's translation of this passage is given on p. 577.

21. This is the same Thersites who spoke out of turn in the assembly of the Greeks in Book 2 of the *Iliad*.

22. Ajax is the Latin form of the Greek Aias. For the metamorphosis of Hyacinthus, see pp. 184–185.

23. Being descended from one of the heroes shut up in the wooden horse was one of the marks of the *crème de la crème* of the Greek nobility.

24. His sacrilege had a strange historical consequence; for a thousand years the Locrians annually sent two daughters of noble families to serve as temple servants of Athena at Troy (i.e., the later foundations after the fall of Priam's city) as a penance for Ajax's crime. If any of these girls was caught by the Trojans before she reached the temple, she was put to death. This penance was ended not long before A.D. 100. There is a connection between the name Oileus and the Greek name for Troy, Ilium.

25. The gods are here called by their Latin names.

Notes to Chapter 18

1. The summary is ascribed to the fifth century A.D. scholar Proclus, who names Agias of Troezen as the author of the *Nostoi*. A useful discussion is by G. L. Huxley, *Greek Epic Poetry* (Cambridge: Harvard University Press, 1969), chap. 12.

2. For the story that Helen was in Egypt during the Trojan War see pp. 352–353.

3. Pindar, *Nemean Odes* 10. 7. Among the many narratives of the legend of Diomedes are those of Vergil (*Aeneid* 11. 243–295) and Ovid (*Metamorphoses* 14. 460–511).

4. Said by Ovid to be "next in shape to swans." What these birds were can only be guessed.

5. He is also associated with Colophon in Asia Minor.

6. Many attempts have been made to follow the route of Odysseus. See T. Severin, *The Ulysses Voyage: Sea Search for the Odyssey* (London: Hutchinson, 1987). Compare T. Severin, *The Jason Voyage: The Quest for the Golden Fleece* (New York: Simon and Schuster, 1985).

7. According to the conventions of Homeric society the liaisons with Calypso and Circe did not make Odysseus unfaithful. Cf. Mary R. Lefkowitz, *Women in Greek Myth* (London: Duckworth, 1986), p. 64: "[Penelope] does not demand strict fidelity; neither she nor Helen object to their husbands' liaisons with other women, so long as they are temporary." The same point is made by Sarah Pomeroy, *Goddesses, Whores, Wives, and Slaves* (New York: Schocken, 1975), pp. 26–27, and by Marilyn Katz, *Penelope's Renown* (Princeton: Princeton University Press, 1991), p. 13.

8. The Greek word *polytropos* (of many ways) means a combination of complexity, intelligence, and being widely traveled.

9. A powerful adaptation of this legend is the Circe episode in James Joyce's *Ulysses*.

10. The adventures of Odysseus subsequent to the *Odyssey* were narrated in the lost epic *Telegonia* by Eugammon of Cyrene. It ends with Telegonus conveying Odysseus' body with Penelope and Telemachus to Circe, who

makes them immortal. Telegonus then marries Penelope and Circe marries Telemachus.

Notes to Chapter 19

1. For Proetus and Bellerophon see pp. 502–504.
2. The Roman poet Horace (*Odes* 3. 16) changed Danaë's prison to a brazen tower, which has become the traditional version.
3. The Athenian historian Pherecydes (early fifth century B.C.) is an early authority for the saga.
4. The word *kibisis* is not Greek and in antiquity was believed to be Cypriote.
5. Hermes wears the Cap of Darkness in the Gigantomachy and is regularly portrayed with winged sandals. Athena wore the Cap of Invisibility at Troy (*Iliad* 5. 844–845).
6. It is also placed by others in the far north, among the Hyperboreans, or in the far south, among the Ethiopians.
7. For their origin, see p. 114.
8. The Gorgon Euryale is mourning for her dead sister, Medusa.
9. In the first century A.D. the marks of Andromeda's fetters were still being shown on the rocks near the city of Joppa.
10. The legends of these heroes are discussed on pp. 494–495 (Melampus), 329–333 (the Seven), and 392 (Diomedes).

Notes to Chapter 20

1. The Greek form of his name, which means "glory of Hera," is used here. Its Latin form is Hercules. He is also called Alcides (i.e., descendant of Alcaeus) and sometimes Amphitryoniades (i.e., son of Amphitryon).
2. Licymnius, surviving son of Electryon, was later killed by a son of Heracles.
3. According to Apollodorus, Amphitryon was helped by Creon after ridding Thebes of a monstrous fox with the aid of Cephalus and his magic hound (see pp. 453–454).
4. Eileithyia sat outside Alcmena's door with her hands clasped around her knees in a gesture of sympathetic magic. Alcmena's servant Galanthis broke the spell by rushing out crying "My mistress has borne a son!" Eileithyia leaped up and unclasped her hands, and the birth took place, She punished Galanthis by turning her into a weasel.
5. Eurytus was grandson of Apollo and king of the Euboean city of Oechalia. See p. 437 for his death at the hands of Heracles.
6. The Cattle of Geryon, the Apples of the Hesperides, and Cerberus.
7. Although female the hind is always shown with horns. Euripides makes the hind destructive, and some authors call it the Cerynitian hind, from the Achaean river Cerynites.
8. Atlas was the name of a mountain in Arcadia as well as of the more famous range in North Africa.
9. The hind is shown beside the tree of the Hesperides in a vase painting.

10. *Parerga* are adventures incidental to the labors.

11. Pausanias attributes the founding of the games to "Heracles the Dactyl," an attendant of the great Cretan goddess. He had nothing to do with the Greek hero Heracles.

12. The attributes of the birds vary with the imagination of individual authors. See D'Arcy W. Thompson, *Glossary of Greek Birds*, 2d ed. (New York: Oxford University Press, 1936), p. 273. The birds are later encountered by the Argonauts on the Island of Ares (see p. 479).

13. The killing of Cacus is one of the *parerga* to this labor. It is told by Vergil (see pp. 521–522).

14. The Agathyrsi and Geloni were tribes to the north of Scythia, which was the area between the Danube and the Don.

15. His name means "the house of Osiris." Herodotus points out that the Egyptians did not practice human sacrifice.

16. In another version Zeus throws a thunderbolt between Cycnus and Heracles.

17. Vergil describes this in the sixth *Eclogue* (6. 44): *ut litus Hyla, Hyla omne sonaret*).

18. There are many variants of the legend of Telephus, about whom both Sophocles and Euripides wrote tragedies.

19. This is the *cornu copiae* (horn of plenty). Amalthea is the name of a goddess of Plenty and of the goat that suckled the infant Zeus. Ovid says that the horn of Acheloüs became the cornucopia when the Naiads picked it up and filled it with fruit and flowers.

20. Walter Burkert, *Structure and History in Greek Mythology and Ritual* (Berkeley: University of California Press, 1979), p. 94.

21. Xenophon, *Memorabilia* 2. 21–34; Cicero, *De Officiis* 1. 118. The parable has been very important in Western art: see E. Panofsky, *Hercules am Scheideweg* (Leipzig, 1930).

22. For further discussion see L. R. Farnell, *Greek Hero-cults and Ideas of Immortality* (New York: Oxford University Press, 1921), chaps. 5–7; G. Karl Galinsky, *The Herakles Theme* (Oxford: Basil Blackwell, 1972). The best discussion is that of Burkert, *Structure and History*. For Heracles in art see Frank Brommer, *Herakles*, 2 vols. (Darmstadt: Wissenschaftliche Buchgesellschaft, 1972–1984); vol. 1 has been translated by Shirley J. Schwarz as *Heracles: The Twelve Labors of the Hero in Ancient Art and Literature* (New Rochelle: Caratzas, 1984). See also Jane Henle, *Greek Myths: A Vase Painter's Notebook* (Bloomington: Indiana University Press, 1973), pp. 231–238.

23. For the different versions of her myth see J. G. Frazer's notes on pp. 181–182 and 303 in vol. 1 of his edition of Apollodorus (Cambridge: Loeb Classical Library, Harvard University Press, 1961 [1921]).

Notes to Chapter 21

1. They saw either a pair of snakes or Erichthonius with his snakelike lower half. Ovid makes Athena punish Aglauros.

2. Euripides, *Erechtheus,* frag. 18, 94–98.

3. The sacrifice of a virgin was the original form of the legend. Later versions give her the name of Chthonia (which means "earth woman") and have her sisters take an oath to kill themselves so as to die with her.

4. Euripides' *Erechtheus* survives only in fragments; its ending (including a long speech from Athena), first published in 1967, has helped fill out many of the missing details of the relationship between the myth of Erechtheus and his cult. Erechtheus took the title of the god who caused his death (i.e., he became Poseidon-Erechtheus). His original status as a hero, with a cult located at the place of his burial, was later confused with that of the god. His daughters had become goddesses with the title Hyacinthides, to be worshiped with annual sacrifices and dances.

5. The lines are sung just after Medea has secured the promise of protection from Aegeus.

6. Pandrosos had her own shrine and cult on the Acropolis, close to the Erechtheum. She was the one of the three daughters of Cecrops, to whom, in some versions, Athena had entrusted Erichthonius. Aglauros was worshiped in a cave on the north side of the Acropolis, while the name *Herse* had been connected etymologically with the festival of the *Arrephoria,* in which two specially chosen young girls carried mysterious objects from the Acropolis by night down to the sanctuary of Aphrodite and Eros, which was also on the north side of the Acropolis.

7. Ovid plays on words with a double meaning, literal and erotic, for which English has no adequate equivalent.

8. In another version Procris was discovered by Cephalus with a lover. She fled to Minos, king of Crete, who himself fell in love with her. He had been bewitched by his wife, Pasiphaë, so that whenever he lay with a woman he discharged snakes and other creatures. Procris cured him and then lay with him, being rewarded with the gift of the hound and the javelin. Later she returned to Athens and was reconciled with Cephalus.

9. There is a pun here on Ion's name, which is also the Greek word meaning "going."

10. The legend of Ion stems almost entirely from Euripides' play. It explains the historical fact of the colonization of Ionia by mainland Greeks (principally from Athens) during the unsettled period after the collapse of the Mycenaean civilization.

11. The chief source is Plato's *Phaedrus* 229, where Socrates rationalizes the legend: "I would say that the North Wind pushed her, as she was playing, down from the nearby rocks. She died in this way; but her death was described as her being ravished by Boreas."

12. And by his link with the cult of Apollo Delphinius, i.e., Apollo as a god of spring, when the sea becomes navigable and the dolphins appear as portents of good sailing weather. See pp. 174 and 196–198.

13. The oracle is difficult to reconcile with this story if the "home" referred to should be Athens. Euripides has Medea cure Aegeus of his sterility after she has joined him in Athens.

14. Theseus was idealized in the latter part of the sixth century B.C. when Pisistratus was tyrant of Athens, and again immediately after the Persian Wars (ca. 475).

15. The most complete source for the legend of Theseus is Plutarch's *Life of Theseus* (early second century A.D.). This biography blurs the lines between

mythology, history, and philosophy. A useful collection of essays on the saga of Theseus is Anne G. Ward, ed., *The Quest for Theseus* (New York: Praeger, 1970). For Theseus in ancient art, see Frank Brommer, *Theseus, die Taten des griechischen Helden in der antiken Kunst und Literatur* (Darmstadt: Wissenschaftliche Buchgesellschaft, 1982).

16. Sciron originally had his own legend and cult at Megara, on the island of Salamis, and in Attica where there were limestone outcrops (his name means "limestone").

17. Procrustes is also called Damastes (Subduer), Procoptes (Slicer), and Polypemon (Troubler).

18. According to the fifth-century historian Hellanicus, Minos himself chose the victims and took them on his ship back to Crete.

19. Respectively, in the tenth letter of the *Heroides;* in *Ars Amatoria* 1. 527–564; and in *Metamorphoses* 8. 174–192.

20. This dance was represented on the François vase (ca. 575 B.C.); see pp. 489–499. At Athens Theseus instituted the *Oschophoria* (carrying of branches) in which two boys disguised as girls carried vine branches in a procession to honor Bacchus and Ariadne.

21. In Athens the battle with the Amazons was depicted in the Hephaesteum and in the Stoa Poecile (Painted Colonnade); it was one of the subjects of the metopes of the Parthenon and was depicted on the shield of Pheidias' statue of Athena Parthenos. It also appeared on the pedestal of the statue of Zeus at Olympia.

22. They were called by the title of *Anakes* or *Anaktes* (Kings), and their temple was called the *Anakeion.*

23. Poseidon was said to have granted Theseus three wishes, of which this was the third. The others were to escape from the Labyrinth and to return from Hades.

24. Twentieth-century dramatic adaptations of the myth include *The Cretan Woman* by Robinson Jeffers, and *Desire Under the Elms* by Eugene O'Neill.

25. Mary Renault, in *The King Must Die* (New York: Pantheon Books, 1958), recreates the early life of Theseus and deals with political and religious issues, like that of patriarchy and matriarchy in the Minoan-Mycenaean period. Her *The Bull from the Sea* (1962) depicts the life of the Amazons, one of whom becomes the mother of Hippolytus.

26. He was said to have succeeded Menestheus as Athenian leader at Troy and to have brought his grandmother Aethra back to Athens.

27. The boy is also called Talus and his mother, Daedalus' sister, Perdix.

28. Homer *(Odyssey* 19. 178–179) describes him as the intimate friend of Zeus; and Hesiod (frag. 103) calls him "the most kingly of mortal kings, who ruled over most subjects and held his scepter from Zeus."

29. In the opening lines of the sixth book of Vergil's *Aeneid,* Daedalus comes to Cumae in Italy.

30. Two other sisters are mentioned: Aerope, who became the wife of a Mycenaean prince (either Pleisthenes or Atreus); and Clymene, who became the wife of Nauplius and the mother of Palamedes.

31. Forgetfulness induced by spitting is a folktale motif, as is also the seer who can understand the ways of birds and snakes.

32. Its identification is unknown. According to Aeschylus, Scylla was bribed by Minos with a golden necklace to betray Nisus.

Notes to Chapter 22

1. Sources for the saga are the Greek epic *Argonautica* by Apollonius of Rhodes (third century B.C.) and the Latin epic *Argonautica* by Valerius Flaccus (late first century A.D.). Pindar's complex fourth *Nemean Ode* (ca. 460 B.C.) is the most poetic account, and Ovid (early first century A.D.) has a brief narrative in Book 7 of the *Metamorphoses*.
2. Her name is also given as Alcimede or Amphinome.
3. He was the son of Poseidon and the husband of Cleopatra, daughter of Boreas. Different reasons are given for his blindness.
4. Clashing rocks called *Planctae* (Wanderers) appear in the Argonauts' return voyage and in the *Odyssey*. Herodotus calls them *Cyaneae* (Dark-rocks).
5. The teeth came from the Theban dragon killed by Cadmus (see p. 320), and had been given to Aeëtes by Athena.
6. Apollodorus has Medea take Apsyrtus on the *Argo* and delay the pursuers by cutting him up and throwing his limbs piecemeal into the sea.
7. The earliest epic narratives of the saga were part of the *Corinthiaka* and *Naupaktika* of the Corinthian poet Eumelos (ca. 730 B.C.). Only a few lines survive.
8. Triton gave a clod of earth to the Argonaut Euphemus as a token that his descendants would rule in Libya. From it grew the island of Thera, from which eventually the Greek colony of Cyrene was founded in Libya by the descendants of Euphemus.
9. There are many different accounts of the origin, functions, and death of Talus.
10. See Janet R. Bacon, *The Voyage of the Argo* (London: Methuen, 1925), chap. 9. For an attempt to retrace the journey see T. Severin, *The Jason Voyage: The Quest for the Golden Fleece* (New York: Simon and Schuster, 1985).
11. Michael Grant, *Myths of the Greeks and Romans* (London: Weidenfeld and Nicolson, 1962; New York: Mentor Books, 1964), p. 302 of the London edition. A modern verse epic is by John Gardner, *Jason and Medeia* (New York: Alfred A. Knopf, 1973).

Notes to Chapter 23

1. He taught Achilles, Jason, and Asclepius.
2. Pindar calls her Hippolyta. Similar stories are those of Bellerophon and Stheneboea and the biblical Joseph and Potiphar's wife (Genesis 39).
3. The magic sword is a folktale element in the legend.
4. Either by dipping him in the river Styx or by burning away his mortality (see p. 257 for the similar story of Demophoön).
5. Homer (*Iliad* 11. 682–704) says that Neleus survived into old age.
6. For her recovery from the Underworld by Heracles see p. 428.
7. There are many folktale elements in the legend, for example, the bridegroom's

task; the magician who can understand the speech of animals; the cure of disease by sympathetic magic (cf. Telephus, pp. 370–371).

8. In the *Homeric Hymn to Apollo* (see p. 194) the god himself lays the foundations of the temple.

9. According to the sixth-century poetess Telesilla, Alpheus loved Artemis herself.

10. Divination was practiced by inspecting entrails of victims sacrificed at the altar, and Iamus was asked for omens.

Notes to Chapter 24

1. Because of the demands of the Latin hexameter, the gods are not named in order of importance. Ennius' forms are given, but we refer to Mercury and Jupiter (for Mercurius and Iovis).

2. Augustus continued to live on the Palatine Hill after he became Pontifex Maximus in 12 B.C.

3. Her name seems to be connected wuth the Latin words for mind (*mens*) and remembering (*meminisse*).

4. Some years after the great fire of A.D. 64 the emperor Domitian set up altars to Vulcan in every one of the fourteen districts of Rome.

5. Ovid tells the same story of Priapus and Vesta at *Fasti* 6. 319–346. The story of Lotis is the subject of Bellini's painting, *The Feast of the Gods* (see Color Plate 9).

6. These ships reached Italy and were turned into sea-nymphs by Cybele, who, as the Phrygian goddess, protected ships made from Phrygian trees (*Aeneid* 10. 220–231).

7. See p. 519 for Ovid's account of Aeneas' death and his epithet. The meaning of the title *Indiges* is not certain. A group of gods were called the *Di Indigetes*, and certain gods (e.g., Jupiter and Sol) were sometimes worshiped with this epithet. Aeneas was sometimes called *Pater Indiges*.

8. The etymology of *Quirites* is unknown. It has the same root as the god Quirinus and the Quirinal Hill. The Romans wrongly connected it with the Sabine town Cures.

9. See Georges Dumézil, *Archaic Roman Religion*, trans. P. Knapp, 2 vols. (Chicago: University of Chicago Press, 1970). For further reading in Roman mythology we recommend the following: Michael Grant, *Roman Myths* (Harmondsworth and Baltimore: Penguin Books, 1973; reprint, New York: Dorset, 1984); G. Karl Galinsky, *Aeneas, Sicily, and Rome* (Princeton: Princeton University Press, 1969); L. Richardson, *A New Topographical Dictionary of Ancient Rome* (Baltimore: Johns Hopkins University Press, 1992). The last-named work gives much valuable information about the religious significance of places and buildings in the city.

Notes to Chapter 25

1. *Gala* is the Greek word for milk, hence *Galaxy* for the Milky way.

2. Chapter 18 in the Phillips manuscript of Caxton's translation now at Magdalene College, Cambridge. Transcribed from the facsimile edition published by G. Braziller (New York, 1968).

3. Taken from *Recuyell*, ed. H. Oskar Sommer (London: D. Nutt, 1894), p. 604.

4. For the transmission of Greek and Latin literature see L. D. Reynolds and N. G. Wilson, *Scribes and Scholars*, 3d ed. (Oxford: Oxford University Press, 1991). Chapter 4 is valuable for the revival of Greek studies.

5. See D. T. Starnes and E. W. Talbert, *Classical Myth and Legend in Renaissance Dictionaries* (Chapel Hill: University of North Carolina Press, 1955; reprint, Westport, Conn.: Greenwood Press, 1973).

6. Reissued in facsimile, ed. Karl K. Hulley and Stanley T. Vandersall (Lincoln: University of Nebraska Press, 1970).

7. See Richard Jenkyns, *The Victorians and Ancient Greece* (Cambridge: Harvard University Press, 1980), especially pp. 174-191 ("The Gods of Greece") and Chapter 9 ("Homer"). Less spirited but more thorough is Frank Turner, *The Greek Heritage in Victorian Britain* (New Haven: Yale University Press, 1981), especially Chapters 3 ("Greek Mythology and Religion") and 4 ("The Reading of Homer"). Both books deal with the decades before and after the Victorian Age.

8. See Meyer Reinhold, *Classica Americana* (Detroit: Wayne State University Press, 1984) and (for the eighteenth century) *The Classick Pages* (University Park, Pa.: American Philological Association, 1975).

Notes to Chapter 26

1. For the history of the musical treatment of Vergilian themes and characters, see A. E. F. Dickinson, "Music for the Aeneid," *Greece & Rome* 6 (1959): 129-147; and James S. Constantine, "Vergil in Opera," *Classical Outlook* 46 (1969): 49 ff. Cavalli wrote *La Didone* in 1641. A libretto by Metastasio, *Didone Abbandonata,* was first set to music by D. A. Sarro (1724); subsequently many other composers set this same poem to music, among them Luigi Cherubini (1786).

2. See Michael Ewans, *Wagner and Aeschylus: The Ring and the Oresteia* (London: Faber & Faber, 1982). Of historical interest is a mammoth work inspired by Wagner's *Ring,* a cycle of operas entitled *Homerische Welt* by August Bungert (1845-1915), which failed to win favor.

3. The choreography is by George Balanchine. The wealth of mythological repertoire in ballet must be omitted from this brief survey. But it is worthwhile to single out the dynamic and imaginative works for dance theater of this century by Martha Graham on Greek themes, for example, *Clytemnestra, Phaedra, Alcestis, Night Journey, Cave of the Heart*, and *Errand into the Maze*. The last three, available on video, are described on p. 608.

4. It is worthwhile to be in touch with a company that offers access to a large video catalogue, such as Facets Multimedia Inc. in Chicago. Prices and availability vary considerably; also to be consulted are Educational Video Network, Huntsville, Texas, and, especially for rare operatic performance, Lyric Distribution Incorporated, Roslyn Heights, New York.

5. In the catalogue of Ivy Classics Video, New York City.

6. In the catalogue of Films for the Humanities, Princeton; also listed are several educational titles on mythological subjects. A catalogue of a similar nature is available from Insight Media, New York City.

7. The New York Greek Drama Company also offers *Songs of Sappho,* a recreation in ancient Greek of excerpts.

8. For an intelligent assessment see Peter W. Rose, "Teaching Greek Myth and Confronting Contemporary Myths," in Martin M. Winkler, ed., *Classics and Cinema* (Lewisburg: Bucknell University Press, 1991 [*Bucknell Review* 35, no. 1]), pp. 17–39.

9. Erling B. Holtsmark, *Tarzan and Tradition: Classical Myth in Popular Literature* (Westport, Conn.: Greenwood Press, 1981).

SELECT BIBLIOGRAPHY

Only a few of the basic works in English have been listed. Subsidiary references will be found in the text and in the notes; see in particular the bibliographies at the end of the Introduction and Chapters 14, 25, and 26.

Handbooks and Surveys

Gayley, Charles Mills. *The Classic Myths in English Literature and in Art.* New ed. New York: Ginn & Co., 1939 [1911].

Grant, Michael. *Myths of the Greeks and Romans.* London: Weidenfeld and Nicolson, 1962; New York: Mentor Books, 1964.

Graves, Robert. *The Greek Myths.* 2 vols. Baltimore: Penguin Books, 1955.

Hamilton, Edith. *Mythology.* New York: Mentor Books, 1953 [1942].

Hathorn, Richmond Y. *Greek Mythology.* Beirut: American University of Beirut, 1977.

Kerenyi, C. *The Heroes of the Greeks.* New York: Grove Press, 1960.

Kirkwood, G. M. *A Short Guide to Classical Mythology.* New York: Holt, Rinehart & Winston, 1959.

Larousse Encyclopedia of Mythology. New York: Prometheus Press, 1960.

Lefkowitz, Mary R. *Women in Greek Myth.* Baltimore: Johns Hopkins University Press, 1986.

Mayerson, Philip. *Classical Mythology in Literature, Art, and Music.* Waltham, Mass.: Xerox College Publishing, 1971.

Reinhold, Meyer. *Past and Present: The Continuity of Classical Myths.* Toronto: Hakkert, 1972.

Rose, H. J. *A Handbook of Greek Mythology: Including Its Extension to Rome.* 6th ed. London: Methuen, 1958; New York: Dutton, 1959.

Sergent, B. *Homosexuality in Greek Myth,* with a preface by G. Dumézil. London: Athlone Press, 1987.

THE GREEK SPELLING OF NAMES

In the transliteration of Greek into English, the letter upsilon (u) usually appears as y. The letter chi usually becomes ch but sometimes kh; both forms are given below. The following changes are to be noted in the Latin and English spelling of Greek words:

Greek   i (as consonant) = j: Iason = Jason
        k = c: Kastor = Castor
        ai = ae, or e: Graiai = Graeae;
                       Klytaimnestra =
                       Clytaemnestra,
                       Clytemnestra
        ei = e or i: Medeia = Medea;
                     Kleio = Clio
        ou = u: Medousa = Medusa
        oi = oe: Kroisos = Croesus
        oi = i: Delphoi = Delphi
        final e – a: Athene = Athena
        final on = um: Ilion = Ilium
        final os = us: Hyllos = Hyllus

Achaia, Akhaia = Achaea
Acheloos, Akheloos = Achelous
Acheron, Akheron = Acheron
Achilleus, Akhilleus = Achilles
Admetos = Admetus
Adrastos = Adrastus
Agathyrsos = Agathyrsus
Agaue = Agave
Aglaia = Aglaea
Aglauros = Aglaurus
Akamas = Acamas
Akarnania = Acarnania
Akastos = Acastus
Akestes = Acestes
Akis = Acis
Akontios = Acontius
Akrisios = Acrisius
Aktaion = Actaeon
Aia = Aea
Aiaia = Aeaea
Aiakos = Aeacus
Aias = Ajax

Aietes = Aeetes
Aigeus = Aegeus
Aigialeia = Aegialia
Aigimios = Aegimius
Aigina = Aegina
Aigis = Aegis
Aigisthos = Aegisthus
Aigyptos = Aegyptus
Aineias = Aeneas
Aiolos = Aeolus
Aipytos = Aepytus
Aisakos = Aesacus
Aison = Aeson
Aithra = Aethra
Aitolia = Aetolia
Alekto = Alecto
Alexandros = Alexander
Alkestis = Alcestis
Alkibiades = Alcibiades
Alkeides = Alcides
Alkinoos = Alcinous
Alkmaion = Alcmaeon

Alkmene = Alcmena
Alkyone = Alcyone
Alkyoneus = Alcyoneus
Alpheios = Alpheus
Althaia = Althaea
Althaimenes = Althaemenes
Amaltheia = Amalthea
Amphiaraos = Amphiaraus
Amyklai = Amyclae
Amykos = Amycus
Anios = Anius
Ankaios = Ancaeus
Antaios = Antaeus
Anteia = Antea
Antikleia = Anticlea
Antilochos, Antilokhos = Antilochus
Antinoos = Antinous
Apsyrtos = Apsyrtus
Arachne, Arakhne = Arachne
Areion = Arion
Areiopagos = Areopagus
Arethousa = Arethusa
Argos = Argus
Aristaios = Aristaeus
Arkadia = Arcadia
Arkas = Arcas
Askanios = Ascanius
Asklepios = Asclepius
Asopos = Asopus
Atalante = Atalanta
Athene = Athena
Augeias = Augeas
Autolykos = Autolycus

Bakchos, Bakkhos = Bacchus
Boiotia = Boeotia
Briareos = Briareus

C, see K

Chairephon, Khairephon = Chaerephon
Chalkiope, Khalkiope = Chalciope
Chariklo, Khariklo = Chariclo
Cheiron, Kheiron = Chiron
Chimaira, Khimaira = Chimaera
Chronos, Khronos = Chronus
Chrysippos, Khrysippos = Chrysippus
Chthonios, Khthonios = Chthonius

Daidalos = Daedalus
Danaos = Danaus
Dardanos = Dardanus
Deianeira = Deianira, Dejanira
Deidameia = Deidamia
Delphoi = Delphi
Deukalion = Deucalion
Dikte = Dicte
Dionysos = Dionysus
Dioskouroi = Dioscuri
Dirke = Dirce

Echemos, Ekhemos = Echemus
Elektra = Electra
Elysion = Elysium
Epeios = Epeus
Epigonoi = Epigoni
Epikaste = Epicasta
Erebos = Erebus
Erytheia = Erythia
Eteokles = Eteocles
Euadne = Evadne
Euboia = Euboea
Eumaios = Eumaeus
Euneos = Euneus
Europe = Europa
Eurykleia = Euryclea
Eurydike = Eurydice

Gaia = Gaea
Galateia = Galatea
Ganymedes = Ganymede
Glauke = Glauce
Glaukos = Glaucus
Graiai = Graeae

Haides = Hades
Haimon = Haemon
Hekabe = Hecabe, Hecuba
Hekate = Hecate
Hekatoncheires, Hekatonkheires =
    Hecatonchires
Hektor = Hector
Helenos = Helenus
Helios = Helius
Hephaistos = Hephaestus
Herakles = Heracles, Hercules
Hippodameia = Hippodamia
Hippolyte = Hippolyta
Hippolytos = Hippolytus
Horai = Horae
Hyakinthos = Hyacinthus
Hyllos = Hyllus

Iakchos, Iakkhos = Iacchus
Iason = Jason
Ikarios = Icarius
Ikaros = Icarus
Ilion = Ilium
Inachos, Inakhos = Inachus
Iokaste = Jocasta
Iolaos = Iolaus
Iolkos = Iolcus
Iphigeneia = Iphigenia
Iphikles = Iphicles
Iphiklos = Iphiclus
Iphimedeia = Iphimedia
Iphitos = Iphitus
Ithaka = Ithaca

J, see I

Kadmos = Cadmus
Kaineus = Caeneus

Kalchas, Kalkhas = Calchas
Kallidike = Callidice
Kalliope = Calliope
Kallisto = Callisto
Kalypso = Calypso
Kanake = Canace
Kapaneus = Capaneus
Kassandra = Cassandra
Kassiepeia = Cassiepea
Kastor = Castor
Kerkops = Cercops
Kelaino = Celaeno
Keleus = Celeus
Kentauros = Centaurus, Centaur
Kephalos = Cephalus
Kerberos = Cerberus
Kerkopes = Cecropes
Kerkyon = Cercyon
Keto = Ceto
Keyx = Ceyx
Kirke = Circe
Kithairon = Cithaeron
Kleio = Clio
Klymene = Clymene
Klytaimnestra = Clytaemnestra, Clytemnestra
Knossos = Cnossus
Kodros = Codrus
Koios = Coeus
Kokytos = Cocytus
Kolchis, Kolkhis = Colchis
Kolonos = Colonus
Komaitho = Comaetho
Korinthos = Corinthus, Corinth
Koronis = Coronis
Kreon = Creon
Kreousa = Creusa
Kroisos = Croesus
Kronos = Cronus
Kybele = Cybele
Kyklops = Cyclops
Kyknos = Cycnus
Kyparissos = Cyparissus
Kypros = Cyprus
Kythera = Cythera
Kytisoros = Cytisorus
Kyzikos = Cyzicus

Labdakos = Labdacus
Laios = Laius
Lakedaimon = Lacedaemon
Laodameia = Laodamia
Learchos, Learkhos = Learchus
Leukippe = Leucippe
Leukippos = Leucippus
Leukothea = Leucothea
Leukothoe = Leucothoe
Likymnios = Licymnius
Linos = Linus
Lykaon = Lycaon
Lykia = Lycia
Lykomedes = Lycomedes

Lykurgos = Lycurgus
Lykos = Lycus
Lynkeus = Lynceus

Makareus = Macareus
Makaria = Macaria
Machaon, Makhaon = Machaon
Mainas = Maenas, Maenad
Medeia = Medea
Medousa = Medusa
Meleagros = Meleager
Meliai = Meliae
Melikertes = Melicertes
Menelaos = Menelaus
Menoikeus = Menoeceus
Minotauros = Minotaurus, Minotaur
Moira, Moirai = Moera, Moerae
Musaios = Musaeus
Mousa, Mousai = Musa, Musae, Muse, Muses
Mykenai = Mycenae, Mycene
Myrtilos = Myrtilus

Narkissos = Narcissus
Nausikaa = Nausicaa
Neoptolemos = Neoptolemus
Nessos = Nessus
Nykteus = Nycteus

Oidipous = Oedipus
Oileus = Oeleus
Oinomaos = Oenomaus
Okeanos = Oceanus
Olympos = Olympus
Orchomenos, Orkhomenos = Orchomenus
Oreithyia = Orithyia
Orthros = Orthrus
Ourania = Urania
Ouranos = Uranus

Palaimon = Palaemon
Palladion = Palladium
Panathenaia = Panathenaea
Parnassos = Parnassus
Parthenopaios = Parthenopaeus
Patroklos = Patroclus
Pegasos = Pegasus
Peisistratos = Pisistratus
Peneios = Peneus
Penthesileia = Penthesilea
Peloponnesos = Peloponnesus, Peloponnese
Periklymenos = Periclymenus
Persephone = Proserpina
Perikles = Pericles
Phaiakes = Phaeaces, Phaeacians
Philoktetes = Philoctetes
Phoibe = Phoebe
Phoibos = Phoebus
Plouton = Pluton, Pluto
Ploutos = Plutus
Podaleirios = Podalirius
Poias = Poeas

Polybos = Polybus
Polydeukes = Polydeuces
Polyneikes = Polynices
Polyphemos = Polyphemus
Priamos = Priamus, Priam
Prokne = Procne
Prokris = Procris
Prokrustes = Procrustes

Rheia = Rhea
Rhesos = Rhesus

Salmakis = Salmacis
Satyros = Satyrus, Satyr
Schoineus, Skhoineus = Schoeneus
Seilenos = Silenus
Seirenes = Sirenes, Sirens
Sibylla = Sibylla, Sibyl
Sisyphos = Sisyphus
Skeiron = Sciron

Skylla = Scylla
Stheneboia = Stheneboea

Tantalos = Tantalus
Tartaros = Tartarus
Telemachos, Telemakhos = Telemachus
Teukros = Teucer
Thaleia = Thalia
Thorikos = Thoricus
Thrinakie = Thrinacia
Tityos = Tityus
Troizen = Troezen

U, see Ou

Xanthos = Xanthus
Xouthos = Xuthus

Zephyros = Zephyrus, Zephyr
Zethos = Zethus

INDEXES

▨ INDEX OF AUTHORS, ARTISTS, COMPOSERS, AND TITLES

This index is particularly useful for finding information about material in Chapters 25 and 26 (on the survival of Greek and Roman mythology) and identifying the ancient sources used throughout the book. Section numbers of specific works translated are indicated within parentheses under authors' names.

Apollo and Daphne. See Andrejevic
Apollodorus, *Bibliotheca*, 28–29, 321, 424, 447, 456, 560
Apollo et Hyacinthus. See Mozart
Apollo of Bellac, The. See Giraudoux
Apollon Musagète. See Stravinsky
Apollonius of Rhodes, *Argonautica*, 27, 483–484, 488–489, 558
Apology. See Plato
Apuleius, 29, 151, 155, 309–310, 566; *Metamorphoses* (*The Golden Ass*), (11. 5; 11. 16) 310; (11. 23) 311; (6. 23–24) 155
Arab manuscripts, 563, 586; Arabs, 585, 588
Aratus, *Phaenomena*, 561, 585
Ares, Homeric Hymn to, 90
Argonautica. See Apollonius, Valerius Flaccus
Ariadne. See Maconchy, Vanderlyn
Ariadne auf Naxos. See Strauss
Arianna. See Monteverdi
Aristophanes, 143, 147, 442; *Birds* (683 ff.), 39; *Clouds*, 557; *Frogs*, 297, 442
Aristotle, 4, 7, 241; *Poetics* (17), 393, 442
Arnold, Matthew, *Culture and Anarchy*, 578–579
Ars Amatoria. See Ovid
Artemis, Homeric Hymns to, 157–159
Ascanio in Alba. See Mozart
Asclepius, Homeric Hymn to, 186
Astronomica. See Manilius
Athena, Homeric Hymns to, 116, 125
"Atlas, Der." *See* Schubert
Attone. See Handel
Atys. See Lully
Augustine, St., 545, 562–563, 580; *De Civitate Dei* (7. 18), 559
Aulularia. See Plautus

Bacchae. See Euripides
Bacchanal. See Hesselius
Bacchantes (film), 611
Bacchus. See Massenet
Bacchus and Ariadne. See Hesselius
Bacchylides of Cos, 27, 430, 459, 497, 500; *Dithyramb*, (17. 92–116) 461; (18. 16–60) 459–460; *Epinician Ode*, (5. 93–154) 497; (5. 172–175) 430
Bach, Johann Sebastian, *Der Streit zwischen Phoebus und Pan; Hercules auf dem Scheidewege*, 597
Bakchantinnen, Die. See Wellesz
Ballanchine, George, 646 n. 3
Banks, Tony, "The Waters of Lethe," 605
Barber, Samuel, *Andromache's Farewell*, 602–603
Basilica of St. Peter, 307, 584
Beautiful Galatea, The. See Suppé
Bedford, David, *The Odyssey*, 605
Beethoven, Ludwig van, *Coriolanus, The Creatures of Prometheus*, 599–600
Belle Hélène, La. See Offenbach
Bellerophon. See Euripides

Bellini, Giovanni, *Feast of the Gods*, 587
Bellini, Vincenzo, *Norma*, 600
Berlioz, Hector, *Les Troyens*, 600, 609
Bibliotheca. See Apollodorus
Birds. See Aristophanes
Birth of Tragedy. See Nietzsche
Birth of Venus. See Botticelli
Birtwistle, Harrison, *Nenia, The Death of Orpheus*, 604
Black Orpheus (film), 612
Blegen, Carl, 21, 23
Bliss, Arthur, *Hymn to Apollo; Morning Heroes; The Olympians*, 603
Blow, John, *Venus and Adonis*, 597
Boccaccio, *De Genealogia Deorum*, 566–567; *Teseida* (*Theseid*), 567–568
"Book of the Dead," *Nekuia*, see Homer, *Odyssey*, Book 11 and Vergil, *Aeneid*, Book 6
Borges, Jorge Luis, *Labyrinths* ("The Immortal"), 583
Botticelli, *Birth of Venus; Pallas and the Centaur; Primavera; Venus and Mars*, 587
Boucher, François, 572, 591
Braque, Georges, 592
Breuer, Lee. *See* Telson
Britten, Benjamin, *Death in Venice; Phaedra; The Rape of Lucretia; Six Metamorphoses after Ovid; Young Apollo*, 602
Brot und Wein. See Hölderlin
Bulfinch, Thomas, *Age of Fable*, 580
Burkert, Walter, 13–14, 442
By Jupiter. See Rogers
Byzantium, Byzantine manuscripts, 566

Caccini, Giulio, 596
Cacoyannis, Michael, 611
Cadmus et Hermione. See Lully
Callimachus, 27, 557; *Aetia* (*Causes*), 557–558; *Hymns*, 27, 558
Calzabigi, Raniero, 598–599
Cambert, Robert, *Pomone*, 572
Camerata, 595–596
Campbell, Joseph, 16
Canterbury Tales. See Chaucer
Carmen Saeculare. See Horace
Carracci brothers, 587
Cartari, Vincenzo, *Le Imagini degli Dei Antichi*, 567
Castor and Pollux. See Partch, Rameau
Catasterisms. See Pseudo-Eratosthenes
Cato the Elder, 538, 551; *Origines*, 538
Catullus, 536, 558, 625 n. 6 (ch. 7); (64. 52–59) 462; (66. 51–56, "Berenice's Lock") 558
Cavalli, *Ercole Amante; Giasone*, 596–597
Cave of the Heart. See Graham
Caxton, William, *Ovyde Hys Booke of Metamorphose*, 564; *Recuyell of the Historye of Troye*, 565–566

GLOSSARY/INDEX OF MYTHOLOGICAL AND HISTORICAL PERSONS, PLACES, AND SUBJECTS

A simple guide to pronunciation follows most words in this index. The long vowels are to be pronounced as follows: ā (cape), ē (bee), ī (ice), ō (boat), and ū (too). Syllabification is marked by a prime mark (′) and a hyphen (-). Syllables that precede the prime are stressed.

Aeolians (ē-ō'li-anz), division of the Greek people, 62 n. 23

Aeolus (ē'ō-lus), son of Hellen and eponymous ancestor of the Aeolians, 473, 621 n. 23; keeper of the winds, encountered by Odysseus, 71, 170, 395–396, 405, 493, 496, 501, 504, 541

Aepytus (ē'pit-tus), son of Cresphontes and Merope, 447–448; Evadne's foster father, who brings up Iamus, 505

Aërope (ā-er'o-pé), Atreus's wife, seduced by Thyestes, 343

Aesacus (ē'sa-kus), Trojan soothsayer, 638 n.5

Aesculapius (es-ku-lā'pi-us), Latin name for Asclepius, 535

Aeson (ē'son), son of Cretheus and Tyro, and Jason's father, rejuvenated by Medea, 473, 482, 484, 494, 562

Aether (ē'ther), upper atmosphere, offspring of Night and Erebus 38, 306

Aethra (ē'thra), daughter of Pittheus and mother of Theseus, 334, 457, 465, 467

Aetna (et'na), mountain in Sicily, 55, 521

Aetolia (e-tō'li-a), region in central Greece, 448, 496–500

Agamedes (ag-a-me'dēz), skilled builder, along with his brother Trophonius, 194, 496

Agamemnon (ag-a-mem'non), king of Mycenae, leader of the Greeks against Troy, and murdered by his wife Clytemnestra, 21, 272, 276, 282, 338, 343–347, 352, 363–366, 369, 371–373, 375, 377–379, 388, 391, 399, 506, 562, 577

Agathon (ag'a-thon), poet, host of Plato's *Symposium*, 143, 147

Agathyrsus (ag-a-thir'sus), son of Geryon and Echidna, 429

Agave (a-gā'vē), daughter of Cadmus and Harmonia and mother of Pentheus, 224, 228–230, 233, 235–236, 321

Agenor (a-jē'nor), king of Tyre and father of Cadmus and Europa, 223, 317–318, 420, 418

Ager Laurens (ag'er law'renz), territory in Italy, where Aeneas founded Lavinium, 538–546

Aglaea (ag-lē'a), one of the Graces, 623 n. 16

Aglauros (a-glaw'ros), "Bright," daughter of Cecrops, 452–453

Agriania (a-gri-an'i-a), festival connected with the Bacchic madness of the daughters of Proetus, 495

Agyrtes (a-jer'tēz *or* a-gir'tēz), trumpeter who tricked Achilles on Scyros, 368

Aias (ī'as), the Greek name of Ajax

Aidos (ī'dos), Modesty, a concept or goddess, 60

Ajax (ā'jax), the great or greater, Telamon's son (Telamonius), who committed suicide, 274–275, 282, 362, 364–365,

376, 378, 384–385, 399, 475; the less or lesser, Oileus' son, who raped Cassandra, 364–365, 388, 391, 475

Akragas (a-kra'gas), city in Sicily, 413

Alba, Alba Longa (al'ba lon'ga), Latin city, founded by Iulus, 521, 536, 538–539, 541, 546–548, 552–553

Alcaeus (al-sē'us), father of Amphitryon and grandfather of Heracles, 420

Alcestis (al-ses'tis), wife of Admetus, who offers to die in his place, 187, 428, 443, 494

Alcibiades (al-si-bī'a-dēz), Athenian statesman, accused of mutilation of the herms and desecration of the mysteries, 630 n. 12

Alcides (al-sī'dēz), name of Heracles as grandson of Alcaeus, 424, 671

Alcinoüs (al-sin'ō-us), king of the Phaeacians and father of Nausicaä, 271, 277, 402, 483

Alcmaeon (alk-mē'on), Amphiaraüs' son, who led the Epigoni against Thebes and murdered his mother, 334–335

Alcmena (alk-mē'na) or Alcmene (alk-mē'nē), seduced by Zeus to become the mother of Heracles, 61, 410, 420–423, 439, 444, 446–447

Alcyone (al-sī'ō-nē), wife of Ceyx, turned into a sea bird ("halcyon"), 493

Alcyoneus (al-sī-on'us *or* al-sī-on'e-us), brigand and giant killed by Heracles, 429, 434

Alexander, another name for Paris, 317, 352, 358

Alexander the Great, son of Philip II of Macedon and Greek conqueror in the fourth century B.C., 557, 561

Alexandria (a-lex-an'dri-a), city in Egypt, with a library, founded by Alexander the Great, 557; Alexandrian, Alexandrianism, 27, 557–561

Algol (al'gol), Arabic, Demon's head, 585

Allecto (a-lek'tō), a Fury, 296, 540

Aloeus (a-lō'us *or* a-lō'e-us), father of Otus and Ephialtes, the Aloadae (al-ō'a-dē *or* al-ō'a-dī), 290, 634 n. 15; brother of Aeëtes, 485

Alpheus (al-fē'us), river at Olympia and its god, who pursued Arethusa, 80, 203, 209, 237, 340, 426, 505

Althaea (al-thē'a), mother of Meleager, 496–497

Althaemenes (al-thē'me-nēz), Catreus' son, destined to kill his father, 470

Amalthea (am-al-thē'a), the goat whose milk nurtured the infant Zeus, 51, 436

Amata (a-ma'ta), mother of Lavinia, 540

Amaurus (a-maw'rus), river in Thessaly, 432

Amazons (a'ma-zonz), warlike women from the northern limits of the world, 119–120, 362, 383, 432, 457, 465, 469, 503–504, 584

Apples of the Hesperides, eleventh labor of Heracles, 426, 429–430, 580

Apsyrtus (ap-sir′tus), brother of Medea, whom she (or Jason) murdered, 482–483

Apulia (a-pū′li-a), a region in Italy; Apulian, 392

Arachne (a-rak′nē), "Spider," the woman who challenged Athena in spinning and weaving and was turned into a spider, 123–125, 569–571

Ara Maxima (a′ra mak′sim-a), "Greatest Altar," cult site in Rome for the worship of Hercules, 522, 533–534

Arcadia (ar-kā′di-a), a region in the Peloponnesus, 163, 200, 244- 245, 316, 329, 335, 339, 425, 485, 575; Arcadian(s), 146, 163, 331, 479, 500, 525, 545

Arcas (ar′kas), the son of Zeus and Callisto, who was turned into the constellation, Bear Warden, 164–165

Arcesilas (ar-ke′si-las), king of Cyrene to whom a Pindaric Ode is addressed, 492

Archemorus (ar-kem′or-us), "Beginner of Death," another name given to Opheltes, 330

Ardea (ar′de-a), Rutulian capital, 553

Ardiaeus (ar-di-ē′us), a tyrant hurled down into Tartarus forever, 278–279

Areopagus (ar-ē-op′a-gus), the Athenian court, originally constituted by Athena for the trying of Orestes, 127, 296, 346

Ares (ar′ēs), son of Zeus and Hera, god of war, equated by the Romans with Mars, 22, 46, 58, 76, 82, 86–90, 94, 125, 143, 193, 320, 332, 364, 366, 432, 473, 502, 513–515, 570; island of, 479

Arete (a′re-tē), Greek concept of excellence, valor, and virtue, 362, 372, 475, 579; Phaeacian queen, wife of Alcinoüs, 402, 483

Arethusa (ar-e-thū′sa), nymph, pursued by Alpheus and turned into a fountain in Syracuse, 505, 578

Argei (ar-jē′ī), straw dummies offered to propitiate the god of the Tiber, 528

Argeiphontes (ar-ge-i-fon′tēz), "Slayer of Argus," epithet of Hermes, 68. See also Argus Panoptes

Arges (ar′jēz), "Bright," one of the three Cyclopes, 40

Argo (ar′gō), "Swift," the ship of Jason and the Argonauts, built by Argus, 400, 434, 472–473, 475, 479, 480, 483–484

Argolid (ar′go-lid), region in the northern Peloponnese, 409

Argonauts (ar′gō-notz), "the sailors of the Argo," 25, 27, 367, 434, 456, 473, 475–480, 482–484; Argonaut, Argonautic, 304, 467, 472, 500, 565

Argos (ar′gos), a city and its region (Argolid) in the northern Peloponnese, 80, 95, 186, 316, 329–330, 392, 409–410, 416–419, 420, 422, 428, 434, 447–448, 471, 502; Argive(s), 99–100, 274, 317, 330, 333–334, 345, 349, 356, 364, 409, 419, 441, 467, 496, 501, 507

Argus (ar′gus), Arestor's son, builder of the Argo, 475; Argus Panoptes (pan-op′tēz), the "all-seeing" guardian of Io, killed by Hermes, 63–64, 68, 78, 83, 139, 141–142, 200, 202, 207, 209, 259, 261, 417; Odysseus' dog, 403; son of Phrixus and Chalciope, 473, 479

Ariadne (ar-i-ad′nē), daughter of Minos and Pasiphaë, abandoned by Theseus on Naxos and saved by Dionysus, 240, 307, 461–463, 466, 469–470, 558, 580, 584, 592

Aricia (a-ri′si-a), town in Italy, site of a precinct and cult of Diana, 529–530

Arion (a-rī′on), Adrastus' horse, offspring of Poseidon and Demeter, 333, 624 n. 4; of Lesbos, a famous musician, saved by a dolphin, 504–505

Arisba (a-ris′ba), first wife of Priam, 358

Aristaeus (ar-is-t-ē′us), keeper of bees, son of Apollo and Cyrene, husband of Autonoë, and father of Actaeon, 180, 302

Aristodemus (a-ris-to-dē′mus), Heraclid leader, 447

Aristonice (a-ris-to-nī′se), Pythian prophetess at Delphi, 638, n. 13

Aristophanes (a-ris-to′pha-nēz), Greek comic playwright, speaker in Plato's Symposium, 143, 147

Armenius (ar-mē′ni-us), father of Er, 277

Arruns (ar′runz), Etruscan, killed by Opis for killing Camilla, 545; son of Tarquinius Priscus and husband of Tullia, 553

Arsinoë (ar-si′no-ē), wife of Ptolemy II and deified as Aphrodite Zephyritis, 558

Artemis (ar′te-mis), daughter of Zeus and Leto, virgin goddess of chastity, the hunt, childbirth, and the moon, and equated by the Romans with Diana, 22, 46, 76, 81–82, 127, 136–139, 157–160, 163, 165–168, 169, 173, 186, 189, 193, 244, 262, 310, 343, 348, 369, 425–426, 453, 463, 466, 476, 496–497, 505–506, 513, 530, 536–546, 569, 578

Ascanius (as-kā′ni-us), Aeneas' son, also called Iulus, 386, 389- 389, 536, 538, 541

Asclepius (as-cle′pi-us), son of Apollo and Coronis and Greek god of medicine (Aesculapius for the Romans), 185–186, 267, 370, 366, 535

Asopus (a-sō′pus), river and its god in Boeotia and father of Aegina, 234, 502

Assaracus (as-sar′a-cus), king of Troy, 291

Astarte (as-tar′tē), Phoenician goddess, resembling Aphrodite, 132, 418, 526

Astyanax (as-tī'a-naks), infant son of Hector and Andromache, thrown to his death from the walls of Troy, 360, 375–376, 386, 388, 572

Astydamia (as-ti-da-mē'a *or* as-ti-da-mī'a), wife of Acastus, king of Iolcus; she fell in love with Peleus, 485

Atalanta (at-a-lan'ta), daughter of Schoeneus or Iasus, virgin huntress, participant in the Calydonian boar hunt and Argonautic quest, and great runner, defeated in a foot-race by Milanion (or Hippomenes), 282, 497–501

Atargatis, (a-tar'ga-tis), Syrian mother-goddess of mysteries, 309

Ate (a'tē), goddess of destruction, 107, 385

Athamas (ath'a-mas), husband of Nephele and Ino and father of Phrixus and Helle, 473, 501, 630 n. 3

Athena (a-thē'na), born from Zeus' head after he had swallowed Metis; virgin goddess of wisdom, war, and weaving, equated by the Romans with Minerva, 22, 62–64, 76, 81, 83–84, 89, 94–95, 113, 116–123, 125–127, 136–138, 187,195, 241, 310, 320, 332, 335–336, 346, 348, 353–356, 361, 364, 372, 374, 380, 384–386, 391–392, 394, 406, 409, 412–415–416, 419, 425–426, 429–430, 432, 435, 449, 451–453, 475, 478, 480, 503, 513, 520–521; Athena Parthenos, Pheidias' statue of Athena in the Parthenon, 119–120

Athloi (ath'loy), Labors of Heracles, 424

Atlantis (at-lan'tis), mythical island, 20–21

Atlas (at'las), son of Iapetus and Clymene, punished by Zeus with the task of holding up the sky, 53, 55, 60, 165, 200, 216, 400, 415–416, 426, 429–430, 432, 531

Atreus (ā'trūs *or* ā'tre-us), king of Mycenae, son of Pelops, brother of Thyestes, and father of Agamemnon and Menelaus, 21, 27, 338, 342–347, 363, 366, 377–378, 531, 581

Atropos (at'rō-pos), "Inflexible," the one of the three fates who cuts off the thread of a person's life, 91, 279–280, 282

Attica (at'ti-ka), region in Greece where Athens is located, 21, 113, 119, 124, 141, 310, 316, 327, 329, 333–334, 348, 446, 449, 456–457, 460, 465–466, 468, 471, 567

Attis (at'tis), Cybele's beloved, who was driven mad, castrated himself, died and became a resurrection-god of a mystery religion, 107, 135–136, 264–265, 307–308, 514, 536

Atys (ā'tis), son of Croesus, accidentally murdered by Adrastus, 99, 101–104, 107

Auge (aw'jē), mother of Odysseus' son Telephus, 435

Augeas (aw-jē'as *or* aw'jē-as), son of Helius and king of Elis, 80, 426, 434, 475, 496; Augean (aw-jē'an) Stables, fifth labor of Heracles, 80, 426

Augurs (aw'gurs), group of Roman priests, 535; augury, interpreting omens from the flight of birds, 548

Augustus (aw-gus'tus), first Roman emperor and a great patron of the arts, 514–516, 527, 530, 533, 535, 539, 560

Aulis (aw'lis), port on the coast of Boeotia, from which the Greeks sailed against Troy, 348, 369–370

Aura (aw'ra), Latin word for "breeze," 453–454

Aurora (aw-ror'a), the Roman name of Eos, goddess of the dawn, 46, 384, 453–454

Autochthonous (aw-tok'tho-nus), "sprung from the earth," 310, 449, 452

Autolycus (aw-tol'i-kus), Hermes' son, a master-thief, father of Anticlea and grandfather of Odysseus, 272, 403, 424, 502

Autonoë (aw-ton'ō-ē), daughter of Cadmus and Harmonia, wife of Aristaeus, and mother of Actaeon, 161, 224, 229, 236, 321

Aventine (a'ven-tīn), one of the hills of Rome, 521–522, 530, 548–549

Avernus (a-ver'nus), "birdless," a lake associated with the Underworld, 284–285, 289, 299

Baal (bā'al), Syrian sky god, 309

Bacchae (bak'kē), female followers of Bacchus (Dionysus), 219, 221, 225, 229–230, 232–233, 235, 238; Bacchant (male), Bacchante (female), 224, 227

Bacchus (bak'kus), name for Dionysus preferred by the Romans, 76, 124, 218, 223–224, 226, 228, 236, 455; Bacchic, 220, 222, 224, 227, 230, 232–235, 239, 241, 244, 245, 247, 301, 304, 455, 461–463, 523, 562, 592

Baucis (baw'kis), she and her husband Philemon, a pious old couple, entertained Zeus and Hermes and were rewarded, 508–509, 581, 593

Bebryces (be-brī'sēz), Bithynian tribe, ruled by king Amycus, 478

Bellerophon (bel-ler'ō-fon), Sisyphus' grandson, who tamed Pegasus and killed the Chimaera, 127, 362, 413, 490, 495, 503–504

Bellona (bel-lō'na), Roman war goddess, identified with the Greek Enyo, 516

Belus (bē'lus), father of Aegyptus and Danaüs, 299, 418

Berenice, wife of Egyptian king Ptolemy III; *coma Berenices,* lock of Berenice's hair and a constellation, 558

Bia (bi'a), "Force," a character in Aeschylus' *Prometheus Bound*, 65

Bias (bi'as), brother of Melampus, who helped him win Pero, 494–495

Biton (bi'ton), he and his brother Cleobis were judged the second happiest of men by Solon, 99–100, 496

Black Sea, 384, 473, 475, 478. *See also* Euxine

Boeotia, (bē-ō'shi-a), region in Greece, north of Attica, 72, 316, 333, 369, 441, 479, 495–496; Boeotian, 26, 276, 473, 497, 500

Bona Dea (bo'na de'a), "Good Goddess," Roman goddess, worshiped only by women, 525

Boreas (bō'rē-as), North Wind, 56, 71, 73, 456, 478

Brauron (braw'ron), a town in Attica where Iphigenia was priestess of Artemis, 348

Briareus (brī-ā're-us), one of the three Hecatonchires, 41, 54, 286

Briseïs (brī-sē'is), Achilles' beloved, taken by Agamemnon, 371–372, 375, 377–379

Bromia (bro' mi-a), servant of Alcmena in Plautus, 422

Bromius (bro'mi-us), an epithet of Dionysus, 230

Brontes (bron'tēz), "Thunder," one of the three Cyclopes, 40, 521

Bronze Age, historical period between the neolithic and iron ages, 19–21, 23–25; third of the legendary four Ages, 57–59

Brutus (brū'tus), Lucius Junius, liberator of Rome from the tyranny of King Tarquin Superbus, 555

Busiris (bū-sī'ris), king of Egypt, killed by Heracles, 430

Byblis (bib'lis), Miletus' daughter who fell in love with her brother Caenus and was turned into a fountain called by her name, 510

Cabiri (ka-bi'rī), great gods of a mystery cult, 506, 636 n. 13

Caca (ka'ka), "Bad," sister of Cacus,

Cacus (ka'kus), "Bad," Italian fire-god, Vulcan's son, who stole Heracles' cattle and was killed by him, 521–522, 533, 545; Scalae Caci (scā'lī ka'kī), "Steps of Cacus," pathway leading up to the Aventine hill, 522

Cadmeia (kad-mē'a), city founded by Cadmus, later named Thebes with only its citadel called Cadmeia, 317, 320, 323, 331, 446

Cadmus (kad'mus), Theban king, son of Agenor, brother of Europa, and husband of Harmonia, 25, 59, 160, 218, 220–225, 235, 243, 317, 319–323, 332, 402, 418, 473, 495, 595

Caduceus (ka-dū'se-us), herald's wand, especially that of Hermes, 213

Caeneus (sē'ne-us). *See* Caenis

Caenina (sē'ni-na), Sabine town, 549

Caenis (sē'nis), a Lapith girl, turned into a man named Caeneus, 288, 492

Caesar, Julius (sē'sar jū'li-us), Roman statesman and general, assassinated in 44 B.C., 527

Calabria (Cal-a' bri-a), region in Italy, 392

Calaïs (kā'la-is), he and his brother Zetes were winged sons of Boreas and Orithyia and Argonauts, 456, 476, 478

Calchas (kal'kas), Greek prophet in the Trojan war, 360, 369–370, 372

Callidice (kal-lid'i-sē), daughter of Celeus and Metaneira, 254–255

Calliope (ka-lī'ō-pē), Muse of epic poetry, 43, 90, 304, 571

Callirhoë (kal-lir'ō-ē), an Oceanid, wife of Chrysaor and mother of Geryon and Echidna, 114, 428; daughter of Acheloüs and wife of Alcmaeon, 335

Callisto (kal-lis'tō), daughter of Lycaon and Artemis' follower, who mated with Zeus, bore Arcas, was turned into a bear, and became the constellation Ursa Major, 12, 163–165, 560

Callithoë (cal-li'thō-ē), daughter of Celeus and Metaneira, 254

Calydon (kal'li-don), a city in Aetolia in western Greece, 496; Calydonian (ka-li-dō'ni-an) boar hunt, 107, 367, 467, 475, 492, 496–500

Calypso (ka-lip'sō), Atlas' daughter, who detained Odysseus on her island, Ogygia, 393–394, 400–401, 405

Camenae (ka-mē'nē), Roman water nymphs identified with the Muses, 529, 561

Camilla (ka-mil'la), Etruscan, warrior maiden, killed by Arruns, 545

Camillus (ca-mil'lus), Roman hero, 519

Camirus (ca-mī'rus), city of Rhodes, 506

Canace (kan'a-sē), mother of a child by her brother Macareus, 507

Cancer, constellation of the crab Hera sent to help the Lernaean Hydra, 425

Canens (ka'nens), "Singer," nymph, Picus' wife, who became only a voice, 516

Capaneus (kap'a-nūs), Evadne's husband, one of the seven against Thebes, struck down by Zeus, 330–332, 334, 467

Caphareus (ka-far'ūs), cape in Euboea, 391

Capitoline (ka'pi-to-līn), Capitol, one of Rome's hills, 184, 515, 526, 535, 549, 549; Capitoline triad, Jupiter, Juno, and Minerva, 517, 519–520

Capture of Cerberus, twelfth labor of Heracles, 430

Capua (kap'u-a), a city in Campania, 530

Carmentis (kar-men'tis), or Carmenta, prophetic water nymph associated with the Camenae, 529

Carthage (kar'thij), city in north Africa, kingdom of Dido, and enemy of Rome, 539, 541–543, 545–546

Cassandra (kas-san'dra), daughter of Priam and Hecuba and Apollo's beloved, whose true prophecies were never believed; raped by Ajax the less and murdered by Clytemnestra, 179, 344–345, 347, 360, 365, 386, 388, 583

Cassiepea (kas-si-e-pē'a), Cepheus' wife and Andromeda's mother, who boasted she was more beautiful than the Nereids, 415

Castalian (kas-tā'li-an), spring at Delphi, 175

Castor (kas'tor), horse-tamer and rider, son of Zeus and Leda, and brother of Polydeuces (Pollux), 348, 350–352, 476, 529, 534. See also Dioscuri

Catreus (kā'tre-us or ka'trūs), son of Minos and Pasiphaë and fated to be killed by his son Althaemenes, 470

Cattle of Geryon, tenth labor of Heracles, 428, 521

Caunus (caw'nus), Miletus' son who fled from the love of his sister Byblis, 510

Cecropia (se-kro'pi-a), early name of Attica, founded by Cecrops, 449

Cecrops (sē'kropz), early, autochthonous king of Athens, 449, 452, 456; Cecropian, 310

Cclaeno (se-lē'nō), Harpy who prophecied to Aeneas, 539–540

Celeus (sē'lē-us or sē'lūs), king of Eleusis and husband of Metaneira, 254–258, 263

Centaur (sen'tawr), centaurs, creatures with a human head and torso and the legs and body of a horse, 6, 80, 119–120, 186, 190, 205, 286, 367–368, 426, 431, 465, 473, 491–492; Centaurus (sen-taw'rus), monstruous offspring of Ixion and Nephele and father of the centaurs, 491

Ceos (sē'os), Aegean island, 506

Cephalus (sef'a-lus), son of Hermes and Herse, lover of Eos, and husband of Procris, 453–454, 620 n. 15

Cepheus (sē'fe-us or sē'fūs), husband of Cassiepea and father of Andromeda, 415

Cephisus (se'fi-sus), Boeotian river, father of Narcissus, 193, 246

Cerberus (ser'ber-us), the hound of Hades, offspring of Echidna and Typhon, 81, 115, 154, 288, 428, 430; twelfth labor of Heracles, 428, 430

Cercopes (ser-kō'pēz), two dwarfs, who attempted to steal Heracles' weapons, 433–444

Cercyon (ser'si-on), a brigand wrestler, killed by Theseus, 459

Ceres (sē'rēz), Roman agricultural goddess equated with Demeter, with a temple on the Aventine, 76, 301, 310, 513, 522–523, 535, 562

Cerynea (se-ri-nē'a), mountain in Arcadia, 425; Cerynean Hind or Stag, third labor of Heracles, 425–426

Cerynites (ser-i-nī'tēz), a river in Achaea

Ceto (sē'tō), daughter of Pontus and Ge, wife of Phorcys, and mother of the Graeae, Gorgons, and Ladon, 113–114

Ceyx (sē'iks), king of Trachis, husband of Alcyone, friend of Heracles and Deïanira, and turned into a seabird, 437, 446, 493

Chaerephon (kēr'e-fon), friend of Socrates, 177

Chalciope (kal-sī'o-pē), daughter of Aeëtes and wife of Phrixus, 473, 479

Chalcis (kal'kis), city on the island of Euboea

Chalybes (kal'i-bēz), iron-working people, 479

Chaos (kā'os), a "Yawning Void," the first principle for Hesiod, 38–39, 42, 54, 57, 285, 306

Chariclo (ka-rik'lō), nymph, mother of Tiresias, 335–336

Charis (ka'ris), "Grace," one of the Graces, or a name or epithet of Aphrodite, 623 n. 16

Charites (kar'i-tēz) See Graces

Charon (ka'ron), the ferryman of the Underworld, 154, 286, 287, 295, 532

Charybdis (ka-rib'dis), monstrous daughter of Poseidon and Ge; a dire obstacle, with Scylla, in the Straits of Messina, 113, 400, 405, 483, 539

Chimaera (kī-mī'ra), offspring of Typhon and Echidna with a lion's head, a goat's body, and a serpent's tail, killed by Bellerophon, 115, 286, 503

Chione (kī'o-nē), daughter of Boreas and Orithyia and mother of Eumolpus, 456

Chios (kī'os or kē'os), island off the coast of Asia Minor, 24, 165, 170, 173

Chiron (kī'ron), a wise centaur, tutor of heroes, 70, 186, 367- 368, 426, 430, 473, 491–492

Christ, the founder of a mystery religion, dominant in the western world, 134, 236, 307, 545, 580; Christian, Christianity, 96, 134, 192, 268–269, 284, 296–297, 307–309, 559, 562–564, 569, 570–571, 574, 584–585, 588

Chronus (kron'us), "Time," the first principle in the Orphic theogony, 305–306

Chrysaor (kri-sā'or), "He of the golden sword," son of Medusa and Poseidon, and father of Geryon and Echidna, 114–115, 413, 428

Chryse (krī'sē), island in the Aegean, 370

Chryseïs (krī-sē'is), Chryses' daughter who was taken captive by Agamemnon during the Trojan war, 370–372

Chryses (krī'sēz), father of Chryseïs, and Apollo's priest, who was insulted by Agamemnon, 189, 371–372

Chrysippus (krī-sip'pus), Pelops' son, abducted by Laius, 324

Chthonia (thŏ'ni-a), "Earth woman," daughter of Erechtheus,

Chthonian (thŏ'ni-an), chthonic, chthonius, "of the earth," an epithet for deities of the earth and Underworld, 22, 93, 120, 295, 327–328, 333, 345, 452, 496

Chthonius (thŏ'ni-us), one of the five Spartoi, king of Thebes, and father of Lycus and Nycteus, 321

Cicones (sik'kō-nēz), people of Ismarus in Thrace, encountered by Odysseus, 298, 394, 405; Ciconian, 301

Cilicia (si-li'shi-a), region in southern Asia Minor, 510

Cimmerians (sim-mē'ri-anz), inhabitants of a remote land, where Odysseus entered the Underworld, 271

Cimon (sī'mon), or Kimon (ki'mon), Athenian statesman and general of the fifth century B.C., 269, 467

Cinyras (sin'i-ras), son of Pygmalion and Galatea, seduced by his daughter Myrrha, and father of Adonis, 132, 133, 524

Cios (si'os), city on the Asiatic shore of the Propontis, where Heracles lost Hylas and was left behind by the Argonauts, 434, 478

Circe (sir'sē), daughter of the Sun (Helius) and a sorceress on the island of Aeaea, who turned men into swine; Odysseus overcame her and she gave him directions, 272, 397–400, 405, 408, 473, 479, 483, 516, 571, 582, 584

Cithaeron (si-thē'ron), a mountain between Thebes and Corinth, where Bacchic revels where held and where the infant Oedipus was exposed and rescued, 221, 230, 234, 236, 324, 326, 424, 575

Claros (klar'os), city in Asia Minor with a temple and oracle of Apollo, 157–158, 170, 181, 201

Cleisidice (clī-si'di-sē), daughter of Celeus and Metaneira, 254

Cleitus (klī'tus), beloved of Eos, 620 n. 15

Cleobis (klē'o-bis), he and his brother Biton were judged the happiest of men by Solon, 99–100, 496

Cleopatra (klē-ō-pat'ra), daughter of Boreas and Orithyia and wife of Phineus, 456; wife of Meleager, 497

Clio (klī'ō), Muse of history or lyre playing, 90

Clivus Urbius (clī'wus ur'bi-us), street in Rome, whose name was changed to

Vicus Sceleratus (Crime Street), because of Tullia's murder and desecration of her father Servius Tullius, 553

Cloaca (clō-ā'ca). Roman goddess of the drainage system; Cloacina (clo-a-si'na), epithet of Venus, 527

Cloanthus (clo-an'thus), victor in a boat-race in Vergil's Aeneid, after a prayer to Fortunus, 528

Clotho (klō'thō), "Spinner," the one of the three fates who spins out the thread of a person's life, 91, 279–280, 282

Clymene (klim'e-nē), wife of Helius and mother of Phaëthon 44, 495; wife of Iapetus and mother of Atlas, Menoetius, Prometheus and Epimetheus 60; wife of Iasus and mother of Atalanta, and of Pheres, 495

Clytemnestra (klī-tem-nes'tra), daughter of Zeus and Leda; she took Aegisthus as her lover, murdered her husband Agamemnon, and was killed by Orestes, 274, 343–347, 350, 352, 360, 388, 391, 582

Clytië (klī'ti-ē or klī'shi-ē), an Oceanid, jealous lover of Helius who turned into a sunflower, 495

Cnossus (knos'sus), site of Minos' palace in Crete, excavated by Sir Arthur Evans, 18, 20, 274, 196, 198, 469

Cocalus (kok'a-lus), king in Sicily, who received Daedalus, and whose daughters killed Minos, 470

Cocytus (kō-sī'tus), river of "Wailing" in the Underworld, 153, 286, 295

Codrus (kod'rus), last king of Athens, who sacrificed himself for his city, 468

Coeus (sē'us), one of the twelve Titans, father of Leto, 42, 170

Colchis (kol'kis), a city at the eastern end of the Black Sea, to which Jason sailed for the golden fleece, 317, 473, 479, 488; Colchian(s), 480, 482–483, 562

Collatia (kol-lā'she-a), town where Lucretia was violated, 555

Collatinus, (col-lā-tī'nus), Tarquinius, husband of the beautiful and virtuous Lucretia, who was raped, 554

Colonus (ko-lō'nus), region (deme) in Attica, where Oedipus died, 327, 329, 333

Colophon (ko'lo-fon), city in Asia Minor, 123

Comaetho (ko-mē'thō), Pterelaüs' daughter, who fell in love with Amphitryon, 420–421

Compitalia (kom-pi-tā'li-a), crossroads festival honoring the Lares, 532–533

Constantine (con'stan-tīn), the Great, 584–585; Roman emperor, fourth century A.D., 23

Consus (kon'sus), Italian harvest god, whose Roman festival was the Consualia (kon-swā'li-a), 549; cult partner of Ops, 523

Corcyra (kor-sī′ra), an island off the west coast of northern Greece, now called Corfu (kor′fu), 82

Corinth (kor′inth), city in the northern Peloponnesus, 129, 324–326, 330, 340, 349, 356, 409, 429, 447, 458, 467, 484–486, 490, 501–504, 573; Corinthian(s), 174–175, 324, 485

Corniculum (kor-ni′cu-lum), city where Ocrisia came from, Cornu copiae (kor′nū kōp′i-ē), "Horn of Plenty," 641 n. 19

Corona (ko-rō′na), the wreath of Ariadne, which became a constellation, 461–463

Coronis (ko-rō′nis), unfaithful beloved of Apollo and mother of Asclepius, 185–186

Corybantes (kor-i-ban′tēz), followers of Cybele, 222, 631 n. 5

Corycus (kor′i-kus), mountain on Delos, 170

Corynetes (kor i-nē′tēz), "Club Man," a name for Periphetes, 458

Cos (kos), island in the Aegean, 170, 186

Cottus (kot′tus), one of the three Hecatonchires, 41, 54

Cranaë (Kra′na-ē), island in the Aegean, 374

Crane dance (geranos), dance of Theseus on Delos, 463–464

Creon (krē′on), son of Menoeceus, brother of Jocasta, husband of Eurydice, and father of Haemon and Menoeceus, 32, 325, 327, 329, 332–334, 337, 420, 424, 467; king of Corinth, father of Glauce, whom Jason married, 485, 562

Cresphontes (kres-fon′tēz), Heraclid, who got Messene, 447

Cressida (cres′si′da), beloved of Troilus in medieval legend, 638 n. 8

Cretan Bull, seventh labor of Heracles, 428

Crete (krēt), large island in the Aegean, centre of Minoan civilization and birthplace of Zeus, 6, 18–19, 21, 50–51, 174, 198, 222, 239, 255, 316–31, 319, 352, 391–392, 460 ; Cretan(s), 161, 174, 196, 198–199, 289, 310, 317, 365, 392, 418, 418, 460–461, 463, 466, 468–469, 484, 539

Cretheus (krē′the-us or krē′thūs), king of Iolcus, husband of Tyro, and father of Aeson, Pheres, and Amythaon, 473, 494, 501

Creusa (krē-ū′sa), Aeneas' first wife, who died during Troy's capture, 389–390; daughter of Erechtheus and mother of Ion, 452, 456; another name for Glauce, whom Jason married, 485

Crisa (kri′sa), site of Delphi, 173–174, 194, 197

Crius (krī′us), one of the twelve Titans, 42

Crocale (cro′ka-lē), a nymph of Diana

Croesus (krē′sus), wealthy king of Lydia, and Atys' father, who was defeated by Cyrus and learned wisdom after his encounter with Solon, 27, 98–107, 175

Crommyon (krom′mi-on), a village near Megara, home of a huge, man–eating sow, killed by Theseus, 459

Cronus (krō′nus), sky-god, son of Uranus and Ge, and Rhea's husband, overthrown by his son Zeus, 6, 16, 41, 45–51, 53, 58–59, 61–63, 66, 75, 77–79, 84–85, 87, 92, 135, 137, 195, 200–202, 205, 207, 209, 212, 237, 252–254, 259, 261, 263, 306, 352, 404, 423, 444, 490–491, 502, 513, 559

Cumae (kū′mē), city in Italy, north of Naples, 177, 178, 284, 540

Cumaean Sibyl (kūc-mē′an sib′il), Deiphobe, Sibyl of Cumae, prophetic priestess of Apollo, and Aeneas' guide in the Underworld, 177–179, 284–291, 293, 534–535, 540

Cupid (kū′pid), the Roman name of Eros, 29, 151–155, 180, 215

Curetes (kū-rē′tēz), "Young Men," who hid the cries of the infant Zeus and were associated with the frenzied worship of the mother goddess, 51, 222, 632 n. 5; people who warred with the Calydonians, 497

Curiatii (kūr-i-ā′shi-ī), three champions from Alba Longa who fought against the Roman Horatii, 552–553

Cybele (sib′e-lē), Phrygian mother goddess, sprung from the earth, who loved Attis and with him was associated with a mystery religion, 41, 50–52, 135–136, 221, 239, 264–265, 307–310, 501, 535–536

Cycladic (sik′la-dēz), pertaining to the islands in the Aegean encircling Delos, 19

Cyclopes (sī-klō′pēz), "Orb-Eyed," three sons of Uranus and Ge, with one eye in the middle of their forehead, assistants of Hephaestus, who forged the thunder and lightening bolts of Zeus, 40–41, 47–48, 53, 83, 291, 521; the giants whom Odysseus and his men encountered, including Polyphemus who fell in love with Galatea, 394–395, 539; Cyclops (sī′klopz), the singular of Cyclopes, 108, 110–111, 187, 405, 542; Cyclopean (sī-klō-pē-an) walls, 21

Cycnus (sik′nus), Trojan, Poseidon's son and Phaëthon's cousin, turned into a swan, 371, 619 n. 13; a robber, son of Ares, encountered by Heracles, 432

Cydippe (si-dip′ē), priestess of Hera and mother of Cleobis and Biton, 623 n. 3; beloved of Acontius, 506

Cyllene (sil-lē′nē), mountain in Arcadia, 70, 200, 208; Cyllenian (sil-lē′ni-an), an epithet of Hermes, 203, 207, 209

Cynossema (si-nos-sē′ma), "Dog's Tomb," the burial place of Hecuba, turned into a bitch, 388

Cynthus (sin'thus), a mountain on Delos, 170;
Cynthian (sin'thi-an), 169, 172
Cyparissus (si-pa-ris'sus), boy loved by Apollo
and turned into a cypress tree, the
meaning of his name, 506
Cyprus (sī'prus), island in the eastern
Mediterranean, associated with the
birth of Aphrodite and a center for her
worship, 48, 128, 130–131, 133,
137–138, 142, 243, 463, 507; Cyprian
(sip'ri-an), Cyprogenes (sip-ro'je-nēz),
epithets of Aphrodite, 48, 137; Cypris
(sī'pris), another name for Aphrodite,
128
Cyrene (sī-rē'nē), nymph, loved by Apollo,
mother of Aristaeus, and eponymous
ancestor of the city Cyrene in Libya,
179–180, 482, 635 n. 3
Cyrus (sī'rus), the Great, king of the Persians,
who defeated Croesus, 98, 104–107
Cythera (sith'e-ra), an island off the southern
coast of the Peloponnesus, associated
with Aphrodite's birth, 48, 128;
Cytherea, an epithet of Aphrodite, 48,
87, 128, 130, 137, 140, 142
Cytisorus (si-tis-o'rus), son of Phrixus and
Chalciope, 473
Cyzicus (siz'i-kus), city (and its king) on the
Asiatic shore of the Propontis where
the Argonauts stopped, 477–478

Daedalus (dē'da-lus), artisan and inventor,
Icarus' father, who devised the
labyrinth, a hollow cow for Pasiphaë to
satisfy her passion, and wings for
flying, 468–470
Daimon (dī'mōn), divine spirit, divinity, 282
Damastes (da-mas'tēz), "Subduer," another
name for Procrustes, 643 n. 17
Danaë (da'na-ē), Acrisius' daughter and
Perseus' mother, destined to bear a son
who would kill her father, 12, 410–412,
416
Danai (dā'na-ī or da'na-ē), Danaans (dan'a-
anz), subjects of Danaüs, the Greeks,
418
Danaids (dan'ā-idz), Danaüs' fifty daughters,
who married Aegyptus' fifty sons, 290,
299, 418–419, 634 n. 21
Danaüs (dā'na-us), Egyptian Belus' son and
Aegyptus' brother, who became king of
Argos and had fifty daughters, 409,
418–419, 507
Daphne (daf'nē), "Laurel," Peneus' daughter,
who rejected Apollo's advances and
was turned into his sacred laurel tree,
29, 180–184, 564, 581, 594
Dardanelles (dar'da-nelz), the straits between
Europe and Asia, 473
Dardanus (dar'da-nus), son of Zeus and king
of Troy; from him the land was called
Dardania and its people Dardani, 140,
291, 508, 537, 539

Daunus (daw'nus), king of Apulia, 392
Day, offspring of Night and Erebus, 38
Death, 362, 428, 502, 532, 582. See also
Thanatos
Deianira (dē-ya-nī'ra), daughter of Oeneus,
wife of Heracles, and responsible for
his death by means of Nessus' blood,
424, 430, 435–437, 439, 496–497
Deidamia (dē-i-da-mī-a), daughter of
Lycomedes, king of Scyros and mother
of Achilles' son Neoptolemus, 368
Deiphobe (dē-if'ō-bē). See Cumaean Sibyl
Deiphobus (dē-if'ōbus), son of Priam and
husband of Helen, after Paris' death,
289, 360, 380
Deliades (dēl-ī'ad-ēz), a maiden chorus,
serving Apollo at Delos, 172–173
Delos (dē'los), island in the Aegean,
birthplace of Apollo and Artemis, and a
sanctuary of Apollo, 95, 159, 169–172,
174, 189, 192, 463, 465, 469, 506, 539;
Delian (dēl'i-an), 173
Delphi (del'fī), panhellenic sanctuary sacred to
Apollo, centre for games and contests
and his oracle, 69, 82, 95, 98, 104, 157,
173–177, 181, 190, 266, 319–320, 324,
346, 348–349, 393, 414, 424, 432, 43,
447, 456, 472, 492, 575; Delphic
(del'fic), 105, 324, 349, 371, 456–457,
467, 473, 482, 496, 505, 536
Delphinius (del-fin'i-us), a title of Apollo, 174,
198, 460
Demeter (de-mē'ter), daughter of Cronus and
Rhea, goddess of the ripe grain,
vegetation, agriculture, and the
Eleusinian Mysteries, and Persephone's
mother, equated with Ceres by the
Romans, 13, 41, 49, 52–53, 76, 112,
241, 251–254, 256–259, 261–270, 284,
307–310, 328, 340, 418, 446, 467, 513,
523, 559
Demo (dem'ō), daughter of Celeus and
Metaneira, 254
Demodocus (de-mo'do-kus), a bard in
Homer's Odyssey, 87
Demophoön (de-mof'ō-on) or Demophon
(dem'o-fon), son of Celeus and
Metaneira and nursed by Demeter,
256–257, 264, 266
Demophon (dem'o-fon), son of Theseus and
Phaedra and king of Athens, 446, 466,
468. See also Demophoön
Desire, Himeros, an attendant of Aphrodite,
357
Deucalion (dū-kā'li-on), son of Prometheus
and husband of Pyrrha, the Greek
Noah of the archetypal flood story, 70,
72–75; son of Minos and Pasiphaë and
father of Idomeneus, 365, 470
Dexamenus (dek-sa'me-nus), "Receiver," a
prince, whose daughter Heracles
helped, 426

Dia (dī'a), an early name for Naxos, 461–462; the daughter of Eïmoneus and wife of Ixion, 491

Diana (dī-an'a), goddess, equated by the Romans with Artemis, 46, 76, 160–166, 215, 310, 513, 529–530, 543, 545, 553, 567, 569–570

Dicte (dik'tē), mountain in Crete, where the infant Zeus was hidden, 51

Dictys (dik'tis), "Net," fisherman, savior of Danaë and Perseus and brother of Polydectes, 412, 416

Dido (dī'dō), Phoenician queen of Carthage, who loved Aeneas and committed suicide when he left her, 28, 288, 292, 538, 539–546, 580

Diocles (dī'o-klez), Dioclus (dī'o-klus), prince in Eleusis, 255, 263

Diomedes (dī-ō-mē'dēz), son of Tydeus, king of Argos and often teamed with Odysseus at Troy; exchanged armor with Glaucus, 361, 363–364, 366, 368, 370, 391–392, 409, 419, 502, 521; son of Ares, owner of mares, encountered by Heracles, 428, 431; mortal turned into a sea-god, rejected lover of Scylla, 624 n. 5

Dione (dī-ō'nē), mate of Zeus and mother of Aphrodite Pandemos, Common Aphrodite, 128, 171

Dionysus (dī-ō-nī'sus), son of Semele and reborn from Zeus' thigh, savior of Ariadne, god of the grape and the vine, vegetation, wine, intoxication, sex, irrationality, music, dancing, ecstacy, drama, and mysteries (Roman Bacchus), 22, 27, 76, 98, 130, 155, 190–191, 218–254, 264, 268, 294, 297, 304–307, 461–463, 476, 495, 504–506, 523, 561, 575, 584–585

Dioscuri (dī-os-cū'rī), "Sons of Zeus" and Leda, Castor, and Polydeuces (Pollux), patron deities of ships and sailors, 346, 350–352, 365, 529, 534, 560

Diotima (dī-o-tī'ma), woman from Mantinea and Socrates' teacher about love, 148–150

Dirae (dī'rī or dī'rē), avenging goddesses, 543

Dirce (dir'sē), fountain in Thebes, wife of Lycus, persecutor of Antiope, and killed by Amphion and Zethus, 220, 320, 323, 332

Discord, Eris. See Eris

Dis Pater (dis pat'er), Roman name for Pluto, 28, 49, 264, 285, 289, 295, 532. See also Hades

Dithyramb (dith'i-ramb), choral song, especially one in honor of Dionysus, 504–505, 630 n. 2

Dius Fidius (dī'us fī'di-us), Sabine god of Good Faith (Fides) identified with Jupiter, 418

Dodona (do-dō'na), sanctuary and oracle of Zeus, in northern Greece, 69, 78, 82, 348, 475

Dolichus (dol'i-kus), prince in Eleusis, 255

Doliones (dol-i'o-nēz), inhabitants of Cyzicus, visited by the Argonauts, 477–478

Dolon (dō'lon), a Trojan spy, killed by Diomedes and Odysseus, 363–364

Dorian (dō'ri-an), Dorians, a division of the Greek people, 435, 441, 447–448

Doris (dō'is), an Oceanid and wife of Nereus, 108

Dorus (dō'us), son of Hellen and eponymous ancestor of the Dorians, 621 n. 23

Doso (dō'sō), name of Demeter, disguised as an old woman in Eleusis, 255

Dryad (drī'ad), Dryads, nymphs of trees, 249, 302, 304, 623 n. 1

Dryope (drī'o-pē), Dryops' daughter and mother of Pan, 244–245

Dryopes (drī'o-pēz), Thessalian tribe hostile to Aegimius, 435

Dryops (drī'opz), father of Dryope, 244–245

Ea (e'a), a Babylonian god, 75

Earth, Gaia, Gaea, and Ge, sprung from Chaos, mother goddess of earth and fertility and wife of Uranus, 38–42, 45–51, 54–55, 57, 108, 113, 117, 171, 173, 195, 252, 285, 294, 306, 320, 328, 429–430

Ecastor (e-kas'tor), women's oath, calling on Castor and Pollux

Echemus (ē'ke-mus), king of Tegea, who killed Hyllus, 447

Echidna (e-kid'na), half nymph and half snake, mate of Typhon and her son Orthus, and mother of monsters, 115; Snake Woman who bore Heracles three sons, 429

Echion (e-kī'on), husband of Agave and father of Pentheus, 224, 228, 236

Echo, a nymph who became only a voice; she was pursued by Pan and rejected by Narcissus, 29, 244–250

Eëtion (e-ē'ti-on), Andromache's father, killed by Achilles, 360

Egeria (e-jē'ri-a), water nymph, helpful to pregnant women and counselor of king Numa, 518, 529–530

Egesta (e-jes'ta), city in Sicily, 5400

Egypt, country in northern Africa, 27, 68, 237, 243, 317, 353, 391, 409, 417–418, 430, 441, 507; Egyptian(s), 310, 417–418, 496, 507, 561–562

Eidothea (ī-do'thē-a), sea goddess, who helped Menelaus consult her father Proteus, 391

Eileithyia (ī-lī-thī'ya or ī-li'thīa), goddess of childbirth and daughter of Zeus and Hera, 22, 82, 171–172, 422

Eïoneus (i-yō'ne-us), father of Dia, murdered by her husband Ixion, 491

Elaïs (e'la-is), "Olive Girl," daughter of Anius, turned into a dove, 506

Electra (e-lek'tra), Clytemnestra's daughter, who hated her mother for the murder of her father Agamemnon and waited for the return of her brother Orestes to seek vengeance, 8, 26, 346–349; an Oceanid, wife of Thaumas and mother of Iris and the Harpies, 113; daughter of Atlas, 508

Electryon (e-lek'tri-on), king of Mycenae, uncle of Amphitryon, who married his daughter Alcmena, 420, 422

Eleusis (e-lū'sis), a town west of Athens, center for the Mysteries of Demeter, 52, 99, 254, 259, 264–266, 269–270, 308, 334, 452, 459, 467; Eleusinians (el-ū-sin'i-anz), Eleusinian, 319, 452, 523; Mysteries, 264–270; Eleusinion, sanctuary of Demeter, 267

Eleuthia (e-lū'thi-a), the name of Eileithyia in Linear B, 22

Elis (ē'lis), region in the western Peloponnesus, 80, 324, 338–339, 342, 426, 434, 493

Elissa (e-lis'sa), another name of Dido, 543, 545

Elpenor (el-pē'nor), Odysseus' comrade, who fell off Circe's roof, died, and in the Underworld asks Odysseus for burial, 272, 287

Elysium (e-liz'i-um), the Elysian Fields, paradise in the realm of Hades, the Elysian Fields, 267, 277, 289–294, 295, 321, 392, 446–447, 571

Enceladus (en-sel'a-dus), defeated giant under Mt. Aetna, 55

Endymion (en-dim'i-on), the beloved of Selene, Artemis (Diana), 45–46, 578

Enipeus (e-nip'e-us), river and its god in Thessaly, in whose disguise Poseidon loved Tyro, 493–494

Enualios (en-y-al'i-os), word in linear B, later associated with Ares, 22

Eos (ē'os), daughter of Hyperion and Theia and amorous goddess of the "Dawn," 43–44, 46, 89, 141, 204, 384, 453

Eosphoros (ē-os'for-us), Lucifer, the Morning Star, father of Ceyx, 93

Epaphus (ep'a-fus), "He of the Touch," the son of Zeus and Io, 68–69, 409, 417–418

Epeus (e-pē'us), son of Panopeus, 282; builder of the Trojan horse, 386

Ephesus (ef'e-sus), city in Asia Minor, 165

Ephialtes (ef-i-al'tēz), a giant who stormed heaven, 144, 290, 634 n. 15. See also Aloadae

Ephyra (e'fi-ra), another name for Corinth, 349, 501

Epicasta (ep-i-kas'ta), Homer's name for Jocasta, 325

Epidaurus (ep-i-daw'rus), city in the northern Peloponnesus, 457

Epigoni (e-pig'o-nī), sons of the seven against Thebes led by Alcmaeon, who made a second and successful attack, 334–335, 337

Epimetheus (ep-i-mē'thē-us or ep-i-mē'thūs), "Afterthinker," Prometheus' brother, who accepted Pandora from Zeus, 60, 64, 70, 620 n. 9

Epirus (e-pī'rus), region in northern Greece, 360, 393, 539

Epops (ep'ops), Hoopoe, the bird into which Tereus was transformed, 455

Er, son of Armenius, who died and came back to life to present the vision of the Afterlife recorded by Plato, 28, 277, 279, 280–283

Erato (er'a-tō), Muse of love poetry or hymns to the gods and lyre playing, 90

Erebus (er'e-bus), the darkness of Tartarus or Tartarus itself, 38–39, 60, 91, 259, 272, 275, 285, 301, 306

Erechtheum (e-rek-thē'um), Ionic temple on the Acropolis of Athens, dedicated to Poseidon-Erechtheus and Athena Polias, 119, 451

Erechtheus (e-rek'the-us or e-rek'thūs), early king of Athens, associated with Poseidon and father of Procris, Orithyia, and Creusa, 119–120, 451–453, 456–457

Eretria (e-re'tri-a), a city on the island of Euboea

Erginus (er-jī'nus), father of the builders Trophonius and Agamedes, 194, 496

Eriboea (e-ri-bē'a), Athenian maiden attacked by Minos, 460

Erichthonius (er-ik-thōn'i-us), early Athenian king, confused with Erectheus, sprung from the earth, and raised by Athena, 449, 452–454

Eridanus (e-rid'a-nus), river in the Underworld, 45, 291, 483

Erigone (e-rig'ō-nē), daughter of Icarius, who hanged herself upon finding her father dead, 241

Erinyes (e-rin'i-ēz), the Furies or Eumenides, dread daughters of Earth or Night, avengers of blood guilt, and punishers of sinners in the Underworld, 48, 346, 348

Eriphyle (e-ri-fī'lē), Amphiaraüs' wife, bribed by Polynices to persuade her husband to go to his death, and murdered by her son Alcmaeon, 288, 330, 334–335

Eris (er'is), goddess of "Discord," 353, 492

Forum Boarium (bo-ar'i-um), commercial quarter of Rome, where there was a cult of Hercules, 533–534

Fields of Mourning, a region in Vergil's Underworld, 288, 294

Flora (flo'ra), Roman agricultural goddess of flowering, consort of Zephyrus, 516, 523–524, 558

Fortuna (for-tū'na), Fortune, a goddess of chance or fate, 543, 553

Furies, Fury, 71, 127, 166, 289, 296, 46, 540. *See also* Erinyes and Eumenides

Gabii (gab'i-ī), Latin town, 555

Gaea (jē'a *or* gē'a) *or* Gaia (gī'a). *See* Earth

Galatea (gal-a-tē'a), Nereid, in love with Acis and wooed by Polyphemus, 108, 110–111; beloved of Pygmalion, 132, 507

Galaxy, the Milky Way, 560

Galli (gal'lī), eunuchs, priests of Cybele, 135, 308, 536

Ganymede (gan'i-mēd), Trojan prince carried off by Zeus to become the cupbearer of the gods on Olympus, 82–83, 140–141, 155, 340, 574, 586

Garden of Eden, the paradise of Adam and Eve, 571

Gargaphie (gar-gā'fi-ē), vale sacred to Diana, 160

Ge (jē *or* gē). *See* Earth

Gegeneis (je'je-nīs *or* gā'ge-nays), "Earth-born" Giants, 55. *See also* Giants

Gelonus (je-lō'nus), son of Heracles and Echidna, 429

Gemini (jem'i-nī), the "Twins," the Dioscuri, a constellation, 560

Genius (jen'i-us), a man's creative power, 533

Geryon (jer'i-on), three-bodied son of Chrysaor and Callirhoë, killed by Heracles, who took Geryon's Cattle, 115, 286, 413, 428–429, 432, 495, 521, 533

Giants, 48, 434, 477. *See also* Gegeneis

Gigantomachy (jī-gan-to'mak-ē), battle of the giants against Zeus and the Olympians, 55–57, 119–129, 434, 561

Gilgamesh (gil'ga-mesh), Mesopotamian hero, linked to Heracles, 441

Girdle of Hippolyta, ninth labor of Heracles, 428

Glauce (glaw'sē), or Creusa, Creon's daughter, whom Jason married and Medea murdered, 485, 562

Glaucon (glaw'kon), person addressed by Socrates, 277–278, 280, 283

Glaucus (glaw'kus), mortal turned into a sea-god, lover of Scylla of whom Circe was jealous, 578; Hippolochus' son, who exchanged his golden armor for the bronze armor of Diomedes, 361–364, 502–503; son of Minos and Pasiphaë;

he fell into a vat of honey and was brought back to life by Polyidus, 470–471; son of Sisyphus and father of Bellerophon, 501

Glaukopis, epithet of Athena, 125–126

Golden Age, the Age of Paradise, 57–58, 306

Gordias (gor'di-as), the father of the Adrastus who killed Atys, 102, 104

Gorgon, Gorgons (gor'gonz), three daughters of Phorcys and Ceto, so terrifying in appearance that those who looked upon them were turned into stone; only Medusa was mortal and beheaded by Perseus, 94, 114, 125, 286, 364, 389, 399, 409, 412–416, 503, 585

Graces, Charites (Latin, Gratiae), lovely attendants of Aphrodite, 64, 89, 129, 137–138, 155, 157, 193, 357, 409, 491, 524

Graeae (grī-ī *or* grē'ē), or Graiai (grī'ī), "Aged Ones," three sisters of the Gorgons, "Old Women," sharing one eye and one tooth, who helped Perseus, 412–413, 580

Graioi (grī'oi), Hellenes who provided the designations Greek and Greece, 621 n. 23

Gyes (jī'ēz *or* guy'ēz), one of the three Hecatonchires, 41, 54

Hadad (ha'dad), Semetic sky-god, 309

Hades (hā'dēz), Greek god of the Underworld and his realm, son of Cronus and Rhea, and husband of Persephone (Roman Pluto), 53, 56, 59, 76, 139, 154, 166, 212–213, 232, 251–254, 258–261, 264, 269, 271–276, 284, 295, 296–297, 304, 344–345, 371, 377, 389, 392, 398–399, 405, 430, 434–435, 466, 495, 497, 502. *See also* Pluto

Hadrian (hay'dri-an), Roman emperor, second century A.D., 269, 309, 527

Haemon (hē'mon), son of Creon and Eurydice, who kills himself to die with his beloved Antigone, 334

Haemus (hē'mus), mountain in Thrace, 301

Halae (hal'ē), town in Attica, 348

Halicarnassus (hal-i-kar-nas'sus), city in Asia Minor

Hamadryads (ham-a-drī'adz), nymphs of oak trees, 623 n. 1

Hamaxa (ha'mak-sa), the "Wain," another name for Ursa Major

Harmonia (har-mō'ni-a), the wife of Cadmus, 320; a goddess, 193, 320–321, 323, 329–330, 334–335

Harpies (har'pēz), the "Snatchers," dread daughters of Thaumus and Electra, 94, 113–114, 286, 478; Harpy Celaeno, 539

Harpocrates (har-pok'ra-tēz), another name for Horus

Hebe (hē'bē), "Youthful Bloom," daughter of Zeus and Hera, cupbearer to the gods, and wife of Heracles, 82, 193, 423, 439, 446

Hebrus (hē'brus), river in Thrace, 302, 432

Hecabe (hek'a-bē), Greek name of Hecuba, 353

Hecale (hek'a-lē), old woman encountered by Theseus, 460

Hecalus (hec'a-lus), epithet of Zeus in Hecale's honor, 460

Hecate (hek'a-tē), goddess of the moon, ghosts, and witches and a dread fury in the Underworld, 166, 253, 262, 264, 285, 289, 310, 479–480, 530, 543

Hecatonchires (hek-a-ton-kī'rēz), "Hundred-Handed or-Armed," offspring of Uranus and Gaia, 41, 48, 53–55

Hector (hek'tor), son of Priam and Hecuba, husband of Andromache, and father of Astyanax; greatest Trojan hero, killed by Achilles and ransomed by Priam, 348, 360–362, 371, 373–383, 385–386, 521, 537, 541, 561–562, 577, 583

Hecuba (hek'ū-ba), Priam's wife, who bore him many children and was changed into a bitch, 352–353, 358, 361, 375, 382, 384, 386, 388

Helen (hel'en), daughter of Zeus and Leda and wife of Menelaus, whom she left for Trojan Paris, 59, 289, 317, 345, 348, 352–353, 356–358, 360–361, 363–366, 373–375, 377, 382, 386, 391–392, 465, 570, 574–575, 583

Helenus (hel'e-nus), Trojan prophet who married Andromache, 178, 360, 370, 385, 388, 393, 539

Helicon (hel'i-kon), a mountain in Boeotia, 37, 112, 317, 413

Helius (hē'li-us), sun-god, son of Hyperion and Theia, father of Phaëthon, and grandfather of Medea, 43–46, 87, 119, 165, 190, 197–202, 208, 253, 271, 394, 400, 405, 428, 469, 473, 483, 485, 489, 495–496, 501, 506–507

Hell, 267, 622, 671. See also Tartarus

Hellas (hel'las), ancient Greek name of Greece, 75, 432; Helladic, 19, 20–21

Helle (hel'lē), daughter of Athamas and Nephele and Phrixus' sister, who fell off the ram at the Hellespont, 473

Hellen (hel'len), son of Deucalion and Pyrrha and eponymous ancestor of the Hellenes, 75, 621 n. 23

Hellenes (hel'lēnz), Greeks, inhabitants of Hellas, 102, 220, 227; Hellenic (hel-len'ic), 174, 214, 265, 304

Hellenistic (hel-len-is'tic), period from the death of Alexander the Great from 323 to 146 B.C., 217, 557, 561

Hellespont (hel'le-spont), Dardanelles, where Helle fell off the ram, 473, 508, 527–528

Hephaestus (he-fēs'tus), son of Zeus and Hera or Hera alone; lame, artisan god, husband of Aphrodite, he was equated with Vulcan by the Romans, 62–63, 66, 76, 82–89, 95, 117–118, 125, 127, 146–147, 195, 203, 320, 379, 449, 457, 479, 482, 513, 521

Hera (hē'ra), daughter of Cronus and Rhea, sister and wife of Zeus, and queen of the gods; the Romans equated her with Juno, 22, 41, 49, 52, 53, 68–69, 76, 78–80, 95, 100, 111, 118, 129, 166, 171, 195, 200–201, 218, 237, 241, 310, 325, 353–356, 409, 417, 422–424, 429, 434, 439, 441, 475, 478–479, 485, 490, 493, 513, 560, 592; Heraeum, Hera's sanctuary in Argos, 409

Heracles (her'a-klēz), son of Zeus and Alcmena, he performed many deeds and twelve labors and won immortality among the gods on Olympus, 9, 12, 21, 58, 61, 70, 80, 95, 187, 276, 287, 296, 358, 364, 370, 409, 417, 419, 420–447, 457, 460, 465–466, 475, 477–479, 488, 495–497, 505, 533, 559, 560, 571, 592, 620 n. 4; Pillars of, 429, 467

Heraclidae (her-a-klī'dē), Heraclids, descendants of Heracles, 349, 446–448

Hercules (her'kū-lēz), the Roman name of Heracles; for the Romans Hercules (like Mercury) was especially a god of commerce and profit, 28, 127, 521–522, 525, 533–534, 545, 551, 580, 585, 588

Hermaphroditus (her-ma-frō-dī'tus), Hermaphrodite, son of Hermes and Aphrodite, he became one with Salmacis and turned into a hermaphrodite, 214–217

Hermes (her'mez), son of Zeus and Maia, trickster god of thieves, who stole Apollo's cattle (Roman Mercury), 22, 63, 66, 76, 78, 81, 83, 88, 130, 139, 141, 200–214, 244–245, 259, 261, 295, 342, 353–355, 371, 382, 398, 400, 412, 415–417, 422, 430, 446–447, 453, 456, 470, 473, 502, 508, 513, 530–531, 559–560

Herm(s), phallic pillars, topped by the head of Hermes, then phallic pillars topped by the head of anyone, 213–214, 515

Hermione (her-mī'ō-nē), daughter of Menelaus and Helen and wife of Neoptolemus and Orestes, 348–349, 352, 393, 492

Hero, Aphrodite's priestess, who committed suicide when her lover Leander drowned, 508

Heroic Age, Hesiod's fourth of his five Ages, 59–60

Herse (her'sē), "Dew," daughter of Cecrops, 452–453

Hersilia (her-sil'i-a), wife of Romulus, 551

Hesione (hē-sī′o-ne), Laomedon's daughter, rescued by Heracles, 358, 428, 488

Hesperides (hes-per′i-dēz), "Daughters of Evening," three guardians of the tree with golden apples at the ends of the earth, 61, 114–115, 426, 429–430, 483, 580

Hestia (hes′ti-a), daughter of Cronus and Rhea and goddess of the hearth; the Romans equated her with their Vesta, 49, 53, 76–78, 136–137, 513

Hiera (hī′er-a), "Holy Things," 266–268; Hierophant (hī′er-o-fant), "He who reveals holy things," a priest, 266, 269–270

Hieros gamos (hī′e-ros ga′mos), "Sacred or Holy Marriage," between a sky-god and earth-goddess, 40–41

Hippasus (hip′pa-sus), Leucippe's son, who was torn to pieces like Pentheus, 631 n. 7

Hippocoön (hip-po′ko-on), Spartan king, attacked by Heracles, 435

Hippocrates (hip-pok′ra-tez), physician and writer, fifth century B.C., 186

Hippocrene (hip-po-krē′nē), "Horse's Fountain," fountain (created by Pegasus' hoof) on Mt. Helicon, home of the Muses, 90, 413

Hippodamia (hip-pō-da-mē′a or hip-pō-da-mī′a), Oenamaüs' daughter, whom Pelops won through treachery, 80, 338–342; wife of Pirithoüs, 491–492

Hippolochus (hip-pol′o-kus), son of Bellerophon and father of Glaucus, who exchanged armor with Diomedes, 503

Hippolyta (hip-pol′i-ta), queen of the Amazons, 428

Hippolytus (hip-pol′i-tus), follower of Artemis, son of Theseus and Antiope; he rejected Aphrodite and the love of his stepmother Phaedra and was killed, 166–168, 186, 457, 465–466, 530, 572, 581

Hippomedon (hip-po′me-don), one of the seven against Thebes, 330–332

Hippomenes (hip-po′me-nēz). See Milanion

Holy Spirit, 564

Homole (ho′mo-lē), mountain in Thessaly, 431

Hope, 64–65

Hora Quirini (ho′ra qwi-ri′nī), Hersilia as deified wife of Romulus, 551

Horae (hō′rī or hō′rē), "Hours," the Seasons, daughters of Zeus and Themis and attendants of Aphrodite, 64, 92, 129–130, 155, 193, 524, 623 n. 21

Horatii (ho-rā′shi-ī), three Roman brothers who fought against the three Curatii from Alba Longa, 552–553

Horatius (ho-rā′shi-us), one of the three Horatii who murdered his unpatriotic sister, Horatia, 552–553

Horus (hō′rus), child sought for by the Egyptian goddess Isis

Hound of Hell. See Cerberus

Hours. See Horae

Hubris (hū′bris), "Excessive Pride," often mortal arrogance, a sin against the gods, 107, 224, 347, 378

Hyacinthus (hī-a-sin′thus), Hyacinth, Spartan youth, loved and accidently killed by Apollo, 184–185, 384–385, 524, 578, 581; Hyacinthia, festival honoring Hyacinthus, 185

Hydra (hī′dra), "Water Snake," in particular the dragon-like monster with poison blood, offspring of Echidna and Typhon, encountered by Heracles at Lerna, 115, 432, 436, 441, 584

Hygeia (hī-jē′a) or Hygieia (hī-ji-ī′a), "Health," daughter of Asclepius, 196

Hylas (hī′las), Argonaut, beloved of Heracles, who was seized by water nymphs, 434, 478

Hyllus (hil′lus), son of Heracles and Deïanira and husband of Iole, 436, 439, 447

Hymen (hī′men), god of marriage, 298, 357, 370, 463

Hypaepa (hi-pē′pa), a town in Lydia, 123, 188

Hyperboreans (hi-per-bor′ē-anz), mythical people in a paradise in the far north, 413, 425–426

Hyperion (hī-pēr′i-on), Titan, husband of Theia and father of Helius, Selene and Eos, 42–43, 45–46, 116, 190, 253–254, 394

Hypermnestra (hi-perm-nes′tra), Hypermestra (hi-per-mes′tra), Danaïd, who did not kill her husband Lynceus, 409, 418

Hypsipyle (hip-sip′i-lē), daughter of Thoas and Lemnian queen, who bore Jason twin sons, 476, 488; nurse of Opheltes, 330

Hyrieus (hī′ri-ūs), Boeotian king, 496

Iacchus (i-ak′kus), name of Dionysus, 230, 523

Ialysus (i-al′i-sus), city of Rhodes, 506

Iambe (i-am′bē), servant of Celeus and Metaneira, who jests with Demeter, 256

Iamus (ī-am′us), son of Apollo and Evadne with oracular powers, 505

Ianthe (ī-an′thē), wife of Iphis, 298

Iapetus (ī-ap′e-tus), Titan, father of Prometheus, Epimetheus, Atlas, and Menoetius, 42, 57, 60–63

Iarbas (i-ar′bas), suitor, rejected by Dido, 543, 546

Iasion (i-as′i-on), son of Zeus and father of Plutus, 264, 508

Iasus (ī'a-sus), Arcadian, father of Atalanta, 500

Icarius (i-kar'i-us), Erigone's father who received Dionysus hospitably in Attica, 241

Icarus (ik'a-rus), Daedalus' son, who given wings by his father, disobeyed his instructions and drowned, 469–470; Mare Icarium, the sea into which Icarus fell, 469

Ichor (ī'kor), the clear blood of the gods, 93

Ida (ī'da), mountain near Troy, 137–138, 170, 215, 353–354, 356, 358, 362

Idas (ī'das), son of Aphareus and Lynceus' brother, and Argonaut who wooed and won Marpessa, 350, 476

Idmon (id'mon), of Colophon, father on Arachne, 123; seer and an Argonaut, 476, 479

Idomeneus (ī-dom'e-ne-us or ī-dom'e-nūs), king of Crete, 392; ally of the Greeks at Troy, 365

Iepaean (i-ē-pē'an). See Paean

Ilia (il'i-a), another name for Rhea Silvia, 541, 546

Ilissus (i-lis'sus), river in Attica, 456

Ilium (il'i-um), another name for Troy, 375

Illyrians (il-li'ri-anz), 321

Ilus (ī'lus), early king of Troy, 291

Inachus (in'ak-us), river of Argos, father of Io and Phoroneus, 69, 409, 417, 419

Indiges (in'dig-ēz), epithet of Jupiter, associated with the River Numicus, and a divine title of Aeneas, 518–519, 545

Ino (ī'nō), daughter of Cadmus and Harmonia, Semele's sister, who cared for the infant Dionysus, and wife of Athamas, 218, 224, 229, 321, 402, 630 n. 3

Io (ī'ō), Inachus' daughter, loved by Zeus, turned into a cow, and mother of Epaphus, 12, 68–69, 317, 417–418, 582

Iobates (ī-ōb'a-tēz), king of Lycia, father of Stheneboea, and taskmaster of Bellerophon, 503

Iolaüs (ī-ō-lā'us), nephew and helper of Heracles, 425, 432, 446

Iolcus (ī-ol'kus), city in Thessaly, 193, 316, 472–473, 476, 484, 494

Iole (ī'ō-lē), Eurytus' daughter, with whom Heracles fell in love, 435–437, 439, 447

Ion (ī'on), son of Apollo and Creusa and eponymous ancestor of the Ionians, 452, 456

Ionia (ī-ōn'i-a), region in Asia Minor, 456; Ionians (ī-ō'ni-anz), division of the Greeks, 456

Iphicles (if'i-klēz), son of Amphitryon and Alcmena and father of Iolaüs, 422, 425, 435, 592

Iphiclus (if'iklus), son of Phylacus, cured of impotence by Melampus, 494–495

Iphigenia (if-i-je-nī'a), daughter of Agamemnon and Clytemnestra, she was sacrificed by her father at Aulis or saved by Artemis to become her priestess in Tauris, 343, 369–370, 384, 574

Iphimedeia (if-i-me-dē'a or if-i-me-dī'a), mother of the Aloadae, she claimed Poseidon was their father, 634 n. 15. See also Aloadae

Iphinoë, (i-fi'no-ē), daughter of Proetus, 495

Iphis (ī'fis), girl, changed by Isis, into a boy who married Ianthe, 298, 507–508; scorned lover of Anaxarete, 507, 524

Iphitus (if'i-tus), son of Eurytus, brother of Iole, and killed by Heracles, 434, 437

Iris (ī'ris), daughter of Thaumas and the Oceanid, Electra, goddess of the "Rainbow" and messenger of the gods, especially Juno, 72, 113–114, 259, 171, 478, 545; a woman's Genius, 533

Iron Age, follows the historical Bronze Age 24–25, the last of the legendary Ages of humankind, 57, 59–60

Irus (ī'rus), beggar, who insulted Odysseus, 403

Isandrus (i-sand'rus), son of Bellerophon, 503

Isis (ī'sis), Egyyptian goddess of mysteries, equated with Io, 309–310, 417–418, 507–508, 561

Islands of the Blessed, 50, 295

Ismarus (is'mā-rus), Thracian city, home of the Cicones, sacked by Odysseus, 394

Ismene (is-mē'nē), Antigone's sister and foil, 325, 333

Ismenus (is-mē'nus), river of Thebes, 220, 333

Isthmian (isth'mi-an) Games, Panhellenic festival in honor of Poseidon, founded by Sisyphus and refounded by Theseus, 465, 501

Ithaca (ith'a-ka), island off the west coast of Greece, home of Odysseus, 271, 366, 393–394, 396, 398, 400, 403, 406, 408, 573

Itys (īt'is), son of Tereus and Procne, who is murdered by his mother and served up to his father, 454–455

Iulus (ī-ū'lus), another name for Ascanius, as ancestor of the gens Julia, the family of Julius Caesar and Augustus, 389–390, 536, 538, 540–541, 544

Ixion (ik-sī'on), king of the Lapiths and sinner in Tartarus, bound to a revolving wheel, 6, 290, 295, 299, 465, 490–491, 504

Janus (jā'nus), Roman god of bridges, entrances, and archways, 515, 550–551; Curiatius (cū-i-ā'ti-us), 552

Jason (jā'son), son of the deposed king of Iolcus, Aeson, husband of Medea and Glauce, and the hero of the Argonautic

Machaon (ma-kā'on), son of Asclepius, 186, 370

Maenad (mē'nad), Maenads, female followers of Dionysus, usually possessed by their god, 222, 224, 232, 234–236, 238, 261, 301, 304–305, 463, 585

Maenalus (mē'na-lus), mountain in Arcadia, 70, 163

Magna Mater (mag'na ma'ter), "Great Mother," Roman name for Cybele, 535

Maia (mī'a *or* mā'a), one of the Pleiades, mother of Hermes, 78, 200–202, 204–205, 207, 209–213

Maira (mī'ra), Erigone's dog, 242

Mamurius (ma-mū'ri-us), craftsman who made the false ancilia, 518

Manes (mā'nez), Roman spirits synonymous with the dead; all persons have their own Manes, 531–532

Marathon (mar'a-thon), site, in Attica, of the Athenian victory against the Persians in 490 B.C., 107, 457; Bull of Marathon, labor of Theseus, 428, 460

Marcus Curtius (mar'kus kur'ti-us), Roman, who sacrificed himself to close the chasm, Lacus Curtius, 550

Marduk (mar'duk), Babylonian god, 75, 586

Mares of Diomedes, eighth labor of Heracles, 428

Mariandyni (ma-ri-an-di'nī), people who received the Argonauts, 479

Marica (ma-rī'ca), Italian birth goddess, 525

Maron (mar'on), Apollo's priest, who gave Odysseus wine, 394–395

Marpessa (mar-pes'sa), Evenus' daughter, who preferred Idas to Apollo, 179

Mars (marz), Mavors, equated by the Romans with Ares, who loved Rhea Silvia and became the father of Romulus and Remus, 76, 480, 456, 513–516, 518, 520–521, 526, 541, 551, 567; Campus Martius (kam'pus mar'shi-us *or* mar'ti-us), the "Field of Mars," a region in Rome, 516, 528, 532, 550

Marsyas (mar'si-as), satyr, took Athena's flute and, losing in a contest with Apollo, was skinned alive and turned into a river, 187–188

Matronalia (ma-tro-nā'li-a), festival of Juno Lucina, 519

Meda (me'da), unfaithful wife of Idomeneus, 392

Medea (me-dē'a), daughter of Aeëtes, wife and helper of Jason, priestess, sorceress, and murderer, 317, 460, 467, 479–489, 501, 562, 572, 580–582

Medicus (me'di-cus), "Healer," epithet of Roman Apollo. *See* Paean

Medon (mē'don), son of Pylades and Electra, 349

Medus (mē'dus), son of Aegeus and Medea, he established the kingdom of Media, 460, 486, 488

Medusa (me-dū'sa), Gorgon, loved by Poseidon and mother of Chrysaor and Pegasus, and beheaded by Perseus, 114, 120, 125, 409, 413–416, 592

Megaera (me-jē'ra), a Fury, 296

Megalensia (me-ga-len'si-a), festival of Cybele at Rome, 536

Megapenthes (meg-a-pen'thēz), son of Proetus and king of Tiryns, 417

Megara (me'ga-ra), wife of Heracles, whom he killed, 424, 430; city in the northern Peloponnesus, 457, 460, 471, 573; Megarid, area around Megara, 459

Melampus (mel-am'pus), Amythaon's son and a seer, who got for his brother Bias the cattle of Phylacus and Pero, 419, 490, 494–495, 631 n. 7

Melas (mē'las), son of Phrixus and Chalciope, 473

Meleager (mel-ē-ā'jer), son of Oeneus and Althaea, brother of Deïanira, and hero of the Calydonian boar hunt, 13, 430, 435, 475, 496–500; Meleagrides, women who mourned Meleager, transformed into guinea fowl, 497

Meliae (mē'li-ē), nymphs of ash trees, 48, 623 n. 1

Melicertes (mel-i-ser'tēz), son of Athamas and Ino, he became the god Palaemon and the Isthmian games were instituted in his honor, 501, 630 n. 3

Melita (me'li-ta), Malta, 546

Melkart (mel'kart), Phoenician god identified with Heracles, 441

Melpomene (mel-pom'e-nē), Muse of tragedy or lyre playing, 90

Memnon (mem'non), son of Eos and Tithonus, Ethiopian leader, killed by Achilles, 384, 558

Memphis (mem'fis), city in Egypt, 418

Menelaus (men-e-lā'us), king of Sparta, husband of Helen, and father of Hermione, 289, 345, 348, 352–353, 356, 358, 363–366, 369, 374, 391–393, 403, 583

Menestheus (me-nes'the-us *or* me-nes'thūs), usurper of Theseus' power and leader of the Athenians at Troy, 465, 467

Menoeceus (me-nē'sūs *or* me-nē'se-us), father of Creon, 325; son of Creon, 332

Menoetius (me-nē'shi-us), son of Iapetus and Clymene, 60

Mentha (men'tha), maiden transformed into "Mint," 133

Mercury (mer'kūr-i), Mercurius (mer'kūr-i-us), Roman god of commerce and profit, equated with Hermes, 76, 215, 422, 513, 530–531, 534, 539, 542–543, 586

Naiads (nī'adz), nymphs of waters, 215, 249, 302, 527, 623 n. 1

Nana (na'na), mother of Attis, made pregnant from the blossom of Cybele's almond tree, 135

Narcissus (nar-sis'sus), son of Lirope and Cephisus, he rejected the love of many (including Echo), died of unrequited love for his own reflection, and was turned into a flower, 29, 245–250, 524; narcissim, 250, 578, 582

Nauplius (naw'pli-us), father of Palamedes, 391, 475

Nausicaä (naw-sik'a-a), Alcinoüs' daughter, who helps Odysseus, 402

Naxos (nak'sos), island in the Aegean where Theseus abandoned Ariadne, 170, 240, 461–463

Nebo (ně'bō), Babylonian god, 586

Nebrophonus (ne-brof'o-nus), or Thoas, son of Jason and Hypsipyle, 476

Necessity. See Ananke

Nectar, the drink of the gods, 93, 206

Neleus (něl'ūs or něl'e-us), son of Poseidon and Tyro, father of Nestor, and king of Pylos, 364, 434–435, 437, 496, 494–495

Nemea (nem'ě-a), city in the northern Peloponnesus, 330; Nemean Games, founded in honor of Opheltes, 330, 476; Nemean Lion, offspring of Echidna and Orthus and first labor of Heracles, 81, 115, 425

Nemesis (nem'e-sis), goddess of retribution, 60, 98, 100, 310, 413

Nemi (ně'mī), lake near Aricia, known as "Diana's mirror," 529

Neolithic, pertaining to the "New Stone" Age, 18–19

Neoptolemus (ně-op-tol'e-mus), also called Pyrrhus, son of Achilles and Deidamia, 275, 348–349, 368, 376, 385–386, 393, 492–493

Nephele (nef'e-lě), "Cloud," wife of Athamas and mother of Phrixus and Helle, 473; mother of Centaurus, 491

Neptune (nep'tūne), Neptunus, the Roman name for Poseidon, 72, 76, 110, 124, 389, 513, 528, 562, 576

Nereids (ně'rē-idz), sea nymphs, daughters of Nereus and Doris, 108, 111, 415

Nerio (něr'i-ō), Sabine fertility goddess, associated with Minerva and consort of Mars, 516, 520

Nereus (něr'e-us or něr'ūs), son of Pontus and Ge, and a prophetic old man of the sea, 94, 108, 112–113, 195, 367, 391, 429, 461

Nero (něr'ō), Roman emperor, first century A.D., 29, 535

Nessus (nes'sus), centaur killed by Heracles for trying to rape Deïanira, 436, 437

Nestor (nes'tor), son of Neleus, king of Pylos, and wise orator in the Trojan War, 21–22, 364, 403, 434, 494

Night, sprung from Chaos or a daughter of Phanes, 38–39, 91, 285, 306

Nike (nī'kē), "Victory," a goddess, and an epithet of Athena, 81, 90, 125; temple of, 125

Niobe (nī'ō-bē), Amphion's wife; hubris against Leto caused Apollo and Artemis to kill her seven sons and seven daughters, 81, 159–160, 189, 323

Nisus (nī'sus), son of Pandion, king of Megara, and father of Scylla, who cut off his purple lock of hair; he was turned into a sea eagle, 457, 460, 471; lover of Euryalus, 545. See Euryalus

Nobody, Outis, name Odysseus gives to the Cyclops Polyphemus, 395

Notus (nō'tus), South Wind, 56, 71

Numa (nū'ma), Roman king, responsible for religious innovations, 518, 520, 525, 529, 553

Numicus (nū'mi-kus), a river in Latium, 519, 546

Numitor (nū'mi-tor), brother of Amulius, father or Rhea Silvia, restored as king in Alba Longa by Romulus and Remus, 546–547

Nycteus (nik'tūs or nik'te-us), brother of Lycus and father of Antiope, 323

Nymph (nimf), nymphs, spirits of nature, 45, 51, 94, 138, 142, 188, 201, 215, 218, 237, 244–245, 384, 391, 400, 413, 416, 425, 454, 527–528

Nysa (nī'sa), legendary mountain associated with Dionysus, 218, 237; Nysaean (nī'sē'an), 252

Ocean, Oceanus (ō-sē'a-nus), a Titan, god of the stream of water encircling the earth, husband of Tethys, 37, 39, 42–44, 46, 54, 56, 59, 108, 141, 202, 204, 251, 271, 273, 276, 428, 483

Oceanids (ō-sē'a-nidz), children of Oceanus and Tethys, 42–43, 65, 94, 108, 165

Ocrisia (ō-krī'si-a), mother of Servius Tullius, 553

Odysseus (ō-dis'se-us or ō-dis'ūs), son of Laertes (or Sisyphus) and Anticlea, husband of Penelope, father of Telemachus, and a hero in the Trojan war; his journey home to regain his kingdom in Ithaca is the theme of Homer's Odyssey, 64, 112, 127, 213, 271–277, 282, 287, 289, 316, 335, 344, 352, 360, 363–368, 370–371, 376–377, 382–386, 388, 391, 393–408, 424, 483, 539–541, 565, 570, 581

Oeagrus (ē-ag'rus), Thracian river-god, perhaps father of Orpheus, 302

Oechalia (ē-kal'i-a), city in Boeotia, 437, 671

Oedipus (ē'di-pus *or* e'di-pus), "Swellfoot," son of Laius and Jocasta, who murdered his father, married his mother and found redemption at Colonus, 7–9, 11, 14, 17, 21, 59, 94, 99, 324–329, 331–333, 336–337, 467, 582–583

Oeneus (ē'nūs *or* ē'ne-us), king of Calydon and father of Meleager and Deïanira, 435, 496

Oeno (ē'nō), "Wine Girl," daughter of Anius, turned into a dove, 506

Oenomaüs (ē-nō-mā'us), king of Pisa in Elis, who pursued suitors for the hand of his daughter Hippodamia, 80, 338, 340–342

Oenone (ē-nō'nē), nymph with the gift of healing who loved Paris, 358, 592

Oenopion (ē-nō'pi-on), "Wine-Face," king of Chios and father of Merope, 165

Oeta (ē'ta), mountain in Trachis, site of Heracles' funeral pyre, 439, 571

Ogygia (ō-jij'i-a), the island of Calypso, 393–394, 400, 405

Oileus (o-il'us *or* o-il'e-us), father of Ajax the less, from Locris, 364–365, 388, 475

Olympia (ō-lim'pi-a), the panhellenic sanctuary of Zeus, in the western Peloponnesus, 78, 80–82, 118–119, 175, 190, 266, 338, 340, 425–426, 429, 492, 558, 592; Olympiads, Olympic, 340, 426

Olympus (ō-lim'pus), mountain in northern Greece, home of the Olympian deities, 37, 53–54, 56, 60, 64, 70, 79, 83–86, 88–90, 93, 95, 116, 155, 171, 173, 188–189, 192–193, 195, 198, 207, 211, 237, 243, 245, 254–255, 259, 262–263, 290, 296, 304, 339, 340, 372–373, 422, 434, 439, 446, 493, 504, 505, 575; mountain in Mysia, 102–103; Olympian(s), 22, 26, 28, 61, 64, 67, 84–86, 93, 95, 119, 210, 119, 352, 353, 452, 513–514, 541

Omophagy (ō-mo'fa-jē), eating of an animal's raw flesh in Bacchic ritual, 238

Omphale (om'fa-lē), Lydian queen, whom Heracles served as a slave, 428, 437, 525–526

Omphalos (om'fa-los), "navel," egg-shaped stone marking Delphi as the center of the earth, 174

Onchestus (on-kes'tus), a city in Boeotia, with a precinct of Poseidon, 193, 202, 204–205

Opheltes (ō-fel'tēz), "Snake Man," whose name was changed to Archemorus, 330

Opis (ō'pis), Diana's follower, who killed Arruns, 545

Oppian (op'pi-an), one of the hills of Rome, 551

Ops, Roman fertility goddess, linked with Saturn, equated with Rhea, and cult partner of Consus, 523

Orchamus (or'ka-mus), Persian king, father of Leucothoë, 495

Orchomenus (or-ko'men-us), city of Boeotia, 316, 424. 495–496

Orcus (or'kus), Roman name for Hades and the Underworld, 285, 295

Orestes (o-res'tēz), son of Agamemnon and Clytemnestra, he murdered his mother and was tried and acquitted by the Areopagus, 13, 127, 296, 345–349, 447, 492

Orion (ō-rī'on), a hunter and lover, who was turned into a constellation with his dog Sirius, 165, 275, 560, 620 n. 15

Orithyia (or-ī-thī'ya), wife of Boreas and mother of Zetes, Calaïs, Cleopatra, and Chione, 456

Oropus (ō-rō'pus), city in Attica, 333

Orpheus (or'fe-us *or* or'fūs), son of Apollo or Oeagrus and an archetypal poet, musician, and religious teacher, who won his wife Eurydice back from Hades, only to lose her again because he looked back too soon, 18, 39, 241, 265, 282, 284, 291, 298–305, 307, 475 571, 582, 584; Orphic(s), 28, 52, 142, 267, 283, 294, 305–306, 581, 593; Orphism (orf'ism), mystery religion, founded by Orpheus, 39, 268–269, 305–307

Orthus (or'thus), or Orthrus, the two-headed hound of Geryon, offspring of Echidna and Typhon, 428

Ortygia (or tij'i a), "Quail Island," perhaps Delos, birthplace of Apollo and Artemis, 169

Osiris (ō-sī'ris), Egyptian god, husband and brother of Isis, 309,

Ossa (os'sa), mountain in northern Greece, 56

Othrys (ōth'ris), the mountain from which Cronus and the Titans fought against Zeus and his allies on Olympus, 53

Otreus (ōt'rūs *or* ot're-us), Phrygian father of Aphrodite, according to her fictional biography for Anchises, 139

Otus (ō'tus), a giant who stormed heaven, 56, 144, 290. *See also* Aloadae

Oxylus (ok'si-lus), the "three-eyed man" of the oracle, who helped the Heraclids, 447

Pactolus (pac-tō'lus), a river near Sardis, into which Midas washed the power of his golden touch, 242

Paean (pē'an), a song, especially associated with Apollo, and his epithet meaning Healer (Roman, Medicus), 22, 535; also Iepaean, 194, 199, 291

Palaemon (pa-lē'mon), Melicertes as a god, 501

Palamedes (pal-a-mē'dēz), Nauplius' son, to whom Odysseus was hostile, 366, 391, 475, 638 n. 11

Palatine (pal'a-tīn), one of the hills of Rome, 522, 525, 530, 535- 536, 547, 549, 551

Paleolithic, pertaining to the "Old Stone" Age, 18

Pales (Pal'ēz), Roman deities of livestock, with a festival called Parili or Palilia, 524–525

Palinurus (pal-i-nū'rus), helmsman, who meets Aeneas in the Underworld and requests burial, 287

Palladium (pal-lā'di-um), statue of Pallas, which was linked to Troy's destiny, 123, 364, 521

Pallanteum (pal-len-tē'um), city of Evander on the future site of Rome, 528–529, 540, 542, 547

Pallas (pal'las), "Maiden," daughter of Triton, and friend and epithet of Athena 62–63, 116, 122–123, 125, 262, 320, 364, 389, 406, 414; son of the Titan Crius, 203; son of Pandion and brother of Aegeus, 457, 460; son of Evander and Aeneas' friend, killed by Turnus, 540, 542–543

Pamphylia (pam-fil'i-a), region in Asia Minor, 278; Pamphylian, 277

Pan, goat-like god of the forests, who invented the pan–pipe(s) and lost in a contest with Apollo, 130, 153, 155, 188–189, 218, 244–245, 233, 244–245, 525. See also Faunus

Panathenaea (pan-ath-e-nē'a), festival at Athens in honor of Athena, 119, 449; Panathenaic, 460

Pandemos (pan-dēm'os), "Of all the people," epithet of Common Aphrodite, daughter of Zeus and Dione, 128

Pandia (pan-dī'a), daughter of Zeus and Selene, 45

Pandion (pan-dī'on), king of Attica and father of Procne, Aegeus, Pallas, Nisus, and Lycus, 241, 454–457

Pandora (pan-dōr'a), woman or the first woman, who brought to mankind a jar of evils, 57, 63–65, 120

Pandrosos (pan'dro-sos), "All-Dew," daughter of Cecrops, 452–453

Panopeus (pan'ō-pūs), father of Epeus, 282

Paphos (pā'fos), a city in Cyprus, favored by Aphrodite, 89, 128, 137; son of Pygmalion and Galatea, who gave his name to the city, 132, 507

Paradise, 267. See also Elysium and Islands of the Blessed

Parcae (par'kī or par'sē), Roman birth goddesses, identified with the three fates, 529

Parergon (par-er'gon), pl. parerga, incidental adventures of Heracles, 426, 429, 442

Parentalia (par-en-tā'li-a), Italian festival propitiating the spirits of dead ancestors, 531–532

Paris (par'is), son of Priam and Hecuba, who won Helen from Menelaus, 289, 317, 352–360, 364, 366, 370, 375, 384, 386, 492. See also Alexander

Parnassus (par-nas'sus), mountain near Delphi, 173–174, 188, 194, 196, 199, 212, 575

Parnes (par'nēz), mountain of Boeotia, 317

Paros (par'os), island in the Aegean, 170, 263, 470

Parthenon (par'the-non), the temple of Athena Parthenos on the Acropolis of Athens, 80, 113, 118–121, 452, 492

Parthenopaeus (par-then-ō-pē'us), Atalanta's son, one of the seven against Thebes, 288, 330–332, 500

Parthenos (par'the-nos), "Virgin," epithet of Athena, 118, 123

Pasiphaë (pa-sif'a-ē), "All Shining," daughter of Helius and Minos' wife, who mated with a bull and bore the Minotaur, 288, 468–469, 473

Patavium (pa-tā'vi-um), city Padua in Italy

Patrae (pa'trē), city in northern Peloponnesus, 447

Patroclus (pa-tro'klus), Achilles' companion, killed by Hector, 274, 362, 365, 368–369, 379, 381, 383, 503

Pausanias (paw-sā'ni-us), speaker in Plato's Symposium, 143, 147

Pegasus (peg'a-sus), winged horse, offspring of Poseidon and Medusa, associated with Perseus, but mastered by Bellerophon, 114, 413, 503–504, 558

Peisistratos (pī-sis'tra-tus), 269. See also Pisistratus

Peleus (pē'le-us or pēl'ūs), Aeacus' son, husband of Thetis, and father of Achilles, 95, 108, 274, 348, 353, 367, 369, 371, 373, 380, 475, 492–493, 500

Pelias (pē'li-as), son of Poseidon and Tyro, he usurped the throne of Iolcus from Aeson and Jason and was killed by Medea, 473–475, 482, 484–485, 494; daughters of, 484

Pelion (pē'li-on), mountain in northern Greece, 56, 170, 431–432, 491–492

Pelopia (pe-lō-pī'a), daughter of Thyestes, by whom he had a son Aegisthus, 343

Pelopion (pelō-pī'on), shrine of Pelops at Olympia, 340

Peloponnesus (pel-o-pon-nē'sus), "Pelops' Island," Peloponnese, Peloponnesian(s), 194, 197, 316, 321, 340, 412, 417, 425, 437, 447, 468, 475, 495, 505, 557

Pelops (pē′lops), king of Elis, who won Hippodamia in a chariot race, and father of Chrysippus, 80, 324–325, 338–343, 356

Penates (pe-nā′tēcz), Roman household spirits of the store cupboard (penus), family and the state, 520–521, 539

Penelope (pe-nel′ō-pē), faithful wife of Odysseus, 366, 393–394, 398, 401, 403–405

Peneus (pe-nē′us), river in the Peloponnesus and its god, father of Daphne, 180–181, 192, 393, 426, 431

Penia (pen′i-a), "Poverty," mother of Eros in the *Symposium*, 148

Penthesilea (pen-thes-i-lē′a), queen of the amazons, killed by Achilles, 383

Pentheus (pen′thūs *or* pen′the-us), "Sorrow," king of Thebes, who opposes Dionysus and is killed by his mother Agave, 221–236, 308, 321

Perdix (per′diks), "Partridge," nephew and assistant of Daedalus, who killed him; he was turned into a partridge, 468

Periander (per-i-an′der), tyrant of Corinth, ca. 600 B.C., 504–505

Pericles (per′ik-lēz) or Perikles, Athenian statesman and general, fifth century B.C., 269

Periclymenus (per-i-kli′me-nus), Argonaut who could change shape, and Neleus' son, killed by Heracles, 434, 476

Perimedes (per-i-mē′dēz), comrade of Odysseus, 271

Periphetes (per-i-fē′tēz), brigand, son of Hephaestus, armed with a club (called Corynetes ["Club Man"]), and killed by Theseus, 457–458

Pero (pēr′ō, daughter of Neleus, wooed by Bias

Persaeus (per-sē′us) or Perses (per′sēz), son of the Titan Crius and father of Hecate, 253

Perse (per′sēz), son of Perseus and Andromeda, 415

Persephone (per-sef′ō-nē), or Kore, goddess of the budding grain, Demeter's daughter, abducted by Hades to be his wife (Roman Proserpina, Proserpine), 123, 133–134, 154, 241, 251–253, 258–264, 268, 272, 274, 297, 298, 306, 310, 430, 446, 465, 523

Perseus (per′se-us), son of Zeus and Danaë, he beheaded the Gorgon Medusa and married Andromeda, whom he rescued from a sea monster, 12, 127, 298, 409–417, 585

Persian Wars, Wars between the Persians and the Greeks, early fifth century B.C., 107, 118, 317, 365, 467

Pessinuntia (pes-si-nun′ti-a), Phrygian goddess equated with Isis, 310

Pessinus (pes′si-nus), city in Phrygia, from which Cybele (as a black stone) came to Rome, 536

Petasus (pet′a-sus), traveler's hat, especially the winged hat of Hermes, 213

Phaeacians (fē-ā′shi-anz), people of Scheria, who receive Odysseus hospitably, 271, 401–403, 405–406, 483

Phaedra (fē′dra), "Bright," daughter of Minos, wife of Theseus, and stepmother of Hippolytus, with whom she falls in love, 16, 288, 466, 572, 581–582

Phaëthon (fā′e-thon), "Shining," son of Helius and Clymene, he drove the chariot of the sun-god disastrously and was struck down by Zeus, 44–45, 131

Phanes (fā′nēz), epithet of Eros, 39, 306

Phasis (fa′sis), river of Colchis, 479

Phegeus (fē′jus), king, whose daughter married and whose sons killed Alcmaeon, 335

Pheres (fē′rēz), father of Admetus and founder of Pherae, city in Thessaly, 187, 428, 494

Phidippides (fī-di′pid-dēz), Athenian runner who encouted Pan, 632 n. 20

Philemon (fī-lē′mon). *See* Baucis

Philoctetes (fe-lok-tē′tēz), received Heracles' bow and arrows from his father Poeas, abandoned on Lemnos because of a snake bite, and at Troy killer of Paris, 358, 364, 370, 385–386, 392, 582

Philomela (fil-ō-mē′la), daughter of Pandion, sister of Procne, violated by Tereus, and turned into a swallow or nightingale, 454–455

Philyra (fil′i-ra), mother of the centaur Chiron, 473, 491

Phineus (fin′e-us *or* fīn′us), Cepheus' brother, betrothed to Andromeda, 415; blind prophet, plagued by the Harpies and rescued by the Argonauts, 478

Phlegethon (flej′e-thon *or* fleg′e-thon), River of the Underworld, 285, 289, 295. *See also* Pyriphlegethon

Phlegyas (fle′ji-as), father of Coronis and Ixion and a sinner in Tartarus, 186, 290, 490

Phocis (fō′sis), region where Delphi is located, 72, 320, 346

Phocus (fō′kus), half brother of Peleus, 492

Phoebe (fē′bē), "Bright," a Titan moon goddess, and an epithet for Artemis, 42, 46

Phoebus (fē′bus), "Bright," epithet of the sun-god, especially Apollo, 46, 157, 169–170, 172, 178, 184, 186, 188–189, 192, 194, 196, 203, 207–209, 211, 243, 290–291, 302, 372, 380, 578

Phoenix, (fē′niks), tutor and companion of Achilles, 368, 376, 378

Pholus, (fō′lus), centaur encountered by Heracles, 426

Phorcys (for'sis), son of Pontus and Ge, mate of Ceto and Hecate and father of the Graeae, Gorgons, Ladon, and Scylla, 113–114, 400, 412, 415–416

Phoroneus (fo-rō'ne-us, *or* fō-rō'nŭs), first man in Argive saga, 409, 417

Phrixus (frik'sus), son of Athamas and Nephele; a golden fleeced ram took him to Colchis, 473, 475, 479; Phrixius, epithet of Zeus as god of escape, 473, 482

Phrontis (fron'tis), son of Phrixus and Chalciope, 473

Phthia (thī'a), area in central Greece, 348, 367–368, 379, 393, 492, 494; Phthians, 367

Phylacus (fī'la-kuus), owner of cattle, won by Melampus as a bride–price for Pero, 494–495

Phylake (fī'la-kē), city in Phthia, 494

Phyleus (fī'lūs), son of Augeas, 426

Phyllis (fil'lis), beloved of the Athenian Demophon, she committed suicide and turned into an almond tree, 468

Picus (Pī'kus), "Woodpecker," Latin king, husband of Canens, 516, 518, 525

Pieria (pī-ēr'i-a), Thessalian home of the Muses, near Olympus, 90, 193, 202, 205

Pierides (pī'er-i-dēs), name for the Muses or their rivals, 623 n. 19

Pietas (pi-ē'tas), Roman virtue exemplified by Aeneas: dutiful devotion to the gods, family, and the state, 540–541, 543

Pirene (pī-rē'nē), Corinthian spring, 503

Pirithoüs (pī-rith'ō-us), son of Ixion and leader of the Lapiths and Deidamia's husband, who defeated the centaurs at his wedding; Theseus' friend, who got left behind in Hades, 80, 287, 290, 328, 430, 465–466, 491–492

Pisa (pī'za), city in the western Peloponnese, 338, 340, 342

Pisistratus (pī-sis'tra-tus), or Peisistratos, tyrant of Athens, sixth century B.C., 26

Pittheus (pit'the-us), king of Troezen, host of Aegeus, and father of Aethra, 457

Pityocamptes (pit-io-kamp'tēz), "Pine Bender," name of the robber Sinis, encountered by Theseus, 458–459

Pitys (pī'tis), nymph pursued by Pan and turned into a "Pine Tree," 632 n. 21

Planctae (plank'tē), two wandering rocks, a threat to Odysseus and Jason, 400, 405, 483

Pleiades (plē'a-dēz), daughters of Atlas and Pleione, pursued by Orion and changed into a constellation, 165, 200

Pleione (plē'ī-nē), Oceanid, mother of the Pleiades, 165

Pluto (plū'tō), another name for Hades, used by the Romans, 76, 287, 291, 295, 532. *See also* Dis Patur

Plutus (plū'tus), "Wealth," son of Demeter and Iasion, 263–264

Po (pō), river in Italy, 634 n. 18

Podalirius (pō-da-lī'ri-us), son of Asclepius, 370

Podarces (pō-dar'sēz), name of Priam, 358, 428, 494

Poeas (pē'as), Philoctetes' father, who lit the funeral pyre of Heracles and received his bow and arrows, 370, 439

Polias (pol'i-as), epithet of Athena as guardian of the city, 451

Pollux (pol'luks) or Polydeuces, boxer, son of Zeus and Leda and brother of Castor, 350–352, 476, 529, 534. *See also* Dioscuri

Polybus (pol'i-bus), king of Corinth and husband of Merope, who brought up Oedipus, 324–326

Polydamas (po-lid'a-mas), friend of Hector

Polydectes (pol-i-dek'tēz), king of Seriphos, brother of Dictys, lover of Danaë and killed by Perseus, 412, 415–416

Polydeuces (pol-i-dū'sēz). *See* Pollux

Polydorus (pōl-ĭ-dor'us), son of Hecuba, who took vengeance on Polymestor for his murder, 388

Polyhymnia (pol-i-him'ni-a), Muse of sacred music or dancing, 90

Polyidus (pol-i-ī'dus), seer who brought Glaucus back to life, 470–471

Polymede (pol-i-mē'dē), mother of Jason, 473

Polymestor (pol-i-mes'tor), king in Thrace, upon whom Hecuba took vengeance for the murder of her son Polydorus, 388

Polynices (pol-i-nī'sez), killed by his brother Eteocles, while attacking Thebes, and later buried by his sister Antigone, 325, 329–334

Polypemon (pol-i-pē'mōn), "Troubler," another name for Procrustes, 459, 643 n. 17

Polyphemus (po-li-fē'mus), Cyclops, son of Poseidon and blinded by Odysseus; also the wooer of Galatea, 112, 395, 403, 539

Polyphontes (pol-i-fon'tēz), Heraclid, who killed Cresphontes, 447–448

Polyxeinus (po-lik-sī'nus), prince in Eleusis, 255, 263

Polyxena (po-lik'se-na), daughter of Priam and Hecuba, sacrificed on Achilles' tomb, 360–361, 384

Pomona (po-mō'na), Roman goddess of fruit that can be picked from trees, who married Vertumnus, 524, 572

Pompey (pom'pē), Roman general and statesman, first century B.C., 527

Pons Sublicius (sub-lic'i-us), bridge over the Tiber, 528

Silenus (si-lē'nus), Sileni (si-lē'ni *or* si-lē'nī), another name for satyrs, particularly old ones; one (named Silenus) was particularly wise and philosophized to Midas, 142, 238, 242, 244, 528

Silvanus (sil-vā'nus), "Forester," Roman god of forests, 516, 525

Silver Age, second of the legendary four Ages, 57–58

Sinis (sī'nis). *See* Ptyocamptes

Sinon (sī'non), treacherous Greek, who convinced the Trojans to accept the wooden horse, 386

Sintian (sin'ti-an), inhabitants of Lemnos, 86–87

Sipylus (si'pi-lus), mountain in Asia Minor, 626 n. 3

Siren (sī'ren), Sirens, mythological women who, by their song, enticed sailors to their deaths, 279–280, 399–400, 405, 483, 570

Sirius (sir'i-us), Orion's dog turned into the constellation Dog Star, 165

Sisyphus (sis'i-fus), Aeolus' son, who outwitted Death and, for telling Zeus' secret, was punished in the Underworld by rolling a huge stone up a hill forever; he, not Laertes, was reputed by some to be father of Odysseus, 276, 290, 296, 299, 485, 501–502

Sleep, 293

Smyrna (smir'na), city in Asia Minor with a temple of Artemis, 157–158

Socrates (sok'ra-tēz), Athenian philosopher of the fifth century B.C., speaker in Plato, *Symposium*, 143, 147–148, 277, 279, 557

Solon (sō'lon), Athenian statesman and poet of the sixth century B.C., who advised Croesus, 27, 98–101, 105–106, 175, 238

Solymi (sol'i-mī), mighty people against whom Bellerephon fought, 503–504

Sophia (so-fē'a), second wife of Schliemann, 23

Sosia (sō'si-a), servant of Amphitryon in Plautus, 422

Sparta (spar'ta), city in the southern Peloponnese, 316, 351–353, 357, 391, 403, 435, 447–448, 465, 575; Spartan(s), 146, 161, 317, 349, 356, 374, 579

Spartoi (spar'toy), five men sprung from the serpent's teeth sown by Cadmus, 320, 332, 335, 446

Spermo (sper'mo), "Seed Girl," daughter of Anius turned into a dove, 506

Sphinx (sfinks), "Strangler," offspring of Echidna and Orthus, with a woman's face, a lion's body, and bird's wings; Oedipus answered her riddle, 81, 115, 120, 325

Steropes (ster'o-pēz), "Lightning," one of the three Cyclopes, 40, 521

Stheneboea (sthen-e-bē'a), daughter of Iobates and Proetus' wife, who fell in love with Bellerophon, 495, 503–504

Sthenelus (sthen'e-lus), father of Erystheus, 420, 422–423

Stheno (sthē'no), one of the three Gorgons, 114

Strophius (strō'fi-us), king of Phocis and father of Pylades; he took in the exiled Orestes, 346, 348; son of Pylades and Electra, 349

Stymphalus (stim-fā'lus), Arcadian lake, 427; Stymphalian (stim-fā'li-an) Birds, sixth labor of Heracles, 427, 479

Styx (stiks), river of "Hate" in the Underworld, 44, 171, 211, 249, 257, 286–288, 295, 297, 298, 367; Stygian (stij'i-an), 285, 287, 310

Sychaeus (si-kē'us), husband of Dido, killed by Pygmalion, 288, 546

Syleus (si'lūs), robber, killed by Heracles, 432

Symaethis (si-mē'this), sea-nymph, mother of Acis, 110; Symaethian, 111

Symaethus (si-mē'thus), river-god in Sicily, father of Symaethis, 110

Symplegades (sim-pleg'a-dēz), Clashing Rocks at the western end of the Black Sea; a hazard for the Argonauts, 478

Syncretism, "growing together," harmonizing of different myths, cults, and deities, 307, 310

Synoecism (sinē'sism), union of Attica into the city-state of Athens, 465

Syracuse, city in Sicliy, 505

Syrinx (sir'inks), "Pan-pipe(s)," nymph who rejected Pan and was turned into marsh reeds, out of which he fashed his pipe(s), 244

Syrtes (Sir'tēz), treacherous shoals near Libya, 483

Taenarum (tē'na-rum), southern cape of the Peloponnesus, 197, 505

Taenarus (tē'na-rus), Laconian town, site of an entrance to the Underworld, 298

Talus (tā'lus), bronze giant on Crete, killed by the Argonauts, 484

Tammuz (tam'muz), consort of Astarte and Atargatis, 309, 625 n. 5 (ch. 7)

Tanaquil (tan'a-kwil), wife of Tarquinius Priscus, 553

Tantalus (tan'ta-lus), punished in the Underworld by being tantalized by water and fruit just beyond his reach, 275, 290, 296, 299, 338–342, 504, 563

Tarchon (Tar'chon), Etruscan leader, 540

Tarentum (ta-ren'tum), precinct of a cult of Dis Pater and Persephone in the Campus Martius, 532; city in southern Italy, 534

of Artemis and king among the Taurians, 348, 478; son of Jason and Hypsipyle, also called Nebrophonus, 476

Thoricus (thŏ'ri-kus), 255; rock of, in Colonus, 328

Thrace (thrās), region north of Greece, 89, 119, 301–302, 363, 428, 454, 456, 468; Thracian(s), 170, 291, 298–299, 301–302, 304–305, 362–363, 388, 394, 428, 452, 454–455, 468, 476, 539

Thriae (thri'ē), "Pebbles," three nymphs with the gift of prophecy, 212, 630 n. 10

Thrinacia (thri-nā'shi-a), island where the Sun (Helius) pastured his herds, 400

Thyestes (thī-es'tēz), Aegisthus' father and brother of Atreus, whom he cursed, 339, 342–344

Thyone (thī-ō'nē), another name for Semele, 237, 241

Thyrsus (thir'sus), pole, wreathed with ivy or vine leaves with a pine cone atop its sharpened tip, and used in Bacchic rituals for miracles and murder, 220–222, 224, 227, 229–231, 234–235

Tiber (tī'ber), river in Rome 515, 522, 525, 535–536, 540, 546, 548; Tiberinus (ti-be-rī'nus), god of the Tiber, 528, 534, 540

Tifata (ti-fā'ta), mountain near Capua, where Diana was worshiped, 530

Tigillum sororium (ti-gil'lum so-rō'rium), yoke associated with Horatius, involving a ritual passing under the yoke, 552

Tiphys (tī'fis), helmsman of the Argonauts, 476, 479

Tiresias (ti-rē'si-as), Theban priest and prophet, 222–225, 246, 271–274, 332, 334–338, 398, 405, 406–408, 422–423, 583

Tiryns (tī'rinz), a Mycenaean citadel in the Argolid, associated with Heracles and excavated by Schliemann, 18, 21, 316, 409, 417, 424, 435, 437, 439, 441, 503–504, 507

Tisamenus (ti-sam'en-us), son of Orestes and Hermione and leader against the Heraclidae, 348, 447

Tisiphone (ti-sif'ō-nē), a Fury, 289, 296

Titanomachy (tī-tan-o'ma-kē), battle in which Zeus and the Olympians defeat Cronus and the Titans, 53–57

Titans (tī'tanz), twelve children of Uranus and Ge, 40, 42, 47, 53 56, 66, 241, 290, 294, 305; Titan, 46, 65, 74, 165, 184, 195, 301, 306

Tithonus (ti-thō'nus), brother of Priam, beloved of Eos, and turned into a grasshopper, 46, 141, 384

Titus Tatius (tī'tus tā'ti-us or tā'shi-us), Sabine leader, who became Romulus' colleague, 515, 549, 551–552

Tityus (tit'i-us), killed by Apollo for his attempt to rape Leto, and punished in the Underworld by vultures devouring his liver forever, 189, 275, 290, 295, 299, 563

Tlepolemus (tle-pol'e-mus), Heracles' son, who led the Rhodian contingent in the Trojan War, 507

Tmolus (tmō'lus), mountain in Lydia and its god, who judged in favor of Apollo in his contest with Pan, 123, 188–189, 221, 226

Trachis (trā'kis), region in northern Greece, associated with the last years of Heracles' life, 437, 439, 493

Tree of Life, the tree with golden apples in the garden of the Hesperides, 429–430

Triptolemus (trip-tol'e-mus), prince in Eleusis and Demeter's messenger, 255, 263–264

Tritogeneia (trī-tō-je-nī'a or tri-to-je-nē-a), epithet of Athena, 116–117, 121–123

Triton (trī'ton), son of Poseidon and Amphitrite, merman, trumpeter of the sea, 73, 111–112, 484, 576–577; Tritons, 568

Triton (trī'ton) or Tritonis, river or lake in Boeotia or Libya, associated with Pallas and Athena, 121, 483; Tritonian, 389

Troezen (trē'zen), city in the Argolid, associated with the saga of Theseus, 457, 466

Troïlus (trō'i-lus), Priam's son, killed by Achilles, 360, 565–566

Trophonius (tro-fō'ni-us), "He who fosters growth," builder, brother of Agamedes, and chthonic hero or god with an oracle, 194, 496

Tros (trōs), son of Dardanus, king of Troy, and father of Ganymede, 82–83, 141, 289

Troy, situated near the Dardanelles and first excavated by Schliemann; there were nine settlements on the site, including that of Priam and the Trojan War, 18, 23–24, 59, 119, 189, 289, 291, 338, 344, 348–349, 352–353, 356–358, 360–368, 370–373, 375–376, 382, 384, 386, 388–389, 391, 394, 403, 437, 447, 503, 506, 521, 531, 536, 538–539, 542–543, 545, 561, 565, 572; Trojan(s), 46, 82, 84, 123, 138–139, 316–317, 343, 357–380, 383–384, 465, 470, 519, 527, 540, 586; Trojan (trō'jan) War, 23–24, 26, 60, 179, 287–288, 335, 338, 345, 350, 353, 360, 365, 393, 419, 434, 447, 472, 475, 492, 506, 536–539, 583

Tuculcha (tu-kul'ka), an Etruscan demon of the Underworld, 432

Tullia (tul'li-a), daughter of king Servius Tullius, who murdered her father,